Lecture Notes in Computer Science 6101

Commenced Publication in 1973
Founding and Former Series Editors:
Gerhard Goos, Juris Hartmanis, and Jan van Leeuwen

Alessandro Acquisti   Sean W. Smith
Ahmad-Reza Sadeghi (Eds.)

Trust
and Trustworthy
Computing

Third International Conference, TRUST 2010
Berlin, Germany, June 21-23, 2010
Proceedings

 Springer

Volume Editors

Alessandro Acquisti
Carnegie Mellon University, Heinz College
5000 Forbes Avenue, HBH 2105C, Pittsburgh, PA 15213, USA
E-mail: acquisti@andrew.cmu.edu

Sean W. Smith
Dartmouth College, Department of Computer Science
6211 Sudikoff Laboratory, Hanover, NH 03755-3510, USA
E-mail: sws@cs.dartmouth.edu

Ahmad-Reza Sadeghi
Ruhr University Bochum, System Security Lab
Universitätsstr. 150, 44780 Bochum, Germany
E-mail: ahmad.sadeghi@trust.rub.de

Library of Congress Control Number: 2010928338

CR Subject Classification (1998): C.2, K.6.5, E.3, D.4.6, J.1, H.4

LNCS Sublibrary: SL 4 – Security and Cryptology

ISSN   0302-9743
ISBN-10   3-642-13868-3 Springer Berlin Heidelberg New York
ISBN-13   978-3-642-13868-3 Springer Berlin Heidelberg New York

springer.com

© Springer-Verlag Berlin Heidelberg 2010
Printed in Germany

Typesetting: Camera-ready by author, data conversion by Scientific Publishing Services, Chennai, India
Printed on acid-free paper   06/3180

Preface

This volume contains the proceedings of the Third International Conference on Trust and Trustworthy Computing (TRUST), held at the Ritz-Carlton hotel in Berlin, Germany, June 21–23, 2010.

TRUST is a rapidly growing forum for research on the technical and socio-economic aspects of trustworthy infrastructures. TRUST provides an interdisciplinary forum for researchers, practitioners, and decision makers to explore new ideas and discuss experiences in building, designing, using, and understanding trustworthy computing systems.

The third edition of TRUST welcomed manuscripts in two different tracks: a Technical Strand and a Socio-economic Strand. We assembled an engaging program with 21 peer-reviewed technical papers and nine peer-reviewed socio-economic papers; eight keynotes from industry, academia, and government; and panel discussions on privacy and standards. In addition, this year, TRUST was co-located with four workshops: Trust in Cloud, Hardware Security, Emerging and Future Risks, and Anonymous Signatures.

We would like to thank numerous individuals for their effort and contribution to the conference and for making TRUST 2010 possible: the Organizing Committee members—Nadine Palacios and Marcel Winandy—for their tremendous help with all aspects of the organization; the Technical and Socio-economic Program Committee members, whose names are listed on the following pages, together with the names of external reviewers who helped us in the process of selecting manuscripts to be included in the conference proceedings; the keynote and invited speakers; and the invited panel speakers.

Finally, we express our gratitude to our sponsors, whose support was crucial to the success of TRUST 2010: Microsoft Research, Intel, Hewlett-Packard, TCG (Trusted Computing Group), Sirrix AG security technologies, Intrinsic ID, and CASED (Center for Advance Security Research Darmstadt).

June 2010

Alessandro Acquisti
Sean W. Smith
Ahmad-Reza Sadeghi

.

Organization

TRUST 2010

The Third International Conference on Trust and Trustworthy Computing was held at the Ritz-Carlton hotel in Berlin, Germany, June 21–23, 2010.

General Chair

Ahmad-Reza Sadeghi   Ruhr University Bochum, Germany

Program Chairs

Technical Strand

Sean W. Smith   Dartmouth College, USA

Socio-economic Strand

Alessandro Acquisti   Carnegie Mellon University, USA

Organizing Committee

Nadine Palacios   Ruhr University Bochum, Germany
Marcel Winandy   Ruhr University Bochum, Germany

Program Committees

Technical Strand

N. Asokan   Nokia Research Center, Finland
Sergey Bratus   Dartmouth College, USA
Liqun Chen   HP Laboratories, UK
David Grawrock   Intel, USA
Cynthia Irvine   Naval Postgraduate School, USA
Bernhard Kauer   Technische Universität Dresden, Germany
Michael LeMay   University of Illinois Urbana-Champaign, USA
Michael Locasto   George Mason University, USA
Andrew Martin   University of Oxford, UK
Jon McCune   Carnegie Mellon University, USA
Chris Mitchell   Royal Holloway University, UK
David Naccache   ENS, France
Dimitris Pendarakis   IBM T.J. Watson Research Center, USA
Graeme Proudler   HP Laboratories, UK
Anand Rajan   Intel, USA
Scott Rotondo   Sun, USA

Ahmad-Reza Sadeghi   Ruhr University Bochum, Germany
Radu Sion   Stony Brook University, USA
Sean W. Smith   Dartmouth College, USA
Christian Stüble   Sirrix, Germany
G. Edward Suh   Cornell University, USA
Leendert van Doorn   AMD, USA
Claire Vishik   Intel, UK

Socio-economic Strand

Alessandro Acquisti   Carnegie Mellon University, USA
Andrew A. Adams   Reading University, UK
Ian Brown   University of Oxford, UK
Johann Cas   Austrian Academy of Science, Austria
Lorrie Faith Cranor   Carnegie Mellon University, USA
Tamara Dinev   Florida Atlantic University, USA
Peter Gutmann   University of Auckland, New Zealand
Tristan Henderson   St Andrews University, UK
Adam Joinson   Bath University, UK
Eleni Kosta   Katholieke Universiteit Leuven, Belgium
Meryem Marzouki   French National Scientific Research Center
                              (CNRS), France
Tyler Moore   Harvard University, USA
Deirdre Mulligan   UC Berkely, USA
Anne-Marie Oostveen   University of Oxford, UK
Andrew Patrick   Carleton University, Canada
Angela Sasse   University College London, UK
Jonathan Zittrain   Harvard University, USA

Steering Committee

Alessandro Acquisti   Carnegie Mellon University, USA
Boris Balacheff   Hewlett Packard, UK
Andrew Martin   University of Oxford, UK
Chris Mitchell   Royal Holloway University, UK
Sean Smith   Dartmouth College, USA
Ahmad-Reza Sadeghi   Ruhr University Bochum, Germany
Claire Vishik   Intel, UK

Additional Reviewers

Ellick Chan   Ravinder Shankesi
Matthew Hicks   Anna Shubina
Hans Löhr   Wattana Viriyasitavat
John Lyle   Christian Wachsmann
Cornelius Namiluko   Marcel Winandy
Thomas Schneider

Sponsors

Microsoft Research
Intel
Hewlett-Packard
TCG (Trusted Computing Group)
Sirrix AG security technologies
Intrinsic ID
CASED (Center for Advance Security Research Darmstadt)

Table of Contents

Technical Strand—Full Papers

Technical Strand—Short Papers

Socio-Economic Strand

Workshop on Trust in the Cloud

Workshop on Security Hardware

Beyond Kernel-Level Integrity Measurement: Enabling Remote Attestation for the Android Platform

Mohammad Nauman[1], Sohail Khan[2], Xinwen Zhang[3], and Jean-Pierre Seifert[4]

[1] Department of Computer Science, University of Peshawar, Pakistan
recluze@gmail.com
[2] School of Electrical Engineering and Computer Science, NUST, Pakistan
sohail.khan@seecs.edu.pk
[3] Samsung Information Systems America, San José, USA
xinwen.z@samsung.com
[4] Technische Universität Berlin & Deutsche Telekom Laboratories
jean-pierre.seifert@telekom.de

Abstract. Increasing adoption of smartphones in recent times has begun to attract more and more malware writers towards these devices. Among the most prominent and widely adopted open source software stacks for smartphones is Android that comes with a strong security infrastructure for mobile devices. However, as with any remote platform, a service provider or device owner needs assurance that the device is in a trustworthy state before releasing sensitive information to it. Trusted Computing provides a mechanism of establishing such an assurance. Through remote attestation, TC allows a service provider or a device owner to determine whether the device is in a trusted state before releasing protected data to or storing private information on the phone. However, existing remote attestation techniques cannot be deployed on Android due to the unique, VM-based architecture of the software stack. In this paper, we present an attestation mechanism tailored specifically for Android that can measure the integrity of a device at two levels of granularity. Our approach allows a challenger to verify the integrity of Android not only at the operating system level but also that of code executing on top of the VM. We present the implementation details of our architecture and show through evaluation that our architecture is feasible both in terms of time complexity and battery consumption.

1 Introduction

Mobile devices are becoming more powerful and are offering new functionalities that go well beyond the traditional use of cell phones such as making and receiving calls. More and more services are being deployed on these devices leading them to their use as a PC on the go. However, this rapid growth in smartphone usage and their evolving capabilities have made this technology more vulnerable

A. Acquisti, S.W. Smith, and A.-R. Sadeghi (Eds.): TRUST 2010, LNCS 6101, pp. 1–15, 2010.
© Springer-Verlag Berlin Heidelberg 2010

to today's sophisticated malware and viruses. PandaLabs [1] has identified applications downloaded from the Internet as one of the main causes of propagation of malware on mobile phones.

According to Gartner Research [2], smartphones sales and usage has increased by 12.7% in the first quarter of 2009. One of the driving reasons of this growth is the introduction of open source platforms for mobile devices. In this arena, Android [3] is the most prominent and leading open source platform which has succeeded in attracting a large number of individuals and organizations. In fact, Android OS share in terms of web requests had already surpassed that of Windows Mobile by June 2009 [4]. The growing popularity of Android is attracting more and more enterprises to deploy their custom applications for Android and to allow employees to download data for viewing or editing on their smartphones. On the other hand, the open source nature of Android is also attracting more and more malware writers. Hence, the growing security problems of smartphones are becoming a real concern for users. Service providers need assurance that if sensitive data is released to a smartphone, it will not be compromised due to the presence of a malware on the phone. Similarly, users save highly sensitive information such as their contacts and personal messages on the phone. In case of Android (and other GPS-enabled devices), the phone also has access to real-time information about the owner's location. A compromised device can lead to severe financial losses or even social threats.

To alleviate these problems, there is a need for the creation of a mechanism that can securely establish the trustworthiness of an Android-based device, providing remote parties assurance that the data released to the phone will not be compromised. The traditional approach towards solving this problem is by signing applications as being trustworthy. This approach is followed by many Symbian- and J2ME-based software stacks. A trusted application can perform all tasks, whereas an untrusted application is either sandboxed or severely restricted from accessing any sensitive resource. However, there are several problems with this approach in the context of Android. First, Android does not distinguish applications as being trusted or untrusted – *all applications are created equal*. Secondly, the open source nature of Android means that Android's infrastructure can be changed arbitrarily, thus making any security infrastructure unreliable. Finally, it has been shown in the past [5] that an assurance of trustworthiness of a device cannot be provided through the use of software-based solutions alone. Software is inherently mutable and can be modified to report inaccurate information about the hosting device. To solve this problem, Trusted Computing [6] provides the mechanism of *remote attestation* that allows a *challenger* to establish the trustworthiness of a remote *target* platform. Existing remote attestation techniques mainly aim to measure all the executables loaded on a platform and reporting them to the challenger during attestation. The challenger can then verify, using the reported measurements, whether any of the applications loaded on the platform were malicious. However, these techniques fail to cater to the unique architecture of Android because of the presence of a Virtual Machine (VM) that is responsible for executing all code. As far as the integrity measurement entity is concerned, the VM is just another executable. Even if the VM is known to be benign, there is no assurance that the code it loads for execution will behave as expected. Note that it has been shown that user-space code (including that executed by a VM) can also lead to severe vulnerabilities in a system [7,8,9].

In this paper, we present an efficient integrity measurement mechanism aimed specifically at Android that allows integrity verification of code loaded on top of the VM as well as that running on the operating system level.

Contributions: Our contributions in this paper are as follows: (1) We design an integrity measurement architecture which ensures that all the executable code loaded on Android is measured, (2) We provide two alternative solutions for the deployment of our integrity measurement mechanism, which cater to different real-world use cases, and (3) We describe the details of implementation of both alternatives and provide evaluation results to show that the technique is highly feasible both in terms of time taken for integrity measurement and battery overhead caused by it.

Outline: The rest of the paper is organized as follows: Section 2 provides real-world use cases for motivating the need for integrity measurement and gives a brief summary of the background on Android. In Section 3, we provide the details of our architecture covering the two alternative solutions in 3.2 and 3.3. Section 4 outlines the verification mechanism. Detailed evaluation results are presented in Section 5. Sections 6 and 7 reflect upon pros and cons of our technique and the conclusions drawn respectively.

2   Background

2.1   Motivating Examples

We motivate the need for the measurement of integrity of an Android-based smartphone through the use of two real-world use cases. The first use case is similar to those presented as a motivation for remote attestation in the PC world, whereas the second is more relevant to the personal nature of a smartphone.

Use case #1: Consider an organization that provides its employee – Alice – with a G1 handset running several applications that she might require for carrying out her job responsibilities. The employer, being the owner of the device, allows Alice to install applications that she might need for her daily use. However, since the organization releases sensitive information to Alice's mobile, it wants to ensure that the integrity of Android is intact and that there is no malicious software or application running on the mobile device.

Use case #2: Emma, on the other hand, is a self-employed IT consultant who has bought her own smartphone running Android. Knowing that a smartphone in general [10] and Android in particular [9,8] is much more likely to be affected by a virus threat, she decides to take preventive measures against such attacks. While the smartphone is better than her old cell phone, it is still dependent on a battery source, and if Emma were to run a dedicated antivirus software on the device, its battery would drain a lot sooner than she would like. Therefore, she decides to use remote attestation as a virtual antivirus. She remotely attests the integrity of her smartphone periodically and after she installs a new application. This ensures that her mobile device is not running any malicious software while still keeping it free of a battery-hungry antivirus software.

2.2   Android Architecture

Android is an emerging open source platform for mobile devices like smartphones and netbooks. It is not just an operating system but provides a complete software stack including a middleware and some built in applications. Android architecture is composed of different layers, with the Linux kernel layer at the bottom. This layer provides various hardware drivers and acts as a hardware abstraction layer. It is also responsible for memory and power management functionalities of Android. The Android native libraries written in C and C++ sit above the kernel layer. These libraries provide some core functionalities. For example, the Surface Manager libraries are responsible for composing graphics onto the screen, SGL and OpenGL enable graphics processing capabilities, webkit provides HTML rendering and SQLite is used for data storage purposes.

Next is the Android runtime layer which is composed of two principle components namely *Dalvik Virtual Machine* and *Android core libraries*. Android runtime is specifically designed as an optimized environment to meet the requirements of running on an embedded system i.e., limited battery life, CPU speed and memory. Dalvik virtual machine executes its own bytecode represented by *dex files*. The second component of Android runtime is the collection of class libraries written in Java programming language, which contains all of the collection classes and I/O utilities.

Class loaders: Android framework and applications are represented by classes composed of `dex` code. One or more class loaders are used to load these classes from a repository. These class loaders are called when the runtime system requires a particular class to be loaded. All of the class loaders are systematized in a hierarchical form where all requests to child class loaders are first delegated to the parent class loader. The child class loader only tries to handle a request when the parent class loader cannot handle it.

Android comes with several concrete implementations of the abstract class – `ClassLoader` [11] – which implement the necessary infrastructure required by all of the class loaders. Of these, the `PathClassLoader` will be of particular importance to us.

3   System Architecture

In Section 2.1, we presented two real-world use cases for motivating the creation of an integrity measurement system on Android devices. In this section, we present an architecture that provides two levels of granularity, each catering to one of the use cases presented. Figure 1 shows the high-level architecture of our approach.

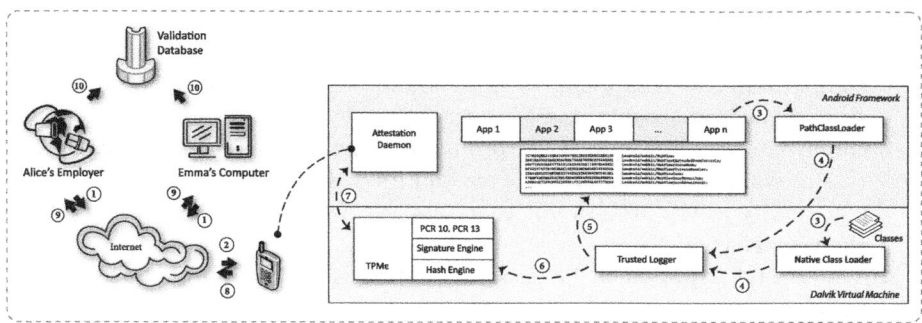

Fig. 1. Android Integrity Measurement Architecture

The attestation challenge begins at Alice's employer's system (or Emma's PC – depending on the scenario). The challenge is sent to the *Attestation Daemon* running on the Android device. On the device, one of the two integrity measurement systems must be in place: (1) Application-level attestation or (2) Class-level attestation. In either case, the measuring entity reports the measurements to a trusted logger that maintains an integrity measurement log and extends a PCR with the hashes of these measurements. When an attestation challenge is received, the attestation daemon reads the log and requests a quote over the PCR in which the measurements have been recorded by the logger. Both of these trust tokens – measurement log and PCR quote – are returned to the challenger as the attestation response. The challenger can then verify the trustworthiness of the platform based on these measurements using a *validation system*.

Both application-level attestation and class-level attestation require the presence of a *root-of-trust*. The chain of trust must be extended from this root-of-trust to the Dalvik VM and then to the measuring entities within the virtual machine. For this purpose, we need: (1) an implementation of a TPM, either hardware or software; (2) a device driver library for communicating with the TPM and; (3) a Trusted Software Stack (TSS) for providing high-level APIs for accessing the low-level functionality of the TPM. Below, we first briefly describe the creation of a minimal subset of the TPM and the TSS that is required for our implementation since a hardware TPM does not exist for mobile phones.

3.1 Chain-of-Trust

For the establishment of a chain of trust, there are two requirements:

1. A root-of-trust that acts as an anchor for the chain. It must be immutable and, according to [5], hardware-based. The TCG has defined a specification for a hardware root-of-trust – called *Mobile Trusted Module* (MTM) [12] – specifically aimed at mobile platforms. To date, no agreed-upon and widely deployed implementation of the MTM exists. We have therefore abstracted away the details of the MTM implementation and built our approach on top of the

TCG specification. This allows us to decouple our integrity measurement architecture from any specific prototype *implementation* and assures forward compatibility by complying with the standards. It should also be noted that since a hardware root-of-trust is currently not available, our implementation cannot, as yet, be deployed in production environments. However, the successful standardization of the MTM and its wide acceptance by the scientific community leaves little doubt that MTM hardware will be made available in the very near future.

2. The second requirement for a chain of trust is making all links in the chain integrity-aware. The BIOS, bootloader and the operating system all need to be modified so that they measure the integrity of every loaded executable before passing control on to it.

Below, we take a look at how we have addressed the aforementioned problems.

Emulating the Trusted Platform Module: One of the most important aspects of our architecture is the presence of a root-of-trust that can securely save the hashes of the measurements and report them to the challenger in a trustworthy manner. The absence of a hardware TPM mandates the creation of a minimal implementation of a software emulator that can act as a prototype until a hardware root-of-trust becomes available. Software emulators of both TPM [13] and MTM [14] already exist. An implementation of MTM has also been proposed recently [15]. However, we decided not to use either of these. The reason is that they are complex softwares that aim to implement the whole TPM/MTM specifications. We, on the other hand, need only protected storage (i.e. PCRs) and the PCR quote operation. Implementing the complete specifications not only gives rise to complexity in the software but also taxes the limited resources of the phone device. We have therefore created a simplified *mini* TPM *emulator* (TPM_ϵ) that provides only these two functionalities and is optimized for use on a mobile device to consume as little computational cycles and battery power as possible.

We implement TPM_ϵ as part of the kernel instead of as a module so that it can measure all the modules loaded by the kernel. TPM_ϵ uses facilities provided by the Linux kernel code for auxiliary operations, such as random number generation.

Each of the entities performing measurements needs to communicate with TPM_ϵ. The communication aspects of each of these entities are discussed in their relevant sections below.

Establishing the Chain-of-Trust: In PC world, the first link in the chain of trust is the BIOS. However, in the case of mobile and embedded devices, there is no BIOS. Device initialization is performed by the bootloader instead. Therefore, the chain of trust in our architecture begins with the bootloader. Moreover, as discussed earlier, no hardware root-of-trust is available on the Android device and consequently, there is no protected storage available for storing the hashes measured before the kernel. Therefore, as yet, the bootloader has to remain outside the chain of trust in our architecture.[1]

---

[1] We discuss the implications of this aspect in Section 6.

The chain begins at the kernel level with our TPM_ϵ loaded as part of the kernel. Since TPM_ϵ is a part of the kernel itself, it can be used to securely save the hashes of loaded executables. Integrity measurement is performed by Integrity Measurement Architecture that we have ported to the Android kernel. We have tried to keep the changes to IMA at a minimum so as to ensure backward and forward compatibility with IMA code that has now been incorporated in the Linux kernel. However, since our architecture uses TPM_ϵ and not a hardware TPM, we have had to make some changes regarding the communication of the integrity measurement code with the TPM. Other than the aspects concerning the communication with TPM, we have not modified any functionality of IMA. It therefore measures all executables loaded on the Android platform by the Linux operating system. This includes the Android VM as well as any libraries (such as `libdvm.so`, `libandroid-runtime.so` and `libandroid-system.so`). This ensures that all the executables loaded outside the Dalvik virtual machine as well as the native code of Dalvik itself gets measured and stored in the Stored Measurement Log (SML).

Similarly, the semantics of SML are also unmodified. This is because we opt not to interleave the Linux executable hashes with the Dalvik executable hashes but keep the two logs separate. The aggregate up to the point of the Dalvik load is stored in the *Android Measurement Log* (AML).

Once the chain of trust up to the Dalvik virtual machine is established, we provide two alternatives for measurement of code that is loaded on top of the VM. These two alternatives form the core part of our contribution and are discussed at length in the following sections.

3.2   Application-Level Attestation

For coarse-grained attestation of the Android Software Stack that can cater to the requirements of Use case #1 (cf. Section 2.1), we have implemented a binary attestation mechanism that can measure all loaded *applications*. Recall that in the first use case, the employer is only interested in finding out if any malicious application is executing on Alice's phone.

In Android, applications are distributed as `.apk` files that can be downloaded or copied onto the phone and installed through the `PackageInstaller` activity. These *package* files contain the `AndroidManifest.xml` file (that defines the permissions requested by the application), resource files and the `.dex` files that consist of the actual application code. All `.apk` files are stored in the `/system/app` folder in the Android filesystem. Whenever the user starts an application that isn't already loaded, Android looks up the class required for loading that application and calls the `PathClassLoader`. The name of the required class is passed to the class loader that loads the class file from the `.apk` file of that application.

We have inserted an integrity measurement hook in the `findClass()` function of the `PathClassLoader` that ensures that whenever an application gets loaded, the complete apk file corresponding to the application is measured and an entry is made to the AML. The hash of the apk is extended in PCR-11 to ensure that the log can be trusted at verification time. The implementation of the SHA-1 hashing mechanism is based on the `MessageDigest` algorithm provided by the Java Cryptography Extensions (JCE).

For communicating with TPM_ϵ, the measurement function requires an implementation of the Trusted Software Stack (TSS). As with the TPM and MTM emulators, we have opted not to use any of the existing TSS implementations due to performance concerns. For this coarse-grained measurement, we have implemented a minimal implementation of the TSS specifications – called TSS_ϵ – that allows only two operations: (1) PCR extend – allowing the measurement function to communicate the measured hash to the TPM_ϵ and (2) PCR quote – that allows trustworthy reporting of the PCR values to the challenger. Since the measurement functions operate below the Android application framework layer i.e. in the Java library layer (cf. Section 2.2), TSS_ϵ is implemented as a Java class (`edu.android.aim.TssE`) that exposes two functions for the aforementioned operations – `pcrExtend()` takes a hash and a PCR number as input for extending the PCR and `quote` takes a collection of PCRs, a nonce, an AIK label and the associated authorization secrets as input and returns the quote performed by TPM_ϵ over the PCR values and nonce using the AIK associated with the label. Each PCR extend operation must be matched by an entry made in the AML. This is also implemented as a class in the Java libraries (`edu.android.aim.TrustedLogger`) that exposes two operations – (1) `logEvent()` that creates a new entry in the AML with the provided entry description and hash and; (2) `retrieveLog()` that returns the complete AML. The AML is stored in the filesystem in an unprotected space (`systemdir/aml_measurements`) since its correctness can be ensured through the measurements in the protected storage of TPM_ϵ.

This coarse-grained approach has several advantages in the context of a mobile platform. Firstly, it only requires the measurement of `apk` files of applications that are loaded. For a typical smartphone user, this number is usually quite small. This ensures that the computational requirements for integrity measurement are keep to a minimum. Moreover, the AML is fairly small and thus aids in keeping the communication overhead to a minimum. Likewise, the battery consumption during calculation of hashes is also fairly small. In Section 5, we discuss the performance issues associated with this approach.

The major drawback of attestation at this level of granularity is that it is not complete! It does not measure the system classes which form an essential part of Android's trusted computing base. Ignoring these classes removes the possibility of ensuring that, for example, the Android permission mechanism will be enforced by the mobile device – which in turn reduces the level of trust that can be placed in the correct enforcement of the security mechanisms that are expected by the challenging party. To alleviate this drawback, we have implemented a finer-granular integrity measurement approach as defined in the following section.

3.3   Class-Level Attestation

To cater to fine-grained requirements of attestation for the Android platform, we go a step beyond just measuring the applications that are loaded on the device and propose a solution that provides completeness in integrity measurement. This level of attestation can measure all executables loaded on top of the Dalvik VM and can thus cater to the requirements of Use case #2.

Class-level attestation aims to measure all executables (i.e. classes) loaded on top of the Dalvik VM. While this approach is similar to IMA in essence, it differs significantly in the semantics of measurement. Moreover, since the loading mechanism of Dalvik is, at its core, different from that of the Linux kernel, our binary integrity measurement has major differences in what and how it measures.

As mentioned in Section 2.2, there are two ways in which classes may be loaded into Dalvik. The mechanism mentioned earlier is that which uses `ClassLoaders` executing on top of the VM itself. These class loaders are themselves classes and thus need to be loaded too. Moreover, there are several classes that are 'system classes' and are required for the proper functioning of Java code (e.g. `java.lang.Object`). These classes cannot be loaded by Java-based class loaders and have to be loaded by the native code in the VM itself. Another issue with `ClassLoaders` is their unrestrictive nature. Applications are allowed to write their own class loaders to load classes from arbitrary sources. For example, an application may write a class loader that reads from a byte stream to load a class. This is substantially unlike the Linux/IMA scenario in which all executables are loaded from the filesystem. It is therefore possible in Linux to measure an executable before it is loaded. In case of Dalvik (or any Java-based VM), this is not always possible due to the potentiality of arbitrary class loaders. It is for this reason that the semantics of our binary attestation are that we measure a class *after* it is loaded but before it can be executed.

In Dalvik, the code responsible for calling class loaders is present in three major files – `Class.c`, `InternalNative.c` and `JNI.c` The two broad categories of classes in Dalvik are *system classes* and (what we informally term as) *standard classes*. These are loaded by `dvmFindSystemClassNoInit()` and `dvmFindClassFromLoaderNoInit()` respectively. Both of these functions are present in `Class.c` and are called from a single point – `dvmFindClassNoInit()`. The 'no-init' functions are responsible for loading classes (either directly or by calling a class loader) *without* initializing them. By placing the integrity measurement hooks in `dvmFindClassNoInit()`, we ensure that (1) the measurement is complete i.e. all the classes that are loaded get measured and (2) that classes are measured immediately after they are loaded and before they can be executed.

After a class is loaded, it is returned to Dalvik in a structure that encapsulates the methods, fields, loader details and other information about the class. This is a highly complex structure and includes pointers to many internal structures representing detailed information about the class. Including all this information in the hash of the class would cause severe performance bottlenecks without adding much to the utility of measurement. In our integrity measurement mechanism, we include only those parts of this structure that may influence the dynamic behavior of the class. We define these parts in three categories:

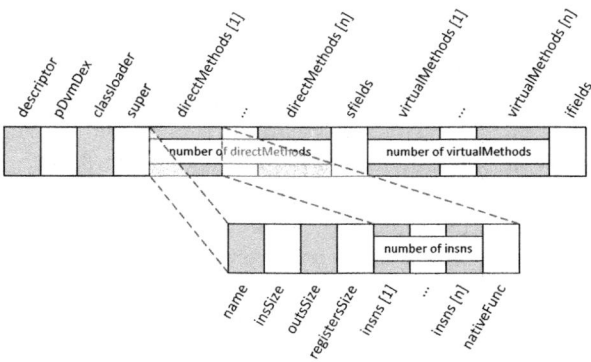

Fig. 2. Subset of a Class Structure for Hash

1. **Meta-information:** This information does not directly influence the execution of a class but is helpful in unique identification of the class. Included in this category are the *descriptor* i.e. fully qualified name of a class, the source dex filename, the *class loader* and parent class etc.
2. **Passive entities:** These are static portions of the class that, while non-executable, may affect the execution of the class. Passive entities include *static and instance fields, method names* and *instruction and register size* etc.
3. **Executable code:** This is the most important aspect of the measurement and includes the instructions present in the method bodies of a class. Note that, since inner (and anonymous) classes are measured separately, their methods and instructions will be included in their respective measurements and can thus be verified.

Figure 2 shows the precise structure over which the hash is calculated during class-level integrity measurement and Figure 3 shows the integrity measurement log. Each class is represented in the log by its descriptor and is preceded by the hash of the structure described above. Note that since this fine-grained level of integrity measurement computes the hash of *all* loaded classes, it may cause some performance hit but as we discuss in Section 5.2, the performance hit is minimal and with some performance enhancement can be successfully deployed in production settings.

Note that the TSS_ϵ solution proposed in Section 3.2 cannot be utilized at this level of attestation as it operates *above* the VM level, whereas measurement in this fine-grained approach is being done at the VM level. For this level of integrity measurement, we have implemented TSS_ς in the Dalvik VM itself. TSS_ς only performs one operation i.e. saving an entry in the AML. The AML is stored in the same location as in the application-level attestation. It does not provide a function for reading the AML because that functionality is required only at the application level of the Android framework and can be taken care of by the TSS_ϵ's retrieveLog(() function. The details of this retrieval operation follow.

```
133A57C0CB942D5F74376BD6A89A3DD98EAB4886 vmaggregate
...
4FC88626E94A631D9FF4BD7C39C57F6EA8847C3F Landroid/widget/AbsListView;
FC060385A2B800175CE68D96AFC4A49E965A8E8F Landroid/widget/AbsListView$CheckForLongPress;
59517950D7280DC0CB4517B40E812D9E2B1BAFB2 Landroid/widget/AbsListView$SavedState$1;
69CEB9E9ED1398EFFF0C2C0705C7D45506481BA1 Landroid/widget/AbsoluteLayout;
457F0C258A8B76B4C03C3A89B1B7BAC8E306ECA1 Landroid/widget/AbsoluteLayout$LayoutParams;
8E84D83A9BFE50BDC7F41714769AB48CE55E208D Landroid/widget/AdapterView;
AE8BB8B2E8585395EB697DC8403C3EC1E2BFF7ED Lcom/android/internal/telephony/Phone;
5CB11877BF82DA663722AFBF19CB3DE2DBC03F3B Lcom/android/internal/telephony/Phone$State;
...
```

Fig. 3. ASCII representation of the Android Measurement Log: Capturing the hash of the class and the class descriptor

4   Verification

Once the attestation tokens i.e. PCR quote and measurement logs are received at the challenger side, they need to be verified to establish the trustworthiness of the remote platform. The first step in the procedure is to validate the digital signature on the quote structure to verify that a genuine TPM vouches for the measurement logs. This is a simple procedure and requires only the knowledge of the AIK which can be provided by a PrivacyCA [16]. Afterwards, the integrity of each loaded executable reported in the measurement log is verified individually. The Android Market [17] is by far the largest and most reliable source of applications. The basic verification mechanism involves creation of a database of *known-good* and *known-bad* hashes of executables retrieved from the Android Market. For instance, currently our database includes information about our own versions of the *Intent Fuzzer* and *Intent Sniffer* tools [9] that may be used to maliciously monitor and/or modify the operation of Android's intent model. If the hash associated with one of these tools is found in the AML reported by the target device, the challenger may conclude that the device is compromised and take preventive measures.

5   Evaluation

In the context of mobile devices, computational complexity and battery consumption are two essential factors that need to be considered when making any changes to the software stack on these devices. We have evaluated both these aspects for the two options of attestation presented in this paper. As a test system, we have taken the Android cupcake branch, operating on the HTC G1 handset. Evaluation of the two levels of attestation is presented below.

5.1   Application-Level Attestation

In general, application-level attestation imposes little overhead on both the computational capabilities and battery consumption of Android.

Time: The average time for measurement of an application on our testbed was 1631ms. This is a rather large number but note that we cache the results of measurement and only measure an application on subsequent loads if it has changed. This caching, coupled with the facts that mobiles are 'always-on' and application apks are unlikely to change frequently, makes the average time fairly acceptable. Moreover, since the largest portion of this time is taken by the hashing algorithm, a faster Java implementation of this function may significantly improve this time.

Log size: Since this coarse-grained attestation only reports the hashes of loaded applications, the log size is extremely small and is dependent only on the number of applications executed on the target device. The size L in bytes of the reported log is given as:

$$L = nL_h + \sum_{i=1}^{n} (L_{a_i}) + L_q + L_s$$

where n is the number of applications loaded, L_h is the size of the application's hash, L_{a_i} is the length of ith application name, L_q is the size of the data structure representing the PCR quote signed by TPM$_\epsilon$ and L_s is the size of IMA's SML.

In our evaluation, L_h and L_q were constants (i.e. 20 bytes and 64 bytes) respectively, the average number of applications loaded on the device was 28, the average length of the application name was 11.2 bytes and the size of the SML was 4998 bytes. The total size of the log for application-level attestation was therefore:

$$L = (20 + 11.2) \times 28 + 64 + 4998 = 5935.6$$

which is less than 6KB of data per attestation request for application-level attestation.

Power: Measurement of battery consumption on Android is difficult due to the fact that the battery *charge level* reported by the Android hardware is at a very coarse grained level. Using software for measurement of battery consumption during hash calculation simply yields 'no change' in battery level. However, note that since the attestation techniques only use the CPU and do not tinker with parameters of radio communication, the battery overhead caused by integrity measurement is directly proportional to the time taken. Therefore, using the same arguments as those for time consumption, we can conclude that the battery consumption overhead caused by our integrity measurement mechanism is also bearable.

5.2   Class-Level Attestation

Class-level attestation is performed at a finer-grained level and thus might be expected to have slightly larger overhead in terms of both time and battery.

Time: Figure 4 shows the evaluation results of the time taken for performing this level of integrity measurement. As can be seen, using native C/C++ code for calculating SHA-1 has improved performance by three orders of magnitude. The average time for integrity measurement of a class is 583 μs. Integrity measurement of a few classes took more than a second but these were only around

1% of all the classes measured. Moreover, similar to application-level attestation, caching has been employed for class-level attestation to ensure that after a class has been measured, it is not re-measured on subsequent loads unless it has changed. Moreover, taking only a subset of the structure of the class (cf. Section 3.3) also increases the performance of attestation.

Log size: The length of the log at this fine-grained level of attestation was rather large. The average number of loaded classes during our tests was 1941 and the average length of class names was 35.67. Using the same method of calculation as for application-level attestation, the log size was:

$$L = (20 + 35.67) \times 1941 + 64 + 4998 = 113117.47$$

The log size of around 110KB is not completely insignificant for the a mobile device. However, since we do not require real-time results, attestation can be carried out when the device is connected to the enterprise server or PC through a high-speed connection such as WiFi, thus reducing the time taken for transmission of the log.

Power: Similar to application-level attestation, battery consumption overhead of this finer granular integrity measurement is also directly proportional to the time taken. Moreover, since the time taken by class-level attestation is quite small, battery consumption is also much more acceptable than that for application-level attestation.

6   Discussion

In this paper, we have presented the first attempt at measuring the integrity of the Android platform using the concepts of Trusted Computing. The two levels of granularity presented in the paper both have their pros and cons as discussed earlier. However, there are a few issues that inhibit the deployment of either of the techniques in production environments just yet. First of all, there is the lack of a hardware root-of-trust. A hardware TPM or MTM does not exist for any mobile device. We currently use an emulator for the demonstration of our technique and rely on the assumption that it is only a matter of time before an MTM becomes available for mobile devices. Note that we have designed the architecture in such a way that our technique would be able to use an MTM

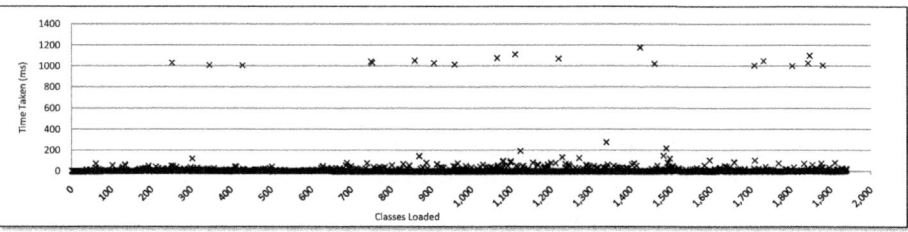

Fig. 4. Class-level Attestation Results

directly without any change to its working. We envision the deployment of our attestation technique probably as a separate trusted sub-system [18] that acts on behalf of either the service provider or the local owner of the device to provide attestation responses.

Finally, we discuss the issue of *time of measurement, time of use race conditions* [19] that was a major concern in the original IMA technique. The issue is that when reading from a filesystem, the file may change after it is measured but before it gets loaded for execution. Since we measure classes or applications only after they are loaded and not from the filesystem, our architecture does not suffer from this drawback.

7   Conclusion and Future Work

The personal and ubiquitous nature of mobile phones poses serious security concerns regarding data that is stored on these devices. Measuring the integrity of a smartphone can ensure that sensitive information accessible to applications running on the device will not be compromised. Android is among today's most popular smartphone platforms. It is backed by a vast majority of industry leaders and is made available as open source, thus leading to wide adoption of this software stack. In this paper, we have proposed the design and implementation of an integrity measurement mechanism aimed specifically at the unique architecture of Android's software stack. We have described our architecture at two levels of granularity catering to different real world use cases. We have shown our architecture to be efficient both in terms of time complexity and battery consumption – two critical factors for any architecture targeting mobile devices.

One of the more important usages of our attestation technique, that we can foresee, is for ensuring 'copy protection' of paid applications for Android phone. Paid applications that are not allowed to be moved from one device to another are protected by the Android system. However, due to the presence of 'rooted' phone devices, it is possible for a malicious user to bypass copy protection [20]. Using our attestation technique before releasing a copy-protected application may provide assurance to Android Market that the target device is in a trusted state and will thus enforce copy protection as expected. Formalizing the semantics and procedure of this mechanism forms part of our future work.

References

1. PandaLabs: PandaLabs Q1 2008 report (2008),
   http://pandalabs.pandasecurity.com/blogs/images/PandaLabs/2008/04/01/
   Quarterly_Report_PandaLabs_Q1_2008.pdf
2. Gartner Research (2009) Press Release, http://www.gartner.com/it/page.jsp?
   id=985912
3. Google: Android Home Page (2009), http://www.android.com.
4. AdMob Mobile Metrics: Mobile Metrics Report (June 2009), http://metrics.
   admob.com/2009/07/june-2009-mobile-metrics-report/.

5. Pearson, S.: Trusted Computing Platforms: TCPA Technology in Context. Prentice Hall PTR, Upper Saddle River (2002)
6. TCG: Trusted Computing Group (2010), http://www.trustedcomputinggroup.org/
7. Zovi, D.A.D.: Advanced Mac OS X Rootkits. In: Black Hat Technical Security Conference USA (2009), https://www.blackhat.com/html/bh-usa-09/bh-usa-09-archives.html
8. Miller, C., Mulliner, C.: Fuzzing the Phone in your Phone. In: Black Hat Technical Security Conference USA (2009), https://www.blackhat.com/html/bh-usa-09/bh-usa-09-archives.html
9. Burns, J.: Exploratory Android Surgery. In: Black Hat Technical Security Conference USA (2009), https://www.blackhat.com/html/bh-usa-09/bh-usa-09-archives.html
10. Evers, J.: Russian Phone Trojan Tries to Ring Up Charges – Zdnet Australia (2006), http://www.zdnet.com.au/news/security/soa/Russian-phone-Trojan-tries-to-ring-up-charges/0,130061744,139240795,00.htm
11. Google: Android Abstract ClassLoader (2009), http://developer.android.com/reference/java/lang/ClassLoader.html
12. Mobile Phone Work Group Mobile Trusted Module Overview Document, http://www.trustedcomputinggroup.org/resources/mobile_phone_work_group_mobile_trusted_module_overview_document
13. Strasser, M., Stamer, H., Molina, J.: Software-based TPM Emulator, http://tpm-emulator.berlios.de/
14. Ekberg, J., Kylaanpaa, M.: Mobile Trusted Module (MTM)–An Introduction (2007)
15. Ekberg, J.E., Bugiel, S.: Trust in a Small Package: Minimized MRTM Software Implementation for Mobile Secure Environments. In: STC 2009: Proceedings of the 2009 ACM workshop on Scalable trusted computing, pp. 9–18. ACM, New York (2009)
16. IAIK: About IAIK/OpenTC PrivacyCA (2010), http://trustedjava.sourceforge.net/index.php?item=pca/about.
17. Google: Android Market (2009), http://www.android.com/market.html.
18. Schmidt, A., Kuntze, N., Kasper, M.: On the deployment of Mobile Trusted Modules. Arxiv preprint arXiv:0712.2113 (2007)
19. Sailer, R., Zhang, X., Jaeger, T., van Doorn, L.: Design and Implementation of a TCG-based Integrity Measurement Architecture. In: SSYM 2004: Proceedings of the 13th Conference on USENIX Security Symposium (2004)
20. Oberheide, J.: A Look at a Modern Mobile Security Model: Google's Android Platform. In: Annual CanSecWest Applied Security Conference (March 2009), http://jon.oberheide.org/research/

SBAP: Software-Based Attestation for Peripherals

Yanlin Li, Jonathan M. McCune, and Adrian Perrig

CyLab, Carnegie Mellon University
4720 Forbes Avenue, Pittsburgh, PA, United States
{yanlli,jonmccune,perrig}@cmu.edu

Abstract. Recent research demonstrates that adversaries can inject malicious code into a peripheral's firmware during a firmware update, which can result in password leakage or even compromise of the whole host operating system. Therefore, it is desirable for a host system to be able to verify the firmware integrity of attached peripherals. Several software-based attestation techniques on embedded devices have been proposed as potentially enabling firmware verification. In this work, we propose a Software-Based Attestation technique for Peripherals that verifies the firmware integrity of a peripheral and detects malicious changes with a high probability, even in the face of recently proposed attacks. We implement and evaluate SBAP in an Apple Aluminum Keyboard and study the extent to which our scheme enhances the security properties of peripherals.

1 Introduction

Recent research shows that adversaries can subvert keyboards by injecting malicious code into a keyboard's firmware during firmware update [1]. The injected code can compromise users' privacy and safety, such as eavesdropping a user's bank account password or credit card number, or embedding a kernel-level rootkit into a clean re-installed operating system through some software vulnerabilities in the host operating system. Similar attacks can happen on other peripherals, such as a mice or a game controller. Peripheral manufacturers enable updating of firmware to fix firmware bugs. However, due to constrained computation and memory resources, the low-speed embedded microcontroller on many peripherals cannot verify complex cryptographic signatures or message authentication codes. Consequently adversaries can inject malicious code into peripheral firmware during a firmware update. Therefore, a legacy computer is potentially under serious attacks due to vulnerabilities on widely used peripherals. We take the position that it is desirable for a host machine to verify the firmware integrity on peripherals.

Software-based attestation schemes on embedded systems [2,3,4] have been proposed as potentially enabling firmware verification, which enables an external trusted verifier to verify the firmware integrity on peripherals. However, recent research [5] suggests that it may be feasible to hide the malicious code from an attestation through a return-oriented attack or a compression attack.

A. Acquisti, S.W. Smith, and A.-R. Sadeghi (Eds.): TRUST 2010, LNCS 6101, pp. 16–29, 2010.

In addition, constrained computation and memory resources in the low-speed peripherals limit the implementation of the software-based solutions. For example, some software-based attestation schemes [2] require hardware multiplication units or a large amount of data memory that is not available on all peripherals, especially on low speed peripherals such as mice or keyboards. Therefore, peripheral firmware integrity verification remains an important challenge.

In this paper, we propose Software-Based Attestation for Peripherals (SBAP) to verify peripherals' firmware integrity. Similar to previous proposals, SBAP is based on a challenge-response protocol between a trusted verifier and an untrusted peripheral, and a predicted computation time constraint. It verifies the contents of both program and data memory on the peripheral and can detect any malicious changes with arbitrarily high probability, even in the face of recently-proposed attacks. In this paper, we make the following contributions:

1. We propose a software-only solution to verify the firmware integrity of peripherals, that can be implemented via a software upgrade to the peripherals and avoid a costly hardware upgrade.
2. We propose an approach to verify the code or data integrity on both program memory and data memory in peripherals that can prevent all known attacks.
3. We design, implement, and evaluate a prototype of SBAP using an Apple Aluminum Keyboard.

We organize the remainder of this paper as follows. In Section 2, we provide the background on software-based attestation and related attacks. Section 3 presents the problem definition, assumptions, and the attacker model. In Section 4, we describe the system design including the system architecture, attestation protocol and verification function design. Section 5 details our SBAP implementation on an Apple Aluminum Keyboard and Section 6 gives our experimental results. We discuss our work in Section 7 and describe related work in Section 8. Finally, we offer our conclusions and identify future work in Section 9.

2   Background

2.1   Software-Based Attestation for Embedded Devices

SWATT. SoftWare-based ATTestation for embedded devices (SWATT) is based on a challenge-response protocol between a trusted verifier and an untrusted embedded device, and a predicted computation time constraint. First, the verifier sends a random nonce to the embedded device. Using this nonce as a seed, a verification function in the embedded device computes a checksum over the entire memory contents and returns the checksum result to the verifier. The verifier has a copy of the expected memory contents of the embedded device, so it can verify the checksum result. Also, the verifier knows the exact hardware configuration of this untrusted embedded device, enabling the verifier to exactly predict the checksum computation time. Because the checksum function is well optimized, the presence of any malicious code in memory will either invalidate the checksum result or introduce a detectable time delay. Therefore, only the checksum result received within the expected time range is valid. During checksum computation, the checksum function reads memory in a pseudo-random traversal, thus preventing an attacker from precomputing the checksum result. SWATT requires that the embedded device can only communicate with the verifier during attestation. This prevents a malicious device from communicating with a faster machine to compute the checksum.

ICE. Indisputable Code Execution (ICE) sets up a dynamic root of trust in the untrusted device through a challenge-response protocol between a trusted verifier and an untrusted embedded device, and a predicted computation time constraint. The dynamic root of trust also sets up an untampered execution environment, which in turn is used to demonstrate verifiable code execution to the verifier. As in SWATT, the verifier first sends a random nonce to the untrusted device. Upon receiving the random nonce, the verification function in the untrusted device sets up an untampered execution environment. The verification function includes code to set up an ICE environment by disabling interrupts, a checksum function that computes a checksum over the contents of the verification function, a communication function (send function) that returns computation results to the verifier, and a hash function that computes a hash of the executable that will be invoked in the untampered environment. After checksum computation, the send function sends the checksum result to the verifier. As in SWATT, the verifier can verify the checksum result and predict the checksum computation duration. If the verifier receives the correct checksum within the expected time, the verifier obtains assurance that the untampered execution environment (dynamic root of trust) has been set up in the untrusted device. The send function invokes the hash function to compute a hash of the executable in the embedded device and sends the hash result to the verifier. Then the verification function invokes the executable on the untrusted device. Simultaneously, the verifier obtains the guarantee of the integrity of the executable through verifying the hash of the executable.

Discussion. Both ICE and SWATT implement code integrity verification through a software-only approach. However, there are several challenges to implement ICE on embedded devices. In ICE, CPU registers describing code location (e.g., the program counter) and interrupt status information are included in the checksum to confirm the intended code location and interrupt status. However, not all microcontrollers provide instructions to directly access the values of the PC or interrupt status registers. For instance, on the CY7C63923 microcontroller [6] in the Apple Aluminum Keyboard, there is no instruction to read the value of the PC, although the CY7C63923 does provide instructions to access the Flag register containing interrupt status information. Moreover, the code size of verification function in ICE is larger than the code size of the checksum routine in SWATT.

On some embedded devices, there are very constrained memory resources for the implementation of the verification function. For example, on an Apple Aluminum Keyboard, the size of Flash memory is only 8 KB and there is only about 1 KB of free Flash memory for the implementation of our verification function.

2.2   Attacks on Existing Proposals

Memory Copy and Memory Substitution Attack. In a memory copy attack, the attacker modifies the checksum code in program memory while keeping a correct copy of the original code in unused memory. In a memory substitution attack, the attacker keeps the correct code in the original memory location, but deploys the malicious code in unused memory. In both attacks, the malicious code computes the checksum when expected. To obtain the correct checksum result, the malicious code redirects the location of the memory read operation to the correct code. On common embedded devices, the values in empty program memory are constant (i.e., 0xFF, which is the uninitialized value of Flash memory). Thus, the malicious code can predict such constant values and use them during checksum computation. SWATT and ICE prevent a memory copy or memory substitution attack by reading the program memory in a pseudo-random fashion so that the malicious code cannot predict the memory address to read, and has to add additional instructions to check and redirect the memory address. Such operations result in a detectable time overhead. On a Harvard architecture embedded device, the read latency of data memory is much smaller than the read latency of program memory. Thus, the malicious code can minimize the computation overhead of a memory copy attack by having a copy of the original code in data memory and redirecting the location of checksum memory read operations to data memory instead of program memory.

Compression Attack. One important enabler of a memory copy or memory substitution attack is that the malicious code can remember or predict the constant values of empty memory during attestation. Therefore, Seshadri et al. [2] propose to fill the empty space of program memory with pseudo-random values and leave no available free space for attackers to make a memory copy or memory substitution attack. However, an attacker can still create free space through compressing the existing code on program memory. Some compression algorithms, such as the Canonical Huffman Encoding [7], can decompress the compressed stream from an arbitrary position. Thus, the malicious code can decompress the compressed steam on-the-fly during attestation and obtain the correct checksum result though the checksum code reads memory in a pseudo random traversal. The decompression procedure causes a detectable computation overhead because of the complexity of the decompression algorithm.

Return Oriented Programming Attack. Return oriented programming (ROP) [8, 9,10] performs computation on a system by executing several pieces of code that are terminated by a return instruction. These pieces of code are executed through well-controlled stack content. If there is sufficient existing binary code in the system, an adversary can execute arbitrary computations through a ROP attack without injecting any code, except for overwriting the stack with well-designed content. Castelluccia et al. [5] present that an adversary can use a ROP attack to protect malicious code from being detected by software-based attestation schemes. Briefly, the adversary code first saves a copy of the adversary code on data memory before attestation. Then the adversary code modifies the contents of data memory by embedding ROPs on the stack. Through these ROPs, the attacker erases all the malicious code in program memory and restores the original code before checksum computation. Then, during checksum computation, the contents of program memory are exactly as expected. After attestation, the attacker restores malicious code in program memory through an additional ROP. The ROP attack generates little computation overhead. For example, in the attack described by Castelluccia et al. [5], the computation overhead caused by a ROP attack is undetectable, only 0.3% of the expected checksum computation time.

Attack Analysis. As described above, an attacker can hide malicious code from an attestation through a compression attack or a ROP attack. However, both attacks modify the contents of data memory, by storing either malicious code or ROP data. Thus, a checksum function can detect such malicious changes by verifying the contents of both program memory and data memory. However, it is challenging to verify the contents of data memory, since the content is unpredictable to the verifier. To verify it, the verifier must be able to reset data memory into a known or predictable state before attestation. The verification function can reset data memory into a known state by erasing the contents of data memory. To prevent attacker from predicting or compressing the contents of data memory, the data memory should be filled with pseudo-random values before attestation.

3   Problem Definition, Assumptions and Attack Mode

Problem Definition. We consider the problem of how a host machine can verify the firmware integrity of a peripheral attached to it without any dedicated hardware, i.e., using a software-only approach that can detect arbitrary malicious changes.

Assumptions. We assume that the verifier knows the exact hardware configuration of the peripheral, such as the CPU model, the CPU clock speed, the size of program memory, and the size of data memory. We also assume that the verifier has a copy of the expected contents of the program memory of the peripheral. We assume that the communication channel between the peripheral and the verifier can provide message-origin authentication. We also assume that the peripheral can only communicate with the verifier during the attestation, which prevents the peripheral from communicating with a faster machine to compute the checksum (this attack is called a proxy attack). This can be implemented through a physical connection, such as USB cable.

Attacker Model. We assume that an attacker cannot change the hardware configuration of peripherals, such as speeding up the CPU clock, or adding additional program memory or data memory. However, the attacker can make arbitrary changes to the peripheral software. We assume that there are software vulnerabilities in the peripheral firmware, through which an attacker can attempt a compression or ROP attack.

4   SBAP: Software-Based Attestation for Peripherals

4.1   System Overview

Similar to previous proposals [2, 3], SBAP verifies the firmware integrity of a peripheral through a challenge-response protocol and a predicted computation time constraint. To prevent known attacks, SBAP leaves no available empty space in memory for attackers by filling all unused space in program and data memory with pseudo-random values, and verifying the integrity of both program and data memory. Also, different from SWATT and ICE, SBAP utilizes an efficient pseudo-random number generator, which is mainly designed for low-speed devices with constrained computation and memory resources. Figure 1 depicts an overview of the system setup as well as the protocol steps. On the peripheral, the verification function is responsible for disabling all interrupts in the microcontroller, filling the data memory with pseudo-random values, computing the checksum over the entire contents of data memory and program memory, and sending the final checksum result to the verifier. Before peripheral deployment, available free space in program memory must be filled with pseudo-random values. On the verifier, a nonce generator generates random nonces to seed the untrusted peripheral and a timer measures the verification time. A checksum simulator on the verifier computes the expected checksum result by simulating the checksum procedure.

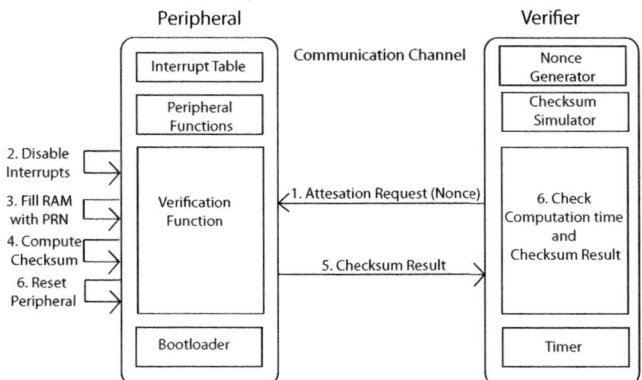

Fig. 1. System Overview and Protocol

4.2   Protocol

To verify the firmware integrity on a peripheral, SBAP performs the following steps:

1. The verifier sends the attestation request to the untrusted peripheral. An 8-byte random nonce is included in this request as a seed to the verification function.
2. Upon receiving the attestation request, the verification function first disables all interrupts on the peripheral to set up an untampered execution environment.
3. The verification function fills the entire data memory with pseudo-random values generated using the nonce as a seed.
4. The verification function computes a checksum over the entire contents of both program memory and data memory. Our checksum function uses part of data memory to store variables. The values of these variables are predictable to the verifier though they change dynamically during checksum computation.
5. The verification function sends the checksum result to the verifier.
6. The verifier verifies the checksum result as well as the computation time. If the verifier receives the expected checksum result within predicted time, the verifier trusts the attached peripheral. Otherwise, the verifier rejects the attached peripheral. At the same time, the peripheral is reset so that the pseudo-random values in data memory are cleaned, and the registers of the peripheral are restored to their default states.

After the attestation, since data memory is filled with pseudo-random values, the peripheral should be reset before being used. Additionally, during the reset, some of the registers should be restored to their default states. Otherwise, an attacker may get a chance to hide malicious data in the register space for future attacks. An attacker may store the malicious data in some IO data or control registers that are never used by the peripheral. For example, on a CY7C63923 microcontroller, there are 17 bytes of IO data registers that an attacker can use to hide malicious data for future attacks. In general, a power on reset is always enabled on a peripheral, during which all the registers are restored to their default values. A software-based reset function is also a solution if the function can prevent an attacker from hiding any malicious data in register space.

4.3   Verification Function

Due to the constrained computation and memory resources in the simple microcontrollers that are deployed on low-speed peripherals, the verification functions that are used in previous proposals cannot be deployed directly in SBAP. In this section, we detail the verification design in SBAP by describing the pseudo-random number generator, our design for filling data memory with pseudo-random values, and our checksum function.

Pseudo-Random Number Generator (PRNG). In the verification function, the PRNG is used for two purposes:

1. output PRNs to fill the data memory;
2. output PRNs to construct memory address to read in a pseudo-random fashion.

In previous proposals [2], T-functions [11] or RC4 [12] are used to output PRNs. However, on low speed peripherals, it is challenging to implement the same PRNGs efficiently due to constrained computation or memory resources. T-functions need a multiplication unit to generate PRNs efficiently. However, a hardware multiplication unit is not available in many low-speed microcontrollers that are used in peripherals. Software-based multiplication is too slow to be a viable option. For instance, on a CY7C63923 microcontroller [6], a software-based multiplication requires thousands of cycles to complete a 16-bit multiplication. An RC4-based PRNG outputs pseudo-random numbers through simple arithmetic and logical operations. However, RC4 requires at least 256 bytes of RAM, which consumes all memory resource on some microcontrollers (such as the CY7C63923). Laszlo et al. [13] propose several efficient PRNGs that are primarily designed for low speed embedded devices. The PRNGs proposed by Laszlo et al. only require simple addition, XOR, or shift operations and few memory resources to output PRNs efficiently. From the PRNGs that Laszlo et al. propose, we select a 2-stage PRNG in our SBAP design. Other PRNGs that have the same features are also potential choices for SBAP. The PRNG we select outputs PRNs as follows:

$$x[i + 1] = x[i - 1] + (x[i] \oplus rot(x[i - 1], 1)) \tag{1}$$

$\oplus$ is the logical XOR operation and *rot* is the left rotation shift operation. x is the output of this PRNG, a 32-bit long stage. The value of one stage is updated based on the values of the previous two stages in each iteration.

Filling Data Memory With Pseudo-Random Values. The verification function fills data memory in a pseudo-random fashion. Such a design is required to prevent an attacker from reserving one small block at the end of data memory to store malicious data, and then generating the PRNs that are expected to be in that small block of data memory on-the-fly when they are needed by the checksum routine. In our design, the verification function determines the data memory addresses to be filled based on the outputs of the PRNG. Each address is then filled using the XOR of two bytes of PRNG output. This prevents the attacker from generating the PRNs that are expected in data memory based on the values of existing PRNs in other locations in data memory, since only XOR results are stored in data memory. To make sure that all data memory is filled, the verifier can obtain the number of loop iterations upon which all data memory has been filled. This value is determined by simulating the filling procedure before sending the attestation request.

Checksum Function Design. The checksum function computes a fingerprint over the entire contents of both program memory and data memory. As in SWATT or ICE, the checksum is computed through a strongly ordered sequence of addition, XOR, and rotation shift operations. If the sequence of the operations is altered or some operations are removed, the checksum result will be different with a high probability. Also, the checksum function reads memory in a pseudo-random traversal. If the memory size is N bytes, each memory location is accessed at least once after $O(NlnN)$ memory read with a high probability [2]. The input to the checksum function is a 16-byte pseudo-random value, which is used to seed the PRNG (i.e., to provide stages $x[0]$ and $x[1]$) and to initialize an 8-byte checksum vector. The output of the checksum function is also an 8-byte checksum vector. Each byte of the checksum vector is called a checksum state. For each iteration of the checksum function, the value of one checksum state is updated based on the current memory contents, the pseudo-random value, and the values of other checksum states. Following is the pseudo code of one iteration of the checksum function:

```
/* C is the checksum vector, i is its current index. */
/* PRN is the pseudo-random number */
/* addr is the memory address */
   addr = PRN & MASK      /* Construct memory address */
/* update one checksum state */
   C[i] = C[i] + ( Mem[addr] xor C[(i-2) mod 8] )
   C[i] = left rotate one bit (C[i])
   i = (i + 1) mod 8             /* update the index i */
```

To optimize the computation time of the checksum, we unroll the checksum loop eight times and each time one checksum state is updated by either the contents of program memory or the contents of data memory, which can be adjusted based on the memory size proportion of each. For example, on a peripheral that has 8 KB of programmable Flash and 256-bytes of RAM, seven checksum states can be updated based on the contents of Flash memory while one checksum state can be updated based on the contents of RAM.

5   Implementation

In this section, we detail the implementation of SBAP on a wired Apple Aluminum Keyboard.

5.1   The Apple Aluminum Keyboard

The Apple Aluminum Keyboard connects to a computer via a USB interface. Inside the Apple Aluminum keyboard, a Cypress CY7C63923 microcontroller controls the keyboard matrix. During a firmware update, the firmware on the CY7C63923 microcontroller is updated. The Cypress CY7C63923 microcontroller belongs to the Cypress enCoReTM II family and is primarily designed for low-speed USB peripheral controllers, such as mice, keyboards, joysticks, game pads, barcode scanners, and remote controllers. The Cypress CY7C63923 is a Harvard Architecture, 8-bit programmable microcontroller with 256 bytes of RAM and 8 KB of Flash. Five registers on this microcontroller control the operations of its CPU. These five registers are the Flag register (F), Program Counter (PC), Accumulator Register (A), Stack Pointer (SP), and Index Register (X). PC is 16-bits in length, while all the other registers are 8-bits long. A and I are used during arithmetic or logical operations on this microcontroller.

5.2 Verification Function

Following a keyboard firmware update, the Flash memory from 0xe00 to 0x1300 (1280 bytes) is available free space, where we implement our verification function. Figure 2 shows the final memory layout of keyboard Flash memory. The verification function is located at addresses 0x0e00 – 0x1268 in the Flash memory. The Flash memory from 0x1268 to 0x1300 is filled with pseudo-random values. In the verification function, a 'Send Function' is the communication module that handles the attestation request from the verifier and returns checksum results through the USB channel to the verifier following checksum computation. Before the attestation, the contents of RAM is unpredictable to the verifier. Therefore, an 'Initial Function' sets the contents of data memory to a known state by filling the data memory with pseudo-random values (we fill data memory in a linear sequence instead of in a pseudo-random fashion as designed). The data memory from 0x18 to 0xff is filled with with pseudo-random values, while the data memory from 0x00 to 0x17 is used to store variables for the verification function. Also, the 'Initial Function' disables all interrupts on the CY7C63923 microcontroller, which prevents the contents of data memory from being modified by an interrupt call during checksum computation. A 'Checksum Function' is implemented, which computes a checksum over the entire contents of both program memory (Flash) and data memory (RAM). After attestation, we reset the Apple Aluminum Keyboard. A two-stage pseudo-random number generator (PRNG) is implemented in both the 'Initial Function' and 'Checksum Function'. The 8-byte nonce sent by the verifier is used to seed the PRNG in the 'Initial Function'. After filling RAM, the PRNG in 'Initial Function' outputs a 16-byte random number to serve as input to the 'Checksum Function', which is used to seed the PRNG in 'Checksum Function' and to initialize the 8-byte checksum vector. All of these functions are implemented in assembly. The two-stage PRNG is implemented using 23 assembly instructions. It outputs 4 bytes of pseudo-random values every 157 CPU cycles on the Apple Aluminum Keyboard. We unroll the checksum iteration eight times. Each time one checksum state is updated. The first seven checksum states are updated based on the content of Flash memory while the last checksum state is updated based on the content of RAM. Including the two-stage PRNG, 'Checksum Function' only requires 19.5 instructions and 133.5 CPU cycles on the average to update one checksum state on the Apple Aluminum Keyboard. Following is the assembly we implement to update one checksum state:

```
; [0x00] to [0x07] saves outputs of PRNG
; [0x08] to [0x0f] saves temp variables, such as counter
; [0x10] to [0x17] saves checksum states
; ROMX is the instruction to read flash memory
; CPU loads memory address from register A
; and register X when ROMX is executed
; the result of ROMX is saved in register A automatically by CPU
; Update checksum[0]
MOV X, [0x00]      ; read pseudo-random values
MOV A, [0X01]      ; to register X and A
AND A,0X1F         ; construct memory address
ROMX               ; read Flash memory, result is saved in A
XOR A, [0x16]      ; Mem[addr] xor checksum[6]
ADD [0x10], A      ; add previous checksum value
ASL [0x10]         ; left shift 1 bit
ADC [0x10],0x00    ; add flag (equal to rotation shift)
```

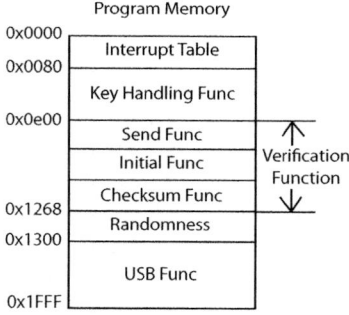

Fig. 2. Memory layout of program memory

6   Experimental Results

Verification Time. Figure 3 shows the verification time for 40 trials. In each trial, the verifier measures the entire verification time between sending a nonce to the Apple Aluminum Keyboard and receiving the checksum result from the keyboard. The average verification time of the 40 trials is 1706.77 ms while the standard deviation is only 0.18 ms.

USB Communication Overhead. In this experiment, the verifier first sends an attestation request to the Apple Aluminum Keyboard. Upon receiving a request from the verifier, the verification function on the Apple Aluminum Keyboard returns an 8-byte value to the verifier immediately without computing the checksum. To obtain accurate experimental results, the verifier measures the entire

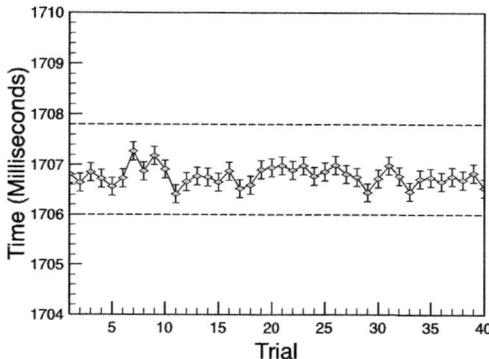

Fig. 3. Verification Time

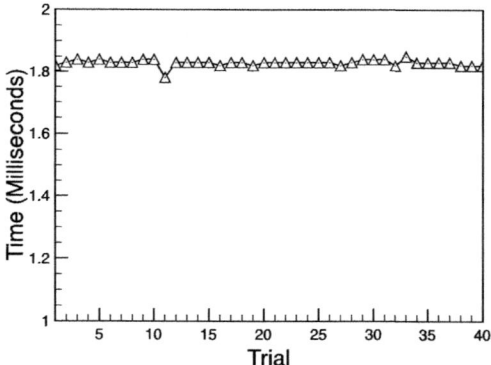

Fig. 4. USB Communication Overhead

time of 1000 runs of the communication in each trial. Figure 4 shows the average communication time of the 1000 runs in each trial. The average value of the USB communication overhead for all the experiments is 1.83 ms and the standard deviation is only 0.01 ms.

Analysis. The experimental results show that the verification procedure is very stable. As shown in Figure 3, the verification time for all 40 trials varies from about 1706 ms to about 1708 ms. An attacker cannot hide malicious code from an attestation unless the malicious code computes the correct checksum result with a computation overhead less than 3 ms, which is only about 0.2 percent of the verification time. This kind of attack is extremely challenging for the attacker since there is not any free space left in program or data memory. Also, the experimental results show that the communication overhead does not affect the detection of the computation overhead caused by malicious code, since the communication is also very efficient and stable. Another important result we obtain from the system evaluation is that SBAP is an efficient and realistic solution to solve the peripheral integrity verification problem. In our prototype, a verifier (a user) only needs to wait about 2 seconds for the entire verification procedure, which is acceptable if run in response to being connected to a host.

7   Discussion

To the best of our knowledge, there is no efficient attack against SBAP. One possible attack is that an attacker performs a compression attack or ROP attack and stores the malicious data or code in data memory, then generates the pseudo-random values that should be filled in data memory on-the-fly during the checksum computation. However, this attack causes large computational overhead due to the complexity of the PRNG. Another attack is that an attacker performs a memory copy attack by having a copy of the original code or pseudo-random values that should be in data memory in the register space of the microcontroller. This attack can be detected by the verifier since a memory copy attack causes a detectable computation overhead. In fact, there is very low likelihood that an attacker can perform this attack because there is not much register space available for an attacker to perform a memory copy attack on a peripheral. For example, we find that on a CY7C36923 microcontroller there are about 30 registers (30 bytes) that can be used for a memory copy attack by an attacker. However, once the attacker changes the checksum loop, the attacker needs hundreds of bytes memory to store the original copy of the checksum function. Finally, an attacker can hide some malicious data that can be used for future attacks in the register space of a peripheral. SBAP prevents this attack by resetting the peripheral after an attestation.

8   Related Work

Several software based attestation technologies on embedded devices have been proposed. Seshadri et al. propose SWATT [2], ICE, SCUBA [3], and SAKE [4], as discussed in Section 2. However, as discussed in this paper, it is challenging to implement ICE in resource-constrained embedded devices. To prevent adversary from hiding malicious code in the empty memory, Yang et al. suggest filling the available empty space with pseudo-random values [14]. However, a compression attack [5] can create free space by compressing the original code in program memory.

9   Conclusions and Future Work

We propose SBAP, a software-only solution to verify the firmware integrity of peripherals. SBAP verifies the contents of both program memory and data memory in a peripheral and detects malicious changes with high probability in the face of recently proposed attacks (e.g., a memory copy or memory substitution, a compression attack, and a ROP attack). We implement and evaluate SBAP on an Apple Aluminum Keyboard. One area of future work is to implement and evaluate SBAP on other peripherals, especially high-speed peripherals such as a network interface. The hardware architecture and configuration of a high-speed peripheral is different from those of a low speed peripheral. Therefore, there will likely be new challenges when we evaluate SBAP on a high-speed peripheral.

References

1. Chen, K.: Reversing and exploiting and apple firmware update. In: Black Hat. (July 2009)
2. Seshadri, A., Perrig, A., van Doorn, L., Khosla, P.: Swatt: Software-based attestation for embedded devices. In: Proceedings of the IEEE Symposium on Security and Privacy (2004)
3. Seshadri, A., Luk, M., Perrig, A., van Doorn, L., Khosla, P.: Scuba: Secure code update by attestation in sensor networks. In: ACM Workshop on Wireless Security (WiSe 2006) (2006)
4. Seshadri, A., Luk, M., Perrig, A., Van Doorn, L., Khosla, P.: Sake: Software attestation for key establishment in sensor networks. In: Nikoletseas, S.E., Chlebus, B.S., Johnson, D.B., Krishnamachari, B. (eds.) DCOSS 2008. LNCS, vol. 5067, pp. 372–385. Springer, Heidelberg (2008)
5. Castelluccia, C., Francillon, A., Perito, D., Soriente, C.: On the difficulty of software-based attestation of embedded devices. In: Proceedings of ACM Conference on Computer and Communications Security (CCS) (November 2009)
6. CYPRESS: Cypress encore ii low-speed usb peripheral controller (cy7c639xx)
7. Huffman, D.: A method for the construction of minimum redundancy codes. In: Proceedings of the IRE 40 (1962)
8. Buchanan, E., Roemer, R., Shacham, H., Savage, S.: When good instructions go bad: Generalizing return oriented programming to risc. In: Proceedings of the ACM Conference on Computer and Communications Security (CCS) (October 2008)
9. Hund, R., Holz, T., Freiling, F.: Return oriented rootkit: Bypassing kernel code integrity protection mechanisms. In: Proceedings of the 18th USENIX Security Symposium (August 2009)
10. Shacham, H.: The geometry of innocent flesh on the bone: Return into libc without function calls (on the x86). In: Proceedings of the ACM Conference on Computer and Communications Security (CCS) (2007)
11. Klimov, A., Shamir, A.: A new class of invertible mappings. In: Kaliski Jr., B.S., Koç, Ç.K., Paar, C. (eds.) CHES 2002. LNCS, vol. 2523, pp. 470–483. Springer, Heidelberg (2003)
12. wikipedia, http://en.wikipedia.org/wiki/rc4
13. Hars, L., Petruska, G.: Pseudo-random recursions: Small and fast pseudo-random number generator for embedded applications. EURASIP Journal on Embedded Systems (2007)
14. Yang, Y., Wang, X., Zhu, S., Cao, G.: Distributed software-based attestation for node compromise detection in sensor networks. In: Proceedings of IEEE International Symposium on Reliable Distributed Systems (2007)

Key Attestation from Trusted Execution Environments

Kari Kostiainen[1], Alexandra Dmitrienko[2], Jan-Erik Ekberg[1],
Ahmad-Reza Sadeghi[2], and N. Asokan[1]

[1] Nokia Research Center, Helsinki, Finland
{kari.ti.kostiainen,jan-erik.ekberg,n.asokan}@nokia.com
[2] Horst Görtz Institute for IT Security, Ruhr-University Bochum, Germany
alexandra.dmitrienko@rub.de, ahmad.sadeghi@trust.rub.de

Abstract. Credential platforms implemented on top of Trusted Execution Environments[1] (TrEEs) allow users to store and use their credentials, e.g., cryptographic keys or user passwords, securely. One important requirement for a TrEE-based credential platform is the ability to *attest* that a credential has been created and is kept within the TrEE. Credential properties, such as usage permissions, should be also attested. Existing attestation mechanisms are limited to attesting which applications outside the TrEE are authorized to use the credential. In this paper we describe a novel key attestation mechanism that allows attestation of both TrEE internal and external key usage permissions. We have implemented this attestation mechanism for mobile phones with M-Shield TrEE.

1 Introduction

Cryptographic protocols use credentials to authenticate users to various security sensitive services, including on-line banking and corporate network access. Traditional credential solutions fall short. Software credentials, such as passwords, are vulnerable to on-line fraud [4] and software attacks [12]. Dedicated hardware tokens, such as SIM-cards used for authentication in cellular networks, provide higher level of security, but are expensive to manufacture and deploy, and a separated hardware token is typically needed for each service, which forces users to have multiple tokens.

Recently, hardware-based commodity general-purpose Trusted Execution Environments (TrEEs), such as Trusted Platform Module (TPM) [17], JavaCard [6], M-Shield [14] and ARM TrustZone [1], have started to become widely deployed. TPMs are already available on many high-end personal computers while several mobile phone models are based on TrEEs like M-Shield and TrustZone. Credential platforms implemented on top of these TrEEs, including On-Board Credentials [7] and Trusted Execution Module [3], provide higher level of security compared to software credentials, and easier deployment and better usability compared to dedicated hardware tokens.

---

[1] A trusted EE is a computing environment where execution takes place as expected.

A. Acquisti, S.W. Smith, and A.-R. Sadeghi (Eds.): TRUST 2010, LNCS 6101, pp. 30–46, 2010.

Credential platforms [7,3] allow third-parties to implement their own "credential programs" that are executed within the TrEE in a controlled manner. These credential programs may generate new asymmetric keys within the TrEE. One important requirement for a credential platform is the ability to *attest* that a key has been created and is kept within the TrEE. Additionally, the attestation should prove key properties, such as usage permissions. A straightforward approach would be to limit the usage permissions of such keys only to the credential program that generated the key. However, in some cases the developer of the credential program should be able to authorize other credential programs to use the key. Then the credential platform should be able to enforce specified by the developer key usage permissions and to provide an attestation of these permissions to an external verifier.

The following use case provides an example: IT department of a company creates a credential program that generates an asymmetric key within the TrEE and performs (possibly proprietary) corporate network authentication operation. The employees of the company may use this credential program to create themselves a corporate network authentication credential and enroll it to the authentication system of the company. Later, the same IT department wants to issue another credential program to their employees; this time for email signing. The email signing credential program should be allowed to operate on the same, already enrolled key, to save the employees from enrolling multiple keys (typically each enrollment operation requires some user interaction). At the same time credential programs developed by other companies should not be able to use this key. The credential platform should provide an attestation of these key properties to the enrollment server of the company, so that only compliant keys are enrolled to the authentication system of the company.

Contribution. In this paper we describe an extension to On-board Credentials platform [7] that enables credential program developers and applications to define which other entities both within the TrEE and externally are authorized to use the asymmetric keys they generate and for which operations these keys may be used. We also describe a key attestation mechanism that provides evidence on internal and external key usage permissions to a verifier. To the best of our knowledge, no other credential platform provides similar functionality. We have implemented the key attestation mechanism and matching key property enforcements for Symbian mobile phones with M-Shield TrEE.

2   Requirements and Assumptions

Requirements. The main objective is to design a framework for a credential platform that allows credential programs, written by third-parties, to generate new asymmetric keys within the TrEE and to prove certain properties of these keys to any (correct) verifying entity. More concretely, the credential platform should support the following features:

R1: Key usage and usage permission definition. The *key creator*, i.e., the entity who generates a new key, should be able to define (i) key usage, i.e., allowed key operations (e.g., signing, decryption) and (ii) key usage permissions by defining entities, both internal and external to TrEE, which are authorized to use the key. In particular, the key creator should be able to authorize key usage for an entity whose exact identity is not known at the time of key generation (e.g., other credential programs written by the same credential developer in future).

R2: Key usage permissions update. The key creator should be able to update key usage permissions after the key has been generated. Such a possibility should be optional and be allowed or restricted at the time of key generation.

R3: Key usage enforcement. The credential platform should enforce key usage and key usage permissions defined by the key creator.

R4: Attestation coverage. The credential platform should provide an (externally) verifiable evidence/proof that the *subject key* was created and is accessible only within the TrEE. Additionally, the attestation should provide evidence on the following subject key properties: (i) key creator, (ii) key usage (signing, decryption), (iii) key usage permissions (entities which are authorized to use the key), and (iv) indication whether the key creator is allowed to update key usage permissions.

R5: Attestation unforgeability. The credential platform should only attest credentials it has generated itself and which are under its control. In other words, an attacker should not be able to fool the credential platform to attest keys generated by the attacker.

R6: Attestation freshness. In case the creator of the key is allowed to update key usage permissions (R2), an external verifier should not trust previous (old) attestations (the key creator might have changed key usage permissions after the old attestation was created). Thus, the key attestation mechanism should provide freshness guarantee.

Assumptions. We make some assumptions regarding underlying hardware and operating system level security:

A1: Trusted execution environment. We assume availability of a hardware-based TrEE that provides: (i) isolated code execution (by means of separation of processing and memory), (ii) secure storage (by ensuring integrity and confidentiality of persistent data), (iii) integrity protection of secure execution environment for credential programs.

A2: OS security. We assume existence of operating system level platform security framework with the following features: (i) availability of the secure storage for OS level applications/processes, (ii) access control on inter-process communication, (iii) integrity protection of security critical components, (iv) isolation of application/process execution, and (v) access control model that allows only trusted (e.g. signed) OS-level components to communicate with TrEE.

Note that these assumptions are reasonable in the context of our primary implementation platform: We utilize M-Shield [14] security hardware and Symbian [10] operating system. M-Shield provides all required features for TrEE. First, it supports secure boot[2] which ensures integrity of TrEE. Second, M-Shield supports secure code execution in hardware by means of separation of processing and memory. Third, it provides the secure storage by means of sealing all data with a device-specific symmetric key which is protected by the TrEE. The Symbian OS provides the application-specific secure storage and process execution isolation, and enforces control on inter-process communication via capability mechanism[3]. Moreover, the integrity of security critical OS components is ensured with secure boot that utilizes M-Shield hardware.

Adversary Model. We assume the following adversary capabilities:

AC1: Communication channel attacks. The adversary has access to communication channel between the attesting device and the external verifier and is able to eavesdrop, reply, relay or alert any network traffic.

AC2: End-point software attacks. The adversary can launch software attacks targeting the ObC platform. The execution of the OS-level components cannot be affected and OS-level secure storage cannot be accessed **if** the adversary is not able to compromise OS platform security at runtime. Assuming inability to compromise OS security framework may not be realistic due to the large size of modern operating systems and in Section 6 we discuss the implications of OS security compromise to our proposal.

AC3: End-point hardware attacks. The adversary can launch limited subset of hardware attacks on a circuit board level. We assume that the adversary is not able to tamper with chips and launch side-channel attacks, but can eavesdrop on the conductor wires connecting components or try to modify data or program code stored on the device (e.g., via programming interface).

3   On-Board Credentials Platform

In this section we give a brief overview of the On-board Credentials (ObC) platform. Figure 1 describes the parts of the ObC platform architecture that are relevant to key usage control and attestation. For more detailed description of the ObC platform see [7].

Interpreter. The core of the ObC platform is a trusted Interpreter that can be executed within the TrEE. The trust on the Interpreter can be based on code signing, i.e., only authorized code is allowed to be executed within the TrEE. Interpreter provides a virtualized environment where "credential programs", i.e., scripts developed by untrusted third-parties, can be executed. When a credential program is executed, the Interpreter isolates it from secrets that are stored within the TrEE and from the execution of other credential programs.

---

[2] Secure boot means a system terminates the boot process in case the integrity check of a component to be loaded fails [5].

[3] A capability is an access token that corresponds to access permissions[10].

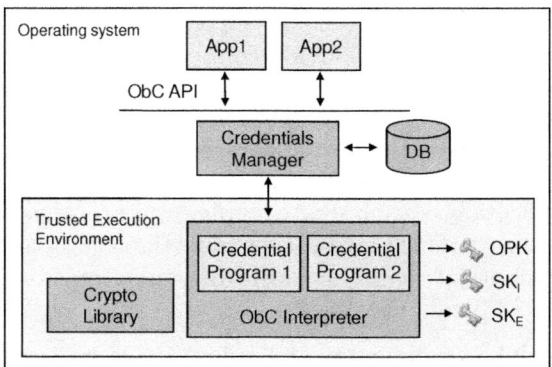

Fig. 1. On-board Credential architecture

The Interpreter provides a sealing[4]/unsealing function for ObC programs, which can be used to protect secret data stored persistently outside the TrEE. Additionally, the Interpreter provides common cryptographic primitives, such as encryption, decryption and hash functions, for credential program developers. The credential programs are written using (a subset of) Lua scripting language [8] or in assembler.

The ObC platform supports three types of credentials: (1) credential programs that operate on symmetric secrets provisioned by an external provisioner, (2) credentials programs that locally generate and operate on asymmetric keys, and (3) asymmetric keys locally generated by applications without involvement of credential programs. In this paper we focus on two latter credential types.

The ObC platform supports a concept of "credential families". A family is defined by a credential provisioner (full description of credential provisioning and families can be found in [7]). Credential programs belonging to the same family may share sealed and persistently stored data.

Credential Manager. The ObC platform includes a trusted operating system level component called Credentials Manager *CM*. The trust in *CM* can be provided, e.g., based on secure boot. *CM* provides an API for third-party developed applications. Using the API the applications can execute credential programs, and create and use new asymmetric keys. *CM* maintains a database, in which credentials and key properties are stored. *CM* also enforces that only authorized applications are allowed to use credentials.

Device Keys. The ObC platform uses three device specific keys (which are only accessible within the TrEE) for key generation and attestation:

- **ObC platform key** (*OPK*) is a symmetric device key. The Interpreter uses *OPK* for sealing/unsealing function.

---

[4] Protecting an object so that only a certain set of OS-level or TrEE-level entities can access or use it.

- **Internal device key** (PK_I, SK_I) is an asymmetric device key. The public part of this key is certified as an "internal device key" by the device manufacturer. The Interpreter uses this key only to sign data that originates from within the TrEE, or data whose semantics or structure it can verify.
- **External device key** (PK_E, SK_E) is an asymmetric device key. The public part of this key is certified as an "external device key" by the device manufacturer. The Interpreter uses this key to sign data that originates from outside the TrEE. Using secure boot and OS-level security framework, we limit the use of the external device key to *CM* only.

4   Key Attestation Design

Key attestation protocols involve the following entities: (i) attestor A, i.e., ObC platform which attests to properties of the locally generated *subject* key, (ii) the platform manufacturer M which certifies device specific keys of A, (iii) a server S which aims to get assurance regarding subject key properties, and (iv) certification authority *CA* which may issue subject key certificate.

We utilize the following notations: A signature scheme consists of algorithms (GenKey(), Sign(), Verify()). Here $(SK, PK) \leftarrow$ GenKey() is the key generation algorithm that outputs signing key (private key) SK, and the corresponding verification key (public key) PK, $\sigma \leftarrow$ Sign(SK, m) is the signature algorithm on message m which outputs a signature σ, and $ind \leftarrow$ Verify(PK, σ, m) is the signature verification algorithm with $ind \in \{0, 1\}$.

An authenticated encryption[5] scheme consist of algorithms (Enc(), Dec()). Here $c \leftarrow$ Enc(K, m) is the encryption algorithm on a message m using K as the symmetric key which outputs an encrypted message c, and $(ind, m) \leftarrow$ Dec(K, c) is the decryption algorithm on c using K as the symmetric key with $ind \in \{0, 1\}$ indicating integrity of c.

A hash algorithm is denoted by H().

4.1   Key Generation by Credential Programs

Key generation by a credential program is illustrated in Figure 2. We describe the main steps in the following:

Step 1: A credential program requests the Interpreter to generate the subject key. It may authorize other credential programs to use this key in two ways:

(i) **Credential Program Identifiers** are used to define zero or more identifiers of credential programs that are authorized to use the generated key. In ObC platform, credential programs are identified by the hash of the program code; (ii) **Family Identifiers** are used to define zero or more identifiers of credential families that are authorized to use the generated key. Credential families are

---

[5] We use authenticated encryption AES-EAX for various needs including sealing/unsealing operations to keep code and memory footprint minimal.

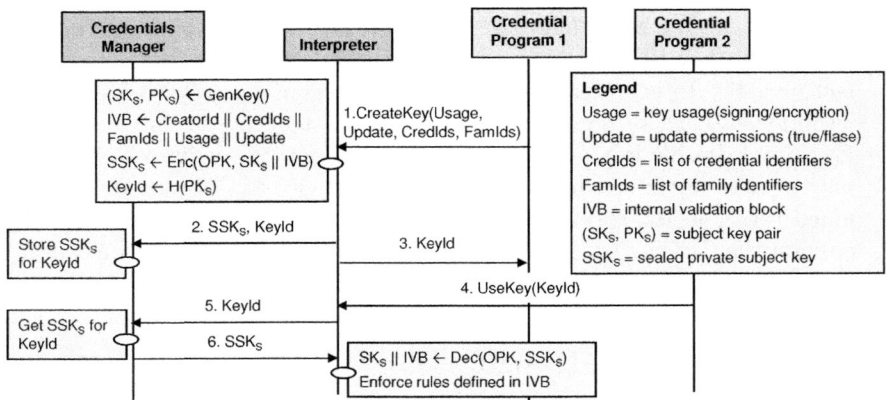

Fig. 2. Key generation by a credential program

identified by the hash of family key[6]. The credential program also defines key usage and whether key usage permissions are allowed to be updated.

Step 2: The Interpreter generates a new subject key (SK_S, PK_S) and creates a structure called *internal validation block* (IVB). IVB contains (i) the identifier *CreatorId* of the credential program that created the key, (ii) a list of credential program identifiers *CredIds*; (iii) a list of family identifiers *FamIds*, (iv) an indication whether credential program identifiers and family identifiers may be updated by the key creator *Update* and (v) the allowed key operations *Usage*. The Interpreter seals the private part of the subject key SK_S and IVB using platform key OPK. Then it derives the key identifier *KeyId* by hashing the public key PK_S. The resulting sealed key SSK_S and *KeyId* are stored on the operating system side by CM.

Step 3: The key identifier *KeyId* is returned to the credential program that may, e.g., export it to the application that triggered the credential program execution, so that the same key can be used later (from the same or another credential program).

Steps 4-6: The next time the key is used, the Interpreter requests, and obtains the sealed key from CM on operating system side based on *KeyId*, and unseals it using OPK. The Interpreter unseals SSK_S and verifies IVB components and performs the requested key operation only if the key usage is allowed, and the calling credential program is either the creator of the key or its identifier, or family is listed as authorized to use the key.

4.2   Key Generation by Applications

The Credentials Manager CM provides an API for creating and using asymmetric keys directly from applications. Figure 3 illustrates key generation by an application.

---

[6] Family key is used in credential provisioning.

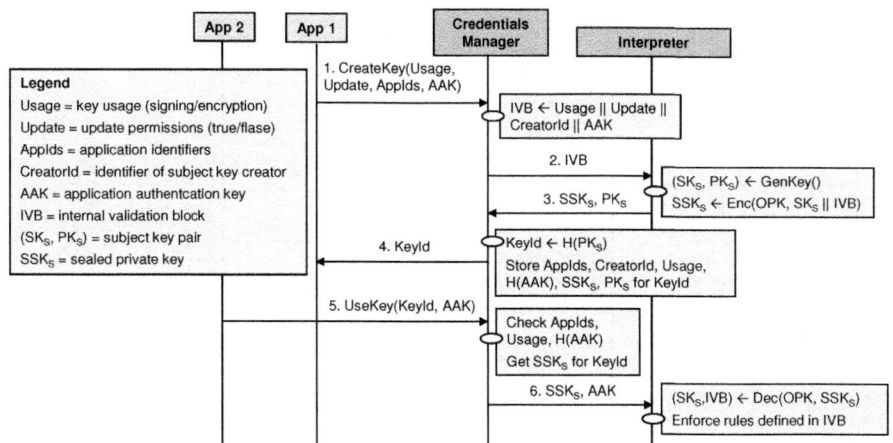

Fig. 3. Key generation by an application

Step 1: An application calls the key creation function over the API provided by *CM*. The application may authorize other applications to use the generated key in two ways: (i) to define zero or more **application identifiers**. The listed applications are permitted to use the key. This method requires that the underlying OS can provide reliable information about the identity of the calling application to *CM*[7]; (ii) to define that an authorization token called **application authentication key** (AAK) is required to use the key. In such a case the generated key may be only used if the correct AAK is provided by the application to *CM*. AAK may be shared among several applications.

When an application creates a new key, *CM* constructs *IVB*. Application identifiers *AppIds* are not included in *IVB*, since those cannot be reliably verified within the TrEE. If AAK is used, it is included in *IVB* together with the key usage *Usage*, the identity of the application that generated the key *CreatorId* and a flag *Update* that defines whether key usage permissions can be updated.

Step 2: *CM* loads *IVB* to the TrEE, in which the Interpreter generates the subject key (SK_S, PK_S), and seals the private part together with *IVB* to SSK_S.

Steps 3-4: PK_S and SSK_S are returned to *CM*. *CM* stores them together with hash of AAK, the list of application identifiers *AppIds*, the key creator *CreatorId*, and the key usage *Usage*. A key identifier *KeyId* is returned to the application.

Steps 5-6: When the same or another application requests to use the subject key, *CM* verifies the identifier of the calling application with respect to locally stored *CreatorId* and *AppIds*. *CM* also checks key usage *Usage* and hash of AAK if needed. If these checks pass, *CM* loads the sealed private key SSK_S

---

[7] For example, in Symbian OS each process has a unique identifier which can be verified for each inter-process function call.

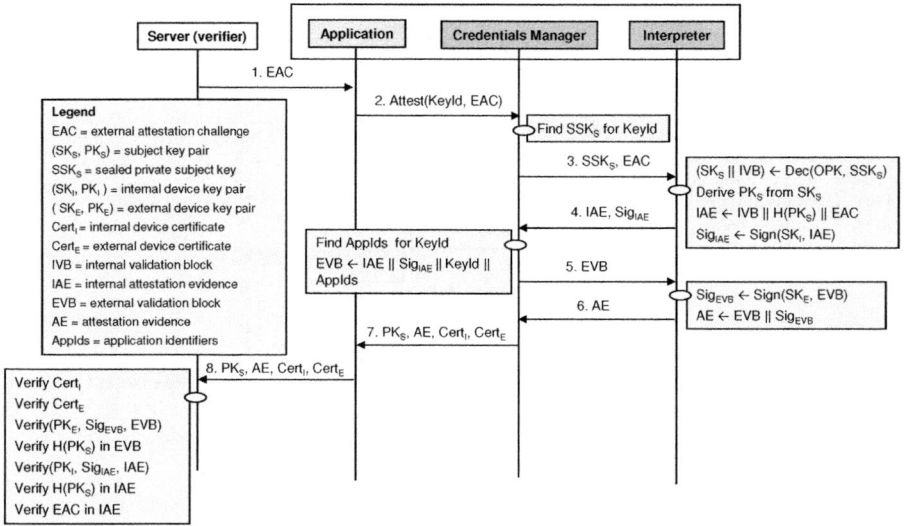

Fig. 4. Interactive key attestation

and possible AAK to the TrEE in which the Interpreter unseals the key and checks that AAK matches the one defined in IVB (if used), and that key usage is allowed before performing the private key operation.

4.3   Interactive Key Attestation

The attestation process must be interactive in case the key creator is authorized to update key usage permissions during key life time (as required by the objective (R2)). In interactive scenario, the attestation evidence must be verified by the server S. Figure 4 illustrates this attestation protocol.

Steps 1-2: S picks a random nonce called *external attestation challenge* (EAC) and sends it to an application on the target device. The application identifies the subject key to attest (typically based on information originating from S) and triggers the attestation. CM retrieves the sealed subject key SSK_S from local storage.

Steps 3-4: CM loads SSK_S and EAC to TrEE. Inside the TrEE the Interpreter first unseals SSK_S, derives PK_S from SK_S[8] and then creates an *internal attestation evidence* (IAE). IAE is a concatenation of IVB, hash $H(PK_S)$ of a subject public key and EAC. Then IAE is signed using the internal device key SK_I. The Interpreter returns IAE and signature Sig_{IAE} to CM.

Steps 5-6: CM constructs an *external validation block* EVB. EVB is a concatenation of IAE, Sig_{IAE}, $KeyId$ (hash of public subject key $H(PK_S)$), and a list of

---
[8] PK_S can be derived from SK_S efficiently in our implementation.

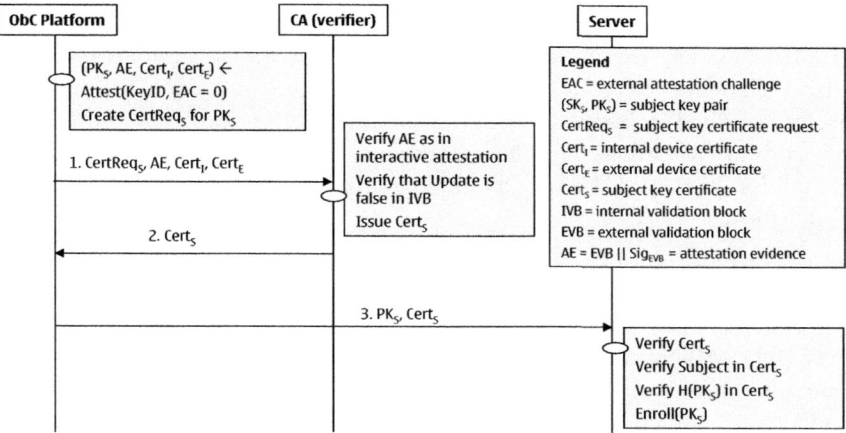

Fig. 5. Non-interactive key attestation

application identifiers *AppIds*. *CM* loads *EVB* to TrEE in which the Interpreter signs it using the external device key SK_E. The resulting *attestation evidence AE* is sent back to *CM*.

Steps 7-8: *CM* returns *AE* together with the subject public key PK_S and certificates of both internal and external device keys (*Cert_I*, *Cert_E*) to the application. The application forwards this data to the server S which verifies the following: (i) *AE* has been signed with a key that has been certified as an external device key by a trusted authority, and (ii) the public key hash in *EVB* matches the received subject public key PK_S. If these two conditions hold, S can parse the external key usage permissions and based on that determine which OS level key usage permissions are enforced by *CM*.

To verify the internal attestation, S checks that (i) *IAE* contains signature made with a key that has been certified as internal device key, (ii) the public key hash inside *IAE* matches the received subject public key, and (iii) *EAC* inside *IAE* matches the one picked by S earlier. If these three conditions hold, S can determine from *IVB* the key usage permissions enforced by the Interpreter within the TrEE.

4.4 Non-interactive Key Attestation

Non-interactive key attestation can be used when key usage permissions are not allowed to be updated and freshness guarantee is not needed. Figure 5 depicts non-interactive attestation. In this scenario a certification authority *CA* validates the attestation evidence and issues a subject key certificate that other servers can verify. The main steps of the protocol are described below:

Steps 1-2: The credential platform triggers attestation with fixed challenge (e.g., $EAC = 0$). *CM* and Interpreter create the attestation evidence as in interactive key attestation. *CM* generates also a certificate request containing the public part of subject public key, subject identity and proof-of-possession of the subject key[9]. The certificate request, attestation evidence and internal and external device key certificates are submitted to *CA*. *CA* validates *AE* using the fixed challenge (verification is performed in the same way as in interactive scenario described in Section 4.3). Additionally, *CA* verifies that the key usage permissions are not allowed to be updated, i.e., the field *Update* in *IVB* structure is set to false. Finally, *CA* issues a subject certificate *Cert$_S$* and returns it to the ObC platform.

Step 3: The ObC platform submits the key enrollment request to *S*. The request includes *PK$_S$* and *Cert$_S$*. *S* validates *Cert$_S$*, and if it is correct, enrolls the subject key. In this scenario, *S* relies on *CA* to verify the attestation evidence. However, since X.509 certificates do not have standard place to indicate if the attestation evidence has been validated by *CA*, *S* must have out of band knowledge that the particular *CA* always validates the attestation evidence before the public key certificate is issued.

Another approach for non-interactive attestation assumes that *CA* issues public key certificate omitting attestation evidence validation, then attestation evidence is incorporated into subject key certificate. The TCG SKAE [16] defines a X.509 certificate extension for this purpose. In this approach verification of the attestation evidence is left for the server.

Note, that in both scenarios communication between ObC platform and *CA* must be secured so that *CA* can associate the submitted public key with the correct authorizations allowed for the submitter.

5   Implementation

We have implemented the described attestation mechanism for Nokia N96 mobile phone with M-Shield TrEE. In M-Shield architecture trusted (signed) code can be executed within the TrEE isolated from the rest of the system. The trusted code is implemented as so called "protected applications" (PAs) in C. The maximum size of each PA is very limited (in terms of both implementation footprint and runtime memory) and for this reason we had to implement the Interpreter, key generation and attestation functionality as three separate PAs: (i) Interpreter PA, (ii) RSA PA and (iii) Attestation PA. Because in M-Shield architecture the communication between different PA invocations must be mediated by an operating system level component (*CM* in our architecture), the data that is transfered from one PA to another one must be protected.

Interpreter PA is the component that handles credential program execution. When Interpreter PA encounters key creation macro it constructs *IVB*, creates a fresh session key and seals *IVB* and the current state of the program execution using the session key. The Interpreter PA saves the session key to volatile secure memory inside the TrEE and returns *IVB* and program state in sealed format.

CM on the OS side saves sealed program execution state temporarily and loads RSA PA to the TrEE together with the sealed *IVB*. RSA PA unseals *IVB*,

---

[9] E.g., a signature created using the subject key within the TrEE.

generates a new RSA key and seals *IVB* and private part of the generated key using *OPK* for future use. RSA PA calculates key identifier (hash of public key) and returns this sealed with the session key. *CM* loads Interpreter PA to TrEE together with the sealed key identifier and sealed program execution state. The Interpreter PA can unseal the state and the key identifier using the session key and continue credential program execution.

Asymmetric key operations are handled in similar fashion. When Interpreter PA encounters key operation in credential program execution it seals key operation parameters and current state with the session key. *CM* triggers RSA PA which unseals parameters, performs the operation and seals the results for Interpreter PA. Key attestation and application triggered key operations are handled by Attestation PA which requires no communication with other PAs.

The operating system side *CM* component is implemented as a Symbian OS server in C++. Using Symbian OS platform security framework *CM* can check unique identifier of calling application for each function call. *CM* maintains a database in its private directory which is not accessible by other applications (except few trusted system components).

In our implementation, the device keys (internal and external) are generated when the credential platform is first taken into use. The keys are created within the TrEE and sealed using *OPK* for storage in *CM* database. When the device keys are created, a key type *tag* is included to the seal. With the tag, the key type can be determined when the key is later unsealed inside the TrEE.

In our implementation, the internal validation block (*IVB*) is a binary structure with fixed format, to keep the TrEE side implementation minimal. *IVB* can contain up to five identifiers which are used to define credential programs, families and *AAK*. A bitfield in the header defines the types of these identifiers. *IVB* header also defines the key creator, usage and whether usage permission can be updated. We have implemented the external validation block using ASN.1 formatting (similar to TCG SKAE [16]) to make external attestation flexible and easy to implement. For non-interactive attestation our *CM* implementation can generate standard X.509 certificate requests into which the attestation evidence is included as an extension.

We have not implemented a mechanism to update key usage permissions. Currently, key usage permissions are always defined as unchangeable at the time of key generation.

6   Security Analysis

Based on the assumptions on the underlying hardware platform (A1) and on the OS security framework (A2) (see Section 2), in the following we will give an informal security analysis of our proposal.

Our design and implementation provide key usage definition (R1) for keys generated both from within or outside the TrEE. The internal key usage permissions are defined in terms of credential program and family identifiers. The external key usage permissions are defined in terms of application identifiers and by means of applying the application authentication tokens. Allowed key operations are defined in *Usage*.

Key usage enforcement (R3) is provided in the following way: the allowed key operations *Usage* and internal usage permissions are enforced by the trusted Interpreter. Note that the Interpreter resides within TrEE. Moreover, the underlying hardware provides secure execution. Hence, the integrity of the Intepreter is ensured both statically and in run-time.

In case of external usage permissions, rules defined through application identifiers are enforced by CM. Note that CM is a trusted OS-level component, and hence its integrity is provided based on the assumptions regarding OS security framework, so that CM can enforce the usage permission rules specified for each credential., e.g., in EVB.

Key usage permissions update (R2) can be supported, because the key creator can be always identified via key creator identity *CreatorId* included into *IVB*. Also, the attestation evidence creation is not bound to time of the key generation, thus it can reflect changes made during key life time. Possible solutions for the key usage permissions update mechanism are discussed in Appendix B..

Attestation coverage (R4) is simply realized by including all required statements into the attestation evidence. Attestation unforgeability (R5) is ensured through the use of the device keys for attestation those are protected by the TrEE and their genuineness is certified by the trusted device manufacturer. Attestation freshness (R6) is guaranteed with inclusion of the challenge in the internal attestation evidence.

Discussion on Run-Time Compromise. As mentioned in Section 2, we cannot generally assume that the adversary cannot compromise OS-level security framework. In this section we discuss implications of OS compromise to our solution.

First, we consider credential program generated keys. As shown in Figure 2, OS-level components including CM do not have access to the key properties in unsealed form during key generation process. A compromised CM is able to forge an external attestation for credential program generated key with false application level usage permissions, but it does not allow CM to use the key since the Interpreter inside the TrEE will deny the key operation invoked by the CM for a key generated by a credential program. Internal attestation can be trusted, since it is performed internally by Interpreter within the TrEE. Also, a malicious CM is not able to invoke SK_I usage to sign forged IVB since the Interpreter will not use this key to sign data that originates outside the TrEE. The external attestation evidence cannot impersonate the internal attestation evidence since they are signed with different keys, SK_E and SK_I respectively.

Next, we consider application created keys. Again, a compromised CM is able to forge external attestation evidence and specify usage permissions for false OS-level applications. If the key usage permissions are defined in terms of application identifiers, a compromised CM can allow key usage for unauthorized applications. If the key usage permissions are defined in terms of AAK a compromised CM cannot use the key without knowledge of valid AAK. However, one should note that if the adversary is able to compromise *CM* he most likely can read *AAK* from the storage of the authorized application as well, and thus use the key. Internal attestation can be trusted for application generated keys, only if *CM* has been compromised *after* the key was generated. If *CM* was compromised before key generation, even internal attestation cannot be trusted for application generated keys.

As a conclusion, our design and implementation can only partly address the problem of runtime compromise of OS-level security framework[10]. Thus in real life scenarios the verifier should take into account the discussed arguments and define the trust to the attestation created by the ObC platform according to its security policy.

7 Related Work

Trusted Computing Group (TCG) [15] has specified a mechanism called Subject Key Attestation Evidence (SKAE) [16] for attesting TPM generated asymmetric keys. In short, a SKAE attestation contains the public part of the attested subject key and the platform configuration (in terms of platform configuration register values) under which the subject key can be used, signed with a certified and device-specific attestation identity key. A typical use of SKAE is to include it as an extension to a certificate request; the SKAE extension proves to the certificate authority that the subject key was created and is kept within a TPM and specifies the application(s) that can use the key by defining the platform configuration.

The TCG SKAE is limited to attesting which applications *outside* the TrEE are allowed to use the attested subject key whereas our attestation mechanism provides evidence on TrEE-internal key usage permissions as well. Moreover, the TCG SKAE is a non-interactive mechanism, and thus not applicable to attesting keys which usage setting may be updated (R2).

The work closest to ours is "outbound authentication" (OA) architecture [13] for IBM 4758 programmable secure coprocessors. IBM 4758 is TrEE with layered security architecture: layers 0-2 boot up the coprocessor and run an operating system. Applications originating from different (possibly mutually distrusting) sources can be loaded to the coprocessor and executed on layer 3. External parties should be able to verify which of the applications within the coprocessor performed certain operation. The OA architecture uses certificate chaining to achieve this. Layer 0 has a root key (certified by a trusted authority) which is used to certify higher layers. When an application is executed, the operating system layer creates a key for the application and certifies this key. The application may authenticate itself to an external verifier using its key.

---

[10] It should be noted that handling runtime compromise is still an open research problem and the existing solutions such as Runtime Integrity Monitors either require extra hardware support (e.g., [9]) or utilize virtualization technology to run the system under inspection within a virtual machine (e.g., [2]) which is hard affordable for mobile devices due to the corresponding overhead.

Our attestation mechanism and OA architecture address essentially the same problem — providing evidence on which entity within a TrEE is allowed to access a certain key. However, our attestation mechanism supports certain features that fall outside the scope of OA. First, the ObC architecture supports sharing of keys between entities within the TrEE and our attestation mechanism provides evidence on this in terms of credential programs and family identifiers. Second, our attestation mechanism provides also evidence on TrEE external access.

KeyGen2 [11] is a proposal for provisioning of asymmetric keys to devices, such as mobile phones. In KeyGen2 asymmetric keys are created inside the TrEE of the client device. To enroll a key to a server, the client creates an attestation of the key by signing it with a device key. To distinguish this attestation signature from other signatures made with the *same* device key, special padding (reserved for this use only) is applied.

The key attestation in KeyGen2 does not include information about software that is authorized to use the key neither in terms of platform configuration (as it is done in the TCG SKAE), nor in form of TrEE internal key usage permissions (as in our proposal). The attestation only proves that the to-be-enrolled key was created and is kept within the TrEE.

8   Conclusion

In this paper we have described a key attestation mechanism that allows a platform to attest to a verifier key usage permissions and properties of both (internal) programs residing in a Trusted Execution Environment (TrEE) as well as OS-side applications outside the TrEE. We have implemented this key attestation mechanism and matching local enforcements as an extension to the existing on-board Credentials platforms for mobile phones based on M-Shield secure hardware. To the best of our knowledge, this is the first credential platform that efficiently provides such an enhanced attestation functionality.

References

1. ARM. Trustzone technology overview (2009), http://www.arm.com/products/security/trustzone/index.html
2. Baiardi, F., Cilea, D., Sgandurra, D., Ceccarelli, F.: Measuring semantic integrity for remote attestation. In: Chen, L., Mitchell, C.J., Martin, A. (eds.) Trust 2009. LNCS, vol. 5471, pp. 81–100. Springer, Heidelberg (2009)
3. Costan, V., Sarmenta, L.F.G., van Dijk, M., Devadas, S.: The trusted execution module: Commodity general-purpose trusted computing. In: Grimaud, G., Standaert, F.-X. (eds.) CARDIS 2008. LNCS, vol. 5189, pp. 133–148. Springer, Heidelberg (2008), http://people.csail.mit.edu/devadas/pubs/cardis08tem.pdf
4. Internet Crime Complaint Center. Internet crime report (2008), http://www.ic3.gov/media/annualreport/2008_IC3Report.pdf
5. Itoi, N., Arbaugh, W.A., Pollack, S.J., Reeves, D.M.: Personal secure booting. In: Varadharajan, V., Mu, Y. (eds.) ACISP 2001. LNCS, vol. 2119, pp. 130–144. Springer, Heidelberg (2001)

6. JavaCard Technology, http://java.sun.com/products/javacard/
7. Kostiainen, K., Ekberg, J.-E., Asokan, N., Rantala, A.: On-board credentials with open provisioning. In: Proc. of ACM Symposium on Information, Computer & Communications Security, ASIACCS 2009 (2009)
8. The Programming Language Lua, http://www.lua.org/
9. Petroni Jr., N.L., Fraser, T., Molina, J., Arbaugh, W.A.: Copilot - a coprocessor-based kernel runtime integrity monitor. In: Proceedings of the 13th USENIX Security Symposium, August 2004, pp. 179–194. USENIX (2004)
10. Nokia. Symbian OS platform security, http://www.forum.nokia.com/Technology_Topics/Device_Platforms/S60/Platform_Security/
11. Rundgren, A.: Subject key attestation in keygen2 (2009), http://webpki.org/papers/keygen2/keygen2-key-attestation-1.pdf
12. SANS Institute. SANS Top-20 2007 Security Risks (November 2008), http://www.sans.org/top20/2007/top20.pdf
13. Smith, S.W.: Outbound authentication for programmable secure coprocessors. International Journal of Information Security 3, 28–41 (2004)
14. Srage, J., Azema, J.: M-Shield mobile security technology, TI White paper (2005), http://focus.ti.com/pdfs/wtbu/ti_mshield_whitepaper.pdf
15. Trusted Computing Group, https://www.trustedcomputinggroup.org/home
16. TCG Infrastructure Workgroup. Subject Key Attestation Evidence Extension Specification Version 1.0 Revision 7 (June 2005), https://www.trustedcomputinggroup.org/specs/IWG/
17. Trusted Platform Module (TPM) Specifications, https://www.trustedcomputinggroup.org/specs/TPM/

Appendix A.   Device Key Alternatives

The key attestation mechanism described in the paper requires two device keys: Internal device key is used to sign internal attestation and external device key is used to sign external attestation. Both of them must be certified by a trusted authority, such as the device manufacturer. The device keys can be created either during device manufacturing or when the credential platform is first taken into use. In the latter case, the device key certification is an on-line protocol between the TrEE and the device manufacturer – we assume that the device manufacturer may authenticate its own TrEEs in reliable fashion.

Creating asymmetric keys is a time consuming process on TrEEs with limited resources. Thus, the need to have two certified device keys increases the device manufacturing time and cost, or alternatively decreases credential platform installation user experience. In this appendix we discuss two alternative approaches to device key creation and certification to address this problem.

Single Device Key. Instead of creating two separate device keys, a single device key could be used for signing both internal and external attestations. In such a case, signatures made over IVB and EVB should be distinguishable from each other to prevent EVB to be interpreted as IVB by the verifier. To distinguish different type of signatures made with the same key, one of the following two techniques could be applied.

First, the Interpreter could apply distinguishable formatting to IVB and EVB before signing them. The Interpreter could, e.g., concatenate a tag to these elements before signing. If such an approach were used, the device key should never sign anything else except an attestation evidence, otherwise the specific formatting can be forged. Thus, such a solution does not scale well since may require new device keys for other operations.

Second, the signatures can be made distinguishable by applying different padding schemes or hashing algorithm as proposed in [11]. For example a unique padding could be used for internal attestation signatures, another unique padding for external attestation signatures, and standard padding could be used for normal signatures. The disadvantage of this approach is that the external verifier is required to understand these non-standard padding schemes which can be an obstacle for wide scale deployment.

Device Key Chaining. Another alternative would be to use certificate chaining. In this approach two separate device keys would be used for signing the attestations, but the device manufacturer would have to certify only *one* device key which in turn could certify the second needed device key locally on the platform. The benefit of such an approach is that only one device key has to be created when the device is manufactured or when the credential platform is taken into use. The second device key can be generated and certified later, e.g., when the device is in idle state, but before the device is used for attestation. This approach would also scale better, if more than two device keys are needed.

Appendix B.   Key Usage Permissions Update

The task of updating key usage permissions can be seen as consisting of two subtasks: (i) to grant usage rights to new credential programs and applications; (ii) to revoke usage rights granted before.

One alternative would be to provide the key creator the possibility to do both, to grant and to revoke key usage permissions. In this way, lists of credential programs and applications authorized to use the key may be freely modified by the key creator.

Another alternative would be to provide the key creator the only possibility to revoke key usage permissions. In this way, identities of credential programs and applications may be excluded from the lists defined before, but new identities may not be added. In this situation, key usage permissions can be granted via utilization of already available mechanisms: Family paradigm can be used to grant usage permissions to additional credential programs, and application authentication token can be used to grant usage permissions to new applications.

The former design solution provides better flexibility, since family identifiers and application tokens can be added and updated by the key creator. The latter design solution is less flexible, but it does not require to ensure attestation freshness. Indeed, if the old attestation is satisfactory for the verifier, the new one would be also for sure accepted because it has reduced list of authorized entities compare to the old version. When freshness is not required, the attestation could be always performed in non-interactive manner, that is an advantage of this scheme.

Anonymous Authentication with TLS and DAA*

Emanuele Cesena[1], Hans Löhr[2,**], Gianluca Ramunno[1],
Ahmad-Reza Sadeghi[2,**], and Davide Vernizzi[1]

[1] Dip. di Automatica e Informatica – Politecnico di Torino, Italy
{emanuele.cesena,gianluca.ramunno,davide.vernizzi}@polito.it
[2] Horst Görtz Institute for IT Security – Ruhr-University Bochum, Germany
{hans.loehr,ahmad.sadeghi}@trust.rub.de

Abstract. Anonymous credential systems provide privacy-preserving authentication solutions for accessing services and resources. In these systems, copying and sharing credentials can be a serious issue. As this cannot be prevented in software alone, these problems form a major obstacle for the use of fully anonymous authentication systems in practice. In this paper, we propose a solution for anonymous authentication that is based on a hardware security module to prevent sharing of credentials. Our protocols are based on the standard protocols *Transport Layer Security (TLS)* and *Direct Anonymous Attestation (DAA)*. We present a detailed description and a reference implementation of our approach based on a *Trusted Platform Module (TPM)* as hardware security module. Moreover, we discuss drawbacks and alternatives, and provide a pure software implementation to compare with our TPM-based approach.

1 Introduction

Anonymous authentication (see, e.g., [13,26,22,21]) is a widely studied cryptographic concept that allows to authenticate users (e.g., check authorization to access a service) while maintaining their privacy (i.e., their identities are not disclosed). As an application scenario, consider an online subscription service where users can access contents, such as a service for real-time information about stock market prices or news. Service provider and users have different objectives, which intuitively may seem to be in conflict: The service provider requires that only subscribed users access the service; users desire to be anonymous because access details are personal and sensitive information (e.g., which stocks they are interested in). Anonymous authentication resolves this tension by providing both authentication (provider's requirement), and user privacy.

A particularly powerful means for anonymous authentication are anonymous credential systems (see, e.g., [13,10]): Users obtain credentials from an issuer and can use them to access (online) services from different providers, but their communication remains unlinkable even in case the providers collude with the

---

* Full version available at http://security.polito.it/tc/daa/anon_auth_full.pdf
** Partially supported by the European projects CACE (IP) and ECRYPT2 (NoE).

A. Acquisti, S.W. Smith, and A.-R. Sadeghi (Eds.): TRUST 2010, LNCS 6101, pp. 47–62, 2010.
© Springer-Verlag Berlin Heidelberg 2010

issuer. Basing on such systems, it is possible to extend classical authentication primitives to take into account the privacy aspects of the users.

Unfortunately, the direct application of fully anonymous credential systems in practice, e.g., for online subscription services, poses a serious problem: Dishonest users can share their credentials with others, hence allowing a potentially very large group of (actually unauthorized) users to access the service. With a fully anonymous solution implemented in software, this cannot be prevented, because users can just copy all necessary authentication data (i.e., the credential).

To some extent, this threat can be mitigated by using pseudonyms instead of full anonymity: The service provider might detect if a pseudonym is used too often within a short period of time and thus conclude that the credential has been shared. As an alternative, a valuable secret (e.g., a key that is important to the user) can be embedded into the credential such that users have to share this secret in order to share credentials. For this to work as intended, all users of the system need to have such a valuable secret that they do not want to share.

As we elaborate in *related work* below, current solutions either do not consider sharing of credentials explicitly [26,21,22], they offer the possibility to use pseudonyms [5,3,13], or they support all-or-nothing sharing [10,5].

As another solution, hardware security modules can be used to prevent users from copying credentials. At a first glance, this approach seems to be an expensive special-purpose solution with limited applicability. However, current PCs are already equipped with a cost-effective security chip, the *Trusted Platform Module (TPM)* [30]; this device implements a hardware security module specified by the *Trusted Computing Group (TCG)*.[1] The TPM supports a cryptographic protocol called *Direct Anonymous Attestation (DAA)* [8,30] that is a kind of anonymous credential system. DAA mitigates a major privacy issue: Each TPM is endowed with an encryption key, called Endorsement Key (EK), which is embedded at manufacturing time and, together with its certificate, represents a unique cryptographic identity for the TPM. DAA allows the TPM to create anonymous signatures based on a "credential" that has been issued by a Trusted Third Party, the DAA issuer, which must inspect the EK certificate of the TPM in order to ensure that only genuine TPMs can obtain credentials.

Contribution. In this paper, we propose a generic framework that combines TLS with DAA for implementing an anonymous authentication system: A hardware security module is employed to prevent unauthorized sharing of credentials.

Our framework is flexible to adapt to different scenarios with different security requirements. We provide a high-security solution based on a TPM as security module, which prevents the sharing of authentication credentials. We also present a pure software implementation (based on a newer version of the DAA protocol [15]), which has better performance, but where sharing of credentials is possible unless additional countermeasures are taken.

---

[1] Although recent news about attacks (e.g., [24]) show that TPM chips cannot guarantee security against highly determined and well-equipped adversaries, they still offer security against software attacks as much as any highly secure smart card, and against basic hardware attacks that do not require costly specialized equipment.

Our framework supports both full anonymity and pseudonymity, allowing for different business models and enhancements: For instance, it can be combined with remote attestation (a feature to report the integrity state of a platform, supported by the TPM) to achieve an *anonymous trusted channel*[2]. We present our solution based on OpenSSL and the TPM, with experimental results.

Related Work. Anonymous authentication is a topic extensively studied in the scientific literature (see, e.g., [13,26,22,21]), indeed a plethora of cryptographic protocols have been proposed. Although there exist proposals to use secure hardware tokens such as smart cards for anonymous authentication (see, e.g., [21]), to our knowledge the question of preventing clients from cloning authentication credentials has not been considered widely. However, some authors (e.g., in [10]) propose all-or-nothing sharing. In contrast, our proposal for anonymous authentication is the first including detailed protocols and an implementation that prevents cloning using widely deployed security hardware: The TPM.

Since their introduction by Chaum [13], various anonymous credential systems have been proposed: Camenisch-Lysyanskaya (CL) [10] is of particular importance for this paper. This scheme forms the basis for all DAA schemes, and hence also for our proposal. Variants of CL credentials based on the strong RSA[3] assumption [10], and based on pairings over elliptic curves [11] exist.

Recently, a credential system using strong RSA-based CL credentials, called Idemix, has been implemented within the PRIME project [5,1]. Compared to Idemix, we employ a hardware security module to prevent credential sharing, and our software implementation uses a more efficient pairing-based variant of DAA than the Idemix implementation, which is based on RSA. Moreover, Idemix' protocols have to be executed over a TLS connection (or another implementation of a secure channel), whereas our solution explicitly combines TLS and DAA. On the other hand, the objectives of PRIME (and Idemix) are set in a much wider scope than just anonymous authentication (which is the topic of this paper).

Bichsel et al. [6] present an implementation of CL credentials that uses a JavaCard as hardware module, providing portable credentials and multi-application support. This solution prevents credential sharing, provided the JavaCard is secure. However, users need additional hardware (JavaCard and card reader), whereas our solution uses TPMs that are integrated in many recent computers.

Leung and Mitchell [20] introduce an anonymous authentication protocol based on DAA, as in our proposal, for client authentication and conventional public key cryptography (based on X509 certificates) to authenticate the server. However, they discuss neither copying of credentials (although by using TPMs their solution prevents this), nor the combination with a standard protocol for a secure channel (such as TLS). Further, they do not present an implementation.

Balfe et al. [3] propose pseudonymous authentication in peer-to-peer networks by using DAA with TLS and IPsec, but they only sketch how such results can be achieved. Instead, we provide a detailed design and implementation.

---

[2] A trusted channel is a secure channel ensuring integrity of its endpoints (e.g., [18,2]).

[3] The strong RSA assumption was introduced in [4].

Finally, we note that some vulnerabilities have been found in DAA which may lead to privacy violation (e.g., [27]), and fixes have been proposed. However, since we focus on the design of a general framework that allows to use a generic DAA scheme together with TLS, any strict improvement of DAA that counters these vulnerabilities can be included in our framework, by only fixing DAA implementation without affecting the rest of the system. Other fixes not strictly related to the DAA core (e.g., choice of parameter values) might also require a review of our protocols. However, our design approach (see Sect. 4) enables easy protocol updates and flexible DAA version negotiation.

Anonymous communication is required by all schemes that are supposed to provide anonymous authentication, otherwise information from the communication system could be used to break the anonymity of the authentication scheme. Various solutions for anonymous communication have been proposed and implemented, including mix networks [12], onion routing [19,28], and Crowds [23]. Our proposal does not address the problem of anonymous communication, instead, it can be implemented on top of any such system.

Structure. The remainder of this paper is organized as follows: Sect. 2 introduces objectives and model of our solution, Sect. 3 provides a background on TLS and DAA, and Sect. 4 presents our work in more details. In Sect. 5, we sketch a security analysis, while Sect. 6 describes our implementation and experimental results. Finally, Sect. 7 concludes the paper and mentions future works.

2 Anonymous Authentication: Objectives and Model

Requirements. A practical anonymous authentication system should satisfy the following requirements[4]:

R1. (Correctness) Users with valid credentials must be able to (anonymously) authenticate to the server.
R2. (Unforgeability) Users must not be able to forge an authentication, i.e., they must not be able to authenticate without having obtained a valid credential.
R3. (Unclonability) Valid credentials must be unclonable, i.e. cannot be copied.
R4. (Unlinkability, or full anonymity) Unlinkable sessions must be possible.
R5. (Pseudonymity) Alternatively, it must be possible to link sessions.
R6. (Viability) All protocols should be based on well-established standards, and implemented upon widely used software libraries and hardware components.

R4 and R5 are (mutually exclusive) privacy requirements and express the properties of anonymous authentication. A real system should be flexible and implement both options, to be chosen at runtime. R1, R2 and R3 are security requirements that, in general, should be met by any authentication scheme. Anyway, non-anonymous ones, even if using weak credentials like username and password, could allow to identify intrusions and misuse – e.g., by performing a

---

[4] Note: full user anonymity (or pseudonymity) requires the prevention of traceability at all communication layers. However, this work focuses on the transport layer only.

statistical analysis of the accesses – and to revoke the related credentials. With anonymous systems, instead, misuse detection is much more difficult; therefore for an anonymous authentication scheme, R3 is mandatory while it could be optional for non-anonymous systems. R6 emphasizes that realistic solutions must be based on standards, otherwise it is unlikely that they are ever deployed in practice. Further, they should allow simple retrofitting of existing applications.

Model and Overview. We give a model and high-level overview of our solution for anonymous (or pseudonymous) authentication, based on the joint usage of the TLS protocol and DAA (see Sect. 3). The protocols are detailed in Sect. 4.

Figure 1 presents our model: A security module $\mathcal{M}$, a host $\mathcal{H}$, an issuer $\mathcal{I}$ and a verifier $\mathcal{V}$. The user $\mathcal{U}$ owns a platform based on the DAA design: $\mathcal{M}$ carries out the security critical operations, while $\mathcal{H}$ computes the more computationally intensive ones. The service provider plays the role of $\mathcal{I}$ to issue credentials (Join protocol) and of $\mathcal{V}$ to authenticate $\mathcal{U}$ (TLS-DAA Handshake). Here, we consider client anonymous authentication only, though our design can be extended with server anonymous authentication (e.g., for peer-to-peer scenarios).

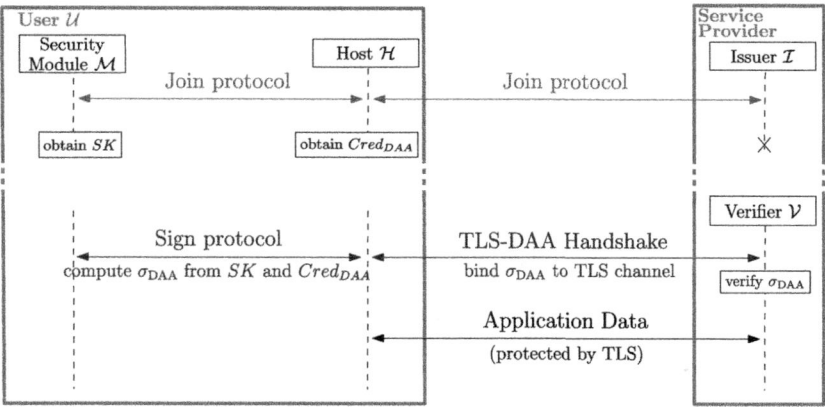

Fig. 1. Model for anonymous authentication based on TLS and DAA

The Join protocol runs only once at time of subscription. $\mathcal{M}$ and $\mathcal{H}$ interact with $\mathcal{I}$ to obtain a secret key SK, and a DAA credential $Cred_{DAA}$ on SK.

When $\mathcal{U}$ wants to anonymously authenticate to a service, $\mathcal{H}$ engages a TLS-DAA Handshake with $\mathcal{V}$. During the execution of the protocol, $\mathcal{M}$ and $\mathcal{H}$ compute a DAA signature σ_{DAA} using SK and $Cred_{DAA}$, binding together DAA authentication and TLS session (see Sect. 4 for details). After successful verification of σ_{DAA}, $\mathcal{H}$ and $\mathcal{V}$ can exchange data over the secure TLS channel.

Our framework design is flexible enough to support several DAA variants and many designs or implementations of $\mathcal{M}$. In our solution, $\mathcal{M}$ is instantiated by the TCG-proposed TPM, whose design ensures that the DAA credentials are bound to the TPM and a valid signature cannot be generated without its usage.

3   Background

Transport Layer Security (TLS). TLS [16] is a protocol that provides a secure channel (data authentication, integrity and confidentiality) between a client $\mathcal{C}$ initiating the communication and a server $\mathcal{S}$ listening for incoming connections. TLS is composed of several sub-protocols. In the following, we will only focus on the Handshake, because the other sub-protocols are not affected by our proposal.

To add functionality to TLS, *Hello Extensions* [7,16] have been standardized: $\mathcal{C}$ can propose one or more extensions and $\mathcal{S}$ may accept them or not. Since Hello Extensions may deeply change the Handshake flow and affect its security, new extensions must be defined via RFC to be validated. Furthermore, Hello Extensions are backward compatible: By specification, $\mathcal{S}$ must ignore any extension it does not know. Hello Extensions are carried over `ClientHello` and `ServerHello` messages (of limited size) in a single client-server interaction.

Supplemental Data [25] have been standardized as new Handshake messages `SupplementalData` (client and server) to transmit supplemental application data during the Handshake, for instance data useful to take authentication and authorization decisions. By specification, Supplemental Data can carry multiple data, `SupplementalDataEntry`, for different applications; they must be negotiated through a Hello Extension, and must be processed only after the Handshake finishes. Figure 2 shows the Handshake messages relevant for our framework.

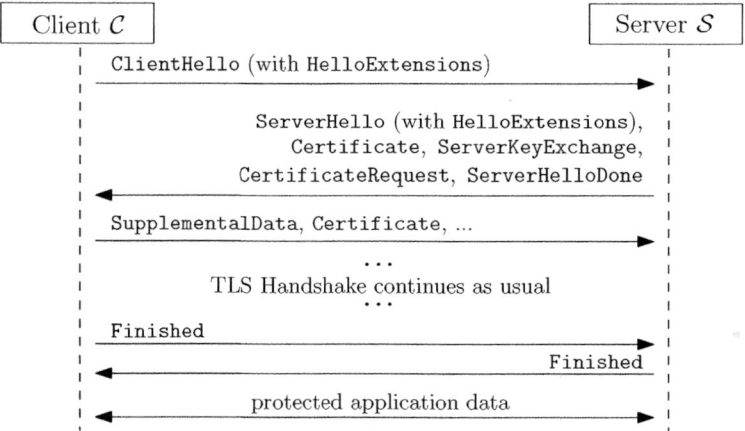

Fig. 2. TLS Handshake with Hello Extensions and client Supplemental Data messages

Direct Anonymous Attestation (DAA). DAA [8,30] is an anonymous credential system that has been designed specifically to encapsulate security-critical operations in a cost-effective secure hardware module. DAA offers various features, such as linking signatures and tagging rogue participants. Here, we concentrate on the most relevant components for our purpose.

A DAA scheme involves the following parties: A DAA issuer $\mathcal{I}$ which issues DAA credentials; a security module $\mathcal{M}$ (e.g., a TPM) and a host $\mathcal{H}$ which generate a secret key SK, obtain DAA credentials and create DAA signatures whose correctness is checked by a verifier $\mathcal{V}$. DAA consists of these sub-protocols:

- Setup: On input of a security parameter, $\mathcal{I}$ uses this algorithm to generate a secret key $SK_{\mathcal{I}}$ and a set of public parameters, including the issuer public key $PK_{\mathcal{I}}$. In practical schemes, $\mathcal{I}$ must prove the validity of $PK_{\mathcal{I}}$. We denote by $Cred_{\mathcal{I}}$ the set of $PK_{\mathcal{I}}$ and such a proof of validity (this is a public parameter).
- Join: This protocol runs between $\mathcal{I}$ that issues a credential, and $\mathcal{H}$ and $\mathcal{M}$ that work together to obtain this credential. $\mathcal{M}$ generates a secret key SK and, supported by $\mathcal{H}$, a commitment com on SK. On input of com and $SK_{\mathcal{I}}$, $\mathcal{I}$ generates $Cred_{DAA}$, a DAA credential associated with SK. The value $Cred_{DAA}$ is given to $\mathcal{H}$[5], while SK is only known to $\mathcal{M}$. In practical schemes, $\mathcal{M}$ must append a proof that it is a genuine security module to com (e.g., a TPM must include its EK certificate). In this case, $\mathcal{I}$ has to validate such a proof (e.g., the EK certificate) before issuing $Cred_{DAA}$.
- Sign: On input of SK, $Cred_{DAA}$, a basename bsn (the name of $\mathcal{V}$ for pseudonymity, or the empty string for full anonymity), the verifier's nonce $n_{\mathcal{V}}$ (for freshness) and a message m, $\mathcal{M}$ and $\mathcal{H}$ run this protocol to obtain a signature σ_{DAA} on m. In fact, σ_{DAA} is a signature proof of knowledge demonstrating that $\mathcal{M}$ and $\mathcal{H}$ possess a valid credential, which does not include any information about their identities.
- Verify: On input of a message m, a candidate signature σ_{DAA} for m, a basename bsn, a nonce $n_{\mathcal{V}}$ and the issuer public key $PK_{\mathcal{I}}$, $\mathcal{V}$ runs this algorithm to return either *accept* or *reject*. Note that σ_{DAA} does not include any information about the signer. In practical schemes, this algorithm gets a list of rogue participants as input to avoid accepting a signature made by a rogue $\mathcal{M}$. How to deal with such a list is out of the scope of this paper.
- Link: On input of two signatures σ_{DAA} and σ'_{DAA}, $\mathcal{V}$ runs this algorithm to return *linked, unlinked* or *invalid signatures*.

Different DAA variants have been proposed [8,9,15,14]. For our purpose [8] and [15] are particularly relevant and will be considered in Sect. 6: The original DAA scheme based on the strong RSA assumption – which has been specified by the TCG and implemented in TPM v1.2 – and a recent proposal based on elliptic curve cryptography and asymmetric pairings.[6]

4 Protocols for TLS-Based Anonymous Authentication

In this section, we describe our enhancement of TLS based on Hello Extensions and Supplemental Data (cf. Sect. 3) to incorporate DAA for anonymous authentication. We detail the Join protocol and the TLS-DAA Handshake, using the

---

[5] Depending on the underlying DAA protocol, $Cred_{DAA}$ may also be forwarded to $\mathcal{M}$. However, we omit this technical detail in the following.

[6] Security flaws were found in this scheme, and a preprint of a fixed version is available at eprint.iacr.org/2009/198. Our current implementation is based on [15].

TPM as $\mathcal{M}$. $\mathcal{I}$ must run DAA Setup (cf. Sect. 3) before the Join protocol starts. Usually one party, the service provider, will play the roles of both $\mathcal{I}$ and $\mathcal{V}$.

Join Protocol. This protocol is executed only once, between $\mathcal{U}$ and $\mathcal{I}$, to let $\mathcal{U}$ obtain DAA credentials: More specifically, $\mathcal{M}$ will generate a secret key SK, and $\mathcal{H}$ will obtain the associated DAA credential $Cred_{DAA}$. The latter can be used for multiple anonymous TLS sessions with possibly distinct servers. Basically, $\mathcal{H}$ and $\mathcal{I}$ open a standard TLS session, without modification, that is used to encapsulate a DAA Join providing integrity and confidentiality of messages exchanged over the network and authentication of $\mathcal{I}$. We recall that in this phase anonymity is not required (in fact, $\mathcal{U}$ must be often identified, e.g. to collect payments).

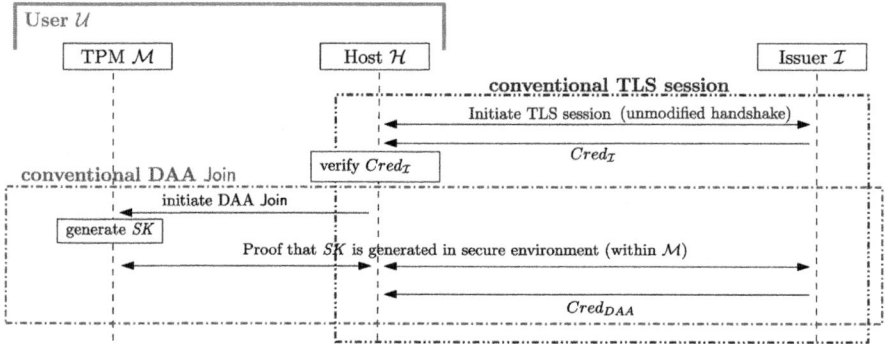

Fig. 3. Join protocol with a TPM as security module: a conventional TLS session is used to protect the communication between host and issuer during the (unmodified) DAA Join protocol. For clarity, a simplified abstract version of DAA Join is shown.

Our protocol is shown in Fig. 3 and proceeds as follows:

1. A conventional TLS session is initiated to protect all subsequent messages from outside adversaries (i.e., attackers that cannot compromise $\mathcal{H}$ or $\mathcal{I}$).
2. $\mathcal{H}$ retrieves $\mathcal{I}$'s credential $Cred_{\mathcal{I}}$ and verifies its validity.
3. $\mathcal{M}$, $\mathcal{H}$ and $\mathcal{I}$ execute the DAA Join protocol as specified by the TCG (cf. Sect. 3). For brevity, we only show the main steps here:
   (a) $\mathcal{M}$, instructed by $\mathcal{H}$ to initiate the DAA Join, generates SK.
   (b) $\mathcal{M}$ and $\mathcal{H}$ together prove to $\mathcal{I}$ that SK has been generated in a secure environment, i.e. a genuine TPM (cf. Sect. 3).
   (c) If the proof is correct, $\mathcal{I}$ issues $Cred_{DAA}$ to $\mathcal{H}$.

TLS-DAA Handshake. Our approach combines DAA and TLS protocols by defining appropriate Hello Extensions and Supplemental Data for client authentication. In our scenario, the DAA verifier $\mathcal{V}$ plays the role of TLS server $\mathcal{S}$ and anonymously authenticates $\mathcal{H}$ (i.e., the TLS client $\mathcal{C}$) and $\mathcal{M}$.

We first give an overall description of our solution, then we detail the protocol. $\mathcal{H}$ and $\mathcal{V}$ negotiate the usage of the anonymous authentication via TLS Hello Extensions. Then $\mathcal{H}$ performs a TLS client authentication using $SelfCert_{\mathcal{S}}$, an X509

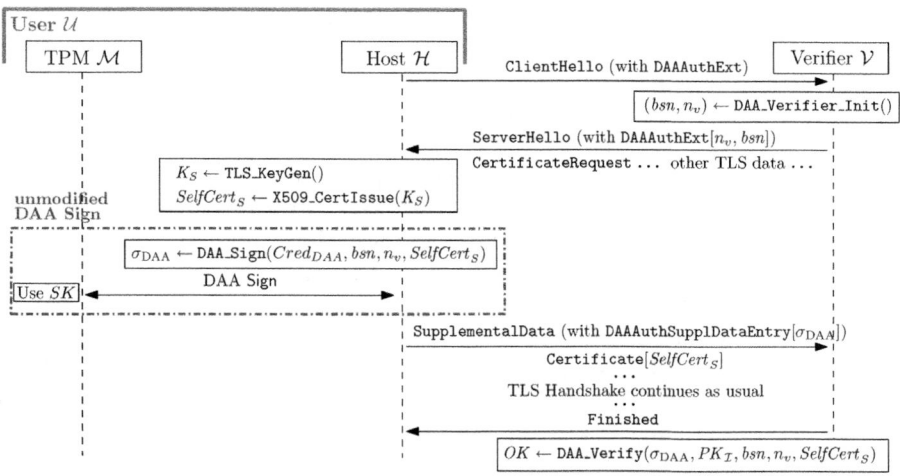

Fig. 4. Our anonymous authentication protocol based on TLS (cf. Fig. 2) and DAA. For clarity, the (conventional, unmodified) DAA Sign protocol is shown without details.

certificate that must be freshly-generated (and signed by a freshly-generated key) for each different TLS session to guarantee anonymity. Further, $\mathcal{H}$ and $\mathcal{M}$ run the DAA Sign protocol: They compute σ_{DAA} over $SelfCert_S$ to prove possession of credentials issued by $\mathcal{I}$ during Join protocol. Finally, $\mathcal{H}$ sends σ_{DAA} to $\mathcal{V}$ via a Supplemental Data message to be verified.

Our protocol relies on the following functions as an interface to DAA[7]:

- $(bsn, n_\mathcal{V}) \leftarrow$ DAA_Verifier_Init() is run by $\mathcal{V}$ to generate a nonce $n_\mathcal{V}$ (used for freshness) and the basename bsn, that can be either fixed for pseudo-nymity, or the empty string for full anonymity.
- $\sigma_{\mathrm{DAA}} \leftarrow$ DAA_Sign($Cred_{DAA}, bsn, n_\mathcal{V}, m$) is run by $\mathcal{H}$ to initiate the DAA Sign protocol with $\mathcal{M}$ and obtain a DAA signature σ_{DAA} on the message m.
- $OK \leftarrow$ DAA_Verify($\sigma_{\mathrm{DAA}}, PK_\mathcal{I}, bsn, n_\mathcal{V}, m$) is run by $\mathcal{V}$ to invoke DAA Verify.

The details of our anonymous authentication protocol are shown in Fig. 4 and its flow is described below:

1. $\mathcal{H}$ starts the TLS Handshake by sending a ClientHello message containing a Hello Extension DAAAuthExt which informs $\mathcal{V}$ to use DAA for anonymous authentication. According to TLS best practices, DAAAuthExt contains a list of supported DAA protocols (allowing for future extensions) and DAA operation modes (full anonymity or pseudonymity).
2. $\mathcal{V}$ uses the function DAA_Verifier_Init to generate $n_\mathcal{V}$ and bsn. Then, in the ServerHello message, $\mathcal{V}$ sends to $\mathcal{H}$ the Hello Extension DAAAuthExt, that contains the chosen DAA protocol, operation mode, $n_\mathcal{V}$ and bsn. For full anonymity, bsn is left empty. Moreover, $\mathcal{V}$ requests the TLS client authentication by sending a CertificateRequest message.

---

[7] For TPMs, the TCG specifies these as part of the TCG Software Stack (TSS) [29].

3. $\mathcal{H}$ prepares for the anonymous authentication by generating a new key pair K_S for TLS client authentication (e.g., an RSA or DSA key pair), and issuing a self-signed certificate $SelfCert_S$ for this key[8]. For full anonymity, $SelfCert_S$ must not contain any data that might identify $\mathcal{U}$; for pseudonymity, it may contain additional data useful to link $\mathcal{U}$'s sessions.

4. $\mathcal{H}$ invokes the DAA_Sign function, resulting in running the DAA Sign protocol between $\mathcal{H}$ and $\mathcal{M}$ to obtain a signature σ_{DAA} on $SelfCert_S$. For this, $\mathcal{H}$ and $\mathcal{M}$ use respectively $Cred_{DAA}$ and SK obtained during the Join protocol.

5. $\mathcal{H}$ sends σ_{DAA} to $\mathcal{V}$ in a DAAAuthSupplDataEntry carried by the client SupplementalData message, and sends $SelfCert_S$ in the ClientCertificate message (as during the standard TLS Handshake).

6. Then the TLS Handshake continues as usual. As in a conventional TLS session, $\mathcal{H}$ authenticates by computing a signature with K_S over all messages previously exchanged between $\mathcal{H}$ and $\mathcal{V}$.

7. After the Finished messages have been exchanged, $\mathcal{V}$ verifies σ_{DAA} by invoking DAA_Verify to validate the anonymous authentication[9]. We assume $\mathcal{V}$ has its own list of trusted DAA issuers, including the issuer's key $PK_{\mathcal{I}}$.

In case of pseudonymity, $\mathcal{V}$ runs the DAA Link algorithm with input σ_{DAA} and signatures previously received. How $\mathcal{V}$ handles the output of such an algorithm is application-dependent and out of the scope of this paper.

Discussion. We chose to use Supplemental Data instead of other possibilities (e.g., defining a new ciphersuite for TLS) mainly for flexibility reasons: Different versions of DAA have different optional features that may require to exchange additional data (e.g., the TCG specifications [29] offer the possibility to selectively reveal attributes of the credential in which case additional information must be exchanged). Moreover, our framework is adaptable to scenarios which require to transport additional data between client and server (e.g., information about the platform configuration). Finally, encapsulating the DAA signature into Supplemental Data allows to define a specific optimization for reconnecting to the same hostname (see Sect. 6 for details).

5 Sketch of Security Analysis

As explained in the following, the security of our solution is based on the security of DAA and TLS. For both protocols, security proofs in (idealized) formal models exist (see, e.g., [8,17]). In this section, we give an informal analysis of

---

[8] It is possible to precompute and store several keys K_S with their certificates $SelfCert_S$ for use in later sessions. If pseudonymity is in use, the process can be optimized by generating only one single $K_{\mathcal{V}}$ and $SelfCert_{\mathcal{V}}$ per-verifier instead of per-session.

[9] The verification of σ_{DAA} is delayed until this step to comply with [25]: To prevent a modification of the normal protocol flow, it mandates that the Supplemental Data are ignored until the TLS handshake finishes; any action involving the data carried by SupplementalData must be performed after the handshake is completed.

our protocols with respect to the requirements listed in Sect. 2, based on the assumption that DAA and TLS are secure (and are used in a secure mode).

Assumptions. For this analysis, we assume that it is infeasible for the adversary $\mathcal{A}$ to compromise $\mathcal{M}$. This assumption is motivated by the fact that current TPMs provide (limited) tamper-evidence and tamper-resistance.

Moreover, we do not consider so-called relay attacks, i.e., attacks where $\mathcal{A}$ poses as a man-in-the-middle between $\mathcal{H}$ and $\mathcal{V}$ and simply forwards all data that is relevant for authentication. Note that although this allows some limited shared use of credentials among users, it still requires (online) interaction of an authorized $\mathcal{M}$ with $\mathcal{V}$ for each authentication. Since $\mathcal{H}$ could also forward all traffic that it obtains over an authenticated link, this kind of "online sharing" cannot be prevented by an authentication mechanism alone.

Informal Security Analysis. During the Join protocol, $\mathcal{I}$ must verify that $\mathcal{M}$ is genuine and guarantees unclonability of credentials. With TPM, this is done by verifying the EK certificate (cf. Sect. 3 and 4). Since the EK is unique to a specific TPM, it is privacy-sensitive data which must not be disclosed to outsiders. Our protocol protects via TLS the EK certificate, as all Join messages.

Our protocols fulfill requirements R1 and R2, because authentication is successful only when the DAA signature σ_{DAA} can be verified correctly. σ_{DAA} is used to authenticate the certificate $SelfCert_S$ used for TLS, hence it is bound to the TLS channel. Thus, the unforgeability of DAA signatures implies that only users with valid DAA credentials can authenticate successfully to $\mathcal{V}$. Breaking requirement R2 implies forging a DAA credential, which would also break the security of the underlying DAA scheme.

Unclonability of credentials (requirement R3) is achieved based on the assumption that $\mathcal{A}$ cannot attack $\mathcal{M}$. When using a TPM, the DAA secret key SK is protected by the TPM (i.e., when stored outside the chip, it is always encrypted with a key only the TPM can access), and unless the TPM can be attacked successfully (e.g., by hardware attacks), the secret is never disclosed to $\mathcal{H}$ and thus cannot be copied. Therefore, our solution meets requirement R3.

Unlinkability (requirement R4) follows from the unlinkability of DAA signatures and from the fact that $SelfCert_S$ and the corresponding key K_S are freshly generated for distinct TLS sessions and do not contain any identifying information. In addition, no other data that allows linking is transmitted.

However, in [27], the authors discovered a weakness in the DAA protocol for the case when $\mathcal{I}$ and $\mathcal{V}$ collude or are under the control of a single party, as in our subscription service scenario. To fix this issue, as suggested in [27], bsn must be chosen properly, which requires additional steps in the protocol ($\mathcal{H}$ must either choose bsn, or verify that it has been formed correctly). Such fixes can be incorporated into our solution, but are not implemented yet.

The possibility of DAA to provide pseudonymity instead of full anonymity means that, in such case, DAA signatures can be linked to a pseudonym. This implies that our protocols also offer pseudonymous authentication (requirement R5) by using the same bsn for multiple authentications.

6 Architecture and Implementation

To support a large number of applications, we chose a widely used library implementing TLS and based our work on OpenSSL[10] v1.0: libcrypto and libssl have been extended to support, respectively, DAA and the DAA enhancement to TLS. Applications not directly using OpenSSL can also be supported via local proxy that first sets up a TLS-DAA channel, then carries data over this tunnel.

In order to put our framework[11] to use, applications require very limited modifications. Moreover, legacy applications which cannot be modified may establish an anonymous TLS channel by exploiting a legacy mode which automatically triggers the anonymous channel and allows to set the necessary parameters via environment variables or a configuration file.[12]

Software-Only Anonymous Authentication. Beside the solution described in Sect. 4, we also offer a purely software implementation based on elliptic curves cryptography (ECC) and pairings [15]. The main motivation for such an implementation is demonstrating the flexibility of our framework, that allows to easily switch between different cryptographic modules (RSA-DAA based on TPM/TSS and purely software ECC-DAA). Moreover, the pure software version allows to analyze the impact of DAA on TLS handshake avoiding the overhead due to the TPM (see below for details). However, a software-only implementation cannot provide unclonability of DAA credentials. In the future, we will explore the possibility of using a combination with other hardware and software security mechanisms to protect the credentials.

Efficiency Aspects. We performed experiments with two HP Compaq DC7700 with Intel Core2 Duo 2.13GHz CPU, 2GB of RAM and Infineon TPM 1.2, both running Linux (Fedora 12), using OpenSSL s_server on the server and OpenSSL s_time on the client to measure the number of connections per second. We remark that measures are taken from a client perspective and we are not benchmarking the server, which is left as future work.

The TPM operations are very slow, while the software implementation performs reasonably well: We can see the impact of DAA on the TLS handshake.[13]

In Fig. 5, we present two data sets to support the feasibility of our solution: The number of connections per second (table on the left) and the total number of bytes transmitted during a handshake (chart on the right). We compare TLS without and with client authentication to the TLS-DAA channel, using the ECC and TPM/TSS implementations.

Table on the left in Fig. 5 reports the number of connections per second for initiating new connections (new/s) and resuming previous TLS sessions (res./s). The DAA enhancement introduces a considerable latency in the TLS handshake: The TPM is really slow, while the pure software implementation provides

---

[10] Currently, OpenSSL implements TLS v1.1.

[11] Available at http://security.polito.it/tc/daa/

[12] Details of our framework architecture are available in the full paper.

[13] In Appendix A of the full paper we provide timings of the DAA primitives.

Protocol	Connections	
	new/s	res./s
TLS (no client auth.)	91.62	690.8
TLS (with client auth.)	80.23	495.3
TLS-DAA (ECC)	3.22	493.1
TLS-DAA (TPM/TSS)	0.03	456.3

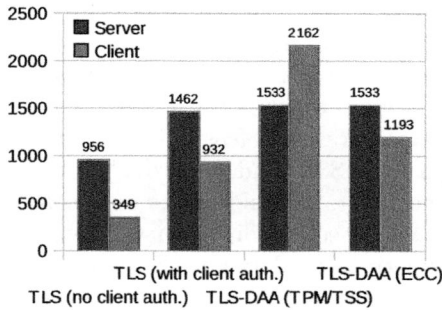

Fig. 5. (Left) Number of new connections/sessions resumed per second for TLS and DAA-TLS. (Right) Total number of bytes sent by client and server during a handshake.

reasonable timings (around 300ms for a connection) from the perspective of a user wanting to anonymously access a service. Further, the use of TLS session resumption guarantees almost no loss in performance for all following accesses. Indeed the number of resumed connections with the DAA enhancement (both ECC and TPM/TSS) is close to that one for standard TLS with client authentication.

Enhancing TLS with Supplemental Data instead of introducing a new ciphersuite for DAA (cf. Sect. 4) allows the client, after a successful connection, to reconnect to the same server with a full TLS handshake (using client authentication with the same X509 certificate previously signed with DAA), without the DAA overhead, i.e. recomputing the DAA signature and sending it via supplemental data.[14] This use of multiple connections to a single host is common practice, e.g., by browsers to speed up the loading of web pages' resources.[15]

We finally examine the amount of data transmitted during the handshake (Fig. 5, chart on the right). This may be a relevant aspect for the deployment in constrained environments, such as mobile or wireless sensor networks. We consider a simple scenario where the client's certificate is only 512 bytes long and no certificate chain is transmitted. As we are performing only client anonymous authentication, the amount of data sent by the server with the DAA enhancement is almost unchanged, compared to standard TLS with client authentication. On the client side, the TPM/TSS version implements the RSA-based DAA whose signature is 1225 bytes long. Nevertheless, the ECC version provides a very efficient solution, as the DAA signature is only 256 bytes long in this case.

7 Conclusion and Future Work

In this paper, we designed and implemented an anonymous authentication system combining TLS with DAA. Our system supports both full anonymity and

---

[14] Of course, such a reconnect is linkable to the first connection.

[15] Whilst HTTP/1.1 recommends to open only two connections per hostname, recent browsers use more, e.g. 6 for Firefox 3.0 (see http://www.browserscope.org/).

pseudonymity, and prevents credential cloning by employing a hardware security module. We designed our framework to be flexible enough to support different variants of DAA, as well as multiple designs and implementations of the security module – which is instantiated by the TCG-proposed TPM in our solution. To demonstrate the feasibility of our solution, we implemented a prototype based on OpenSSL, and we provided two implementations for DAA: one employing the TPM, and another as pure software implementing a more recent version of DAA based on elliptic curves cryptography and pairings. For both, we provided experimental data and discussed efficiency aspects.

As future work, we plan extensions and improvements of our framework. As already mentioned, we will consider the extension of anonymous authentication to the server side (e.g., for peer-to-peer scenarios) and the coupling of our pure software implementation of DAA with security mechanisms to guarantee credential unclonability, with (hopefully) better performance than our current TPM-based solution. Moreover, we are working to enhance our framework with remote attestation to provide anonymous trusted channels. Finally, we plan an implementation on embedded hardware (e.g. smartphones), as well as more detailed benchmarking and a formal security analysis.

References

1. Ardagna, C., Camenisch, J., Kohlweiss, M., Leenes, R., Neven, G., Priem, B., Samarati, P., Sommer, D., Verdicchio, M.: Exploiting cryptography for privacy-enhanced access control: A result of the PRIME project. Journal of Computer Security 18, 123–160 (2010)
2. Armknecht, F., Gasmi, Y., Sadeghi, A.R., Stewin, P., Unger, M., Ramunno, G., Vernizzi, D.: An efficient implementation of Trusted Channels based on Openssl. In: Proceedings of the 3rd ACM Workshop on Scalable Trusted Computing (STC 2008), pp. 41–50. ACM, New York (2008)
3. Balfe, S., Lakhani, A.D., Paterson, K.G.: Securing peer-to-peer networks using Trusted Computing. In: Trusted Computing, pp. 271–298. IEEE Press, Los Alamitos (2005)
4. Barić, N., Pfitzmann, B.: Collision-free accumulators and fail-stop signature schemes without trees. In: Fumy, W. (ed.) EUROCRYPT 1997. LNCS, vol. 1233, pp. 480–494. Springer, Heidelberg (1997)
5. Bichsel, P., Binding, C., Camenisch, J., Groß, T., Heydt-Benjamin, T., Sommer, D., Zaverucha, G.: Cryptographic protocols of the identity mixer library. Technical Report RZ 3730 (#99740), IBM Research (2009)
6. Bichsel, P., Camenisch, J., Groß, T., Shoup, V.: Anonymous credentials on a standard Java Card. In: Proceedings of the 16th ACM Conference on Computer and Communications Security (CCS 2009). ACM Press, New York (2009)
7. Blake-Wilson, S., Nystrom, M., Hopwood, D., Mikkelsen, J., Wright, T.: Transport Layer Security (TLS) Extensions. RFC 4366 (Proposed Standard), Obsoleted by RFC 5246 (April 2006)
8. Brickell, E., Camenisch, J., Chen, L.: Direct Anonymous Attestation. In: Proceedings of the 11th ACM Conference on Computer and Communications Security (CCS 2004), pp. 132–145. ACM Press, New York (2004)

9. Brickell, E., Chen, L., Li, J.: Simplified security notions of Direct Anonymous Attestation and a concrete scheme from pairings. International Journal of Information Security 8(5), 315–330 (2009)
10. Camenisch, J., Lysyanskaya, A.: An efficient system for non-transferable anonymous credentials with optional anonymity revocation. In: Pfitzmann, B. (ed.) EUROCRYPT 2001. LNCS, vol. 2045, pp. 93–118. Springer, Heidelberg (2001)
11. Camenisch, J., Lysyanskaya, A.: Signature schemes and anonymous credentials from bilinear maps. In: Franklin, M. (ed.) CRYPTO 2004. LNCS, vol. 3152, pp. 56–72. Springer, Heidelberg (2004)
12. Chaum, D.: Untraceable electronic mail, return addresses, and digital pseudonyms. Commun. ACM 24(2), 84–88 (1981)
13. Chaum, D.: Security without identification: Transaction systems to make big brother obsolete. ACM Commun. 28(10), 1030–1044 (1985)
14. Chen, L.: A DAA scheme requiring less TPM resources. In: Proceedings of the 5th China International Conference on Information Security and Cryptology, Inscrypt 2009 (2010); Also available at Cryptology ePrint Archive, Report 2010/008
15. Chen, L., Morrissey, P., Smart, N.: Pairings in Trusted Computing. In: Galbraith, S.D., Paterson, K.G. (eds.) Pairing 2008. LNCS, vol. 5209, pp. 1–17. Springer, Heidelberg (2008)
16. Dierks, T., Rescorla, E.: The Transport Layer Security (TLS) Protocol Version 1.2. RFC 5246 (Proposed Standard) (August 2008)
17. Gajek, S., Manulis, M., Pereira, O., Sadeghi, A.R., Schwenk, J.: Universally composable security analysis of TLS. In: Baek, J., Bao, F., Chen, K., Lai, X. (eds.) ProvSec 2008. LNCS, vol. 5324, pp. 313–327. Springer, Heidelberg (2008)
18. Goldman, K., Perez, R., Sailer, R.: Linking remote attestation to secure tunnel endpoints. In: Proceedings of the first ACM workshop on Scalable Trusted Computing (STC 2006), pp. 21–24. ACM, New York (2006)
19. Goldschlag, D.M., Reed, M.G., Syverson, P.F.: Onion routing. ACM Commun. 42(2), 39–41 (1999)
20. Leung, A., Mitchell, C.J.: Ninja: Non identity based, privacy preserving authentication for ubiquitous environments. In: Krumm, J., Abowd, G.D., Seneviratne, A., Strang, T. (eds.) UbiComp 2007. LNCS, vol. 4717, pp. 73–90. Springer, Heidelberg (2007)
21. Lindell, A.Y.: Anonymous authentication. Aladdin Knowledge Systems Inc. (2006), http://www.aladdin.com/blog/pdf/AnonymousAuthentication.pdf
22. Nguyen, L., Safavi-Naini, R.: Dynamic k-times anonymous authentication. In: Ioannidis, J., Keromytis, A.D., Yung, M. (eds.) ACNS 2005. LNCS, vol. 3531, pp. 318–333. Springer, Heidelberg (2005)
23. Reiter, M.K., Rubin, A.D.: Crowds: Anonymity for web transactions. ACM Trans. Inf. Syst. Secur. 1(1), 66–92 (1998)
24. Robertson, J.: Supergeek pulls off 'near impossible' crypto chip hack. News article at NZ Herald (February 2010), http://www.nzherald.co.nz/technology/news/article.cfm?c_id=5&objectid=10625082&pnum=0
25. Santesson, S.: TLS Handshake Message for Supplemental Data. RFC 4680 (Proposed Standard) (October 2006)
26. Schechter, S., Parnell, T., Hartemink, A.: Anonymous authentication of membership in dynamic groups. In: Franklin, M.K. (ed.) FC 1999. LNCS, vol. 1648, pp. 184–195. Springer, Heidelberg (1999)

27. Smyth, B., Ryan, M., Chen, L.: Direct Anonymous Attestation (DAA): Ensuring privacy with corrupt administrators. In: Stajano, F., Meadows, C., Capkun, S., Moore, T. (eds.) ESAS 2007. LNCS, vol. 4572, pp. 218–231. Springer, Heidelberg (2007)
28. Syverson, P.F., Tsudik, G., Reed, M.G., Landwehr, C.E.: Towards an analysis of onion routing security. In: Federrath, H. (ed.) Designing Privacy Enhancing Technologies. LNCS, vol. 2009, pp. 96–114. Springer, Heidelberg (2001)
29. Trusted Computing Group: TCG Software Stack Specification Version 1.2, Level 1, Errata A
30. Trusted Computing Group: TCG TPM Specification, Version 1.2, Revision 103

Group-Based Attestation: Enhancing Privacy and Management in Remote Attestation

Sami Alsouri, Özgür Dagdelen, and Stefan Katzenbeisser

Technische Universität Darmstadt
Center for Advanced Security Research Darmstadt - CASED
Mornewegstraße 32, 64293 Darmstadt, Germany
{sami.alsouri,oezguer.dagdelen}@cased.de,
katzenbeisser@seceng.informatik.tu-darmstadt.de

Abstract. One of the central aims of Trusted Computing is to provide the ability to attest that a remote platform is in a certain trustworthy state. While in principle this functionality can be achieved by the remote attestation process as standardized by the Trusted Computing Group, privacy and scalability problems make it difficult to realize in practice: In particular, the use of the SHA-1 hash to measure system components requires maintenance of a large set of hashes of presumably trustworthy software; furthermore, during attestation, the full configuration of the platform is revealed. In this paper we show how chameleon hashes allow to mitigate of these two problems. By using a prototypical implementation we furthermore show that the approach is feasible in practice.

1 Introduction

One of the main functionalities of the Trusted Platform Module (TPM), as specified by the Trusted Computing Group (TCG), is the ability to attest a remote system, i.e., to verify whether the system is in a well-defined (trustworthy) state. The TCG specified a measurement process that uses the TPM as a *root of trust* and employs a *measure-then-load* approach: Whenever control is passed to a specific system component, its executable code is hashed and the hash is added to a tamper-resistant storage (the Platform Configuration Registers, PCRs) within the TPM in the form of a hash chain: the hash value of the program to be executed is concatenated with the current values in the PCR register, the resulting string is hashed and stored in the PCR. The content of the PCR registers therefore can be considered to reflect the current state of the system. In the process of *remote attestation*, this state is signed and transferred to a remote entity (called challenger), who can subsequently compare the provided measurements with a list of trusted measurements (Reference Measurement List, RML) and decide about the trustworthiness of the remote platform.

Research has identified several problems with the remote attestation process as specified by the TCG. These problems include privacy [1] and scalability issues [2,3], problems with the sealing functionality [4] and high communication

A. Acquisti, S.W. Smith, and A.-R. Sadeghi (Eds.): TRUST 2010, LNCS 6101, pp. 63–77, 2010.

and management efforts [3]. In this paper we deal with these aforementioned problems. Remote attestation discloses full information about the software running on the attested platform, including details on the operating system and third-party software. This may be an unwanted privacy leak, as it allows for product discrimination (e.g., in a DRM context a party can force the use of a specific commercial software product before certain data is released, thereby limiting freedom of choice) or targeted attacks (e.g., if a party knows that someone runs a specifically vulnerable version of an operating system, dedicated attacks are possible). Thus, attestation methods are required that do not reveal the full configuration of the attested platform but nevertheless allow a challenger to gain confidence on its trustworthiness. The second major problem of TCG attestation is the scalability of Reference Measurement Lists [2]. The large number of software products and versions of operating systems makes maintenance of the lists cumbersome. For instance, [5] notes that a typical Windows installation loads about 200 drivers from a known set of more than 4 million, which is increasing continuously by more than 400 drivers a day. The large number of third-party applications aggravates the problem further. Scalability of the remote attestation process is sometimes seen as a major limiting factor for the success of Trusted Computing [3].

In this paper, we propose novel attestation and integrity measurement techniques which use chameleon hashes in addition to SHA-1 hash values or group signatures in the integrity measurement and attestation process. Even though this increases the computational complexity of the attestation process, we show that the presented mechanisms increase the scalability of remote attestation, while providing a fine-grained mechanism to protect privacy of the attested platform. One construction uses chameleon hashing [6], which allows grouping sets of software and hardware versions, representing them through one hash value. For instance, all products of a trusted software vendor or versions of the same software can be represented by one hash value. On the one hand, this reduces the management effort of maintaining RMLs, and on the other hand increases privacy, as the challenger is not able to see any more the exact configuration of the attested platform, but only the installed software groups. At the same time, the challenger system can be assured that all running software comes from trusted software groups. We show that the proposed system can easily be integrated into an architecture similar to the TCG, with only minor modifications. We have implemented the attestation process in a prototypical fashion and show that the approach is feasible in practice. Finally, we show that a very similar attestation technique can be implemented by group signatures instead of chameleon hashes as well.

This paper is organized as follows. In Section 2 we briefly review the mechanism provided by the TCG standards to measure system integrity and to perform remote attestation. In addition, we give background material about chameleon hashes and discuss its security. Furthermore, we discuss the problems with remote attestation and outline solutions proposed in related work. In Section 3 we outline our Chameleon Attestation approach to integrity measurement and remote attestation and also propose an alternative using group signatures. Section 4 provides details on our implementation, and Section 5 discusses the advantages of Chameleon Attestation and details our experimental results. Finally, we conclude the paper in Section 6.

2   Background and Related Work

2.1   Integrity Measurement and Remote Attestation

One of the main goals of Trusted Computing is to assure the integrity of a platform. This is done by measuring every entity (such as BIOS, OS kernel and application software) using the SHA-1 hash before its execution. All measurements are securely stored by extending values in a particular PCR register by a hash chain. To allow the challenger to recompute the hash values, information on the measured entities is stored in form of a Measurement Log (ML). To prevent malicious software behavior, the TPM chip only allows to extend the PCR registers, so that PCRs can not be reset as long as the system is running (the only way to reset the registers is to reboot).

A practical attestation framework called IMA, an extension of the Linux kernel, was developed by IBM research [2]. IMA measures user-level executables, dynamically loaded libraries, kernel modules and shell scripts. The individual measurements are collected in a *Measurement List* (ML) that represents the integrity history of the platform. Measurements are initiated by so-called *Measurement Agents*, which induce a measurement of a file, store the measurement in an ordered list into ML, and report the extension of ML to the TPM. Any measurement taken is also aggregated into the TPM PCR number 10. Thus, any measured software can not repudiate its existence.

Signed measurements can be released to third parties during the process of "remote attestation". For this purpose, the challenger creates a 160-bit *nonce* and sends it to the attested platform. The attestation service running on that host forwards the received nonce and the PCR number requested by the challenger to the TPM chip, which signs the data using the *TPM_Quote* function. After signing, the results are sent back to the attestation service. To protect identity privacy, only the *Attestation Identity Keys* (AIKs) can be used for the signing operation. The attestation service sends the signed data together with the ML back to the challenger. Using the corresponding public key AIK_{pub}, the challenger verifies the signature and the nonce, and re-computes the hash chain using the ML. If the re-computed hash value equals the signed PCR value, then ML is untampered. Finally, the challenger determines whether all measurements in ML can be found in the trusted Reference Measurement List (RML); in this case the attested platform is considered as trusted.

2.2   Chameleon Hashing

Chameleon hashing was introduced by Krawczyk and Rabin [6]. Unlike standard hash functions, chameleon hashes utilize a pair of public and private keys.

Every party who knows the public key is able to compute the hash value on a given message. The possession of the private key enables collisions to be created. However, chameleon hash functions still provide collision-resistance against users who have no knowledge of the private key.

A chameleon hash function is defined by a set of efficient (polynomial time) algorithms [7]:

Key Generation. The probabilistic key generation algorithm $\mathbf{Kg} : 1^\kappa \to (\mathbf{pk}, \mathbf{sk})$ takes as input a security parameter κ in unary form and outputs a pair of a public key $\mathbf{pk}$ and a private key (trapdoor) $\mathbf{sk}$.

Hash. The deterministic hash algorithm $\mathbf{CH} : (\mathbf{pk}, m, r) \to h \in \{0,1\}^\tau$ takes as input a public key $\mathbf{pk}$, a message m and an auxiliary random value r and outputs a hash h of length τ.

Forge. The deterministic forge algorithm $\mathbf{Forge} : (\mathbf{sk}, m, r) \to (m', r')$ takes as input the trapdoor $\mathbf{sk}$ corresponding to the public key $\mathbf{pk}$, a message m and auxiliary parameter r. $\mathbf{Forge}$ computes a message m' and auxiliary parameter r' such that $(m, r) \neq (m', r')$ and $\mathbf{CH}(\mathbf{pk}, m, r) = h = \mathbf{CH}(\mathbf{pk}, m', r')$.

In contrast to standard hash functions, chameleon hashes are provided with the **Forge** algorithm. By this algorithm only the owner of the trapdoor ($\mathbf{sk}$) can generate a different input message such that both inputs map to the same hash value. In some chameleon hashes the owner of the private information can even choose himself a new message m' and compute the auxiliary parameter r' to find a collision $\mathbf{CH}(\mathbf{pk}, m, r) = h = \mathbf{CH}(\mathbf{pk}, m', r')$. This is a powerful feature since anyone who knows the private information can map arbitrary messages to the same hash value.

We desire the following security properties to be fulfilled by a chameleon hash function (besides the standard property of collision resistance):

Semantic Security. For all message pairs m, m', the hash values $\mathbf{CH}(\mathbf{pk}, m, r)$ and $\mathbf{CH}(\mathbf{pk}, m', r)$ are indistinguishable, i.e., $\mathbf{CH}(\mathbf{pk}, m, r)$ hides any information on m.

Key Exposure Freeness. Key Exposure Freeness indicates that there exists no efficient algorithm able to retrieve the trapdoor from a given collision, even if it has access to a **Forge** oracle and is allowed polynomially many queries on inputs (m_i, r_i) of his choice.

Any chameleon hash function fulfilling the above definitions and security requirements can be used in our approach; our particular choice of a chameleon hash is detailed in [7].

2.3   Group Signatures

Group signatures were introduced by Chaum and van Heyst [8] and allow a member of a group to anonymously sign a message on behalf of the group. A group has a single group manager and can have several group members. Unlike standard digital signatures, signers of a group are issued individual signing keys

gsk[i], while all members share a common group public key **gpk** such that their signatures can be verified without revealing which member of the group created the signature. This provides anonymity. However, the group manager is assigned with a group manager secret key **gmsk** and is able to discover the signer (traceability).

Basically, a group signature scheme $\mathcal{GS} = (\mathbf{GKg}, \mathbf{GSig}, \mathbf{GVf}, \mathbf{Open})$ is defined by a set of efficient algorithms (for more details, we refer to [8] and [9]):

Group Key Generation. The probabilistic group key generation algorithm $\mathbf{GKg} : (1^\kappa, 1^n) \rightarrow (\mathbf{gpk}, \mathbf{gmsk}, \mathbf{gsk})$ takes as input the security parameter κ and the group size parameter n in unary form and outputs a tuple $(\mathbf{gpk}, \mathbf{gmsk}, \mathbf{gsk})$, where **gpk** is the group public key, **gmsk** is the group manager's secret key, and **gsk** is an vector of n secret signing keys. The group member $i \in \{1, \ldots, n\}$ is assigned the secret signing key **gsk**[i].

Group Signing. The probabilistic signing algorithm $\mathbf{GSig} : (\mathbf{gsk}[i], m) \rightarrow \sigma_i(m)$ takes as input a secret signing key **gsk**[i] and a message m and outputs a signature $\sigma_i(m)$ of m under **gsk**[i].

Group Signature Verification. The deterministic group signature verification algorithm $\mathbf{GVf} : (\mathbf{gpk}, m, \sigma) \rightarrow \{0, 1\}$ takes as input the group public key **gpk**, a message m and a signature σ and outputs 1 if and only if the signature σ is valid and was created by one of the group members. Otherwise, the algorithm returns 0.

Opening. The deterministic opening algorithm $\mathbf{Open} : (\mathbf{gmsk}, m, \sigma) \rightarrow \{i, \bot\}$, which takes as input a group manager secret key **gmsk**, a message m and a signature σ of m. It outputs an identity $i \in \{1, \ldots, n\}$ or the symbol $\bot$ for failure.

Join. A two-party protocol **Join** between the group manager and a user let the user become a new group member. The user's output is a membership certificate $cert_i$ and a membership secret **gsk**[i]. After an successful execution of **Join** the signing secret **gsk**[i] is added to the vector of secret keys **gsk**.

In order to allow revocation of users, we require an additional property:

Revocability. A signature produced using **GSig** by a revoked member must be rejected using **GVf**. Still, a signature produced by a valid group member must be accepted by the verification algorithm.

2.4 Attestation Problems and Related Work

Integrity measurement according to the TCG specification seems to be a promising way to check the trustworthiness of systems. However, the suggested remote attestation process has several shortcomings:

- *Privacy.* We can distinguish between identity privacy (IP) and configuration privacy (CP). IP focuses on providing anonymity for the attested platform. This problem can be solved by Direct Anonymous Attestation (DAA) [1, 10, 11]. On the other hand, CP is concerned with keeping configuration details of an attested platform secret, since disclosure may lead to privacy violations. Still, the challenger system must be assured that the attested platform indeed is in a trustworthy state. In this paper we focus on providing CP. (However, since CP and IP are orthogonal problems, our solution can be used in conjunction with mechanisms that guarantee IP).

- *Discrimination and targeted attacks.* By using remote attestation, product discrimination may be possible. For example, in the context of DRM environments, large operating system vendors and content providers could collaborate and force usage of specific proprietary software, which restricts the freedom of choice. Furthermore, an adversary could leverage the precise configuration of the attested platform and perform a specific targeted attack [12].
- *Scalability.* A further drawback lies in the scalability of Reference Measurement Lists [2]. The TCG attestation requires the challenger to maintain a Reference Measurement List, which contains hashes of all trustworthy software, to validate the received measurements. Consequently, software updates or patches require distribution of new hash values. For this reason, the management overhead increases to a point where attestation becomes impractical. Consequently, keeping these RML lists up-to-date involves high management and communication efforts.
- *Sealing.* Besides remote attestation, TCG offers the ability to seal data to the configuration of a specific platform. Again, any software update or configuration change can lead to a completely new platform configuration state and consequently hinder unsealing [4].

Sadeghi and Stüble [4] approached the above mentioned problems by the introduction of Property-based Attestation (PBA). By applying PBA, the attested platform proves that it fulfills certain semantic security requirements, called "properties". This way, the concrete configuration of a platform does not need to be disclosed. However, PBA requires an extension of TPM or alternatively a Trusted Third Party along with a Trusted Attestation Service, which is responsible for translations between properties and software. Semantic attestation [13] verifies that the behavior of a platform fulfills given particular high-level properties. WS-Attestation proposed by Yoshihama et al. [14] employs PCR obfuscation to hide software versions; however, scalability remains a problem [15].

3   Group-Based Attestation

In this section we propose three novel attestation techniques, which are based on either chameleon hashes or group signatures. The first and second technique allow balancing configuration privacy with the control precision of the attestation process and substantially decrease the overhead for maintaining RMLs, while the third one provides more flexibility for the challenger in control precision but offers no privacy advantage when compared with the TCG attestation.

3.1   Chameleon Attestation I

In this section we describe a novel remote attestation approach, which makes it possible for the challenger to decide on the trustworthiness of the attested platform, without knowing its detailed configuration. The assumptions listed in [2] about the attacker model are also the basis of our approach. In particular we assume that once a measurement is stored in an RML, the corresponding software is considered trusted; additional security mechanisms must be in place to secure the integrity of the RML (this is out of scope of this work).

To reduce the management overhead, we propose the concept of *software groups*; according to the precise scenario, these groups may e.g. contain all software products of the same vendor, compatible software products or all versions of one specific software. We design the attestation process in such a way that we assign the same hash value to all members of a software group. To achieve this, we make use of a chameleon hash function. As mentioned in Section 2.2, any party who knows the public key **pk** is able to compute the hash value for a given message. In contrast, only the trusted instance holding the private key **sk** can create collisions. Based on the idea of software groups sharing the same hash value, we describe in the following a novel remote attestation we call *Chameleon Attestation I*.

Setup phase: For each group, a trusted instance (such as a software vendor) runs the key generation algorithm **Kg** to obtain a public/private key pair $(\mathbf{pk}, \mathbf{sk})$. When establishing a new software group, the software vendor picks for the first product contained in the new software group a random r and makes it available to the attested platform by delivering it with the software. Furthermore, he hashes the code m of the software with the chameleon hash to obtain $h = \mathbf{CH}(\mathbf{pk}, m, r)$; for performance reasons the SHA-1 hash value of the software is taken as m. The obtained chameleon hash is made public in a trusted RML. Subsequently, to add a new software m' to the same software group, he uses the algorithm **Forge** to find a new r' so that $\mathbf{CH}(\mathbf{pk}, m', r') = h$ and distributes the new r' alongside the software. Step 1 in Figure 1 (a) shows the parameters distributed to the attested platform by a software vendor.

Integrity measurement: On the attested platform, the operation proceeds in a similar way as in the original integrity measurement process, see Figure 1 (a). In particular, the software is first hashed using SHA-1 (step 2). Subsequently, the attested platform computes in step 3 the chameleon hash value h of the software using the public key **pk** and the random value r distributed alongside the software. Since the PCRs in the TPM accept only a 160-bit message to be extended to a particular register, the chameleon hash value is hashed again using SHA-1 in step 4 and the corresponding information is stored in the ML in step 5. The resulting value is finally extended to a PCR register (step 6).

Remote attestation: The attestation process of Chameleon Attestation I is very similar to the standard TCG attestation process. In step 1 in Figure 1 (b) the challenger sends a *nonce* and the PCR numbers whose content has to be signed by the TPM. In step 2 the Attestation Service forwards the request to the TPM, and in step 3 the TPM signs the desired PCRs values and the *nonce*, and sends them back to the Attestation Service. In step 4, the attested platform sends the ML containing the chameleon hash values instead of SHA-1 values. In steps 5-7 the challenger verifies the signature, validates the PCRs values against ML, and checks the trustworthiness of the sent measurements. Only if ML contains trustworthy measurements the attested platform is considered trusted.

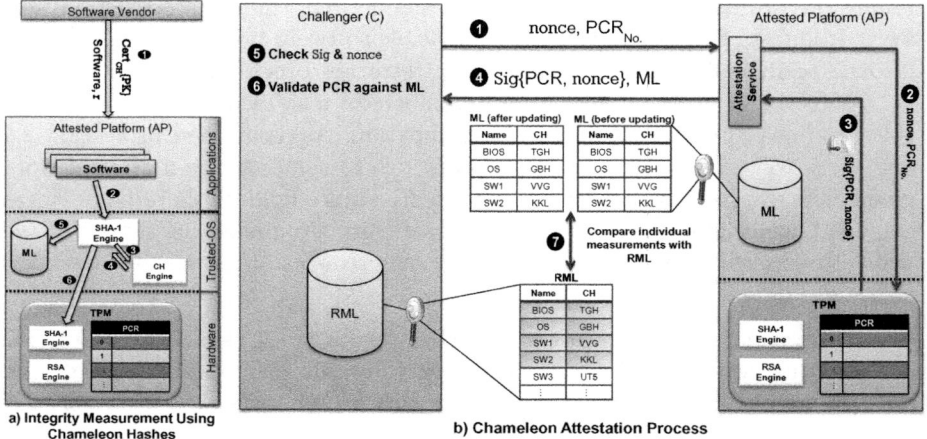

Fig. 1. Chameleon Integrity and Attestation

Chameleon Attestation I is flexible in the sense that the granularity of the software groups can easily be chosen to balance privacy and control precision: If more privacy is desired, then larger software groups may be formed; on the other hand, if distinction between different software versions is an issue, smaller groups can be maintained. Note that the decision of how granular a group is, can be made only by the software vendor. Without modifying the TPM, Chameleon Attestation I supports only the *static chain of trust*, since the TPM itself does not provide functionalities to calculate chameleon hashes.

3.2   Group Signatures Based Attestation

An alternative approach to improve the remote attestation process in terms of privacy and scalability is possible by applying digital signatures, in particular group signatures. This requires the following modifications to the integrity measurement architecture:

Setup phase: We again use the concept of software groups. This time, we use group signatures; each software in the software group has its own private signature key $\mathbf{gsk}[i]$, while all share a common verification key $\mathbf{gpk}$. Whenever a new product or an update of software is published, the software is first hashed with SHA1 to obtain $h = $ SHA-1(SW), where SW is the code of the software. Then, the hash value h is signed by the private key **gsk**$[i]$, i.e. $\sigma = $ **GSig**(**gsk**$[i], h$). The public verification key and the signature is distributed alongside the software. Furthermore, the public keys of all trusted software groups are stored in the RML.

Integrity measurement: Whenever a software is loaded, it is hashed with SHA-1 and its signature is checked with the included public key using the group signature verification algorithm **GVf**. If the signature is valid, the attesting platform hashes the public key and extends the particular PCR with the hash value of the public key of the verified software (instead of the hash value of the software). Afterwards, a corresponding information item containing the name of the software group and its public key **gpk** is stored in the Measurement Log (ML). If any failure occurs, similar to the process of IMA, the corresponding PCR is set to an invalid state.

Remote attestation: The remote attestation works exactly as described in Section 2.1 up to the point where the challenger receives the answer from the attested platform. Then, the challenger verifies the signed PCR and his chosen nonce, validates the hash chain of the PCR against the public keys contained in the ML and checks whether they are all listed in the trusted RML. If all checks succeed, the system is considered trustworthy.

Using group signatures instead of chameleon hashes provides some advantages. While in Chameleon Attestation I a revocation of chameleon hash value requires the revocation of all group members, using group signatures allows the revocation of specific members of the group without the need to revoke the whole group. A second advantage lies in the ability of fitting a group signature hierarchy to an organization structure. That is, every product realm or series could have its own private key, while verification is performed with one single public key.

On the other hand, Chameleon Attestation I outperforms group signature based attestation in terms of performance. While fast group signature schemes (like [16]) need about six exponentiations for signing and verification, chameleon hash functions require much less computations. For instance, our particular choice of a chameleon hash detailed in [7] performs only two exponentiations. To the best of our knowledge there exists no group signature which require less than three exponentiations.

3.3   Chameleon Attestation II

The remote attestation proposed above can be used to mitigate the privacy problem. However, there is a tradeoff between privacy and *control precision* of the approach: as the challenger is only able to see the software groups running on the attested system, the challenger cannot distinguish individual software versions any more: Assume a software vendor has developed a product $SW_{v.1}$ which is later updated to $SW_{v.2}$ because of disclosed security vulnerabilities. By applying the technique mentioned above, a challenger cannot distinguish platforms where $SW_{v.1}$ or $SW_{v.2}$ is run. When using Chameleon Attestation I we lose the possibility to efficiently revoke certain members of a software group. A software vendor can only declare the old chameleon hash value for the group as invalid and publish a new one. However, this requires an update to the challenger's RML. That is, revocation in this context means revocation of the whole software group with all of its members and not revocation of a certain member or even a subgroup.

In this section we show how chameleon hashes can be used to reduce the management overhead of maintaining large RMLs in scenarios where configuration privacy is not an issue. Instead of computing chameleon hashes on the attested platform, we can move this calculation to the challenger side. As in the system described in Section 3.1, the manufacturer picks one chameleon hash for each software group, publishes the hash value of each group in an RML, and sends alongside the software random values r required to compute the chameleon hash. On the attested system, the standard integrity measurement process is performed (in which SHA-1 hashes of loaded executables are stored into PCRs), except that the random values r required to compute the chameleon hashes and the SHA-1 hashes are both saved in the ML. The remote attestation process proceeds as in the standard TCG attestation, i.e., the challenger receives the signed PCR values. Subsequently, the challenger verifies the signed PCR and his chosen nonce and validates the contents of the PCR against the ML containing all SHA-1 values. Finally, for each entry in ML, the chameleon hash is computed to build software groups and validated against the RML.

Applying Chameleon Attestation II makes revocation of specific software group members easier. Unlike Chameleon Attestation I and group signatures based attestation, the challenger himself can refuse untrusted software versions by simply validating the SHA-1 values of these members against blacklists of revoked or untrusted group members. This leads to more flexibility for the challenger and gives him a tradeoff between scalability and control precision.

4   Implementation

In this section we describe the changes we made to the Linux system during the implementation of both variants of Chameleon Attestation as proposed in Sections 3.1 and 3.3.

In order to support a trusted boot we use the Grand Unified Bootloader (GRUB) version 0.97 with the TrustedGrub extension 1.13. All measurements taken are stored in the Intel iTPM. As Linux distribution, we used Fedora 10 with the kernel version 2.6.27.38. The kernel contains the Integrity Measurement Architecture (IMA), which measures all executables and stores the measurements in the Measurement Log (ML). For Trusted Computing support we use the Java based jTSS in version 0.4.1. Because jTSS supports only one measurement log, we modified it to also support reading the measurement log created by IMA. For the remote attestation process, we implemented a Java based server and client. jTSS is used by the server to access the functions of the TPM such as reading PCR registers, signing PCR content, etc. The client also uses the functionalities provided by jTSS to verify signatures and recompute PCR contents. In addition, a MySQL database management system was used on the client side to store the Reference Measurement List (RML).

Implementation of Chameleon Attestation I. For the first variant described in Section 3.1, it is necessary to calculate our chosen chameleon hash function described in [7], denoted as **CH**, on the attested platform. For that reason, we extended IMA such that the **CH** value is calculated after measuring every executable. We assume that the parameters required to calculate **CH** are delivered with the executable and stored. We first created a special measurement list ML_{CH} which contains the chameleon hashes of measured executables. We also modified the standard ML to store the public **CH** parameters J, r, e and N. In particular, in order to store these parameters we extended the struct *ima_measure_entry*. Afterwards, to read these parameters again from ML, we implemented a new function in the file */security/ima/ima_main.c*, which is called from the functions that are responsible for measuring executables, namely *ima_do_measure_file* and *ima_do_measure_memory*. To calculate the **CH** value, we created a new function in the file */ima/ima_main.c*, which also stores the resulting **CH** value in ML_{CH} and the SHA-1 value in standard ML. Note that the standard ML is used only for internal purposes, whereas the ML_{CH} is sent to the challenger during the attestation process. For the implementation of **CH** we used a slightly changed version of the RSA patch for avr32linux.

Implementation of Chameleon Attestation II. In the second variant described in Section 3.3 we need to calculate the chameleon hash on the platform of the challenger. We thus modify the measurement process in a way that the parameters J, r, e and N are added to ML, as in Chameleon Attestation I. Furthermore, we extended the package *iaik.tc.tss.impl.java.tcs.evenmgr* of jTSS such that the new chameleon hash parameters can be read from ML in addition to SHA-1 values. To calculate the chameleon hash on the challenger side, we modified the server such that the SHA-1 values and the corresponding new parameters can be delivered to the challenger. We implemented the RSA based chameleon hash function using OpenSSL on the side of the challenger to enable it to calculate the hash value and verify it against the RML.

5 Experimental Results

In this section we show that Chameleon Attestation significantly reduces the number of the reference measurements required to decide the trustworthiness of the attested system. Subsequently, we discuss the performance of our approach.

Scalability. To test the scalability of Chameleon Attestation, we first created an RML by measuring a fresh installation of Fedora 10 (kernel version 2.4.27.5), but neglecting the content two folders: the folder */var/* which contains variable data that can be changed or deleted at runtime, and the folder */usr/share/* which contains the architecture-independent data. Since it is difficult in retrospect to

Table 1. Reduction of measurements in RML

Packages	Measurement	Fresh installation	Update	Total	Statistics	
					% Fresh installation	% Update
kernel	TCG	1,820	1,816	3,636	50.1 %	49.9 %
	CA	1	0	1	100.0 %	0.0 %
samba-comomn	TCG	18	15	33	54.5 %	45.5 %
	CA	1	0	1	100.0 %	0.0 %
samba	TCG	24	26	50	48.0 %	52.0 %
	CA	1	0	1	100.0 %	0.0 %
httpd (Apache)	TCG	71	72	143	49.7 %	50.3 %
	CA	1	0	1	100.0 %	0.0 %
⋮	⋮	⋮	⋮	⋮	⋮	⋮
All	TCG	8,268	5,448	13,716	60.3 %	39.7 %
	CA	981	37	1.018	96.3 %	3.7 %
	ratio	8.5:1	147:1	13.5:1		10.7:1

group packages by manufacturer (because the package manager of Fedora does not store information about the author/manufacturer of a package), we grouped software products by packages and assigned each file in a package its appropriate random r. Table 1 shows how our approach reduces the number of entries in the RML. The table shows that we need 8,268 different entries in RML for the fresh installation when we employ classic TCG attestation (one for each file). In the contrast, we only need to store 981 measurements in the RML by applying our approach (one for each package in case of grouping by packages).

To test the management overhead when updating packages, we performed another experiment by updating the Linux distribution and its installed packages to newer versions. For instance, the kernel is updated from version 2.6.27.5 to 2.6.27.41, the package samba-common from 3.2.4 to 3.2.15, the package samba from 3.2.4 to 3.2.15, and the package httpd from 2.2.10 to 2.2.14. Table 1 shows that in case of using the classic TCG attestation 1,816 new SHA-1 measurements (49.9 % of the total measurements for the kernel) have to be distributed and published in RMLs. Conversely, by employing Chameleon Attestation no new measurements have to be distributed or published. For the overall distribution and its installed packages, we only need to update 37 chameleon hashes rather than 5,448. These hashes mainly account for newly added packages. Thus, the management and communication effort is significantly reduced.

Privacy. The configuration privacy of the attested platform is substantially enhanced by the use of Chameleon Attestation I: the challenger can decide on the trustworthiness of the attested platform without knowing the exact details of the configuration. Since there is a tradeoff between privacy and control precision, the scheme can be applied on different granularities: depending on the choice of the manufacturer, software groups may encompass different versions of individual files, packages, software systems or even software of a specific vendor (see

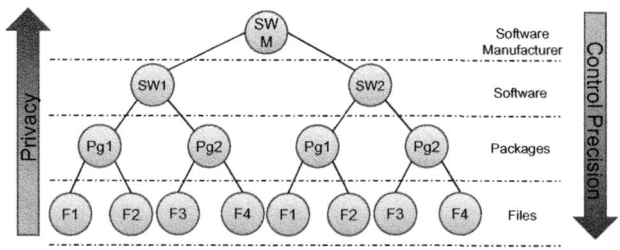

Fig. 2. Levels of privacy and control precision

Figure 2). The higher the level, the more privacy can be protected; on the downside, less information on the platform is available, i.e., the control precision is lower. Our approach can be easily combined with other identity privacy approaches, such as a Privacy CA and DAA.

Sealing. In a similar manner, the sealing problem can be avoided, since different versions of the same software will have the same chameleon hash value; consequently, data can be bound to this value without risking data unavailability when updating to the next version.

Performance evaluation. To evaluate the performance of Chameleon Attestation, we measure the timing difference compared to the standard TCG measurement process. Our experiments were performed on a Lenovo W500 with the following main components: Intel CPU Core 2 2.8 Ghz, 1066 Mhz FSB, a HD of 250 GB SATA 7200 rpm, 4 GB SDRAM, Fedora 10, and kernel version 2.6.27.41.

The calculation of **CH** in Chameleon Attestation I (see Section 3.1) is performed in the kernel space and requires 4,674 μs, while the calculation of **CH** in Chameleon Attestation II (see Section 3.3) is done in the user space and requires 896 μs, i.e., the fifth of the time needed for the first variant. The calculation of collisions takes 899 μs in the user space. All measurements were taken using the function *gettimeofday* in both the kernel space and the user space. Note that all measurements we present in this section aim at giving a gross overview on the overhead of applying public-key schemes in the attestation process. We expect that significant performance improvements can be obtained using highly optimized code also in kernel space.

We used bootchart[1] to determine the boot time of a standard kernel, a kernel with IMA, and a kernel with **CH**. While a standard kernel takes 30s to finish booting, a kernel with IMA takes 33s and a kernel with **CH** takes 44s.

The times required to measure individual files give more insight into the performance. Table 2 illustrates the performance of **CH** in the measurement process. Obviously, the size of the measured files influences the required time significantly. For instance, the calculation of SHA-1 of a 1 KB file takes approx. 20.1 μs, while

---

[1] http://www.bootchart.org

Table 2. Performance of **CH** depending on SHA-1 and different file sizes

Measurement method	2 byte	1 KB	1 MB
SHA-1	2 μs	20 μs	18,312 μs
SHA-1 + **CH**	4,677 μs	4,694 μs	22,986 μs
CH fraction	99.8 %	99.6 %	20.3 %
SHA-1 + extend	9,972 μs	9,989 μs	28,281 μs
SHA-1 + **CH** + extend	14,646 μs	14,663 μs	32,955 μs
CH fraction	31.9 %	31.9 %	14.2 %

measuring a 1 MB file takes 18,312.3 $\mu s \approx 18.3\ ms$. Note that the time required to compute **CH** is constant, as it is only applied to a SHA-1 value. Table 2 also gives timing measurements for the whole process of computing the SHA-1 and chameleon hashes and extending the PCR register with the newly created hashes. The measurements show that for a file of 1 MB 14.2% of the total time required to extend a particular PCR is taken for computing the **CH** value. This percentage falls further when larger files are executed. Thus, we believe that Chameleon Attestation can be implemented in current Trusted Computing platforms with reasonable overhead.

6   Conclusion

In this paper we have considered the problem of privacy and scalability in remote attestation, as standardized by the Trusted Computing Group. In particular, the use of SHA-1 hashes to measure the integrity of programs and system components creates a large management overhead; in addition, remote attestation causes privacy problems, as the full state of the system is disclosed. To mitigate these problems we proposed Chameleon Attestation, where we can assign a single hash value to sets of trusted software. By a prototypical implementation we show that the performance overhead of using public-key operations in the attestation process is acceptable.

Acknowledgments. The authors would like to thank Carsten Büttner who helped in the implementation of our approaches. A special thank goes to Bertram Poettering who had early access to this paper and made valuable comments. The feedback and comments from all members of the SECENG group were much appreciated.

References

1. Brickell, E., Camenisch, J., Chen, L.: Direct Anonymous Attestation. In: Proceedings of the 11th ACM Conference on Computer and Communications Security, Washington DC, USA, pp. 132–145. ACM, New York (2004)
2. Sailer, R., Zhang, X., Jaeger, T., van Doorn, L.: Design and implementation of a TCG-based integrity measurement architecture. In: 13th USENIX Security Symposium, San Diego, CA, USA, August 2004, USENIX Association (2004)

3. Lyle, J., Martin, A.: On the feasibility of remote attestation for web services. In: 2009 International Conference on Computational Science and Engineering, Vancouver, BC, Canada, pp. 283–288 (2009)
4. Sadeghi, A., Stüble, C.: Property-based attestation for computing platforms: caring about properties, not mechanisms. In: Proceedings of the 2004 Workshop on New Security Paradigms, Nova Scotia, Canada, pp. 67–77. ACM, New York (2004)
5. England, P.: Practical techniques for operating system attestation. In: Lipp, P., Sadeghi, A.-R., Koch, K.-M. (eds.) Trust 2008. LNCS, vol. 4968, pp. 1–13. Springer, Heidelberg (2008)
6. Krawczyk, H., Rabin, T.: Chameleon hashing and signatures. In: Proceedings of the Network and Distributed System Security Symposium, pp. 143–154. The Internet Society, San Diego (2000)
7. Ateniese, G., de Medeiros, B.: On the key exposure problem in chameleon hashes. In: Blundo, C., Cimato, S. (eds.) SCN 2004. LNCS, vol. 3352, pp. 165–179. Springer, Heidelberg (2005)
8. Chaum, D., van Heyst, E.: Group signatures. In: Davies, D.W. (ed.) EUROCRYPT 1991. LNCS, vol. 547, pp. 257–265. Springer, Heidelberg (1991)
9. Bellare, M., Micciancio, D., Warinschi, B.: Foundations of group signatures: Formal definitions, simplified requirements, and a construction based on general assumptions. In: Biham, E. (ed.) EUROCRYPT 2003. LNCS, vol. 2656, p. 644. Springer, Heidelberg (2003)
10. Brickell, E., Li, J.: Enhanced privacy ID: a direct anonymous attestation scheme with enhanced revocation capabilities. In: Proceedings of the 2007 ACM Workshop on Privacy in Electronic Society, Alexandria, Virginia, USA, pp. 21–30. ACM, New York (2007)
11. Chen, X., Feng, D.: A new direct anonymous attestation scheme from bilinear maps. In: International Conference for Young Computer Scientists, pp. 2308–2313. IEEE Computer Society, Los Alamitos (2008)
12. Kühn, U., Selhorst, M., Stüble, C.: Realizing property-based attestation and sealing with commonly available hard- and software. In: STC 2007: Proceedings of the 2007 ACM Workshop on Scalable Trusted Computing, pp. 50–57. ACM, New York (2007)
13. Haldar, V., Chandra, D., Franz, M.: Semantic remote attestation: a virtual machine directed approach to trusted computing. In: Proceedings of the 3rd Conference on Virtual Machine Research And Technology Symposium, San Jose, California, vol. 3, p. 3. USENIX Association (2004)
14. Yoshihama, S., Ebringer, T., Nakamura, M., Munetoh, S., Maruyama, H.: WS-Attestation: efficient and Fine-Grained remote attestation on web services. In: Proceedings of the IEEE International Conference on Web Services, pp. 743–750. IEEE Computer Society, Los Alamitos (2005)
15. Alam, M., Nauman, M., Zhang, X., Ali, T., Hung, P.C.: Behavioral attestation for business processes. In: IEEE International Conference on Web Services, pp. 343–350. IEEE Computer Society, Los Alamitos (2009)
16. Boneh, D., Boyen, X., Shacham, H.: Short group signatures. In: Franklin, M. (ed.) CRYPTO 2004. LNCS, vol. 3152, pp. 41–55. Springer, Heidelberg (2004)

Towards a Trusted Mobile Desktop

Marcel Selhorst, Christian Stüble, Florian Feldmann, and Utz Gnaida

Sirrix AG Security Technologies,
Lise-Meitner-Allee 4, 44801 Bochum, Germany
{m.selhorst,c.stueble}@sirrix.com
http://www.sirrix.com
Federal Office for Information Security,
Godesberger Allee 185-189, 53175 Bonn, Germany
{florian.feldmann,utz.gnaida}@bsi.bund.de
http://www.bsi.bund.de

Abstract. Today's mobile phone platforms are powerful enough to be used as personal assistants that render and edit even complex document formats. However, short development cycles in combination with high complexity and extendability make these devices not secure enough for security-critical tasks. Therefore, end-users either have to use another secure device, or to accept the risk of losing sensitive information in the case of a loss of the device or a successful attack against it.

We propose a security architecture to operate on security-critical documents using a commercial off-the-shelf (COTS) mobile phone hardware platform offering two working environments. The first one is under full control of the user while the second is isolated and restricted by additional security and mobile trusted computing services.

The realizability of such an architecture has been proven based on a 'TrustedSMS' prototype developed on top of an OMAP-35xx development board, a hardware platform similar to many actual mobile phone platforms. The prototype includes nearly all components required to securely isolate the two compartments and implements use cases such as SMS writing, signing, receiving, verification, and key management.

1   Introduction

Nowadays, mobile phones are the most used mobile computing devices in the world. The Global System for Mobile Communications standard (GSM) and its successors define a mobile telephone communication system that is used by over 4 billion people[1] in over 200 countries[2].

Due to the increasing bandwidth and the possibility to connect to the Internet via GSM or UMTS, more and more devices are used as personal assistants. In the past, tethering techniques have been used in order to connect a computer to the Internet or a closed enterprise network. Today, the performance and form

---

[1] http://www.bitkom.org/60614_60608.aspx

[2] http://www.prnewswire.com/cgi-bin/stories.pl?ACCT=109&STORY=/www/story/06-13-2006/0004379206&EDATE=

A. Acquisti, S.W. Smith, and A.-R. Sadeghi (Eds.): TRUST 2010, LNCS 6101, pp. 78–94, 2010.

factor of mobile devices allows users to directly view and edit even complex document formats: End-users are able to read mail, edit documents, or browse in the Internet while traveling.

On the one hand, the increased flexibility and performance of modern mobile devices allows users to individualize their devices, e.g., by installing additional third party software such as iPhone Apps. However, third party software often comes from untrusted or unknown sources and thus should not have access to security-critical information. On the other hand, users also want to use their devices to operate on security-critical and/or private documents, or to access restricted enterprise networks (e.g., VPNs). However, the increasing list of known exploits and malicious software shows that this gap between extendable and configurable end-user systems and high trustworthiness to operate on sensitive information cannot be solved by today's mobile operating systems. The reasons for the low assurance on their security and reliability are well-known but hard to solve: Short development cycles due to the feature pressure of the market and the high complexity of the underlying software components are only two of them [7, 9].

However, today's mobile processors in combination with today's efficient microkernels [8, 17, 18] are powerful enough to execute (para-) virtualized operating systems offering isolated working environments. Moreover, these devices provide enough memory to run two or more operating systems in parallel, and many state of the art mobile devices are shipped with open operating systems such as Android or Maemo which are based on the Linux operating system and thus provide a higher level of flexibility and configurability than the legacy operating systems used in the past.

Therefore, it is our goal to offer on top of a COTS mobile device a trustworthy communication and working environment that is executed in parallel to another legacy operating system that fulfills user requirements regarding configurability, extendability, and individualization. Both working environments are executed on top of a microkernel-based security kernel providing different security services and Trusted Computing technology provided by a Mobile Trusted Module (MTM). Parts of this work have been initiated by the BSI-Project *MoTrust*[1].

Contribution and Outline. After a short discussion of related work in the following section, section 3 describes the general design and the security components required to realize the security kernel and the Trusted Mobile Desktop (TMD) on top of an existing mobile phone platform.

Then, section 4 describes the demonstration prototype, a trusted SMS application, that has been implemented based on an OMAP-35xx development board. This prototype includes two virtualized Linux instances, a TrustedGUI, an Attestation Service, and a Software-MTM implementation used to sign and attest SMS.

This paper concludes with an analysis of the implementation in section 5 as well as an outlook of open issues and possible enhancements in section 6.

2   Related Work

The design and the implementation of a minimal MTM is proposed in [11]. This work is especially to be used in the context of embedded and/or mobile systems.

The Software-MTM implementation used in the TrustedSMS prototype has not been optimized with the focus on resource consumption, but on an easy design and an easy API. However, the usage of a more efficient MTM implementation is possible.

Two MTM designs and implementations are proposed by the authors of [10]. The first MTM design uses the ARM TrustZone [4] technology to provide a hardware-supported isolation of the MTM state and the legacy operating system. The second proposal is the use of a smartcard as a trust anchor to realize an MTM. In contrast, our approach uses the isolation mechanisms of the underlying microkernel to protect the MTM state, but an adoption to one of the other proposals would also be possible.

An isolation mechanism between security domains in a distributed IT infrastructure is described in [2]. The architecture proposed in this paper only provides isolation between two working compartments executed on one mobile platform. However, the basic idea behind the Trusted Mobile Desktop was to connect it to an existing security-critical infrastructure. Thus, the proposed architecture could be used to extend the Trusted Virtual Domains (TVD) used in [2] by mobile platforms.

Several publications discuss designs and realizations of secure user interfaces, a good overview is provided by Epstein [12]. The secure user interface implemented for the proposed prototype is an embedded version of the secure GUI of the Turaya Security Kernel [20, 21]. In contrast to, e.g., Nitpicker [14] that allows to show different compartments on one screen, the embedded secure user interface strictly isolates compartments using different virtual desktops and a fixed TrustBar (see section 3.1).

3   Design of a Trusted Mobile Desktop

This section introduces the required building blocks to realize a Trusted Mobile Desktop (TMD) in parallel to a regular operating system (see Figure 1). While,

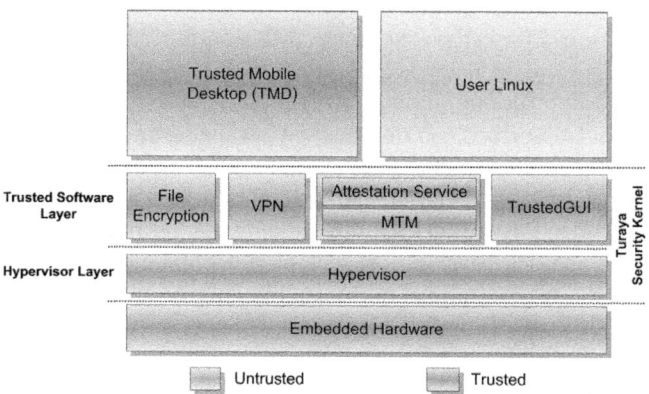

Fig. 1. High-level architecture of the Trusted Mobile Desktop

in general, the protected compartment can be used in a similar way to the User Linux compartment, the main focus is to have the TMD compartment under control of the organization the TMD is connected to. In an enterprise environment, e.g., the TMD compartment would be connected to the internal enterprise network if allowed by the enterprise's security policy. Moreover, the enterprise's security policy defines the allowed information flows between user compartment and TMD compartment. This way, the Trusted Mobile Desktop compartment can be seen as a part of the enterprise's network.

The resulting architecture includes a mobile version of the Turaya Security Kernel (which will be introduced in subsection 3.1), different security-critical Turaya services, as well as the "Trusted Mobile Desktop" compartment and the "User Linux" compartment.

3.1 Turaya Security Architecture

Turaya is a security architecture providing strong isolation and multilaterally secure policy enforcement of legacy applications [3, 21]. As illustrated in Figure 1, a Turaya-based security architecture consists of three layers: (i) an Embedded Hardware Layer, including conventional components such as memory and CPU; (ii) the Turaya Security Kernel, including a Hypervisor Layer and a Trusted Software Layer; (iii) applications and legacy operating systems that are executed in parallel and isolated from each other.

Hypervisor Layer. The Hypervisor Layer of the Turaya Security Kernel acts as a traditional Virtual Machine Monitor (VMM) by managing the hardware resources and providing basic virtualization support. Due to the modular concept of the Turaya architecture, different VMMs and microkernels can be used. Here, the PikeOS microkernel P4 is used [8], which has been ported to the ARM-based hardware target within the Trusted Embedded Computing (TECOM) project[3]. On top of the P4 microkernel, fundamental services dedicated to resource management are executed. These include services for the management of processes, memory, interrupts, as well as those providing device drivers and enforcing system-wide security policies. Depending on the used security associations of the Turaya Security Kernel, the Hypervisor Layer enforces the communication policies between isolated partitions. This is achieved by providing unidirectional communication channels between the corresponding entities. Access to these channels is only permitted to the assigned partitions thus enabling a system wide information flow control enforced by the microkernel.

Trusted Software Layer. The Trusted Software Layer is located directly above the Hypervisor Layer and provides high-level security services, such as a secure user interface (TrustedGUI) or a file encryption service. Turaya services as well as user processes and virtualized operating systems are isolated in so-called compartments based on a mandatory security policy.

---

[3] See http://www.tecom-project.eu

The provided security services are explained in the next subsections.

Secure User Interface. A secure user interface [12, 13, 15, 23] is an essential prerequisite of the trustworthiness of the Trusted Mobile Desktop. The embedded version of a secure GUI, called 'm-gui', is a slightly adapted version of its desktop pendant, the TrustedGUI [21]. The m-gui is a native Turaya service providing a trusted path to users.

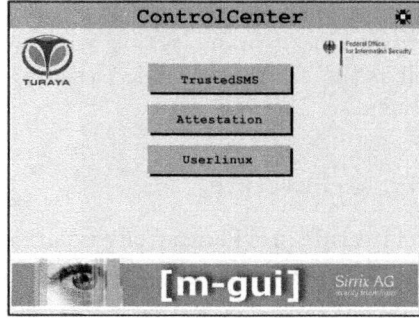

Fig. 2. Screenshot of the m-gui control center showing buttons for the available compartments

In order to ensure that only the m-gui has access to the physical graphic memory, each compartment receives its own virtual isolated framebuffer to be used for graphics output. Due to the isolation of memory regions enforced by the microkernel, different kinds of attacks, e.g., "Overlaying Attacks" where a password dialog window is overlayed by a fake window to retrieve the user input are prevented.

The actual graphic resolution of the framebuffer is reduced by a small region that is explicitly used by the m-gui to show a trusted status bar (TrustBar). This TrustBar is under full control of the m-gui and indicates the currently active compartment. Since the information displayed in the TrustBar cannot be modified by the client, "Look-Alike Attacks", where an application looks like another one, can be identified. Additionally, further information about the compartment's trust state is shown by the TrustBar using colors. An accessory icon symbolizes the trust state, in case one cannot distinguish between the colors red and green.

Furthermore, the m-gui realizes a secure input channel between a compartment and the user by controlling the input hardware and forwarding user inputs only to the active compartment. This allows users to always identify the current communication endpoint of their inputs (such as passwords).

The m-gui offers different ways of switching the focus of the currently displayed compartment. The m-gui main screen (cmp. Figure 2) shows buttons for each registered compartment, i.e., it is possible to select the compartment by clicking on the button. Moreover, the TrustBar shows the title of the currently active compartment and provides a button in the upper left corner to return to the main overview screen of the m-gui[4]. In addition, the m-gui allows to iterate through the available compartments by clicking onto the TrustBar.

Attestation Service. The Attestation Service provides to the application layer interfaces for key management and remote attestation. For this purpose, the Attestation Service internally uses the Mobile Trusted Module to manage cryptographic keys and to attest the security kernel and application-level compartments. However, the application interfaces are kept general enough to be able to support alternative hardware security modules.

In the context of the TrustedSMS prototype introduced in section 4, for example, the Attestation Service manages the signature key to sign the SMS and the Attestation Identity Key to perform remote attestation. Further, the Attestation Service creates a platform certificate, called trust state, uniquely identifying the state of the signing platform in order to allow external entities the verification of the platform state, the configuration of the TrustedSMS application, and the signed SMS. The invoked commands of the MTM include a quote over the Platform Configuration Register (PCR) values of the MTM. The Attestation Service is also used to manage public keys required for verification of incoming data.

MTM. The Mobile Trusted Module is a trust anchor defined and specified by the Trusted Computing Group (TCG) [19]. It can be seen as a specialization of a Trusted Platform Module (TPM) [25], coping the needs for mobile devices. In contrast to a TPM, an MTM can be realized as a software component, in this case a dedicated MTM service running in a separate compartment. The MTM command set is extended in a way to fulfill the requirements of local parties as well as external parties such as mobile device vendors, software, or - in case of mobile phones - network providers.

Within the Trusted Mobile Desktop, the MTM is used for different purposes: Firstly, it is used to verify Reference Integrity Metrics (RIM) certificates of trusted compartment to realize "Secure Boot" based on the command MTM_VerifyAndExtend. Secondly, the MTM is used to attest to a remote entity a compartment configuration including the underlying security kernel. Thirdly, the MTM is used instead of a smartcard to create, manage, and operate on cryptographic keys.

In order to ease the usage of the MTM, an embedded Trusted Software Stack (eTSS) [16, 24] for embedded devices has been developed. The eTSS is an object-oriented implementation of a TCG Software Stack (TSS) and is compatible with the TCG's TPM specification version 1.2. Furthermore, it supports new features from the current TCG's MTM specification version 1.0.

VPN Client. The network encryption module of the Turaya Security Kernel realizes VPN tunnels using the remote attestation functionality of the Attestation Service. It establishes a so-called trusted channel [5, 22] that links a secure VPN connection to the result of a remote attestation of the underlying Turaya system and the according Trusted Mobile Desktop. This way, remote communication

---

[4] Note: The button is not present in the m-gui overview screen.

partners can derive the trustworthiness of the compartments that want to establish a connection, e.g., to the enterprise server. The used protocols can also be combined with Trusted Network Connect (TNC) technology as specified in [26].

File Encryption. The file encryption service acts as a virtual file system by offering a file system interface to the Trusted Mobile Desktop. This enables the usage of the persistent file system provided by the (untrusted) User Linux to permanently store the encrypted files. The use of such a trusted file encryption service has several advantages:

- Permanent changes of the TMD compartment are not required. This allows to mount the TMD image read-only.
- The available storage can be used more efficiently, since it does not have to be split into a secure and an insecure part.
- Users can operate on the encrypted files as usual, e.g., they can send or store them using different untrusted services such as Bluetooth, USB, or backup clients.

The file encryption module uses the Mobile Trusted Module to bind the master encryption key to the configuration of the TMD. This way, a manipulated Trusted Mobile Desktop cannot access the encrypted data.

3.2   User Linux

The User Linux represents the common working environment of the user, e.g., a MAEMO[5] or Android[6]. Due to the strict isolation of security-critical applications (e.g., the Attestation Service and the Mobile Trusted Module), no security-related harm can be done to the system by malicious software or bugs.

The main benefit from the isolation is that users can have full control over their User Linux, that is, they can install any software and configure the whole (untrusted) working environment to their needs. However, access to critical information, e.g., to enterprise-related documents, will not be possible.

3.3   Trusted Mobile Desktop

In parallel to the User Linux compartment, another virtualized and isolated Linux operating system is executed. The Trusted Mobile Desktop includes software that is typically used in business environments, such as an Email client, an SMS messenger, and/or a VoIP telephony software.

The Trusted Mobile Desktop can indirectly use services offered by the User Linux via trusted modules of the Turaya Security Kernel. For example, it can access the network through the VPN module, and access the User Linux file system through the file system encryption module. However, the underlying security

---

[5] http://www.maemo.org
[6] http://www.android.com

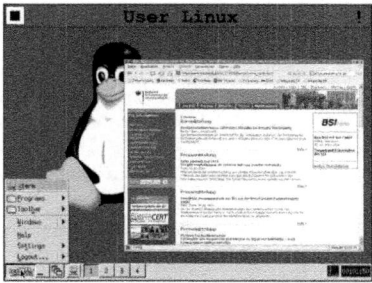

Fig. 3. Screenshot of the User Linux

policies enforced by the Turaya Security Kernel ensure that a direct communication between the User Linux and the Trusted Mobile Desktop is impossible.

During startup of the TMD, the Turaya Security Kernel measures the TMD image and stores the result into the MTM. Since all user data is stored outside of the TMD using the file encryption module, the TMD image can be mounted read-only.

4   Prototype Implementation: TrustedSMS

For evaluation purposes of the concept of a Trusted Mobile Desktop, a prototype has been developed based on an OMAP-35xx development board[7]. The prototype is capable of sending and receiving SMS messages by using the security services provided by the Turaya Security Kernel. Figure 4 illustrates the corresponding high-level architecture of this demonstrator.

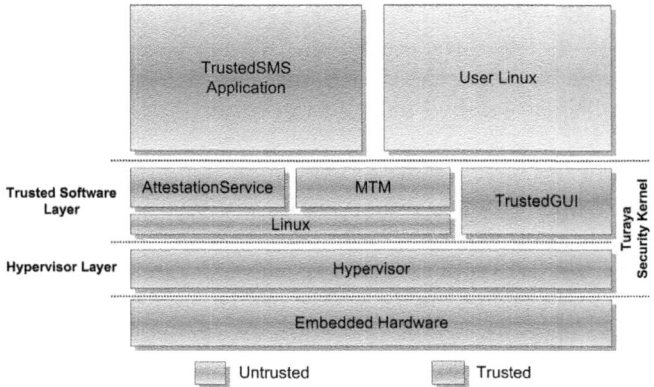

Fig. 4. Architecture of the TrustedSMS Demonstrator

---

[7] http://www.mistralsolutions.com/products/omap_3evm.php

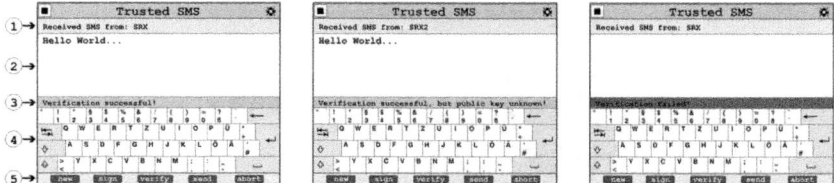

Fig. 5. Screenshot of the TrustedSMS application indicating the different trust states of an SMS

In contrast to the TMD design discussed in section 3, the TrustedSMS prototype is realized by a native application running on top of the underlying microkernel. The Attestation Service and the Software-MTM, however, are in this prototype realized based on an isolated Linux kernel.

Due to the trusted path concept of the m-gui, all user inputs (here coming from a touchpad) will directly be forwarded to the TrustedSMS application, when it has focus. Additionally, the TrustedSMS application uses Inter-Process Communication (IPC) mechanisms[8] to communicate with the necessary security services required for signing, verifying, and attesting the SMS.

The TrustedSMS application makes use of the Attestation Service and the MTM in two ways: Firstly, the cryptographic key used to sign the SMS is stored within the MTM and bound to the configuration of the security kernel and the TrustedSMS application itself. Secondly, the public part of the signature key is certified using the TPM_CertifyKey command to enable remote parties to check the trustworthiness of the security kernel and the TrustedSMS application.

It was also planned to realize secure boot based on the M-Shield functionality [6] of the base board together with the MTM_VerifyAndExtend functionality of the MTM. However, the M-Shield functionality is disabled on all available development boards. Therefore, the current prototype does not include a Root of Trust for Verification (RTV) and thus cannot fully implement secure boot.

The TrustedSMS application itself does not include support for accessing the GSM stack. Instead, it uses the communication mechanisms offered by the User Linux. This is possible, since the User Linux neither has access to the signature key, nor to the display used to indicate the result of the signature verification process.

A screenshot of the current TrustedSMS implementation is shown in Figure 5. The TrustedSMS application is running in its own virtual framebuffer. The trust state of the application can be seen in the TrustBar in the upper area of the display, the TrustedSMS application itself can only access the area below that bar. The main application screen consists of five areas: The grey TrustedSMS

---

[8] By using PikeOS as a microkernel, this is realized by creating unidirectional channels between dedicated ports of the according partitions. In order to setup the communication channels, one has to connect two ports (one of each partition) in a static channel list before building the software image, thus a manipulation at runtime is impossible.

status bar (1) in the upper screen (right under the TrustBar) displays current activities and additional information. The white input box (2) below is used as an editor / displaying window. Directly in the middle of the window is an SMS status bar (3) indicating the trust state of the currently displayed SMS. Due to the positioning in the middle of the screen, the trust state is always in the focus of the user. The last two sections contain a virtual keyboard (4) as well as buttons (5) for the according functionalities provided by the TrustedSMS application (e.g., to sign or verify an SMS).

In the following, we describe the implemented use cases of the TrustedSMS application:

4.1 Sending SMS

Figure 6 describes the internal communication between components to implement the "Send SMS" use case.

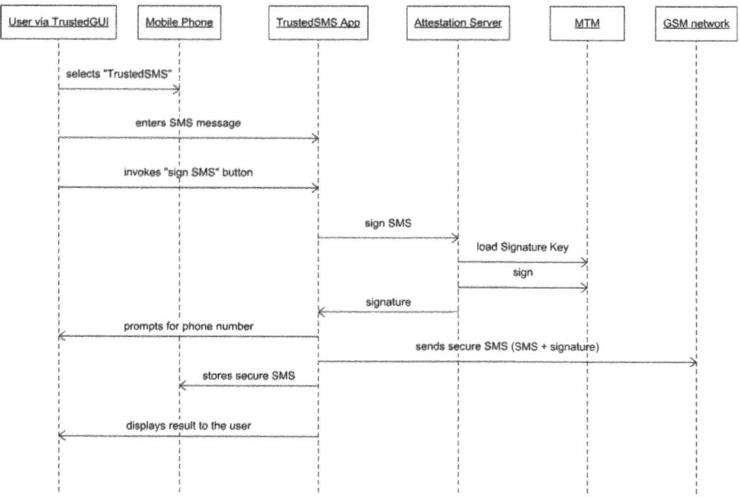

Fig. 6. Sequence of sending a signed SMS within the Trusted Mobile Desktop prototype

Assuming a user wants to send a secure SMS, he can switch the focus to the TrustedSMS application by selecting the TrustedSMS button on the m-gui overview screen. Within the TrustedSMS application, a click on the "new" button allows the user to insert the message. As soon as he is finished, the entered SMS can be signed by clicking on the "sign" button. The TrustedSMS application will now send the SMS to the Attestation Service, which itself will invoke the Mobile Trusted Module in order to load an Attestation Identity Key (AIK) and sign the SMS. Afterwards, the signature is returned to the TrustedSMS application and can be verified manually by pressing the "verify" button.

After pressing the "send" button, the user has to enter the telephone number and acknowledge it with the "send" button, which will finally send the SMS along with the signature to the User Linux. A daemon inside the User Linux will receive the SMS and send it via the GSM network to the dedicated recipient.

Typically, an SMS can contain up to 160 7-bit characters, 140 8-bit characters, or 70 16-bit characters (including spaces). The signature scheme used in this prototype is TPM_SS_RSASSAPKCS1v15_SHA1. In case a 512-Bit key is used, a 64-Byte signature is generated leaving about 70 Bytes for the actual SMS. In case a user requires more SMS space, the current GSM specification allows the sending of multiple, concatenated SMS (currently up to ten SMS). The usage of a signature key with 2048-Bit produces a 256-Byte signature, which would implicitly require to send at least two SMS.

4.2   Receiving SMS

Figure 7 shows the required steps to implement the "Receive SMS" use case.

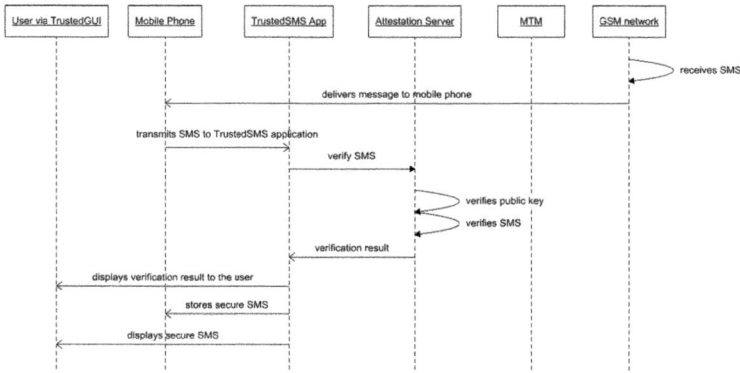

Fig. 7. Sequence of verifying a received trusted SMS within the Trusted Mobile Desktop prototype

As soon as an incoming SMS is detected, it is transmitted from the User Linux to the TrustedSMS application. This will invoke the Attestation Service for a verification process. The Attestation Service will first browse its local key storage to check for a matching public key. In case a key is found and the SMS was successfully verified, the SMS will be displayed within the TrustedSMS application and the trust indicator bar will switch to green. In case no public key was found, but a public key was sent along with the SMS, the SMS will be displayed with a warning, that the public key is unknown and the SMS therefore is not trustworthy. In case the incoming SMS does not match the attached signature, the trust bar will turn red and display an error message. The SMS itself will not be displayed.

4.3   Public Key Import

In order to verify signed SMS created by a remote peer, the TrustedSMS application provides functions to import the corresponding verification key. The

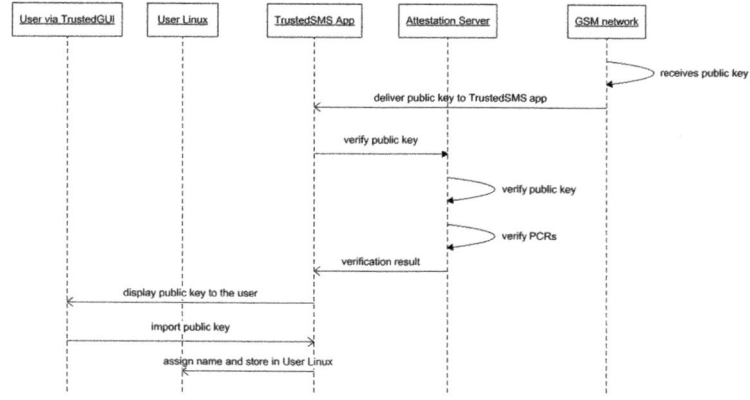

Fig. 8. Sequence of importing a public key

public key is received via an untrusted SMS, thus it needs to be verified before it will be imported.

Figure 8 describes the required steps to implement the "Import Public Key" use case. As soon as a public key is received, it is transmitted to the TrustedSMS application, which itself will invoke the Attestation Server to verify the public key. In case a platform certificate including the current configuration of the remote peer has also been received, it is compared against valid reference values. Afterwards, the origin of the public key and its fingerprint are displayed to the user, along with the verification result of the remote platform. If the user is willing to accept the public key, he can assign a name to it and click on an "import" button, which will store the public key. In the current prototype, the imported public keys are stored within the Attestation Linux, such that the Attestation Server can directly access the public keys without interacting with the TrustedSMS application during the verification process. This has the additional benefit that the TrustedSMS application does not require a persistent storage and is therefore read-only.

However, in order to enhance the usability, a full-featured key management component handling the mappings between human-readable names, telephone numbers, and public keys is required. In order to keep the TrustedSMS application (and thus the TCB) small, the management can be outsourced into either a native application with persistent and secure storage or into the User Linux. The latter would allow to re-use the already existing addressbook of the user by adding the public key information as payload. However, due to the security impact of this task, the stored information needs to be integrity-protected. One way of achieving this is to have the TrustedSMS application setup the mapping between a public key and the according user and have it signed by the Software-MTM through the Attestation Service. The resulting signed mapping can then be stored inside the addressbook of the user inside the User Linux. Upon reception of a signed SMS, the corresponding public key is retrieved from the addressbook of the user. First, the signature on the key mapping is verified followed by the verification of the signed SMS.

4.4 Resource Considerations

Due to the limited resources of the target OMAP-35xx platform, resource restrictions needed to be taken into account during the development of the prototype presented. The used hardware target has 128MB RAM and is running with 600MHz. The executed software is isolated in five individual compartments:

1. **System Software Partition:** The PikeOS system software is installed in a special system partition with highest privileges. The executed code has a size of 292kB for system software, network drivers and a debugging console.
2. **Turaya Partition:** This partition contains the m-gui. The executed code inside this partition has about 1MB, containing of the actual m-gui application, the LCD- and touchpad drivers for the OMAP board as well as the background images and a small widget library to draw text and buttons on the screen. The memory consumption of this application is depending on the maximum amount of concurrent clients. Each client of the m-gui requires about 0.5 MB RAM for its virtual framebuffer.
3. **Attestation Partition:** The first Linux instance is running in this partition. On top of it, the Software-MTM and the Attestation Service are executed. The executed code in this partition has a size of 2.4MB for the Linux kernel + 3MB Software-MTM + 1MB Attestation Service.
4. **TrustedSMS Partition:** The TrustedSMS application runs within this partition. The size of the executed binary is 590kB, consisting of the TrustedSMS application, required figures and a small widget library to draw text and buttons on the framebuffer.
5. **User Linux Partition:** The last partition contains the User Linux. All the remaining resources are assigned to this partition.

5 Analysis

This section analyses the impact of possible threats to the TrustedSMS application. Further, it is argued how the introduced architecture prevents them.

– *The content of the SMS is changed without the knowledge of the user, before the SMS is signed by the user.*
One possible way to execute this attack is to undetectably modify the TrustedSMS application on the mobile client. This is prevented in our prototype, since the corresponding signature key can only be used by an unmodified TrustedSMS application. Another way to perform this attack is intercepting user inputs in order to send fake keystrokes to the application or, more generally, internally modify the message while in transit between processes. This attack is prevented due to the strong isolation of communication paths by the underlying microkernel as well as the trusted path between the m-gui and the TrustedSMS application.

- *The displayed content of the SMS deviates from the actual content of the SMS.*
  This attack is eliminated by the usage of a secure user interface, such as the m-gui, provided by the underlying security layer.
- *An SMS is generated, signed, and sent by an untrusted application.*
  In order to eliminate this attack, two security measures are in place. On the one hand, an untrusted application does not have the permission to communicate with the Attestation Service and the Mobile Trusted Module. Further, the cryptographic key material used for generating the signature is not accessible from outside. Therefore, even if an attacker is able to launch an untrusted application, it will not be able to generate a valid signature on the SMS, since it has no access to the key material.
- *A secure SMS is generated by a malicious application sending keystrokes to the TrustedSMS application.*
  This attack is avoided by strongly isolating the keypad from other functions by the usage of a trusted path between the m-gui and the TrustedSMS application. This way, even if the untrusted mobile phone's operating system is compromised, it cannot send malicious inputs to the SMS editor application, since the input device is explicitly owned by the m-gui and therefore isolated from the User's operating system.
- *The displayed result of the signature verification deviates from the actual result of the verification.*
  By strongly isolating the verification process from the mobile phone's untrusted operating system and by using the m-gui provided by the underlying security layer, this attack can be prevented.
- *The underlying security kernel is maliciously or accidentally modified.*
  By using mechanisms such as trusted boot or secure boot on an embedded platform, it is possible to measure and verify each security-critical application before execution. In case the verification fails, the application is not executed. Moreover, the platform certificate created by the MTM allows remote parties to derive the trustworthiness of the TrustedSMS application in use.

The threats for signature generation and verification can then be derived into the following security requirements:

i Trusted path to the TrustedSMS application.
ii TrustedGUI for displaying the content of the SMS editor application.
iii TrustedGUI for displaying the content of the SMS signature application.
iv Strict isolation of the Attestation Service and the Mobile Trusted Module from other running applications.
v Strict isolation of the keypad input driver from other running applications while enforcing a strict communication scheme with software entities.
vi Platform integrity checks during startup.
vii Secure Storage of cryptographic keys.

As argued above nearly all requirements (except a full implementation of secure boot) are already implemented by the TrustedSMS prototype.

6   Outlook and Conclusion

In this document, we have proposed a security architecture allowing end-users to view and to edit security-critical documents using a commercial off-the-shelf (COTS) mobile phone hardware platform. The general idea behind this architecture is to split the operation software into two compartments, one compartment under full control of the user and another isolated and restricted compartment for security-critical tasks.

Such a design allows users to operate on security-critical documents, e.g., in a business environment, but still provides an untrusted working environment that can be configured by users according to their needs. In our opinion, such a design increases the acceptance of security-critical mobile devices, especially because it supports actual mobile phone hardware.

The complexity of the Trusted Mobile Desktop compartment has been reduced by replacing many operating system services (such as the file system, the network stack, and the GSM stack) by a small encryption layer of the security kernel that reuses untrusted services of the User compartment. In this context, the underlying security kernel ensures that the User Linux cannot access code and data outside of its own environment. Moreover, the Trusted Mobile Desktop can be mounted read-only, measured using a cryptographic hash function, and remotely attested using the provided MTM functionality.

We have proven the realizability of our design based on a TrustedSMS prototype developed on top of an OMAP-35xx development board, a hardware platform similar to many actual mobile phone platforms. The realized TrustedSMS prototype implements the most important use cases, such as SMS writing, SMS receiving, and key management, and includes nearly all components required to securely isolate the User Operating System and the Trusted Mobile Desktop from each other, including a TrustedGUI, an Attestation Service, and a Software-MTM. Several extensions of that prototype are already under development or will start in the near future:

- First of all, the TrustedSMS application will be replaced by a shrinked Linux compartment, the Trusted Mobile Desktop, executing existing communication software such as an Email-client and a web browser. Since the existing prototype already includes a second Linux instance, this enhancement will be finished in the near future.
- Another task currently under development is the implementation of the Attestation Service and the MTM as native applications such that the underlying Linux kernel can be removed. This step will heavily reduce the complexity of security-critical components of the Turaya Security Kernel.
- Furthermore, we are looking for a development platform providing a working Root of Trust for Verification (RTV) allowing the realization of secure boot based on the MTM functionality.
- Finally, it is planned to port the existing prototype in the near future to an existing mobile phone – allowing an evaluation of the resulting Trusted Mobile Desktop in a realistic environment and by normal end-users. Devices

currently under consideration are the *Google phone* HTC G1[9] and the Nokia N900[10]. Based on the underlying hardware, it will also be decided whether the User Linux will be based on Android or Maemo.

Our experience with the development based on the OMAP-35xx board has shown that a good vendor support and documentation drastically reduces the required efforts to develop such a solution. Therefore, the platform decision will mainly be based on the offered support and the availability of documentations and specifications.

References

1. Alkassar, A., Gnaida, U., Quirin, T.: MoTrust-TCG: Manipulationsschutz für mobile Signaturanwendungen mittels Trusted Computing. In: Sicherheit 2008, pp. 575–580 (2008)
2. Alkassar, A., Husseiki, R.: Data Leakage Prevention in Trusted Virtual Domains. In: Pohlmann, N., Reimer, H., Schneider, W. (eds.) Information Security Solutions Europe (ISSE 2009). Vieweg + Teubner Verlag (2009)
3. Alkassar, A., Scheibel, M., Sadeghi, A.-R., Stüble, C., Winandy, M.: Security architecture for device encryption and VPN. In: Information Security Solution Europe (ISSE 2006). Vieweg Verlag (2006)
4. Alves, T., Felton, D.: TrustZone: Integrated hardware and software security. Technical report, ARM (July 2004)
5. Armknecht, F., Gasmi, Y., Sadeghi, A.-R., Ramunno, G., Vernizzi, D., Stewin, P., Unger, M.: An Efficient Implementation of Trusted Channels based on OpenSSL. In: Proceedings of ACM STC 2008 (2008)
6. Azema, J., Fayad, G.: M-Shield: Mobile Security Technology: making wireless secure. Technical report, Texas Instruments (June 2008)
7. Basili, V., Perricone, B.: Software Errors and Complexity: An Empirical Investigation. Communications of the ACM, 42–52 (1984)
8. Brygier, J., Fuchsen, R., Blasum, H.: PikeOS: Safe and Secure Virtualization in a Separation Microkernel. Technical report, Sysgo (September 2009)
9. Cheng, Z.: Mobile Malware: Threats and Prevention (2007), http://www.mcafee.com/us/local_content/white_papers/threat_center/wp_malware_r2_en.pdf
10. Diedrich, K., Winter, J.: Implementation Aspects of Mobile and Embedded Trusted Computing. In: Chen, L., Mitchell, C.J., Martin, A. (eds.) Trust 2009. LNCS, vol. 5471, pp. 29–44. Springer, Heidelberg (2009)
11. Ekberg, J.-E., Bugiel, S.: Trust in a small package: minimized MRTM software implementation for mobile secure environments. In: STC 2009: Proceedings of the 2009 ACM workshop on Scalable Trusted Computing, pp. 9–18. ACM, New York (2009)
12. Epstein, J.: A bibliography of windowing systems and security. ACM SIGSAC Review 10(4), 7–11 (1992)
13. Epstein, J., McHugh, J., Orman, H., Pascale, R., Marmor-Squires, A., Danner, B., Martin, C.R., Branstad, M., Benson, G., Rothnie, D.: A high assurance window system prototype. Journal of Computer Security 2(2), 159–190 (1993)

---

[9] http://www.htc.com/www/product/g1/specification.html
[10] http://maemo.nokia.com/n900/specifications/

14. Feske, N., Helmuth, C.: A nitpicker's guide to a minimal-complexity secure GUI. In: 21st Annual Computer Security Applications Conference. ACM, New York (2005)
15. Fischer, T., Sadeghi, A.-R., Winandy, M.: A Pattern for Secure Graphical User Interface Systems. In: 3rd International Workshop on Secure Systems Methodologies Using Patterns (2009)
16. Forler, C., Käß, S.: D03.5 - Embedded TSS: Technical specification. Technical report, Trusted Embedded Computing (January 2009)
17. Heiser, G., Elphinstone, K., Kuz, I., Klein, G., Petters, S.M.: Towards trustworthy computing systems: taking microkernels to the next level. ACM Operating Systems Review 4, 3–11 (2007)
18. Liedtke, J.: Towards real micro-kernels. Communications of the ACM 39(9) (1996)
19. Mobile Phone Working Group. TCG Mobile Trusted Module Specification. Technical Report version 1.0, Trusted Computing Group (June 2008)
20. Pfitzmann, B., Riordan, J., Stüble, C., Waidner, M., Weber, A.: The PERSEUS system architecture. Technical Report RZ 3335 (#93381), IBM Research Division, Zurich Laboratory (April 2001)
21. Sadeghi, A.-R., Stüble, C., Pohlmann, N.: European multilateral secure computing base - open trusted computing for you and me. Datenschutz und Datensicherheit DuD, Verlag Friedrich Vieweg & Sohn, Wiesbaden 28(9), 548–554 (2004)
22. Schulz, S., Sadeghi, A.-R.: Extending IPsec for Efficient Remote Attestation. In: 14th International Conference on Financial Cryptography and Data Security, FC 2010 (2010)
23. Shapiro, J.S., Vanderburgh, J., Northup, E.: Design of the EROS trusted window system. In: Proceedings of the 13th USENIX Security Symposium, August 2004, USENIX (2004)
24. Stüble, C., Zaerin, A.: μTSS - A Simplied Trusted Software Stack. In: Acquisti, A., Smith, S.W., Sadeghi, A.-R. (eds.) TRUST 2010. LNCS, vol. 6101, pp. 124–140. Springer, Heidelberg (2010)
25. Trusted Computing Group. TPM main specification. Main Specification Version 1.2 rev. 85, Trusted Computing Group (February 2005)
26. Trusted Computing Group. Trusted Network Connect. Specification Version 1.2 (2007)

Application of Trusted Computing in Automation to Prevent Product Piracy

Nora Lieberknecht

Research Center for Information Technology
Embedded Systems and Sensors Engineering (ESS)
Haid-und-Neu-Str. 10-14, 76131 Karlsruhe, Germany
lieberknecht@fzi.de

Abstract. Product piracy has become a serious threat for automation and mechanical engineering in recent years. Therefore effective protection measures are desperately needed. Especially the software has to be protected since it determines the machine's functionality and without software the machine (and the imitations) cannot work. Thereby it has to be prevented that software can be copied from one machine to another and that it can be manipulated in order to activate additional machine functionalities. Moreover the unauthorized replacement of software-equipped machine components must be prohibited. This can be achieved by applying Trusted Computing and TPMs to this new field of application.

Keywords: Product Piracy, Automation, Mechanical Engineering, Trusted Computing, Trusted Platform Module (TPM).

1 Introduction

Product piracy is a serious problem today not only for the consumer goods industry but also for the capital goods industry. The mechanical engineering and automation field for instance is highly affected by piracy, covering the imitation of spare parts and the reproduction of complex plants. Product piracy leads to an immense loss of sales and profits for machine manufacturers, to the loss of jobs and the insolvency of whole companies in the worst case. This is why effective countermeasures against product piracy in mechanical engineering are desperately needed that prevent—or at least complicate—the production of imitations and pirate copies.

Nowadays machines consist of hardware and software and both have to be protected against piracy. Since the machine depends on the software and without software the hardware (i.e. the mechanics) cannot work, it is especially important to protect the software. This holds particularly since many machine manufacturers sell different machine variants in different prize categories on the market concurrently, which sometimes differ only in the software that runs on them. In this case the machine's functionality is only determined by software and not by hardware and thus it has to be prevented that one can copy the software from a more expensive machine variant to a cheaper one.

A. Acquisti, S.W. Smith, and A.-R. Sadeghi (Eds.): TRUST 2010, LNCS 6101, pp. 95–108, 2010.

Furthermore it has to be prevented that software-equipped machine components are exchanged without permission e.g. for imitated ones. It must be achieved that the machine "behaves" only in the intended manner after it has been sold and delivered i.e. that it only works if its hardware/software-configuration has not been changed illegally.

By applying Trusted Computing (TC) and Trusted Platform Modules (TPM) to automation and mechanical engineering, these goals can be achieved and effective protection measures against product piracy can be implemented as described in Section 4. Trusted Computing was primarily intended to be used in general-purpose computing systems like desktop PCs, laptops and mobile devices, and a lot of work has been done in this area in recent years. The related work covers e.g. an architecture that enables arbitrary applications to perform remote platform attestation, allowing them to establish trust based on their current configuration, as proposed in [1]. In [2], approaches for mobile TPMs have been introduced since in contrast to common TPMs, TPMs for mobile platforms do not need to be implemented as microcontrollers, leading to different security assumptions. In [3] the use of TPMs in embedded systems is described in detail. This is quite different from its use in ordinary PC environments as described in Section 3.

The application of Trusted Computing and TPMs to industrial environments like mechanical engineering and automation is a new field of application and is thus challenging (see Section 3). The ordinary applications of TPMs for general-purpose computing systems do not apply here due to different hardware platforms and specific constraints. In the following, several approaches will be introduced how Trusted Computing and TPMs can be applied to this field in order to prevent product piracy.

The remainder of this paper is organized as follows: in Section 2 an overall introduction to Trusted Computing is given, including its aims, benefits and criticism. Section 3 outlines the challenges of using Trusted Computing in mechanical engineering. In Section 4 the implementation of several protection measures against product piracy is introduced that achieve the desired protection goals, machine manufacturers have today. Finally Section 5 briefly concludes the paper.

2   Aims and Criticism of Trusted Computing

The Trusted Computing (TC) concept was developed and promoted by the Trusted Computing Group (TCG), an international not-for-profit industry standards organization of leading hardware and software manufacturers, including AMD, HP, IBM, Microsoft, Infineon, Intel, Sun Microsystems et al. Its aim is to increase the security and trustworthiness of IT-systems. "Trust" in the TCG's terminology means "the expectation that a device will behave in a particular manner for a specific purpose" [4].

The basic element of Trusted Computing is a special crypto-chip, the so called Trusted Platform Module (TPM), which is usually mounted on the mainboard of a computer platform and fulfills several cryptographic functions. Due to its integrated hardware random number generator it can be used e.g. to generate random keys for the (symmetric) encryption of data. Moreover it can generate pairs of keys for asymmetric RSA [5] encryption and securely store these keys.

By the use of a TPM data can be bound to a specific platform by encrypting it with a key stored in the TPM so that it can only be decrypted by this specific TPM. Moreover the encrypted data can be bound ("sealed") to a specific TPM "state" which corresponds to a specific hardware/software-configuration of the platform. Therefor "measurements" of the configuration are taken by computing hash values of the program code and storing them in special registers of the TPM, the so called Platform Configuration Registers (PCR). The contents of these registers are then incorporated into the sealing-operation. In doing so, the encrypted data can later only be decrypted if the hash values in these registers are the same as during encryption.

The Trusted Computing concept has been highly controversial ever since its development. Those critics and opponents object that it was intended to be used by device and software manufacturers to enforce software usage rights, to control the user and to achieve monopolization. Many users feared that they could be controlled and supervised e.g. when surfing the Internet with a TPM equipped device since it would be possible to unambiguously identify a platform (and thus also the user if the hardware platform is always used by only one user) due to the TPM's unique Endorsement Key.

In cases where privacy and anonymity play an important role for the users (e.g. when surfing the Internet for private purposes) it is important to protect their right to "informational self-determination" which belongs to the German data privacy law. This right states that "[...] in the context of modern data processing, the protection of the individual against unlimited collection, storage, use and disclosure of his/her personal data is encompassed by the general personal rights of the [German Constitution]. This basic right warrants in this respect the capacity of the individual to determine in principle the disclosure and use of his/her personal data. Limitations to this informational self-determination are allowed only in case of overriding public interest." [6].

Hence the user concerns and critics about Trusted Computing in regard to privacy are indeed comprehensible, but they do not apply to industrial environments like mechanical engineering and automation, in which software and devices are used for production and not for private purposes. Beyond that machines are often not connected to the Internet. Machines are no multi-purpose devices (like desktop PCs, laptops etc.) but they are usually designed for one purpose only and it is not intended to change this purpose afterwards. Hardware and software of machines today are usually developed by the same manufacturer and they are designed to work only in conjunction. Thus an inseparable binding of both is reasonable in this case.

For these reasons it is feasible and practicable to apply Trusted Computing to this field of application in order to achieve effective protection against product piracy.

3 Challenges in Using Trusted Computing in Mechanical Engineering

Using Trusted Computing in mechanical engineering and automation is different from its use in general-purpose computing systems and challenging due to different hardware platforms and additional requirements that apply specifically to this field of application.

Machines mostly consist of an industrial PC (IPC), which is the superordinate machine control unit, and several connected "embedded devices" like sensors, actuators etc. The IPC executes complex software programs like the stored program control and HMI[1] programs, whereas the embedded devices are usually equipped with less complex firmware. When using Trusted Computing in this field of application, both types of platforms (IPCs and embedded systems) and different kinds of software and firmware have to be considered.

Industrial PCs are basically similar to ordinary "x86" Personal Computers (PCs) concerning the hardware components and they can also be run with the same software. However they have to meet high demands on robustness, reliability and stability. Today there are already IPCs with TPM available in the market and the usage of the TPM as well as its integration into the software development processes in IPCs is similar to its use in desktop PCs.

Just like desktop PCs, industrial PCs mostly have a BIOS[2], an operating system, device drivers etc. Today most TPM manufacturers deliver device drivers for the common operating systems together with their devices and sometimes even own implementations of the TCG Software Stack (TSS) [7]. This is the software specification that provides a standard API for accessing the functions of the TPM. There is also a free and open-source TSS implementation available for Linux systems (TrouSerS [8]) and several commercial implementations like the NTRU Core TCG Software Stack (CTSS) [9]. Moreover common operating systems like Windows and Linux meanwhile support TPMs, e.g. some versions of the Windows operating system provide the TPM Base Services (TBS) [10] for this purpose. Furthermore there are also approaches for a Trusted BIOS e.g. in [11] and the SecureCore BIOS from Phoenix [12].

Thus the basic software support for TPMs is at hand for manufacturers, software developers and users, but nevertheless TPMs are hardly used so far. The only (user) application, the TPM is actually used for, is the BitLocker Drive Encryption [13] in the Windows operating system. Hence there is still a lack of user experience in the practical application of Trusted Computing and TPMs in the desktop PC world and also in industrial PC environments.

Using TPMs in embedded systems is even more challenging since embedded systems often do not have a BIOS, an operating system, device drivers or software stacks, which could facilitate the access to and the communication with the TPM. In this case the communication with the TPM has to take place "directly" i.e. by sending the appropriate byte sequences that correspond to the TPM

---

[1] Human-machine interface.

[2] Basic Input/Output System.

commands in [14] via the LPC[3]- or SMBus[4] to the TPM. Therefor the concrete byte sequences have to be figured out first, which is more laborious than using an API like the TSS.

Moreover embedded systems often do not have powerful CPUs and hence cannot execute extensive encryption and decryption operations in suitable time. Since TPMs were originally designed to be used in general-purpose computing systems with one or more powerful CPU(s) and sufficient memory, its use in embedded systems with limited processing and storage capabilities is not possible in the same manner.

By using Trusted Computing in mechanical engineering, the following protection goals have to be met: firstly software programs on the IPC and firmware in the embedded devices must be protected against copying and unauthorized manipulation. Secondly the unauthorized exchange of software-equipped (embedded) machine components has to be prevented or at least detected. In the following, possible approaches are described how this can be achieved.

4   Implementation of Anti-piracy Measures for Machines Using TPMs

As described in Section 1 there is a high demand for machine manufacturers to implement (software) protection measures against product piracy in their machines. So far TPMs are not used for this purpose in this domain yet, although TPMs meanwhile have become a quasi-standard and many platforms already are or easily can be equipped with a TPM. Today there are both industry PCs and various embedded platforms with TPM in the market.

The TPM can be used to prevent that software on one machine can be copied to another machine (e.g. to an imitation), that it can be manipulated (e.g. to activate additional features) and that individual machine components can be replaced without permission. In the following it is described how this can be achieved.

4.1   Data Sealing

To protect software like machine control programs from being copied to another machine, the programs (or parts of it) could be encrypted and bound to a specific hardware platform during manufacturing using a TPM, so that they are protected when the machine is sold and delivered to a customer.

Large amounts of data are usually encrypted using a symmetric encryption algorithm like the Advanced Encryption Standard (AES) [15] and later the used symmetric key is itself encrypted by an asymmetric key pair from the TPM using RSA. The symmetric key is usually a random number, which can be generated using the random number generator of the TPM. This is done by sending the

---

[3] Low-Pin Count.
[4] System Management Bus.

command *TPM_GetRandom()* with the appropriate parameters (e.g. the desired length) to the TPM which thereupon generates and returns a random number [14].

After the symmetric encryption of the data using AES and the random key, an RSA key pair is generated within the TPM, triggered by the command *TPM_CreateWrapKey()*. This command both generates and creates a secure storage bundle for asymmetric keys in the TPM. The created key can be locked to a specific PCR value by specifying a set of PCR registers [14]. Using this RSA key, the AES key is encrypted and optionally bound to a specific platform configuration (represented by the PCR values) by using the command *TPM_Seal()*. The input parameters of this command are the data to seal (in this case the symmetric key), the RSA key that should be used to encrypt the data and one or more PCR indices which represent the platform configuration the data is sealed to. In doing so the data is bound to a specific platform since the decryption key resides only within the TPM and is never revealed. Beyond that it is also bound to a specific platform configuration and it can only be decrypted by the TPM if the platform configuration is unchanged.

After sales and delivery of the machine, the software programs have to be decrypted before or during execution. To decrypt the sealed data the command *TPM_Unseal()* is sent to the TPM, together with the sealed data block and the key handle of the key that was used to encrypt the data. The TPM thereupon checks the content of the PCRs that were used during encryption and if they match the current values, the TPM unseals the symmetric key. If the PCR contents do not match, this implies that the platform configuration has changed and thus the TPM will not reveal the key. After the TPM has unsealed the AES key, the data (i.e. the program) can be decrypted and executed.

The introduced data sealing approach using the TPM is similar to the sealed storage concept introduced by Microsoft in its Next-Generation Secure Computing Base (NGSCB). Thereby information can be stored in such a way that only the application from which the data is saved (or a trusted designated application or entity) can open it [16]. Therefor a key is generated within the TPM during manufacturing which can later be used by applications to encrypt data so that it can only be decrypted by the TPM. The decrypted data will only be passed to authenticated, trusted applications and it is inaccessible both to other applications and the operating system.

The NGSCB should have been integrated into the next generations of the Windows operating system but it seems that Microsoft gave up these plans due to unknown reasons [17] since in the two major versions Windows Vista and Windows 7 none of the principal features described in the NGSCB has appeared. Thus in case there is no support for sealed storage by the operating system, our approach to encrypt and seal data to a specific platform configuration using the TPM could be used instead.

4.2 Software Integrity Verification

To prevent or at least detect the unauthorized alteration of software program code (e.g. so as to activate additional features) and to prevent the execution of manipulated or malicious software, an approach is needed that first checks the integrity and authenticity of the software program code before it is executed. This can be done by a "trust measurement" approach as described in [11]. The measurement has to be done by a separate entity that is reliably always executed at first after the platform is turned on. In the Trusted Computing Terminology this separate entity that does the integrity measurement is called Core Root of Trust for Measurement (CRTM). The CRTM has necessarily to be trusted and must be implemented in an immutable part of the storage so that it cannot be manipulated, overwritten or circumvented by means of software. Ideally the CRTM should be implemented in the TPM according to [18] but in this case the microprocessor reset vector has to point to the TPM which is not yet possible with existing computer architectures [11].

Thus the CRTM has to be implemented in a separate storage outside the TPM e.g. in an (OTP-)ROM[5]. This ROM contains the first instructions that are executed by the microprocessor after start-up. Usually this is done by making the CRTM part of the BIOS and storing it together with the BIOS firmware in the Boot-ROM. The CRTM starts the so-called Chain-of-Trust by measuring the next stage of the boot process (which is typically the rest of the BIOS) before passing control to this stage. "Measuring" in this case means to compute a hash value of the program code using a hash algorithm like SHA-1 [19]. The measurement results i.e. the computed hash values are usually stored in the Platform Configuration Registers (PCRs) of the TPM. Therefrom they can trustworthily be reported to a remote entity like a communication partner who then can verify the computed hash values and thus the current platform configuration by comparing the received hash values with the values he expects. This process is called "Remote Attestation".

In our use case there is no remote entity or communication partner which could verify the integrity of the platform and the loaded software programs since the machines are usually stand-alone and not connected to others. Thus the integrity verification has to be done within the system itself e.g. by the CRTM program. One possibility to realize this is to verify the digital signature of the software program code in case the software manufacturer generated a signature and attended it to the software. This is done by computing a hash value of the program code and signing this hash value with the private part of an RSA key that only the manufacturer knows. To be able to verify the signature, the CRTM must have access to the corresponding public part of this RSA key i.e. the public key has to be stored within the system.

In order to prevent an attack, in which an attacker signs his own (malicious) code using his own private RSA key and replaces the public key that is needed for verification with his own public key as described in [11], the public key should be stored securely e.g. in the TPM. In this case the signature could be verified by the TPM's internal RSA engine.

In case the software program does not contain a digital signature (e.g. in small microcontroller platforms that are only equipped with a firmware in the

---

[5] One Time Programmable Read-Only Memory.

flash memory) another approach could be used to verify the firmware integrity. Therefor a hash value of the firmware code is computed by the CRTM which is afterwards compared to a reference value that is the expected value if the firmware code has not been altered. This reference value has to be stored within the system as well, which could also be done using the TPM. The TPM has therefor a special-purpose register, the so called Data Integrity Register (DIR), which is part of the non-volatile storage within the TPM and can hold digest values of usually 160 bit. During manufacturing, when the platform is equipped with the firmware, the reference value has to be computed and securely stored in the DIR using the TPM command *TPM_DirWriteAuth()* which requires user authorization. The user authorization data must only be known to authorized people e.g. the manufacturer in this case.

After sales and delivery of the device respectively the machine, the CRTM has to compute a hash value of the firmware code and compare this to the reference value at each start-up before the software is to be executed. To read the content of the DIR the command *TPM_DirRead()* is used. So the following operations have to be executed after power-on, every time before the software program is to be executed as illustrated in Fig. 1:

1. The CRTM program computes a hash value of the software program code
2. The command *TPM_DirRead()* is sent to the TPM
3. The TPM sends the content of the DIR (which is the stored reference value) back to the CRTM program
4. The CRTM program compares the computed hash value to the reference value
5. If both values match, the software program is executed

If the computed hash value and the reference value do not match (in step 4), the software is not executed. The problem with this approach (marked with the red arrow) is that the TPM's return to the command *TPM_DirRead()* in step 3 contains no user authorization [14] and thus the receiver (in this case the CRTM program) cannot be sure if the message block he receives really comes from the TPM or not. This could be exploited by an attacker in that he intercepts the *TPM_DirRead()* command that is sent from the CRTM program to the TPM in step 2 and sends a message block with a chosen hash value back to the CRTM program (step 3). The CRTM program would not notice that the response in fact does not come from the TPM but that a wrong value has been foisted on it.

So if an attacker had the ability to alter the software program code and to foist a wrong reference value on the CRTM program he could deceive the system and circumvent the protection measure. Therefore it must be ensured that the CRTM program always receives the correct reference value that really comes from the TPM. An alternative approach to securely store the reference value and to ensure that it is trustworthily reported to the CRTM program, is to encrypt it with a private key from the TPM and seal it to a specific platform configuration i.e. to a specific PCR value. This PCR value could for instance be the hash value of the unchanged software program code.

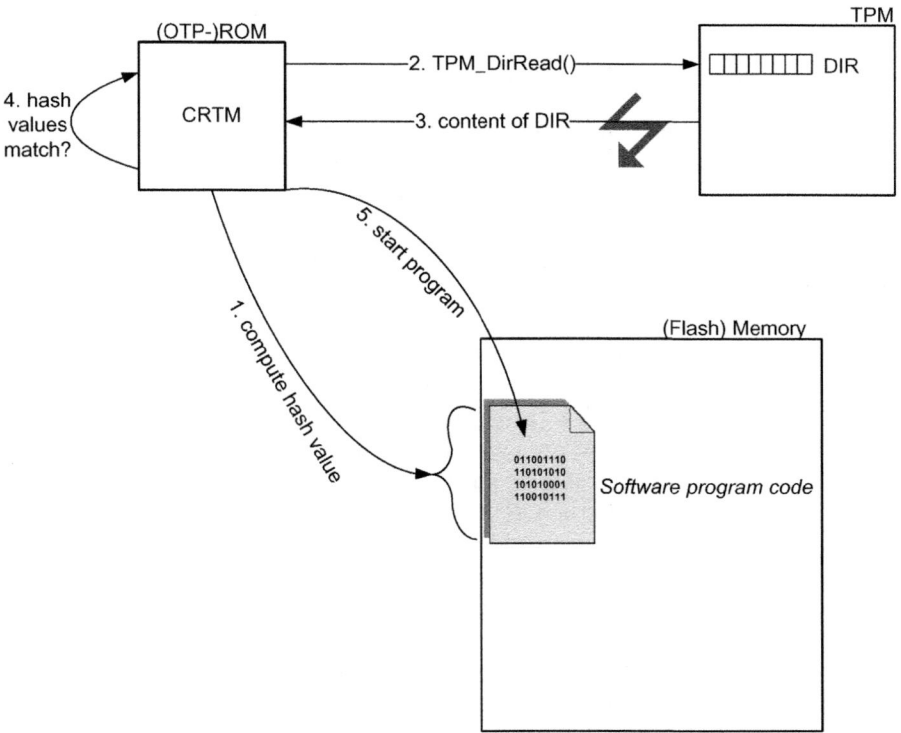

Fig. 1. Software Integrity Verification Process Using DIR

Thus the determination and secure storage of the reference value can be improved in the following way:

1. Compute a hash value h_1 of the program code and write it to PCR_i
2. Create an RSA key pair $k_1 = (k_1^{priv}, k_1^{pub})$ within the TPM
3. Call *TPM_Seal()* with k_1, h_1 and PCR_i as arguments
4. Get the sealed data block b_1 from the TPM
5. Store b_1

Each time the software program is to be executed, the following steps have to be done to check the software integrity (see Fig. 2):

1. The CRTM program computes the current hash value h_2 of the software program code
2. The CRTM program writes h_2 to PCR_i
3. The CRTM program reads the sealed data block b_1 from the memory
4. The command *TPM_Unseal()* with k_1, b_1 and PCR_i as arguments is sent to the TPM
5. The TPM checks the content of PCR_i
6. If the value of PCR_i (i.e. h_2) is equal to h_1, the TPM decrypts the sealed data block using k_1^{priv} and sends it back

7. The CRTM program compares the computed hash value to the decrypted reference value
8. If both values match, the software is executed

If h_2 does not match h_1 in step 6, the reference value is not decrypted and the TPM sends an error code back. In this case the software should not be executed. Step 7 could also be omitted since the reference value is only decrypted by the TPM in step 6 if the value of PCR_i (which is the currently computed hash value) matches the value it had during encryption. So if the reference value is decrypted by the TPM, this implies that both hash values match and the software code has not been altered.

The introduced approach works as long as no firmware update is necessary. In case of an update, a new reference value has to be sealed to the TPM and stored at the place, the CRTM program expects it. Thereby it must be ensured that an attacker cannot foist an own reference value to the system. To seal data to the TPM using *TPM_Seal()* an authorization value is needed (see [14]). The same value is used later by the CRTM program when sending *TPM_Unseal()* to the TPM. If these values are not identically, the TPM will not unseal the data and return an error code. Thus in this case the CRTM program will not execute the software program. So if an attacker does not know the correct authorization value, he cannot seal his reference value to the TPM in such a way it is expected by the system i.e. with the same authorization value that is used by the CRTM program. Hence the authorization value must be kept secret within the CRTM program as well.

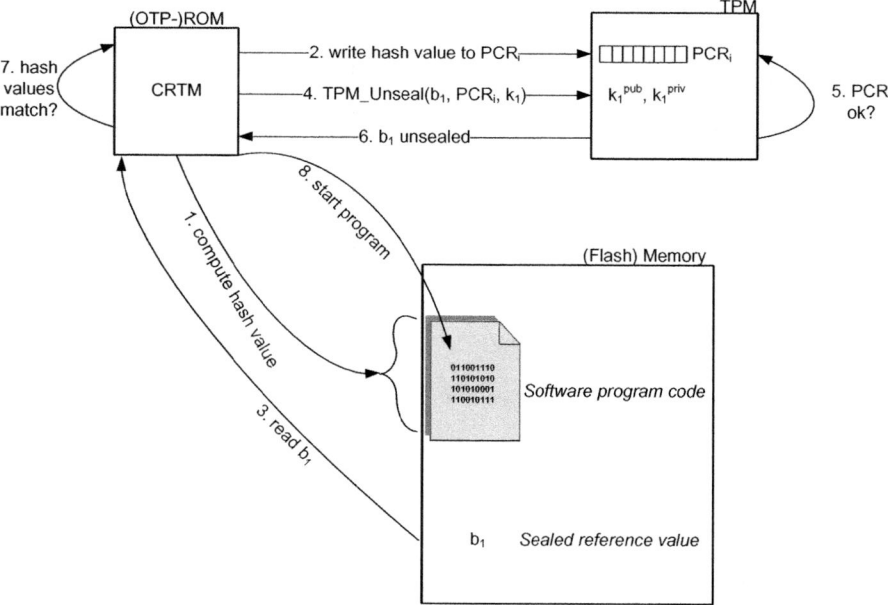

Fig. 2. Software Integrity Verification Process using *TPM_Seal()*

4.3   Mutual Authentication between Machine Components

If machine manufacturers want to ensure that no machine component can been replaced without permission, an approach for the mutual authentication between the machine components can be implemented in such a way that the superordinate control unit (i.e. the IPC) first checks the authenticity of the connected embedded devices and vice versa before the whole system starts working.

This could be done by implementing a Challenge-Response protocol between the IPC and the connected embedded devices using TPMs as illustrated in Fig. 3. For this a pair of RSA keys has to be generated in the TPM of the IPC as well as in the TPMs of each embedded device during manufacturing. Afterwards the public parts of the key pairs are interchanged between IPC and embedded devices and stored respectively.

After delivery of the machine the following steps are executed by the IPC at each start-up of the machine:

1. The IPC generates a nonce (i.e. a random number e.g. by using the random number generator of its TPM)
2. The nonce is sent to all embedded devices with the request to sign it with the private parts of their particular RSA key
3. The embedded devices i.e. their TPMs each sign the nonce with their private RSA key and send it back to the IPC
4. The IPC compares the received nonces to the sent one
5. If the numbers match, the IPC verifies the signatures using the public part of the appropriate RSA keys

If the signatures could successfully be verified, the IPC knows that the embedded devices are authentic since otherwise they would not have the correct private key to generate the correct signature. Thus the illegitimate replacement of an embedded machine component would be detected by the IPC.

The other way round the embedded devices can also verify the authenticity of the IPC by each generating a nonce and sending it to the IPC with the request to sign it. The IPC thereupon sends *TPM_Sign()* for each nonce to its TPM which signs all the nonces with its private RSA key and sends them back so that the devices can verify the signature by using the IPC's public key. If the signatures could successfully be verified by the embedded components, the IPC has proved his authenticity since only the authentic IPC has the correct private key within its TPM to generate the correct signatures.

Assuming there are n embedded components in the machine, the IPC—its TPM respectively—has to generate n signatures for n different nonces, which might perhaps be too time-consuming in some cases, depending on how often the authentication should take place. Hence an alternative approach would be to use a (symmetric) Message Authentication Code (MAC) instead of the asymmetric signature generation and verification method.

For this purpose a shared symmetric key has to be stored securely both in the IPC and the embedded devices during manufacturing. When the mutual authentication takes place, the IPC generates a nonce (to prevent replay-attacks)

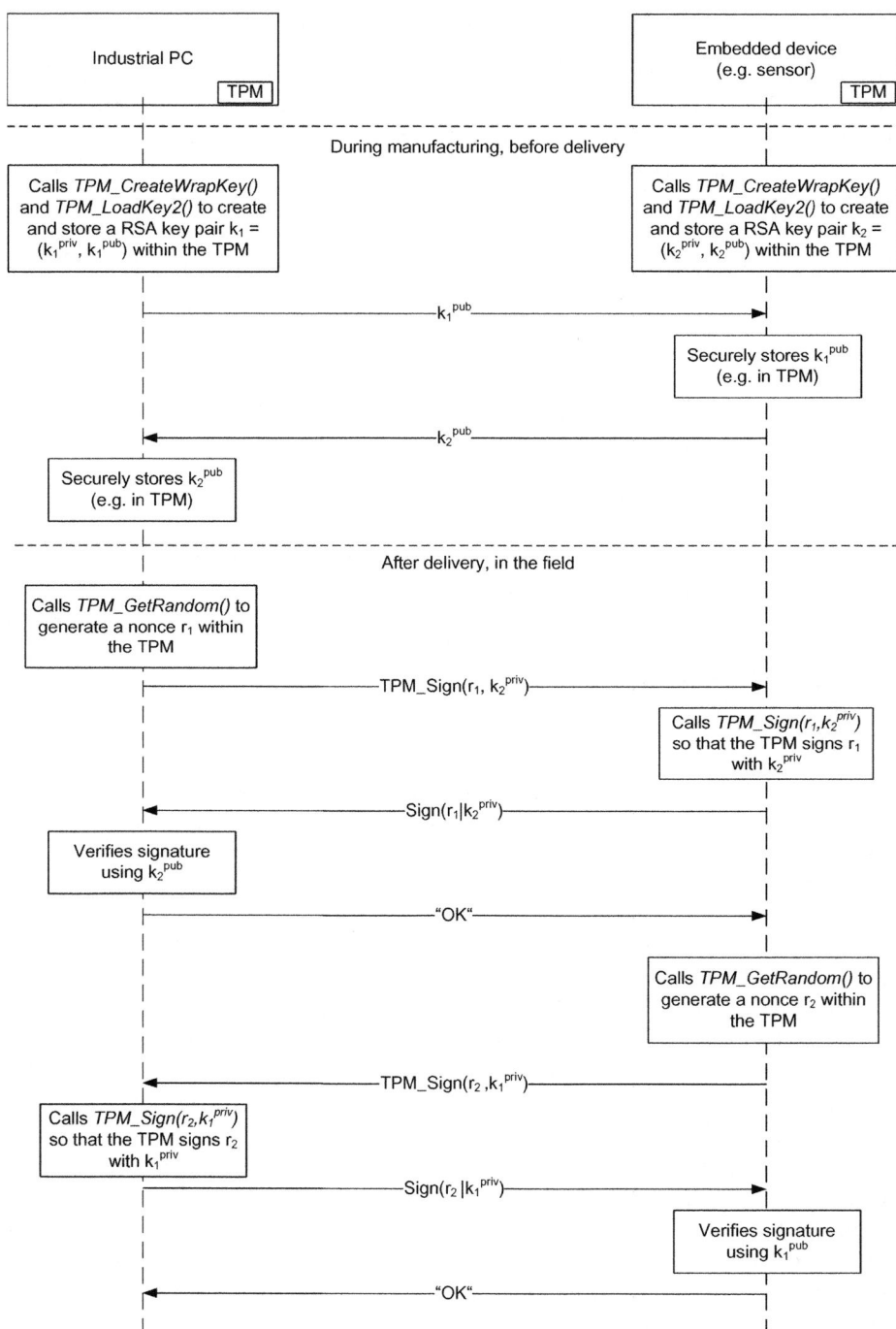

Fig. 3. Mutual Authentication Between Machine Components Using a Challenge-Response Protocol and TPMs

and computes a MAC for this nonce using the symmetric key. The nonce and the computed MAC is then sent to all the embedded devices which can verify that the MAC is correct by computing the MAC to the message (i.e. the nonce) on their part using the symmetric key and comparing the computed MAC to the received one. If both MAC values match, this implies that the message has probably not been altered and the MAC really comes from the IPC since an attacker would probably not be able to guess the correct symmetric key.

5 Conclusion

In this paper, several approaches have been introduced how Trusted Computing and TPMs can be applied to the mechanical engineering and automation field in order to prevent product piracy.

Copy protection of software programs like machine control programs can be achieved by encrypting these programs (or parts of it) during manufacturing and sealing it to a specific platform configuration using the TPM. During runtime, the symmetric key has to be unsealed by the TPM which is only done if the platform configuration has not been changed. Afterwards the program can be decrypted and executed.

The unauthorized manipulation of software programs can be prevented by first verifying the integrity of the program code before the program is executed. This is done by the Core Root of Trust for Measurement (CRTM) that computes a hash value of the program code and compares it to a reference value which is encrypted and stored within the system. If both values match, the software (or firmware) is executed otherwise not.

To prevent or at least detect the unauthorized replacement of software-equipped (embedded) machine components, a mutual authentication between the superordinate machine control (i.e. the industrial PC) and the connected embedded devices (sensors, actuators etc.) can be executed. This can be done using a Challenge-Response protocol and asymmetric generation and verification of signatures or—in case this is too time-consuming—by using Message Authentication Codes (MAC).

With the introduced approaches, Trusted Computing and TPMs can be reasonably applied in the mechanical engineering and automation field to prevent product and software piracy. To our knowledge there are so far no applications of Trusted Computing in this field yet, although there is a great demand for effective countermeasures against product piracy, particularly in this domain. Thus a new field of application for Trusted Computing and TPMs has been depicted that has to be explored doing further research.

Acknowledgments

This work has been supported by the German government BMBF project Pro-Protect.

References

1. Dietrich, K., Pirker, M., Vejda, T., Toegl, R., Winkler, T., Lipp, P.: A practical approach for establishing trust relationships between remote platforms using trusted computing. In: Barthe, G., Fournet, C. (eds.) TGC 2007 and FODO 2008. LNCS, vol. 4912, pp. 156–168. Springer, Heidelberg (2008)
2. Dietrich, K., Winter, J.: Implementation aspects of mobile and embedded trusted computing. In: Chen, L., Mitchell, C.J., Martin, A. (eds.) Trust 2009. LNCS, vol. 5471, pp. 29–44. Springer, Heidelberg (2009)
3. Kinney, S.: Trusted Platform Module Basics: Using TPM in Embedded Systems. Elsevier, Burlington (2006)
4. Trusted Computing Group: TCG Glossary,
   http://www.trustedcomputinggroup.org/developers/glossary
5. RSA Laboratories: PKCS #1 v2.1: RSA Cryptography Standard,
   http://www.rsa.com/rsalabs/node.asp?id=2125
6. Rouvroy, A., Poullet, Y.: The Right to Informational Self-Determination and the Value of Self-Development: Reassessing the Importance of Privacy for Democracy. In: Gutwirth, S., Poullet, Y., de Hert, P., de Terwangne, C., Nouwt, S. (eds.) Reinventing Data Protection? pp. 45–76. Springer, Netherlands (2009)
7. Trusted Computing Group: TCG Software Stack (TSS) Specification Version 1.2 Level 1 Errata A Part1: Commands and Structures,
   http://www.trustedcomputinggroup.org/files/resource_files/
   6479CD77-1D09-3519-AD89EAD1BC8C97F0/TSS_1_2_Errata_A-final.pdf
8. IBM: TrouSerS - An open-source TCG software stack implementation,
   http://sourceforge.net/projects/trousers/
9. Security Innovation: Core TCG Software Stack (CTSS),
   http://www.securityinnovation.com/pdf/collateral/
   trusted-software-stack.pdf
10. Microsoft Developer Network: TPM Base Services,
    http://msdn.microsoft.com/en-us/library/aa446796%28VS.85%29.aspx
11. Zhou, Z., Xu, R.: BIOS Security Analysis and a Kind of Trusted BIOS. In: Qing, S., Imai, H., Wang, G. (eds.) ICICS 2007. LNCS, vol. 4861, pp. 427–437. Springer, Heidelberg (2007)
12. Phoenix Technologies: Phoenix SecureCore,
    http://www.phoenix.com/ptec/docs/securecore_ds_en.pdf
13. Microsoft: BitLocker Drive Encryption: Technical Overview,
    http://technet.microsoft.com/en-us/library/cc732774.aspx
14. Trusted Computing Group TPM Working Group: TPM Main Part 3 Commands Specification Version 1.2 Level 2 Revision 103,
    http://www.trustedcomputinggroup.org/files/static_page_files/
    ACD28F6C-1D09-3519-AD210DC2597F1E4C/mainP3Commandsrev103.pdf
15. FIPS: Specification for the Advanced Encryption Standard (AES), In: Federal Information Processing Standards Publication 197,
    http://csrc.nist.gov/publications/fips/fips197/fips-197.pdf
16. Microsoft: Next-Generation Secure Computing Base General Information
    http://technet.microsoft.com/en-us/library/cc723472.aspx
17. Mueller, T.: Trusted Computing Systeme. Springer, Heidelberg (2008)
18. Trusted Computing Group: TCG Specification Architecture Overview
    http://www.trustedcomputinggroup.org/files/resource_files/
    AC652DE1-1D09-3519-ADA026A0C05CFAC2/TCG_1_4_Architecture_Overview.pdf
19. Eastlake III, D., Jones, P.: US Secure Hash Algorithm 1 (SHA1). RFC 3174 (2001)

Lagrangian E-Voting:
Verifiability on Demand and Strong Privacy*

Łukasz Krzywiecki and Mirosław Kutyłowski

Institute of Mathematics and Computer Science, Wrocław University of Technology, Wybrzeże
Wyspiańskiego 27, 50-370 Wrocław, Poland
Lukasz.Krzywiecki@pwr.wroc.pl, Miroslaw.Kutylowski@pwr.wroc.pl

Abstract. We propose a new approach to verifiability of Internet e-voting procedures: correct counting of each single ballot can be checked, but verification is
a zero-knowledge court procedure. After verification period is over, certain keys
are destroyed and breaking vote privacy becomes substantially harder.

Our main goal is to provide a framework for the political situation in which
the voters are more concerned about disclosure of their preferences than about
the correctness of the results. Our approach also responds to threats of coercion
exercised by a physically present coercer.

Our approach can be used on top of most previous schemes to improve their
privacy features. It is limited to the cases when the voters hold electronic ID cards.

Keywords: remote e-voting, electronic ID card, anonymity, verifiability,
Lagrangian interpolation, zero-knowledge proof, undeniable signature.

1 Introduction

There is a growing demand for remote electronic voting procedures that could be applied safely in major political elections. Growing mobility of voters makes it inevitable
to admit methods such that physical presence at the polling station at the election day
is no longer a precondition to cast a vote. Unfortunately, designing a good e-voting system turns out to be an extremely difficult task, perhaps one of the most difficult ones for
trust and privacy protection technologies.

History of e-voting is not only history of developing new ideas and techniques, but
also continuous evolution of requirements for e-voting systems and growing awareness
of diversity and complexity of the problem. Numerous and sometimes spectacular failures follow from misunderstanding or neglecting critical design factors. One of them is
technical security of the system, however, not the only one. It is equally important how
the voters perceive their personal security and how they are influenced by their understanding of security problems. In particular, a voter may believe that a cryptographic
ballot betrays her or his vote, despite of a formal security proof.

One of the sources of problems in e-voting design is insufficient information flow
between computer systems designers and specialists in sociology and political sciences

---

* Partially supported by Polish Ministry of Science and Higher Education, grant N N206 2701
  33. The second author has been also supported by Foundation for Polish Science within the
  MISTRZ Programme.

A. Acquisti, S.W. Smith, and A.-R. Sadeghi (Eds.): TRUST 2010, LNCS 6101, pp. 109–123, 2010.

[5]. This concerns also information flow between different fields of computer science. For instance, some people claim that disclosing the code and the algorithm is enough to achieve transparency of the voting process. This is not, since for instance the trapdoors may be installed by a compiler (see e.g a textbook [12]).

Also, it is necessary to have in mind that due to very different voting mechanisms in different countries there is no unique model of voting, no universal set of requirements for such a system. A good example would be a comparison between the British and the German voting system. In the first case, it is necessary to provide mechanisms for disclosing the votes and recounting them openly after a court decision. This eliminates, for instance, any cryptography without a trapdoor (for the entitled authorities). On the other hand, even possibility of existence of such a trapdoor eliminates immediately such an e-voting system in Germany, due to the rules contained in the German constitution.

Verifiability versus privacy. We focus on the problem of voters concerned that verifiability, which became a must-to-be condition in serious e-voting procedures, may be feared by the voters as a source of information endangering secrecy of their voting preferences in a long run. So far, most authors and political activists, especially from Anglo-American countries, follow the opinion that after elections as much information should be published as possible (a notable exception is [11]). "As possible" means here that the published information must not violate privacy of votes. However, the real purpose of publishing voting information is to guarantee that the published election results match the voter's decisions. So according to standard information processing rules, the system should reveal the minimal amount of information to achieve the goal and not the maximal one that does not violate other rules.

In some societies the voters are more interested in their long term privacy than in the election results. They fear that the information published can be reused for linking the votes to the voters. In fact, this is justified, since progress in cryptanalysis may provide necessary tools in the future. We have to keep in mind that time horizon is here quite long – breaking after, say 20 years, is a serious concern. On the other hand, nobody can provide security guarantees for cryptographic methods for such a long time. Current e-voting schemes disregard this issue; it seems to be the main weakness of most e-voting schemes compared with paper-based methods.

The problem described above has been reported for voters behavior in case of verifiable paper audit trails. Use of cryptography in the paper trials and hiding information there can be a source of distrust - the voter may believe that their votes are encoded there so that some authorities may read it.

In principle, the only function of verification is to enable checking correctness of the results by the voters and election observers. It does not mean that a verification procedure must be really executed – the threat of inevitable detection of frauds makes participants of the process behave correctly. So, without endangering the role of verification, we might limit information disclosure as long as fraud detection is possible. The goal of this paper is to design alternative and privacy aware means of verifiability.

Trust issues. One of the major problems in designing e-voting systems is to convince general public that the system can be really trusted. Certainly, declarations of the system providers are not enough, even if they are honest. For instance, the declaration concerning the Estonian system is not much useful, as securing e-elections from malicious PC's was not a part of the specification.

There are multiple issues that lead to citizens' acceptance or distrust in e-voting systems. The main issues from the point of view of a single voter is not only correctness of the results but also confidentiality of his voting decisions. In a long run even a threat to break voter's privacy may severely influence voter's choice: a voter may abstain from voting or cast the votes as expected by a ruling party. There are many examples in history and in present political situation that this is one of the key issues – it is the crucial issue to convince the voter about security of a system.

1.1   State of the Art

End-to-end systems.   Recent history of deployment of electronic voting systems is full of failure stories of systems that miss to reach a decent security level. A typical mistake is to relay solely on the declarations of the manufacturers about security and safety of their systems in the case when security requirements have not been even formulated (a good source of examples of this kind is the California Report [3]).

It is often assumed that certain e-voting participants or protocol agents are honest. In particular, most authors of academic papers made no distinction between the voter and her or his computational devices as different protocol participants. A hidden assumption was that hardware and software components used for voting are secure, non-malicious, and under full control of the voter. Unfortunately, attacking election software, providing fake election equipment and even installing trapdoors to the system are relatively easy. Currently available techniques are quite effective, e.g. kleptographic techniques by Young and Yung can be easily applied against e-voting schemes [14] revealing completely voters' choices to the attacker. Certainly, some problems can be avoided thanks to deployment of TPM's. However, it turns out that the protection offered by TPM's is not unbreakable (see e.g. [21]) and TPM's can be both fooled about the state of the system and allow extraction of their private keys. Similarly, in some opinions, using smart cards prevents attacks due to Trojan software and unwelcome dependence on general purpose operating systems, allowing more reliable inspection of the hardware used. While this is true, one has to keep in mind that it is quite easy to replace original smart cards with malicious ones: due to black box principle it is almost impossible to detect the fraud in a normal use. Also, usage of smart cards with a single e-voting functionality may facilitate vote selling - so in fact reaching reverse effect than intended.

There is growing consensus about necessity to design *end-to-end systems*, where security is examined not for chosen components (including both protocol participants and hardware/software components), but for the system as a whole, including all kinds of threats, including for example socio-technical attacks (see Dagstuhl Accord [1]).

So far, design of end-to-end voting systems was quite successful in the area of paper based methods (Prêt à Voter [9], Punchscan [6], Scantegrity [8], VAV [20] and their variations). Surprisingly, it has turned out that one can achieve verifiability of the election result without violating privacy requirements (let us remark that the traditional way of voting offers almost no verifiability). The first elections of this kind already took place in Takoma Park in Maryland.

Systems for remote voting over computer networks. There is a vast literature concerning remote e-voting systems. Here we point only to a few recent trends.

Remote voting is more challenging that designing systems for a polling station. The problem is that one has no control over the equipment used by a voter to create and send a ballot. Moreover, one cannot assume that cryptographic operations are performed by the voter manually, so he must use some computing devices.

If computer networks are used for communication only, like in [19], the situation is somewhat easier: a voter can fetch a ballot electronically, print it, fill it and send to the election committee via a different channel (per post or by faxing the ballot). In this scenario we avoid the problem of a malicious PC leaking information on voter's preferences. On the other hand, selling votes becomes easier even than for mail-in systems, as a ballot can be sold with no physical contact between the seller and the buyer.

Paper [16] states a security model for remote e-voting and proposes scheme for this model. The solution is based on credentials, but validity of a credential cannot be determined by a PC or a coercer. The idea is that each vote comes together with a credential and that the votes with invalid credentials are removed during the final stage just before vote counting. Moreover, the credentials are not published in plaintext, therefore coercion is almost impossible. This conceptually simple and elegant solution is inefficient for large scale elections. Paper [22] shows that efficiency can be improved. However, there are major security problems with this scheme when applied in real life elections. The main concern is that the PC (or the PC's) used by the voter may cheat and send a vote for a different candidate than indicated by the voter – the scheme assumes silently that the voter's computer is honest. The voter has no possibility to check his vote. Second, the registrar $\mathcal{R}$ can cast additional votes for candidates of his choice through an anonymous channel re-using the credentials of the voters. The duplicates are removed according to some policy, but it seems to be inevitable that some votes cast by the registrar will remain.

The scheme [17] provides a solution in which the PC used by a voter cannot determine the meaning of a ballot, even if it has been prepared by the PC. So, it cannot break privacy of the vote. Coercion is excluded by a mechanism of anti-votes: if a vote is cast, it can be later disabled by the same voter (after appropriate authentication). Moreover, the fact of canceling the vote is not visible for a coercer, so the voter can do it safely. Nevertheless, the voter can cast the vote once more after sending an anti-vote. Therefore, the voter can cheat and sell its vote many times and finally vote as he wishes. The scheme splits a vote into parts that are re-encrypted during the mixing process - which makes verification of mixes fairly simple and efficient. However, the scheme is conceptually too complex to be accepted even by very well educated voters, even the process of vote casting is not a simple one. So it does not satisfy "transparency" requirement and is a purely academic solution.

The recent Helios [4] is an example of a system, where threats of coercion and attacks by infecting PC are simply ignored (see [10]). Despite this the system has been used in practice in university elections in Belgium.

The scheme SC&V presented in paper [18] reuses the ideas of Threeballot, Punch-scan, and Prêt à Voter. It offers immunity against malicious PC used by a voter - the idea is that the PC performs some operations for the voter, but it is unaware about the meaning of the vote, even if it knows the ballot cast by the voter. Manipulating the ballot is hard, since it is unclear which configurations of the "marks" on the ballot are valid for a vote. So, with a substantial probability misbehavior of the PC would be immediately detected. The construction depends on an additional information channel inaccessible for the PC, through which the voter gets information necessary to fill the ballot. The scheme is relatively friendly and transparent, but certainly too complex for a certain voters. Its prototype has been tested in real life elections (elections of student representatives in a university). The main drawback is that vote selling and coercion is possible, when the buyer or coercer appears in person – only online coercion is prevented.

Remote e-voting in political elections in practice. The systems deployed so far in practice for political elections are far away from fulfilling minimal security requirements. The system in Estonia assumes that user's PC and electronic ID card are secure, and that the mixing authorities (there are just two!) do not cooperate. In Switzerland, a version of SureVote is used: computer of the voter need not to be trusted, however secrecy of voter's preferences against election authorities is quite limited. Even less secure methods has been deployed in Austria in student elections, and in France for AFE (the assembly that represents French nationals living abroad). These schemes are not immune against malicious PCs and offer limited privacy of votes.

On the other hand, there is an e-voting project in Norway [2], where the set of requirements well describes necessary security goals. However, the system to be deployed gives no guarantee of voters' privacy against her or his computer – the computer learns the option chosen by the voter. On the other hand, the voter gets a receipt that makes it possible to detect that the vote has been changed by the computer. The mechanism is similar to SureVote.

Deploying a good system is however a non-trivial task, as so far no system really fulfills all conditions. Sometimes problematic issue is not only security, for instance it might be electronic authentication of voters and their education level. In particular, formal security proofs of voting protocols have mainly academic value, what it really needed is a convincing security argument for non-specialists.

Our contribution. In this paper we show how to build an extra layer on top of remote voting schemes such as SC&V in order to provide better privacy guarantees and coercion resistance. The method is quite general and can be viewed as a plug-in solution for schemes where vote casting is performed by setting a number of binary values in a specific way. Namely, our approach is to show how to set the binary values when casting a vote using any other remote voting scheme. So, thereby we get a scheme that inherits all positive security features of the main scheme, but adds an additional one:

- verification can be performed only in an election court and the evidence cannot be used outside the court due to its zero knowledge properties,
- verification requires cryptographic keys of the election authorities; so it is possible to destroy the keys and thereby prevent any investigations once the election results are irrevocable (for instance, when the term of elected persons is over).

On the other hand, each binary value is encoded by several ciphertexts created with asymmetric methods. So, it increases communication complexity, but on the other hand any usable e-voting scheme must not require too much manual work, and in particular clicking too many buttons. So the number of binary values is restricted by design of the background scheme.

2 Method Description

In order to make description easier to follow we formulate it as a stand-alone scheme were the voter has to choose between two values ("yes" or "no"). However, we have in mind that the scheme serves as a subprocedure for other algorithms.

2.1 Personal Identity Cards

In the European Union there are decisions to introduce electronic personal identity cards for citizens. Potentially, these cards can be used for remote e-voting schemes. Its primary use for e-voting is reliable remote authentication and verification of voting rights (i.e. citizenship and age). However, using personal identity card for e-voting has an additional advantage. Any special purpose e-voting smart card can be given to a vote buyer. This is not the case for personal identity card, since it might be misused by the vote buyer for other purposes, like taking a cash credit. Moreover, it is a well learned behavior of the voters, to refuse to give anybody own personal identity card. It will be even stronger if more functionalities appear on the personal identity card.

From now on, a smart card that is non-transferable and able to authenticate the voter will be called *ID card* of the voter.

2.2 Registration

Before the election day, a voter has to register with his ID card. Registration is necessary anyway, since we have to admit both remote voting and voting at polling stations. In order to generate the list of voters eligible to cast votes in a traditional way, we need to get a list of the voters that cast the votes electronically. (In countries like USA or Australia, there is almost no voter verification and casting many votes is possible. However, our goal is to design a system that each voter has a single vote.)

During registration a voter receives a *voting token* necessary for casting a vote (and sometimes for verification purposes). A token x is constructed in the following way:

1. The ID card of a voter generates at random a pair of keys for some signature scheme. For the purpose of description, let cs denote here the secret key, and cp denote the public key generated.
2. The ID card encapsulates cp preparing a request for a blind signature of the Registration Authority. The request is signed digitally by the card with a regular digital signature of the voter.
3. The request is passed to the Registration Authority through a PC, or through an e-government kiosk installed by public authorities.
4. Registration Authority checks the signature on the request and marks the voter as registered for electronic elections. Then it blindly generates a signature s over cp.
5. The blind signature is delivered back to the ID card.

6. The ID card recovers the signature s and creates a token $x = (cp, s)$.
7. The ID card sends a confirmation to the Registration Authority about receiving the token.

If the Registration Authority does not receive the confirmation from the last step, then the voter is asked to resend it. If the confirmation is still not received, then the voter is asked to appear in person with the card. Then the blind signature can be loaded directly into the card. If the voter does not appear, then the token is regarded as delivered, but simultaneously the public signature key of the voter is revoked for the further use. So if the voter does not cooperate, his ID card becomes blocked for electronic use. For the voter, the only way to avoid responsibility (the ID card has to be protected by its owner, with penalties for not doing this), is to show up claiming that the ID card has been lost. In this case the inconvenience for the voter is so high, that it is reasonable to assume that in practice he would better confirm receiving the token. Note that he would not be admitted to cast a vote in a traditional way after loosing identification document.

2.3 Ballot Structure

In the next subsections we explain in detail the role of each component of a ballot. Now we only sketch the general structure:

- A voter sends triples of the form (x, y, z) , where x is the token mentioned above.
- The voter may send many such triples, but still casting one vote. This prevents vote selling and coercion – the voter can change how her vote is counted as long as she holds her ID card.
- Parameter z is an *activation counter* chosen at random (except for a few occasions). The numbers x and y are used for Lagrangian interpolation of some polynomial used for counting the results. The point x is the argument, while y together with x is used by an election authority to determine the value of the polynomial at x.
- The ID card computes y in a deterministic and verifiable way:
  $y = \text{hash}(\text{sign}_{ID}(x, z))$. The signature is created with a key used only for creating the parameters y (for some discussion see Sect. 3.7).

2.4 Casting a Vote

During counting procedure two polynomials will be constructed: one for "yes" and one for "no" option. The degree of each polynomial will represent the number of votes cast for its option.

All triples (x, y, z) with the same first component x (sent by the same voter) are used to construct a single point of one of the polynomials. Which polynomial is used depends on the values of the activation counters. Now we describe some details of the procedure:

- The ID card creates some number of triples of the form (x, y, z) with different numbers z and the fixed x, it sends them to (possibly different) Electronic Ballot Boxes. The triples must be sent via an anonymous channel or via a proxy, no authentication of the sender is necessary. The triples can be created at different times and sent via different computers. However, at least two such triples must be sent. This may be guaranteed by the property that for each demand the ID card creates two triples.

- To each triple (x, y, z) the ID card attaches a signature created with the key cs. Recall that cp is contained in x, so Electronic Ballot Box can verify this signature.
- The triple (x, y, z) and its signature are encrypted with probabilistic encryption scheme with designated receiver. The designated receiver is, in this case, the tallying authority. As usual, many layers of encryption may be used in case of multiple tallying authorities, each layer to be removed by one authority.
- Each Electronic Ballot Box sends a signed confirmation of each packet received. In this way it may also confirm receiving junk, since the decoding is done later by the tallying authorities. An important feature is that the same encrypted triple can be sent to many Electronic Ballot Boxes – there is no problem with duplicates during vote counting. In this way, one can deal with denial of service problem or lack of confirmations due to communication system failures.
- If a voter sends some number of triples of the form (x, y, z), say (x, y_1, z_1), ..., (x, y_k, z_k), then the vote will be counted for the "yes" option provided that $\sum z_i = 0 \bmod m$ (where m is some sufficiently big number) – via creating a point for Lagrangian interpolation of the "yes"- polynomial. Otherwise, the point will be used for the "no"-polynomial.

Note that the card can easily turn a vote cast to *no* by sending an additional triple (x, y, z) with z generated at random. Since the voter may send the triples from different locations and different PC's, a coercer or vote buyer would have to retain the personal ID of the voter in order to prohibit him from revoking a *yes* vote.

Similarly, if the ID card keeps the sum of different numbers z from the triples already sent to the Electronic Ballot Boxes, then the card can turn a "no" vote to a "yes" vote.

2.5   Ballot Mixing and Decryption

The ballots are processed via a cascade of tallying authorities in an conventional way, each tallying authority removes one layer of encryption. In order to avoid any later dispute in case of fraud detection, when a tallying authority outputs partially decrypted ballots to the next authority in the cascade, then the set of ballots is signed by both authorities and retained in a safe place. No procedure to check the mixing and decoding is necessary due to other integrity mechanisms implemented by our scheme.

2.6   Counting the Votes

After the final decryption of ballots, Counting Authority gets a set of triples with signatures. It verifies the signatures and discards any triple with an invalid signature. Then it groups all triples with the same x. Say, for a given x there are triples (x, z_1, y_1), ..., (x, z_k, y_k) properly signed. The triples with x are processed as follows:

- Counting Authority computes $z := \sum_{i=1}^{k} z_i$.
- If $z \bmod m = 0$, then the point $(x, F(\sum y_i))$ is used for Lagrangian interpolation of the "yes"-polynomial (for the definition of F see below). Otherwise, $(x, F(\sum y_i))$ is used for Lagrangian interpolation of the "no"-polynomial.

Function $F(y)$ is an undeniable signature of Counting Authority created for y. For this purpose, the scheme proposed in e.g. [7] can be used. The key properties of such a scheme are that:

- verification of the signature requires cooperation with Counting Authority,
- verification takes the form of a zero-knowledge proof (hence a transcript of the proof is meaningless for the third party),
- Counting Authority can either prove that the signature is correct (if it is so), or prove that it is invalid (if the signature is false). (The proof might be probabilistic.)

After computing all these points Counting Authority uses Lagrangian interpolation to compute polynomials W_{yes} and W_{no} that go through all these points.

2.7   Publishing the Results

Counting Authority publishes the polynomials W_{yes} and W_{no} constructed in the counting phase. For instance, if the degree of W equals N, then Counting Authority may present the values of W for the arguments $0, 1, 2, \ldots, N$.

The triples used to compute the results are not published.

2.8   A Sketch of the Verification by a Voter

The scheme offers possibility to check that each single vote has been properly counted. The procedure is executed on demand of a voter in a court. The only participants of the procedure are the judge, the voter (appearing in person) and perhaps independent and trusted election observers (e.g. from OECD). The Counting Authority provides access to electronic interface with the judge.

- The voter presents the triples sent and their confirmations to the judge.
- The triples are sent by the judge through the cascade of tallying authorities in order to decrypt them.
- Counting Authority is asked about the number of triples with x.
  - If it is larger than the number of confirmations shown by the voter, then Counting Authority is asked to present additional triples with the same x, if they are used in the counting process. Since each ballot is self-signed, it is evident that they come from the same ID card. If Counting Authority presents such triples, it means that the voter provides incomplete data and the case is closed.
  - If the number of triples obtained by Counting Authority is lower than the number of confirmations obtained by the voter, then all triples are decrypted by Tallying Authorities under supervision of the judge. The judge finds out which Tallying Authority has removed a triple from the list of intermediate results in the original process by checking for their presence on the original list. The case is closed by finding the cheating authority.
- The judge computes $z = \sum z_i$, where the values z_i are taken from all triples provided by the voter.

- Based on the value of z, a vote for the "yes"- option or for the "no"-option is checked. That is, either $W_{yes}(x)$ or $W_{no}(x)$ should take the value $F(\sum y_i)$. Let us assume that $W_\bullet(x) = F(\sum y_i)$ should hold. Since $W_\bullet$ has been published as the voting result, one can compute the value $W_\bullet(x)$. On the other hand, recall that $F(\sum y_i)$ is a deterministic undeniable signature of the Counting Authority for $\sum y_i$. So, in order to check the equality $W_\bullet(x) = F(\sum y_i)$ an interactive zero knowledge verification protocol is executed by the Counting Authority and the judge. For the polynomial $W_\circ$ that does not correspond to the voter's choice, a repudiation protocol is executed to show that $W_\circ(x) \neq F(\sum y_i)$.

This procedure ensures that it is risky for Counting Authority and Tallying Authorities to modify any vote cast or not to include it in the tally in the correct way. On the other hand, the value $F(\sum y_i)$ is proved in the court only in the electronic procedure initiated by the judge with the electronic interface of Counting Authority. Even if the session is recorded by the voter, it has no value for a vote buyer due to the properties of the zero knowledge proofs.

During the procedure the judge usually learns the value chosen by the voter ("yes" or "no"). However, the judge and the Counting Authority can easily cheat the coercer showing him a fake zero-knowledge proof. The only problematic case is is when the judge himself is the coercer. However, recall that the whole procedure (setting binary values) is designed as a plug-in to another protocols (like SC&V, Threeballot, ...), where the voter may show some number of her binary choices without revealing her vote. In fact, these schemes even provide explicit receipts with binary values signed by the election authorities. For the reason mentioned, the voter is allowed to challenge Counting Authority on a limited number of binary values. Their exact number depends on the scheme used.

Apart from the checking procedure initiated by a voter, there might be an additional checking procedure. There are M special ID cards that can only cast a "yes" vote, and M special ID cards that can only cast a "no" vote. They are used by audit bodies just as regular ID cards (and cannot be distinguished from them), but do not influence the election results as M values are given to each option. The difference is that afterward the checking procedure is executed openly. The number M is chosen so that from statistical point of view any attempt of the election authorities to change the election result would require to manipulate such a subset of vote that at least one of M special votes has to be manipulated as well with a fairly high probability.

2.9   Destroying Verification Material

After the period, during which the voters are allowed to challenge the election results, all keys used for verification are destroyed. This concerns in particular the keys used to prove the values of F. This is to prevent any attempt to break voting privacy in the future, when the control over voting data becomes weaker.

2.10   Verification of the Number of Votes Cast

The main purpose of the procedure described here is to avoid casting additional votes by the Counting Authority. We have to make sure that if additional votes have been cast, they have no influence on the final election outcome.

For each token x, used for counting the votes, Counting Authority publishes $u(x)$, which is a cryptographic commitment to token x. Of course, the number of these signatures must be equal to the sum of degrees of W_{yes} and W_{no}.

Depending on the election result, some number of entries $u(x)$ is checked. The exact number of entries to be verified is determined according to the rules of statistics. Verification is executed with election observers and an election court, but the results may be published. First, the value of x is revealed. Then one of the triples containing x together with the signature created by the ID card is shown by the Counting Authority. Since the token x contains the verification key signed by Registration Authority, we can therefore check the signature and assure ourselves that the token x has been really used for casting a vote.

3   Discussion of Security Features

In this section we discuss some of the features of our approach. We do not provide complete assumptions and risk analysis, since our method is thought to be used jointly with other schemes. As experience shows, most vulnerabilities arise on the boundary between different design layer, so such an analysis is useful only if performed on a complete system.

Of course, the scheme proposed does not offer unconditional correctness of the results. The authorities may create virtual voters and let them vote. However, this is the problem of any voting procedure including the traditional ones, where a person may appear in multiple polling stations, each time with a different personal ID. Note that some number of such ID's are issued by security agencies for operational purposes.

3.1   Vote Selling and Coercion

Vote buying and coercion does not work, since the voter can always send an additional triple to flip the vote value. Moreover, the additional triple can be sent <u>before</u> selling the vote. So it does not change the situation, if the ID card of the voter gets locked just after selling the vote, and remains inaccessible until the end of the election day.[1]

If the ID-card remembers the sum of values z_i sent so far, then it would be possible to turn the vote in both directions: from "yes" to "no" and from "no" to "yes". There is a technical aspect that the card must not reveal the status of the sum of all z_i.

If Counting Authority is the coercer, then he can ask the voter to send some big number of triples in order to recognize the voters contribution by the number of triples. This may be defended in a number of ways. One of them is that each binary value is submitted to a different counting authority, so the counting authorities would have to cooperate to coerce. If counting authorities are under supervision of different parties, this becomes hard. Another method is to limit the number of triples that may be sent by each ID card and keep it in a reasonable range so that quite many repetitions regarding the number of sent triples must occur. The voter can cheat the coercer about the admissible number of triples and send some triples before.

---

[1] In Estonia, one can cancel a vote, but it requires using personal ID card. So a vote buyer may put the ID card in a special envelope and leave it to its owner, he pays after the election day if the envelope has not been opened.

3.2 Malicious Computers

No cryptographic operation is computed on a PC, it is used only for communication. So it cannot encode the voter's choice with techniques such as kleptographic codes. Of course, the PC can inform an attacker about:

- transmitting a ballot from this computer,
- the serial number of the ID card (unless the card is configured very carefully),
- the choice of the voter entered on the keyboard.

However, a voter may use different PC's for sending triples. Then, the attacker does not get information about the voters choice unless all computers used are under his control. Moreover, the background scheme should be designed in such a way that even revealing all choices of the voter at the keyboard does not reveal the vote.

An additional countermeasure would be that together with the ID card a voter gets information about which key is regarded to be "yes" and which is regarded to be "no". This information can be delivered like PIN codes for the ATM cards. So, even if the machine can see the stroked key, it does not know if it stands for "yes" or "no". Since there are not many public elections during a typical lifetime of an ID card (say, 5–10 years), one can even provide a different translation scheme for each election! So the adversary cannot even learn if a particular voter changes her or his preferences.

3.3 Voter's Privacy

Thanks to the blind signatures, the ID card authenticates only against Registration Authority, vote casting is via anonymous channel without any authentication against Electronic Ballot Box. The cascade of mix servers run by Tallying Authorities ensures disruption of the link between a voter casting an encrypted ballot and the triples in the plaintext form. However, there are additional points that make the algorithm stronger:

- The published results do not reveal the data obtained from the Tallying Authorities. The polynomials published are checked against this data on demand only.
- The link between a token x and the voter getting it is untraceable as long as the blind signature scheme is secure, or Registration Authority remains honest and the communication between the voter and Registration Authority is well protected against eavesdropping.

Additionally, breaking privacy of the votes becomes even harder after destroying the keys used for computing F and proving its values.

3.4 Decline of Cryptographic Strength of Algorithms

Due to improvements of cryptanalytic techniques, one may fear that some day her or his ballot encoded cryptographically will be readable to everybody. This is a serious threat to any scheme where the encoded ballots are presented on a bulletin board.

In this sense, the scheme presented in this paper reduces the problems compared to other solutions for remote voting presented in the literature. The information about the encoded ballots publicly available is very limited. The verification procedure can be performed on demand, but again the data processed is not published.

Of course, some data may be retained by dishonest election authorities. However, since we assume that the keys for F are stored in an HSM, we can destroy them without leaving any information.

3.5 Dishonest Authorities

Serious problems occur, if all authorities are controlled by a malicious party. Since the authorities are issuing the ID cards as well, then the system becomes broken completely. However, this is the case also for traditional paper based voting.

On the other hand, Tallying Authorities can be supervised by different parties and one honest mix guarantees privacy of mixing. Registration Authority may collaborate with Counting Authority, however it does not break the system, since Registration Authority does not know the token signed for a given user. The crucial part is security of the ID cards. However, as we explain below, to some extent they can be verified as well.

3.6 Dishonest Judge

During the court procedure, the judge learns identity of a voter and some of his voting choices. Therefore, at the first look it seems that the judge can leak sensitive information. However, if we use a proper background scheme, then verification may be performed so that no information on voter's preference is revealed. In fact, this is the main idea of Threeballot [20] and the schemes following it.

3.7 Verifiability of ID Cards

The main idea is to make the work of an ID card deterministic, so that it can be checked for correctness and lack of any hidden information (for instance a kleptographic channel). This is important, since the ID card knows everything about voting preferences of its owner. (Note that due to simplicity of the system on the card it is technically feasible to implement a procedure for cleaning up the card from any information on past elections.)

As explained, we have to use cryptographic schemes that are immune against kleptography. There are the following key moments:

– the choice of (cs, cp),
– generating a request for a blind signature (for instance the choice of the blinding factor used),
– the choice of the "random" parameters z,
– the choice of the encoding for the cascade of mixes.

Designing methods resistant against kleptography is known in some cases (e.g. for DH key exchange [15]).

The issue of choosing the parameters z is relatively easy. We can assume that each "fresh" value z_i (i.e. the one that does not convert the sum to zero) is related with the last "fresh" value z_j already used in such way that $z_j = \text{HASH}(z_i)$, where HASH is a secure hash function. This enforces the ID card to choose a *root* value and compute the values z_i on demand by hashing repeatedly the root value appropriate number of times. Note that then irregularities can be detected at the stage of vote counting – the parameters z have to be related as described. Of course, the ID cards can be tested in trial elections where all data are accessible. We note also that the described way of creating strings z leaves not much room for kleptographic tricks.

Similarly, the blinding factor can be verified in a cut and choose fashion: after a request is stated the card might be asked to reveal the blinding factor and generate the keys (cs, cp) once more. The blinding factor itself can be generated as a deterministic digital signature (with the keys used for this purpose only), so that it remains unpredictable for a third party while it can be easily verified after revealing.

Encrypting for a cascade of mixes can be done with a deterministic public key scheme.

Final Remarks and Acknowledgments

The framework proposed in this paper is just a first step in a new direction - finding a new balance between privacy and correctness of results. Of course, many details, like cryptographic building blocks, should be adjusted to suit particular requirements.

Finally, we would like to thank anonymous referees for helpful suggestions. We also thank Witold Drożdż, former Undersecretary of State in Polish Ministry of Interior and Administration, for encouragement to do this work.

References

1. Dagstuhl Accord (2007), http://www.dagstuhlaccord.org/
2. The E-vote 2011-project Electronic Voting. 2011,
   http://www.regjeringen.no/en/dep/krd/kampanjer/election_
   portal/electronic-voting.html?id=437385
3. Top-to-bottom Review. Top-to-bottom Report Conducted by Secretary of State Debra Bowen of Many of the Voting Systems Certified for Use in California (2007),
   http://www.sos.ca.gov/elections/elections_vsr.htm
4. Adida, B.: Helios: Web-based Open-Audit Voting. In: USENIX Security Symposium 2008, USENIX Association, pp. 335–348 (2008), ISBN 978-1-931971-60-7
5. Baer, W.S., Borisov, N., Danezis, G., Guerses, S.F., Klonowski, M., Kutyłowski, M., Maier-Rabler, U., Moran, T., Pfitzmann, A., Preneel, B., Sadeghi, A.-R., Vedel, T., Westen, T., Zagórski, F., Dutton, W.H.: Machiavelli Confronts 21st Century Digital Technology: Democracy in a Network Society. In: Social Science Research Network, 1521222 (2009),
   http://ssrn.com/abstract=1521222
6. Chaum, D.: Punchscan (2005), http://www.punchscan.org
7. Chaum, D., Antwerpen, H.V.: Undeniable Signatures. In: Brassard, G. (ed.) CRYPTO 1989. LNCS, vol. 435, pp. 212–216. Springer, Heidelberg (1990)
8. Chaum, D., Essex, A., Carback, R., Clark, J., Popoveniuc, S., Rivest, R.L., Ryan, P.Y.A., Shen, E., Sherman, A.: Scantegrity II: End-to-End Voter-Verifiable Optical Scan Election Systems Using Invisible Ink Confirmation Codes. In: USENIX/ACCURATE EVT 2008 (2008)
9. Chaum, D., Ryan, P.Y.A., Schneider, S.: A Practical Voter-Verifiable Election Scheme. In: di Vimercati, S.d.C., Syverson, P.F., Gollmann, D. (eds.) ESORICS 2005. LNCS, vol. 3679, pp. 118–139. Springer, Heidelberg (2005)

10. Desmedt, Y., Estehghari, S.: Hacking Helios and its Impact. CRYPTO 2009 rump session (2009), http://www.cs.ucl.ac.uk/staff/Y.Desmedt/IACR/
11. Desmedt, Y., Kurosawa, K.: Electronic Voting: Starting Over? In: Zhou, J., López, J., Deng, R.H., Bao, F. (eds.) ISC 2005. LNCS, vol. 3650, pp. 329–343. Springer, Heidelberg (2005)
12. Garrido, J.M., Schlesinger, R.: Principles of Modern Operating Systems. Jones and Barlett Publishers (2008), ISBN 0-7637-3574-4
13. Gjøsteen, K.: Analysis of an Internet Voting Protocol,
    http://www.regjeringen.no/en/dep/krd/kampanjer/election_
    portal/electronic-voting/news-about-the-e-vote-2011-project/
    year/2010/Description-of-cryptografhic-protocol-.html?
    id=594906
14. Gogolewski, M., Klonowski, M., Kutyłowski, M., Kubiak, P., Lauks, A., Zagórski, F.: Kleptographic Attacks on E-voting Schemes. In: Müller, G. (ed.) ETRICS 2006. LNCS, vol. 3995, pp. 494–508. Springer, Heidelberg (2006)
15. Gołębiewski, Z., Kutyłowski, M., Zagórski, F.: Stealing Secrets with SSL/TLS and SSH – Kleptographic Attacks. In: Pointcheval, D., Mu, Y., Chen, K. (eds.) CANS 2006. LNCS, vol. 4301, pp. 191–202. Springer, Heidelberg (2006)
16. Juels, A., Catalano, D., Jakobsson, M.: Coercion-Resistant Electronic Elections. In: ACM Workshop on Privacy in the Electronic Society, pp. 61–70. ACM, New York (2005)
17. Kutyłowski, M., Zagórski, F.: Coercion-free Internet Voting with Receipts. In: Miyaji, A., Kikuchi, H., Rannenberg, K. (eds.) IWSEC 2007. LNCS, vol. 4752, pp. 199–213. Springer, Heidelberg (2007)
18. Kutyłowski, M., Zagórski, F.: Scratch, Click & Vote: E2E Voting over the Internet'. Cryptology ePrint Archive: Report 2008/314. In: Towards Trustworthy Election Systems, in State-of-the-Art Survey Series. Springer, Heidelberg (2008) (to appear), http://eprint.iacr.org/2008/314
19. Popoveniuc, S., Lundin, D.: A Simple Technique for Safely Using Punchscan and Pret a Voter in Mail-in Elections. In: Alkassar, A., Volkamer, M. (eds.) VOTE-ID 2007. LNCS, vol. 4896, pp. 150–155. Springer, Heidelberg (2007)
20. Rivest, R.L., Smith, W.D.: Three Voting Protocols: Threeballot, Vav, and Twin. In: EVT 2007: Proceedings of the USENIX/Accurate Electronic Voting Technology on USENIX/Accurate Electronic Voting Technology Workshop. USENIX Association (2007)
21. Tarnovsky, C.: Hacking the Smartcard Chip. A presentation at Black Hat DC (2010), http://www.blackhat.com/html/bh-dc-10/bh-dc-10-briefings.html
22. Weber, S., Araujo, R., Buchmann, J.: On Coercion-Resistant Electronic Elections with Linear Work. In: ARES, Proceedings of the 2nd International Conference on Availability, Reliability and Security, pp. 908–916. IEEE Computer Society, Los Alamitos (2007)

µTSS – A Simplified Trusted Software Stack

Christian Stüble and Anoosheh Zaerin

Sirrix AG
Lise-Meitner Allee 4,
44801 Bochum, Germany
{stueble,zaerin}@sirrix.com

Abstract. The TCG Software Stack (TSS) specifies the software layer
for application developers to use functions provided by a Trusted Platform Module (TPM). However, the current TSS interface is highly complex, which makes its usage very difficult and error-prone, and the high
complexity makes it unsuitable for embedded devices or security kernels.

We present a simplified TSS design and implementation (µTSS) providing a lightweight and intuitive programming interface for developers
based on the TPM main specification. The major principles of the µTSS
design are a reduced complexity, obtaining type safety, object encapsulation, and a simple error handling. These principles ensure that the
resulting µTSS is maintainable and easy to use. Moreover, the modular
architecture of the µTSS allows using only a subset of the provided functionality as it is required, e.g., for embedded systems, mobile devices, or
in the context of a security kernel. This paper discusses experiences with
the µTSS, based on several projects such as the TCG TPM compliance
test suite and a Mobile Trusted Module (MTM) implementation.

1 Motivation and Problem Description

Trusted Computing is a technology allowing parties of an electronic infrastructure to verify the integrity of remote computing platforms. The Trusted Computing Group (TCG) is an industry-consortium of important IT-enterprises that
has published a list of documents specifying building blocks to realize a trusted
IT-infrastructure.

The main documents include the TPM specification [1] defining a hardware
module providing protected keys and cryptographic functions, the Trusted Network Connect (TNC) specification [2] defining protocols and formats on the network level, and the TCG Software Stack (TSS) specification [3] defining software
layers to access the TPM. Based on these building blocks (hardware, software,
network protocols), a trusted IT-infrastructure can be built where access to critical information is only permitted after a successful authentication and integrity
verification of the involved computing platforms.

Trusted Computing is an evolving technology and in the near future, many
new applications that are using this technology as a building block are expected
to come into the market. Example applications currently under development are

A. Acquisti, S.W. Smith, and A.-R. Sadeghi (Eds.): TRUST 2010, LNCS 6101, pp. 124–140, 2010.
© Springer-Verlag Berlin Heidelberg 2010

security kernels [4,5], VPN gateways [6], and security add-ons such as TPM-based hard-disk encryption systems [7,8].

However, the trust in an IT-infrastructure depends on the trust in its building blocks including the TPM, the TSS, and the used protocols. The TSS has especially to be trusted by the user, since it (i) has access to many cryptographic keys used to encrypt user-data and (ii) it can violate anonymity requirements. Moreover, the TSS specification is very complex[1], since it includes about 750 pages containing a huge number of structures, constants and function definitions (see Section 2 for more details) distributed over several architectural layers. This results in three main disadvantages: Firstly, the high complexity of the TSS API makes it hard for developers to profit from its security functions. Secondly, the high complexity decreases the maintainability and increases the probability of internal bugs and wrong or insecure implementations of application developers. Thirdly, the TSS specification includes functions that are not required or even not available, especially in small execution environments such as embedded systems, mobile devices, or security kernels. In some environments, for instance, persistent memory to realize an object storage is not available.

Contribution. We define requirements to be fulfilled by a software stack compatible with the TPM Main Specification and to be used in the context of small and security-critical environments such as embedded systems, security kernels, and MTM/TPM realizations. Based on these requirements, we propose an object-oriented TSS interface and the corresponding implementation providing a light-weight interface to developers that is more intuitive and easier to use than the flexible but complex interface of the existing TSS specification. The μTSS design is directly based on the TPM Specification and thus covers the full TPM functionality without adding the overhead required for a full TSS implementation. Moreover, the object-oriented design of the μTSS hides the complexity of the TPM Specification by automating functions such as key loading, unloading, or the creation of authentication sessions. Finally, the μTSS design is modular allowing the use of only a subset of the provided functionality as it is required, e.g., for embedded systems or mobile devices. The μTSS implementation has already been successfully used in different projects: The TCG TPM Compliance Test Suite used for certification of TPMs[2], a Software-TPM as well as a Software-MTM implementation, and the TPM Manager [9], an open-source graphical TPM management tool based on the Qt widget-library[3].

It is important to mention that the proposed μTSS design is not intended to replace the existing TSS specification. However, it is rather a suggestion of an alternative design allowing a more intuitive and easier usage of the functionality provided by the TPM. When meaningful, we decided not to support specific functions required by the TSS specification (e.g., the object storage) in favor of

---

[1] The term complexity is used in this paper to point that something is not easy to understand and is hard to deal with. This may be substituted by the term complicated.

[2] http://www.trustedcomputinggroup.org/certification/

[3] https://projects.sirrix.com/trac/tpmmanager

an easier and less complex software architecture and to make it modular enough to allow an integration into standalone binaries such as a boot loader.

Outline: This paper is structured as follows: The next section introduces the TSS as specified by the TCG. Section 3 outlines the deficiencies we identified during our experiences with the existing TSS and defines our requirements for our own TSS design. The design of the μTSS is explained in Section 4, followed by a usage example shown in Section 5. Section 6 summarizes our experiences with our μTSS implementation. A short reference of related work is given in Section 7. Section 8 concludes this work with a short summary.

2   TSS Basics

In the following, we give a short overview of the architectural layers, components, and responsibilities of the TSS as defined in its specification [3].

The main purpose of the TSS is to multiplex access to the TPM, since a TPM has limited resources and can only communicate with one client at a time. Moreover, not all functions related to Trusted Computing require TPM access. These functions are located within the TSS to allow a reduction of the complexity of the TPM.

As illustrated in Figure 1, the TSS is comprised of the three layers TSS Service Provider (TSP), TSS Core Services (TCS), and the TSS Device Driver Library (TDDL) respectively their public interfaces TSPi, TCSi, and TDDLi.

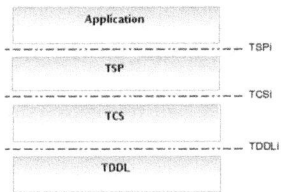

Fig. 1. Architectural layers of the TCG Software Stack (TSS)

TSP and TSPi: An application employing TPM functionality has to use a TSP via its interface, the TSPi. Every application uses its own TSP that is loaded as a library into the application process using it. The TSP provides high-level TCG functions as well as auxiliary services such as hashing or signature verification.

One important aspect of the TSP is the TSP Context Manager (TSPCM), which provides dynamic handles allowing efficient usage of multiple TSPs and application resources. The managed context provides a connection to a TSS Core Service, which itself provides functions for resource management such as freeing of memory, creating working objects, establishing a default policy for working objects, and providing functionality to access the persistent storage database. However, providing all these functions means an enormous increase in complexity.

A second aspect is regarding the TSP Cryptographic Functions (TSPCF), which are provided to make full use of the protected functions in a TPM. In its specification, the TSPi is defined as a C interface.

TCS and TCSi: The TCS provides a common set of operations to all TSPs running on a platform. Since there is only one instance of a TCS per TPM, the main task of the TCS is to multiplex TPM access. Moreover, the TCS provides operations to store, manage, and protect keys as well as privacy-sensitive credentials associated with the platform. The TCS also includes more sophisticated functions to manage TPM resources such as key management.

TDDL and TDDLi: The TDDL, accessed via the TDDLi, provides a unique interface to different TPM driver implementations. Moreover, it provides a transition between kernel mode and user mode[4]. The TDDL provides functions (e.g. Open(), Close(), GetStatus()) to maintain communication with the device driver. Additionally, it provides functions (e.g. GetCapability(), SetCapability()) to get and set attributes of the TSP as well as direct functions (e.g. Transmit(), Cancel()) to transmit and cancel TPM commands.

For each of these layers, the TSS specifies several data types, flags, constants, and functions. Collectively the TSS specification contains more than 716 definitions, data types, flags, constants, and 317 functions.

3   Requirements

The requirements have mainly been derived from Trusted Computing scenarios where the usage of a full TSS implementation is difficult or even impossible:

Trusted Boot Loader: If a trusted boot loader needs TPM commands that are not supported by the BIOS, the corresponding functions have to be integrated into the boot loader binary. In this scenario, a direct TPM access (using BIOS functionality without `tcsd` or external TPM driver) is required.

Mobile and Embedded Devices: When integrating Trusted Computing functionality such as remote attestation into a mobile phone, only a small subset of TPM commands are required and a multiplexing of different clients, as it is done by the `tcsd`, is not necessary.

TPM/MTM Implementation: By implementing a Software-TPM or a Software-MTM, the commands and structures defined by the TPM specification and not those of the TSS specification are required.

To use Trusted Computing functionality in these scenarios, a TSS is required that fulfills the following requirements:

1. *Compliance:* The μTSS should be compatible with the TCG TPM Main Specification [1]. Moreover, it would be helpful if the μTSS could be used as the basis of an MTM/TPM implementation.

---

[4] The current TSS design assumes a monolithic operating system including device drivers running in kernel mode.

2. *Completeness:* The μTSS should provide all mandatory functions defined by the TCG TPM Main Specification [1].

3. *Portability:* The μTSS should be usable under different operating systems such as Linux and Windows. Moreover, different hardware architectures, especially embedded platforms such as ARM architectures, should be supported.

4. *Security:* The API as well as the implementation should prevent typical implementation errors such as buffer overflows by offering intuitive interfaces and type safety.

5. *Usability:* The API should be easy and intuitive allowing application developers to use TPM features without much effort in reading and understanding the specification. Moreover, the μTSS interfaces should hide complexity by automating steps (e.g., key loading or opening of session) and hiding version-specific details (e.g., TPM_CertifyKey vs TPM_CertifyKey2).

6. *Maintainability:* The design should prevent code redundancies to allow an easy maintenance of the code, especially in the context of specification updates.

7. *Modularity:* Software components should be decoupled to reduce both functionality and size for usage in small and security-critical environments such as embedded systems and security kernels. Moreover, it should be possible to embed the μTSS, or parts of it, into single binaries without a runtime environment, e.g., in the context of a boot loader.

8. *Small code basis:* Finally, the μTSS should have as few dependencies as possible. This makes it possible to have a small code basis and therefore it would be suitable to be integrated in security kernels or embedded systems.

The focus of all above requirements is to prevent implementation errors of the TSS itself and of developers using the TSS in their own applications.

4   μTSS Design

In the following, we describe design and implementation aspects of the μTSS, an object-oriented TCG Software Stack that fulfills the requirements defined in Section 3.

We have chosen C++ as the programming language, since it allows on the one hand to realize maintainable code because, e.g., of its support for an object-oriented implementation and exceptions. On the other hand, C++ only requires a small runtime environment in contrast to higher-level languages such as Python, Java, or C#.

The μTSS design includes, similar to the TSS specification, the object-oriented architectural layers oTSP, oTCS, and oTDDL which are described in the following. However, in contrast to the TSS specification, it is an orthogonal design decision of whether these layers should all be included into one application (i.e., creating an application that is directly using the TPM device), or whether they are split into different components to allow multiplexing (i.e., implementing a tcsd).

4.1   oTSP Design

Similar to the TSP specification, the oTSP layer provides the high-level interface used by application developers to use TPM functions. The main goal of the oTSP is to provide an object-oriented abstraction of the TPM functionality that is more intuitive than the specified TSS interface and hides as much complexity as possible. The underlying idea behind the design is to model all objects and relations of the TPM specification that are directly visible for an application developer, such as the TPM, Keys, Counters, NV-Space, etc.

The TPM class. The main component of the oTSP design is the class TPM providing the main interface to the physical TPM. The class TPM includes methods to obtain general information about the physical TPM (e.g. the vendor name, version and revision) as well as the possibility to read and write TPM capabilities.

Moreover, the TPM class provides access to the TPM-internal keys, namely the Storage Root key (SRK) and the Endorsement Key (EK). Furthermore, it offers methods to manage Platform Configuration Registers (PCR), create monotonic counters, or manage non-volatile memory (see Figure 2(a)).

Cryptographic keys. One major task of a TPM is to manage cryptographic keys (e.g., encryption keys and signature keys). The TPM distinguishes a variety of key types (e.g., Endorsement Key, Binding Key, Legacy Key, etc.) that are directly represented by the oTSP through an assortment of C++ classes such as StorageKey, SigningKey, UnbindingKey and their public counterparts, e.g., VerificationKey and BindingKey.

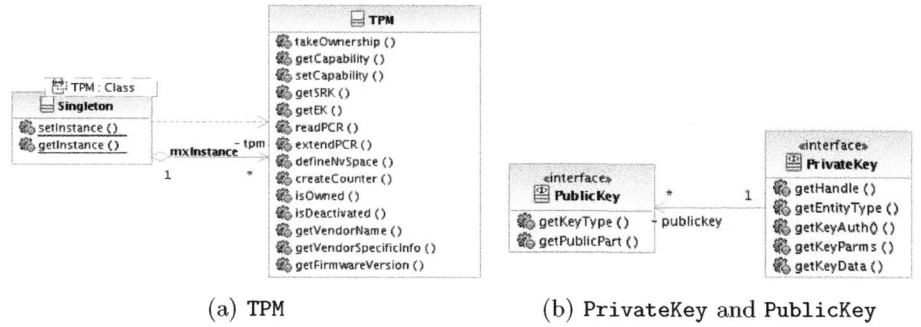

(a) TPM   (b) PrivateKey and PublicKey

Fig. 2. The public interfaces of base classes TPM, PrivateKey and PublicKey

Depending on the sensitivity of the key data, all oTSP keys are derived from one of the two base classes, PrivateKey and PublicKey (refer to Figure 2(b)). However, due to the fact that variant key types may implement different functions (e.g. an attestation key can be used to certify other keys and to quote, whereas a signing key can also be used to sign arbitrary data), the functionality to be realized by cryptographic keys has been split into different interfaces to be derived by concrete public key or private key instances.

Moreover, the base class `PrivateKey` hides the complexity of loading and flushing the key. The implementation ensures that the key data is loaded whenever needed, which allows a key manager to flush any key when all key slots are in use. The key data is flushed from the TPM automatically in the destructor of the `PrivateKey`.

Figure 3(a) defines the available interfaces to be used as base classes of private keys and Figure 3(b) defines the appropriate public counterparts.

Concrete TPM key types, such as `SigningKey`, `SRK` or `BindingKey` implement those interfaces that provide a functionality to be used with that key. For instance, the key type `PrivateLegacyKey` is derived from all private interfaces except `Storage`, since it can be used for certification, signing, quoting and

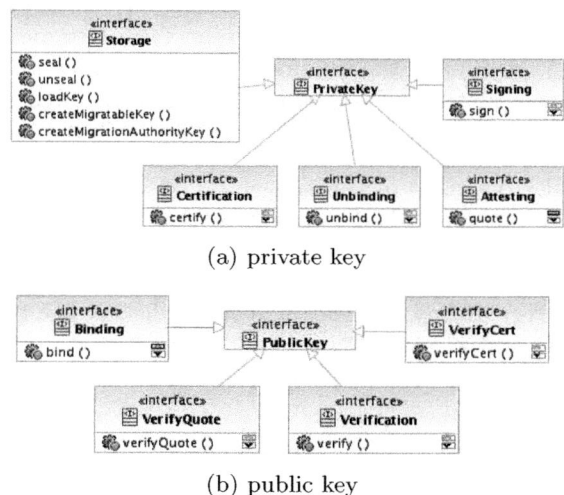

Fig. 3. The interfaces to be implemented by public and private keys

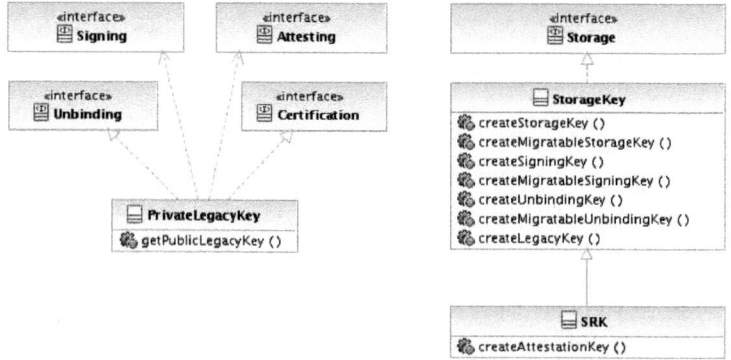

Fig. 4. `PrivateLegacyKey` is realized by deriving from all usable private key interfaces and the `SRK` is realized by deriving from the storage interface

unbinding but can neither seal nor unseal. Figure 4 shows two examples of concrete key instances, namely `PrivateLegacyKey` and `SRK`.

Other key types are constructed in a similar fashion. This type safe design prevents misuse of the keys, e.g., a `SigningKey` cannot be used by mistake for a binding operation, and the design provides a better overview of operations which the `SigningKey` can perform, namely, signing, certification and attestation.

Monotonic counters. The TPM methods `createCounter()` and `getCounter()` are used to create and instantiate monotonic counters represented by the class `Counter`.

The counter method `increase()` is used to increase the value of the counter, while the method `readValue()` reads the current counter value from the TPM. The method `readLastValue()` returns the last value that was read from the TPM (without querying the TPM).

4.2 oTCS Design

The architectural layer oTCS implements the TCS providing TPM commands, sessions, and the `CommandExecutor` interface, to execute TPM commands. Moreover, this layer defines elementary data types and structures of the TPM specification.

One of the principal design directives characterizing this layer is to realize each TPM command as a separate C++ class to allow more flexibility in supporting various specifications and minimizing the interface. By implementing this so-called command pattern [10], such a design allows the modification of single command implementations (e.g., in the case of a specification update), or the removal of all unneeded commands (e.g., to use a selection of commands in an embedded environment).

TPM commands The main classes of the oTCS layer are `Command` and `Result` representing a command sent to a TPM and the result returned by a TPM, respectively (refer to Figure 5).

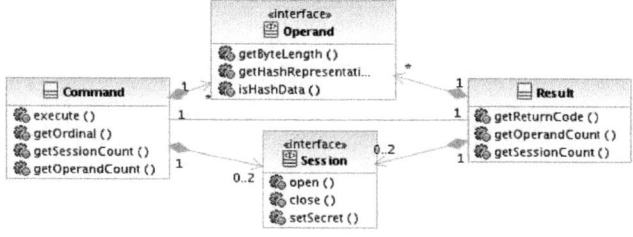

Fig. 5. Interface of the classes `Command` and `Result` including a list of `Operand` types and `Session` types

The method `execute()` of the class `Command` executes a TPM command and returns the associated instance of a class derived from `Result`. For example, a result of type `GetCapabilityResult` is returned by the command `GetCapability` implementing the `TPM_GetCapability` command.

Both, commands and results, consist of attributes derived from the operand base class `Operand` or `Session`. These operands represent the parameters sent to, or returned from, the TPM, while session objects are responsible for the authentication of TPM objects or roles. The inclusion of a session object in a command causes the appropriate operands (handle, nonces, etc.) to be included with the command.

Commands as well as operands implement a streaming interface allowing objects to be converted into a binary stream. The resulting binary stream can be sent directly to a TPM. This way, the complex marshalling and unmarshalling process of commands and their operands has to be implemented only once in the `Command` and `Result` base class and will be inherited by derived commands. This also includes the complex calculation of the session authentication when sending commands as well as authentication verification and consistency checks of data received from the TPM. If the TPM returns an `TPM_AUTHFAIL` error code, e.g., the `Result` automatically throws an appropriate exception of the same name to be handled by the application.

Secret Provider. The secret provider interface manages the authentication information to be used by the TPM. All authentication data, e.g. of owners, keys, or other objects are saved and managed by the `SecretProvider`. Users of the μTSS can derive their own implementation that, e.g., implements a secure storage, a password cache, or a GUI dialog to allow users to enter the secrets.

Sessions. Sessions are used within a TPM command to authenticate the usage of specific objects such as cryptographic keys and to authenticate a specific role, e.g., the TPM owner. Figure 6 illustrates the available session types provided by the oTCS layer.

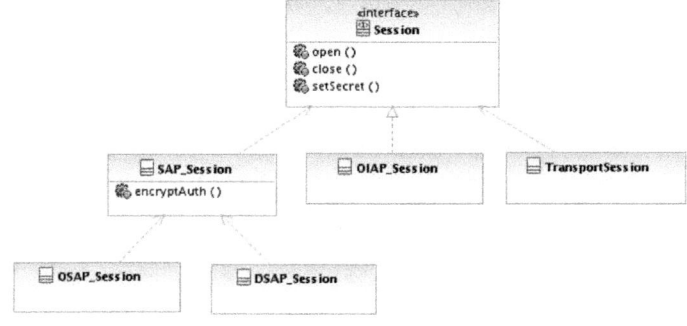

Fig. 6. The implementation of the session types OSAP, DSAP, OIAP and Transport

Depending on the specific TPM command, the number and the type of sessions may vary, just as in the specification. For example, the TPM command TPM_Quote accepts one session or no session at all, and the session can be of the type OSAP or OIAP. To be able to handle this, the interface Session provides the public interface of all session objects.

Separate classes are dedicated to the various session types: OIAP_Session for OIAP sessions, OSAP_Session for OSAP sessions, DSAP_Session for DSAP sessions, TransportSession for transport sessions.

Command executor. The oTCS provides the CommandExecutor interface (see Figure Figure 7) as the central instance used to handle the execution of TPM commands as well as select the backend for execution (e.g., TDDL or tcsd). A typical responsibility of the command executor is the handling of non-fatal errors returned by the TPM. For example, the command executor catches the non-fatal TPM errors TPM_RETRY and waits an appropriate amount of seconds, until it tries to resend the command to the TPM. This way, the command executor handles many exceptional TPM states that normally had to be handled by the application developer.

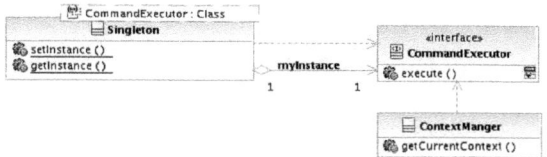

Fig. 7. Interface and available instances of the command executor

The TCS framework allows stacking of different command executor implementations. This way, an implementation that handles certain TCS or TPM errors, or an implementation that audits the TPM commands and responses, can be added to the existing functionality.

4.3 oTDDL Design

The oTDDL implements the TDDL interface, i.e., the interface to the TPM device driver. As illustrated in Figure Figure 8, the singleton TDDL implements the TDDLi interface used to send TPM commands, and the associated TPM response, using the method transmit() based on byte streams. The static method getInstance() provides access to the singleton by returning a reference to the TDDL implementation.

Different back-ends implementing the TDDLi interface are provided. The class SocketTDDL uses a TCP/IP connection to send TPM commands to a remote service. The class DeviceTDDL, however, accesses the TPM of the local platform under different operating systems such as Linux or Windows.

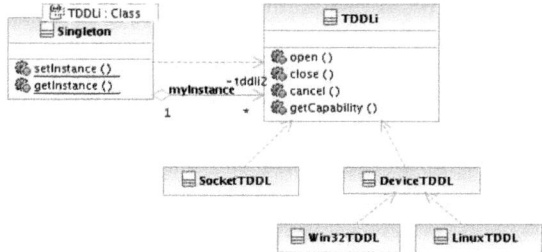

Fig. 8. Interfaces and implementations of the architectural layer oTDDL

Multiplexer. To allow multiple applications to access the TPM, a `tcsd`-like multiplexer has been implemented. The multiplexer acts upon the TDDL byte streams and isolates clients using the class `Context` implemented based on the TPM commands `TPM_LoadContext` and `TPM_SaveContext`.

Since the multiplexing is done on the TDDL layer, every client can use the multiplexer through the `SocketTDDL` backend.

The multiplexer itself has been implemented by only 180 code lines, including the management of different command line options.

5   Binding Usage Example

In this section we are going to give an illustrative example to show how the μTSS is used. Listing 1.1 shows how to bind some data to the TPM and how to unbind it.

Listing 1.1. Binding Example

```
try {
  RND<BYTEARRAY>  plain ( 204 );
  cout << "Plain: " << plain << endl;

  /// Create unbinding key
  TPM             &tpm  = TPM::getInstance ();
  SRK             srk   = tpm.getSRK ();
  UnbindingKey ubKey = srk.createUnbindingKey ();
  /// Extract binding key from unbind key
  BindingKey    bKey = ubKey.getBindingKey ();

  /// Bind the data
  BYTEARRAY     cipher = bKey.bind ( plain );
  cout << "Cipher: " << cipher << endl;

  /// Unbind the data
  BYTEARRAY     result = ubKey.unbind ( cipher );
  cout << "Result: " << result << endl;
}
catch ( TPM_Error &e ) {
  cerr << "TPM Error: " << e << endl;
}
catch ( TCS_Exception &e ) {
  cerr << "TCS Exception: " << e << endl;
}
```

In the first line we create a random plaintext of length 204 used for encryption. Then, an unbinding key is created by the method `createUnbindingKey()` of the SRK which itself was obtained from the TPM singleton. The invoked method internally uses the TPM command `TPM_CreateWrapKey` with the correct parameters, and returns the created UnbindingKey (ubKey).

In order to bind the plaintext, first the method `getBindingKey()` is used to retrieve the public key part bKey which is then used to bind the plaintext by invoking the method `bind()`.

When invoking the method `unbind()` to unbind the ciphertext, the created key data stored within the class `UnbindingKey` is automatically loaded into the TPM.

In general, the application developers neither have to care about occurring TPM or TCS errors, nor do they have to free allocated resources explicitly, because both are automatically done by the exception system in combination with appropriate destructors. For example, if the TPM returns the error `TPM_INVALIDKEYHANDLE`, because the used unbinding key is not loaded (or has been unloaded in between), this error is caught by the unbinding key which then loads the key data into the TPM and re-invokes the failed command.

For comparison, we provided 2 examples in the appendix of the extended version of this paper (to be found on the Sirrix publication page[5]). The first example shows an implementation of the same functionality using TrouSerS and the other example is the implementation based on jTSS. Both examples are from the standard test suite implementations and are not provided by the authors of this paper.

The TrouSerS example uses the TSP API and requires 146 source lines of code (LOC) versus 18 LOC using the μTSS[6].

The jTSS example requires slightly more LOC, namely 30, than the μTSS-based implementation. However, it provides less type-safety for the key object. The same key data object is used for binding and unbinding, as well as for binding and signing. Thus, the wrong key usage will result in failures during runtime instead of compile time.

6 Evaluation

As shown in the example of Section 5, using the μTSS is very easy, since it hides many details behind simple interfaces.

A performance analysis showed that a comparison with other software solutions is irrelevant, due to the fact that the TPM itself is much slower than the software. However, comparing an implementation of the binding example explained in Section 5 and the binding example based on TrouSerS (explained in the extended version of the paper to be found on the Sirrix publication page[7]) shows that the implementation based on the μTSS implementation takes 1.7 seconds, while the example based on TrouSerS takes 2.00 seconds.

---

[5] http://www.sirrix.com/content/pages/publications.htm

[6] Measured by sloccount http://www.dwheeler.com/sloccount/

[7] http://www.sirrix.com/content/pages/publications.htm

The μTSS is tested extensively and used in several applications. Section 6.1 gives an overview of the most important applications that are based on the μTSS.

6.1   Applications

The following applications are implemented based on the μTSS.

To further test the extensibility and flexibility of the μTSS design, we decided to develop a *Software-TPM* based on it. We hoped that the Software-TPM could be developed without much effort, since nearly all the required data types and the specification of commands already exist. In fact our expectations have been completely satisfied. The development of the Software-TPM is limited to the implementation of the concrete command (according to the TPM specification), by overwriting the method `execute()` of each Command object using a derived class.

Based on the Software-TPM described before, an *MTM Software Stack* and *Software-MTM* were implemented. An MTM [11] is a security extension specified by the TCG which is similar to the TPM but intended for use in embedded and mobile devices. An MTM command set is similar to the TPMs, but some differences exist: On the one hand, some TPM commands are not available on an MTM and on the other hand, the MTM has some additional commands such as `MTM_VerifyAndExtend()`. As at the moment no hardware support for MTM exists, this implementation provides a facility to experiment with the basic concepts of the MTM.

The *TrustedVPN* is a TPM-based enterprise VPN solution[8] based on a central management server. The implementation on both the client and server side heavily utilizes TPM functionalities, e.g., to establish a PKI based on TPM-internal keys, to bind data to a platform configuration, and to realize a trusted channel [12,13] between VPN client and management server. The actual implementation of the TrustedVPN solution is based on the μTSS, taking advantage of its easy API, its limited size and complexity due to the fact that only a subset of TPM commands are used, and the capability to use the TPM without the need to start a `tcsd`.

The μTSS has been successfully used to develop a *TPM Compliance Test Suite* including more than 650 test cases and covering nearly all TPM commands that can be tested on a standard PC platform. Here, the oTCS layer has mainly been used to implement the concrete test cases, while the high-level abstractions of the oTSP are used as helper to generate input data etc. The development of the test cases was very easy, since the μTSS hides most of the complexity of the TSS.

Another project that uses the μTSS is the *TPM Manager*, an open-source graphical TPM management tool based on the Qt widget-library. Earlier versions used the TrouSerS library as the backend, while the current developer version has been ported to the μTSS within one to two days. A specific advantage of the μTSS here is the `DeviceTDDL` implementation allowing an application to directly

---

[8] http://www.sirrix.com/content/pages/54608.htm

accessing the TPM driver without the need of a `tcsd` daemon. This was required to keep an `initrd` that includes a TPM Manager as small as possible.

6.2 Overall Evaluation Results

Although the μTSS implementation does not provide the complete functionality required by the TSS specification, our experiences show that a TSS implementation, providing a more intuitive and easier interface, helps developers to successfully use TPM functions. The object-oriented and clean design helped a stable state to be reached in a relatively small time. Finally, the command pattern [10] used to realize the TPM commands allows the easy addition, change, or removal of command implementations.

The μTSS fulfills the requirements defined in Section 3 for the following reasons:

Compliance and Completeness: Since the μTSS has been used to realize the TCG TPM compliance test suite, it obviously fulfills the compliance and completeness requirements. Moreover, the μTSS has been used to develop a software TPM that itself is compatible with the TPM specification.

Portability: The μTSS has been implemented in C++ and is in use on top of the Linux/x86, Linux/ARM, and Windows XP operating systems.

Security: The type safe design of the μTSS reduces the risk of runtime errors and the use of standard data containers instead of C-pointers limits the number of possible buffer and heap overflows. However, C++ is not the ideal programming language for developing secure code but has been chosen, because it allows low-level system implementations.

Usability: The μTSS provides a simple API hiding most of the complexity of the TPM specification. The exception handling capability makes source code easier to read and helps developers to focus on their tasks.

Maintainability: The object-oriented design of the μTSS reduces code redundancies and hides implementation details behind object interfaces.

Modularity: The μTSS can be used in different configurations. E.g., it can directly access a TPM device, use its own TPM driver, or access a network server such as a `tcsd`. Moreover, it can be configured to support only a subset of TPM commands and structures.

Small code basis: The μTSS only includes structures, TPM commands, and logical objects of the TPM specification. While the oTCS layer is a one to one mapping of the TPM specification, the oTSP layer implements the logical TPM objects such as keys, counters, and NV-Space areas.

7 Related Work

In the following, we briefly discuss the related works in the context of the TCG software stack. Moreover, we analyze to which extent these implementations fulfill the requirements of Section 3. To our knowledge none of the existing implementations directly implements the TPM Main Specification [1].

TrouSerS is an open source TSS implementation maintained by IBM since 2004. The latest version released is stable and implements TSS version 1.1 [14] interfacing version 1.1b TPMs. Since the TCG has released a new version of the TSS specification [3] to support new functionality provided by version 1.2 TPMs, version 0.3.x of TrouSerS was developed. Most of the features are implemented. The source code itself is implemented in ANSI C. Due to the high complexity and the elaborate specification, the implementation of a TSS stack is very challenging. The usability and maintainability requirements as described in Section 3 cannot be achieved using TrouSerS.

The *Trusted Platform Agent* (TPA) [15] is an open source library, which is designed to minimize the effort of writing applications that use Trusted Computing technology and employ the TPM. According to the website, the TPA hides the complexity of the TSS interface. The library provides a small set of functionalities such as binding, sealing, TPM management (takeownership and is-owned), PCR (reading and extending). The TPA library has dependencies on TrouSerS, TrouSerS tpm-tools, OpenSSL, SQLite and libcurl.

The IAIK *jTSS* is developed and maintained at the Institute for Applied Information Processing and Communication at Graz University of Technology [16]. The IAIK jTSS stack is a new implementation of the TCG Software Stack for the Java^{TM}programming language. IAIK has initialized a Java Specification Request (JSR 321) in the Java Community Process (JCP). The current status of the specification process is outlined in the recent paper of the JSR 321 group [17]. However, the need to use a Java runtime environment for running the jTSS violates our requirement of a small code basis.

TPM/J [18] is an object-oriented API using Java for low-level access to the TPM. It was developed as part of the research project on Trusted Computing at MIT. TPM/J treats TPM low-level commands (i.e., the commands directly given to the TPM chip itself), and the response data structures of these commands, as first-class Java objects. The TPM/J stack does not provide full functionality for TPM commands such as Quote2, Delegation commands, NV write commands, CertifyKey commands, CMK commands and DSAP sessions.

Another library provided by IBM [19], *libtpm*, is implemented to communicate with TPMs according to the TCG specifications. The library supports TPM v1.1b and therefore it is not fully functional with TPMs of version 1.2. For instance, TPM_RESET and TPM_LOADKEY are not working anymore. libtpm contains a small set of most important TPM commands such as TPM_Seal, TPM_Unseal, TPM_Bind, TPM_Unbind, and has been used in the past as basis for a security kernel [5]. As libtpm only provides a limited functionality and is not properly functional with TPM v1.2, it does not fulfill our requirements.

The *Minimized MRTM* [20] is a software implementation of a minimal MRTM that runs in hardware-enforced isolation inside the trusted execution environment of a Nokia N96 handset. The code is, with a few minor exceptions, compatible with the MTM v1.0 specification, and as a monolithic compilation it can execute in 20kB of RAM encompassing both code and data. This is achieved by reducing the data structures to a specification compliant minimum and by optimizing the command logic to comply with the highly specialized demands of an MRTM. However, it is not the goal of the μTSS to realize a minimal MTM. Instead, a TSS should be implemented that provides the basis for many different application scenarios including the development of a Software-MTM.

8 Conclusion

This paper presented the μTSS, an object-oriented TSS design and implementation providing developers an intuitive and easy to use interface. We have analyzed in Section 1 the deficiencies of a complex and difficult to understand software architecture. Based on three example scenarios, Section 3 identified requirements of a TSS to be used in specific environments such as embedded platforms or boot loaders.

The major principles behind our μTSS design are reduced complexity to simplify the interface and the implementation, type safety to prevent runtime errors and potential programming errors, object encapsulation to hide the complexity of the implementation, and meaningful error handling to prevent resource leaks. The design of the μTSS prevents code redundancies and makes maintenance of the code easier and thus the implementation more stable. The μTSS design is scalable allowing the use of only a subset of the provided functionality as it is required, e.g., for embedded systems or mobile devices. We discussed in Section 6 our positive experiences with our μTSS based on several projects such as the TCG TPM compliance test suite, the TPM Manager, and a Software-TPM as well as a Software-MTM implementation.

References

1. Trusted Computing Group. TPM main specification. Main Specification Version 1.2 rev. 103, Trusted Computing Group (July 2007)
2. Trusted Computing Group. Trusted network connect. Specification Version 1.2 (2007)
3. Trusted Computing Group. TCG Software Stack specification. Version 1.2 (January 2006), http://trustedcomputinggroup.org
4. Löhr, H., Sadeghi, A.-R., Stüble, C., Weber, M., Winandy, M.: Modeling Trusted Computing Support in a Protection Profile for High Assurance Security Kernels (2009)
5. Sadeghi, A.-R., Stüble, C., Pohlmann, N.: European Multilateral Secure Computing Base - Open Trusted Computing for You and Me 28(9), 548–554 (2004)
6. Alkassar, A., Scheibel, M., Sadeghi, A.-R., Stüble, C., Winandy, M.: Security Architecture for Device Encryption and VPN. In: Information Security Solution Europe (ISSE 2006). Vieweg Verlag (2006)
7. Microsoft. BitLocker drive encryption, http://www.microsoft.com/windows/windows-vista/features/bitlocker.aspx
8. Wave Systems Corp. EMBASSY Trust Suite, http://www.wave.com/products/ets.asp

9. Stüble, C., Zaerin, A.: The TPM Manager Software Architecture. Sirrix AG (2008)
10. Gamma, E., Helm, R., Johnson, R., Vlissides, J.: Design Patterns. Addison-Wesley Professional Computing Series (1995)
11. Mobile Phone Working Group. TCG Mobile Reference Architecture. Technical Report Version 1.0, Trusted Computing Group (June 2007)
12. Armknecht, F., Gasmi, Y., Sadeghi, A.-R., Ramunno, G., Vernizzi, D., Stewin, P., Unger, M.: An Efficient Implementation of Trusted Channels based on OpenSSL. In: Proceedings of ACM STC 2008 (2008)
13. Schulz, S., Sadeghi, A.-R.: Extending IPsec for Efficient Remote Attestation. In: 14th International Conference on Financial Cryptography and Data Security, FC 2010 (2010)
14. Trusted Computing Group. TCG Software Stack specification. Version 1.1 (August 2003), http://trustedcomputinggroup.org
15. Trusted Platform Agent - The open source library for Trusted Computing, http://security.polito.it/tc/tpa/
16. IAIK jTSS - TCG Software Stack for the Java (tm) Platform, http://trustedjava.sourceforge.net/
17. Toegl, R., Winkler, T., Nauman, M., Hong, T.: Towards platform-independent trusted computing. In: STC 2009: Proceedings of the 2009 ACM workshop on Scalable trusted computing, pp. 61–66. ACM, New York (2009)
18. TPM/J Java-based API for the Trusted Platform Module (TPM), http://projects.csail.mit.edu/tc/tpmj/
19. libtpm - a small, low-level TPM access library, http://domino.research.ibm.com/comm/research_projects.nsf/pages/gsal.TCG.html
20. Ekberg, J.-E., Bugiel, S.: Trust in a small package: minimized MRTM software implementation for mobile secure environments. In: STC 2009: Proceedings of the 2009 ACM workshop on Scalable Trusted Computing, pp. 9–18. ACM, New York (2009)

Requirements for an Integrity-Protected Hypervisor on the x86 Hardware Virtualized Architecture

Amit Vasudevan[1], Jonathan M. McCune[1], Ning Qu[2],
Leendert van Doorn[3], and Adrian Perrig[1]

[1] CyLab, Carnegie Mellon University, Pittsburgh, PA, USA
[2] Nvidia Corp., Santa Clara, CA, USA
[3] Advanced Micro Devices (AMD) Corp., Austin, TX, USA

Abstract. Virtualization has been purported to be a panacea for many security problems. We analyze the feasibility of constructing an integrity-protected hypervisor on contemporary x86 hardware that includes virtualization support, observing that without the fundamental property of hypervisor integrity, no secrecy properties can be achieved. Unfortunately, we find that significant issues remain for constructing an integrity-protected hypervisor on such hardware. Based on our analysis, we describe a set of *necessary* rules that must be followed by hypervisor developers and users to maintain hypervisor integrity. No current hypervisor we are aware of adheres to all the rules. No current x86 hardware platform we are aware of even allows for the construction of an integrity-protected hypervisor. We provide a perspective on secure virtualization and outline a research agenda for achieving truly secure hypervisors.

1 Introduction

Virtualization allows a single physical computer to share its resources among multiple *guests*, each of which perceives itself as having total control of its *virtual machine* (VM) [30]. Virtualization is an effective means to improve hardware utilization, reduce power and cooling costs, and streamline backup, recovery, and data center management. It is even making inroads on the client-side. However, in all of these roles, the *hypervisor* (or *Virtual Machine Monitor (VMM)*) becomes yet another maximally privileged software component from the perspective of the guest's trusted computing base (TCB). This stands in direct violation of several well-known principles of protecting information in computer systems [36]. In many scenarios, the hypervisor may support guests for two or more mutually distrusting entities, thereby putting to the test the hypervisor's ability to truly protect its own integrity and isolate guests [7].

Unfortunately, today's popular hypervisors are not without their share of vulnerabilities (e.g., [4,49]), and appear to be unsuitable for use with highly sensitive applications. Despite recent enhancements to hardware support for virtualization [6,21,32], low-level systems problems (e.g., System Management Mode exploits [12,50] and vulnerable BIOSes [26,35]) continue to plague existing solutions. We distinguish between threats to *hypervisor integrity* and threats to hypervisor and guest data secrecy, observing that an integrity-protected hypervisor is a necessary, but not sufficient, condition for

A. Acquisti, S.W. Smith, and A.-R. Sadeghi (Eds.): TRUST 2010, LNCS 6101, pp. 141–165, 2010.

maintaining data secrecy in the face of mutually distrusting guests. We define *integrity-protected* to mean that the hypervisor's code cannot be modified in any fashion and the hypervisor's data cannot be maliciously changed. The secrecy of guests' data is explicitly defined to be outside the scope of the current paper.

Are today's virtualization and security extensions to the x86 platform sufficient to maintain the integrity of a hypervisor? This is a challenging question to answer for current platforms due to their high complexity. Challenging practical issues that we consider include per-device idiosyncrasies that arise from devices that are not completely standards-compliant, and the need to offer the precise (i.e., bug-compatible) environment expected by unmodified guest operating systems.

Given the challenges in designing and implementing an integrity-protected hypervisor, we define threats to data secrecy and availability (such as covert channels, side channels, timing channels, and resource exhaustion attacks) to be outside the scope of this paper. Data secrecy and availability can be ensured only if the fundamental property of hypervisor integrity is realized. For example, without integrity-protection, portions of the hypervisor that manage the isolation of memory pages between guests may be maliciously modified, thereby allowing one guest to make modifications to the code or data of another guest. These modifications may include releasing secrets.

We enumerate core system elements (e.g., buses and system components) required to protect the integrity of the hypervisor in §2, and present rules for an integrity-protected hypervisor in §3. In §4, we discuss specific details of AMD's and Intel's hardware virtualization support in the context of an integrity-protected hypervisor. We believe our rules represent a strong first approximation of the necessary requirements for an integrity-protected hypervisor on today's x86 hardware. We write these rules as hypervisor developers with years of experience investigating hypervisor integrity. We leave for future work the demonstration that these rules are also sufficient.

Given the complexity of the current x86 hardware virtualization architecture and the plethora of available devices, it may be difficult to conclude definitively that an integrity-protected hypervisor can be created when its VMs are commodity operating systems expecting a rich set of peripheral devices and capable of running arbitrary code. Thus, in §5, we also describe a spectrum of different VM environments, illustrating why it may be non-trivial to ensure that some combinations of OSes can execute unmodified on an integrity-protected hypervisor. Further, in §6 we describe the design of several popular hypervisors and discuss the adherence of their design to our integrity-protected hypervisor rules. This section also includes a table summarizing our rules and the level of adherence of these popular hypervisors.

To summarize, this paper makes the following contributions: (1) an analysis of the platform elements that must be properly managed to integrity-protect a hypervisor, (2) a set of rules that hypervisor developers must follow, (3) the manifestation of these rules on contemporary systems, (4) the implications of these rules with respect to supporting concurrent VMs on top of the hypervisor, and (5) an analysis of the adherence of existing hypervisor designs to these rules. While we believe our results are interesting in their own right, we also intend this paper to serve as a call to action. Significant additional research is needed to determine whether the rules presented here are not just necessary but also sufficient. We also hope to inspire subsequent investigations to

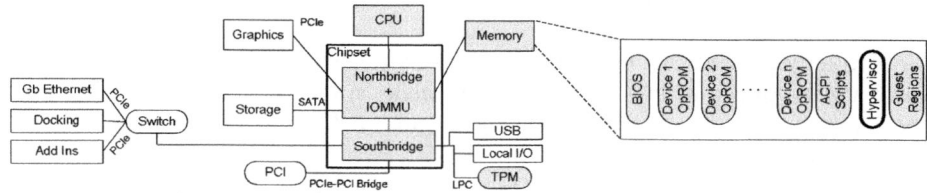

Fig. 1. Elements of today's x86 hardware virtualization architecture. Shaded regions represent elements that *must* be access-controlled to ensure hypervisor integrity. We discuss the TPM in §3.1.

ascertain the data secrecy properties attainable with commodity virtualization solutions, particularly given the effectiveness of recently disclosed attacks (e.g., [31]).

2   Elements of x86 Hardware Virtualization

Our goal is to preserve the integrity of a hypervisor, i.e., preventing inadvertent or malicious manipulation of hypervisor memory regions (both code and data). Consequently, only system components that can directly access memory or mediate memory accesses become critical to preserving hypervisor integrity. AMD and Intel—the two major x86 CPU vendors that support hardware virtualization—design their CPUs to work with the Peripheral Component Interconnect Express (PCIe [10]) system architecture and build on the existing non-hardware virtualized x86 architecture. Both the PCIe and x86 architectures define precise methods for moving data to and from system memory. This standardization serves as a guide for the remainder of this section. To maintain generality, where applicable, we adhere to the PCIe terminology instead of using CPU/vendor specific terms.

2.1   Overview

Current x86 hardware virtualization encompasses both hardware and software elements (Figure 1). The hardware elements are connected via the PCIe bus (though both Intel and AMD employ proprietary buses – Quick Path Interconnect and Hypertransport, respectively – to connect the northbridge and southbridge).

The Northbridge (or Memory Controller Hub – MCH – on recent Intel-VT platforms) connects the CPU(s) (which include an integrated Memory Management Unit, or MMU) and Memory/Cache. The northbridge also supports other performance-critical components such as the graphics controller. Recent Intel-VT platforms use the term Graphics and Memory Controller Hub (GMCH) to describe a MCH with integrated graphics controller. The northbridge further contains an IO Memory Management Unit, or IOMMU, which is responsible for managing Direct Memory Access (DMA) transactions between the Memory and all attached peripherals without intervention by the CPU.

The Southbridge (or IO Controller Hub – ICH) supports less performance-critical IO capabilities such as some types of disk and network interfaces, USB, audio, and legacy ports such as the serial and parallel port. The southbridge also connects an optional

Trusted Platform Module (TPM) which is used to measure a dynamic root of trust (which we treat in §2.2 and §3.1).

The software elements in the x86 hardware-virtualized architecture are the system boot and runtime firmware (BIOS), firmware code on various peripherals, power management scripts within the BIOS, memory regions belonging to individual VMs, and the hypervisor itself.

Throughout this paper we use the terms northbridge, southbridge and IOMMU functionally rather than referring to physical components. As an example, on the recent AMD-V and Intel-VT architectures the northbridge and IOMMU are physically a part of the CPU. However, their functionality remains the same. The following sections discuss these hardware and software elements in the context of an integrity-protected hypervisor.

2.2   Hardware Elements

The hardware elements in the context of preserving hypervisor integrity are the CPU, Northbridge and Southbridge.

CPU. An x86 hardware virtualization-capable CPU, like a normal x86 CPU, includes registers, caches, and an instruction set. The CPU has two over-arching operating modes: host (more privileged) and guest (less privileged). The guest mode is used to execute a guest OS environment in a controlled manner, i.e., in a virtual machine. The host mode can *intercept* certain critical operations that are performed in guest mode such as accessing CPU control registers and performing IO. There can be multiple concurrent guest instantiations, but only one host mode execution environment. Both host and guest modes can further execute in any of four privilege *rings* 0 (most privileged) through 3.

System Management Mode (SMM). SMM code (part of the BIOS) executes at the highest privilege level and is used to handle system events such as system and CPU temperature control, and legacy support for USB input devices. SMM is entered whenever a System Management Interrupt (#SMI) occurs. The #SMI is an external hardware interrupt and can occur at any point during system operation. When SMM is entered, all normal execution state is suspended (including host and guest modes) and firmware code (#SMI handler) is executed with full access to system physical memory. The #SMI handlers are stored in a special memory region called the System Management RAM (SMRAM) which is only accessible by programming certain CPU registers or IO locations within the southbridge (§2.2).

Memory Management Unit (MMU). The MMU is the CPU component that enables virtual memory management and handles all memory accesses from the CPU. Its main function is to translate virtual addresses to physical addresses using paging structures while enforcing memory protections, in both the host and guest modes. Recent x86 hardware-virtualized CPUs introduce the concept of hardware physical memory virtualization where memory addresses are separated into guest virtual, guest physical, and system physical. The guest virtual addresses are translated to guest physical addresses using guest paging structures. The guest physical addresses are translated into system physical addresses using another set of paging structures within the hypervisor.

Microcode. CPU microcode resides in a special high-speed memory within the CPU and translates instructions into sequences of detailed circuit-level operations. Essentially, microcode enables the CPU to reconfigure parts of its own hardware to implement functionality and/or fix bugs in the silicon that would historically require procuring a new unit. Microcode updates are loaded by the BIOS or the OS into the CPU dynamically.

All CPU(s) are shared between the hypervisor and the VM(s) that it runs, as the portion of the hypervisor that handles guest intercepts will always execute on the same CPU as the VM that generated the intercept. This can lead to hypervisor integrity compromise if not managed properly. As an example, a malicious VM may attempt to manipulate CPU cache contents so that unintended code runs as if it is hypervisor code (e.g., [50]). An attacker may also change existing SMI handlers in BIOS so that the malicious handlers execute as SMM code with sufficient privileges to modify hypervisor physical memory regions [12,50]. An attacker can also alter a legitimate microcode[1] update to execute a CPU instruction that would normally be illegal and instead "trick" the memory caches into thinking the CPU is in host mode [37]. From there, the attacker can gain access to hypervisor memory regions.

Northbridge. A *northbridge* (aka memory controller hub, MCH, or memory bridge) typically handles communication between the CPU, memory, graphics controller, and the southbridge (§2.2). The northbridge handles all transactions to and from memory. The northbridge also contains an IO Memory Management Unit (IOMMU) that is responsible for managing direct device accesses to memory via DMA.

IOMMU. An IO Memory Management Unit (IOMMU)[2] manages Direct Memory Accesses (DMA) from system devices. It allows each device in the system to be assigned to a specific *protection domain* which describes the memory regions that are accessible by the device. When a device attempts to access system memory, the IOMMU intercepts the access and determines whether the access is to be permitted as well as the actual location in system memory that is to be accessed. In systems with multiple physical CPUs, there may be multiple IOMMUs, but logical CPUs on a single die currently share an IOMMU.

Most devices today perform DMA to access memory without involving the CPU. DMA increases system performance since the CPU is free to perform computations, but a malicious device may attempt DMA to hypervisor memory regions, potentially compromising its integrity. As an example, Firewire is a serial bus that allows endpoints to issue remote DMA requests. One system may be able to issue DMA requests on the other system via the Firewire controller, thereby gaining read/write access to the full memory contents of the target and compromising its integrity [8].

---

[1] Intel digitally signs microcode updates and hence altering a legitimate microcode update is not straightforward. However, AMD microcode updates are not signed, thereby allowing an attacker to freely modify bits [37].

[2] x86 CPUs also include a more limited graphics-related address translation facility on-chip, called a GART. However, unlike the IOMMU, the GART is limited to performing address translation only and does not implement protections.

Southbridge. The *southbridge* (also known as the IO Bridge) is a chip that implements the lower-bandwidth IO in a system, e.g., USB, hard disks, serial ports, and TPM. It is also responsible for providing access to the non-volatile BIOS memory used to store system configuration data. The southbridge contains certain IO locations that may be used to compromise hypervisor integrity. For example, SMRAM access and SMI generation are controlled by IO locations that reside within the southbridge. An attacker could implant a malicious SMI handler by enabling SMRAM access [12] and execute the handler by generating a SMI. The malicious SMI handler then has unrestricted access to hypervisor memory regions. Similarly, system configuration data copied from firmware into system memory at boot time can be manipulated using the southbridge, potentially preventing the BIOS from setting the system to a known correct state during boot-up.

2.3   Software Elements

In addition to the hardware elements that comprise the current x86 hardware virtualization architecture, there are various software elements. The software elements include firmware such as the BIOS, option ROMs, power management scripts that are embedded into the platform hardware, and OS and applications that run within a VM on top of the hypervisor. These software elements can contain bugs or can be altered to compromise the integrity of a hypervisor. Further, certain software elements such as the BIOS and option ROMs execute even before a hypervisor is initialized and can set the system into a malicious initial state that compromises hypervisor integrity.

BIOS / UEFI. The Basic Input and Output System (BIOS) is by far the most prevalent firmware interface for x86 platforms. The BIOS prepares the machine to execute software beginning from a known state – a process commonly known as system bootstrapping. The Universal Extensible Firmware Interface (UEFI) is a specification that defines a software interface between an operating system and platform firmware [23]. UEFI is a much larger, more complex, OS-like replacement for the older BIOS firmware interface but is only recently making its way into commodity platforms.

The BIOS is typically stored on a Flash (EEPROM) chip that can be programmatically updated. This allows for BIOS vendors to deliver BIOS upgrades that take advantage of newer versions of hardware or to correct bugs in previous revisions. Unfortunately, this also means that a legitimate BIOS can be overwritten with a malicious one that may compromise hypervisor integrity, e.g., hardware virtualization rootkits such as BluePill [34] that emulate nested hypervisor functionality. Thus, an integrity protected hypervisor thinks it is executing at the lowest level; BluePill code however has complete control over hypervisor memory regions.

Note that certain bootstrapping firmware such as Intel's EFI [23] and Phoenix's SecureCore BIOS [41] only allow signed updates to the relevant Flash chip. However, since they have to include OEM customizable sections, parts of the BIOS image are not signature verified. Such areas (e.g., the BIOS boot logo) have been successfully changed by attackers to run malicious code [18].

Option ROMs. A system can contain several BIOS firmware chips. While the primary BIOS typically contains code to access fundamental hardware components, other devices such as SCSI storage controllers, RAID devices, network interface cards, and video controllers often include their own BIOS, complementing or replacing the primary BIOS code for the given component. These additional BIOS firmware modules are collectively known as *Option ROMs*, though today they are rarely implemented as read-only, instead using Flash to support updates.

The BIOS invokes option ROM code for all system devices during bootstrapping. This gives the option ROMs the chance to intercept system interrupts and occupy system memory, in order to provide increased functionality to the system at runtime. The option ROM code is often legacy code that accesses physical memory directly. An attacker may replace a legitimate option ROM with a malicious one which may then be invoked at runtime by an OS running within a VM [16]. This code can then have unrestricted access to hypervisor physical memory regions, thereby compromising its integrity. Certain BIOS code (e.g., Intel Active Management Technology) execute on a seperate processor in parallel to the main CPU and can be used to compromise hypervisor integrity via DMA.

Power Management Scripts. Most systems today are equipped with power management capabilities where the entire system, including devices, can be transitioned into a low-power state to conserve energy when idle. Power management on current commodity systems is governed by the Advanced Configuration and Power Interface (ACPI) specification [20]. With an ACPI-compatible OS, applications and device drivers interact with the OS kernel, which in turn interacts with the low-level ACPI subsystem within the BIOS.

An ACPI subsystem provides an OS with certain power management data structures in memory. A Differentiated System Descriptor Table (DSDT) provides power management code for system devices in a bytecode format called the ACPI Machine Language (AML). The OS kernel typically parses and executes the DSDT scripts to set device and CPU power states. Popular OSes such as Windows parse AML scripts in a CPU mode that allows accessing physical memory directly. An attacker that can insert malicious code within AML scripts will then have unrestricted access to physical memory when executed [17].

Other Code. A VM running on a hypervisor can run a full commodity OS. The OS itself may be subverted and may attempt to attack the hypervisor. As an example, malicious code within a VM may attempt to manipulate the caching policies of hypervisor memory, thereby effectively gaining access to hypervisor memory regions.

3   Integrity-Protected Hypervisor

We now present our assumptions and the rules an integrity-protected hypervisor must observe, with related discussion. For the hypervisor to protect its integrity, it must ensure that it starts up in an unmodified fashion and continues to run without any inadvertent modifications to its code and data.

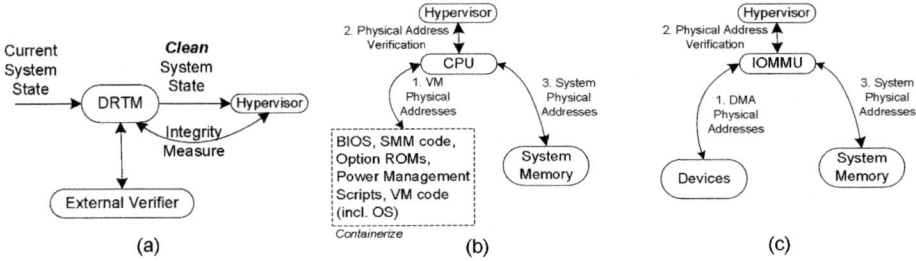

Fig. 2. An integrity-protected hypervisor: (a) must use a dynamic root of trust to startup, (b) must protect itself against any code via physical memory virtualization, and (c) must prevent any device in the system from directly accessing hypervisor memory. Finally, the hypervisor itself must be free of vulnerabilities.

We assume that: *The target system on which an integrity-protected hypervisor runs is physically protected.* An attacker who can physically tamper with or replace with malicious versions system components such as the northbridge, southbridge, CPU, or TPM may successfully compromise hypervisor integrity. As an example, commands generated by the CPU during *dynamic root of trust* establishment (see §3.1) must reach the TPM with their integrity intact. The TPM connects via the Low Pin Count (LPC) bus to the southbridge. The LPC bus is a relatively inexpensive and low-speed bus in modern systems, and is thus susceptible to physical tampering. Therefore, the platform on which an integrity-protected hypervisor runs must be physically protected at all times.

The rules for an integrity-protected hypervisor can be divided into rules that must be followed for (a) startup, (b) runtime, and (c) hypervisor design (Figure 2). From §2 we note that there are only two ways in which hypervisor memory regions can be accessed on an x86 hardware-virtualized platform: (a) via code executing on the CPU,[3] and (b) via system devices performing DMA operations. Accordingly, we present the *exact* rules that must be followed by an integrity-protected hypervisor during startup and runtime, and consider its design in the context of cases (a) and (b) above. Consequently, a hypervisor that follows these rules is automatically protected from integrity compromise.

3.1   Startup Rules

These rules allow for the requirement that an integrity-protected hypervisor must start up in an unmodified fashion.

Definition 1. *A* dynamic root of trust *(DRT) is an execution environment created through a disruptive event that synchronizes and reinitializes all CPUs in the system*

---

[3] This includes code executing from the CPU caches. For example, an attacker could attempt to tamper with the execution of the hypervisor not by changing the memory of the hypervisor directly, but by changing the view of the hypervisor's code when it is executed on the CPU by tampering with the values stored in the CPU code caches.

to a known good state. It also disables all interrupt sources, DMA, and debugging access to the new environment. An explicit design goal of a DRT mechanism is to prevent possibly malicious firmware from compromising the execution of a hypervisor.

Rule 1. *An integrity-protected hypervisor* **must** *be initialized via the creation of a dynamic root of trust.*

Discussion. The traditional BIOS initialization and boot sequence is plagued by having existed for several decades. As such, modern security requirements and virtualization capabilities did not exist when it was first conceived. The result of this is that there may exist legacy code in a system's BIOS that should not be trusted, since it was never subjected to rigorous analysis for security issues.[4] Further, many devices have option ROMs (§2.3) that are invoked by the system's BIOS at boot time. Thus, a malicious option ROM may take control of a platform before the hypervisor can be initialized. The dynamic root of trust mechanism provides a means for integrity-protected hypervisor initialization without breaking compatibility with myriad legacy devices.

Rule 2. *A dynamic root of trust mechanism* **must** *allow for an external verifier to ascertain the identity (e.g., cryptographic hash) of the memory region (code and data) in the new execution environment.*

Discussion. In some cases the DRT establishment can be unsuccessful (e.g., not all CPUs were able to synchronize). Further, if the DRT is successful, it only guarantees that the environment that is initialized is clean. The code that executes within the new environment may be a hypervisor whose integrity is already compromised. Therefore, there must be a mechanism to securely communicate to an external verifier whether a DRT was successfully established, as well as a cryptographic hash of the code and data in the clean execution environment, so that the identity of the loaded hypervisor can be verified to be one known to enforce integrity protections. There are currently both hardware (TPM-based [44]) and software [38] based hardware mechanisms for DRT establishment. The dynamic root of trust mechanism available on today's systems from AMD and Intel also includes a facility to perform an *integrity measurement* of the new environment using the platform's TPM chip.

3.2 Runtime Rules

Once an integrity-protected hypervisor has started in an unmodified form, it must continue to run without any inadvertent modifications to its memory regions (code and data). The following are the set of rules that must be followed at runtime by a hypervisor to ensure its integrity protection.

Rule 3. *An integrity-protected hypervisor* **must** *employ physical memory virtualization to prevent any code executing within a VM from accessing hypervisor memory regions.*

---

[4] For a closed system where only known firmware is executed at boot-time, a dynamic root of trust may not be necessary. However, most (if not all) x86 systems do not fall under this category.

Discussion. A VM running on top of an integrity-protected hypervisor can run any commodity OS and applications. Such an OS can use the BIOS, option ROM, and Power Management Script code during runtime. E.g., Windows uses PCI BIOS functions during startup and employs the video BIOS to control the video subsystem during runtime. Further, it parses and executes Power Management Scripts as a part of system power management.

Code running within a VM may manipulate the MMU's virtual memory data structures to map and access hypervisor memory regions. Further, it may disable virtual memory support and directly access system physical memory. Therefore, an integrity-protected hypervisor must verify any physical address originating from a VM before it reaches the memory controller. Consequently, an integrity-protected hypervisor must virtualize physical memory.

Definition 2. *We define a* hypervisor core *to be the part of a hypervisor that is responsible for initializing, creating, and terminating VMs and for handling any intercepts that occur during VM execution.*

Definition 3. *We define* critical system operations *as operations that can result in compromising hypervisor integrity, e.g., changing page tables mapping within a VM to map and access memory regions belonging to the hypervisor.*

Rule 4. *An integrity-protected hypervisor* **must** *execute its core in the highest privilege level so it can interpose on critical system operations.*

Discussion. An integrity-protected hypervisor is responsible for setting up guest environments, running them, and tearing them down. These operations require execution of privileged instructions and hence the hypervisor must be in an operating mode that allows the use of such instructions. Further, an integrity-protected hypervisor must be able to detect any attempts to modify its memory regions by any other code within the system (e.g., code within the guest environments or device firmware). Thus, an integrity-protected hypervisor must execute in a CPU mode that enables the hypervisor to intercept and handle critical system operations such as device IO and writing to CPU control registers. Other parts of the hypervisor can execute at lower privilege levels contingent on hypervisor design.

Definition 4. *Critical CPU registers are the set of CPU registers that can be used to compromise the integrity of a hypervisor. On the x86 hardware virtualized architecture they can be divided into: (i) control registers – used for controlling the general behavior of the CPU such as interrupt control, switching the addressing mode (16/32/64-bit), and floating-point/multimedia unit control, (ii) segment registers – used to define the memory region and access type for code, data and stack segments, (iii) debug registers – used for debugging purposes, and (iv) machine specific registers (MSR) – special-purpose control registers exposing CPU implementation-specific features. E.g., MSR_EFER is used on both Intel-VT and AMD-V CPUs to enable extended features such as NX (no-execute) memory protections.*

Rule 5. *An integrity-protected hypervisor* **must** *have an independent set of critical CPU registers and* **must** *sanitize values of CPU data registers during control transfers to and from VMs.*

Discussion. Sharing critical CPU registers between the hypervisor and a VM can lead to hypervisor integrity compromise. Code within a VM may use the control registers to turn off MMU-based virtual memory and set the data segment to address all of physical memory to gain access to hypervisor physical memory regions. Certain MSRs are employed by the CPU to save host mode state. As an example, on AMD-V CPUs, the VM_HSAVE MSR is used to set the host mode save area which describes the physical memory region used to save certain host mode runtime state. A guest environment that can change the contents of this MSR can then change the host mode registers and compromise hypervisor integrity. Memory Type Range Registers (MTRRs) are another type of MSR which are used to set caching policy for a range of physical memory. A guest environment can setup the MTRRs such that the CPU cache contents can be accessed and manipulated at runtime [50]. Since parts of hypervisor code and data will often be in the CPU cache, such MTRR manipulation can be used to compromise hypervisor integrity if the hypervisor's page tables for a guest map hypervisor code or data with read permissions.[5] Therefore, an integrity-protected hypervisor must have an independent set of critical CPU registers which are *always* in effect when the CPU is operating in the host mode.

The CPU data registers are used for data movements to and from system memory. Data registers can be divided into: integer, floating-point, and multimedia registers. Guest modes can run a full-fledged OS which typically use these data registers for their functioning. If a hypervisor uses these registers (or a subset of them) for its operation, values of these registers carried over from the guest environment during an intercept can result in the compromise of hypervisor data integrity. Therefore, an integrity-protected hypervisor must either set data registers to a defined state (e.g., zero them) or save and restore contents of used data registers during control transfers to and from guest modes.

Rule 6. *An integrity-protected hypervisor* **requires** *the MMU to maintain independent states for the hypervisor and guest environments.*

Discussion. The MMU is the CPU component that includes support for virtual memory (using paging) and memory access protections. The MMU interface is exposed via a set of CPU registers. The MMU also employs a Translation Lookaside Buffer (TLB) for caching address translations when using virtual memory. Since the MMU is involved in nearly every instruction that is executed by the CPU, a guest environment can compromise hypervisor memory regions if the MMU register set and internal states are shared between host and guest modes. As an example, if a hypervisor does not have its own TLB, the TLB entry loaded in guest mode can lead to unexpected address translations or access permissions. Therefore, an integrity-protected hypervisor needs the MMU on the CPU to maintain independent states for the hypervisor and guest environments.

Rule 7. *An integrity-protected hypervisor* **must** *intercept all x86 hardware virtualization instructions.*

---

[5] Note that an adversary cannot exploit cache synchronization protocols in multi-core CPUs in order to manipulate CPU cache contents. All current x86 CPUs supporting hardware virtualization implement cache coherency in hardware, thereby maintaining a uniform view of main memory.

Discussion. An x86 hardware virtualized CPU provides a set of virtualization specific instructions that are used to create, modify, run and terminate guest environments and to save and load guest environment states. A hypervisor can be compromised if these instructions are allowed to execute within a guest environment. For example, a guest environment could load its own state devoid of protections set by the hypervisor. However, an integrity-protected hypervisor can choose to implement recursive virtualization by emulating such instructions.

Definition 5. *We define* containerization *as the process by which a hypervisor isolates some given code and associated data and executes them under complete control.*

Rule 8. *An integrity-protected hypervisor* **must** *containerize any System Management Mode code and BIOS, option ROM or Power Management Scripts it uses.*

Discussion. SMM code, BIOS, option ROMs, and Power Management Scripts are low-level code that have unrestricted access to all system resources such as critical CPU registers, memory, and device IO locations. A buggy or malicious #SMI handler can therefore access memory regions belonging to the hypervisor and compromise its integrity [12,50]. Malicious code can be embedded within the BIOS, option ROM, or Power Management Scripts [16,17,18] and these in turn can alter hypervisor memory regions. Therefore, if an integrity-protected hypervisor requires the use of BIOS, option ROM, or Power Management Script code, it must run them in isolation (e.g., in a VM). Further, since #SMIs can occur at any point during system operation, an integrity-protected hypervisor must always containerize any SMM code regardless of the CPU operating mode.

Rule 9. *An integrity-protected hypervisor* **must** *prevent system devices from directly accessing hypervisor memory.*

Discussion. An integrity-protected hypervisor can choose to let a VM use a physical device without employing any form of device virtualization. Alternatively, the hypervisor might need to virtualize a physical device and let the VM use a virtual device. As an example, in many systems, a single physical USB controller device controls all the available USB ports. The only way to share the USB ports between VMs would be to present each VM with its own virtual USB controller device that then controls a subset of the physical USB ports on the system. The virtual USB controller devices reside within the hypervisor and interpose on the USB protocol and direct the requests to the appropriate physical USB controller.

USB, Firewire, Storage and Network devices can directly access physical memory via DMA, potentially bypassing the hypervisor. These devices can be programmed by an attacker to access any portion of the physical memory including those belonging to the hypervisor [8]. Malicious firmware on a device can also accomplish the same goal by replacing legitimate physical memory addresses passed to it with hypervisor physical memory regions. Therefore, an integrity protected hypervisor must prevent devices from directly accessing its memory regions.

Rule 10. *An integrity-protected hypervisor* **must** *enumerate all system devices at startup and be able to detect hot-plug devices at runtime.*

Discussion. As discussed in the previous rule, an integrity-protected hypervisor must restrict devices from accessing hypervisor memory regions. This requires the hypervisor to configure memory access restrictions for every device within the system. Consequently, the hypervisor needs to uniquely identify each device. While a device can be uniquely identified (e.g., the bus, device and function triad on a PCIe bus), the identification can change depending on system configuration. As an example, the triad on the PCIe bus is dependent on the physical location of the device on the system board, which may change between hardware upgrades. Therefore, an integrity-protected hypervisor must always enumerate all system devices during its startup to configure permissible memory regions for each device. Further, with hot-plugging capabilities in current systems (where a device can be added or removed from the system at runtime), an integrity-protected hypervisor must be able to dynamically detect such additions and removals and enforce memory access restrictions for such devices. (An alternative, non-technical solution is to maintain stringent physical security to prevent devices from being hot-plugged. This may not be economical in practice.)

Definition 6. *We define critical system devices to be devices that must be properly managed to prevent hypervisor integrity compromise. On the x86 hardware-virtualized architecture, these devices are the functional equivalents of the northbridge, southbridge, and IOMMU, as they can constrain the behavior of all other devices.*

Rule 11. *An integrity-protected hypervisor* **must** *prevent access to critical system devices at all times.*

Discussion. Critical system devices, like any other device, can expose their interface through either legacy IO or memory-mapped IO. For example, Intel-VT systems expose the IOMMU as a DMA device through ACPI while AMD-V systems expose the IOMMU as a PCI device. A VM on top of the hypervisor may perform direct IO to these devices, effectively compromising the integrity of the hypervisor. Therefore, an integrity-protected hypervisor *must* prevent access to these critical system devices at all times.

3.3 Design Rule

A hypervisor's runtime integrity can be compromised by manipulating its memory regions. On an x86 hardware virtualized platform memory can be accessed either via code executing on the CPU or system devices using DMA. In this section, we discuss the rule governing the design of an integrity-protected hypervisor in the above context.

Rule 12. *An integrity-protected hypervisors' code* **must** *be free of vulnerabilities.*

Discussion. A hypervisor needs to be configured with guest environment state (guest OS and allocated resources) before a guest environment can be run. Further, contingent on hypervisor design, configuration changes can be needed at runtime during guest environment operation (e.g., adding or removing resources at runtime). Depending on the hypervisor design, inter-VM communication (e.g., drag and drop between different guest environments) and guest runtime interfaces to the hypervisor (e.g., accelerated IO drivers for virtualized devices) might be supported. Such runtime interfaces might also directly access hypervisor data (e.g., accelerated drivers within the guest may access temporary data buffers that are mapped within hypervisor memory regions for fast IO). All these configuration options and interfaces pose significant risk to hypervisor integrity if they are complex [4]. An integrity-protected hypervisor must therefore ensure that such configuration and runtime interfaces are minimal. Further, designers must also ensure that the hypervisor's core operating logic is simple and its code-base is within limits to perform manual and analytical audits to rule out any vulnerabilities [11,14,27].

4   Integrity-Protected Hypervisor on AMD-V and Intel-VT

We present details on *if* and *how* the rules described in §3 can be enforced on AMD-V and Intel-VT.

Rule 1. An integrity-protected hypervisor must be initialized via the creation of a dynamic root of trust. To date, hardware- and software-based [38] mechanisms for creating a dynamic root of trust have been proposed. AMD introduced a new CPU instruction called *SKINIT* [6], and Intel introduced a family of instructions called *GETSEC* [22], where *GETSEC* [*SENTER*] is the most similar to AMD's *SKINIT*.

Rule 2. A dynamic root of trust mechanism must allow for an external verifier to ascertain the identity of the code that executed on a system. The TPM's PCR 17 is reset during the establishment of a DRTM. It resets to 0 (20 bytes of 0x00) during successful establishment, and -1 (20 bytes of 0xff) in the event of an error. The contents of the code to be executed in the new environment are sent to the TPM itself, where they are hashed and extended into the newly reset PCR. On the AMD-V this is PCR 17 while on the Intel-VT it is PCR 18. (An Intel-provided *Authenticated Code Module*, or ACMod, is extended into PCR 17 on Intel systems.)

Rule 3. An integrity-protected hypervisor must virtualize physical memory to prevent access to its memory regions. There are both software and hardware approaches to physical memory virtualization.

Software physical memory virtualization performs guest virtual to system physical address translations on behalf of the guest environment by using shadow page tables within the hypervisor. The shadow page tables are synchronized with the guest page tables during guest page table modifications and are enforced using MMU configuration registers of the guest environment. Note that if the guest environment attempts to run without virtual memory support (e.g., real-mode), the switch must be intercepted and virtual memory support must be enabled transparently.

On both AMD-V and Intel-VT, all guest accesses to MMU registers can be intercepted by the hypervisor, which facilitates enforcement of shadow page tables. Further, TLB flushes are performed using the CR3 and CR4 registers and the INVLPG instruction, all of which can be intercepted by the hypervisor to synchronize shadow page tables. Furthermore, CPU mode switches within a VM can be intercepted by the hypervisor on both architectures, to enable virtual memory transparently.

Both AMD-V and Intel-VT have support for hardware physical memory virtualization in the form of nested page tables and extended page tables, respectively. With hardware physical memory virtualization, the guest has its own set of MMU configuration registers and page tables which need not be tracked by the hypervisor. Instead, the guest page tables translate guest virtual addresses into guest physical addresses. The guest physical addresses are then translated to system physical addresses by the MMU using nested (extended) page tables which reside within the hypervisor for each guest. All page faults incurred in the nested (extended) page tables lead to a control transfer to the hypervisor. This guarantees that the hypervisor has full control over system physical memory.

Rule 4. An integrity-protected hypervisor must execute its core in the highest privilege level to allow it to interpose on critical system operations. Consequently, an integrity-protected hypervisor on AMD-V or Intel-VT must run in the host mode in ring 0. On AMD-V, a CPU can be switched to host mode in ring 0 using the CR0 register and by enabling host mode using MSR EFER (once in host mode, MSR VM_HSAVE_PA should be initialized to point to the host save area). On Intel-VT, a CPU can be switched to host mode in ring 0 using the CR0 register and by initializing VMXON region contents, enabling host mode using the CR4 register, and executing the VMXON instruction.

Rule 5. An integrity-protected hypervisor must have an independent set of critical CPU registers and must sanitize values of CPU data registers during control transfers to and from VMs. Both AMD-V and Intel-VT CPUs provide the host and each guest mode with their own set of control, debug, and segment registers. Thus, guest-mode changes to these registers only impact the guest mode operation and *cannot* result in any changes within the host mode.

On both AMD-V and Intel-VT CPUs, certain MSRs are shared between the host and guest modes. AMD-V has support for an MSR Bitmap structure for every guest mode instance. If a bit corresponding to a particular MSR is set in the bitmap, it results in an intercept to the hypervisor when a guest mode accesses the MSR. Intel-VT has a similar mechanism using MSR Lists for guest mode. On AMD-V CPUs an integrity-protected hypervisor must intercept accesses to VM_HSAVE_PA (used to store host mode state), EFER (used to control enabling/disabling virtualization) and the SMRAM MSR (used to control SMRAM access and SMI generation).

In both AMD-V and Intel-VT, MTRRs are implemented by using a set of MSRs. The MTRRs are divided into fixed range (for setting caching type for 1 MB and below) and variable range (for greater than 1 MB). There is also a default-range MTRR which sets the default caching policy for all other physical memory regions apart from the fixed- and variable-range MTRRs. AMD-V CPUs have another MSR related to the MTRRs which is responsible for global configuration of MTRR registers. An integrity-protected hypervisor must intercept access to all the MTRRs and ensure that the memory ranges specified by guests do not belong to the hypervisor.

Both AMD-V and Intel-VT CPUs share integer registers (except registers R/EAX, R/ESP, and R/EFLAGS), floating-point registers and multimedia registers between the host and guest modes. Thus, if a hypervisor makes use of these registers, it *must* sanitize their values across guest mode switches.

Rule 6. An integrity-protected hypervisor requires the MMU to maintain independent states for the hypervisor and guest environments. Both AMD-V and Intel-VT CPUs provide the host and each guest mode with their own set of MMU-related configuration registers. Thus, any changes to these registers only impact MMU operation within the specific mode. Further, both AMD and Intel support Address Space Identifiers (ASID). With ASID, a unique ID can be assigned for each guest; the host mode is always allocated ASID 0. The ASIDs are then used to isolate TLB entries of the hypervisor and guests.

Rule 7. An integrity-protected hypervisor must intercept all x86 hardware virtualization instructions. Both AMD-V and Intel-VT CPUs cause an unconditional guest mode intercept if any virtualization-specific instructions are used within a guest environment. Therefore, a hypervisor *must* handle guest mode intercepts caused due to such instructions [6,21]. The nature of operations performed on such intercepts is contingent on hypervisor design.

Rule 8. An integrity-protected hypervisor must containerize any System Management Mode code and BIOS, option ROM or Power Management Scripts it uses. Code associated with the BIOS, option ROM, and Power Management Scripts can be contained by running them within a VM. The hypervisor can use a similar technique for SMM code by intercepting SMIs and running the SMI handlers in isolation.

Intel-VT provides support for SMM containerization using *dual-monitor* treatment. With dual-monitor, there is a regular hypervisor and an SMM Transfer Monitor (STM) that is in control of a hardware virtual machine solely for running SMM code. The STM gets control on all SMIs (occurring within the hypervisor as well as guests) and is responsible for running the target SMM code.

SMI handlers in production systems typically need to execute with guaranteed execution response. The fundamental question then with STM is whether it can provide real-time execution guarantees. Given that the STM runs within its own hardware virtual machine, the CPU would have to save and restore entire hardware virtual machine execution contexts, which would incur non-negligible runtime cost. Furthermore, given the fact that there are currently no Intel CPUs that implement STM, it is impossible to precisely evaluate whether the STM model is applicable in practice.

AMD-V on the other hand only supports interception of SMIs occurring in the guest mode. Thus, while an integrity-protected hypervisor on the AMD-V can intercept such guest mode SMIs and run them within a VM, it *must* disable SMI generation when in host mode. This can be done by controlling the SMRAM MSRs. However, disabling SMI generation in such a fashion results in two problems in practice: (i) an SMI can occur during the time taken to perform a transition from guest to host mode and before SMI generation is disabled. Such an SMI results in a SMM handler that executes without any form of isolation, thereby potentially compromising hypervisor integrity, and (ii) disabling SMI altogether would result in a system freeze on most platforms which require certain SMM code to execute periodically (e.g., system temperature sensors).

Rule 9. An integrity-protected hypervisor must prevent system devices from directly accessing hypervisor memory regions. The IOMMU is the only system device that can intervene between DMA transactions occurring between a device and memory and hence must be employed by an integrity-protected hypervisor to protect its memory regions from direct access by devices. Both AMD-V and Intel-VT provide an IOMMU as a part of the northbridge. The IOMMU on both architectures allows each peripheral device in the system to be assigned to a set of IO page tables. When an IO device attempts to access system memory, the IOMMU intercepts the access, determines the domain to which the device has been assigned, and uses the IO page tables associated with that device to determine whether the access is to be permitted as well as the actual location in system memory that is to be accessed. An integrity protected hypervisor *must* instantiate IO page tables such that physical addresses corresponding to hypervisor memory regions are marked as inaccessible to any device.

Rule 10. An integrity-protected hypervisor must enumerate all system devices at startup and be able to detect hot-plug devices at runtime. On the PCIe bus, each device is uniquely identified using the bus, device, and function triad. When a hypervisor starts up, it can iterate through all possible bus, device and function locations and query the PCIe configuration space for the triad. If a device is present, the configuration space access returns a valid device identification.

Hot-plug devices on the PCIe bus can be detected by the hypervisor using ACPI. The Hot Plug Parameters (HPP) table is updated by the ACPI subsystem whenever there is a hot-plug device insertion or removal. A hypervisor can periodically scan the table, and obtain the device identification triad on the PCIe bus.

Rule 11. An integrity-protected hypervisor must prevent access to critical system devices at all times. On both AMD-V and Intel-VT CPUs, devices can be controlled via legacy or memory-mapped IO. Legacy IO is performed using a set of four instructions: IN, OUT, INS, and OUTS. Further, both architectures provide a method for the hypervisor to intercept legacy IO operations on a per-port basis using an IO permission bitmap for each guest. Both AMD-V and Intel-VT support software and hardware physical memory virtualization. An integrity-protected hypervisor can set desired protections using page table entries corresponding to the memory-mapped IO region to intercept accesses.

As seen from the preceding discussions, Rule 1 through Rule 11 depend on the platform hardware and all of them except Rule 8 can be completely implemented on current x86 hardware virtualized platforms. As discussed earlier in this section, Rule 8 cannot be completely implemented as current x86 platforms do not contain adequate hardware support to containerize SMM code. Rule 12 (§3.3) depends on the design of an integrity-protected hypervisor and will be discussed in the following two sections.

5   Guest and Hardware Requirements

In §3, we identified rules that an integrity-protected hypervisor must obey. We further analyzed these rules in the context of commodity hardware from AMD and Intel in §4, and established the feasibility of constructing an integrity-protected hypervisor. In this section, we discuss the impact that such a hypervisor design has on its guests and on hardware requirements. That is, some combinations of guest operating systems may require additional hypervisor functionality that is in conflict with Rule 12.

5.1 Multiple Guests

An integrity-protected hypervisor's ability to support multiple guests is contingent on the hardware and device requirements of the individual guests. For example, an extremely minimal guest that requires only a processor on which to perform basic computations does not introduce any resource contention beyond the CPU time and memory space allocated to it. On the other hand, multiple instances of a fully-interactive, media-rich modern OS may require many of the system's underlying devices to be somehow multiplexed between the guests.

Sharing Devices. On a well-behaved system with sufficient peripherals, each guest running on top of the hypervisor can be granted access to a disjoint set of devices. For example, web servers belonging to mutually distrusting entities can each be allocated their own network interface, disk controller, and set of drives. The hypervisor can protect itself by properly configuring the IOMMU, as previously discussed.

However, in certain cases a hypervisor needs to share a single hardware device between two or more guests. For example, many systems today actually do have multiple USB controllers, each of which controls what are generally (though to our knowledge there is no requirement that this remain so) a small number of physically proximal ports, e.g., front-panel vs. rear-panel ports. It is technically feasible to assign distinct USB controllers to distinct guests. Unfortunately, today it generally requires trial-and-error to determine which controller is responsible for which physical ports. For, e.g., a USB flash drive containing corporate secrets, this level of uncertainty is not acceptable. Thus, one may be tempted to design the hypervisor to interpose on some USB traffic, with the intention of ensuring that certain devices are only accessible from the appropriate guests. In practice, we fear that this will significantly complicate the hypervisor, and risk breaking compliance with Rule 12.

Guest BIOS Calls. Many legacy operating systems – especially closed-source ones – depend on BIOS calls as part of their basic operation. While BIOS calls can be invoked inside of another virtual environment to protect the hypervisor (recall §2.3 and, e.g., Rule 3), these calls can have lasting effects on the relevant devices. In practice, devices manipulated through BIOS calls cannot be shared without a software emulation or virtualization layer to resolve conflicts between multiple guests that attempt to use the device concurrently, or in conflicting operating modes.

A consequence of the above characteristics of many operating systems is that they cannot be readily executed simultaneously on an integrity-protected hypervisor, as the logic necessary to virtualize, emulate, or otherwise multiplex legacy calls such as BIOS calls may drastically increase the complexity of the hypervisor, again threatening Rule 12.

Sharing Between Guests. One solution to sharing a single hardware device between multiple guests is to create an additional guest with the sole responsibility of virtualizing a single physical device and exposing multiple instances of a virtual device. The virtual device may appear identical to the physical device behind it, or the virtual device may expose a different interface. Each option has its advantages. This design space has been explored in great detail as it applies to microkernels [15].

From the perspective of an integrity-protected hypervisor, such an architecture requires a means for sharing information between guests. The primary risk to the hypervisor is the inclusion of a larger configuration interface that enables the creation of, e.g., shared memory and message passing mechanisms for guest intercommunication. We note that any mechanism within the hypervisor that attempts to filter or otherwise restrict traffic between guests will have the effect of further complicating the implementation of the hypervisor. The issue of one guest attacking another via the sharing interface is significant, but it is orthogonal to the hypervisor's ability to protect its own integrity.

5.2   Hardware Considerations

Today, a device is deemed "compatible" with a particular platform architecture and operating system if it implements an interface close enough to the relevant specifications that any differences or discrepancies can be remedied within the relevant device driver. This somewhat sloppy approach has security consequences for an integrity-protected hypervisor. We now discuss the importance of correct hardware, and then relate some examples we have encountered in the wild of devices and systems that do not behave as expected.

To keep the hypervisor minimal, it is of utmost importance that peripheral devices are in compliance with the relevant specification or API. Today, devices abound with bugs or compliance issues that are considered minor from a functionality perspective ("fixed" via a software work-around) but potentially create significant security vulnerabilities.

The problem is that buggy or non-compliant devices generally require a work-around in the form of additional device driver code. In the limit, an integrity-protected hypervisor will need to be aware of these work-arounds, in the form of additional hypervisor code. This effectively bloats the hypervisor codebase and precludes formal or manual verification of the hypervisor's correctness and security properties (i.e., violating Rule 12).

Experiences with Devices.   Here we relate some of our own experience exploring systems built using hardware virtualization and trusted computing support in the context of an integrity-protected hypervisor.

South Bridge Renders DRTM / PCR 17 Unusable.   An integrity-protected hypervisor must initialize itself using a dynamic root of trust mechanism (§3.1). A critical component of the DRTM is its ability to extend the hash of the newly loaded code into a PCR in the system's TPM. In practice, we have encountered systems that do not update PCR 17 correctly. We have received one report that there is a bug in the southbridge that results in data corruption on the LPC bus [13], thereby rendering the resulting PCR value meaningless. This bug renders infeasible on the affected systems an entire class of trustworthy computing systems.

SMRAM locked by the BIOS resulting in no SMI intercept.   Rule 8 states that an integrity-protected hypervisor must containerize any System Management Mode code (§2.2). For a BIOS which does not authenticate SMM code, an integrity-protected hypervisor can containerize SMM code by intercepting #SMIs and executing #SMI handlers within a VM (§4, Rule 8). However, we have encountered systems in the wild where the SMRAM is locked by a non-integrity measured BIOS, thereby preventing an SMI intercept from being generated when the CPU is in guest mode. In other words, an SMM handler (as a result of an SMI) can execute in SMM mode without the hypervisor having any control over it. This leaves a hypervisor on such hardware potentially vulnerable to malicious SMM handler code.

iTPM. The v1.2 TPM specification states that all TPM chips must expose the same, well-defined interface [43]. In practice, this is not the case. For example, the TPM in the Intel GM45 chipset returns an incorrect status message, substituting the VALID TIS status message when it should return the DATA_EXPECT status [42]. This seemingly minor issue can be worked-around in a few lines of code. However, this serves to illustrate the risk posed to an integrity-protected hypervisor by the plethora of devices available today. If each device requires even just a few lines of code in the hypervisor, then the hypervisor's code size is likely to escalate to the point where compliance with Rule 12 (no vulnerabilities in the hypervisor) is intractable.

The Importance of Correct Hardware. If integrity-protection for the hypervisor is a priority, then non-compliant devices are unacceptable. Given that today's market remains largely dominated by features and performance, this situation is troubling. An integrity-protected hypervisor may have to include a blacklist of known non-conformant devices. Or, if blacklists fail to scale, then such a hypervisor may have to include a whitelist of the few hardware devices known to provide the required properties. In practice, this will likely increase the cost of systems.

6   Popular Hypervisors

We now present the designs of popular Type 1 [30] hypervisors and discuss the impact of such designs on the rules discussed in §3. To keep our discussion focused we choose VMware ESX Server, Xen, Hyper-V, L4 and SecVisor as our examples. We believe they encompass the current hypervisor spectrum from general-purpose to ad-hoc.

Figure 3 shows the hypervisors and the integrity rules that each of them adhere to. As seen, no hypervisor adheres to all the rules. None of the hypervisors except Xen and SecVisor load by establishing a dynamic root of trust and hence violate Rule 1. However, adding support to adhere to Rule 1 should be fairly straightforward. More importantly, none of the hypervisors containerize (or can containerize) SMM code (§2.2, §4-Rule 8), thereby violating Rule 8. Finally, implementation of a design of a particular hypervisor leads to increased hypervisor code/data and attack surface that violates Rule 12 as described in the following paragraphs.

A VMware virtual environment consists of the hypervisor and drivers for all supported platform hardware. It also consists of a service console which is used for initial system configuration and ongoing management tasks [45]. The hypervisor also provides a standard API which enables configuration and management via local and/or remote applications. Since the VMware hypervisor is monolithic by design, it results in an increased code base (since all device drivers are present in memory irrespective of the

Integrity Rules	Hypervisors				
	VMware	Xen	Hyper-V	L4	SecVisor
1. An integrity-protected hypervisor must be initialized via the creation of a dynamic root of trust.	✗	✓	✗	✗	✓
2. A dynamic root of trust mechanism must allow for an external verifier to ascertain the identity of the code that has received control in the new execution environment.	✓	✓	✓	✓	✓
3. An integrity-protected hypervisor must employ physical memory virtualization to prevent any code executing within a VM from accessing hypervisor memory regions.	✓	✓	✓	✓	✓
4. An integrity-protected hypervisor must execute its core in the highest privilege level that allows it to interpose on critical system operations.	✓	✓	✓	✓	✓
5. An integrity-protected hypervisor must have an independent set of critical CPU registers and must sanitize values of CPU data registers during control transfers to and from VMs.	✓	✓	✓	✓	✓
6. An integrity-protected hypervisor requires the MMU to maintain independent states for the hypervisor and guest environments.	✓	✓	✓	✓	✓
7. An integrity-protected hypervisor must intercept all x86 hardware virtualization instructions.	✓	✓	✓	✓	✓
8. An integrity-protected hypervisor must containerize any SMM code, BIOS, option ROM or Power Management Script it uses.	✗	✗	✗	✗	✗
9. An integrity-protected hypervisor must prevent system devices from directly accessing hypervisor memory regions.	✓	✓	✓	✓	✓
10. An integrity-protected hypervisor must enumerate all system devices at startup and be able to detect hot-plug devices at runtime.	✓	✓	✓	✓	✓
11. An integrity-protected hypervisor must prevent access to critical system devices at all times.	✓	✓	✓	✓	✓
12. An integrity-protected hypervisors' code must be free of vulnerabilities.	✗	✗	✗	✗	✓*

Fig. 3. No existing hypervisors adhere to all of our integrity rules. In particular, no hypervisor supports (or can support) containerization of SMM code (Rule 8). Note that Xen adheres to Rule 1 using OSLO [26] or tboot [40] at boot time. *SecVisor has gone through a rigorous formal verification process that proves the correctness of its memory protection scheme [14].

platform hardware). The VMware ESX server core is reported to have around 500K lines of code [46]. This can lead to vulnerabilities within the hypervisor core itself [3]. Further, the local and/or remote management interfaces can be exploited in order to execute code with hypervisor privileges [5].

A Xen virtual environment consists of the Xen hypervisor, Domain-0, Domain Management and Control (DMC) software, and paravirtualized and hardware-virtualized guest domains [51]. Domain-0 is a paravirtualized Linux kernel and is a unique virtual machine running on the Xen hypervisor that has special rights to access physical I/O resources as well as interact with the other guest domains. DMC supports the overall management and control of the virtualization environment and executes within Domain-0. Domain-0 and DMC is required to be running before any other guest domains can be started. The Xen hypervisor also exposes a set of hypercalls which can be used by both Domain-0 and guest domains to directly interact with the hypervisor.

Xen Domain-0 uses standard Linux OS drivers to control system hardware. Hence Domain-0 has privileged access to most system hardware. Further, since the Domain-0 TCB is large (due to an entire Linux kernel and supporting drivers) it is easy to exploit vulnerabilities within the OS to gain root access in Domain-0 [1,2]. Once within Domain-0, an attacker can employ DMA accesses, Xen hypercall functionalities and DRAM controller programming in order to access Xen Hypervisor memory regions [47,48].

Hyper-V virtualization consists of *partitions*. A partition is a logical unit of isolation, supported by the hypervisor, in which operating systems execute. The Hyper-V hypervisor must have at least one parent, or root, partition, running Windows Server 2008 [29]. The virtualization stack runs in the parent partition and has direct access to the hardware devices. The root partition then creates the child partitions (using the hypercall API) which host the guest operating systems. Given that the Hyper-V root partition consists of a complete Windows Server 2008 installation, any vulnerability that affects Windows Server 2008 will affect Hyper-V. For example, last fall, a routine Windows patch resulted in the compromise of the Hyper-V parent partition [28].

L4 employs a microkernel approach towards virtualization [19]. It provides basic resource and communication abstractions to which guest OSes need porting. While the current L4 code-base has not been verified, the size of the L4 microkernel (order of 10K) suggests that it should be amenable to formal verification. seL4, an embedded microkernel for ARM processors based on L4 has been mathematically verified for correctness [27]. A guest OS requires considerable changes to be ported to L4. This may not be a viable solution for commodity OSes such as Windows. Also, the seL4 microkernel has been verified only on the ARM architecture and the verification process would reportedly take around 10 person years if done again [27]. Thus, it is unclear whether the verification approach is viable on a much more complex architecture such as x86.

SecVisor is a hypervisor which provides lifetime OS kernel code integrity. It is a *pass-through* hypervisor and does not virtualize system devices or resources. Instead, it manipulates page protections to ensure that only approved kernel-code can execute during runtime [39]. The SecVisor architecture is simple and its code base is very small (around 8000 SLOC). It has been formally verified for correctness [14].

7   Related Work

Karger discusses hypervisor requirements for multi-level secure (MLS) systems [25]. He argues that hypervisors are conceptually divided into Pure Isolation and Sharing hypervisors, with Pure Isolation hypervisors only being practical on extremely expensive hardware. Karger's discussion is largely centered on systems that have received some type of security evaluation, e.g., Common Criteria [24]. Implicit in the ability of a hypervisor to receive such certification is that hypervisor's ability to protect its own integrity, which is the focus of the present work.

Roscoe et al. argue that virtualization research today is clouded by commercial applicability, and has not been sufficiently bold in exploring fundamentally new OS and virtualization designs [33]. They also argue that one of the things enabled by hardware virtualization support today is for research systems to become usable for "real work" much more quickly than was previously possible. While the current paper is guilty of not breaking fundamentally new ground, we feel that it is important to explore the limitations of current hardware so that future researchers are not lulled into a false sense of security.

Bratus et al. argue for a significant architectural change to the MMU in today's systems to better enable integrity measurements to reflect the true state of an executing system, and not just that system's load-time state [9]. Their primary concern is to address the time-of-check, time-of-use (TOCTOU) vulnerability inherent in today's TPM-based integrity measurement solutions. We agree that this is a significant limitation, and believe that solutions to such limitations should be complimentary to secure hypervisor designs.

8 Conclusions

We explored the low-level details of x86 hardware virtualization and established rules that an integrity-protected hypervisor must follow. In the process, we identified a number of discrepancies between specification and practice that can potentially compromise a hypervisor's integrity on these platforms. We conclude that while in theory the latest x86 hardware contains sufficient support to integrity-protect a hypervisor, in practice an integrity-protected hypervisor cannot be realized on today's x86 hardware platforms. As an example, System Management Mode (SMM) code that exists on all x86 platforms runs at a higher privilege than the hypervisor itself. Current x86 platforms do not provide adequate hardware support to isolate such SMM code. We also conclude that an integrity-protected hypervisor will be unable to support arbitrarily many legacy guests. Sharing devices and data between multiple guests coupled with guest BIOS invocations significantly complicates the hypervisor, which can result in vulnerabilities that compromise hypervisor integrity. Also, in constructing a system that truly protects hypervisor integrity, hardware must be selected with great care, as numerous devices that exist in the wild fail to adhere to relevant specifications.

We believe the rules presented in this paper represent a strong first approximation of what is necessary to realize an integrity-protected hypervisor. Such a hypervisor will be capable of maintaining its own integrity and preventing mutually distrusting guests from compromising each other's or the hypervisor's integrity. However, we have not discussed mechanisms required to create a trusted path to the user or administrator of a system equipped with an integrity-protected hypervisor. Further work is also required to provide protection of guests' secrets in a virtualized environment. Recent research [31] reveals that the days of ignoring side channels and timing channels are behind us, as these represent very real and practical threats. We hope that this paper will serve as a solid starting point and a call to action for additional investigation into these significant challenges.

Acknowledgements

This research was supported in part by CyLab at Carnegie Mellon under grants DAAD19-02-1-0389 from the Army Research Office, and by grant CNS-0831440 from the National Science Foundation. The views and conclusions contained here are those of the authors and should not be interpreted as necessarily representing the official policies or endorsements, either express or implied, of ARO, CMU, CyLab, NSF, or the U.S. Government or any of its agencies.

References

1. Elevated privileges. CVE-2007-4993 (2007)
2. Multiple integer overflows allow execution of arbitrary code. CVE-2007-5497 (2007)
3. The CPU hardware emulation does not properly handle the Trap flag. CVE-2008-4915 (under review) (2008)
4. Directory traversal vulnerability in the shared folders feature. CVE-2008-0923 (under review) (2008)
5. Multiple buffer overflows in openwsman allow remote attackers to execute arbitrary code. CVE-2008-2234 (2008)
6. AMD64 virtualization: Secure virtual machine architecture reference manual. AMD Publication no. 33047 rev. 3.01 (2005)
7. Anderson, J.P.: Computer security technology planning study. Technical Report ESD-TR-73-51, Air Force Electronic Systems Division, Hanscom AFB (1972)
8. Boileau, A.: Hit by a bus: Physical access attacks with firewire. RuxCon (2006)
9. Bratus, S., D'Cunha, N., Sparks, E., Smith, S.W.: TOCTOU, traps, and trusted computing. In: Proc. Conference on Trusted Computing and Trust in Information Technologies, TRUST (2008)
10. Budruk, R., Anderson, D., Shanley, T.: PCI Express System Architecture. Addison-Wesley, Reading (2004)
11. Datta, A., Franklin, J., Garg, D., Kaynar, D.: A logic of secure systems and its applications to trusted computing. In: Proc. IEEE Symposium on Security and Privacy (2009)
12. Duflot, L., Levillain, O., Morin, B., Grumelard, O.: Getting into the SMRAM: SMM reloaded. In: Central Directorate for Information Systems Security (2009)
13. Findeisen, R.: Buggy south bridge in HP dc5750. Personal communication (April 2008)
14. Franklin, J., Seshadri, A., Qu, N., Chaki, S., Datta, A.: Attacking, repairing, and verifying SecVisor: A retrospective on the security of a hypervisor. CMU Cylab Technical Report CMU-CyLab-08-008 (2008)
15. Härtig, H., Hohmuth, M., Liedtke, J., Schönberg, S., Wolter, J.: The performance of microkernel-based systems. In: Proceedings of the ACM Symposium on Operating Systems Principles (SOSP) (October 1997)
16. Heasman, J.: Implementing and detecting a PCI rootkit. NGSSoftware Insight Security Research (2006)
17. Heasman, J.: Implementing and detecting an ACPI BIOS rootkit. Black Hat USA (2006)
18. Heasman, J.: Hacking the extensible firmware interface. Black Hat USA (2007)
19. Heiser, G., Elphinstone, K., Kuz, I., Klein, G., Petters, S.M.: Towards trustworthy computing systems: Taking microkernels to the next level. In: Proc. ACM Operating Systems Review (2007)
20. Hewlett-Packard, et al.: Advanced configuration and power interface specification. Revision 3.0b (October 2006)
21. Intel virtualization technology specification for the IA-32 Intel architecture. Intel Publication no. C97063-002 (April 2005)
22. Intel trusted execution technology – measured launched environment developer's guide. Document no. 315168-005 (June 2008)
23. Intel Corporation. The extensible firmware interface specification (2002), http://www.intel.com/technology/efi/
24. International Organization for Standardization. Information technology – Security techniques – evaluation criteria for IT security – Part 1: Introduction and general model, Part 2: Security functional requirements, Part 3: Security assurance requirements. ISO/IEC 15408-1, 15408-2, 15408-3 (1999)

25. Karger, P.A.: Multi-level security requirements for hypervisors. In: Proc. Annual Computer Security Applications Conference (ACSAC) (December 2005)

26. Kauer, B.: OSLO: Improving the security of Trusted Computing. In: Proc. USENIX Security Symposium (August 2007)

27. Klein, G., Elphinstone, K., Heiser, G., Andronick, J., Cock, D., Derrin, P., Elkaduwe, D., Engelhardt, K., Kolanski, R., Norrish, M., Sewell, T., Tuch, H., Winwood, S.: seL4: Formal verification of an OS kernel. In: Proc. SOSP (2009)

28. Microsoft. Microsoft technet MS08-067: Vulnerability in server service could allow remote code execution (2008)

29. Microsoft. Hyper-V architecture. Microsoft Developers Network (2009)

30. Popek, G.J., Goldberg, R.P.: Formal requirements for virtualizable third generation architectures. ACM Comm. 17 (1974)

31. Ristenpart, T., Tromer, E., Shacham, H., Savage, S.: Hey, you, get off of my cloud: exploring information leakage in third-party compute clouds. In: Proc. ACM Conference on Computer and Communications Security, CCS (2009)

32. Robin, J.S., Irvine, C.E.: Analysis of the Intel Pentium's ability to support a secure virtual machine monitor. In: Proc. USENIX Security Symposium (2000)

33. Roscoe, T., Elphinstone, K., Heiser, G.: Hype and virtue. In: Proc. HotOS Workshop (May 2007)

34. Rutkowska, J.: Subverting Vista kernel for fun and profit. SyScan and Black Hat Presentations (2006)

35. Sacco, A.L., Ortega, A.A.: Persistent BIOS infection. Core Security Technologies (2009)

36. Saltzer, J., Schroeder, M.: The protection of information in computer systems. Proc. IEEE 63(9), 1278–1308 (1975)

37. SecuriTeam. Opteron exposed: Reverse engineering AMD K8 microcode updates. SecuriTeam Security Reviews (2004)

38. Seshadri, A., Luk, M., Shi, E., Perrig, A., VanDoorn, L., Khosla, P.: Pioneer: Verifying integrity and guaranteeing execution of code on legacy platforms. In: Proc. SOSP (2005)

39. Sheshadri, A., Luk, M., Qu, N., Perrig, A.: SecVisor: A tiny hypervisor to provide lifetime kernel code integrity for commodity OSes. In: Proc. SOSP (2007)

40. tboot. Trusted boot (2009), http://sourceforge.net/projects/tboot/

41. P. Technologies. Phoenix securecore (2009), http://www.phoenix.com

42. tpmdd-devel. TPM driver problem on GM45. TPM Device Driver Mailing List (December 2008)

43. Trusted Computing Group. PC client specific TPM interface specification (TIS). Ver. 1.2, Rev. 1.0 (July 2005)

44. Trusted Computing Group. Trusted platform module main specification, Part 1: Design principles, Part 2: TPM structures, Part 3: Commands. Version 1.2, Revision 103 (July 2007)

45. VMware. VMware ESX server system architecture (2009),
http://www.vmware.com/support/esx21/doc/
esx21_admin_system_architecture.html

46. VMware Communities. ESX 3.5 or Xen 4.1? (2008),
http://communities.vmware.com/message/900657

47. Wojtczuk, R.: Detecting and preventing the Xen hypervisor subversions. Invisible Things Lab (2008)

48. Wojtczuk, R.: Subverting the Xen hypervisor. Invisible Things Lab (2008)

49. Wojtczuk, R., Rutkowska, J.: Xen 0wning trilogy. Invisible Things Lab (2008)

50. Wojtczuk, R., Rutkowska, J.: Attacking SMM memory via Intel CPU cache poisoning. Invisible Things Lab (2009)

51. XenSource. Xen architecture overview. Version 1.2 (February 2008)

A DAA Scheme Using
Batch Proof and Verification

Liqun Chen

Hewlett-Packard Laboratories
liqun.chen@hp.com

Abstract. Direct anonymous attestation (DAA) is an attractive cryptographic primitive, that is not only because it provides a balance between
user authentication and privacy in an elegant way, but also because it is
a part of the trusted computing technology from the Trusted Computing Group (TCG). However, in the TCG related community, DAA has
a bad reputation of its cost for the Trusted Platform Module (TPM) resources. Researchers have recently worked out a number of DAA schemes,
which require much less TPM resources than the one used by TCG. Our
contribution in this paper is a new DAA scheme that makes use of an
efficient batch proof and verification scheme to reduce the TPM computational workload. In our scheme, for the DAA Signing operation, the
TPM needs only to perform one exponentiation (when linkability is not
required) and two exponentiations (when linkability is required). This
operation requires at least three exponentiations in the existing DAA
schemes that provide the same functionality.

Keywords: direct anonymous attestation, batch proof and verification.

1 Introduction

Direct anonymous attestation (DAA) is a special digital signature primitive,
which provides a balance between signer authentication and privacy in a reasonable and an elegant way. A DAA scheme involves a set of issuers, signers,
and verifiers. An issuer is in charge of verifying the legitimation of signers and
of issuing a DAA credential (also called a DAA membership credential) to each
signer. A signer can prove the membership to a verifier by providing a DAA
signature without revealing the identity of the signer.

A DAA scheme can be seen as a modified group signature scheme, which
provides a number of different degrees of privacy for the signer. More specifically, DAA does not have the feature of opening the signer's identity from its
signature by the issuer. Interactions in DAA signing and verification are anonymous, that means the verifier, the issuer or both of them colluded cannot discover the signer's identity from its DAA signature. Instead of full-traceability as
held in group signatures [2], DAA has user-controlled-traceability, that we mean
the DAA signer and verifier are able to decide whether the verifier enables to
determine if any two signatures have been produced by the same signer.

A. Acquisti, S.W. Smith, and A.-R. Sadeghi (Eds.): TRUST 2010, LNCS 6101, pp. 166–180, 2010.
© Springer-Verlag Berlin Heidelberg 2010

The concept and a concrete scheme of DAA were first introduced by Brickell, Camenisch, and Chen [6] for remote anonymous authentication of a trusted computing platform. Their DAA scheme was adopted by the Trusted Computing Group (TCG) and specified in the TCG TPM Specification Version 1.2 [33]. This specification has recently been adopted by ISO/IEC as an international standard [26]. A historical perspective on the development of DAA was provided by the DAA authors in [7]. Since then, DAA has drawn a lot of attention from both industry and cryptographic researchers, e.g. [10,28,32].

For the purpose of this paper, we are interested in a unique property of DAA: The signer role is split between two entities, a principal signer with limited computational and storage capability, e.g. a trusted platform module (TPM), and an assistant signer with more computational power but less security tolerance, e.g. an ordinary computer platform (namely the Host with the TPM embedded in). It is well-known that the TPM resources are much more expensive, compared with the Host's, because the TPM is a small hardware device and the Host presents the platform software. Therefore, any technique being able to reduce the requirement on the TPM resources is valuable. In a DAA scheme, the TPM is the real signer and holds the secret signing key, whereas the host helps the TPM to compute the signature under the credential. In the condition that the Host is not allowed to learn the secret signing key and to forge such a signature without the TPM involvement, we try to move the workload from TPM to the Host as much as possible.

The original DAA scheme [6] and another DAA scheme by Ge and Tate [23] are based on the strong-RSA problem. We call them RSA-DAA for short. Recently, researchers have been working on how to create DAA schemes with elliptic curves and pairings. We call these DAA schemes ECC-DAA for short. Generally speaking, ECC-DAA is more efficient in both computation and communication than RSA-DAA. The TPM's operation is much simpler and the key/signature length is much shorter in ECC-DAA than in RSA-DAA.

To our best knowledge, there are eight ECC-DAA schemes in the literature. The first one was proposed by Brickell, Chen and Li [8,9]. This scheme is based on symmetric pairings. For the purpose of increasing implementation flexibility and efficiency, Chen, Morrissey and Smart proposed two extensions of this scheme [17,18,19]. Their schemes are based on asymmetric pairings. A flaw in the first one was pointed out by Li and further discussed in [16,19]. Recently, Chen, Page and Smart [21] further improved the performance of the scheme of [19]. Security of these four DAA schemes are based on the LRSW problem [29] and DDH problem. The other four DAA schemes were proposed by Chen and Feng [20], Brickell and Li [11], Chen [14], and Brickell and Li [12], respectively. Security of these four schemes are based on the q-SDH problem [4] and DDH problem.

Our main contribution in this paper is a new ECC-DAA scheme, which is a modification of the Chen, Page and Smart scheme [21]. The most significant advantage of the new scheme is that it requires less TPM resources to create a DAA signature. We will compare the computational cost of the proposed scheme with all the existing DAA schemes, which have the signer splitting property, and show that this new scheme has better performance than all the other schemes. In particular, for the DAA Signing operation, the TPM only performs one exponentiation (when linkability is not required) and two exponentiations (when linkability is required). This computational workload is equivalent to one or two ordinary standard digital signatures, such as EC-DSA or EC-SDSA [27]. This operation requires at least three exponentiations in the existing DAA schemes that provide the same security level.

Our new DAA scheme benefits from the batch verification technology. The original concept and some sample schemes of batch verification were proposed by Bellare, Garay and Rabin [1]. They showed that a batch of similar claims, such as a number of discrete logarithms in modular exponentiation and digital signatures, can be verified in one go; the batch verification requires less cost than that from verifying these claims separately. Since then, a number of researchers published their analysis, improvement and various extensions of the Bellare et al. work, for instance [5,25,30]. In particular, Peng, Boyd and Dawson [30] extended this technique to batch zero-knowledge proof and verification and provided a number of schemes. In this paper, we modify their scheme on proving equality of logarithms with common exponent, and use it in our DAA scheme.

The rest of this paper is organized as follows. We, in the next section, first describe a modified batch proof and verification scheme, which can prove and verify equality of discrete logarithms in an efficient way. We then specify our new DAA scheme in Section 3, including some security analysis and implementation consideration. We show computational efficiency comparison between this scheme and the seven existing DAA schemes with the signer splitting property in Section 4, which demonstrates the proposed scheme is the most efficient DAA scheme so far in the aspect of the TPM computational cost for the signing operation. We conclude the paper in Section 5.

2   Batch Proof and Verification

Throughout the paper, we will use some standard notation as follows. If S is a set, we denote the act of sampling from S uniformly at random and assigning the result to the variable x by $x \leftarrow S$. We let $\{0,1\}^*$ and $\{0,1\}^t$ denote the set of binary strings of arbitrary length and length t respectively. If A is an algorithm, we denote the action of obtaining x by invoking A on inputs $y_1, \ldots, y_n$ by $x \leftarrow A(y_1, \ldots, y_n)$. We denote concatenation of two date strings x and y as $x\|y$. We denote a function of mapping a set X to another set Y as $X \mapsto Y$. For a general cyclic group $\mathbb{G}$, we use $g^x \in \mathbb{G}$ (or simply g^x) to denote the exponentiation of a group element g by some integer exponent x. For an elliptic curve based cyclic group $\mathbb{G}$, we use $[x]P \in \mathbb{G}$ (or simply $[x]P$) to denote the scalar multiplication of an elliptic curve point P by some integer x.

Our DAA scheme makes use of a batch proof and verification scheme, which proves the discrete logarithm equality between two group elements y_1 and y_2 to two bases g_1 and g_2 respectively, i.e., $\log_{g_1} y_1 = \log_{g_2} y_2$ in an efficient way. This scheme is a modification of the batch verification scheme of equality of logarithms with common exponent by Peng, Boyd and Dawson [30]. We call their scheme the PBD scheme. The target of the PBD scheme is given a security parameter L, a prime p, a cyclic subgroup of $\mathbb{Z}_p^*$, namely $\mathbb{G}$, with the prime order q such that $|q| > L$, and the $2n + 2$ group elements $g, y, g_i, y_i \in \mathbb{G}$ for $i = 1, 2, ..., n$, to prove $\log_g y = \log_{g_i} y_i$. The PBD scheme works as follows:

1. The verifier randomly chooses and sends to the prover n integers $t_i \leftarrow \{0, 1\}^L$.
2. The prover randomly chooses an integer $r \leftarrow \mathbb{Z}_q$ and sends the verifier two elements $z_1 \leftarrow (\prod_{i=1}^n g_i^{t_i})^r$ and $z_2 \leftarrow g^r \in \mathbb{G}$.
3. The verifier randomly chooses and sends to the prover an integer $c \leftarrow \{0, 1\}^L$.
4. The prover calculates and sends the verifier an integer $s \leftarrow r - c \cdot \log_g y \bmod q$.
5. The verifier verifies that $(\prod_{i=1}^n g_i^{t_i})^s \cdot (\prod_{i=1}^n y_i^{t_i})^c = z_1$ and $g^s \cdot y^c = z_2$. If any of these two equations does not hold, the verifier outputs Reject; otherwise outputs Accept.

In our DAA signing algorithm, the TPM is required to make a proof of discrete logarithm equality of two group elements y_1 and y_2 to two bases g_1 and g_2 respectively. If we directly use the PBD scheme by selecting either y_1 or y_2 as y, then we cannot get any benefit from the batch proof. For our purpose, we modify the PBD scheme by omitting g, y and z_2 but adding a condition that the prover does not know the discrete logarithm between g_i and g_j, i.e. $\log_{g_i} g_j$, for any $i, j = 1, 2, ..., n$ and $i \neq j$. The modified scheme works as follows:

1. The prover randomly chooses an integer $r \leftarrow \mathbb{Z}_q$ and sends the verifier $z \leftarrow (\prod_{i=1}^n g_i)^r$.
2. The verifier randomly chooses and sends to the prover an integer $c \leftarrow \{0, 1\}^L$.
3. The prover calculates and sends the verifier an integer $s \leftarrow r - c \cdot x \bmod q$, where $x = \log_{g_i} y_i$.
4. The verifier verifies that $(\prod_{i=1}^n g_i)^s \cdot (\prod_{i=1}^n y_i)^c = z$. If this equation does not hold, the verifier outputs Reject; otherwise outputs Accept.

We further use a secure hash-function $H : \{0, 1\}^* \mapsto \mathbb{Z}_q$ to generate the random challenge c in order to change the zero-knowledge proof protocol to the Schnorr-type signature [31] of proof of knowledge. With this change, the security of the scheme is based on the random oracle model [3]. The final modification, which will be used in our DAA scheme in the next section, works as follows:

1. The prover randomly chooses $r \leftarrow \mathbb{Z}_q$ and computes $z \leftarrow (\prod_{i=1}^n g_i)^r$, $c \leftarrow H_2(z)$ and $s \leftarrow r - c \cdot x \bmod q$, where $x = \log_{g_i} y_i$ for $i = 1, 2, ..., n$, and finally sends the verifier the pair (c, s).
2. The verifier computes $z' \leftarrow (\prod_{i=1}^n g_i)^s \cdot (\prod_{i=1}^n y_i)^c$ and then verifiers that $c = H_2(z')$. If this equation does not hold, the verifier outputs Reject; otherwise outputs Accept.

Security of this proof and verification scheme is based on the following discrete logarithm assumption.

Definition 1 (The discrete logarithm assumption). *Given two elements $h_1, h_2 \in \mathbb{G}$, computing $\log_{h_1} h_2$ is computationally infeasible.*

We now address security of the scheme with the following theorem.

Theorem 1. *The above scheme prevents a malicious prover from persuading a verifier to accept the proof if any equation* $\log_{g_i} y_i \neq \log_{g_j} y_j$ *for* $i \neq j$ *and* $i, j = 1, 2, ..., n$ *holds, under the discrete logarithm assumption.*

Proof. We use the following reduction to prove this theorem: if there is a polynomial adversary $\mathcal{A}$, who is able to persuade a verifier to accept the proof if any equation $\log_{g_i} y_i \neq \log_{g_j} y_j$ for $i \neq j$ and $i, j = 1, 2, ..., n$ holds, then $\mathcal{A}$ can be used by another algorithm $\mathcal{B}$ to solve the discrete logarithm problem.

Suppose the algorithm $\mathcal{B}$ has the target that given two elements $h_1, h_2 \in \mathbb{G}$, computing $a = \log_{h_1} h_2$. $\mathcal{B}$ first setups the system parameters for $n = 2$, $g_1 = h_1$ and $g_2 = h_2$, then randomly chooses two different integers $x_1, x_2 \in \mathbb{Z}_q^*$ and computes $y_1 = g_1^{x_1}$ and $y_2 = g_2^{x_2}$. $\mathcal{B}$ runs the above batch proof and verification protocol with $\mathcal{A}$, in which $\mathcal{A}$, given the values $g_1, g_2, y_1, y_2, x_1, x_2$, plays the role of the prover and $\mathcal{B}$ plays the role of the verifier. If $\mathcal{A}$ successfully makes $\mathcal{B}$ accepting the proof, $\mathcal{B}$ rewinds $\mathcal{A}$ to extract the knowledge of the value x by forking on c. Since $x = (x_1 + x_2 \cdot a)/(1 + a)$, $\mathcal{B}$ can compute $a = (x_1 - x)/(x - x_2)$. $\mathcal{B}$ outputs the value a as the result of the target. The theorem follows.

Note that if the two values x_1 and x_2 are chosen by the algorithm $\mathcal{A}$ instead of $\mathcal{B}$, the proof also works as long as $\mathcal{B}$ can obtain these two values from $\mathcal{A}$. $\square$

3   The Proposed DAA Scheme

As mentioned earlier, a DAA scheme involves a set of issuers, signers, and verifiers. An Issuer is in charge of verifying the legitimacy of signers, and of issuing a DAA credential to each signer. A signer, which due to the split role is a pair of Host and associated TPM, can prove to a Verifier that the signer holds a valid DAA credential by providing a DAA signature. The Verifier can verify the DAA credential from the signature, but it cannot learn the identity of the signer. Linkability of signatures issued by a Host TPM pair is controlled by an input parameter bsn (standing for "base name") which is passed to the signing operation. There is assumed to be a list RogueList which contains a list of TPM secret keys which have been compromised. Based on this background information, the rest of this section describes our ECC-DAA scheme.

Throughout the constituent protocols and algorithms, the following notation is used. We let $\mathfrak{I}, \mathfrak{M}, \mathfrak{H}$ and $\mathfrak{V}$ denote the set of all Issuer, Host, TPM and Verifier entities. The value of bsn will be used by the signer/verifier to link signatures, if bsn $=\perp$ then this implies that signatures should be unlinkable.

Our new DAA scheme is based on asymmetric pairings. As discussed in [17], it will avoid the poor security level scaling problem in symmetric pairings and allow one to implement the DAA scheme efficiently at hight security levels. A pairing is a bilinear map $\hat{t} : \mathbb{G}_1 \times \mathbb{G}_2 \rightarrow \mathbb{G}_T$, where $\mathbb{G}_1, \mathbb{G}_2$ and $\mathbb{G}_T$ are groups of large prime exponent $p \approx 2^t$ for security parameter t. All the three groups will be written multiplicatively.

Before proceeding with the description of our scheme, we recall a general issue that needs to be considered throughout. Specifically, every group element received by any entity needs to be checked for validity, i.e., that it is within the correct group; in particular, it is important that the element does not lie in some larger group which contains the group in question. This strict stipulation avoids numerous attacks such as those related to small subgroups. We implicitly assume that all transmitted group elements are elements of the specified groups: within our scheme, the use of Type-III pairings [22] allows efficient methods for checking subgroup membership as described by [15] and expanded upon in [21].

3.1 The Setup Algorithm

To initialise the system, one needs to select parameters for each protocol as well as the long term parameters for each Issuer and each TPM. On input of the security parameter 1^t, the Setup algorithm executes the following steps:

1. *Generate the Commitment Parameters* par_C. In this step, three groups $\mathbb{G}_1, \mathbb{G}_2$ and $\mathbb{G}_T$, of sufficiently large prime order q, are selected. Two random generators are then selected such that $\mathbb{G}_1 = \langle P_1 \rangle$ and $\mathbb{G}_2 = \langle P_2 \rangle$ along with a pairing $\hat{t} : \mathbb{G}_1 \times \mathbb{G}_2 \mapsto \mathbb{G}_T$. Next, two hash functions $H_1 : \{0,1\}^* \mapsto \mathbb{Z}_q$ and $H_2 : \{0,1\}^* \mapsto \mathbb{Z}_q$ are selected and par_C is set to $(\mathbb{G}_1, \mathbb{G}_2, \mathbb{G}_T, \hat{t}, P_1, P_2, q, H_1, H_2)$. Note that in our scheme, as the same as in [21], the TPM operations are strictly limited to $\mathbb{G}_1$. This allows a subset of par_C, namely par_T, to be set to $(\mathbb{G}_1, P_1, q)$ and installed on the TPM in preference to par_C.
2. *Generate Signature and Verification Parameters* par_S. Three additional hash functions are selected, namely $H_3 : \{0,1\}^* \mapsto \mathbb{G}_1$, $H_4 : \{0,1\}^* \mapsto \mathbb{Z}_q$ and $H_5 : \{0,1\}^* \mapsto \mathbb{Z}_q$, and par_S is set to (H_3, H_4, H_5).
3. *Generate the Issuer Parameters* par_I. For each $i \in \mathfrak{I}$, the following steps are performed. Two integers $x, y \leftarrow \mathbb{Z}_q$ are selected, and the Issuer private key isk is set to (x, y). Next, the values $X = [x]P_2 \in \mathbb{G}_2$ and $Y = [y]P_2 \in \mathbb{G}_2$ are computed; the Issuer public key ipk is set to (X, Y). Then an Issuer value K_I is derived from the Issuer public values. Finally, par_I is set to $(\{\mathsf{ipk}, \mathsf{K}_I\})$ for each Issuer $i \in \mathfrak{I}$. In our scheme K_I is a representation of $\mathsf{par}_T{}^1$.
4. *Generate TPM Parameters*. The TPM generates a public/private key pair $(\mathsf{PK}, \mathsf{SK})$, which can be authenticated based on the associated endorsement key. In addition, it generates the private secret value $\mathsf{DAAseed}$. We assume that the private key SK along with the secret $\mathsf{DAAseed}$ is embedded into the TPM (e.g., in non-volatile memory) and that each Issuer has access to the corresponding public endorsement key PK. We also assume either a public key IND-CCA encryption/decryption scheme ($\mathsf{ENC}/\mathsf{DEC}$) along with a MAC algorithm (MAC) or a digital signature/verification scheme ($\mathsf{SIG}/\mathsf{VER}$) has been selected for use with the keys in order to achieve an authentic channel between the TPM and Issuer.
5. *Publish Public Parameters*. Finally, the public system parameters par are set to $(\mathsf{par}_C, \mathsf{par}_S, \mathsf{par}_I, \mathsf{par}_T)$ and published.

---

[1] If the same par_T is used by multiple issuers, in order to limit K_I to a single issuer, the issuer value K_I can be set by using both par_T and a unique issuer name.

Note that each TPM has a single DAAseed, but can create multiple DAA secret keys, even associated with a single issuer. To allow this, a number cnt (standing for "counter value") is used as an additional input to DAA secret key generation, as described in the Join protocol of the next section.

3.2   The Join Protocol

This is a protocol between a given TPM $m \in \mathfrak{M}$, the corresponding Host $\mathfrak{h} \in \mathfrak{H}$ and an Issuer $i \in \mathfrak{I}$. The protocol is identical to either that of [21] if using an encryption-based authentic channel or that of [19] if using a signature-based one. Here we only give an overview of how a general Join protocol proceeds. For the details, see these two papers. There are 4 main stages to a Join protocol.

1. The TPM m and Issuer i first establish an authentic channel, which allows the Issuer to be sure that he only creates the DAA credential for a genuine TPM. The authentic channel is built by using either the ENC/DEC algorithm and MAC algorithm, or the SIG/VER algorithm under the key pair (SK, PK).
2. The TPM m generates a DAA secret key, $sk_T \leftarrow H_1(\text{DAAseed} \| K_I \| \text{cnt}) \in \mathbb{Z}_q$, then computes a commitment on this value, i.e. $Q_2 = [sk_T]P_1 \in \mathbb{G}_1$, along with a proof of possession of this value. The commitment and proof are sent to the Issuer via the authentic channel.
3. The issuer performs some checks on the commitment and proof and, if these correctly verify, computes a credential, cre $= (A, B, C) \in \mathbb{G}_1^3$, which is a blindly signed CL signature [13] of sk_T via Q_2, and then sends it to the host.
4. The Host with the help from the TPM by computing $D = [sk_T]B \in \mathbb{G}_1$, verifies the correctness of the credential.

3.3   The Sign/Verify Protocol

This is a protocol between a given TPM $m \in \mathfrak{M}$, Host $\mathfrak{h} \in \mathfrak{H}$ and Verifier $\mathfrak{v} \in \mathfrak{V}$ as described in Figure 1. We give an overview of the protocol with the following three steps:

1. The Host $\mathfrak{h}$ and Verifier $\mathfrak{v}$ first agree the content of the signed message msg and the base name bsn.
2. The TPM m and Host $\mathfrak{h}$ then work together to produce a DAA signature on msg and associated with bsn. The signature should prove knowledge of a discrete logarithm sk_T, knowledge of a valid credential cre and that this credential was computed for the same value sk_T by a given Issuer $i \in \mathfrak{I}$. In the signing procedure between the two parts of the signer, the TPM uses the value of sk_T and the Host uses the value of cre. We note that the Host will know a lot of the values needed in the computation and will be able to take on a lot of the computational workload. However, if the TPM has not had its secret sk_T published (i.e. it is not a rogue module) then the Host $\mathfrak{h}$ will not know sk_T and will be unable to compute the whole signature without the aid of the TPM. Therefore, we say that the TPM is the real signer and

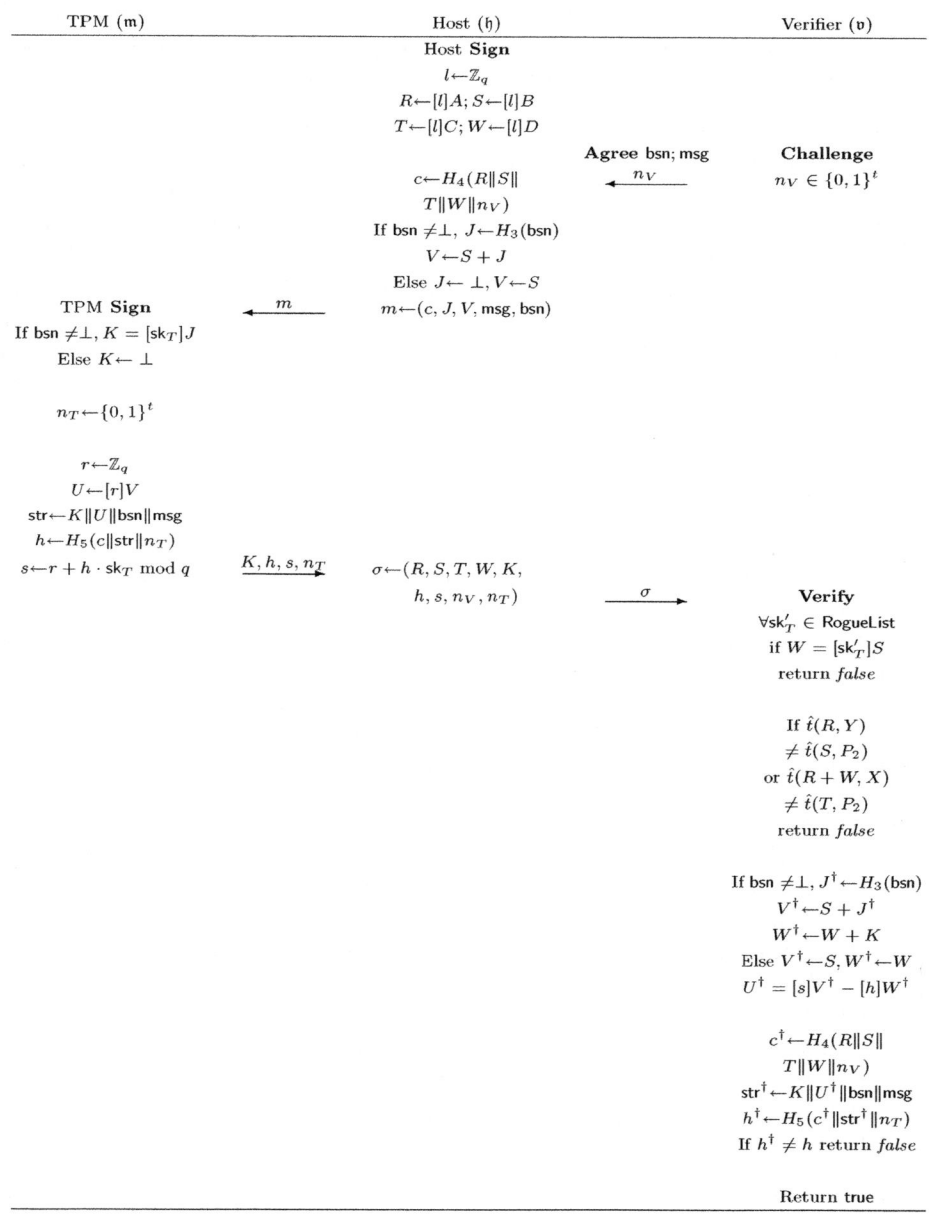

Fig. 1. The Sign/Verify protocol

the Host is a helper. We also note that the four scalar multiplications in $\mathbb{G}_1$ by the Host are independent to the signed message msg or the base name bsn, so they can be precomputed.

3. Upon the receipt of the DAA signature, the Verifier $\mathfrak{v}$ checks the RogueList first, then checks whether the agreed bsn was used correctly. After these

two checks pass successfully, $\mathfrak{v}$ verifies whether (R, S, T, W) is a valid CL signature on an unopened data string sk_T and this data string is used as a private signing key to sign the agreed message msg and $\mathfrak{v}$'s fresh nonce n_V.

There are two major differences between this version and the protocol in [21]. At first, the values of J and K are omitted when $\mathsf{bsn} = \perp$, and the function of checking the RogueList is done with the pair of (S, W) rather than (J, K). Secondly, it makes use of a new process of batch proof and verification to compute the value $U = [r]V$, as opposed to the two values $R_1 = [r]J$ and $R_2 = [r]S$. This makes the total number of scalar multiplications in $\mathbb{G}_1$ by the TPM in the signing algorithm from 3 to 1 if $\mathsf{bsn} = \perp$ or to 2 if $\mathsf{bsn} \neq \perp$. This change comes at some modification in the host signing process and verification side. However, the total computational cost for the Host is not increased and the total computational cost for the Verifier is reduced, from that of [21].

3.4   Security of the DAA Scheme

Instead of providing a formal security proof of the proposed DAA scheme, we discuss the reason why the modification to the Sign/Verify protocol made in this paper has no affect on the security proof from [19]. This discussion follows a similar argument made in [21]. Let us take a look at the similarity and distinction between the three DAA schemes respectively in [19,21] and this paper, from the Verifier point of veiw. The similarity is that given a DAA signature σ and an Issuer's public key ipk, the Verifier (from any of the three DAA schemes) verifies the following three things addressed within σ:

1. A DAA credential cre. It is a Camensich-Lysyanskaya signature [13] $\mathsf{cre} = (A, B, C)$ under ipk, and the signed message sk_T is not revealed. The verification tells that the value of sk_T was authorized by the Issuer to be a DAA secret, and that this value is not listed in the RogueList.
2. A proof of knowledge of a discrete logarithm. This shows someone knows the discrete logarithm of a group element K to a based J, which is specially generated from a base name $\mathsf{bsn} \neq \perp$. By using the same bsn, two DAA signatures show whether they were signed by the same signer or not.
3. A proof of connection between the above two items. This proves the value sk_T hidden in cre is equal to $\log_J K$. Therefore the owner of sk_T is uniquely bound with (J, K, bsn).

The distinction is that the three DAA schemes have different approaches from each other in order to deal with these three verifications.

- In [19], the three verifications are mixed together in a traditional method. This DAA scheme has a formal security proof.
- In [21], the three verifications are performed in two distinct steps: (i) a proof of the fact that the signature σ includes a valid cre on sk_T if and only if $\mathsf{sk}_T = \log_S W$ for two group elements S and W, and (ii) a proof of equality of two discrete logarithms, $\log_S W = \log_J K$. As suggested in [21],

this modification makes the overall protocol structure simpler to understand, but has no affect on the security proof from [19].

- In this paper, the three verifications are performed in a virtually identical way as in [21], except for the following two items: (a) The values of J and K are omitted when bsn $=\perp$, and the function of checking the RogueList is done with the pair of (S, W) instead of (J, K); (b) The step (ii) is replaced with a new process of batch proof and verification.

Based on the similarity and distinction of these three DAA schemes, we now discuss the reasons why these two items (a) and (b) have no affect on the security analysis from [19,21].

Regarding Item (a), in all the existing DAA schemes, the pair of (J, K) (although which might be denoted by using different letters in different papers) offer two functionalities: one is providing user-controlled-linkability and the other is checking the RogueList. They provide evidence whether the linkage between two signatures holds or not only if these two signatures use the same value of bsn and this value is not $\perp$. If bsn $=\perp$, the pair of (J, K) is redundant for the first functionality and contribute to the second functionality only. In the schemes of [21] and this paper, the second functionality, checking the RogueList, can be achieved by using the pair of either (S, W) or (J, K), since $\mathrm{sk}_T = \log_S W = \log_J K$. Therefore, the modification addressed in Item (a) has no affect on the security of the DAA scheme.

Regarding Item (b), we argue that as long as the batch proof and verification process used in our proposed DAA scheme works correctly, the modification addressed in Item (b) also has no affect on the security of the DAA scheme. The correctness of the batch proof and verification scheme follows the discription in Section 2. One point we need to discuss is that the batch proof and verification scheme specified in Section 2 only works under the condition that the prover does not know the discrete logarithms between g_i and g_j for each $i \neq j$. In the proposed DAA scheme, if a malicious signer is able to create a pair of S and J, such that the signer knows the discrete logarithm from each other, i.e. $\log_J S$, then the signer is able to cheat to the verifier by computing K with a different discrete logarithm to the base J from that of W to the base S, but still makes the verifier accepting the signature. Therefore, the signer can make his two signatures with the same bsn $\neq\perp$ unlinked and so can break the property of user-controlled-linkability. We argue that this condition holds in the proposed scheme because of the following theorem.

Theorem 2. *In the proposed DAA scheme, the signer is not able to create a pair of S and J, such that the signer knows the discrete logarithm from each other, under the discrete logarithm assumption and under the random oracle model.*

Proof. If there is a polynomial adversary $\mathcal{A}$, who is able to create a pair of S and J, such that the adversary knows the discrete logarithm from each other, i.e. $\log_J S$, then the adversary $\mathcal{A}$ can be used by another algorithm $\mathcal{B}$ to solve the discrete logarithm problem. See the following for the details.

Suppose the algorithm $\mathcal{B}$ has the target that given two elements $h_1, h_2 \in \mathbb{G}$, computing $a = \log_{h_2} h_1$. $\mathcal{B}$ first setups the system parameters by following the Setup algorithm properly except one bit: letting $P_1 = [1/(r \cdot y)]h_1$ for randomly chosen $r \in \mathbb{Z}_q$ and $y \in \mathbb{Z}_q$, where q is the order of $\mathbb{G}_1$. $\mathcal{B}$ runs the Join protocol and the Sign/Verify protocol with $\mathcal{A}$, in which $\mathcal{A}$ plays the role of the signer (both m and $\mathfrak{h}$) and $\mathcal{B}$ plays the role of the issuer i and the verifier $\mathfrak{v}$ respectively. $\mathcal{B}$ follows these two protocol properly except another bit: $\mathcal{B}$ controls the hash-function H_3 as a random oracle and lets $J = H_3(\text{bsn}) = h_2$ for a randomly selected query $H_3(\text{bsn})$. $\mathcal{B}$ lets the adversary $\mathcal{A}$ take $B = [r \cdot y]P_1 = h_1$ together with $J = h_2$.

If $\mathcal{A}$ successfully makes $W = [x_1]S = [l \cdot x_1]B$, $K = [x_2]J$ and $R = [x]V$, then the equation $x = (x_1 \cdot \log_J S + x_2)/(\log_J S + 1)$ must hold. $\mathcal{B}$ rewinds $\mathcal{A}$ in the TPM Sign algorithm to extract the knowledge of the value x by forking on c. $\mathcal{B}$ also rewinds $\mathcal{A}$ in the TPM Join algorithm to extract the knowledge of the value x_1 by forking on v. Although $\mathcal{B}$ cannot rewinds $\mathcal{A}$ to extract the knowledge of the values x_2 and l, we allow $\mathcal{B}$ to have access to the adversary $\mathcal{A}$'s ephemeral secrets in computing K and randomizing cre, therefore $\mathcal{B}$ knows these two values x_2 and l. Following all of these assumptions, $\mathcal{B}$ can compute $\log_J S = (x_2 - x)/(x - x_1)$ and then $a = \log_{h_2} h_1 = (1/l) \cdot \log_J S$. $\mathcal{B}$ outputs the value a as the result of the discrete logarithm problem. The theorem follows. $\square$

Note that in the proof, $\mathcal{B}$ is allowed to have access to the adversary $\mathcal{A}$'s ephemeral secrets in computing K and randomizing cre. This is reasonable because without the possession of the value x_2 the adversary is not able to compute the value x and without the possession of the value l the adversary is not able to create the valid set of (R, S, T, W). But this is not perfect. We leave a more tightened proof by removing this condition for an open issue.

3.5   Implementation Consideration

Since we follow the approach of [21], i.e. splitting the proof of equality of discrete logarithms from the credential verification step, we enable the use of batch pairing verification techniques as proposed in [21]. The following implementation information is a recall from [21]. In both the Join and Sign/Verify protocols, verification of a blinded Camenisch-Lysyanskaya signature is required. Namely, given $A, B, C, D \in \mathbb{G}_1$ (which are denoted by $R, S, T, W \in \mathbb{G}_1$ in the Sign/Verify protocol) we need to verify whether both

$$\hat{t}(A, Y) = \hat{t}(B, P_2) \quad \text{and} \quad \hat{t}(A + D, X) = \hat{t}(C, P_2).$$

To optimise this operation, we use an analogue of the small-exponent batch verification techniques from [1]. Specifically, we select two small exponents $e_1, e_2 \in \mathbb{Z}_q$ whose bit length is half that of q. To verify the two pairing equations we then verify whether

$$\hat{t}([e_1]A, Y) \cdot ([-e_1]B, P_2) \cdot \hat{t}([e_2](A + D), X) \cdot \hat{t}([-e_2]C, P_2) = 1.$$

Thus the verification involving four pairing computations is replaced by one product of four pairings, plus four (relatively short) multiplications in $\mathbb{G}_1$. As surveyed in [24], computing a "product of pairings" is less expensive than computing the pairings independently; the methods improves verification of a blinded Camenisch-Lysyanskaya signature by around 40%.

4 Performance Comparison

In this section, we compare computational efficiency of the proposed DAA scheme with the seven existing DAA schemes, and show the result in Table 1. In the comparison, we do not include the scheme of [17], since it has a number of security problems as addressed in [16,19]. We do not include the schemes of [11,23] either, since they do not split the signer role between the TPM and Host.

Table 1. Computational Cost of the Eight DAA Schemes

In	Protocol	TPM	Host	Issuer	Verifier
BCC [6]	Join	$3\mathbb{G}_\rho + 2\mathbb{G}_N^3$	$1\mathbb{G}_\rho + 1\mathbb{G}_N^2 + P_v$	$n\mathbb{G}_\rho + 2\mathbb{G}_N + 1\mathbb{G}_N^4 + 1\mathbb{G}_\rho^2 + P_c$	
	Sig/Ver	$3\mathbb{G}_\rho + 1\mathbb{G}_N^3$	$1\mathbb{G}_\rho + 1\mathbb{G}_N + 1\mathbb{G}_N^2 + 2\mathbb{G}_N^3 + 1\mathbb{G}_N^4$		$1\mathbb{G}_\rho^2 + 2\mathbb{G}_N^4 + 1\mathbb{G}_N^6 + n\mathbb{G}_\rho$
BCL [8]	Join	$3\mathbb{G}_1$	$6P$	$2\mathbb{G}_1 + 2\mathbb{G}_1^2$	
	Sig/Ver	$3\mathbb{G}_T$	$3\mathbb{G}_1 + 1\mathbb{G}_T + 3P$		$1\mathbb{G}_T^2 + 1\mathbb{G}_T^3 + 5P + (n+1)\mathbb{G}_T$
CMS [19]	Join	$3\mathbb{G}_1$	$4P$	$2\mathbb{G}_1 + 2\mathbb{G}_1^2$	
	Sig/Ver	$2\mathbb{G}_1 + 1\mathbb{G}_T$	$3\mathbb{G}_1 + 1P$		$1\mathbb{G}_1^2 + 1\mathbb{G}_T^2 + 5P + n\mathbb{G}_1$
CF [20]	Join	$3\mathbb{G}_1^2 + (2P)$	$(2P)$	$1\mathbb{G}_1^2 + 1\mathbb{G}_1^3$	
	Sig/Ver	$2\mathbb{G}_1 + 1\mathbb{G}_T^2$	$1\mathbb{G}_1 + 2\mathbb{G}_1^2 + 1\mathbb{G}_1^3 + 1\mathbb{G}_T^3$		$1\mathbb{G}_1^2 + 2\mathbb{G}_1^3 + 1\mathbb{G}_T^5 + 3P + n\mathbb{G}_T$
Chen [14]	Join	$2\mathbb{G}_1$	$1\mathbb{G}_1 + 2P$	$1\mathbb{G}_1 + 1\mathbb{G}_1^2$	
	Sig/Ver	$2\mathbb{G}_1 + 1\mathbb{G}_T$	$1\mathbb{G}_1 + 1\mathbb{G}_T^3$		$1\mathbb{G}_1^2 + 1\mathbb{G}_2^2 + 1\mathbb{G}_T^4 + 1P + n\mathbb{G}_1$
CPS [21]	Join	$3\mathbb{G}_1$	$1P^4$	$2\mathbb{G}_1 + 2\mathbb{G}_1^2$	
	Sig/Ver	$3\mathbb{G}_1$	$4\mathbb{G}_1$		$2\mathbb{G}_1^2 + 1P^4 + n\mathbb{G}_1$
BL [12]	Join	$2\mathbb{G}_1$	$1\mathbb{G}_1 + 2P$	$1\mathbb{G}_1 + 1\mathbb{G}_1^2$	
	Sig/Ver	$3\mathbb{G}_1$	$1\mathbb{G}_1 + 1\mathbb{G}_1^2 + 1\mathbb{G}_T + 1P$		$1\mathbb{G}_1^2 + 1\mathbb{G}_2^2 + 1\mathbb{G}_T^4 + 1P + n\mathbb{G}_1$
this paper	Join	$3\mathbb{G}_1$	$1P^4$	$2\mathbb{G}_1 + 2\mathbb{G}_1^2$	
	Sig/Ver	$1\mathbb{G}_1/2\mathbb{G}_1$	$4\mathbb{G}_1$		$1\mathbb{G}_1^2 + 1P^4 + n\mathbb{G}_1$

For the computational cost, we consider the Join protocol and the Sign/Verify protocol, with respect to each player. We do not specify the computational cost of the Setup algorithm and its verification, since this is only run once and the resulting parameters are only verified once by each part. We do not specify the cost for the linking algorithm either, as it is closely related to that of the verification algorithm. We also do not specify the cost for the RogueList check in the Join protocol, since it is an optional process. In the table, we let n denote the number of keys in the verifier's rogue secret key list.

For the RSA-DAA scheme, we let $\mathbb{G}_N$ denote the cost of an exponentiation modulo N, and $\mathbb{G}_N^m$ denote the cost of a multiexponentiation of m values modulo

N. Note, that a multiexponentiation with m exponents can often be performed significantly faster than m separate exponentiations, which is why we separate this out. We let $\mathbb{G}_\rho$ denote the cost of an exponentiation modulo Γ (recall $\mathbb{G}_\rho$ is a subgroup of $\mathbb{F}_\Gamma^*$), and $\mathbb{G}_\rho^m$ denote the cost of a multiexponentiation of m values modulo Γ. In addition we let P_c denote the cost of generating a prime number of the required size and P_v the cost of verifying that a given number of the required size is prime.

For the ECC-DAA schemes, we let $\mathbb{G}_i$ ($i = \{1, 2, T\}$) denote the cost of an exponentiation in the group $\mathbb{G}_i$, and $\mathbb{G}_i^m$ denote the cost of a multiexponentiation of m values in the group $\mathbb{G}_i$. We also let P denote the cost of a pairing computation, and let P^m denote the cost of a batch pairing verification of m pairings, as described in Section 3.5. In the signing process of our proposed DAA scheme, if bsn $= \perp$, the TPM computes one scalar multiplication in $\mathbb{G}_1$; if bsn $\neq \perp$, the TPM computes two. We let $1\mathbb{G}_1/2\mathbb{G}_1$ denote the cost of this computation.

We recall the following two observations made in [14]. In [20], the rogue ragging operation is not defined in the Verify algorithm, but it can be easily added in the same way as every existing DAA scheme does. So in Table 1, we add this computation $n \cdot \mathbb{G}_T$. Again in this scheme, the pairing computation in the Join protocol can be done by the Host instead of the TPM, because it is expensive to implement the pairing operation in TPMs. As the same as in [14], we mark this change as $(2P)$ in Table 1.

When a DAA scheme is used in the trusted computing environment, as the original design in [6], the most significant performance is a TPM's computational cost, particularly the TPM's computational cost in the signing algorithm, since obviously the join algorithm is performed only for obtaining the DAA credential, so much less frequently than the signing algorithm is performed. As shown in the table, our proposed DAA scheme has the most efficient computational cost for the TPM in the Sign/Verify protocol. For each signing process, the TPM is only required to compute one exponentiation in $\mathbb{G}_1$ if linkability is not required and two exponentiations in $\mathbb{G}_1$ if linkability is required. But in the other DAA schemes in the table, this cost is at least three exponentiations. Based on this figure, our proposed scheme has the significant advantage compared with all the other DAA schemes in the table.

We do not discuss the communication and storage cost in details. The contribution made in this paper does not change the communication and storage cost from the original scheme in [21] significantly, except a minor improvement that we remove the value J from the signature, since it can be computed by the verifier from the agreed value of bsn.

5   Conclusions

In this paper, we have introduced a new DAA scheme, which is more efficient than all the existing DAA schemes in a particular aspect of reducing the TPM computational cost in the DAA signing operation. This scheme benefits from an efficient batch proof and verification protocol.

Acknowledgements

The author would like to thank Jiangtao Li for pointing out a technical flaw in the early version of this paper, and also to thank the anonymous reviewers of Trust'10 Technical Strand for their valuable comments.

References

1. Bellare, M., Garay, J.A., Rabin, T.: Fast batch verification for modular exponentiation and digital signatures. In: Nyberg, K. (ed.) EUROCRYPT 1998. LNCS, vol. 1403, pp. 236–250. Springer, Heidelberg (1998)
2. Bellare, M., Micciancio, D., Warinschi, B.: Foundations of group signatures: formal definitions, simplified requirements, and a construction based on general assumptions. In: Biham, E. (ed.) EUROCRYPT 2003. LNCS, vol. 2656, pp. 614–629. Springer, Heidelberg (2003)
3. Bellare, M., Rogaway, P.: Random oracles are practical: A paradigm for designing efficient protocols. In: The 1st ACM Conference on Computer and Communications Security, pp. 62–73. ACM Press, New York (1993)
4. Boneh, D., Boyen, X.: Short signatures without random oracles. In: Cachin, C., Camenisch, J.L. (eds.) EUROCRYPT 2004. LNCS, vol. 3027, pp. 56–73. Springer, Heidelberg (2004)
5. Boyd, C., Pavlovski, C.: Attacking and repairing batch verification schemes. In: Okamoto, T. (ed.) ASIACRYPT 2000. LNCS, vol. 1976, pp. 58–71. Springer, Heidelberg (2000)
6. Brickell, E., Camenisch, J., Chen, L.: Direct anonymous attestation. In: The 11th ACM Conference on Computer and Communications Security, pp. 132–145. ACM Press, New York (2004)
7. Brickell, E., Camenisch, J., Chen, L.: Direct anonymous attestation in context. In: Mitchell (ed.) Trusted Computing, ch. 5, pp. 143–174. IEEE, Los Alamitos (2005)
8. Brickell, E., Chen, L., Li, J.: Simplified security notions for direct anonymous attestation and a concrete scheme from pairings. Int. Journal of Information Security 8, 315–330 (2009)
9. Brickell, E., Chen, L., Li, J.: A new direct anonymous attestation scheme from bilinear maps. In: Lipp, P., Sadeghi, A.-R., Koch, K.-M. (eds.) Trust 2008. LNCS, vol. 4968, pp. 166–178. Springer, Heidelberg (2008)
10. Brickell, E., Li, J.: Enhanced privacy ID: A direct anonymous attestation scheme with enhanced revocation capabilities. In: The 6th ACM Workshop on Privacy in the Electronic Society – WPES 2007, pp. 21–30. ACM Press, New York (2007)
11. Brickell, E., Li, J.: Enhanced privacy ID from bilinear pairing. Cryptology ePrint Archive. Report 2009/095, http://eprint.iacr.org/2009/095
12. Brickell, E., Li, J.: A pairing-based DAA scheme furhter reducing TPM resources. In: Acquisti, A., Smith, S.W., Sadeghi, A.-R. (eds.) TRUST 2010. LNCS, vol. 6101. Springer, Heidelberg (2010)
13. Camenisch, J., Lysyanskaya, A.: Signature schemes and anonymous credentials from bilinear maps. In: Franklin, M. (ed.) CRYPTO 2004. LNCS, vol. 3152, pp. 56–72. Springer, Heidelberg (2004)
14. Chen, L.: A DAA scheme requiring less TPM resources. In: The Proceedings of the 5th China International Conference on Information Security and Cryptology – Inscrypt 2009. The full paper is in Cryptology ePrint Archive. Report 2010/008 (2009), http://eprint.iacr.org/2010/008

15. Chen, L., Cheng, Z., Smart, N.P.: Identity-based key agreement protocols from pairings. Int. Journal of Information Security 6, 213–242 (2007)
16. Chen, L., Li, J.: A note on the Chen-Morrissey-Smart DAA scheme (preprint)
17. Chen, L., Morrissey, P., Smart, N.P.: Pairings in trusted computing. In: Galbraith, S.D., Paterson, K.G. (eds.) Pairing 2008. LNCS, vol. 5209, pp. 1–17. Springer, Heidelberg (2008)
18. Chen, L., Morrissey, P., Smart, N.P.: On proofs of security of DAA schemes. In: Baek, J., Bao, F., Chen, K., Lai, X. (eds.) ProvSec 2008. LNCS, vol. 5324, pp. 156–175. Springer, Heidelberg (2008)
19. Chen, L., Morrissey, P., Smart, N.P.: DAA: Fixing the pairing based protocols. Cryptology ePrint Archive. Report 2009/198, http://eprint.iacr.org/2009/198
20. Chen, X., Feng, D.: Direct anonymous attestation for next generation TPM. Journal of Computers 3(12), 43–50 (2008)
21. Chen, L., Page, D., Smart, N.P.: On the design and implementation of an efficient DAA scheme. In: Gollmann, D. (ed.) CARDIS 2010. LNCS, vol. 6035, pp. 223–238. Springer, Heidelberg (2010)
22. Galbraith, S., Paterson, K., Smart, N.P.: Pairings for cryptographers. Discrete Applied Mathematics 156, 3113–3121 (2008)
23. Ge, H., Tate, S.R.: A Direct anonymous attestation scheme for embedded devices. In: Okamoto, T., Wang, X. (eds.) PKC 2007. LNCS, vol. 4450, pp. 16–30. Springer, Heidelberg (2007)
24. Granger, R., Smart, N.P.: On computing products of pairings. Cryptology ePrint Archive. Report 2006/172, http://eprint.iacr.org/2006/172
25. Hoshino, F., Abe, M., Kobayashi, T.: Lenient/strict batch verification in several groups. In: Davida, G.I., Frankel, Y. (eds.) ISC 2001. LNCS, vol. 2200, pp. 81–94. Springer, Heidelberg (2001)
26. ISO/IEC 11889:2009 Information technology – Security techniques – Trusted Platform Module
27. ISO/IEC 14888-3 Information technology – Security techniques – Digital signatures with appendix – Part 3: Discrete logarithm based mechanisms
28. Leung, A., Chen, L., Mitchell, C.J.: On a possible privacy flaw in direct anonymous attestation (DAA). In: Lipp, P., Sadeghi, A.-R., Koch, K.-M. (eds.) Trust 2008. LNCS, vol. 4968, pp. 179–190. Springer, Heidelberg (2008)
29. Lysyanskaya, A., Rivest, R., Sahai, A., Wolf, S.: Pseudonym systems. In: Heys, H.M., Adams, C.M. (eds.) SAC 1999. LNCS, vol. 1758, pp. 184–199. Springer, Heidelberg (2000)
30. Peng, K., Boyd, C., Dawson, E.: Batch zero-knowledge proof and verification and its applications. ACM Trans. Inf. Syst. Secur. Article 6, 10(2) (2007)
31. Schnorr, C.P.: Efficient identification and signatures for smart cards. In: Brassard, G. (ed.) CRYPTO 1989. LNCS, vol. 435, pp. 239–252. Springer, Heidelberg (1990)
32. Smyth, B., Chen, L., Ryan, M.: Direct Anonymous Attestation (DAA): Ensuring privacy with corrupt administrators. In: Stajano, F., Meadows, C., Capkun, S., Moore, T. (eds.) ESAS 2007. LNCS, vol. 4572, pp. 218–231. Springer, Heidelberg (2007)
33. Trusted Computing Group. TCG TPM specification 1.2 (2003), http://www.trustedcomputinggroup.org

A Pairing-Based DAA Scheme Further Reducing TPM Resources

Ernie Brickell and Jiangtao Li

Intel Corporation
ernie.brickell@intel.com, jiangtao.li@intel.com

Abstract. Direct Anonymous Attestation (DAA) is an anonymous signature scheme designed for anonymous attestation of a Trusted Platform Module (TPM) while preserving the privacy of the device owner. Since TPM has limited bandwidth and computational capability, one interesting feature of DAA is to split the signer role between two entities: a TPM and a host platform where the TPM is attached. Recently, Chen proposed a new DAA scheme that is more efficient than previous DAA schemes. In this paper, we construct a new DAA scheme requiring even fewer TPM resources. Our DAA scheme is about 5 times more efficient than Chen's scheme for the TPM implementation using the Barreto-Naehrig curves. In addition, our scheme requires much smaller size of software code that needs to be implemented in the TPM. This makes our DAA scheme ideal for the TPM implementation. Our DAA scheme is efficient and provably secure in the random oracle model under the strong Diffie-Hellman assumption and the decisional Diffie-Hellman assumption.

1 Introduction

The concept and a concrete scheme of Direct Anonymous Attestation (DAA) were first introduced by Brickell, Camenisch, and Chen [5] for remote anonymous authentication of a Trusted Platform Module (TPM). The DAA scheme was adopted by the Trusted Computing Group (TCG) [20], an industry standardization body that aims to develop and promote an open industry standard for trusted computing hardware and software building blocks. The DAA scheme was standardized in the TCG TPM Specification Version 1.2 [19] and has recently been adopted by ISO/IEC as an international standard.

A DAA scheme involves three types of entities: an issuer, signers, and verifiers. The issuer is in charge of verifying the legitimation of signers and of issuing a membership credential to each signer. A signer can prove membership anonymously to a verifier by creating a DAA signature. The verifier can verify the membership of the signer from the DAA signature but he cannot learn the identity of the signer. DAA scheme can be seen as a special group signature scheme without the open feature, i.e., a DAA signature cannot be opened by anyone including the issuer to find out the identity of the signer.

One interesting feature of DAA is that the signer role of DAA is split between two entities: a TPM and a host where the TPM is attached. The TPM is the

A. Acquisti, S.W. Smith, and A.-R. Sadeghi (Eds.): TRUST 2010, LNCS 6101, pp. 181–195, 2010.

main signer but has limited bandwidth, computational capability, and storage. The host is a helper with more computational power but is less trusted. The TPM is the real signer and has the private signing key. The host helps the TPM to compute DAA signatures, but is not allowed to learn the private signing key or forge a DAA signature without the involvement from the TPM.

After DAA was first introduced, it has drawn a lot of attention from both industry and cryptographic community, e.g., in [10,17,1,8,6,12,11], to list a few. The original DAA scheme [5] is based on the strong RSA assumption. Recently several groups of researchers have constructed pairing-based DAA schemes to achieve better efficiency. The first pairing-based DAA scheme was proposed by Brickell, Chen, and Li [6,7]. Chen, Morrissey, and Smart improved the BCL-DAA scheme using asymmetric pairing [12,13]. These DAA schemes are based on the LRSW assumption [18].

Brickell and Li proposed an extension of DAA called Enhanced Privacy ID (EPID) [8] and presented a concrete EPID scheme based on the q-SDH assumption [9]. The EPID schemes focus on the revocation capabilities and treat the signer as a single entity instead of combination of a TPM and a host. Independently Chen and Feng proposed a DAA scheme [15] using q-SDH assumption. Recently, Chen builds a new DAA scheme [11] on top of the EPID scheme [9] by reducing the size of the private signing key. As compared in [11], q-SDH based DAA schemes [15,9,11] are more efficient than LRSW-based DAA schemes [6,7,12,13], especially in the efficiency of the signature verification algorithm.

To the best of our knowledge, Chen's DAA scheme [11] is the most efficient DAA scheme and it requires least amount of TPM resources[1]. In this paper, we give a simple improvement to Chen's DAA scheme. Our DAA scheme is about 5 times more efficient for the TPM implementation using the Barreto-Naehrig curves [2]. In addition, our scheme requires much smaller size of software code that needs to be implemented in the TPM. This makes our DAA scheme ideal for the TPM implementation. More specifically, let $e : G_1 \times G_2 \rightarrow G_T$ be a bilinear map function. The DAA scheme in [11] requires two exponentiations in G_1 and one exponentiation in G_T. Whereas our DAA scheme in this paper requires only three exponentiations in G_1. Our improvement seems to be small, but has significant impact to TPM for the following two reasons:

- Usually operations in G_1 are more efficient than the operations in G_T. According to the arguments in [13], exponentiation in G_1 is about 1/4 the cost of exponentiation in G_T for symmetric pairing. For highly efficient curve choices such as Barreto-Naehrig curves [2] with 128-bit security, G_1 is an elliptic curve group over $\mathbb{F}_q$ while G_T is a subgroup of $\mathbb{F}_{q^{12}}$. Exponentiation in G_1 is about 14 times more efficient than the one in G_T. Thus the computation needed for TPM in our scheme is about 5 times more efficient than the one in DAA scheme [11] using the Barreto-Naehrig curves.

---

[1] The original CMS-DAA scheme [12] requires lesser TPM resources. However, there was a security flaw in their DAA scheme. The patched version [13] has the same computational complexity for TPM as in Chen's DAA scheme [11].

- In our scheme TPM only requires to implement G_1 while the other DAA schemes [13,11,15] require TPM to implement both G_1 and G_T. For small hardware devices such as TPM, more software code means larger firmware image, larger flash storage needed, and more software validation required. Note that if TPM has already implemented EC-DSA or other ECC primitives for other purposes, the additional software code needed for implementing our DAA scheme is very minimum.

Rest of this paper is organized as follows. We first review the formal specification and security requirements of DAA in Section 2. We then review the definition of pairing and related security assumptions in Section 3. We present our DAA scheme in Section 4 and give the security proof in Section 5. We compare our scheme with the existing DAA schemes in Section 6 and conclude our paper in Section 7.

2   Review Security Model of DAA

In this section, we review the specification and security model of DAA proposed in [7]. The security model in [7] is simpler than the original DAA definition [5] and easier to understand the security properties of DAA. There are four types of players in a DAA scheme: an issuer $\mathcal{I}$, a TPM $\mathcal{M}_i$, a host $\mathcal{H}_i$ and a verifier $\mathcal{V}_j$. $\mathcal{M}_i$ and $\mathcal{H}_i$ form a platform in the trusted computing environment and share the role of a DAA signer. A DAA scheme has three polynomial-algorithms (Setup, Verify, Link) and two interactive protocols (Join, Sign):

Setup : On input of a security parameter 1^k, $\mathcal{I}$ uses this randomized algorithm to produce a pair (gpk, isk), where isk is the issuer's secret key, and gpk is the public key including the global public parameters.

Join : This randomized algorithm consists of two sub-algorithms $\mathsf{Join_t}$ and $\mathsf{Join_i}$. $\mathcal{M}_i$ uses $\mathsf{Join_t}$ to produce a pair $(\mathsf{sk}_i, \mathsf{comm}_i)$, where sk_i is the TPM's secret key and comm_i is a commitment of sk_i. On input of comm_i and isk, $\mathcal{I}$ uses $\mathsf{Join_i}$ to produce cre_i, which is a DAA credential associated with sk_i. Note that the value cre_i is given to both $\mathcal{M}_i$ and $\mathcal{H}_i$, but the value sk_i is known to $\mathcal{M}_i$ only.

Sign : On input of sk_i, cre_i, a basename bsn_j (the name string of $\mathcal{V}_j$ or a special symbol $\bot$), and a message m that includes the data to be signed and the verifier's nonce n_V for freshness, $\mathcal{M}_i$ and $\mathcal{H}_i$ use this randomized algorithm to produce a signature σ on m under $(\mathsf{sk}_i, \mathsf{cre}_i)$ associated with bsn_j. The basename bsn_j is used for controlling the linkability.

Verify : On input of m, bsn_j, a candidate signature σ for m, and a set of revoked secret keys RL, $\mathcal{V}_j$ uses this deterministic algorithm to return either 1 (accept) or 0 (reject). How to build the revocation list is out the scope of the DAA scheme.

Link : On input of two signatures σ_0 and σ_1, $\mathcal{V}_j$ uses this deterministic algorithm to return 1 (linked), 0 (unlinked) or $\bot$ (invalid signatures). Link will output $\bot$ if, by using an empty RL, either $\mathsf{Verify}(\sigma_0) = 0$ or $\mathsf{Verify}(\sigma_1) = 0$ holds. Otherwise, Link will output 1 if signatures can be linked or 0 if the signatures cannot be linked.

A DAA scheme is secure if it is correct, user-controlled-anonymous, and user-controlled-traceable.

Correctness. If both the signer and verifier are honest, that implies $\mathrm{sk}_i \notin \mathrm{RL}$, the signatures and their links generated by the signer will be accepted by the verifier with overwhelming probability. This means that the DAA scheme must meet the following consistency requirement.

$$(\mathrm{gpk}, \mathrm{isk}) \leftarrow \mathsf{Setup}(1^k), \ (\mathrm{sk}_i, \mathrm{cre}_i) \leftarrow \mathsf{Join}(\mathrm{isk}, \mathrm{gpk}),$$
$$(m_b, \sigma_b) \leftarrow \mathsf{Sign}(m_b, \mathrm{bsn}_j, \mathrm{sk}_i, \mathrm{cre}_i, \mathrm{gpk})|_{b=\{0,1\}},$$
$$\Longrightarrow 1 \leftarrow \mathsf{Verify}(m_b, \mathrm{bsn}_j, \sigma_b, \mathrm{gpk}, \mathrm{RL})|_{b=\{0,1\}} \ \wedge \ 1 \leftarrow \mathsf{Link}(\sigma_0, \sigma_1, \mathrm{gpk})|_{\mathrm{bsn}_j \neq \perp}.$$

User-Controlled-Anonymity. A DAA scheme is user-controlled-anonymous if no probabilistic polynomial-time adversary can win the following game between a challenger $\mathcal{C}$ and an adversary $\mathcal{A}$ as follows:

- Initial: $\mathcal{C}$ runs $\mathsf{Setup}(1^k)$ and gives the resulting isk and gpk to $\mathcal{A}$.
- Phase 1: $\mathcal{C}$ is probed by $\mathcal{A}$ who makes the following queries:
  - Sign. $\mathcal{A}$ submits a signer's identity S, a basename bsn (either $\perp$ or a data string) and a message m of his choice to $\mathcal{C}$, who runs Sign to get a signature σ and responds with σ.
  - Join. $\mathcal{A}$ submits a signer's identity S of his choice to $\mathcal{C}$, who runs Join_t with $\mathcal{A}$ to create sk and to obtain cre from $\mathcal{A}$. $\mathcal{C}$ verifies the validation of cre and keeps sk secret.
  - Corrupt. $\mathcal{A}$ submits a signer's identity S of his choice to $\mathcal{C}$, who responds with the value sk of the signer.
- Challenge: At the end of Phase 1, $\mathcal{A}$ chooses two signers' identities S_0 and S_1, a message m and a basename bsn of his choice to $\mathcal{C}$. $\mathcal{A}$ must not have made any Corrupt query on either S_0 or S_1, and not have made the Sign query with the same bsn if $\mathrm{bsn} \neq \perp$ with either S_0 or S_1. To make the challenge, $\mathcal{C}$ chooses a bit b uniformly at random, signs m associated with bsn under $(\mathrm{sk}_b, \mathrm{cre}_b)$ to get a signature σ and returns σ to $\mathcal{A}$.
- Phase 2: $\mathcal{A}$ continues to probe $\mathcal{C}$ with the same type of queries that it made in Phase 1. Again, it is not allowed to corrupt any signer with the identity either S_0 or S_1, and not allowed to make any Sign query with bsn if $\mathrm{bsn} \neq \perp$ with either S_0 or S_1.
- Response: $\mathcal{A}$ returns a bit b'. The adversary wins the game if $b = b'$.

Definition 1. *Let $\mathcal{A}$ denote an adversary that plays the game above. We denote by $\mathbf{Adv}[\mathcal{A}_{\mathcal{DAA}}^{anon}] = |\mathbf{Pr}[b' = b] - 1/2|$ the advantage of $\mathcal{A}$ in breaking the user-controlled-anonymity game. We say that a DAA scheme is user-controlled-anonymous if for any probabilistic polynomial-time adversary $\mathcal{A}$, $\mathbf{Adv}[\mathcal{A}_{\mathcal{DAA}}^{anon}]$ is negligible.*

User-Controlled-Traceability. A DAA scheme is user-controlled-traceable if no probabilistic polynomial-time adversary can win the following game between a challenger $\mathcal{C}$ and an adversary $\mathcal{A}$ as follows:

- Initial: $\mathcal{C}$ executes $\mathsf{Setup}(1^k)$ and gives the resulting gpk to $\mathcal{A}$. It keeps isk secret.
- Probing: $\mathcal{C}$ is probed by $\mathcal{A}$ who makes the following queries:
  - Sign. The same as in the game of user-controlled-anonymity.
  - Semi-sign. $\mathcal{A}$ submits a signer's identity S along with the data transmitted from $\mathcal{H}_i$ to $\mathcal{M}_i$ in Sign of his choice to $\mathcal{C}$, who acts as $\mathcal{M}_i$ in Sign and responds with the data transmitted from $\mathcal{M}_i$ to $\mathcal{H}_i$ in the Sign protocol.
  - Join. There are two cases of this query. Case 1: $\mathcal{A}$ submits a signer's identity S of his choice to $\mathcal{C}$, who runs Join to create sk and cre for the signer. Case 2: $\mathcal{A}$ submits a signer's identity S with a sk value of his choice to $\mathcal{C}$, who runs $\mathsf{Join_i}$ to create cre for the signer and puts the given sk into RL. $\mathcal{C}$ responds the query with cre. Suppose that $\mathcal{A}$ does not use a single S for both of the cases.
  - Corrupt. This is the same as in the game of user-controlled-anonymity, except that at the end $\mathcal{C}$ puts the revealed sk into the list of RL.
- Forge: $\mathcal{A}$ returns a signer's identity S, a signature σ, its signed message m and the associated basename bsn. We say that the adversary wins the game if
  1. $\mathsf{Verify}(m, \mathsf{bsn}, \sigma, \mathsf{gpk}, \mathsf{RL}) = 1$ (accepted), but σ is neither a response of the existing Sign queries nor a response of the existing Semi-sign queries (partially); and/or
  2. In the case of bsn $\neq \perp$, there exists another signature σ' associated with the same identity and bsn, and the output of $\mathsf{Link}(\sigma, \sigma')$ is 0 (unlinked).

Definition 2. *Let $\mathcal{A}$ be an adversary that plays the game above. Let $\mathbf{Adv}[\mathcal{A}_{\mathcal{DAA}}^{trace}] = \mathbf{Pr}[\mathcal{A} \; wins]$ denote the advantage that $\mathcal{A}$ breaks the user-controlled-traceability game. We say that a DAA scheme is user-controlled-traceable if for any probabilistic polynomial-time adversary $\mathcal{A}$, $\mathbf{Adv}[\mathcal{A}_{\mathcal{DAA}}^{trace}]$ is negligible.*

3   Pairings and Complexity Assumptions

3.1   Background on Bilinear Maps

Our DAA scheme use bilinear maps as a fundamental building block. We follow the notation of Boneh, Boyen, and Shacham [4] to review some background on pairings. Let G_1 and G_2 to two multiplicative cyclic groups of prime order p. Let g_1 be a generator of G_1 and g_2 be a generator of G_2. We say $e : G_1 \times G_2 \to G_T$ is an admissible bilinear map, if it satisfies the following properties:

1. Bilinear. For all $u \in G_1, v \in G_2$, and for all $a, b \in \mathbb{Z}$, $e(u^a, v^b) = e(u, v)^{ab}$.
2. Non-degenerate. $e(g_1, g_2) \neq 1$ and is a generator of G_T.
3. Computable. There exists an efficient algorithm for computing $e(u, v)$ for any $u \in G_1, v \in G_2$.

We call the two groups (G_1, G_2) in the above a bilinear group pair. In the rest of this paper, we consider bilinear maps $e : G_1 \times G_2 \to G_T$ where G_1, G_2, and G_T are multiplicative groups of prime order p.

3.2   Strong Diffie-Hellman Assumption

The security of our DAA scheme is related to the hardness of the q-SDH problem introduced by Boneh and Boyen [3]. Let G_1 and G_2 be two cyclic groups of prime order p, respectively, generated by g_1 and g_2. The q-Strong Diffie-Hellman (q-SDH) problem in (G_1, G_2) is defined as follows: Given a $(q+3)$-tuple of elements $(g_1, g_1^\gamma, \ldots, g_1^{(\gamma^q)}, g_2, g_2^\gamma)$ as input, output a pair $(g_1^{1/(\gamma+x)}, x)$ where $x \in \mathbb{Z}_p^*$. An algorithm $\mathcal{A}$ has advantage ϵ in solving q-SDH problem in (G_1, G_2) if

$$\Pr\left[\mathcal{A}(g_1, g_1^\gamma, \ldots, g_1^{(\gamma^q)}, g_2, g_2^\gamma) = (g_1^{1/(\gamma+x)}, x)\right] \geq \epsilon$$

where the probability is over the random choice of γ and the random bits of $\mathcal{A}$.

3.3   Decisional Diffie-Hellman Assumption

Let G, generated by g, be a cyclic group of prime order p. The Decisional Diffie-Hellman (DDH) problem in G is defined as follows: Given a tuple of elements (g, g^a, g^b, g^c) as input, output 1 if $c = ab$ and 0 otherwise. An algorithm $\mathcal{A}$ has advantage ϵ in solving DDH problem in G if

$$|\Pr\left[g \leftarrow G, a, b \leftarrow \mathbb{Z}_p : \mathcal{A}(g, g^a, g^b, g^{ab}) = 1\right]$$
$$- \Pr\left[g \leftarrow G, a, b, c \leftarrow \mathbb{Z}_p : \mathcal{A}(g, g^a, g^b, g^c) = 1\right]| \geq \epsilon$$

where the probability is over the random choice of the parameters to $\mathcal{A}$ and over the random bits of $\mathcal{A}$.

Let (G_1, G_2) be a bilinear group pair. Our DAA scheme requires the DDH problem for G_1 to be hard. The DDH assumption on G_1 is often known as the External Diffie-Hellman (XDH) assumption. This assumption is also used in Chen's DAA scheme [11].

4   The Proposed DAA Scheme

In this section, we present our construction of DAA scheme from bilinear maps. Our construction builds on top of the recent pairing-based EPID scheme [9] and Chen's DAA scheme [11]. The DAA scheme has three algorithms Setup, Verify, Link and two interactive protocols Join and Sign which are defined as follows.

4.1   Setup Algorithm

The setup algorithm is exactly the same as the one in [11]. On input of the security parameters 1^t, the setup algorithm takes the following steps:

1. Choose an asymmetric bilinear group pair (G_1, G_2) of prime order p and a pairing function $e : G_1 \times G_2 \to G_T$. Let g_1 and g_2 be the generators of G_1 and G_2, respectively.
2. Choose $h_1, h_2 \leftarrow G_1$, $\gamma \leftarrow \mathbb{Z}_p^*$, and compute $w := g_2^\gamma$.

3. Select five hash functions $H_1 : \{0,1\}^* \rightarrow \mathbb{Z}_p$, $H_2 : \{0,1\}^* \rightarrow \mathbb{Z}_p$, $H_3 : \{0,1\}^* \rightarrow G_1$, $H_4 : \{0,1\}^* \rightarrow \mathbb{Z}_p$, $H_5 : \{0,1\}^* \rightarrow \mathbb{Z}_p$.
4. Compute $T_1 = e(g_1, g_2)$, $T_2 = e(h_1, g_2)$, $T_3 = e(h_2, g_2)$, and $T_4 = e(h_2, w)$.
5. Output the DAA public key and the issuer's private key

$$\text{gpk} := ((G_1, G_2, G_T, p, e, g_1, h_1, h_2, g_2, w, H_1, H_2, H_3, H_4, H_5, T_1, T_2, T_3, T_4)$$
$$\text{isk} := \gamma$$

Note that T_1, T_2, T_3, and T_4 are optional in gpk, as they can be computed from g_1, h_1, h_2, g_2, w by the signers and verifiers. Also note that, in the actual implementation, we can choose the same hash function for H_1, H_2, H_4, and H_5. We use different hash functions in order to prove the security.

4.2   Join Protocol

The join protocol is the same as in [11] as well. This protocol is performed by a TPM $\mathcal{M}$, the corresponding host $\mathcal{H}$, and an issuer $\mathcal{I}$. Assume $\mathcal{M}$ and $\mathcal{I}$ have already established a secure authenticated channel using $\mathcal{M}$'s endorsement key [19]. Let DAAseed be $\mathcal{M}$'s internal secret seed. Let K_I be $\mathcal{I}$'s long term public key. In the join protocol, $\mathcal{M}$ chooses a unique secret key $\text{sk} = f$ and then obtains a credential $\text{cre} = (A, x)$ from $\mathcal{I}$ such that $A = (g_1 \cdot h_1^f)^{1/(x+\gamma)}$. The join protocol takes the following steps.

1. $\mathcal{I}$ chooses a nonce $n_I \in \{0,1\}^t$ and sends n_I as a challenge to $\mathcal{M}$.
2. $\mathcal{M}$ computes $f := H_1(\text{DAAseed}\|\text{cnt}\|K_I)$, where cnt is a count value. $\mathcal{M}$ sets its secret key $\text{sk} := f$. The purpose of using K_I and cnt can be found in the original DAA scheme [5].
3. $\mathcal{M}$ chooses at random $r_f \leftarrow \mathbb{Z}_p$ and computes $F := h_1^f$ and $R := h_1^{r_f}$.
4. $\mathcal{M}$ computes $c := H_2(\text{gpk}\|n_I\|F\|R)$ and $s_f := r_f + c \cdot f \pmod{p}$.
5. $\mathcal{M}$ sets $\text{comm} := (F, c, s_f, n_I)$ and sends comm to $\mathcal{I}$.
6. $\mathcal{I}$ verifies the value of n_I and checks F against the revocation list.
7. $\mathcal{I}$ computes $\hat{R} := h_1^{s_f} \cdot F^{-c}$ and verifies that $c = H_2(\text{gpk}\|n_I\|F\|\hat{R})$. If verification fails, then **abort**.
8. $\mathcal{I}$ chooses at random $x \leftarrow \mathbb{Z}_p$ and computes $A := (g_1 \cdot F)^{1/(x+\gamma)}$.
9. $\mathcal{I}$ sets the DAA credential $\text{cre} := (A, x)$ and sends cre to $\mathcal{M}$.
10. $\mathcal{M}$ forwards F and cre to $\mathcal{H}$.
11. $\mathcal{H}$ verifies that $e(A, wg_2^x) = e(g_1 F, g_2)$. If verification fails, then **abort**.

Note that the TPM $\mathcal{M}$ and the host $\mathcal{H}$ have a DAA signing key (A, x, f) such that $e(A, wg_2^x) = e(g_1 h_1^f, g_2)$. In the DAA schemes [9,15], the signing key is (A, x, y, f) such that $e(A, wg_2^x) = e(g_1 h_1^f h_2^y, g_2)$. Therefore our scheme has a smaller signing key.

4.3   Sign Protocol

This join protocol is performed by a TPM $\mathcal{M}$ and a host $\mathcal{H}$, where $\mathcal{M}$ has the secret key f and $\mathcal{H}$ has the credential (A, x). The other input of the protocol is the DAA public key gpk, a message m to be signed, and a basename bsn and a nonce n_V from the verifier. In this protocol, the signer chooses $B \in G_1$ and computes $K := B^f$, then uses zero-knowledge proof to prove

$$PK\{(A, x, f) : e(A, wg_2^x) = e(g_1 h_1^f, g_2) \wedge K = B^f\}$$

As in most of DAA schemes, the (B, K) pair is used for revocation check. To prove $e(A, wg_2^x) = e(g_1 h_1^f, g_2)$ holds, the signer first computes $T = A \cdot h_2^a$ where a is randomly chosen, then proves the following equation

$$e(T, g_2)^{-x} \cdot e(h_1, g_2)^f \cdot e(h_2, g_2)^{ax} \cdot e(h_2, w)^a = e(T, w)/e(g_1, g_2).$$

The overall approach here is the same as in [11]. The main difference between our scheme and Chen's DAA scheme [11] is on how we divide the computation between $\mathcal{M}$ and $\mathcal{H}$ in a secure way. The sign protocol takes the following steps:

1. If bsn $= \bot$, $\mathcal{M}$ chooses $B \leftarrow G_1$, otherwise, $\mathcal{M}$ computes $B := H_3(\text{bsn})$.
2. $\mathcal{M}$ chooses at random $r_f \leftarrow \mathbb{Z}_p$ and computes

$$K := B^f, \qquad R_1 := B^{r_f}, \qquad R_{2t} := h_1^{r_f}.$$

3. $\mathcal{M}$ sends (B, K, R_1, R_{2t}) to $\mathcal{H}$.
4. $\mathcal{H}$ chooses $a \leftarrow \mathbb{Z}_p$, computes $b := a \cdot x \pmod{p}$, and $T := A \cdot h_2^a$.
5. $\mathcal{H}$ randomly picks

$$r_x \leftarrow \mathbb{Z}_p, \qquad r_a \leftarrow \mathbb{Z}_p, \qquad r_b \leftarrow \mathbb{Z}_p.$$

6. $\mathcal{H}$ computes

$$R_2 := e(T, g_2)^{-r_x} \cdot e(h_1, g_2)^{r_f} \cdot e(h_2, g_2)^{r_b} \cdot e(h_2, w)^{r_a},$$
$$:= e(R_{2t} \cdot T^{-r_x} \cdot h_2^{r_b}, g_2) \cdot T_4^{r_a}.$$

7. $\mathcal{H}$ computes $c_h := H_4(\text{gpk}\|B\|K\|T\|R_1\|R_2\|n_V)$ and sends c_h to $\mathcal{M}$.
8. $\mathcal{M}$ chooses a random nonce $n_T \leftarrow \{0,1\}^t$ and computes $c := H_5(c_h\|n_T\|m)$.
9. $\mathcal{M}$ computes in $s_f := r_f + c \cdot f \pmod{p}$.
10. $\mathcal{M}$ sends (c, n_T, s_f) to $\mathcal{H}$. $\mathcal{M}$ erases r_f after sending this message.
11. $\mathcal{H}$ computes

$$s_x := r_x + c \cdot x \pmod{p}, \quad s_a := r_a + c \cdot a \pmod{p}, \quad s_b := r_b + c \cdot b \pmod{p}.$$

12. $\mathcal{H}$ outputs $\sigma := (B, K, T, c, n_T, s_f, s_x, s_a, s_b)$.

Note that the signing protocol is a three-message protocol: In the first message, $\mathcal{M}$ sends (B, K, R_1, R_{2t}) to $\mathcal{H}$. In the second message, $\mathcal{H}$ sends c_h to $\mathcal{M}$. In the third message, $\mathcal{M}$ sends (c, n_T, s_f) to $\mathcal{H}$. The way we divide the computation between the TPM and the host is similar to the one in the original DAA paper [5].

4.4 Verify Algorithm

On input of a message m, a basename bsn, a nonce n_V, a signature $(B, K, T, c,$ $n_T, s_f, s_x, s_a, s_b)$, the public key gpk, and the revocation list RL (a list of revoked secret keys), the verification algorithm takes the following steps:

1. Verify that $B, K, T \in G_1$ and $s_f, s_x, s_a, s_b \in \mathbb{Z}_p$.
2. Compute $\hat{R}_1 := B^{s_f} \cdot K^{-c}$.
3. Compute

$$\hat{R}_2 := e(T, g_2)^{-s_x} \cdot e(h_1, g_2)^{s_f} \cdot e(h_2, g_2)^{s_b} \cdot e(h_2, w)^{s_a} \cdot (e(g_1, g_2)/e(T, w))^c.$$
$$:= e(T, g_2^{-s_x} \cdot w^{-c}) \cdot T_1^c \cdot T_2^{s_f} \cdot T_3^{s_b} \cdot T_4^{s_a}$$

4. Verify that $c \overset{?}{=} H_5(H_4(\text{gpk}\|B\|K\|T\|\hat{R}_1\|\hat{R}_2\|n_V)\|n_T\|m)$.
5. For each $f' \in$ RL, if $K = B^{f'}$, output 0 (reject).
6. If any of the above verifications fails, output 0 (reject), otherwise, output 1 (accept).

4.5 Link Algorithm

On input of two message-signature pairs (m_0, σ_0) and (m_1, σ_1), a basename bsn, and the public key gpk, the link algorithm performs the following steps:

1. For each signature σ_b where $b \in \{0, 1\}$, run the verify algorithm $\text{Verify}(\sigma_b, m_b, \text{bsn}, \text{gpk})$. If either of two verifications returns 0 (reject), output $\perp$.
2. If $(B, K) \in \sigma_0$ are the same as $(B, K) \in \sigma_1$, return 1 (linked), otherwise return 0 (unlinked).

5 Security Proof

In this section, we prove our DAA scheme is secure under the security definitions stated in Section 2. We show that our DAA scheme is correct, user-controlled-anonymous, and user-controlled-traceable. The security of the DAA scheme based on the q-SDH assumption and G_1-DDH assumption defined in Section 3.

Theorem 1. *The DAA scheme in Section 4 is correct.*

Proof. To show the DAA scheme is correct, we prove that a signature created by a valid and unrevoked signer can be successfully verified by any verifier. In order to have a success signature verification, $\hat{R}_1, \hat{R}_2$ in the verify algorithm must be equal to R_1, R_2 in the sign protocol, respectively. We prove $\hat{R}_1 = R_1$ and $\hat{R}_2 = R_2$ as follows.

$$\hat{R}_1 = B^{s_f} \cdot K^{-c} = B^{r_f} \cdot B^{cf} \cdot (B^f)^{-c} = B^{r_f} = R_1$$

$$\begin{aligned}
\hat{R}_2 &= e(T, g_2)^{-s_x} \cdot e(h_1, g_2)^{s_f} \cdot e(h_2, g_2)^{s_b} \cdot e(h_2, w)^{s_a} \cdot (e(g_1, g_2)/e(T, w))^c \\
&= R_2 \cdot e(T, g_2)^{-cx} \cdot e(h_1, g_2)^{cf} \cdot e(h_2, g_2)^{cb} \cdot e(h_2, w)^{ca} \cdot (e(g_1, g_2)/e(T, w))^c \\
&= R_2 \cdot (e(g_1, g_2) \cdot e(h_1, g_2)^f \cdot e(h_2, g_2)^b \cdot e(h_2, w)^a \cdot e(T, g_2)^{-x} \cdot e(T, w)^{-1})^c \\
&= R_2 \cdot (e(g_1, g_2) \cdot e(h_1, g_2)^f \cdot e(h_2, g_2)^{ax} \cdot e(h_2, w)^a \cdot e(T, g_2^x w)^{-1})^c \\
&= R_2 \cdot (e(g_1 h_1^f, g_2) \cdot e(h_2^a, g_2^x w) \cdot e(A, g_2^x w)^{-1} \cdot e(h_2^a, g_2^x w)^{-1})^c = R_2
\end{aligned}$$

The last equation holds because for a valid private key (A, x, f), $e(A, g_2^x w) = e(g_1 h_1^f, g_2)$ holds. We now show that two signatures created by a single signer using a basename $\texttt{bsn} \neq \bot$ can be linked. This is obvious from the description of the DAA scheme, as two signatures will have the same (B, K) pair if the signatures are created using the same private key f.

Theorem 2. *Under the G_1-DDH assumption, the DAA scheme in Section 4 is user-controlled-anonymous. More specifically, if there is an adversary $\mathcal{A}$ that succeeds with a non-negligible probability to break the user-controlled-anonymity game, then there is a polynomial-time algorithm $\mathcal{B}$ that solves the G_1-DDH problem with a non-negligible probability.*

Proof. Suppose an algorithm $\mathcal{A}$ breaks the user-controlled-anonymity game of the DAA scheme with non-negligible probability. We can build a polynomial-time simulator $\mathcal{B}$ that breaks the G_1-DDH problem as follows. $\mathcal{B}$ is given as input a tuple (u, u^a, u^b, z) where $u \leftarrow G_1$, $a, b \leftarrow \mathbb{Z}_p$, and either $z = u^{ab}$ or z is a random element in G_1. $\mathcal{B}$ decides which z was given by interacting with $\mathcal{A}$ as follows.

We first give an overview of the proof. $\mathcal{B}$ first creates a special signer S^* where its secret key $f = a$, however $\mathcal{B}$ does not know the secret key. $\mathcal{B}$ creates rest of the signers by running the join protocol with $\mathcal{A}$. To respond to a sign query for signer S^*, $\mathcal{B}$ simulates the signature using the (u, u^a) pair. In the challenge phase, if S^* is selected as one of the (S_0, S_1) pair, $\mathcal{B}$ picks S^* for creating a signature by simulating the signature using the (u^b, z) pair, i.e., simulates using the secret key $f = \log_{u^b} z$. If $z = u^{ab}$, then $\log_u(u^a) = \log_{u^b}(z)$, $\mathcal{A}$ has non-negligible advantage guessing the random bit b correctly. If $z \neq u^{ab}$, $\mathcal{A}$ does not have any advantage guessing b or $\mathcal{A}$ may abort the game. $\mathcal{B}$ can use the output of $\mathcal{A}$ to decide whether $z = u^{ab}$.

Setup. Let (G_1, G_2) be a bilinear group pair of prime order p with generator g_1 and g_2, respectively. $\mathcal{B}$ chooses a random $\gamma \leftarrow \mathbb{Z}_p^*$ as $\texttt{isk}$ and sets the public key $\texttt{gpk} = (G_1, G_2, G_T, p, e, g_1, h_1 := u, h_2, g_2, w := g_2^\gamma, H_1, H_2, H_3, H_4, H_5, T_1, T_2, T_3, T_4)$ by running the setup algorithm. $\mathcal{B}$ sends $\texttt{isk}$ and $\texttt{gpk}$ to $\mathcal{A}$.

Hash Queries. We model the hash functions H_2, H_3, and H_5 as three random oracles. $\mathcal{B}$ responds to the hash queries for H_2, H_3, and H_5 as follows.

- $H_2(m)$: If m has not been queried before, $\mathcal{B}$ chooses $H_2(m)$ uniformly at random from $\mathbb{Z}_p^*$ and returns it to $\mathcal{A}$, otherwise $\mathcal{B}$ returns the previously queried result on m to ensure consistency.
- $H_3(m)$: Let q_h be the expected number of unique H_3 queries. $\mathcal{B}$ chooses a random $i \leftarrow \{1, \ldots, q_h\}$. If m has been queried before, $\mathcal{B}$ returns the previously queried result on m to ensure consistency. Otherwise, if m is the i-th unique query on H_3, $\mathcal{B}$ chooses chooses a random $r \leftarrow \mathbb{Z}_p^*$ and sets $H_3(m) := (u^b)^r$. For rest of the queries, $\mathcal{B}$ chooses a random $r \leftarrow \mathbb{Z}_p^*$ and sets $H_3(m) := u^r$. We use $\texttt{bsn}^*$ to denote the i-th unique query.
- $H_5(m)$: $\mathcal{B}$ chooses $H_5(m)$ uniformly at random from $\mathbb{Z}_p^*$ while ensuring consistency.

Join Queries. $\mathcal{A}$ requests for creating a new signer S. Let q_j be the expected number of join requests from $\mathcal{A}$. $\mathcal{B}$ chooses a random $i \leftarrow \{1, \ldots, q_j\}$. There are two cases for $\mathcal{B}$ to respond:

- If the query is the i-th join query: $\mathcal{B}$ sets $F := u^a$ without knowing the secret key $f = a = \log_u(u^a)$, and then forges rest of the join protocol as follows: it chooses randomly $c, s_f \leftarrow \mathbb{Z}_p$ and computes $R = h_1^{s_f} \cdot F^{-c}$. It then patches the oracle by setting $H_2(\mathrm{gpk} \| n_I \| F \| R) := c$. If $H_2(\mathrm{gpk} \| n_I \| F \| R)$ has been queried before, $\mathcal{B}$ quites and outputs "**abortion 0**". $\mathcal{B}$ receives a credential from $\mathcal{A}$. We use S^* to denote the identity of this signer.
- If the query is not the i-th join query: $\mathcal{B}$ chooses a random $f \leftarrow \mathbb{Z}_p^*$, computes $F := h_1^f$. If $F = u^a$, $\mathcal{B}$ quites and outputs "**abortion 0**". $\mathcal{B}$ runs the rest of the join protocol as the signer with $\mathcal{A}$ as the issuer, and obtains a credential $\mathrm{cre} = (A, x)$. $\mathcal{B}$ verifies cre and stores (S, f, A, x) in its log.

Sign Queries. Given a signer's identity S, a message m to be signed, a nonce n_V from $\mathcal{A}$, a basename bsn, $\mathcal{B}$ responds with a signature σ as follows: Assuming the signer S has already joined, if S is not S^*, $\mathcal{B}$ finds the corresponding secret key and credential (f, A, x) associated with S, runs the sign protocol, and outputs σ to $\mathcal{A}$. If $S = S^*$, $\mathcal{B}$ needs to forge a signature as follows:

1. If $\mathrm{bsn} = \bot$, $\mathcal{B}$ chooses $r \leftarrow \mathbb{Z}_p$ and sets $B := u^r$ and $K := (u^a)^r$.
2. If $\mathrm{bsn} = \mathrm{bsn}^*$, $\mathcal{B}$ quits and outputs "**abortion 1**".
3. If $\mathrm{bsn} \neq \{\bot, \mathrm{bsn}^*\}$, $\mathcal{B}$ searches the log of H_3 queries and retrieves r where $H_3(\mathrm{bsn}) = u^r$. $\mathcal{B}$ sets $B := u^r$ and computes $K := (u^a)^r$.
4. $\mathcal{B}$ chooses $T \leftarrow G_1$, $n_T \leftarrow \{0,1\}^t$, and $c, s_f, s_x, s_a, s_b \leftarrow \mathbb{Z}_p$.
5. $\mathcal{B}$ computes $R_1 := B^{s_f} \cdot K^{-c}$.
6. $\mathcal{B}$ computes

$$R_2 := e(T, g_2)^{-s_x} \cdot e(h_1, g_2)^{s_f} \cdot e(h_2, g_2)^{s_b} \cdot e(h_2, w)^{s_a} \cdot (e(g_1, g_2)/e(T, w))^c.$$

7. $\mathcal{B}$ patches the oracle H_5 by setting $H_5(H_4(\mathrm{gpk} \| B \| K \| T \| R_1 \| R_2 \| n_V) \| n_T \| m) := c$. If $H_5(H_4(\mathrm{gpk} \| B \| K \| T \| R_1 \| R_2 \| n_V) \| n_T \| m)$ has been queried before, $\mathcal{B}$ quites and outputs "**abortion 0**".
8. $\mathcal{B}$ outputs the signature $\sigma := (B, K, T, c, n_T, s_f, s_x, s_a, s_b)$.

Corrupt Queries. If a corrupt query is for a signer $S \neq S^*$, then $\mathcal{B}$ responds with the secret key corresponding to S. Otherwise, $\mathcal{B}$ quits and outputs "**abortion 2**".

Challenge. In the challenge, $\mathcal{A}$ outputs a message m, a basename bsn, and two signer's identity S_0 and S_1. If $S^* \notin \{S_0, S_1\}$ or $\mathrm{bsn} \notin \{\bot, \mathrm{bsn}^*\}$, then $\mathcal{B}$ quits and outputs "**abortion 3**". Otherwise, $\mathcal{B}$ picks $b \in \{0,1\}$ such that $S_b = S^*$, and generates a signature σ^* for m as follows:

1. If $\mathrm{bsn} = \bot$, $\mathcal{B}$ chooses $r \leftarrow \mathbb{Z}_p$ and sets $B := (u^b)^r$ and $K := z^r$.
2. If $\mathrm{bsn} = \mathrm{bsn}^*$, $\mathcal{B}$ searches the log of H_3 queries and retrieves r where $H_3(\mathrm{bsn}^*) = (u^b)^r$. $\mathcal{B}$ sets $B := (u^b)^r$ and computes $K := z^r$.
3. The rest of the sign algorithm follows the sign queries above.

$\mathcal{B}$ sends the resulting σ^* to $\mathcal{A}$.

Output. In the end, $\mathcal{A}$ outputs $b' \in \{0,1\}$ as the guess for b or aborts without any output. If $b = b'$, then $\mathcal{B}$ outputs 1, which means that $z = u^{ab}$. Otherwise $\mathcal{B}$ outputs 0, which means that z is a random element in G_1.

We now discuss the probability that algorithm $\mathcal{B}$ does not abort in the above game. There are four cases where $\mathcal{B}$ can abort. We study each case as follows:

1. Abortion 0. The chance of this type of abortion is $O(1/p)$. Since p is a large prime, the probability of this abortion is negligible.
2. Abortion 1. Recall that $\mathcal{A}$ cannot use the same non-empty bsn in the sign query and challenge query for signers S_0 and S_1. In other words, $\mathcal{A}$ cannot query all possible bsn for S^* in the sign queries. The probability that $\mathcal{B}$ does not abort in this case is at least $1/q_h$.
3. Abortion 2. As $\mathcal{A}$ cannot corrupt all the signers, the probability that $\mathcal{B}$ does not abort is at least $1/q_j$.
4. Abortion 3. $\mathcal{B}$ does not abort in this case if $\mathcal{A}$ selects S^* and bsn* in the challenge query. Thus the probability that $\mathcal{B}$ does not abort in this case is $1/(q_h \cdot q_j)$.

$\mathcal{B}$ does not abort if (1) bsn* was not chosen in the sign queries for S^*, (2) S^* was not chosen in the corrupt queries, and (3) S^* and bsn* were chosen in the challenge query. The probability that $\mathcal{B}$ does not abort the above game is roughly $1/(q_h \cdot q_j)$.

Let ϵ be the probability that $\mathcal{A}$ succeeds in breaking the user-controlled-anonymity game. Suppose $\mathcal{B}$ does not abort during the above simulation. If $z = u^{ab}$, then $\log_u(u^a) = \log_{u^b}(z)$, $\mathcal{B}$ simulates the game perfectly, i.e., $\Pr[b = b'] > \frac{1}{2} + \epsilon$. If z is a random element in G_1, then σ^* in the challenge query is simulated using the (u^b, z) pair. In other words, the secret key used in generated σ^* is different from either secret key of S_0 or S_1. Observe that $\mathcal{B}$ in this case does not simulate the game perfectly, especially in the challenge query. $\mathcal{A}$ could abort the game. If $\mathcal{A}$ does not abort the game, $\mathcal{A}$ does not have any advantage guessing b. It follows that $\Pr[b = b'] = \frac{1}{2}$. Therefore, assuming $\mathcal{B}$ does not abort, it has probability at least $\epsilon/2$ in solving the DDH problem in G_1.

Theorem 3. *Under the q-SDH assumption, the DAA scheme in Section 4 is user-controlled-traceable. More specifically, if there is an adversary $\mathcal{A}$ that succeeds with a non-negligible probability to break the user-controlled-traceability game, then there is a polynomial-time algorithm $\mathcal{B}$ that solves the q-SDH problem with a non-negligible probability.*

The proof of this theorem is similar to the user-controlled-traceability proof in Chen's DAA scheme [11]. Due to the space limit, we omit the details.

6   Comparisons with Existing DAA Schemes

In this section, we compare our DAA scheme with several existing pairing-based DAA schemes [6,13,15,11]. Note that we do not include the original CMS-DAA scheme [12] in the comparisons, as it is not secure, instead we compare ours with the patched version [13]. We also do not include the pairing-based EPID scheme [9] in the comparison, because EPID does not have the feature of splitting computation between a TPM and a host.

We compare the credential and signature sizes of our scheme with other DAA schemes in the following table. We use $\mathbb{Z}_q$ to denote the size of an element in $\mathbb{Z}_q$, h to denote the size of a hash result, G_1 to denote the size of an element in G_1, and G_T to denote the size of an element in G_T. For bilinear maps with 128-bit security, G_T needs to be around 3072 bits [16]. Our DAA scheme has the same credential and signature sizes as in Chen's DAA scheme [11]. The credential and signature sizes in our scheme are smaller than other DAA schemes [6,13,15].

DAA Scheme	Credential Size	Signature Size
Scheme of [6]	$3G_1$	$2\mathbb{Z}_q + 3G_1 + 2G_T + 1h$
Scheme of [13]	$3G_1$	$1\mathbb{Z}_q + 5G_1 + 1h$
Scheme of [15]	$2\mathbb{Z}_q + 1G_1$	$6\mathbb{Z}_q + 2G_1 + 2G_T + 1h$
Scheme of [11]	$1\mathbb{Z}_q + 1G_1$	$4\mathbb{Z}_q + 3G_1 + 1h$
Our Scheme	$1\mathbb{Z}_q + 1G_1$	$4\mathbb{Z}_q + 3G_1 + 1h$

We compare the efficiency of signing and verification algorithms of our scheme with other DAA schemes in the following table. We use P to denote a pairing operation, G_1 to denote an exponentiation operation in G_1, G_1^2 to denote a multi-exponentiation operation, and so on. A multi-exponentiation is slightly more expensive than an exponentiation. As we mentioned earlier in Section 1, operations in G_1 are much more efficient than ones in G_T. Therefore, our DAA scheme has significant advantage for computationally weak device such as TPM. The efficiency of the sign protocol for our scheme is approximately 5 times more efficient than the rest of pairing-based DAA schemes [6,13,15,11] using Barreto-Naehrig curves.

DAA Scheme	TPM Sign	Host Sign	Verify
Scheme of [7]	$3G_T$	$3G_1 + 1G_T + 3P$	$1G_T^2 + 1G_T^3 + 5P + (n+1)G_T$
Scheme of [13]	$2G_1 + 1G_T$	$3G_1 + 1P$	$1G_T^2 + 1G_T^3 + 5P + nG_1$
Scheme of [15]	$2G_1 + 1G_T^2$	$1G_1 + 2G_1^2 + 1G_1^3 + 1G_T^3$	$1G_1^2 + 2G_1^3 + 1G_T^3 + 3P + nG_T$
Scheme of [11]	$2G_1 + 1G_T$	$1G_1 + 1G_T^3$	$1G_1^2 + 1G_2^3 + 1G_T^4 + 1P + nG_1$
Our Scheme	$3G_1$	$1G_1 + 1G_1^2 + 1G_T + 1P$	$1G_1^2 + 1G_2^3 + 1G_T^4 + 1P + nG_1$

Observe that the efficiency we gain in TPM comes with a price – the host needs to perform an additional pairing. The total efficiency of the sign protocol is $4G_1 + 1G_1^2 + 1G_T + 1P$ in our scheme, whereas it is $3G_1 + 1G_T + 3G_T^3$ in Chen's DAA scheme [11]. Note that TPM is much slower than the host platform, e.g., probably 100 times slower or more. Based on the performance simulation by Chen, Page, and Smart [14], a pairing operation on a host takes less than 15 millie-seconds for a 64-bit 2.4 GHz Intel Core 2 processor, while $2G_1 + 1G_T$

operation takes more than 3 seconds for a 32-bit 33 MHz simulated TPM. Using these performance data, we estimate that the overall sign protocol will take less than 1 second in our scheme, whereas the sign protocol in [11,13] will take more than 3 seconds.

We did not compare the efficiency of the join protocol because the join protocol is executed much less frequently than the sign protocol or the verification algorithm. Besides the join protocol in our DAA scheme is the same as the one in Chen's DAA scheme [11], thus has the same efficiency.

7   Conclusions

In this paper, we proposed an efficient DAA scheme from bilinear maps. Our new DAA scheme takes much less resources for TPM implementation (both computation and software code size) compared to the existing DAA schemes. We believe our DAA scheme is a good candidate for the next generation of TPM initiated by the TCG TPM working group, assuming that a TPM can support multiple DAA algorithms.

Acknowledgement

We thank Liqun Chen for her helpful discussions and feedback. We also thank the anonymous reviewers for their useful comments.

References

1. Backes, M., Maffei, M., Unruh, D.: Zero-knowledge in the applied pi-calculus and automated verification of the direct anonymous attestation protocol. In: Proceedings of IEEE Symposium on Security and Privacy, pp. 202–215. IEEE Computer Society, Los Alamitos (2008)
2. Barreto, P.S.L.M., Naehrig, M.: Pairing-friendly elliptic curves of prime order. In: Preneel, B., Tavares, S. (eds.) SAC 2005. LNCS, vol. 3897, pp. 319–331. Springer, Heidelberg (2006)
3. Boneh, D., Boyen, X.: Short signatures without random oracles. In: Cachin, C., Camenisch, J.L. (eds.) EUROCRYPT 2004. LNCS, vol. 3027, pp. 56–73. Springer, Heidelberg (2004)
4. Boneh, D., Boyen, X., Shacham, H.: Short group signatures. In: Franklin, M. (ed.) CRYPTO 2004. LNCS, vol. 3152, pp. 41–55. Springer, Heidelberg (2004)
5. Brickell, E., Camenisch, J., Chen, L.: Direct anonymous attestation. In: Proceedings of the 11th ACM Conference on Computer and Communications Security, pp. 132–145. ACM Press, New York (2004)
6. Brickell, E., Chen, L., Li, J.: A new direct anonymous attestation scheme from bilinear maps. In: Lipp, P., Sadeghi, A.-R., Koch, K.-M. (eds.) Trust 2008. LNCS, vol. 4968, pp. 166–178. Springer, Heidelberg (2008)
7. Brickell, E., Chen, L., Li, J.: Simplified security notions of direct anonymous attestation and a concrete scheme from pairings. International Journal of Information Security 8(5), 315–330 (2009)

8. Brickell, E., Li, J.: Enhanced Privacy ID: A direct anonymous attestation scheme with enhanced revocation capabilities. In: Proceedings of the 6th ACM Workshop on Privacy in the Electronic Society, October 2007, pp. 21–30. ACM Press, New York (2007)

9. Brickell, E., Li, J.: Enhanced Privacy ID from bilinear pairing. Cryptology ePrint Archive, Report 2009/095 (2009), http://eprint.iacr.org/

10. Camenisch, J., Groth, J.: Group signatures: Better efficiency and new theoretical aspects. In: Blundo, C., Cimato, S. (eds.) SCN 2004. LNCS, vol. 3352, pp. 120–133. Springer, Heidelberg (2005)

11. Chen, L.: A DAA scheme requiring less TPM resources. In: Proceedings of the 5th China International Conference on Information Security and Cryptology, LNCS. Springer, Heidelberg (2009)

12. Chen, L., Morrissey, P., Smart, N.P.: Pairings in trusted computing. In: Galbraith, S.D., Paterson, K.G. (eds.) Pairing 2008. LNCS, vol. 5209, pp. 1–17. Springer, Heidelberg (2008)

13. Chen, L., Morrissey, P., Smart, N.P.: DAA: Fixing the pairing based protocols. Cryptology ePrint Archive, Report 2009/198 (2009), http://eprint.iacr.org/

14. Chen, L., Page, D., Smart, N.P.: On the design and implementation of an efficient DAA scheme. In: Proceedings of the 9th Smart Card Research and Advanced Application IFIP Conference. Springer, Heidelberg (2010)

15. Chen, X., Feng, D.: Direct anonymous attestation for next generation TPM. Journal of Computers 3(12), 43–50 (2008)

16. Koblitz, N., Menezes, A.: Pairing-based cryptography at high security levels. In: Smart, N.P. (ed.) Cryptography and Coding 2005. LNCS, vol. 3796, pp. 13–36. Springer, Heidelberg (2005)

17. Leung, A., Mitchell, C.J.: Ninja: Non identity based, privacy preserving authentication for ubiquitous environments. In: Krumm, J., Abowd, G.D., Seneviratne, A., Strang, T. (eds.) UbiComp 2007. LNCS, vol. 4717, pp. 73–90. Springer, Heidelberg (2007)

18. Lysyanskaya, A., Rivest, R.L., Sahai, A., Wolf, S.: Pseudonym systems. In: Heys, H.M., Adams, C.M. (eds.) SAC 1999. LNCS, vol. 1758, pp. 184–199. Springer, Heidelberg (2000)

19. Trusted Computing Group. TCG TPM specification 1.2 (2003), http://www.trustedcomputinggroup.org

20. Trusted Computing Group website, http://www.trustedcomputinggroup.org

An Anonymous Attestation Scheme with Optional Traceability

Jiangtao Li and Anand Rajan

Intel Labs, Intel Corporation
jiangtao.li@intel.com, anand.rajan@intel.com

Abstract. Direct Anonymous Attestation (DAA) is a cryptographic scheme designed for anonymous attestation of a hardware device while preserving the privacy of the device owner. Signatures created by a DAA signer are anonymous and untraceable, i.e., cannot be opened to find out the identity of the signer. To prevent abuse of privacy, DAA has a feature called user-controlled-traceability in which the signer and verifier can negotiate whether or not the signatures from the signer can linked. This feature is a preventive mechanism against corrupted DAA signers because they can be prevented from making multiple anonymous authentications. However, it is not a proactive deterrent against such activity as nobody is able to identify the corrupted signer. In this paper, we introduce a new cryptographic scheme called Optionally Traceable Anonymous Attestation (OTAA), in which the signer and verifier can negotiate whether signatures from the signer are traceable to the issuer instead of just being linkable. In the OTAA scheme, if a corrupted signer has produced a traceable signature or published his private key widely, the issuer can identify the signer and effectively revoke him using the verifier-local revocation. We give a construction of an OTAA scheme from bilinear pairing. Our OTAA scheme is efficient and provably secure in the random oracle model under the strong Diffie-Hellman assumption and the external Diffie-Hellman assumption.

1 Introduction

The concept and a concrete scheme of Direct Anonymous Attestation (DAA) were first introduced by Brickell, Camenisch, and Chen [9] for remote anonymous authentication of a hardware module, called Trusted Platform Module (TPM). The DAA scheme was adopted by the Trusted Computing Group (TCG) [31], an industry standardization body that aims to develop and promote an open industry standard for trusted computing hardware and software building blocks. The DAA scheme was standardized in the TCG TPM Specification Version 1.2 [30] and has recently been adopted by ISO/IEC as an international standard. After DAA was first introduced, it has drawn a lot of attention from the industry in general and cryptographic community in particular, e.g., [17,29,10,25,24] are some of the relevant references in this regard.

A DAA scheme involves three types of entities: an issuer, signers, and verifiers. The issuer is in charge of verifying the legitimacy of signers and of issuing

A. Acquisti, S.W. Smith, and A.-R. Sadeghi (Eds.): TRUST 2010, LNCS 6101, pp. 196–210, 2010.

a membership credential to each signer. A signer can prove membership anonymously to a verifier by creating a DAA signature. The verifier can verify the membership of the signer from the DAA signature but cannot learn the identity of the signer. DAA scheme can be seen as a group signature scheme without the traceability feature, i.e., nobody (not even the issuer) can open a DAA signature to find out the identity of the signer.

DAA signatures can be created using one of the two options: random base option and name base option. In the random base option, DAA signatures are unlinkable. In the name base option, two DAA signatures produced by a signer (using one verifier's basename) are linkable. Yet signatures created by a signer using two different basenames are unlinkable. This feature is later referred as user-controlled-traceability [11] (probably user-controlled-linkability is more appropriate), as the signer and verifier can negotiate whether the signatures from the signer can be linked by choosing the appropriate options. This feature can be used to prevent abuse of privacy by a corrupted signer. For example, if a provisioning server wants to issue a key to each valid signer, the server can mandate the name base option to make sure each signer can only get one key at most.

The user-controlled-traceability feature in DAA is a preventive mechanism against corrupted signers but not a proactive one, as a corrupted signer can be prevented from making multiple anonymous authentications to a verifier but he cannot be identified or revoked per the definition of DAA. Brickell and Li have proposed an extension of DAA called Enhanced Privacy ID (EPID) in which the issuer can revoke signatures from corrupted signers without knowing their private keys or identities [12,14]. Tsang et al. proposed a similar revocation mechanism in [32]. However, such a revocation mechanism requires the signer to perform zero-knowledge proof for each revoked signature. This could be too computationally demanding for small hardware devices such as TPM.

In practice, we can separate the use of anonymous attestation into two categories: high-value transactions and low-value transactions. For high-value transactions, such as downloading key materials or accessing medical information, the ability to trace and effectively revoke corrupted signers is required. However, for low-value transactions, such as accessing digital library or proving older than certain age, privacy carries more weight than traceability and revocability. End user may feel more comfortable if his anonymous signatures are untraceable most of the time during his day-to-day transactions, but traceable occasionally for the high-value transactions.

In this paper, we propose a new cryptographic scheme called Optionally Traceable Anonymous Attestation (OTAA) with a concrete construction from bilinear maps. OTAA provides the right balance between privacy and traceability. The difference from DAA is that the signer in OTAA can choose whether or not signatures are traceable instead of linkable. The OTAA scheme has the following features:

1. OTAA signatures are anonymous and unlinkable to the verifiers. However the signer and verifier can negotiate whether or not the signatures are traceable to the issuer.

2. The issuer can open a traceable signature and identify the signer. Furthermore, the issuer can revoke the signer in an efficient way. In addition, if a corrupted signer publishes his private key widely, the issuer can revoke the signer as well. Both revocation checks are performed locally by the verifier. This revocation model is known in the literature as verifier-local revocation.

OTAA can be used in trusted computing as an alternative mechanism for anonymous attestation besides DAA. One of the biggest advantages of OTAA is the revocation method: it is more capable than the original definition of DAA [9,11] and is more efficient than the signature based revocation in EPID [12]. We believe OTAA has wider application beyond the TPM usage, such as in e-commerce, digital content protection, and identity card. Our OTAA construction is very efficient. It has similar efficiency as the DAA schemes [14,24]. Our OTAA scheme becomes a group signature scheme if all the signatures are traceable. We show in Section 6 that our OTAA is more efficient than existing pairing-based group signature schemes [7,20,8,27].

Rest of this paper is organized as follows. We first discuss the related work in Section 2. We then give a formal specification of OTAA and present the security requirements in Section 3. We review the definition of pairing and related security assumptions in Section 4. Next we describe the construction of our OTAA scheme in Section 5. We compare our OTAA scheme with several group signature and DAA schemes in Section 6. We conclude our paper and discuss the future work in Section 7.

2   Related Work

OTAA can be seen as a variant of DAA [9,17,29,3,12,11,25,24]. Many concepts of OTAA borrow from DAA, such as negotiation of different privacy level and revocation if a private key gets revealed publicly. In fact, our construction of OTAA builds on top of the recent pairing-based DAA schemes [14,24]. As we mentioned earlier, DAA signatures cannot be opened. Thus a corrupted signer will not be revoked unless he publishes his private key on the Internet. Such revocation capability in the original definition of DAA [9,11] is limited. OTAA provides a better revocation capability without comprising the efficiency.

OTAA is a special group signatures scheme with the optional traceability feature. In group signature definition [5] and constructions [23,22,1,7,27], all the group signatures are traceable. In most of the group signature schemes, the signer encrypts his identity using the tracing manager's public key in a way that the encryption can be verified by the verifier. To open a group signature, the tracing manager uses his private key to decrypt and find the identity of the signer. Thus, it is not difficult to make a group signature scheme optionally traceable, i.e., the signer can choose whether to encrypt his identity. OTAA is unique in that the issuer not only can open a traceable signature but can also revoke the signer using efficient verifier-local revocation.

Boneh and Shacham proposed an efficient verifier-local revocation group signature scheme [8]. It is not difficult to convert their group signature scheme into an optionally traceable group signature scheme. To make a group signature untraceable in their scheme, the signer simply chooses u and v randomly from G_1 instead of choosing $\hat{u}$ and $\hat{v}$ from G_2. However, such untraceable signatures cannot be revoked in any scenarios, e.g., even if the private key is revealed and widely distributed. Besides, our OTAA scheme is more efficient than the BS group signatures scheme in signature signing, verification, and the revocation check. The revocation check in the BS group signatures scheme requires two pairing operations per revoked key instead of one exponentiation in our OTAA scheme. A pairing operation is about 10 times more expensive than an exponentiation operation. The revocation check in our scheme is fix-base exponentiation which can be further optimized using fast exponentiation technique [16]. Thus the revocation check in our scheme is about two orders of magnitude more efficient than the BS group signatures scheme.

Our OTAA scheme uses verifier-local revocation, a revocation model used widely in all the DAA schemes as well as in some group signature schemes [2,8]. We believe that this revocation model is a practical model, as the revocation lists are only sent to the verifiers. After all, it is in the verifiers' interest to perform the revocation check. This is similar to the revocation model we currently have in the public key infrastructure. Observe that this model adds no burden to the signers. In our OTAA scheme, the revocation check takes n fix-base exponentiations, where n is the size of the revocation list. Using the fast exponentiation technique [16], a verifier can easily process a few thousands revocation checks within one second. Another popular revocation model in the group signatures is to use dynamic accumulators [19,18]. Although dynamic accumulators are very efficient, a limitation of this approach is the infrastructure overhead. Each signer needs to constantly connect to the issuer and update his credentials. This seems to not be practical in the TPM implementation.

3   Specification and Security Requirements of OTAA

In the rest of this paper, we use the following standard notations. Let S be a finite set, $x \leftarrow S$ denotes that x is chosen uniformly at random from S. Let $b \leftarrow A(a)$ denote an algorithm A that is given input a and outputs b. Let $\langle c, d \rangle \leftarrow P_{A,B}\langle a, b \rangle$ denote an interactive protocol between A and B, where A inputs a and B inputs b, in the end A obtains c and B obtains d.

3.1   Specification of OTAA

An OTAA scheme involves three types of entities: an issuer $\mathcal{I}$, platforms $\mathcal{P}$, and verifiers $\mathcal{V}$. There are the following four polynomial-time algorithms Setup, Sign, Verify, and Open, and one interactive protocol Join.

Setup : This setup algorithm for the issuer $\mathcal{I}$ takes a security parameter 1^k as input and outputs a group public key gpk and the issuer's private key isk. The public key gpk includes the global public parameters for the system.

$$(\text{gpk}, \text{isk}) \leftarrow \text{Setup}(1^k)$$

Join : This join protocol is an interactive protocol between the issuer $\mathcal{I}$ and a platform $\mathcal{P}_i$ and consists of two randomized algorithms: $\mathsf{Join_t}$ and $\mathsf{Join_i}$. The platform $\mathcal{P}_i$ uses $\mathsf{Join_t}$ to produce a pair $(\mathsf{sk}_i, \mathsf{comm}_i)$, where sk_i is platform's secret key and comm_i is a commitment of sk_i.

$$(\mathsf{sk}_i, \mathsf{comm}_i) \leftarrow \mathsf{Join_t}(\mathsf{gpk})$$

On input of a commitment comm_i, the group public key gpk, the issuer's private key isk, the issuer $\mathcal{I}$ uses $\mathsf{Join_i}$ to produce cre_i, a membership credential associated with sk_i. The cre_i includes a unique tracing key tk_i. $\mathcal{P}_i$ receives cre_i while $\mathcal{I}$ updates its tracing database dbase by inserting a record of $\mathcal{P}_i$'s identity id_i and the tracing key tk_i.

$$(\mathsf{cre}_i, \mathsf{dbase}) \leftarrow \mathsf{Join_i}(\mathsf{gpk}, \mathsf{isk}, \mathsf{dbase}, \mathsf{comm}_i)$$

The join protocol can be formulated as

$$\langle \mathsf{dbase}, (\mathsf{sk}_i, \mathsf{cre}_i) \rangle \leftarrow \mathsf{Join}_{\mathcal{I},\mathcal{P}} \langle (\mathsf{gpk}, \mathsf{isk}, \mathsf{dbase}), \mathsf{gpk} \rangle$$

Sign : On input of gpk, sk_i, cre_i, a boolean value tr, and a message m, the probabilistic signing algorithm outputs a signature σ. If $\mathsf{tr} = 1$, σ is a traceable signature, otherwise, σ is a non-traceable signature. We often times call $(\mathsf{sk}_i, \mathsf{cre}_i)$ the signing key of $\mathcal{P}_i$.

$$\sigma \leftarrow \mathsf{Sign}(\mathsf{gpk}, \mathsf{sk}_i, \mathsf{cre}_i, \mathsf{tr}, m)$$

Verify : On input of gpk, a message m, a traceable or a non-traceable signature σ, a list of revoked secret keys sRL (the revocation list for non-traceable signatures), and a list of revoked tracing keys tRL (the revocation list for traceable signatures), this verification algorithm outputs valid, $\mathsf{revoked}$, or $\mathsf{invalid}$. We shall discuss how to build the revocation lists in the later sections.

$$\mathsf{valid/revoked/invalid} \leftarrow \mathsf{Verify}(\mathsf{gpk}, m, \sigma, \mathsf{sRL}, \mathsf{tRL})$$

Open : On input of gpk, a message m, a signature σ, and the tracing database dbase, the deterministic tracing algorithm outputs $\mathsf{invalid}$ if the signature is not valid, $\mathsf{untraceable}$ if the signature is not traceable, or $(\mathsf{id}_i, \mathsf{tk}_i)$, the identity and tracing key of the signer.

$$\mathsf{invalid/untraceable/}(\mathsf{id}_i, \mathsf{tk}_i) \leftarrow \mathsf{Open}(\mathsf{gpk}, m, \sigma, \mathsf{dbase})$$

Observe that the revocation lists are only sent to the verifiers. This revocation method is known in the literature as verifier-local revocation [8] and has been used in most of the DAA schemes [9,12,10,25,24]. One implication of verifier-local revocation is the signature is selfless-anonymous, i.e., a platform can tell whether he generated a particular signature σ, but if he did not he learns nothing else about the signer of σ.

3.2   Security Requirements of OTAA

A secure OTAA scheme needs to satisfy the following three requirements: correctness, user-controlled-anonymity, and user-controlled-traceability. We borrow the terms "user-controlled-anonymity" and "user-controlled-traceability" from the definition of DAA [11], as the platform and verifier in OTAA can negotiate the privacy level of a signature, i.e., whether the signatures can be traced. However, the security requirements of OTAA are different from those in DAA [9,11]. Roughly speaking, user-controlled-anonymity guarantees that only the issuer is able to identify the actual signer of a traceable signature and nobody can identify the actual signer of a non-traceable signature, except that if the signer is revoked. User-controlled-traceability guarantees that no one except the issuer is able to successfully add a new platform to the group. Our security requirements follow the framework of Bellare et al. definition of group signatures for dynamic groups [5] and Boneh and Shacham's definition of verifier-local revocation group signatures [8].

Correctness. The correctness requirement states that every signature, no matter traceable or not, generated by a platform can be verified as valid, except when the platform is revoked. It can be formally stated as follows

$$(\text{gpk}, \text{isk}) \leftarrow \text{Setup}(1^k)$$
$$\langle \text{dbase}, (\text{sk}_i, \text{cre}_i) \rangle \leftarrow \text{Join}_{\mathcal{I}, \mathcal{P}} \langle (\text{gpk}, \text{isk}, \text{dbase}), \text{gpk} \rangle$$
$$\sigma \leftarrow \text{Sign}(\text{gpk}, \text{sk}_i, \text{cre}_i, \text{tr}, m)$$
$$\text{Verify}(\text{gpk}, m, \sigma, \text{sRL}, \text{tRL}) = \text{true} \iff$$
$$((\text{tr} = 1) \wedge (\text{tk}_i \notin \text{tRL})) \vee ((\text{tr} = 0) \wedge (\text{sk}_i \notin \text{sRL}))$$

User-Controlled-Anonymity. An OTAA scheme satisfies the user-controlled-anonymity property if no polynomial-time adversary can win the anonymity games. In the anonymity game, the goal of the adversary is to determine which one of two platforms was used in generating a signature. As mentioned earlier, given a signature and a signing key, the adversary could determine whether the signature was generated using the signing key. If the signature is a traceable signature, then the adversary should not be given access to the tracing key of either platform. Otherwise if the signature is non-traceable, the adversary should be given the secret keys of the platforms. The anonymity game between a challenger $\mathcal{C}$ and an adversary $\mathcal{A}$ is defined as follows.

1. Setup. $\mathcal{C}$ runs $(\text{gpk}, \text{isk}) \leftarrow \text{Setup}(1^k)$ and sends gpk and isk to $\mathcal{A}$.
2. Queries. $\mathcal{A}$ can make the following queries to $\mathcal{C}$.
    (a) Join. $\mathcal{A}$ requests for creating a new platform $\mathcal{P}$ by choosing one of the following two types:
        i. $\mathcal{C}$ runs the join protocol as the platform $\mathcal{P}$ by interacting with $\mathcal{A}$ as the issuer. In the end, $\mathcal{C}$ obtains the signing key (sk, cre), while $\mathcal{A}$ only learns the credential cre.
        ii. $\mathcal{C}$ runs the join protocol locally and generates a signing key (sk, cre).

(b) Sign. $\mathcal{A}$ requests a signature on a message m with a traceability option tr for a platform $\mathcal{P}$. $\mathcal{C}$ finds $\mathcal{P}$'s signing key (sk, cre) and computes $\sigma \leftarrow \text{Sign}(\text{gpk}, \text{sk}, \text{cre}, \text{tr}, m)$. $\mathcal{C}$ returns σ to $\mathcal{A}$.

(c) Corrupt. $\mathcal{A}$ requests the signing key of a platform $\mathcal{P}$. $\mathcal{C}$ responds with (sk, cre) of $\mathcal{P}$ to $\mathcal{A}$.

3. Challenge. $\mathcal{A}$ outputs a message m, a traceability option tr, and two platforms $\mathcal{P}_0$ and $\mathcal{P}_1$. $\mathcal{A}$ must have not made a corruption query on either $\mathcal{P}_0$ or $\mathcal{P}_1$. If $\mathcal{A}$ has a membership credential of either $\mathcal{P}_0$ or $\mathcal{P}_1$, the requesting tr must be 0, i.e., $\mathcal{A}$ can only request a non-traceable signature. $\mathcal{C}$ chooses a random bit $b \leftarrow \{0, 1\}$, computes a signature $\sigma \leftarrow \text{Sign}(\text{gpk}, \text{sk}_b, \text{cre}_b, \text{tr}, m)$, where $(\text{sk}_b, \text{cre}_b)$ is the signing key for $\mathcal{P}_b$, and sends σ to $\mathcal{A}$.

4. Restricted Queries. After the challenge phase, $\mathcal{A}$ can make additional queries to $\mathcal{C}$, restricted as follows.

(a) Join. $\mathcal{A}$ can make join queries as before.

(b) Sign. $\mathcal{A}$ can make sign queries as before.

(c) Corrupt. As before, but $\mathcal{A}$ cannot make corrupt queries at $\mathcal{P}_0$ and $\mathcal{P}_1$.

5. Output. Finally, $\mathcal{A}$ outputs a bit b'. The adversary wins if $b' = b$.

Definition 1. *Let $\mathcal{A}$ be the adversary. We use $\mathbf{Adv}[\mathcal{A}_{OTAA}^{An}] = |\Pr[b = b'] - 1/2|$ to denote the advantage of $\mathcal{A}$ in breaking the user-controlled-anonymity game. The probability is taken over the coin tosses of $\mathcal{A}$, of the randomized setup, join, and sign algorithms, and over the choice of b. We say that an OTAA scheme is user-controlled-anonymity if for any probabilistic polynomial-time adversary, $\mathbf{Adv}[\mathcal{A}_{OTAA}^{An}]$ is negligible.*

User-Controlled-Traceability. We say that an OTAA scheme satisfies the user-controlled-traceability property if no adversary can win the following traceability game. In the user-controlled-traceability game, the adversary's goal is to forge a valid non-traceable signature given that all private keys known to the adversary have been revoked or to create a traceable signature that cannot be opened properly. The traceability game between a challenger $\mathcal{C}$ and an adversary $\mathcal{A}$ is defined as follows.

1. Setup. $\mathcal{C}$ runs $(\text{gpk}, \text{isk}) \leftarrow \text{Setup}(1^k)$ and sends gpk to $\mathcal{A}$. $\mathcal{C}$ sets empty revocation lists sRL and tRL.

2. Queries. $\mathcal{A}$ can make the following queries to $\mathcal{C}$.

(a) Join. $\mathcal{A}$ requests for creating a new platform $\mathcal{P}$ by choosing one of the following two types:

   i. $\mathcal{C}$ runs the join protocol as the issuer with $\mathcal{A}$ as the platform $\mathcal{P}$. In the end, $\mathcal{C}$ outputs cre while $\mathcal{A}$ outputs the signing key (sk, cre). $\mathcal{C}$ appends tk in cre to revocation list tRL.

   ii. $\mathcal{C}$ runs the join protocol locally and generates a signing key (sk, cre).

(b) Sign. $\mathcal{A}$ requests a signature on a message m with a traceability option tr for a platform $\mathcal{P}$. $\mathcal{C}$ finds $\mathcal{P}$'s signing key (sk, cre) and computes $\sigma \leftarrow \text{Sign}(\text{gpk}, \text{sk}, \text{cre}, \text{tr}, m)$. $\mathcal{C}$ returns σ to $\mathcal{A}$.

   (c) Corrupt. $\mathcal{A}$ requests the signing key of a platform $\mathcal{P}$. $\mathcal{C}$ responds with (sk, cre) of $\mathcal{P}$ to $\mathcal{A}$. $\mathcal{C}$ also appends sk to sRL and tk from cre to tRL.
3. Response. Finally, $\mathcal{A}$ outputs a message m and a signature σ.

Assuming that $\mathcal{A}$ did not obtain σ by making a sign query on m.

1. If σ is a traceable signature, $\mathcal{A}$ wins if Verify(gpk, σ, m, sRL, tRL) = valid.
2. If σ is a non-traceable signature, $\mathcal{A}$ wins if Verify(gpk, σ, m, sRL, tRL) = valid and $\mathcal{A}$ has never made any type (i) join query.

Note that if $\mathcal{A}$ has made a type (i) join query, it obtained a signing key (sk, cre) such that only the tracing key in cre is known to $\mathcal{C}$. Since $\mathcal{C}$ does not know sk, $\mathcal{A}$ can produce a valid non-traceable signature using the signing key. Thus, if $\mathcal{A}$ outputs a non-traceable signature in the final response, $\mathcal{A}$ wins only if it has not made any type (i) join query.

Definition 2. *Let $\mathcal{A}$ denote an adversary that plays the traceability game above. We use $\mathbf{Adv}[\mathcal{A}_{OTAA}^{\mathrm{Tr}}] = \Pr[\mathcal{A}\ wins]$ to denote the advantage that $\mathcal{A}$ breaks the traceability game. We say that an OTAA scheme is user-controlled-traceability if for any probabilistic polynomial-time adversary, $\mathbf{Adv}[\mathcal{A}_{OTAA}^{\mathrm{Tr}}]$ is negligible.*

4   Pairings and Complexity Assumptions

In this section, we first review the concept of pairings and then discuss some complexity assumptions related to our scheme.

Background on Bilinear Maps. Our OTAA scheme in this paper is based on asymmetric pairings. We follow the notation of Boneh, Boyen, and Shacham [7] to review some background on pairings. Let G_1 and G_2 to two multiplicative cyclic groups of prime order p. Let g_1 be a generator of G_1 and g_2 be a generator of G_2. We say $e : G_1 \times G_2 \to G_T$ is an admissible bilinear map, if it satisfies the following properties:

1. Bilinear. For all $u \in G_1, v \in G_2$, and for all $a, b \in \mathbb{Z}$, $e(u^a, v^b) = e(u, v)^{ab}$.
2. Non-degenerate. $e(g_1, g_2) \neq 1$ and is a generator of G_T.
3. Computable. There exists an efficient algorithm for computing $e(u, v)$ for any $u \in G_1, v \in G_2$.

We call the two groups (G_1, G_2) in the above a bilinear group pair. In the rest of this paper, we consider bilinear maps $e : G_1 \times G_2 \to G_T$ where G_1, G_2, and G_T are multiplicative groups of prime order p.

Strong Diffie-Hellman Assumption. The security of our DAA scheme is related to the hardness of the q-SDH problem introduced by Boneh and Boyen [6]. Let G_1 and G_2 be two cyclic groups of prime order p, respectively, generated by g_1 and g_2. The q-Strong Diffie-Hellman (q-SDH) problem in (G_1, G_2) is defined as follows: Given a $(q+3)$-tuple of elements $(g_1, g_1^{\gamma}, \ldots, g_1^{(\gamma^q)}, g_2, g_2^{\gamma})$ as input, output a pair $(g_1^{1/(\gamma+x)}, x)$ where $x \in \mathbb{Z}_p^*$. An algorithm $\mathcal{A}$ has advantage ϵ in solving q-SDH problem in (G_1, G_2) if $\Pr[\mathcal{A}(g_1, g_1^\gamma, \ldots, g_1^{(\gamma^q)}, g_2, g_2^\gamma) = (g_1^{1/(\gamma+x)}, x)] \geq \epsilon$ where the probability is over the random choice of γ and the random bits of $\mathcal{A}$.

Definition 3. We say that the (q, t, ϵ)-SDH assumption holds in (G_1, G_2) if no t-time algorithm has advantage at least ϵ in solving the q-SDH problem.

External Diffie-Hellman Assumption. Let G, generated by g, be a cyclic group of prime order p. The Decisional Diffie-Hellman (DDH) problem in G is defined as follows: Given a tuple of elements (g, g^a, g^b, g^c) as input, output 1 if $c = ab$ and 0 otherwise.

Definition 4. We say that the (t, ϵ)-DDH assumption holds in G if no t-time algorithm has advantage at least ϵ in solving the DDH problem in G.

Let (G_1, G_2) be a bilinear group pair. Our proposed OTAA scheme requires the DDH problem for G_1 to be hard. The DDH assumption on G_1 is often known as the External Diffie-Hellman (XDH) assumption.

5   The Proposed OTAA Scheme

In this section, we first present our construction of an OTAA scheme from bilinear maps. Our construction builds on top of the recent pairing-based EPID scheme [14] and Chen's DAA scheme [24], and Furukawa and Imai group signatures scheme [27].

5.1   Our OTAA Scheme

The OTAA scheme has the following algorithms Setup, Sign, Verify, and Open and one interactive protocol Join which are defined as follows.

Setup : The setup algorithm takes the following steps:
1. On input of 1^k, it chooses an asymmetric bilinear group pair (G_1, G_2) of prime order p and a pairing function $e : G_1 \times G_2 \to G_T$. Let g_1 and g_2 be the generators of G_1 and G_2, respectively.
2. It selects a collision resistant hash function $H : \{0, 1\}^* \to \mathbb{Z}_p$.
3. It chooses $h_1, h_2 \leftarrow G_1$, $\gamma \leftarrow \mathbb{Z}_p^*$, and computes $w := g_2^\gamma$.
4. It computes $T_1 = e(g_1, g_2)$, $T_2 = e(h_1, g_2)$, $T_3 = e(h_2, g_2)$, $T_4 = e(h_1, w)$, and $T_5 = e(h_2, w)$.
5. It outputs the group public key and private key

$$(\mathtt{gpk}, \mathtt{isk}) := ((G_1, G_2, G_T, e, p, g_1, g_2, h_1, h_2, w, H, T_1, T_2, T_3, T_4, T_5), \gamma)$$

Note that T_1, T_2, T_3, T_4, and T_5 are optional in gpk, as they can be computed from g_1, g_2, h_1, h_2, w.

Join : The join protocol is performed by a platform $\mathcal{P}$ and the issuer $\mathcal{I}$. $\mathcal{P}$ takes
gpk as input and $\mathcal{I}$ has gpk, isk, and dbase as input. The protocol has the
following steps:

1. $\mathcal{I}$ sends a nonce $n_I \in \{0,1\}^t$ as a challenge to $\mathcal{P}$.
2. $\mathcal{P}$ chooses at random $f \leftarrow \mathbb{Z}_p$ and computes $F := h_1^f$.
3. $\mathcal{P}$ sets sk $:= f$ and $\mathrm{id}_{\mathcal{P}} := F$ as its identity.
4. $\mathcal{P}$ chooses at random $r_f \leftarrow \mathbb{Z}_p$ and computes $R := h_1^{r_f}$.
5. $\mathcal{P}$ computes $c := H(\mathrm{gpk}\|F\|R\|n_I)$ and $s_f := r_f + c \cdot f \pmod{p}$.
6. $\mathcal{P}$ sets comm $:= (F, c, s_f)$ as a commitment of its sk, and sends comm to
   $\mathcal{I}$.
7. $\mathcal{I}$ computes $\hat{R} := h_1^{s_f} \cdot F^{-c}$ and verifies $s_f \in \mathbb{Z}_p$ and $c = H(\mathrm{gpk}\|F\|\hat{R}\|n_I)$.
8. $\mathcal{I}$ chooses at random $x, y \leftarrow \mathbb{Z}_p$ and computes $A := (g_1 \cdot F \cdot h_2^y)^{1/(x+\gamma)}$.
9. $\mathcal{I}$ sets tk $:= y$ and cre $:= (A, x, y)$ and sends cre to $\mathcal{P}$.
10. $\mathcal{I}$ updates its tracing database dbase by appending $(\mathrm{id}_{\mathcal{P}}, \mathrm{tk}) := (F, y)$.
11. $\mathcal{P}$ verifies $e(A, wg_2^x) = e(g_1 h_1^f h_2^y, g_2)$ and outputs $(\mathrm{sk}, \mathrm{cre}) := (f, (A, x, y))$.

As in many DAA schemes [9,10,13,24], the above join protocol needs to be
executed in a sequential manner, as comm is a proof of knowledge of the
discrete logarithm of the value F. To support concurrent join, we could use
verifiable encryption [21] of the f value or use the concurrent join technique
described in [28] with some loss of efficiency.

Sign : On input of gpk, sk $= f$, cre $= (A, x, y)$, a tracing option tr $\in \{0,1\}$, a
message $m \in \{0,1\}^*$, this signing algorithm takes the following steps:

1. If tr $= 0$, the algorithm outputs a non-traceable signature on m as
   follows:
   (a) It chooses $B \leftarrow G_1$ and computes $K := B^f$.
   (b) It chooses $a \leftarrow \mathbb{Z}_p$, computes $b := y + ax \pmod{p}$ and $T := A \cdot h_2^a$.
   (c) It randomly picks

   $$r_x \leftarrow \mathbb{Z}_p, \qquad r_f \leftarrow \mathbb{Z}_p, \qquad r_a \leftarrow \mathbb{Z}_p, \qquad r_b \leftarrow \mathbb{Z}_p.$$

   (d) It computes

   $$R_1 := B^{r_f},$$
   $$\begin{aligned}
   R_2 &:= e(T, g_2)^{-r_x} \cdot e(h_1, g_2)^{r_f} \cdot e(h_2, g_2)^{r_b} \cdot e(h_2, w)^{r_a} \\
   &= e(A, g_2)^{-r_x} \cdot e(h_2^a, g_2)^{-r_x} \cdot e(h_1, g_2)^{r_f} \cdot e(h_2, g_2)^{r_b} \cdot e(h_2, w)^{r_a} \\
   &= e(A, g_2)^{-r_x} \cdot T_2^{r_f} \cdot T_3^{r_b - ar_x} \cdot T_5^{r_a}.
   \end{aligned}$$

   (e) It then computes

   $$c := H(\mathrm{gpk}\|B\|K\|T\|R_1\|R_2\|m).$$

   (f) It computes in $\mathbb{Z}_p$

   $$s_x := r_x + cx, \qquad s := r_f + cf, \qquad s_a := r_a + ca, \qquad s_b := r_b + cb.$$

2. If $\mathbf{tr} = 1$, the algorithm outputs a traceable signature on m as follows:
   (a) It chooses $B \leftarrow G_1$ and computes $K := B^y$.
   (b) It chooses $a \leftarrow \mathbb{Z}_p$, computes $b := f + ax \pmod{p}$ and $T := A \cdot h_1^a$
   (c) It randomly picks

$$r_x \leftarrow \mathbb{Z}_p, \qquad r_y \leftarrow \mathbb{Z}_p, \qquad r_a \leftarrow \mathbb{Z}_p, \qquad r_b \leftarrow \mathbb{Z}_p.$$

   (d) It computes

$$R_1 := B^{r_y},$$
$$R_2 := e(T, g_2)^{-r_x} \cdot e(h_2, g_2)^{r_y} \cdot e(h_1, g_2)^{r_b} \cdot e(h_1, w)^{r_a}$$
$$= e(A, g_2)^{-r_x} \cdot e(h_1^a, g_2)^{-r_x} \cdot e(h_2, g_2)^{r_y} \cdot e(h_1, g_2)^{r_b} \cdot e(h_1, w)^{r_a}$$
$$= e(A, g_2)^{-r_x} \cdot T_3^{r_y} \cdot T_2^{r_b - ar_x} \cdot T_4^{r_a}.$$

   (e) It then computes

$$c := H(\mathbf{gpk} \| B \| K \| T \| R_1 \| R_2 \| m).$$

   (f) It computes in $\mathbb{Z}_p$

$$s_x := r_x + cx, \qquad s := r_y + cy, \qquad s_a := r_a + ca, \qquad s_b := r_b + cb.$$

3. It outputs $\sigma := (\mathbf{tr}, B, K, T, c, s_x, s, s_a, s_b)$.

Note that $e(A, g_2)$ in the computation of R_2 can be pre-computed and re-used. Also observe that the traceable and non-traceable signatures have the same size and format. The signature generations for both signature types have the same complexity as well.

Verify : On input of $\mathbf{gpk}$, a message m, a signature $\sigma = (\mathbf{tr}, B, K, T, c, s_x, s, s_a, s_b)$, a list of revoked secret keys $\mathbf{sRL}$, and a list of revoked tracing keys $\mathbf{tRL}$, the verifying algorithm has the following steps:

1. It verifies that $B, K, T \in G_1$ and $s_x, s, s_a, s_b \in \mathbb{Z}_p$.
2. It computes $R_1 := B^s \cdot K^{-c}$.
3. If $\mathbf{tr} = 0$, it computes

$$\hat{R}_2 := e(T, g_2)^{-s_x} \cdot e(h_1, g_2)^s \cdot e(h_2, g_2)^{s_b} \cdot e(h_2, w)^{s_a} \cdot (e(g_1, g_2)/e(T, w))^c$$
$$:= e(T, g_2^{-s_x} \cdot w^{-c}) \cdot T_1^c \cdot T_2^s \cdot T_3^{s_b} \cdot T_5^{s_a},$$

otherwise, it computes

$$\hat{R}_2 := e(T, g_2)^{-s_x} \cdot e(h_2, g_2)^s \cdot e(h_1, g_2)^{s_b} \cdot e(h_1, w)^{s_a} \cdot (e(g_1, g_2)/e(T, w))^c$$
$$:= e(T, g_2^{-s_x} \cdot w^{-c}) \cdot T_1^c \cdot T_3^s \cdot T_2^{s_b} \cdot T_4^{s_a}.$$

4. It verifies that
$$c \stackrel{?}{=} H(\mathbf{gpk} \| B \| K \| T \| \hat{R}_1 \| \hat{R}_2 \| m).$$

5. If any of the above steps fails, it quits and outputs invalid.
6. If $\mathbf{tr} = 0$, for each $f' \in \mathbf{sRL}$, if $K = B^{f'}$, it quits and outputs revoked,

7. If $\text{tr} = 1$, for each $y' \in \text{tRL}$, if $K = B^{y'}$, it quits and outputs `revoked`.
8. If none of the above steps fails, it outputs `valid`.

Open : On input of gpk, a message m, a signature $\sigma = (\text{tr}, B, K, T, c, s_x, s, s_a, s_b)$, a tracing database dbase, the open algorithm has the following steps:

1. If $\text{Verify}(\text{gpk}, m, \sigma, \emptyset, \emptyset) = \text{invalid}$, it quits and outputs `invalid`.
2. If $\text{tr} = 0$, it quites and outputs `untraceable`.
3. For each entry (id, tk) in dbase, it computes $K' = B^{\text{tk}}$. If $K = K'$, it quits and outputs (id, tk).
4. If none of the entry in dbase matches, it outputs `untraceable`.

The above OTAA scheme is secure under the OTAA definition in Section 3. It is correct, user-controlled-anonymous under the XDH assumption, and user-controlled-traceable under the q-SDH assumption. Due to the space limit, the security proof will be given in the full version of this paper.

5.2 Efficiency of Our Scheme

The signing key of the above scheme comprises three elements in $\mathbb{Z}_p$ and one element in G_1. The signature of the above scheme takes one boolean variable, three elements in G_1, and five elements in $\mathbb{Z}_p$. Let p be a 256-bit prime number. Using 256-bit Barreto-Naehrig curves [4], security is approximately 128-bit and is about the same as a standard 3072-bit RSA signature. Each element in G_1 is 257-bit. Thus the signing key is only 1025-bit and the signature is 2052-bit in the above scheme. Using 170-bit MNT curves with approximate 80-bit security, the signing key is 681-bit and the signature is 1364-bit.

The signature generation requires three exponentiations in G_1 and one multi-exponentiation in G_T. The signature verification algorithm requires one multi-exponentiation in G_1, G_2, and G_T, respectively, one pairing operation, and n exponentiations in G_1, where n is the size of the revocation list. The open algorithm includes one signature verification and m exponentiations in G_1, where m is the total number of platforms issued by the issuer.

6 Comparisons with Group Signature and DAA Schemes

As we mentioned earlier, our OTAA scheme becomes a group signature scheme if all the signatures are traceable. Note that the group signature scheme derived from our OTAA scheme does not have the non-frameability property, as the issuer has the tracing keys for all the platforms and can frame any platforms.

We now show that our OTAA scheme is more efficient than the existing group signature schemes [7,20,8,27] in the following table. The BS group signature scheme [8] has a slightly smaller signature size than our OTAA scheme, but is less inefficient. In particular, the revocation check in [8] requires two pairings per revocation item and is much inefficient than our scheme. The FI group signature scheme [27] is more efficient than BBS scheme [7] and CL scheme [20]. The FI scheme is still inefficient than our OTAA scheme. In addition, the FI scheme

Table 1. A comparison between our OTAA scheme and pairing-based group signature schemes and DAA schemes with 80-bit security level, where EXP denotes a exponentiation or a scaler multiplication operation and P denotes a pairing operation.

	sign	verify	signature size
Our OTAA scheme	7 EXP	8 EXP + 1 P	1364-bit
BS Group Signatures [8]	8 EXP + 2 P	9 EXP + 3 P	1192-bit
BBS Group Signatures [7]	14 EXP	17 EXP + 1 P	2057-bit
CL Group Signatures [20]	16 EXP	13 EXP + 5 P	5296-bit
FI Group Signatures [27]	11 EXP	12 EXP + 1 P	1711-bit
BCL DAA scheme [11]	6 EXP + 3 P	5 EXP + 5 P	3063-bit
CMS DAA scheme [26]	5 EXP + 1 P	4 EXP + 5 P	1355-bit
Chen DAA scheme [24]	7 EXP	8 EXP + 1 P	1363-bit
BL DAA scheme [15]	7 EXP + 1 P	8 EXP + 1 P	1363-bit

itself does not support any revocation mechanisms. Revocation could be added to the FI scheme, but with an additional cost.

Our OTAA scheme is efficient than many pairing-based DAA schemes [11,26,15]. It has almost the same complexity as Chen's DAA scheme [24]. Note that in DAA schemes, the sign algorithm is split between a TPM and a host. In the comparison below, we sum up all the computations of the TPM and host.

7   Conclusion and Future Work

In this paper, we have presented a new cryptographic primitive called Optionally Traceable Anonymous Attestation (OTAA). OTAA can be used in trusted computing, content protection, e-commerce, identity cards, and beyond. OTAA is more capable at revocation than DAA, with relatively minimal compromise of privacy to the issuer, e.g., when a platform creates traceable signatures. In most of the transactions, the platform can use non-traceable signatures to safeguard his privacy. We provided an efficient construction of OTAA from bilinear map. The security model and OTAA scheme developed in this paper is a merely first step. There is room for improvement in the following areas.

1. In many group signature schemes such as in [1,27], there is a feature called non-frameability, in which the issuer cannot frame a honest signer for creating a group signature. OTAA does not have this feature. In fact, our OTAA construction is frameable, as the issuer has the tracing keys for all the platforms and can forge a signature using any platform's tracing key. It may be interesting to formally define non-frameability in OTAA and give a corresponding construction.

2. There are features in DAA that can be added to OTAA, such as (1) the signer and verifier can negotiate whether the signature is linkable, and (2) the signer computation can be split between a weak TPM as the main signer and a host. Adding those features to the OTAA scheme is not difficult, but it is a challenge to build a simple security model that captures all the features.

Acknowledgement

We thank Liqun Chen for her helpful discussions and feedback. We also thank the anonymous reviewers for their useful comments.

References

1. Ateniese, G., Camenisch, J., Joye, M., Tsudik, G.: A practical and provably secure coalition-resistant group signature scheme. In: Bellare, M. (ed.) CRYPTO 2000. LNCS, vol. 1880, pp. 255–270. Springer, Heidelberg (2000)
2. Ateniese, G., Song, D.X., Tsudik, G.: Quasi-efficient revocation in group signatures. In: Blaze, M. (ed.) FC 2002. LNCS, vol. 2357, pp. 183–197. Springer, Heidelberg (2003)
3. Backes, M., Maffei, M., Unruh, D.: Zero-knowledge in the applied pi-calculus and automated verification of the direct anonymous attestation protocol. In: Proceedings of IEEE Symposium on Security and Privacy, pp. 202–215. IEEE Computer Society, Los Alamitos (2008)
4. Barreto, P.S.L.M., Naehrig, M.: Pairing-friendly elliptic curves of prime order. In: Preneel, B., Tavares, S. (eds.) SAC 2005. LNCS, vol. 3897, pp. 319–331. Springer, Heidelberg (2006)
5. Bellare, M., Shi, H., Zhang, C.: Foundations of group signatures: The case of dynamic groups. In: Menezes, A. (ed.) CT-RSA 2005. LNCS, vol. 3376, pp. 136–153. Springer, Heidelberg (2005)
6. Boneh, D., Boyen, X.: Short signatures without random oracles. In: Cachin, C., Camenisch, J.L. (eds.) EUROCRYPT 2004. LNCS, vol. 3027, pp. 56–73. Springer, Heidelberg (2004)
7. Boneh, D., Boyen, X., Shacham, H.: Short group signatures. In: Franklin, M. (ed.) CRYPTO 2004. LNCS, vol. 3152, pp. 41–55. Springer, Heidelberg (2004)
8. Boneh, D., Shacham, H.: Group signatures with verifier-local revocation. In: Proceedings of 11th ACM Conference on Computer and Communications Security, October 2004, pp. 168–177 (2004)
9. Brickell, E., Camenisch, J., Chen, L.: Direct anonymous attestation. In: Proceedings of the 11th ACM Conference on Computer and Communications Security, pp. 132–145. ACM Press, New York (2004)
10. Brickell, E., Chen, L., Li, J.: A new direct anonymous attestation scheme from bilinear maps. In: Lipp, P., Sadeghi, A.-R., Koch, K.-M. (eds.) Trust 2008. LNCS, vol. 4968, pp. 166–178. Springer, Heidelberg (2008)
11. Brickell, E., Chen, L., Li, J.: Simplified security notions of direct anonymous attestation and a concrete scheme from pairings. International Journal of Information Security 8(5), 315–330 (2009)
12. Brickell, E., Li, J.: Enhanced Privacy ID: A direct anonymous attestation scheme with enhanced revocation capabilities. In: Proceedings of the 6th ACM Workshop on Privacy in the Electronic Society, October 2007, pp. 21–30. ACM Press, New York (2007)
13. Brickell, E., Li, J.: Enhanced Privacy ID: A remote anonymous attestation scheme for hardware devices. Intel. Technology Journal: Advances in Internet Security 13(2) (2009)
14. Brickell, E., Li, J.: Enhanced Privacy ID from bilinear pairing. Cryptology ePrint Archive, Report 2009/095 (2009), http://eprint.iacr.org/

15. Brickell, E., Li, J.: A pairing-based DAA scheme further reducing TPM resources. In: Acquisti, A., Smith, S.W., Sadeghi, A.-R. (eds.) TRUST 2010. LNCS, vol. 6101, pp. 181–195. Springer, Heidelberg (2010)

16. Brickell, E.F., Gordon, D.M., McCurley, K.S., Wilson, D.B.: Fast exponentiation with precomputation. In: Rueppel, R.A. (ed.) EUROCRYPT 1992. LNCS, vol. 658, pp. 200–207. Springer, Heidelberg (1993)

17. Camenisch, J., Groth, J.: Group signatures: Better efficiency and new theoretical aspects. In: Blundo, C., Cimato, S. (eds.) SCN 2004. LNCS, vol. 3352, pp. 120–133. Springer, Heidelberg (2005)

18. Camenisch, J., Kohlweiss, M., Soriente, C.: An accumulator based on bilinear maps and efficient revocation for anonymous credentials. In: Jarecki, S., Tsudik, G. (eds.) PKC 2009. LNCS, vol. 5443, pp. 481–500. Springer, Heidelberg (2009)

19. Camenisch, J., Lysyanskaya, A.: Dynamic accumulators and application to efficient revocation of anonymous credentials. In: Yung, M. (ed.) CRYPTO 2002. LNCS, vol. 2442, pp. 61–76. Springer, Heidelberg (2002)

20. Camenisch, J., Lysyanskaya, A.: Signature schemes and anonymous credentials from bilinear maps. In: Franklin, M. (ed.) CRYPTO 2004. LNCS, vol. 3152, pp. 56–72. Springer, Heidelberg (2004)

21. Camenisch, J., Shoup, V.: Practical verifiable encryption and decryption of discrete logarithms. In: Boneh, D. (ed.) CRYPTO 2003. LNCS, vol. 2729, pp. 126–144. Springer, Heidelberg (2003)

22. Camenisch, J., Stadler, M.: Efficient group signature schemes for large groups. In: Kaliski Jr., B.S. (ed.) CRYPTO 1997. LNCS, vol. 1294, pp. 410–424. Springer, Heidelberg (1997)

23. Chaum, D., van Heyst, E.: Group signatures. In: Davies, D.W. (ed.) EUROCRYPT 1991. LNCS, vol. 547, pp. 257–265. Springer, Heidelberg (1991)

24. Chen, L.: A DAA scheme requiring less TPM resources. In: Proceedings of the 5th China International Conference on Information Security and Cryptology, LNCS. Springer, Heidelberg (2009)

25. Chen, L., Morrissey, P., Smart, N.P.: Pairings in trusted computing. In: Galbraith, S.D., Paterson, K.G. (eds.) Pairing 2008. LNCS, vol. 5209, pp. 1–17. Springer, Heidelberg (2008)

26. Chen, L., Morrissey, P., Smart, N.P.: DAA: Fixing the pairing based protocols. Cryptology ePrint Archive, Report 2009/198 (2009), http://eprint.iacr.org/

27. Furukawa, J., Imai, H.: An efficient group signature scheme from bilinear maps. IEICE Transactions 89-A(5), 1328–1338 (2006)

28. Kiayias, A., Yung, M.: Group signatures with efficient concurrent join. In: Cramer, R. (ed.) EUROCRYPT 2005. LNCS, vol. 3494, pp. 198–214. Springer, Heidelberg (2005)

29. Leung, A., Mitchell, C.J.: Ninja: Non identity based, privacy preserving authentication for ubiquitous environments. In: Krumm, J., Abowd, G.D., Seneviratne, A., Strang, T. (eds.) UbiComp 2007. LNCS, vol. 4717, pp. 73–90. Springer, Heidelberg (2007)

30. Trusted Computing Group. TCG TPM specification 1.2 (2003), http://www.trustedcomputinggroup.org

31. Trusted Computing Group website, http://www.trustedcomputinggroup.org

32. Tsang, P.P., Au, M.H., Kapadia, A., Smith, S.W.: Blacklistable anonymous credentials: Blocking misbehaving users without TTPs. In: ACM Conference on Computer and Communications Security, pp. 72–81. ACM Press, New York (2007)

Introducing the Trusted Virtual Environment Module: A New Mechanism for Rooting Trust in Cloud Computing

F. John Krautheim[*], Dhananjay S. Phatak, and Alan T. Sherman[*]

Cyber Defense Lab, Dept. of CSEE
University of Maryland, Baltimore County (UMBC)
Baltimore, MD, USA 21250
{john.krautheim,phatak,sherman}@umbc.edu

Abstract. We introduce a new mechanism for rooting trust in a cloud computing environment called the *Trusted Virtual Environment Module (TVEM)*. The TVEM helps solve the core security challenge of cloud computing by enabling parties to establish trust relationships where an information owner creates and runs a virtual environment on a platform owned by a separate service provider. The TVEM is a software appliance that provides enhanced features for cloud virtual environments over existing Trusted Platform Module virtualization techniques, which includes an improved application program interface, cryptographic algorithm flexibility, and a configurable modular architecture. We define a unique Trusted Environment Key that combines trust from the information owner and the service provider to create a dual root of trust for the TVEM that is distinct for every virtual environment and separate from the platform's trust. This paper presents the requirements, design, and architecture of our approach.

Keywords: cloud computing, trust, security, virtualization, TPM.

1 Introduction

Cloud computing is changing the landscape of corporate computing. As companies turn to cloud services to reduce costs compared to their internally managed *Information Technology (IT)* systems, a fundamental shift is occurring in the way IT and computing services are delivered and purchased [1]. With this shift towards *utility computing* [2], new trust relationships arise that force the parties to reconsider the way we handle and manage information in the cloud.

Krautheim, *et al.* [3] define the *Private Virtual Infrastructure (PVI)* cloud trust model describing the unique trust relationships that occur in *Infrastructure as a Service (IaaS)* [4] cloud computing environments. This paper applies the PVI cloud trust model to IaaS clouds with our new *Trusted Virtual Environment Module (TVEM)* and *Virtual Trust Network (VTN)*.

---
[*] Krautheim and Sherman are supported in part by the Department of Defense under grants H98230-08-1-0334 and H98230-09-1-0404.

A. Acquisti, S.W. Smith, and A.-R. Sadeghi (Eds.): TRUST 2010, LNCS 6101, pp. 211–227, 2010.
© Springer-Verlag Berlin Heidelberg 2010

In IaaS cloud computing, an *information owner*, or client, rents virtual computing resources in the form of a *Virtual Machine (VM)* on a host platform operated by a second party *service provider*. The information owner wishes to protect private and sensitive data that are processed in the virtual environment on the rented VM. The *virtual environment* is the entity that is controlled by the information owner and consists of *all* software components, from the *Operating System (OS)* to the applications, that execute on the VM. To assure the information is protected, the client needs to verify the trustworthiness of the host platform and virtual environment. The TVEM and VTN provide the mechanisms to verify the host platform and virtual environment within an IaaS cloud and report the results back to an information owner. No current capability exists to perform these functions.

A current means for establishing trust in computing platforms is the *Trusted Platform Module (TPM)*, a core component of the *root of trust* for the platform. A root of trust is a component of a computing platform that is implicitly trusted to provide a specified set of controlled functions to measure and pass control to other platform components [5]. TPMs are designed to support a single OS on a single platform and typically do not scale well when virtualization is introduced to the platform [6]. Support for multiple virtual environments that simultaneously access TPM resources is required. A *Virtual TPM (VTPM)* that replicates the physical resources of a TPM in software is one method of virtualizing the TPM functions for sharing among multiple virtual environments.

Krautheim's *Locater Bot (LoBot)* [3, 7] uses the VTPM to root trust for a virtual environment in a PVI; however, the VTPM implementation has several issues that make it problematic to use as a root of trust for cloud virtual environments. Three major shortcomings of the VTPM are: the VTPM's trust is rooted to the physical platform on which it is operating, which is typically not owned by the information owner; a VTPM must follow the TPM specification [8], which includes extraneous functionality that is not useful for virtual environments; and a VTPM has non-persistent storage, meaning that it loses all keys, settings, and non-volatile storage upon termination. The TVEM solves these problems through application of the PVI cloud trust model, providing a modular and extensible architecture that allows algorithm and function flexibility, and providing persistent storage for keys, non-volatile memory and settings.

The core challenge in cloud computing that TVEM solves is establishing trust that is distinct for the virtual environment and separate from the hosting platform. *Virtual environment trust* is defined as trust in the virtual environment that is a combination of trust in the service provider's platform and trust from the information owner's domain. Virtual environment trust is necessary to convey ownership and protect information in the cloud. To implement this virtual environment trust, a *Trusted Environment Key (TEK)* is defined and used as the *Endorsement Key (EK)* for the TVEM. The TEK, like the EK, is a unique value used as the *Root of Trust for Reporting (RTR)* to identify the TVEM and attest the virtual environment. The TEK is generated by the virtual environment owner and secured with the service provider's platform storage key creating a *compound trust* distinct and separate from the platform.

The TVEM is a software appliance that is implemented as a helper, or stub, VM. The TVEM is protected by hardware enforced memory and process isolation via

Intel's *Virtualization Technology for Directed I/O (VT-d)* [9] and *Trusted eXecution Technology (TXT)* [10]. The TVEM provides attestation support and trusted storage for the virtual environment similar to functionality provided by VTPM; however, the TVEM does not have to conform to the TPM specification enabling the TVEM to be extensible through functional and cryptographic algorithm flexibility in a configurable modular architecture. The TVEM has multiple interfaces, including an *Application Program Interface (API)*, which moves the *Trusted Software Stack (TSS)* into the TVEM eliminating the burden on the virtual environment to implement the TSS. The API provides for hardened and lightweight environments and reduces the opportunities of implementation errors. These capabilities allow system designers to customize the TVEM and virtual environment to meet their information confidentiality and integrity requirements.

TVEMs are not stand alone devices; they are part of a system to implement trust in cloud computing. The system includes: the TVEM; a TVEM manager in the host hypervisor for host platform TPM access and TVEM provisioning; a VTN control plane that provides system management and support for persistent storage; and a *TVEM Factory (TF)* to manufacture TVEMs, manage keys, and provision TVEMs securely on host platforms.

2 Motivation

Utility cloud computing can provide many benefits to companies wishing to reduce their IT expenses and overhead. Security of information in the cloud and the trustworthiness of the cloud environment is a major concern with IaaS clouds. We describe an example IaaS cloud computing application: a cloud web server. This application benefits from using the TVEM and VTN to manage trust.

A virtual web server in the cloud has many benefits over maintaining a web server locally, a significant advantage being increased availability. The cloud's always-on presence and location flexibility enhance the availability of a web server by providing scalability, migratability, and redundancy. If a server is overwhelmed with requests, it can be migrated to a platform that has increased capacity, or new instances of the server can be instantiated to handle the increased load. Migration and failure restart can be used if host hardware fails or Internet service becomes unavailable.

A server certificate is a critical piece of data on the web server that authenticates its owner. If a company wants to prove that it is the owner of web server, it would obtain an *Extended Validation (EV)* certificate and a *Secure Socket Layer (SSL)* certificate from a certificate authority. The EV and SSL certificates have a public and private key portion that a guest may use to verify the server owner and establish an encrypted SSL session with a server. In a cloud environment, the identity of the web server owner and the service provider needs to be differentiated, which is accomplished via the certificates. The certificates should be accessible only by the web server owner and must be protected from the service provider and other users of the cloud service. If the private portions of the keys are disclosed, anyone who gains access to the private keys can purport to be a valid web server for the information owner. If the private key is stored on a public cloud service, anyone with access to the system could possibly access the key; therefore, the owner of the certificate needs to keep the private key protected from compromise by the service provider, other cloud users, and attackers on the Internet. TVEM protects SSL certificates on a cloud web server by encrypting the certificate such that is accessible only by the TVEM and decrypted inside the host platform's TPM ensuring the plaintext key cannot be observed.

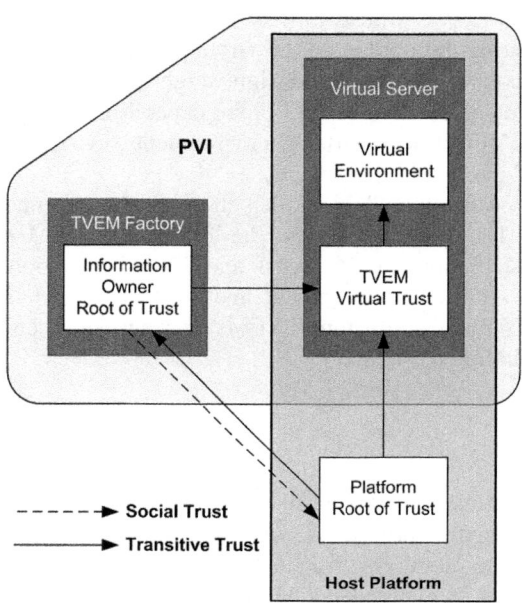

Fig. 1. Trust relationships in a cloud computing environment consist of inferred trust (social trust) and inherited trust (technical trust). The TVEM's virtual trust is a combination of the information owner's trust and host platform trust.

3   Trust in the Cloud

Trust in cloud computing is more complex than in a traditional IT scenario where the information owner owns his own computers. Fig. 1 shows the trust relationships in an IasS cloud as defined by the PVI cloud trust model. The trust chain combines trust from the information owner's domain (or PVI) and trust from the service provider's platform into the virtual environment trust. The information owner has an inferred trust in the platform from a social trust relationship with the service providers. The information owner root of trust is established in the TF and is the core root of trust for the entire PVI. The TF needs to inherit trust from the host platform root of trust measurements to ensure that the PVI is being implemented on a trustworthy platform. The PVI combines the inherited platform trust and information owner trust in a TEK and places it in the TVEM. The TVEM trust is provisioned on the host platform such that it is bound to the platform root of trust, creating the dual rooted virtual environment trust. If either root of trust is revoked, the virtual environment trust is invalidated.

3.1 Social Trust

Social trust is a trust that arises between two entities based upon social relationships. Social trust is established based upon reputations, previous interactions, and contractual obligations. There are two critical social trust relationships that must be established in cloud computing from the perspective of the information owner: service provider trust and cloud user trust. Social trust cannot be measured, but is important to build confidence that an entity is holding up its end of a contract.

Service provider trust lies in the relationship between customer and vendor. If the provider has a good reputation, then there is sufficient reason for customers to trust the provider. A vendor that has questionable service or ethics would not be as trustworthy as a vendor with excellent service and ethics.

Cloud user trust is the amount of trust the user places in the services delivered via the cloud. The user has to be confident that the system is going to protect their data, transactions, and privacy. The user's trust is a social trust in the information owner. The information owner must assure that the services being provided meet the user's expectations.

3.2 Technical Trust

In a cloud computing environment, multiple entities must trust the cloud services: the user of the cloud service or information owner, the provider of the cloud service, and third parties. PVI defined a new paradigm of cloud computing that separates the security responsibility between the service provider and information owner and accounted for third parties. A third party is an outside entity that is providing service to or receiving services from either the user or service provider.

The cloud trust model is based on *transitive trust*, which is the notion that if entity A trusts entity B and entity B trusts entity C, then entity A trusts entity C. This property allows a chain of trust to be built from a single root of trust.

Information owner trust is the foundation of trust that the information owner places in the PVI. Information owner trust is implemented by the TF. Since the information owner has physical control of the TF, the configuration of the TF is a known quantity and can be used as the root of trust for the PVI. As long as the information owner maintains trust in the TF, trust can be established in the PVI and used to build trust chains with cloud host platforms.

Host platform trust lies in the hardware trust of the platform and is measurable. Trustworthiness starts with *Core Root of Trust for Measurement (CRTM)* of the platform. The CRTM is the core set of instructions run at boot or reset that are responsible for establishing trust in the system by measuring the BIOS, and then passing control to the measured BIOS and rest of the *Trusted Computing Base (TCB)* of the platform. The TCB consists of all measured components that provide the foundation of trust in the platform. Platform trustworthiness is determined by an outside entity via attestation from the TPM, which is the *Root of Trust for Reporting (RTR)* on the hosting platform. The TPM also serves as the *Root of Trust of Storage (RTS)* of the platform that is implicitly trusted to store information securely. The attestation from the TPM provides evidence of the state of the platform, from which other entities can decide whether to trust the platform.

Cloud virtual environment trust is the amount of trust placed in the virtual environments created in the cloud. Virtual environment trust is measureable, but there are complications in a cloud environment where the information owner's requirements are different than the platform owner's.

4   Related Work

There are many issues that must be solved to virtualize a TPM. The limited resources of the TPM must be either shared or replicated for each virtualized TPM. Specifically, resources that cannot be shared on the TPM are the EK, *Platform Configuration Registers (PCRs)*, and non-volatile storage. These resources must be replicated by every VTPM implementation.

A common approach to virtualizing the TPM has been to emulate the TPM in software and provide an instance for each virtual environment. The VTPM can be bound to a physical TPM for additional security. Berger, *et al.,* [11] took this approach for their vTPM implementation along with an additional approach of using an IBM 4758 Cryptographic Coprocessor to implement the vTPMs. Scarlata [6] followed with a framework for TPM virtualization, which described a VTPM framework for emulating TPMs in software.

England [12] took a different approach to TPM virtualization with paravirtualized TPM sharing. Paravirtualization is a technique used by the Xen hypervisor [13] to present a software interface to the VM that is similar to the underlying hardware and requires the OS to be modified. This method uses the hypervisor to mediate access to a single hardware TPM. The hypervisor shadows the PCRs for each virtual environment thus overcoming the PCR limitation. This design reduces the ability for migration since the virtualization is done in the hypervisor and uses physical TPM resources that are not transferrable to other platforms.

Another unique approach is property-based TPM virtualization by Sadeghi [14]. This technique uses a different methodology to measure the platform's state and generate keys. Properties are measured for reporting the state of the platform, which are less susceptible to changes in software configuration updates and patches, and makes migration easier.

The Berlios TPM emulator [15] is a form of TPM virtualization, providing a software emulation of a hardware TPM. The TPM emulator can provide TPM services to virtual environments, but does not have any binding to the hardware, limiting its ability for operational use. Consequently, the Berlios TPM emulator is useful for development purposes only.

5   Design Considerations

We explain our design considerations for the TVEM in this section. We considered multiple approaches to implementing a trust module for virtual environments and realized the best way to ensure that each virtual environment has a trust module is for the module to be implemented in software.

By implementing the TVEM in software, we do not have cost, physical, or resource restrictions. The TVEM design is bound by memory and computation restrictions, which are much less restrictive than physical restrictions. On a typical host platform, we can provide multiple fully functional, uncompromised TVEMs for many virtual machines at the same time.

There are several advantages to implementing a trust module in software versus hardware. A software platform can be changed to accommodate vulnerabilities that are discovered after release (*e.g.*, SHA1 collision attacks [16]). A software module can also support different algorithms for different applications and locations, which is important in cloud environments. Export controls on cryptographic algorithms may dictate that a certain algorithm may not be used in certain countries. With the worldwide presence of the cloud, algorithm flexibility is essential. A cloud environment in a restricted country will need an algorithm allowed to be exported, while a stronger algorithm may be used on a system in another country where more security is permitted. An advantage to a modular software design of the TVEM is flexibility to use algorithms that are compatible with the current TPM specification or use new algorithms for future applications and enhanced security. This flexibility allows the TVEM to be used in applications where features of TPM.Next are required, but the hardware does not support TPM.Next.

5.1   Threat Model

The TVEM must protect data and operations from attack. Since the TVEM will be implemented in software, there are multiple attack vectors. Potentially any code running on the host platform could attack the TVEM. We assume VT-d and TXT hardware isolation are in place, which protects the module from attack by entities with access to the platform. The entities that have access to the platform include the following: the service provider, who has root access to the platform; other cloud users on the same system or within the same cloud environment; and outside attackers that access the system via the Internet.

A malicious program may gain access to private data, including keys, inside of the TVEM. The malicious program can then modify and substitute data, to include replacing keys, modifying hashes, and state information. The code of the TVEM could be modified by replacing strong cryptographic algorithms with weaker ones. An attacker could also reduce the entropy of the *random number generator (RNG)* thus reducing the effectiveness of the keys. The state could also be modified to a known or predetermined state to weaken cryptographic results.

The TVEM's main defense against attacks is robust isolation and state verification. Features of the trusted platform can be used to protect against many attacks including: software modification, malicious code, key exposure and modification, and VM isolation and containment attacks, without detection.

The TVEM cannot defend against hardware attacks since it is a software module. A sophisticated attacker with control over hardware would be able to circumvent the TVEMs security, gain access to protected information in the TVEM, and modify state and/or instructions inside the TVEM to alter outcomes of the TVEM's operations.

5.2   Deployment Model

The deployment model for the TVEM is to build and maintain TVEMs on the TF in a secure location that is under the information owner's full physical control. The TF should be isolated and physically separated from the service provider's facility to ensure that it cannot be compromised.

Fully self contained TVEMs images are configured and built in the TF. The TVEM image is provisioned on the service provider's platform through the secure provisioning protocol described in [3] that ensures the TVEM is loaded on the correct host without modification and launched securely. The protocol ensures that the code launched was exactly the code configured by the TF so that the TVEM will operate as intended by its owner.

The service provider needs to accommodate the deployment of TVEMs by providing a TVEM Manager that is accessible by the customer for interfacing with the host TPM. The TPM access can be provided by delegating the customer certain privileged operations to configure the TVEM and interface with the TPM.

6   TVEM System Architecture

The TVEM is a software trust module for providing trust services to a VM or virtual environment in an IaaS cloud computing environment. The TVEM is the protection module and root of trust for a virtual environment that is in a remote location and the virtual environment has the ability to migrate to other platforms; therefore, it is not possible to implement a TVEM in hardware. Thus, a software implementation is the only solution for the TVEM.

Because the TVEM is a cryptographic module and data confidentiality is of utmost importance; we chose for the TVEM to be a self-contained virtual appliance that is implemented in a helper VM or stub domain.

Fig. 2 shows the configuration of a *Host Platform (HP)* with multiple virtual environments that require a TVEM. The virtual environment may be an entire virtualized OS that supports many applications or a special purpose virtual environment that performs a single application. The TVEM lies between the hypervisor and its associated VM. The hypervisor must be aware of TVEMs and provide support via a TVEM manager. The TVEM manager provides mediation for TPM services from each TVEM and other processes that require TPM services. The host platform must provide the TVEM manager and allow access for TVEMs.

The host platform's TPM is used as the RTS to secure the TVEM's private information on the HP. A transitive trust chain is built from the TPM through the hypervisor and TVEM manager to the TVEM ensuring trust in the TVEM is rooted in the hardware trust of the platform.

To ensure that data within the TVEM remains private, several security mechanisms need to be in place on the host platform. An isolating hypervisor such as sHype [17] can be used along with Intel VT-d and TXT to provide additional protection through hardware isolation.

6.1   TVEM Manager

The TVEM manager is the hub for the VTN on the host platform. The TVEM manager is responsible for routing VTN communications between the TF and VTEMs and for arbitrating all access between TVEMs on the platform and the host TPM. The TF communicates with host platforms through the TVEM Managers.

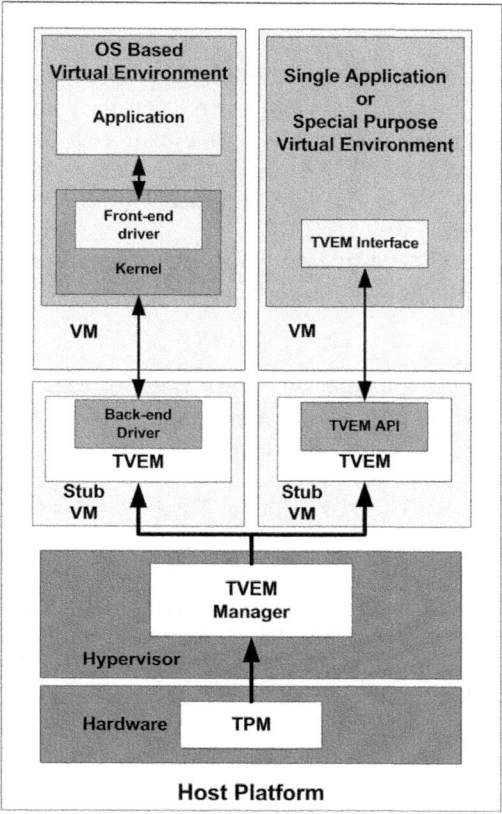

Fig. 2. The host platform has a single TPM, hypervisor, and TVEM manager supporting multiple virtual environments each in its own tightly coupled TVEM

Each host must have a TVEM manager that provides an interface to the host TPM. The TVEM manager must be placed in the hypervisor on the host platform so that it may have access to the host TPM and provide provisioning functions required to support TVEMs. Host TPM access is required for reading the platform PCRs and SRK so that TVEMs may be bound to the host TPM.

Importantly, the TVEM manager is part of the host platform, it is owned by the service provider and is not part of the information owner's domain (see Fig. 2); therefore, the TVEM manager must be a trusted component and part of the measured configuration on the host platform.

A TVEM manager on a host platform may support multiple VTNs from the same information owner or VTNs from other information owners simultaneously. The TVEM manager must be able to isolate communication from multiple VTNs and allow access only to TVEMs associated with the proper VTN.

6.2   Trusted Environment Key

The *Trusted Environment Key (TEK)* is critical in providing security and trust for the TVEM. It prevents cloning of the TVEM and protects the contents of the TVEM from the platform owner and other processes on the platform. The TEK is a unique key generated for a TVEM. The TEK is the TVEM's endorsement key and serves the same purpose as a TPM's EK. The TEK is generated from the VTN root certificate in the *TVEM Factory (TF)*.

The TF generates a VTN certificate, which is the parent for the all TVEM TEKs in a VTN. The VTN certificate is defined as:

$$VTN_{TF} = SRK_{TF}\{VTN\}$$

The TF's TPM generates a unique VTN certificate for each VTN protecting it with the TPM's SRK. The VTN key is a *Migratable Storage Key (MSK)* that can be transferred to other TPMs. The TEK is then generated as a child of the VTN key and is thus a MSK as well. Both keys are transferred to the *Host Platform's (HP)* through the key migration process. The TEK is defined as:

$$TEK_{HP} = MSK_{HP}\{VTN_{TF}\{TEK\}\}$$

The TF migrates the TEK and VTN key to the HP binding the TEK and VTN to the HP's SRK. The TEK is stored in the TVEM, which is a protected partition on the HP, thus it can be unencrypted only by the TVEM using the HP's TPM. The TEK will be protected in the TVEM and exposed on the HP only when requested by the TVEM for necessary operations.

The TEK is effectively "dual rooted" in both the host platform SRK and VTN root. This means that the TVEM cannot be cloned by copying its contents to another machine because the TEK is locked by the host's TPM. The TF maintains the VTN key and TEK root certificates and can revoke the VTN key or TEK at any time effectively removing privileges from TVEMs on rogue hosts.

TVEM migration is achieved by performing a TEK key migration from the current host platform to the new target platform. The TVEM migration is not direct to the target platform; it must go through the TF and verify that the target environment has the same level or greater trustworthiness than does the current host. Once the trustworthiness is determined, the TEK can be migrated to the new host by rewrapping the TEK with the new host's SRK. The TVEM and associated virtual machine can then be migrated to the new host without losing any information sealed by the TVEM.

6.3   Key Hierarchy and Management

The highest level key in a VTN is the master VTN key. All TEKs in the VTN are rooted and secured with the master VTN key. A master VTN key and certificate is generated for each VTN that the factory is responsible for managing. The VTN key is protected and stored with the TF platform's physical TPM SRK. The VTN root certificate along with the host platform SRK are used to generate all TEKs in the VTN.

The TF becomes the root authority for all VTNs under it auspices. TVEMs can be verified by checking their TEK certificates with the TF VTN authority. Since the TF is the root authority, it must maintain a key list of valid and revoked keys for each VTN. Once the VTN is deactivated, the VTN key is destroyed and all keys for that VTN must be revoked. A record of the revoked TEK should be kept to ensure that it will never be used again.

7   TVEM Design

The TVEM design is a set of functions grouped into five categories: legacy TPM functions, TVEM specific functions, storage functions, virtual environment interface, and user interface. Fig. 3 shows a block diagram of the high-level TVEM functions.

7.1   Legacy TPM Functions

The TVEM implements the following TPM functions per the TPM specification [8]: PCRs (as shadow registers), AIK, SRK, public key engine, secure hash, monotonic counter, and RNG.

The PCRs from the TPM are shadowed so that the virtual environment has the ability to read the configuration of the host platform. The virtual environment cannot modify the PCRs because it does not own the TPM. This is an important distinction for cloud computing environments. PCRs are written and modified by the hypervisor and host OS when virtual environments are launched. The configuration of the virtual environment is maintained separately in the *Virtual Environment Configuration Registers (VECRs)*.

The RNG is an important construct for the virtual environment. Since virtual environments have limited ability to generate entropy, an external source for entropy is required. However, the TVEM itself is a virtual environment; therefore, it must also use an external source for entropy. The RNG for the TVEM needs to use the RNG on the host platform TPM to obtain the entropy required to generate encryption keys and nonces. The TPM's hardware based RNG generates sufficient entropy which the TVEM can use for the virtual environment. The latest Linux kernels (2.6.29 and above) support the TPM RNG, which can interface to a TVEM RNG in a VM.

The TPM hash function is implemented in the TVEM as a software module. Since the SHA-1 hash functions will be phased out in 2010 [18], another hash algorithm such as SHA-256 can be easily substituted.

The *Attestation Identity Key (AIK)* and proof is used to provide evidence that an entity is a valid TPM. The AIK is generated in conjunction with a trusted third party privacy authority in a manner that verifying the AIK established that the TPM is valid without revealing which specific TPM is validated. The AIK process can easily be converted to provide proof of a valid TVEM by simply adding the VTN factory's root certificate to the privacy authority's list.

There are also several TPM functions which may not be required at all. These include physical presence, physical maintenance commands (*e.g.*, field upgrade and set redirection) and other functions that are not needed for a software implementation.

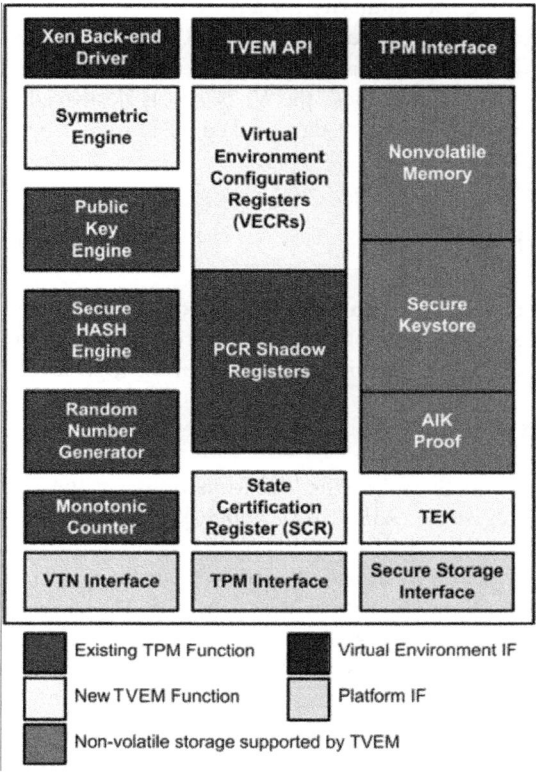

Fig. 3. The TVEM functional block diagram shows legacy TPM functions supported, the new TVEM functions, non-volatile storage, and host and platform interfaces

7.2 New TVEM Functions

Several new TVEM functions have been created to enhance the capability of the TVEM for virtual environments. These new functions include VECRs, the TEK, the *State Certification Register (SCR)*, and a symmetric encryption engine.

VECRs are equivalent to PCRs, and store configuration information of the virtual environment. There are 28 256 bit VECRs to support SHA-1; however, the VECRs can be configured up to 512 bits to support SHA-256. The VECRs are used for the virtual environment exactly as the PCR's for the physical platform. When a virtual environment is configured, the VECRs store configuration information about the virtual environment. The PCRs from the TPM are used; however, they are shadowed and only used for the purpose of determining the configuration of the host platform. The two sets of registers provide the ability to obtain configuration information about the platform and maintain a fine-grain detail about the configuration of the virtual environment. This enhanced view of both environments gives the virtual environment owner the ability to understand the security posture of the cloud.

The TEK is the endorsement key for the TVEM. The TEK functions exactly as the EK on a TPM, providing the master key for all TVEM functions and rooting all other keys. The TEK's dual trust root is essential to establishing trust in a virtual environment on a machine that is not owned by the information owner. Since the key is rooted both in the VTN and host platform, the key can be revoked by a change in configuration on either side thus invalidating the trust in the virtual environment.

A new register called the state certification register is used to verify that the state of the TVEM has not been modified. This feature will be described in a future paper that provides details on state medication and rollback prevention.

Another new feature of the TVEM compared to the VTPM is the addition of a symmetric data encryption engine. Cost is not a limiting factor and symmetric engines are very efficient in software; therefore, we can add an encryption engine and offload encryption tasks for small virtual environments. Providing an encryption engine allows smaller, hardened environments instead of bloated OSes. Additionally, export controls are not a major concern with a TVEM. If a TVEM is to be exported outside of its originating country, the encryption engine can be easily removed or swapped with an engine without export controls. Finally, the encryption engine can provide enhanced security by ensuring that correct and verified implementations are used.

7.3 Non-volatile Storage

To support operation of the TVEM across multiple sessions and migration, the information placed in the non-volatile storage of the TVEM must be persistent. To make the non-volatile memory persistent, the contents of the memory are backed up to the TF where they are stored until the TF is terminated. Each TVEM's non-volatile memory image must be maintained until the TVEM is terminated.

To maintain the image of each TVEM's non-volatile memory, every time the non-volatile memory in the TVEM is updated the TF updates its backup image. The update is done by sending a message with the contents to the TF over the host platform secure storage interface. When the TF receives the message, it updates its backup image for the specified TVM instance accordingly.

An additional benefit of keeping the backup image of the non-volatile memory is the ability to verify the local TVEM image. The TVEM may send the full contents of the TF at any point to request a verification of the content. The TF can compare the sent image with its backup image and verify that both are identical. If the content of the TVEM's memory were tampered, the comparison would be different.

7.4 Virtual Environment Interfaces

One of the biggest differences between a VTPM and a TVEM is the virtual environment interfaces. TVEM virtual environment interfaces on the VM side of the TVEM are designed to accommodate the many types of virtual environments that may need TVEM services. Not all environments will have a full TSS or cryptographic API; therefore, an API on the TVEM provides the cryptographic services for the virtual environment.

The TVEM has three unique interfaces to the virtual environment as shown in Fig. 3: a Xen back-end driver, a TVEM API, and a standard TPM interface for compatibility with TPM 1.2. Each virtual environment that requires a TVEM service has the option to choose the interface it will use. A virtual environment may use multiple interfaces if desired. For example, the OS may use the Xen driver in the kernel and an application may use the TVEM API.

7.5 TPM Interface

The TPM interface will work with any program written to support a TPM 1.2. This interface provides backward compatibility for the TVEM where applications are expecting a TPM or VTPM. The TVEM can appear to be a valid TPM and operate as a TPM replacement.

Note that when accessing a TVEM as a TPM, the VECRs are accessed instead of the PCRs. The VECRs represent the state of the virtual environment, which is the context that the guest is operating.

TVEM API. The TVEM API provides applications a direct interface to the TVEM through a set of function calls. This interface allows OSes and applications without a full TSS or cryptographic library the ability to use the TVEM easily.

The API provides access to extended TVEM functions including the symmetric encryption engine and PCR shadow registers. The interface can also be extended to connect with additional cryptographic hardware such as smartcards and biometrics as well.

Xen Backend Driver. The Xen back-end driver will interface directly to a Xen kernel front-end driver [19]. This capability enables any virtual environment running on a Xen hypervisor the ability to interface to TVEM with the simple addition of the front-end driver to the virtual environment. The Xen interface is an extension of the API and provides a seamless interface for the virtual environment.

7.6 Host Platform Interfaces

The host platform interfaces are to the host platform side of the TVEM. The TVEM interfaces to the host platform differently than a VTPM. The TVEM uses the TPM and host platform as a service to provide functions required for secure operation. The TVEM uses the host interfaces for host TPM services, communicating with the VTN, and for storing non-volatile information.

Host TPM Interface. The TVEM communicates with the host TPM via the TVEM manager. The TVEM manager is responsible for arbitrating access to the TPM. All requests that require host TPM access use this interface including the reading of the TPM's PCRs, storing and retrieving keys to the TPM, and accessing the RNG.

VTN Interface. The VTN interface is used to manage keys and communicate with the TF over the encrypted VTN.

Secure Storage Interface. The secure storage interface is a VTN interface used by the TVEM to store non-volatile memory securely. The secure storage interface uses the VTN to send all non-volatile writes to the TF for backup storage. On provisioning of a TVEM, the secure storage interface is used to populate the non-volatile storage areas on the TVEM from the backup image. The secure storage interface is also used to verify the contents of the non-volatile memory with the backup on the TF.

8 Discussion

The TVEM provides many advantages over a VTPM in a cloud computing environment. The management of TVEM from the TVEM factory provides the ability to control and monitor TVEMs in a VTN and provides enhanced situational awareness to the information owner. The TVEM also provides system designers and information owners support for everything from simple single purpose applications to full OSes. The virtual environment specific functions enable ease of use, and the modular design enables flexibility for deployment. TVEMs provide strong cryptographic support for securing a virtual environment on a cloud host platform. The unique dual rooted key structure provides flexibility to maintain trust in the virtual environment and allows information owners to control the confidentiality of their data on the host platforms.

TVEM configurability is another advantage over VTPMs. By allowing information owners to customize their protection requirements, they have flexibility to use cloud computing services that were previously unavailable.

TVEM improves security in our example web server application by ensuring that the environment is executing on a trustworthy platform and is correctly configured. As the RTS, the TVEM protects the server SSL and EV certificates by encrypting the keys with a unique SRK and storing them in persistent non-volatile memory. For stronger protection, the TVEM can bind the keys to the configuration of the host platform and/or virtual environment. TVEM also provides a high entropy source for random number generation for SSL sessions.

It is important to remember that TVEMs are not designed to defend against hardware based attack. TVEMs are software devices and any attacker with access to certain ports (*e.g.*, PCI, IEEE 1394 FireWire), hardware monitoring devices, emulation and debug equipment, or memory inspection equipment can circumvent the TVEM's security. Since hardware attacks cannot be detected or defended against, physical security of cloud datacenters is of utmost importance.

Another type of attack that TVEM cannot defend against is a dishonest host or service provider. The information owner is at the mercy of the service provider to provide the services agreed upon in a service agreement. If the host platform lies and falsely reports its attestation values to the TF, the TF has no basis for challenging the integrity of the platform. To prevent the dishonest host, social trust must be used as it is likely that once it is detected that the host is falsely reporting, word of the dishonesty will be spread through the community and the service provider's reputation will diminish.

9 Conclusion

TVEM is a new and unique concept for rooting trust in the cloud. The TVEM solves the problem of rooting trust in IaaS cloud computing where a service provider owns the platform on which an information owner's virtual environment is operating. TVEM enhances security by allowing for trust in the virtual environment that is distinct and separate from the hosting platform. The TVEM protects information and conveys ownership in the cloud through the TEK generation process, which creates a dual rooted trust for the virtual environment. This dual rooted trust is necessary to accommodate the unique relationships that occur in cloud computing.

The TVEM gives information owners control of their sensitive and private data in the cloud by providing assurance that their environments are correctly configured and data are kept confidential. The TVEM provides management control of trust through the centralized TVEM factory control facility, key hierarchy, and modular configurable architecture.

This paper introduces the high level system architecture and design concepts of a necessarily somewhat complex TVEM system. The definitions of the TVEM, TVN, and TEK provided here are strong building blocks to continue developing the details of the sub-modules and components. To ensure the TVEM meets the needs of the cloud computing users, the TVEM system should go through a formal specification development cycle with representatives from many stakeholders, including providers, customers, trusted computing experts, and cloud computing researchers. With proper vetting and industry support, the TVEM can be a valuable security component for IaaS cloud computing, enabling a higher adoption rate and a more secure cloud.

The TVEM provides information owners the ability to control their information in the cloud and to realize the savings and benefits that come from the economies of scale that the cloud provides. When combined with other cloud computing security technologies such as Private Virtual Infrastructure and Locator Bots, TVEMs enable a powerful solution to protecting information in cloud computing.

References

1. Carr, N.G.: The Big Switch: Rewiring the World, from Edison to Google. W.W. Norton & Company, New York (2008)
2. Armbrust, M., Fox, A., Griffith, R., Joseph, A.D., Katz, R., Konwinski, A., Lee, G., Patterson, D., Rabkin, A., Stoica, I., Zaharia, M.: Above the Clouds: A Berkeley View of Cloud Computing. University of California, Berkeley (2009),
   http://www.eecs.berkeley.edu/Pubs/TechRpts/2009/
   EECS-2009-28.pdf
3. Krautheim, F.J., Phatak, D.S., Sherman, A.T.: Private Virtual Infrastructure: A Model for Trustworthy Utility Cloud Computing. TR-CS-10-04. University of Maryland Baltimore County, Baltimore, MD (2010),
   http://www.cisa.umbc.edu/papers/krautheim_tr-cs-10-04.pdf
4. Vaquero, L.M., Rodero-Merino, L., Caceres, J., Lindner, M.: A Break in the Clouds: Towards a Cloud Definition. ACM SIGCOMM Computer Communication Review 39, 50–55 (2009)
5. Grawrock, D.: The Intel Safer Computing Initiative. Intel Press, Hillsboro (2006)
6. Scarlata, V., Rozas, C., Wiseman, M., Grawrock, D., Vishik, C.: TPM Virtualization: Building a General Framework. In: Pohlmann, N., Reimer, H. (eds.) Trusted Computing, pp. 43–56. Vieweg+Teubner, Wiesbaden (2008)
7. Krautheim, F.J.: Private Virtual Infrastructure for Cloud Computing. In: Workshop on Hot Topics in Cloud Computing, San Diego, CA (2009)
8. TPM Specification Version 1.2 Revision 103. Trusted Computing Group (2007),
   http://www.trustedcomputinggroup.org/resources/
   tpm_main_specification

9. Abramson, D., Jackson, J., Muthrasanallur, S., Neiger, G., Regnier, G., Sankaran, R., Schoinas, I., Uhlig, R., Vembu, B., Wiegert, J.: Intel Virtualization Technology for Directed I/O. Intel Technology Journal 10, 179–192 (2006)
10. Intel Trusted Execution Technology,
    http://www.intel.com/technology/security/
11. Berger, S., Cáceres, R., Goldman, K.A., Perez, R., Sailer, R., van Doorn, L.: vTPM: Virtualizing the Trusted Platform Module. In: Proceedings of the 15th USENIX Security Symposium, Vancouver, BC (2006)
12. England, P., Loeser, J.: Para-Virtualized TPM Sharing. In: Lipp, P., Sadeghi, A.-R., Koch, K.-M. (eds.) Trust 2008. LNCS, vol. 4968, pp. 119–132. Springer, Heidelberg (2008)
13. Barham, P., Dragovic, B., Fraser, K., Hand, S., Harris, T., Ho, A., Neugebauer, R., Pratt, I., Warfield, A.: Xen and the Art of Virtualization. ACM SIGOPS Operating Systems Review 37, 164–177 (2003)
14. Sadeghi, A.-R., Stüble, C., Winandy, M.: Property-Based TPM Virtualization. In: Wu, T.-C., Lei, C.-L., Rijmen, V., Lee, D.-T. (eds.) ISC 2008. LNCS, vol. 5222, pp. 1–16. Springer, Heidelberg (2008)
15. Strasser, M.: A Software-based TPM Emulator for Linux. Department of Computer Science, Swiss Federal Institute of Technology, Zurich (2004)
16. Wang, X., Yin, Y.L., Yu, H.: Finding Collisions in the Full SHA-1. In: Shoup, V. (ed.) CRYPTO 2005. LNCS, vol. 3621, pp. 17–36. Springer, Heidelberg (2005)
17. Sailer, R., Valdez, E., Jaeger, T., Perez, R., van Doorn, L., Griffin, J.L., Berger, S.: sHype: Secure Hypervisor Approach to Trusted Virtualized Systems. IBM, Yorktown Heights, NY (2005),
    http://www.research.ibm.com/secure_systems_department/
    projects/hypervisor/
18. Dang, Q.: Recommendation for Applications Using Approved Hash Algorithms. NIST Special Publication, vol. 800. NIST, Gaithersburg (2009)
19. Chisnall, D.: The Definitive Guide to the Xen Hypervisor. Prentice Hall, Upper Saddle River (2008)

SegSlice: Towards a New Class of Secure Programming Primitives for Trustworthy Platforms

Sergey Bratus[1], Michael E. Locasto[2], and Brian Schulte[2]

[1] Institute for Security, Technology, and Society, Dartmouth College, Hanover, NH
[2] Computer Science Dept., George Mason University Arlington, VA

Abstract. The TPM is a fairly passive entity. As a result, it can be difficult to involve the TPM in measurements of software trustworthiness beyond simple load-time hashing of static program code. We suggest an approach to dynamic, runtime measurement of software trustworthiness properties as they relate to code-data ownership relationships. We outline a system, SegSlice, that actively involves the TPM in fine-grained labeling and measurement of code slices and the data that these slices operate on. SegSlice requires no changes to x86 hardware, and it relies on the relatively underused x86 segmentation mechanism to mediate access to data events.

1 Introduction

Measuring and enforcing the trustworthiness of a piece of running software is a non-trivial problem to which few satisfactory solutions exist. Being assured that software is behaving as expected (one plausible definition of "trustworthy") faces the central technical problem of defining what behavioral features to measure (and how often to measure them, not to mention the problem of communicating such results to the user in an understandable fashion). Although the TPM provides a tempting, tamper-resistant, high-assurance resource for verifying periodic measurements of system state, to date it has largely been used to verify hashes of static program code at load time.

Assuring that the dynamic properties of a running process are within a particular behavioral envelope presents a much more daunting challenge, and it is unclear how the TPM might be pressed into service to such an end. In this paper, we suggest an architecture for doing so that does not require changes to the TPM or changes to the underlying machine architecture (in this case, x86). We are able to take advantage of the x86 segmentation mechanism, the flexibility of the ELF binary format specification, and small modifications to the Linux kernel to provide a general framework for efficiently measuring and enforcing code-data ownership properties in a running program.

Periodic measurements of program state that are open to TOCTOU attacks; as a result, one closely related piece of prior work suggests an architecture for supplying *selective memory immutability* [1] as a new secure programming primitive for a TCG platform. We propose a new family of runtime primitives that

A. Acquisti, S.W. Smith, and A.-R. Sadeghi (Eds.): TRUST 2010, LNCS 6101, pp. 228–245, 2010.

are intended to build on the same programmer intuitions, and of which selective memory immutability [1] design is strictly a specific case.

1.1 Background and Previous Work

Bratus *et al.* [1] point out one inherent weakness in the TCG approach to software trustworthiness: namely, its lack of OS and hardware support for using the TPM – itself a *passive* security primitive, for programmers to avail themselves of – to enforce dynamic security policies that require preservation of attestable properties (say, integrity of a particular memory region containing a set of critical data structures) throughout a program's runtime. The paper showed that this weakness presents multiple opportunities for TOCTOU attacks.

In order to address this weakness the authors proposed a broad approach to creating TCG architecture-based *runtime* policies, which was to complement the TPM's software measurement support (that is, for cryptographic checksumming of certain memory regions where the software was loaded) with a *memory trapping functionality* that would cause a trap at *memory events* that threatened the integrity of the measured software. The trap handler would take advantage of the (passive) TPM to re-measure software and thus eliminate a potential TOCTOU attack.

Thus a TCG platform with the proposed trapping architecture would go beyond assuming that trustworthiness of software equals its measurement on loading, and become capable of enforcing dynamic properties of software, such as *selective imutability* of memory regions, by making sure that all relevant memory events – in particular, those dealing with page table management and virtual address mapping – are mediated by appropriate, TPM-aware handler logic.

The authors based their prototype implementation on the memory trapping (in particular, page table management mediation) functionality of the Xen, but noted that similar results could be achieved with other general or dedicated hypervisers, or, better yet, with specialized MMU support.

These ideas were developed further in subsequent position papers [2,3], outlining the prospects and promise of how an MMU enhanced with logic for trapping flexibility can bring within reach broad new classes of security policies that cannot be efficiently enforced on modern hardware, but that would allow software developers to express *policy-critical* properties of the software just like they express *correctness-critical properties while debugging* with the modern tools such as DTrace, Pin, SystemTap, etc., at modest hardware and OS support costs.

We believe that the future of trustworthy computing will belong to platforms that support Boolean logic-enhanced, object-granular, and developer-friendly expression of trappable conditions. It may, however, be years until hardware vendors develop and deploy such hardware support. In the meanwhile, we set out to distill the best trustworthiness-related programming practices – especially from such trust- and security-conscious communities as BSD kernel programmers – to the point at which they could be implemented on a modern x86 MMU, albeit with some loss of efficiency.

We propose to extract, allow the developers to specify, and then to enforce at runtime the "ownership" relationships between units of data and code (a.k.a. "slices"). We point out that these relationships are already present in the ELF binary format, between its standard code and data sections, and that their violations are tell-tale signs of attacks. We also describe a mechanism for developers to specify their own code and data units such that their relationships will be enforced throughout runtime, and their violations would be trapped and processed by the TPM-aware handler in a similar manner to [1].

Code–data relationships extend selective immutability. In fact, selective immutability in the sense of [1] can be considered an almost-trivial subcase of a code–data relationship. Namely, selective immutability merely says that *no* code is allowed to write the data other than in select circumstances, thus being, in essence, a simple *write-ownership* policy with an empty set of owners for the selectively immutable data segment.

We explain the rationale for our proposal in the next section, and then describe the prototype implementation in Section 3.

2   Code–Data Relationships and Trustworthiness

Privileges. Trustworthiness of software (and, more generally, the trust we put in software) is ultimately described is terms of its behavior being aligned with our expectations. We point to the arguments in [2,3] noting that debugging and testing can be seen as trust-related activities – because they are essentially *procedures to establish a connection between the expected and the actual behaviors of a program.*

Of course, without a definition of *what behaviors* are relevant to security expectations, such considerations remain theoretical. Classic works define such behaviors as operations on certain systems objects, and formulate expectations in terms of *privileges* to perform these operations. Security models are then equated with privilege management schemes (such as "least" or "role-based" privilege).

However, we believe that such view – despite having worked well in the past, and still working well in environments where security goals can be expressed in terms of read or write access to files – is quite limiting. For example, this view perfectly suited MLS goals ("no read-up, no write-down"), but cannot account for the emerging attacker maxim of "Code running in userspace can always run as Ring0"[1] (implying that the kernel reference monitor itself is in danger if arbitrary code execution can be achieved within a user process), because in fact **none of the behaviors characterising the phases of exploitation leading to the code execution achievement can be described in terms of file access privileges.**

---

[1] See, e.g., DailyDave posting http://lists.immunitysec.com/pipermail/ dailydave/2010-January/006000.html, as based on the recent Linux kernel NULL pointer vulnerability discovered by Tavis Ormandy, e.g., http://blog.cr0.org/2009/08/linux-null-pointer-dereference-due-to.html

In particular, these exploitation steps mostly happen outside of the filesystem namespace, but rather on with the kinds of runtime objects dealt with linkers and loaders, such as such as segments mapped and allocated in the process' virtual memory space.

Even though the underlying OS manages them (e.g., when creating the process from an ELF binary file), it has no system of privileges granular enough to describe "privileges" of operations on them, such as memory mapping operations. **We attach crucial significance to this observation, and posit that to improve trustworthiness, we will need to enforce at runtime known exclusive access relationships between data and code units ("slices") of a program.**

Code–data relations reflected in standard ELF structure. The modern usage of the ELF format as used by GNU/Linux and OpenSolaris makes many fine semantic distinctions between the components of a binary (see, e.g., [4]).

For example, a typical ELF format executable on a modern GNU/Linux system contains about 30 memory sections, which correspond to semantically different contents of contiguous areas of memory to be interpreted by the runtime toolchain (such as GNU binutils, the OS loader, and the dynamic linker). Fundamental shared objects such as /lib/libc.so.6 may contain upward of 70 (!) sections. This semantic diversity, even though not recognized by every runtime tool (which typically requires only one of its facets as represented by the sections' properties for its operation), testified to the granularity of information the OS *could* be using at runtime.

Notably, the relationships between these semantic units are explicitly expressed in the ELF section and segment header tables (specifically, their Info and Link fields). Some of these relationships are "metadata-to-data", specifying that a particular section shall be used to interpret and transform another section, e.g., by way of relocation (say, .rel.text to .text), whereas others are strictly code–data ownership, such as the executable .init and .fini to their respective driving data .ctors and .dtors.

Ultimately, these relationships arise from the programmers' efforts to control program *complexity* such as decomposition of functionality into generic, toolchain-provided, well-tested standard logic (such as .plt dynamic linking stubs and .init) constructor stubs, and their program-specific parametrizations (such as, respectively, .got and .ctors). The very same techniques are used to increase the programs' *trustworthiness* – of which complexity is arguably the worst enemy, and good complexity management is arguably the best cure.

It is no surprise, therefore, that violations of these code–data relationships signal exploitation, from the direct destructor pointer replacement[2] to heap boundary tag manipulation.[3]

---

[2] E.g., http://www.packetstormsecurity.org/papers/unix/
manipulating.dtors.txt,
http://www.securiteam.com/unixfocus/6H00I150LE.html

[3] http://www.phrack.com/issues.html?issue=57&id=8,
http://www.phrack.com/issues.html?issue=57&id=9

2.1 Developer Ways of Keeping Systems Tractable

We further note that the (static) expression of code–data ownership relations has become indispensable to large C projects, in particular, to operating systems kernels. In particular, the use of file-local symbols (both variables and functions) has been steadily growing in the Linux kernel as shown in Table 1.

Table 1. File-scoped symbol declarations in the Linux kernel

	2.0.1	2.2.0	2.4.0	2.6.0
#	736	1833	3336	6675
total lines	512,825	1,205,990	2,241,755	3,853,242
%	.114	.152	.149	.173

We note that the underlying separation is merely static and can only be detected during the build process, not the runtime. We argue, however, that had the kernel runtime permitted it, the enforcement of the same access restrictions would describe a security property of the code's behavior, that is, a useful trustworthiness property, analogous to the "least privilege" at the kernel object level.

We note that one of the earliest Linux kernel explotation techniques was based on patching kernels in such ways that subverted or bypassed loadable kernel module support, or imitated it in case when it was purposefuly disabled.[4] Furthermore, subsequent advanced attacks were based on manipulating virtual memory translation mechanisms through kernel code units that were never meant to affect it, such as, e.g., [5] – which succeeded specifically against an MLS-hardened system. A history sketch of these exploits can be found in [6].

3 Implementation

How can we provide the ability to partition applications at a very fine-grained level, where each "slice" of an application is dynamically defined by the collection of data it "owns"? Slices can cross thread boundaries: we define them to be the elements (instructions, control statements) of a program concerned with the manipulation of a certain exclusive set of data structures and variables. We would like to perform this partitioning without requiring any hardware changes, even though the enforcement of such fine-grained access control seems to entail hardware support that is not currently present in IA-32 or x86_64. Nevertheless, we turn to x86 segmentation for our prototype implementation.

---

[4] http://vxheavens.com/lib/vsc07.html,
http://www.phrack.com/issues.html?issue=58&id=7,
http://www.phrack.com/issues.html?issue=58&id=8

3.1 Isn't x86 Segmentation Dead?

While preparing this paper, we received the following comment that very succinctly summarizes the reasons why x86 segments *as they exist today* are suboptimal for implementing policy mechanisms [7]:

- segmentation makes all memory references slower: using non-flat segments cost a least a cycle on AMD CPUs;
- not all x86_64 CPUs have segmentation support;
- reloading a segment takes a trap/syscall and GDT access;
- only 4 segments (DS, ES, FS, GE) can be accessed at the same time
- only 8K different variables can be protected;
- running with $CPL = 2$ is tricky, as paging assumes superuser privileges in that case;
- the mechanism should guard against attack code loading a flat segment and overwriting the kernel with it;
- wrong error codes in the page fault handler.

We readily agree that the x86 segments would need to change if they were to allow efficient policy enforcement and that their current state does not allow a clean implementation free of ad-hoc fixes. However, we believe that segments are still the closest we have to a more expressive MMU trapping of memory events in x86, and it would probably be good for the security of the platform if the segmentation mechanism were re-optimized to reduce the performance hits and the need for special case band-aids. *The example of x86 virtualization, which arguably started out in a worse state, and – having demonstrated its utility with less-than-perfect prototypes, received great hardware and developer support – gives us hope that segmentation may also be similarly restored and reinvented.*

The paging mechanism might seem to be more appropriate for implementing memory protections within the MMU. However, we believe that a conceptual separation of the MMU's functionality into that supporting security primitives and that focusing on performance is desirable. We also note that natural granularity requirements for strong security *isolation* and multi-level storage *performance optimization* differ substantially, and therefore the paging mechanism should not be overloaded with security functions, as a matter of separating security and performance concerns. The segmentation mechanism appears to offer a more natural expression of any protections granularity required by existing code–data relationships, whereas the size of a page should be determined primarily by performance considerations.

3.2 Prototype Internals

The purpose of this implementation is to augment the Linux kernel's ability to execute 32-bit ELF binaries with a way to automatically wrap individual variables and data structures in their own x86 segment and restrict access to them without hardware modification. We seek to provide a way of mimicking a variable number of "privilege rings" (in IA-32 there are only 4 such rings, limited by the two DPL bits in the segment descriptor and two CPL bits in the CPU). While we could conceptually add a full register for keeping track of these bits, and thus provide 2^{32} possible privilege rings (rather: non-monotonic levels of access), we cannot do this to pre-existing commodity hardware (unless we emulate it in software such as Bochs or QEMU).

Instead, we can modify the OS kernel. The key insight is that if every variable is in its own segment, and we change the DPL bits in the corresponding segment descriptors to be at the privilege level 2 (rather than the normal 3 of user-space), we can trap to the kernel for validation along with a great deal of flexibility to place variables in separate containers. While we cannot directly create new privilege ring levels, we use privilege ring level 2 as a layer of indirection to force a trap and then a subsequent check in the kernel software on whether or not this instruction should be in fact allowed to access the requested data (in essence, we are checking whether the instruction belongs to the "slice" owning that particular data). Thus, we can define per-data instruction slices (a fairly high number of them, limited only by the maximum number of segments on x86 roughly about 8000).

3.3 Segmentation in x86 Linux

Linux's use of segmentation on a 32-bit machine is limited. There are four main segments utilized by the operating system, two for a user and kernel code segment and two for a user and kernel data segment. These entries are contained in the Global Descriptor Table (GDT). In order to keep track of what code

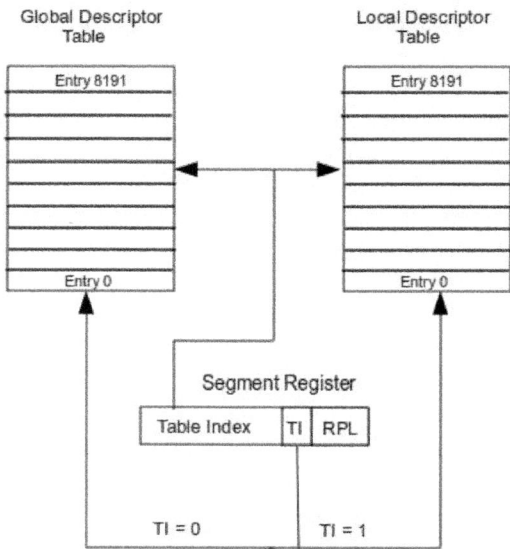

Fig. 1. The x86 segment selectors and tables

and data segments are currently being used by the operating system there is a code and data segment register. These registers contain segment selectors that point to entries inside either the GDT or the Local Descriptor Table (LDT). We summarize this system in Figure 1.

The LDT is a separate descriptor table that is mostly used to hold segments used locally by a particular process. These can be custom segments created by the programming through the system call *modify_ldt*. The *modify_ldt* system call provided with a *user_desc* struct, which is comprised of information about the segment descriptor, creates a new entry in the LDT.

3.4 The Anatomy of the Mechanism

The goal of SegSlice is to protect important variables by having them reside at a privilege level of two instead of the conventional level of three (user land). A check is made by way of a custom system call (for experimental purposes) for the validity of instructions modifying protected variables. This system call will also be responsible for returning the user land process to the default level of three. We recognize that having a custom system call is not the optimal way to handle this, but is most likely the cleanest to experiment with. Other options could be using a hardware exception, taking advantage of certain policies of segmentation and getting the trap for "free", or possibly having a virtual device in */dev* to handle the accesses of protected variables.

Each guarded variable will be provided with its own data segment that encapsulates only itself. These custom segments will be contained inside of the Local Descriptor Table (LDT) of the current process. The system call *modify_ldt* will be used to write these descriptors to the table. In order to allow these segments to reside at ring two, a field in the *user_desc* struct (used by *modify_ldt* to write the LDT entry) had to be created to allow for the modification of the privilege level (by default it is set to three).

Before each attempt to modify the protected variables, a few things have to happen. Eax has to be pushed onto the stack for restoration at a later point. This register is used to hold the segment selector that will be loaded into the data segment register (DS). This is because a direct mov to segment registers is not allowed. Then, the custom system call must be called. The segment selector that is used to access the variable has to be passed as the single, lone parameter.

The custom system call is responsible for performing the check to certify the potentially modifying instruction. There are two ways to perform this check. The first is to see if the instruction in question is in a special hash table in the kernel. The table contains instruction addresses and the corresponding segment selector in the LDT for that particular code segment slice. This table represents code slices that have already proven to be valid. If the instruction is present in the hash table, the corresponding segment selector will be used to overwrite the CS value saved on the stack.

The other check is to see if the instruction is inside the *.text* section of the corresponding ELF. This check only occurs if an entry cannot be found in the hash table for the instruction. In order to perform this check, a modification of the loading of ELFs needs to be made. Inside of the *load_elf_binary* function, each section of the ELF is loaded into memory one at a time. When the *.text* section is loaded, it is copied into a newly added field in the *task_struct* of the process. Then the exception handler will have access to a list of all valid instructions. In order to search the *.text* section in an efficient way, we use the value saved from EIP of the faulting instruction and begin searching there for the instruction we want to validate. If the *.text* section contains the instruction, a new LDT entry is created and an entry is placed in the hash table.

If the instruction is proven to be valid, the process of altering the stack to return to the process at ring two begins. We overwrite the old value of DS on the stack with the value that was passed as a parameter to the system call. From the hash table of instructions and their corresponding segment selectors, the appropriate value is used to overwrite the old CS value on the stack. By overwriting these values, this forces the kernel to perform its normal return to the calling process, but instead of loading the default user land CS and DS, loading our custom segment selectors allowing for execution at ring two.

After the system call is done overwriting DS and CS, we return back to the user land process. After the instructions are finished modifying the now unguarded variable, we make a call to the system call once again. We pass it a special parameter (0 or another value that will not be used as a segment selector) and the system call consequently overwrites CS and DS on the stack (which are now pointing to ring two descriptors) with the default user land selectors for ring three. Returning back to the process after this second call re-armors the variables.

Each protected variables segment has a base of its own address, so some binary rewriting is needed to correct the offsets in the ELF. Originally, the compiler produces and offset from address 0 (the base of the normal data segment). If we leave the original offset in place, it will try to calculate the position of the variable as *[the variable's address + the original offset]* which will undoubtedly lead to a segmentation fault or other unknown results. For beginning experiments, the binary can simply be sifted through for these instructions, and have the offset changed to 0. For a more automated approach, a binary rewriting tool such as Diablo can possibly be used.

Integration with the TCG platforms. The above segmentation-based design provides the trapping framework for capturing and mediating events of code–data accesses of interest, either between the elements of a platform's ELF ABI or between the programmer-defined units.

This SegSlice framework provides a way for measuring related *dynamic* properties of a process throughout its runtime. As mentioned above, the measurement will be invoked by a trapped event, in the corresponding trap handler function.

A TCG platform can take advantage of these measurements in several ways:

1. reset the TPM's PCRs in the trap handler if the measurement suggests violation of the program's desired trustworthiness properties,
2. seal a runtime memory object to the TPM's state, e.g., allowing relinking or re-keying of the program only in trustworthy states, and

3. otherwise maintain a (limited) state record of an application to ensure fulfilment of temporal properties (e.g., enforcing a requirement on the order of certain events).

In all of these cases, the handler will either call on the TPM as a provider of cryptographic services for a TCG-side of a trustworthiness-related multi-step secure computation, or simply signal to the TPM that the trustworthiness property has been irrevocably lost.

3.5 Future Work

Once a working prototype is established for testing, much can be done to improve the project. To move to a more unified mechanism across all machines, a change will have to be made in how the instruction validation is performed. Using a custom system call does not allow for consistency across various systems. Using existing mechanisms in x86 protected mode is an option to allow for a "free" trap to the kernel. The attempt to load a data segment register with a DPL that is lower than the current CPL of the code segment register results in a general protection fault (GPF). This fault is handled by the handler *do_general_protection* where it is possible to intercept the special cases that are caused by SegSlice and handle them appropriately. The clean up process to return to user land is more complicated than a simple system call because the kernel never intends to return from a GPF. For this reason, a custom system call will be used for experimental purposes.

Ideally, this entire process should be transparent to programmers. A dynamic way of identifying particular code slices and important variables through automated binary rewriting would be optimal. Most likely, this would involve a custom binary rewriter that would search through the binary to identify particular code slices that touch important variables in the program. The rewriter would then insert the instructions to encase the to-be guarded variables inside their own segments and also instructions to handle the trap to the kernel and restoration of ring three after the trap.

4   Related Work

We owe our approach to a large quantity of related work. The intuitions on what constitutes an efficient, developer-friendly secure programming primitive tend to travel around a lot, and, before they settle into a successful, productive form of their own, they often make appearances as useful peripheral features of other projects. Thus their full and fair attribution would require a broad survey that is unfortunately beyond the scope of this paper.

We separate this section into two parts: in the first, we discuss the projects that we consider most closely related to ours in either their use of the x86 segmentation or in their emphasis on code and data units in a process. In the second part, we discuss the general trends in related work that we believe support our approach.

4.1   Projects Most Closely Related to SegSlice

We trace the idea of using the program's natural separation into modules as a means of also partitioning it into security-related contexts to [8], in which the authors presented a mechanism to enforce principles of modularity while protecting client code from library code. This is accomplished by two designs: *protected libraries* and *context specific libraries*. When accessing a library routine, through a defined access point, access to the client code is revoked and upon exiting the routine is reinstated. Context-specific libraries (CSL) allow for various sharing policies between client and library code. A CSL may share data with multiple clients, so that each client sees the same data at the same location. CSL's may also share data with a client and service such that the actual contents of the shared region may be associated with either the calling (client) or the called (service) region.

In [9], leading the comparatively recent re-examination of security advantages of segmentation, the authors take advantage of protection mechanisms in segmentation and paging to protection core programs from their extensions, both at the user and kernel level. In the kernel level, kernel service or module's extensions are kept at a privilege level of one, instead of the default level of zero for kernel routines. This protects the kernel services from the extensions, but not vice versa. In order to change the context between the two, a call gate is used which takes advantage of their inter-segment or inter-privilege level procedure calls.

For the user level protection, a combination of segment and paging protection is used. User level applications reside at a privilege level of two from the virtual address space of 0–3GB and have a page protection level (PPL) of zero (more privileged than the other level of one). Extensions are marked with a privilege level of three and a PPL of 1 so that they cannot access the code or data of the original application. In order to have shared code or data, another section is marked to have a privilege level of two but a PPL of one so in order to access it, the software extension must promote itself to privilege level two first.

In the previous sections we consdered the criticism that the x86 segmentation is a relic of the past, and has in fact been substantially deoptimized by CPU makers, who are ready to completely abandon it. While we agree that the danger of such abandonment is real – and believe that it would be griveous to the state of platform security – we do not believe that this mechanism is less than useful, and point to the following work as supporting evidence.

The recent Vx32 [10] is a robust and efficient sandboxing mechanism that utilizes segmentation in the x86 architecture to run guest code safely on top of the host software. No kernel extensions or special privileges are used by vx32. The vx32 sandbox runs standard x86 instruction so any language may be used. Because it is run completely in user land, it cannot rely on the kernel privilege checking mechanism to make sure the guest does not infect the host, so it must translate all operations to "safe" operations at the loss of performance. The guest software is also limited by a restricted system call API. The host decides for each guest what is considered safe and allowed system calls.

The use of segmentation allows each guest to be isolated inside its own segment. Each guest's segment address appears to be at the address of 0 and cannot access beyond its segment (the segment limit). Vx32 uses other data segment registers (FS or GS) to contain the segment selectors for the guests' individual data segments. On 32-bit systems, the code segment register is never changed. When guest code execution begins, it simply jumps to the fragment of code inside the default code segment that contains the guest code. This is safe because vx32 handles any jumps outside of the guest's code, whether it be to other translated code fragments or back to vx32 for operations such as system calls.

Vx32 provides a sandboxing mechanism that can support one or more guest plug-ins, each local to their own specific segments. The control over each guest's system call API provides an extra layer of protection to ensure the host remains isolated. By using x86 architecture to isolate memory accesses and translating instructions to "safe" operations, the authors maintain that vx32 is a lightweight, efficient sandboxing mechanism for the x86 architecture.

The Nooks project [11] makes use of the x86 segmentation system to improve OS reliability through isolation of driver code and data in the kernel, recognizing the fact that driver instability is the leading cause of modern commodity OS instability (as well as of security vulnerabilities). We note that Nooks combines both the idea of code and data isolation and transparent trapping of related (driver) failures, and makes use of the x86 segmentation to achieve this goal.

4.2   Other Related Work

Systems like Valgrind [12] and Pin [13] have recently emerged that enable a programmer or software tester to interweave complex programmatic instrumentation at runtime into an existing software system. These systems use dynamic binary rewriting and do not require access to the source code. Similar environments include the Rio architecture [14] and Dyninst [15].

Program shepherding [16] focuses on ensuring that control flow transfers of a process remain within the bounds of some policy. For example, the technique uses the Rio [14] system to ensure that code in library routines is only accessed via the entry point of the particular library function. Control Flow Integrity (CFI) [17] is a similar idea in which a program's static control flow graph acts like a policy for the runtime behavior of the system.

In what we believe to be a seminal call to action for the operating systems research community, Roscoe *et al.* [18] argue that current OS research utilizing hypervisors should move away from endlessly refining traditional approaches aimed at Unix/Windows ABI model compatibility. In essence, the hypervisor presents a useful backwards-compatible interface, and Roscoe's paper argues that the problems that we currently tackle at the VMM level (such as inter-VM communication, resource sharing among VMs, VM isolation) have all been solved at the OS-level, and adding more functionality in the VMM is largely wasted effort. Furthermore, adding needless functionality to the VMM simply increases the size of the trusted computing base (TCB), and hence it becomes harder to prove VMM correctness or security properties. The size and nature of this complexity are discussed in an article by Karger and Safford [19]; they make many of the same points (and ably illustrate the various interactions) we do with respect to the complexity of VMM I/O systems.

Finally, the object oriented programming discipline is largely concerned with expressing some types of code-data relationships (typically composition and inheritance rules that help govern visibility of data members of classes). Such relationships are typically expressed through the class heirarchy mechanism and the corresponding rules derived from type-checking these relationships at compile time (and in the case of interpreted languages [20], at runtime. Such runtime checking, however, does not incorporate the use of a TPM or other mechanism to provide assurance that the structure and layout of both code objects (methods) and data objects (variables, class instances) remain unmodified by malicious attack (or even random errors [21]).

5   Security Properties of "Slices"

The intention of slices as a programming primitive is to help the programmer decompose the program's code and data units into groups (that is, "slices") of different sensitivity with respect to the programmer's security goals, and to explicitly specify relationships between these groups to be enforced at runtime. When combined with the TCG architecture's measurements, these relationships will constitute an *attestable* property of the system.

In this regard SegSlice can claim descent from a few tried-and-true security primitives, as we explain below.

5.1   UNIX Kernel–Userland Separation

Most importantly, most of UNIX's security and reliability properties ultimately rely on the separation of execution contexts into userland and kernel, with the kernel data being directly accessible only to the trusted kernel code. It is this isolation and the resulting trust in the integrity of kernel data that fueled the subsequent development of UNIX security policy enforcement mechanisms, up to and including SELinux.

"Trustworthy data" became synonymous with "data held by kernel". However, developing new kernel interfaces for each new kind of trust-related data is cumbersome, does not agree with existing application programming practices – essentially, it would imply developing a dedicated companion kernel module for each trusted application, requiring the programmers to become proficient with kernel as well as userland programming environments at the same time. By comparison, SELinux merely requires developers to specify the kernel-loaded companion list of the application's allowed file operations – a sort of a companion program which describes access-focused behaviors of the main program – and even this task has been an obstacle to developers, who had trouble adapting to the specialized language and environment of type/domain specifications.

At the same time, designing a general enough kernel interface for both safe-keeping and application-specific trusted operations on generic application data that would fit a majority of application programming needs appears to be a very hard task – imagine unifying several large *ioctl(2)* and *setsockopt(2)* interfaces into a semblance of coherence!

5.2   Privilege Drop

SegSlice can claim descent from UNIX system calls that allow a process to drop privileges. In particular, such a system call *demarcates code that interacts with certain high-integrity data from the code that is known to have no such need*, and allows the OS to enforce this separation of code into units by access behaviors.

Moreover, an attempt by the process to perform a privileged operation after the privilege drop – that is, a violation of the explicit code boundary set by the call – indicates that the process has entered an untrustworthy state. We also note that the boundary is essentially static.

Unfortunately, even though extremely useful (and widely accepted as a de facto requirement for Internet-facing daemons), such privilege demarcation of code units only lends itself naturally to designs in which the set of privileges "monotonously" shrinks. However, units of code may have other natural sets of privileges than those that nest neatly as subsets of larger sets, and managing them does not fall neatly into the "drop" paradigm.

Even allowing for recovery of privileges (e.g., for temporary drops) opens a can of worms (e.g., [22]), and requires extra care by the programmer that defeats the intuitiveness and ease-of-use (see, e.g., [23], for discussion and proposed solutions). Mechanisms such as *privilege bracketing*[5] aim to solve this problem.

By reformulating "privilege" as code units' enforceable relationship with data units, "slices" offer a model that accommodates non-nesting data access privileges. Slice definitions are contained within the program itself, and thus do not require external configuration of new user accounts with corresponding rights, avoiding additional burden on system administrators (but, as a downside, they are not transparent to the system administrator, unlike user and group definitions).

6   Two Sides of the Same Coin: Slices and Return-Oriented Programming

The formulation of SegSlice presented in this paper (segments denoting code slice ownership of specific data backed by TPM-supported checking of code provenance) is most directly applicable to preventing either foreign injected code or inappropriately re-tasked existing code (a la return-oriented programming) from accessing data and variables that it does not own. In this sense, Segslice provides an automated, finer-grained isolation mechanism supporting legitimate code slices as a defensive technique.

---

[5] See http://docs.sun.com/app/docs/doc/816-1042/6m7g4ma52 in Trusted Solaris Developer's Guide

In contrast, the dynamically composed sequences of executing instructions employed by return-oriented programming (ROP) attacks represent inappropriate or illegitimate "slices" of code functionality: slices which ultimately seek to access or modify data that does not belong to any such slice. Thus, Segslice seeks to enable programmers to define slices of program execution in terms of legitimate data access, whereas ROP-style attacks seek to dynamically compose substrings of existing slices to effect a "malicious computation."

Exploit programming relies on using elements of the target execution environment to accomplish a "malicious computation" (see [24], [25] for discussion of the term) deemed impossible or improbable under the target's trust model.

We found that it helps to think about exploits as programs written in *"weird instructions"* – fragments of standard mechanisms present in the runtime environment, such as libraries, parts of the ABI or calling conventions, dynamic linking logic handling the Global Offset Table (GOT) and Procedure Linkage Table (PLT), compiler-supplied pre-entry and post-exit wrappers for a program, and many other kinds – that are accessible for "off-label" uses unanticipated by the trust model, and accomplish specific tasks, possibly with many side-effects.

The effects of these *weird instructions* could range from overwriting a word at an address controlled vie the input with an integer from a library function's state (e.g., [26,27]) or given by a neighboring word (e.g., [28,29]), to loading and linking an entire missing library via jumping to a part of the dynamic linker code (e.g., [30]). Typically, practical exploits mix and match such "meta-instructions" to both achieve the computation and mitigate its side-effects.

The nature of exploit programming tends to be mischaracterized. The most famous example is probably the historically common association of exploits with introduction of *"malicious code"* into the system, one way or another. This misleading association turned out to be quite tenacious (cf. [24,25]). In fact, the idea that such a computation could be accomplished, with sufficient generality and flexibility, without introducing *any* new executable code into the target can be traced back at least to the 1997 hacker publications [31,32] and the subsequent series of Phrack articles [33,30], and reached its full impact in academic research with [34] (cf. [25], etc.)

We note that a (and, possibly, *the*) hallmark of exploit programming is **violation of expected code–data relationships involved in trustworthiness assumptions**. Each "weird instruction" essentially depends on such violation (or, from the exploit programmer's point of view, creates a new and unanticipated one). It is evident in all examples quoted above. For example, in the case of "double free"-based overrides, heap manager/allocator code writes outside the heap area; "return-to-library"'s sequential calling of the crafted frame chain almost certainly involves some function's code manipulating another function's stack frame, and so do "return-oriented" gadgets.

Our proposed "slice"-based view of trustworthiness acknowledges this hallmark. We recognize that many exploit programming primitives require too granular analysis of the code and data units involved (e.g., at the level of stack frames), which makes their relationships impractical to describe and enforce with

SegSlice. "Slicing" is certainly not a silver bullet that can prevent a malicious computation from happening.

However, SegSlice may provide a programmer with a means of *isolating* a malicious computation, and an indication that the process within which a violation of the SegSlice-enforced properties has occurred is no longer trustworthy.

In a word, slices as a security primitive are informed by exploit programming primitives such as ROP and are, in a sense, dual to them. To summarize,

- ROP gadgets, other "weird instructions" and slices are two sides of the same "programming technique" coin: in one sense, they are all sequences of code units.
- Slices provide a defensive technique that helps define legitimate sequences of code access to specific data, whereas ROP is an attack technique aimed at stitching together sequences of existing "slices" to gain illegitimate access. ROP is possible because programmer-intended code-data relationships (i.e., "slices") are not defined or enforced in current commodity software.
- SegSlice attempts to help define and enforce slice boundaries to frustrate such attacks, and backing them with a TPM is a practical method of *measuring* and *attesting* the runtime preservation of the *dynamic* code–data relationship properties expressed by the programmer via the programming primitive of slices.

7   Conclusion

We define a new class of runtime-measured software trustworthiness properties, based on intended, exclusive relationships between the program's code and data units ("slices"). We describe SegSlice, a trapping framework that supports its measurement and enforcement through using the x86 segmentation system in a "segment virtualization" technique. These units can be defined by the programmer by way of using SegSlice API, or – at a loss of granularity, but still sufficient to capture fairly general kinds of attacks – taken from the semantics of ELF ABI elements. This framework extends the previously proposed TCG platform dynamic secure programming primitive of selective immutability, and provide the TCG with a broader class of trustworthiness properties to be measured throughout the lifetime of a process.

Acknowledgments

Bratus was supported in part by the National Science Foundation, under grant CNS-0524695 and by the U.S. Department of Homeland Security, under grant DHS 2006-CS-001-000001. The views and conclusions do not necessarily represent those of the sponsors. Locasto is supported in part by grant 2006-CS-001-000001 from the U.S. Department of Homeland Security under the auspices of the I3P research program. The I3P is managed by Dartmouth College. The opinions expressed in this paper should not be taken as the view of the authors' institutions, the DHS, or the I3P.

References

1. Bratus, S., D'Cunha, N., Sparks, E., Smith, S.: TOCTOU, Traps, and Trusted Computing. In: Proceedings of the TRUST 2008 Conference, Villach, Austria (March 2008)
2. Bratus, S., Locasto, M.E., Ramaswamy, A., Smith, S.W.: New Directions for Hardware-assisted Trusted Computing Policies (Position Paper). In: Gawrock, D., Reimer, H., Sadeghi, A.-R., Vishik, C. (eds.) Future of Trust in Computing, p. 30. Vieweg+Teubner Verlag, GWV Fachverlage GmbH, Wiesbaden (2009), ISBN 978-3-8348-0794-6
3. Bratus, S., Locasto, M.E., Ramaswamy, A., Smith, S.W.: Traps, events, emulation, and enforcement: managing the yin and yang of virtualization-based security. In: VMSec 2008: Proceedings of the 1st ACM workshop on Virtual machine security, pp. 49–58. ACM, New York (2008)
4. Levine, J.: Linkers & Loaders. Morgan Kaufmann/Academic (2000)
5. Last Stage of Delirium Research Group: Kernel Level Vulnerabilities: Behind the Scenes of the 5th Argus Hacking Challenge. Black Hat Briefings, Amsterdam (November 2001),
   http://www.blackhat.com/presentations/bh-europe-01/LSD/
   bh-europe-01-lsd.ppt
6. Arce, I.: The kernel craze. IEEE Security and Privacy 2, 79–81 (2004)
7. Kauer, B.: Private Communication
8. Banerji, A., Tracey, J.M., Cohn, D.L.: Protected shared libraries: a new approach to modularity and sharing. In: ATEC 1997: Proceedings of the Annual Conference on USENIX Annual Technical Conference, Berkeley, CA, USA, p. 5. USENIX Association (1997)
9. Chiueh, T.C., Venkitachalam, G., Pradhan, P.: Integrating segmentation and paging protection for safe, efficient and transparent software extensions. SIGOPS Oper. Syst. Rev. 33(5), 140–153 (1999)
10. Ford, B., Cox, R.: Vx32: lightweight user-level sandboxing on the x86. In: ATC 2008: USENIX 2008 Annual Technical Conference on Annual Technical Conference, Berkeley, CA, USA, pp. 293–306. USENIX Association (2008)
11. Swift, M.M., Martin, S., Levy, H.M., Eggers, S.J.: Nooks: an architecture for reliable device drivers. In: EW 10: Proceedings of the 10th Workshop on ACM SIGOPS European Workshop, pp. 102–107. ACM, New York (2002)
12. Nethercote, N., Seward, J.: Valgrind: A Framework for Heavyweight Dynamic Binary Instrumentation. In: Proceedings of ACM SIGPLAN 2007 Conference on Programming Language Design and Implementation (PLDI 2007) (June 2007)
13. Luk, C.K., Cohn, R., Muth, R., Patil, H., Klauser, A., Lowney, G., Wallace, S., Reddi, V.J., Hazelwood., K.: Pin: Building Customized Program Analysis Tools with Dynamic Instrumentation. In: Proceedings of Programming Language Design and Implementation (PLDI) (June 2005)
14. Bruening, D., Garnett, T., Amarasinghe, S.: An infrastructure for adaptive dynamic optimization. In: Proceedings of the International Symposium on Code Generation and Optimization, pp. 265–275 (2003)
15. Buck, B., Hollingsworth, J.K.: An API for Runtime Code Patching. The International Journal of High Performance Computing Applications 14(4), 317–329 (Winter 2000)
16. Kiriansky, V., Bruening, D., Amarasinghe, S.: Secure Execution Via Program Shepherding. In: Proceedings of the 11th USENIX Security Symposium (August 2002)

17. Abadi, M., Budiu, M., Erlingsson, U., Ligatti, J.: Control-Flow Integrity: Principles, Implementations, and Applications. In: Proceedings of the ACM Conference on Computer and Communications Security, CCS (2005)
18. Roscoe, T., Elphinstone, K., Heiser, G.: Hype and Virtue. In: Proceedings of the 11th Workshop on Hot Topics in Operating Systems (HOTOS XI) (May 2007)
19. Karger, P.A., Safford, D.R.: Security and Performance Trade-Offs in I/O Operations for Virtual Machine Monitors. In: IBM Research Technical Report RC24500 (W0802-069) (February 2008)
20. Gosling, J., Joy, B., Steele Jr., G.L., Bracha, G.: The Java Language Specification, 3rd edn. Addison Wesley, Reading (2005)
21. Appel, A., Govindavajhala, S.: Using Memory Errors to Attack a Virtual Machine. In: IEEE Symposium on Security and Privacy (2003)
22. Chen, H., Wagner, D., Dean, D.: Setuid demystified. In: Proceedings of the 11th USENIX Security Symposium, Berkeley, CA, USA, pp. 171–190. USENIX Association (2002)
23. Tsafrir, D., Silva, D.D., Wagner, D.: The murky issue of changing process identity: revising "setuid demystified". In: USENIX; login: (June 2008)
24. Buchanan, E., Roemer, R., Shacham, H., Savage, S.: When good instructions go bad: Generalizing return-oriented programming to RISC. In: Syverson, P., Jha, S. (eds.) Proceedings of CCS 2008, October 2008, pp. 27–38. ACM Press, New York (2008)
25. Hund, R., Holz, T., Freiling, F.: Return-Oriented Rootkits: Bypassing Kernel Code Integrity Protection Mechanisms. In: Proceedings of the 18th USENIX Security Symposium (2009)
26. scut / team teso: Exploiting format string vulnerabilities, Version 1.0 (March 2001)
27. gera, riq: Exploiting Format String Vulnerabilities. Phrack 59(7) (July 2002)
28. anonymous author: Once upon a free. Phrack 57(9) (August 2001)
29. MaXX: Vudo malloc tricks. Phrack 57(8) (August 2001)
30. Durden, T.: Bypassing PaX ASLR protection. Phrack 59(5) (July 2002)
31. Designer, S.: Getting around non-executable stack (and fix). Bugtraq mailing list (August 1997)
32. Wojtczuk, R.: Defeating solar designer non-executable stack patch. Bugtraq mailing list (1998)
33. nergal: Advanced return-into-lib(c) exploits (PaX case study). Phrack 58(4) (December 2001)
34. Shacham, H.: The geometry of innocent flesh on the bone: Return-into-libc without function calls (on the x86). In: De Capitani di Vimercati, S., Syverson, P. (eds.) Proceedings of CCS 2007, October 2007, pp. 552–561. ACM Press, New York (2007)

Escrowed Data and the Digital Envelope

King Ables and Mark D. Ryan

University of Birmingham, UK

1 Introduction

1.1 Privacy vs. Security

As computers continue to permeate all aspects of our lives, there is a growing tension between the requirements of *societal security* and *individual privacy*. Societal security encompasses all ways in which we try to make the world more secure, including transport security, financial security, infrastructure security, etc. A prime mechanism for achieving this security involves collecting quantities of data about individuals, for example via ISP logs, mobile phone logs, ticketing systems, and banking systems. As a result, massive databases about every aspect of our lives are being collected by organisations in all the major industrial sectors (financial, transport, retail, telecom, internet, and health care).

These data collection has an impact on individual privacy. The unprecedented **longevity**, **searchability**, and especially the **composability** from different sources of these records imply a radical reduction in the level of individual privacy we can expect to enjoy over the coming decades. Numerous reports have documented this impact and its detrimental consequences to society's well-being (e.g., in the UK, [3,2]).

There is no easy solution to this problem, because the security uses of the data are too important to be denied. Their use in crime detection is an example. About 440,000 requests by the police, local authorities and other permitted organisations to monitor telephone calls, emails and text messages were made in a 15 month period in 2005-06 in the UK [3, pp.32-33]. The "Intercept Modernisation Programme" is a UK Government initiative to centralise electronic communications traffic data in the UK in a single database [5,8]. In another example, the UK intelligence agencies MI5 and MI6 have have sought full automated access to Transport for London's 'Oyster' smartcard database [10]. Debate about balancing security and privacy is taking place at all levels of society [9,3,2,4,1,7], and will likely continue for many more years.

1.2 Escrowed Data

We propose *escrowed data* as an approach that may be capable of providing an appropriate balance between the requirements of individual privacy and societal security. Roughly speaking, data that is collected is held in escrow for a certain period. During that period, the data may be accessed by an authority in order to provide societal security, e.g., for the purposes of crime investigation. It is expected that a minority of the data needs to be accessed in this way, since most

A. Acquisti, S.W. Smith, and A.-R. Sadeghi (Eds.): TRUST 2010, LNCS 6101, pp. 246–256, 2010.

people don't commit crime. After the escrow period is over, the data can be destroyed.

Various kinds of conditions can be put on when and whether the data held in escrow can be accessed by the authorities. Such conditions are likely to vary considerably according to the nature of the data, and we don't consider them in this paper. Instead, we propose a mechanism under which, at the end of the escrow period, the subject of the data can obtain unforgeable evidence about whether the data has been accessed or not. We assume that this fact is sufficient to prevent the authority making unnecessary accesses.

Numerous technical problems need to be solved in order to make this work, including adaptation of the mechanisms by which data is collected and stored, and the ways in which it is used. The core of such a solution needs to provide the following properties:

- Data held in escrow can be accessed by the authority at any time during the escrow period. No cooperation by the subject of the data is required, and the subject is unable to detect whether an access has been made or not, until the end of the escrow period.
- At the end of the escrow period, the subject of the data is able to obtain evidence that says *either* that the data has been accessed; *or* that the data has not been accessed, and has now been destroyed.

This arrangement gives the authority all the power it needs in order to guarantee societal security, while at the same time giving individuals guarantees about their privacy most of the time.

Example 1. In transport charging (for example, London Oyster card, or road usage charging), the data about journeys is held in escrow for a period. In most circumstances, it is never accessed, but under given conditions law enforcement officers can open up data about individual journeys without alerting the individuals involved. After some time-window, still unopened data can no longer be opened, and individuals obtain verifiable evidence about what data has been opened up about them, and what data has been destroyed.

1.3   This Paper: The Digital Envelope

In order to escrow data in the *physical world*, one can store it in a sealed tamper-evident envelope such that it can be opened, but once opened, cannot be resealed. In this paper we present the concept of the *digital envelope* which provides a digital analogue of the envelope in the physical world.

The digital envelope allows Alice to provide digital data to Bob in such a way that Bob has only one of two possible actions available to him:

- He can access the data without any further action from Alice.
- Alternatively, he can revoke his right to access the data, and in this case he is able to prove to Alice that he did not and cannot (any longer) access the data.

Intuitively, it is not possible to achieve this effect using cryptography alone. Alice can encrypt the data and send the ciphertext to Bob. But if she does not send the key as well, then Bob can't unprotect the data without further cooperation from Alice. If she does send the key at the same time as sending the data, then Bob is not ever able to demonstrate that he has not decrypted it. Even if he "returns" the ciphertext to Alice, she has no guarantee that he has not decrypted another copy.

In this paper, we present three mechanisms for achieving the digital envelope in a trusted computing context, and compare them. Section 2 is devoted to background information about trusted computing and the TPM. Section 3 contains our three implementations, and the comparisons. Section 4 considers some modifications of the TPM, and we draw conclusions in Section 5.

2   Background

The *Trusted Platform Module* (TPM) is a commodity chip present on most high-end laptops currently shipped by all the major manufacturers. Through over 100 function calls, it provides protected cryptographic operations to general purpose software that runs on the platform.

In this short version of the paper, we assume readers are knowledgeable about TPM functionality, including platform configuration registers, creation and management of encryption keys, attestation, measurement, identity, monotonic counters, and encrypted transport sessions. A description of all this functionality is available in the longer version of the paper available on the author's web page.

3   Three Implementations of the Digital Envelope Using the TPM

We present three different possible solutions for a digital envelope by using functionality of the Trusted Platform Module. Each solution assumes Bob has a "recipient" computer (his own or a server) containing a functioning TPM. The solutions have varying levels of requirements and thus, a varying level of limitations in usability and functionality. They each have advantages and disadvantages compared to the others. No single solution is clearly superior.

3.1   No Software Required

Somewhat surprisingly, the digital envelope can be implemented directly using the functionality of the TPM, without any trusted software. However, the implementation has some limitations. The idea is to bind the data using a TPM key locked to specific PCR values.

Implementation

Sealing the envelope. Alice creates an encrypted transport session with Bob's TPM and uses it to extend a given PCR with a random nonce n that she has created. She keeps the value of n secret. The transport session is then closed.

Alice or Bob reads the value of the given PCR, finding it to be p, say, and creates a TPM_KEY_BIND key (sk, pk) on Bob's TPM, locked to the PCR value SHA1(p||1). This means that the key can be used only if the value 1 is first extended into the PCR.

Alice encrypts her data with pk, and sends it to Bob. This protocol is illustrated in Figure 1.

Opening the envelope. Bob can use TPM_Extend to extend 1 into the relevant PCR. He can then use TPM_Unbind to decrypt the datagram sent to him by Alice, in order to obtain the data.

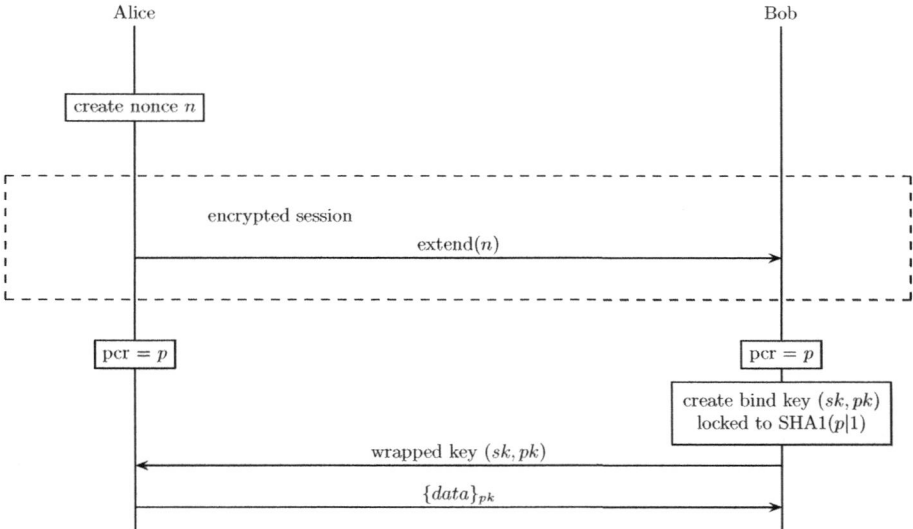

Fig. 1. Solution 1 (no software required): Alice sends envelope

Returning the envelope. Alternatively, Bob can demonstrate that he has given up that possibility. To do that, he extends an agreed value, say 2, into the TPM. Alice may obtain a PCR quote to see that the value of the PCR is now SHA1(p||2). This assures her that Bob can never use the key (sk, pk) to decrypt the datagram. This protocol is illustrated in Figure 2.

Advantages and Limitations. The greatest advantage to this solution is it can be implemented on TPM platforms without requiring any trusted code on Bob's computer. It could be run on a user's personal system or a server system.

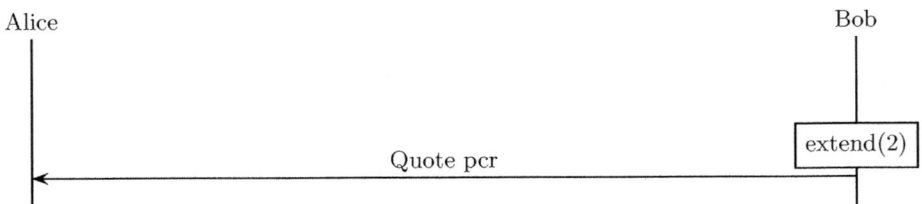

Fig. 2. Solution 1 (no software required): Bob returns envelope

Because the TPM controls access to the encrypted data, no application code requires trust or attestation.

The major disadvantage in using PCRs is that they maintain a volatile state which is lost when the TPM is reset, so this solution can only provide guarantees until the machine is rebooted (including after a crash). Once the system reboots, the PCRs will be reset to their default values and Bob will have lost both his ability to read the encrypted data as well as his ability to prove to Alice that he did not.

3.2   Attestation of Envelope Server Code

Using the TPM and monotonic counters, a digital envelope mechanism can be created that can still be used when the system reboots. However, because monotonic counters are not used to seal the data, all of the code (including the operating system) processing the digital envelope must be attested to by the TPM so it can be trusted by Alice.

To reduce the complexity of the problem, we present a solution that is designed for a limited environment where it runs on a dedicated system. We assume that the system has a TPM and TCG-enabled BIOS and boot loader, and that the application runs native on the hardware with no operating system or virtual machine support. The digital envelope server is capable of processing only one envelope at a time. In addition to these specific assumptions about the platform, some way of obtaining PCR values for various makes and models of hardware platforms is also required.

Implementation. To use the digital envelope server, Alice will create a blob containing the message that can only be opened by a TPM-verified digital envelope server. The procedure she will follow is:

- Request an envelope which includes a TPM-protected key tied to a monotonic counter value.
- Verify the envelope has been created by an authentic TPM running a properly installed and configured digital envelope server application.
- Tie the message to this key (i. e., insert the message into the envelope).
- Send the envelope to Bob.

Then, Bob can, at a time of his choosing, use the digital envelope server to open the envelope or obtain proof that he did not open it and forfeit his ability to ever open it. The act of opening or refusing the message increments the counter so neither operation can be repeated nor can the other operation be performed later.

The digital envelope server runs in two states: initialisation and service. The initialisation state, State 0, starts the service, creates or unwraps keys and data, and prepares to begin servicing envelope requests. The service state, State 1, is the "normal" operational state of the application.

State 0: initialisation. State 0 initialises the environment in which the digital envelope server will run with the following steps:

- Unseal or create the initialisation blob containing the digital envelope server's AIK. If just created, seal the initialisation blob against current PCR values set by State 0.
- Load the digital envelope server AIK into the TPM, and advance to State 1 by extending a particular PCR.

The digital envelope server's *sealing key* can only be loaded during State 0 since it is sealed against the PCR values at the time the application is first executed. The sealing key requires no TPM AuthData because it is stored in a blob which was sealed against PCR values and is only accessible to a measurement-verified digital envelope server in State 0.

State 1: service. In State 1, the digital envelope server waits to provide one of these services upon request:

- Create a new (empty) envelope, *or*
- Open an existing envelope and return the data, *or*
- Return proof of refusal to open an existing envelope.

When creating a new empty envelope, the digital envelope server returns the new public encryption key for the digital envelope, counter information, public digital envelope server AIK and certificate, and signed counter information to the envelope requestor.

Because the initialisation information is sealed against the PCRs at the time the system boots, once the digital envelope server has loaded its data, it extends a particular PCR to enter State 1 to guarantee that no other process may then access the initialisation information.

Operation. When the system boots, the chain of trust is followed all the way to the digital envelope server. The first time the digital envelope server executes, it creates a sealing key using the command TPM_CreateWrapKey (with null AuthData) which will be used to seal the state information blob to State 0 (the current state). It also creates an AIK and random AuthData to be used with all envelope encryption keys using the TPM command TPM_GetRandom. The digital

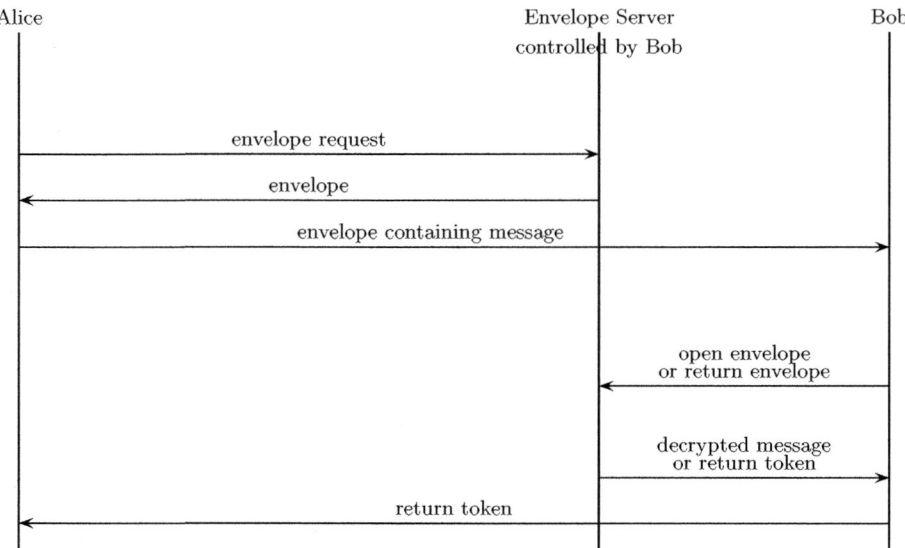

Fig. 3. Solution 2 (monotonic counter): the protocol

envelope server has the TPM sign a digest of PCA information to bind it to the public part of its AIK and submits this with its public EK to the PCA to obtain its AIK certificate. Lastly, the digital envelope server seals a blob containing its AIK, certificate, and a chosen monotonic counter name to the PCR value defining State 0. At this point, it can generate a TPM_Quote of PCR state signed with the digital envelope server AIK and then extend a particular PCR by 1 to advance to State 1.

Subsequent runs of the digital envelope server need only to restore the state, which will only succeed from State 0. This requires loading the digital envelope server sealing key, unsealing the initialisation state blob, loading the digital envelope server AIK into the TPM, generating a signed TPM_Quote of the PCR state, and extending a particular PCR to advance to State 1.

An envelope encryption key is created in State 1, so it is not protected by sealing against PCRs reflecting State 0. The envelope encryption key is protected by a random AuthData value created by the digital envelope server during initialisation and stored in the initialisation state blob. Because the initialisation state is protected by sealing against PCRs reflecting State 0, the AuthData is inaccessible to any other application at any other time. The AuthData for all envelope encryption keys is known only to the digital envelope server.

When Alice needs to send Bob data in a digital envelope, she generates a random nonce and sends the digital envelope server a request for a new envelope with the nonce.

The digital envelope server returns an "empty" digital envelope to Alice consisting of the digital envelope server AIK and certificate, the TPM_Quote of PCR values signed with the digital envelope server AIK, the name and new value of the incremented TPM monotonic counter, the public part of a new envelope encryption key (with AuthData known only to the digital envelope server), and her original nonce.

When Alice has verified the envelope and her nonce, she is ready to send her data to Bob. To do so, she will generate a random symmetric key and encrypt her message with it. She will then use the public part of the envelope encryption key to encrypt the symmetric key and the other parts of the digital envelope. Alice can now send this data to Bob because only the digital envelope server can decrypt the contents of the digital envelope and will only do so if the named counter still has the specified value. Figure 3 shows the generic protocol for the digital envelope server.

Bob can now submit the digital envelope to the server for one of two purposes: to acquire the information sealed in the envelope or to obtain a token proving he has revoked his access. The digital envelope server validates the request, creates the response, increments the monotonic counter, and sends the response back to Bob. The digital envelope is no longer useful and Bob has either the data from Alice or a token he can send her to prove he did not and can no longer access it. The token may include Alice's nonce signed by the digital envelope server or a signed transport session showing the monotonic counter being incremented past the valid envelope value.

Advantages and Limitations. The main advantage of this implementation over the previous one is that it can save the envelope state across reboots of the platform. This comes at the cost of requiring trust in a small amount of software that manages the envelope software. Attestation is used to ensure the integrity of the software. No operating system is present.

The main limitation is that the platform is dedicated to providing the envelope service. Another disadvantage is the digital envelope server can only store and service one envelope at any time. Since each envelope requires its own counter and the TPM only allows the use of a single monotonic counter at any one time, *virtual monotonic counters* must be implemented to support multiple envelopes.

3.3 Flicker Module

Flicker [6] is an infrastructure for executing TPM-attested code in isolation, while allowing a general purpose untrusted operating system with application software to run alongside it. Flicker is able to guarantee the attestation even if the BIOS, the operating system, and DMA-enabled devices are all untrusted. This is achieved by using hardware support for late launch DRTM, which features on high-end processors from AMD and Intel. Flicker works by causing the processor to temporally suspend the operating system, and to enter an attested configuration state where a small kernel, called a Flicker *piece of application logic* (PAL) is executed. The PAL is intended to run for a brief period, and return control to the operating system. It is hoped that the suspension time is short enough not to cause any unrecoverable disruption to the operating system. Before the end of its execution, the PAL is expected to save its state using the TPM's sealing functionality, and to recover its state at the beginning of the next execution. Flicker avoids replay attacks (in which the untrusted environment reverts to an old state of the PAL) by incorporating the current value of a monotonic counter into the saved PAL state, similarly to the way it is done in the previous subsection.

Implementation. The Flicker implementation follows the pattern described for Flicker PALs that save state [6, §6.2]. The pattern focuses on maintaining the integrity of the PAL's state while the untrusted OS operates. To achieve this, the very first invocation of the PAL generates a 160-bit symmetric key based on randomness obtained from the TPM and uses the TPM to seal the key so that no other code can access it. It then performs application specific work. Before yielding control back to the untrusted OS, the PAL computes a cryptographic MAC (HMAC) over its current state. Each subsequent invocation of the PAL unseals the symmetric key and checks the MAC on its state before beginning application-specific work. When the PAL finally finishes its work unit, it extends the results into PCR 17 and exits.

The envelope-specific details are as described in the previous subsection (section 3.2).

Advantages and Limitations. The advantage over the previous implementation (section 3.2) is that the platform does not have to be dedicated to providing the envelope server. It can run a general purpose OS and applications. The cost of this is that the quantity of attested software is greater than that for the previous implementation, because Flicker adds a small additional overhead.

On the negative side, Flicker is currently experimental and has onerous software and hardware requirements, as well as dependency on the underlying processor architecture. These disadvantages can be expected to reduce over time, if continued development of the hardware technologies and of Flicker are made.

4   Suggested TPM Enhancement: Sealing to Monotonic Counters

The ability to seal data to monotonic counters (as well as to PCR values) would allow a significantly improved solution having the simplicity of our first solution (section 3.1) and the flexibility of our second (section 3.2). Such a solution could allow untrusted software to save the envelope state, and the TPM could detect replays that attempt to revert to a previous state.

4.1   New TPM Commands

This can be achieved by providing the following proposed TPM commands.

– TPM_SealByCounter (*key, authdata, data-to-be-sealed, counter-name, counter-value, increment-on-unseal*)

Here, *counter-name*, *counter-value* and *increment-on-unseal* may be represented in a `TPM_COUNTER_INFO` structure, analogous to the `TPM_PCR_INFO` structure used in the existing seal and unseal operations. This command seals arbitrary data with the specified key against a counter name and value just as `TPM_Seal` seals against one or more PCR values. The *increment-on-unseal* is a boolean value which specifies whether or not the specified counter should be incremented when the data is unsealed.

– `TPM_UnsealByCounter` (*key, authdata, data-to-be-unsealed*)
This command obtains the counter name and value from the blob and compares them to the current value of the named TPM counter. If they match, the TPM unseals the data. Upon successful unsealing of the data, but before it is returned to the caller, the named counter is incremented if *increment-on-unseal* was set to `TRUE` when the data was sealed.

4.2 No Software Required, v.2

Using these proposed new TPM commands, the digital envelope could be designed in a much more straightforward manner and could run within an unmeasured and untrusted application under any operating system.

Alice could request an envelope from the desired destination and receive the AIK and certificate as before, a signed log of a transport session proving the current monotonic counter and newly incremented value, two public parts of RSA key pairs, a signed log of a transport session showing these keys being created and sealed against the current monotonic counter (with *increment-on-unseal = TRUE*), and a TPM-signed copy of her nonce.

Alice can verify the envelope and that the keys were sealed properly against the proper counter value. She then encrypts her symmetric key with one public key and a refusal token with the other, encrypts her message with her symmetric key, and sends it all to Bob.

Using `TPM_UnsealByCounter`, Bob can ask his TPM to unseal either of the two envelope keys, but not both. Unsealing either the symmetric key for the message or the refusal token will cause the TPM to increment the monotonic counter which will eliminate the option to ever unseal the other.

5   Conclusion

We have presented the idea of a digital envelope that can provide data escrow in such a way that parties can obtain evidence about whether the data was accessed or not. This idea is expected to have applications in privacy management, and in particular to balancing the often conflicting requirements of individual privacy with societal security.

The Trusted Platform Module provides the primitives necessary to implement a digital envelope in a variety of ways. But the more straightforward the implementation, the more restrictive the functionality. As functionality is expanded to improve usability, security complications increase dramatically.

Due to the rigours of platform attestation, even the simplest solution quickly becomes complex. An additional capability like Flicker significantly minimises the impact of these additional issues.

It has also been shown that a much more straightforward solution could be achieved if the TPM provided a sealing operation using a monotonic counter analogous to the sealing operation it currently provides using Platform Configuration Registers. Therefore, two new TPM commands were proposed for addition to the TPM specification. If the TPM provided these commands in a future version, the measurement and attestation requirement would be eliminated and the digital envelope could easily be implemented in unmeasured code running on any operating system.

References

1. Petition to the UK Prime Minister against the email monitor database,
   http://petitions.number10.gov.uk/privacy-matters/
2. Ball, K., Lyon, D., Wood, D.M., Norris, C., Raab, C.: A Report on the Surveillance Society for the Information Commissioner (September 2006),
   http://www.ico.gov.uk
3. Crossman, G., Kitchen, H., Kuna, R., Skrein, M., Russell, J.: Overlooked: Surveillance and personal privacy in modern Britain (October 2007), Published by Liberty,
   http://www.liberty-human-rights.org.uk
4. Grayling, A.C.: Privacy is a quaint construct in a hyper-connected world,
   http://www.guardian.co.uk/commentisfree/2008/dec/05/humanrights-privacy
5. H. M. Government. The united kingdom security & counter-terrorism science & innovation strategy (2007),
   http://security.homeoffice.gov.uk/news-publications/publication-search/general/science-innovation-strategy1
6. McCune, J.M., Parno, B., Perrig, A., Reiter, M.K., Isozaki, H.: Flicker: An execution infrastructure for tcb minimization. In: Proceedings of the ACM European Conference in Computer Systems (EuroSys) (April 2008)
7. I. of Eduction. Convention on modern liberty (February 28, 2009),
   http://www.modernliberty.net/programme
8. Open Rights Group. Intercept modernisation (2009),
   http://www.openrightsgroup.org/orgwiki/index.php/Intercept_Modernisation
9. Privacy Blog, http://www.theprivacyblog.com
10. The Register. Spooks want to go fishing in Oyster database,
    http://www.theregister.co.uk/2008/03/17/spooks_want_oyster/

Engineering Attestable Services

John Lyle and Andrew Martin

Oxford University Computing Laboratory,
Wolfson Building, Parks Road, Oxford, OX1 3QD
{john.lyle,andrew.martin}@comlab.ox.ac.uk

Abstract. Web services require complex middleware in order to communicate using XML standards. However, this software increases vulnerability to runtime attack and makes remote attestation difficult. We propose to solve this problem by dividing services onto two platforms, an untrusted front-end, implementing the middleware, and a trustworthy back-end with a minimal trusted computing base.

1 Introduction

Web services are a popular way of implementing component-based systems. They have a number of potential advantages, offering higher reliability and integrity due to component reuse and dynamic selection. However, some have significant security concerns, such as those in healthcare and financial scenarios. To fulfil these security requirements, mechanisms are needed to gain assurance in the platforms hosting these services.

One method for assessing a platform is attestation, part of the functionality provided by Trusted Computing. This allows a remote party to find out the exact software configuration being used. If all the software running at a service is well known and trustworthy, then the user can potentially trust it. However, web services use a great deal of complicated software, and little of it may be considered trustworthy. Runtime attacks also remain possible, making remote attestation an impractical solution [1].

The complexity of service middleware, and its position in the trusted computing base (TCB) of a web service, is a significant part of the problem. Service providers require the middleware to provide features such as load balancing and monitoring, along with parsers for complex languages like SOAP. All the libraries that implement these features are of little interest to the end user, but are still part of the TCB and must be attested. This makes it impossible to guarantee the integrity of the service, or the confidentiality of data sent to it, as it all relies on untrustworthy middleware.

The solution we propose is to divide the web service middleware and logic onto different platforms. The middleware platform is then free to implement functionality that the service provider cares about, but remains untrusted by the end user. The integrity of the service application is guaranteed by the second platform, which has a much smaller trusted computing base and is less vulnerable to runtime attack. This makes the service more trustworthy and attestation more practical.

A. Acquisti, S.W. Smith, and A.-R. Sadeghi (Eds.): TRUST 2010, LNCS 6101, pp. 257–264, 2010.

1.1 Trusted Computing

Trusted computing is a paradigm developed by the Trusted Computing Group [2]. It aims to enforce trustworthy behaviour of computing platforms by securely identifying all hardware and software that it uses. If a platform owner can find out what software and hardware is in use, they should be able to recognise and eliminate malware.

The technologies proposed by the TCG are centred around the Trusted Platform Module (TPM). In a basic server implementation, the TPM is a chip connected to the CPU. It provides isolated storage of RSA keys and Platform Configuration Registers (PCRs). These PCRs can be used to hold *integrity measurements*, in the form of 20 byte SHA-1 hash values. They can only be written to in one way: through the extend command. This appends the current register value to the supplied input, hashes it, and stores the result in the PCR. In order to work out what individual inputs have been added to a PCR, a separate log is kept. When this log is replayed, by rehashing every entry in order, the final result should match the value in the PCR.

The limited functionality offered by the TPM can be used to record the boot process. Starting from the BIOS, every piece of code is hashed and extended ('measured') into a PCR by the preceding piece of code. This principle is known as *measure before load* and must be followed by all applications. If so, no program can be executed before being measured, and because the PCRs cannot be erased, this means that no program can conceal its execution from the TPM. A platform is said to support *authenticated boot* when it follows this process.

1.2 Remote Attestation

The TPM allows a platform to report integrity measurements through *remote attestation*. When challenged, the TPM can create a signed copy of its PCRs. This is used by a remote party to verify the platform's measurement log. PCRs are signed using a key held by the TPM, guaranteeing its confidentiality. This Attestation Identity Key (AIK) is certified by an authority (a 'Privacy CA') [2].

The software running at the platform can be identified by matching the hash values in the measurement log with reference data. This requires a list of *reference integrity measurements* (RIMs) contained within a Reference Manifest Database [2].

1.3 Protecting Data and Keys

The TPM can be used to encrypt data and only allow decryption when PCRs are in a predefined state. TPM RSA keys can be created so that they are *bound* to PCR values through the CreateWrapKey command. The private half is then always held securely in the TPM. When it needs to be used, a request ('unbind') is made to apply the private key to the encrypted data. The TPM will only complete the request when the PCRs are in the state defined upon key creation. A credential for the bound key, certifying that the private-half of it is held in the TPM and restricted to certain PCRs, can be generated (using an AIK) through the TPM's CertifyKey operation.

1.4   Why Are Web Services Difficult to Measure and Attest?

Attesting a web service is difficult in practice. The amount of software to measure is surprisingly large – in recent work [3], we found that a typical web service made around 300 integrity measurements, and that, on average, 35 new RIMs were required for updates every month. This is a potentially impractical quantity of software to test and evaluate.

The large TCB is partly due to functional and interoperability requirements. High-level communication protocols [4] used by services require complicated software to process. Servers also have many sophisticated features dedicated to internal requirements such as auditing and management. These are important to the service provider, but not the requester, and yet all must be reported in an attestation. Most operating systems are also guilty of having a large code base, and provide relatively weak isolation. This makes the system error-prone and vulnerable to compromise. Attestation is therefore less valuable, as the chance that a successful runtime attack has been performed is high. Minimizing the trusted computing base appears to be essential.

One component to minimize is middleware. In our experiments, removing it resulted in a 30% fewer integrity measurements [3]. The popular Glassfish application server has around 300 modules (some optional) totalling nearly 100 megabytes of compressed bytecode. Furthermore, middleware is responsible for parsing complex data structures and processing input, obvious targets for attack. Removing it would also reduce the number of features that the operating system has to support, potentially improving efforts to minimize the OS runtime footprint. We believe that this makes a compelling case for removing middleware from the trusted platform. However, middleware provides essential functionality, and it cannot be removed altogether. The next section discusses how to move it away from the TCB without losing any functionality.

2   Removing Web Service Middleware from the Trusted Computing Base

We propose that web services can be deployed so that they support heavyweight protocols and features but have a small TCB. This is achieved by divided them into two components, one trusted and one not. The untrusted component acts as a proxy, and is the perceived endpoint for all web service interactions. It communicates with the outside world through SOAP and XML and performs management functions such as load balancing and auditing. The trusted back-end server provides all the real functionality and logic. In a data processing scenario, the back-end platform could either be a data store, or be responsible for contacting it and forming queries. Communication between the front and back-end is through a simple protocol that requires a less-complex parser, such as Java RMI. Figure 1 illustrates this system.

The advantage of this architecture is that the back-end can attest to a simple configuration. It can also use a minimal operating system, perhaps even a

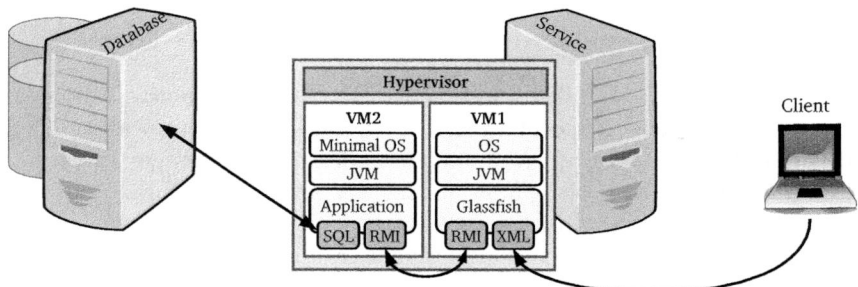

Fig. 1. The split service architecture. Lines show message flow.

bytecode processor. Furthermore, it only needs to parse input from one protocol, and XML does not need to be interpreted. Attestation should therefore be appropriate. Of course, the back-end server has been intentionally designed to not require a web service stack, and therefore attestations must be proxied by the front-end. The rest of this section discusses additional steps and modifications required to realise this proposal.

2.1 Establishing a Secure Channel

Assuming the back-end service is trusted, the next step is to guarantee a secure channel. This is a challenge, as the front-end is proxying all traffic. A *platform in the middle attack* [5] must be avoided, so that the platform that originally attested is the same one that we are then sending requests to. Solutions using transport-level encryption have been discussed before [6], but in our scenario we cannot use TLS with a key held on the back-end, as this would prevent the front-end platform from translating and forwarding requests. Instead, we use message-level cryptography [7]. To do this, the back-end can publish a public key, along with a certificate generated by the TPM's `CertifyKey` command. If the same AIK were used for the attestation process, this establishes that the key belongs to the attested platform. Furthermore, if the key is bound to known-good PCR values, this key can guarantee platform state.

An initial request for a service's public key can follow the WS-Trust specification. The protocol below shows the user (U), credential repository (C), service (S), service public key (S_{pub}) and service AIK (S_{aik}). Line 1 is a request for a service's public, bound TPM key, and line 2 is the response, containing a service key and TPM credential, signed by service's AIK. These steps must be performed in a transport session with a known, trustworthy credential repository:

$$U \rightarrow C : \qquad\qquad\qquad \text{RequestSecurityToken, } S \qquad (1)$$

$$C \rightarrow U : \qquad S_{pub} \text{ , } S_{aik} \text{ , } \{S_{pub}, \text{TPM\_CertifyInfo}\}_{S_{aik}} \qquad (2)$$

Service requesters can use this public key to encrypt messages without fear of loss of confidentiality. Furthermore, any reply message generated by the endpoint can be signed, proving the source of the reply. We propose the following protocol, with the service front- and back- ends denoted as F and S respectively, using an encrypted session key:

$$U \to F : \qquad \text{Method}(\ \{nonce_U, arg_1, arg_2...\}_K\ ), \{K\}_{S_{pub}} \quad \text{(SOAP)} \qquad (3)$$

$$F \to S : \qquad \text{Method}(\ \{nonce_U, arg_1, arg_2...\}_K\ ), \{K\}_{S_{pub}} \quad \text{(RMI)} \qquad (4)$$

$$S \to F : \qquad \text{Reply}, HMAC(nonce_U,\ \text{reply}\ )_{S_{pub}} \quad \text{(RMI)} \qquad (5)$$

$$F \to U : \qquad \text{Reply}, HMAC(nonce_U,\ \text{reply}\ )_{S_{pub}} \quad \text{(SOAP)} \qquad (6)$$

Line 3 is the SOAP method invocation with session key K applied to all field, which is then translated and forwarded via RMI in line 4. The reply is generated in line 5 and translated again to conform to WS standards in line 6. If the TPM key S_{priv} is not bound to PCR values, then an additional WS-Attestation step is required first, which also must be proxied by the front-end.

2.2 Preserving Integrity and Confidentiality

The messages described in lines 3 to 6 of Section 2.1 is simplified in terms of signatures and encryption. Decryption of incoming messages, and signing of the result, must be performed on the back-end, as only it has access to the S_{priv} key. However, this means that only individual fields can be encrypted, not complex XML structures, as the back-end cannot process XML. An attacker now has the opportunity to re-order fields, as nothing binds the content of the field to its location in the document. If the encryption is just of the field itself, then it will also be vulnerable to replay, as no freshness information is present. The same is true for the signed response message from the back-end platform.

To provide both freshness and structure to the elements, without breaking web service standards, fields must be added to the internal methods and the response. The response should contain a hash of the original input, result and a nonce. To avoid the endpoint from needing to process XML, we suggest that a set of identifiers be included internally, linking the expected XML structure to the internal fields. The identifier-result structure is then signed by the endpoint, and included in the response. The example in part 4 of Figure 2 demonstrates this. The verifying party can then compare the request and result against the arguments and result the endpoint believes it has used and computed. We have used XPATHS as IDs, noting that these should be predictable and easy for the verifier to process.

3   Security Analysis

Demchenko et al. [8] and Bhalla and Kazerooni [9] identify threats to XML services. These include misuse of user credentials, unencrypted SOAP messages, maliciously formed input, XML parsers exploits, WSDL enumeration, poor site configuration and error handling. Our proposals reduce the impact of some of these issues, in comparison to a standard Web Service endpoint that also uses message-level encryption.

Threats from SOAP parsers are eliminated in this architecture, as they can only compromise the front-end. These threats are significant as several attacks

```
1) Original SOAP Request
<soap:body ... >
 <m:Entry>
  <m:from>Joe Bloggs</m:from>
  <m:content>...</m:content>
  <m:nonce>36829463846238</m:nonce>
 </m:Entry>
</soap:body>

2) Encrypted SOAP Request
<soap:Header>
 <wsse:Security><xenc:EncryptedKey>
   <ds:KeyInfo ... >
    <ds:KeyName>PubKey X</ds:KeyName>
   </ds:KeyInfo>
   <CipherData><CipherValue>
     [Encrypted Symm Key]
   </CipherValue></CipherData>
   <ReferenceList>
     <DataReference URI='#content'/>
     <DataReference URI='#name'/>
   </ReferenceList>
   <CarriedKeyName>EndpointKey
   </CarriedKeyName>
 </xenc:EncryptedKey></wsse:Security>
</soap:Header>
<soap:Body><m:Entry>
 <m:from>
   <xenc:EncryptedData Id="name">
    <xenc:CipherData><xenc:CipherValue>
      [Encrypted Name]
    </xenc:CipherValue></xenc:CipherData>
   </xenc:EncryptedData>
 </m:from>
 <m:content>
    <xenc:EncryptedData Id="content">
     ...[Encrypted Content]...
    </xenc:EncryptedData>
 </m:content>
 <m:nonce>36829463846238</m:nonce>
</m:Entry></soap:Body>

3) RMI Request
response = endpoint.submit(
 [encSymmKey],       // enc. session key
 "Pub Key X",        // TPM key ID
 [Enc Name],[Enc. Content], //fields
 36829463846238 );  // nonce
```

```
4) ASN.1 style response structure
messageInfo MessageInfo ::= {
  input {
    encrypted-symm-key  [encSymmKey],
    pub-key-id          Pub Key X  ,
    variables {
      { field-xpath       //m:Entry/m:from  ,
        field-value       [Encrypted Name] },
      { field-xpath       //m:Entry/m:content
        field-value       [Encrypted Content] },
      { field-xpath       //m:Entry/m:nonce   ,
        field-value       36829463846238 }},
  result {
      { field-xpath       //m:Response/m:Success,
        field-value  1 }}}

5) RMI Response
return new MessageResponse (
  result,
  messageInfo,
  SHA1( messageInfo ),
  Sign( SHA1( messageInfo ) ) )
  // signed with endpoint private key );

6) SOAP Response
<soap:Header> ...
  <Signature ... >
   <ds:Signature ... >
    <ds:SignedInfo>
     <ds:Reference URI="#MsgVerification">
      <ds:DigestValue>[SHA(messageInfo)]
      </ds:DigestValue>
     </ds:Reference>
    </ds:SignedInfo>
    <ds:SignatureValue>
     [Sign( SHA1( messageInfo ) )]
    </ds:SignatureValue>
   </ds:Signature>
  </Signature>
</soap:Header>
<soap:Body ... >
  <m:Response>
   <m:Success>1</m:Success>
    <m:Verification id="MsgVerification">
     [messageInfo]
    </m:Verification>
   </m:Response>
</soap:Body>
```

Fig. 2. Service request and response transformations

have been published on XML parsers[1]. Of course, vulnerabilities in the parser used to communicate between front and back-end components would still have an impact, but the protocol is less complex, and few vulnerabilities in Java RMI (for example) have been published. Similarly, vulnerabilities in application servers, such as Glassfish and Apache Axis 2, would have a much smaller impact in our system.

Use of poorly-configured services can be avoided through use of remote attestation. This is true of any attestation-enabled platform, but our architecture reduces the number of components to report upon, thus reducing complexity and making it easier for a verifier to establish the properties required. Long-term credentials can also be stored safely using a TPM, reducing this vulnerability.

However, though the front-end service may be untrusted, it can still impact availability, resulting in a denial of service attack. As we have only *split* the

---

[1] For example, Secunia Advisories SA22333 and SA10398.

service into two components, rather than increasing the amount of software, this is no worse than before our modifications. The same is true of error handling.

4   Performance

The proposed architecture will have a performance overhead due to additional RMI requests and TPM operations. Gray [10] provides a performance comparison of RMI and Web Services. His figures show that RMI invocations take around 1ms and are therefore an order of magnitude faster than most WS-Security enabled web services. We would therefore expect the additional RMI step to have a negligible impact on round-trip time. Furthermore, should the front- and back-end services be hosted on the same platform (such as in Figure 1) then we can be even more optimistic.

The impact of using the TPM is more significant. For each message, the TPM must decrypt a symmetric key using a key bound to the TPM, and then sign a digest using another bound key. With an Infineon 1.2 TPM, these operations take 400ms each, addding 800ms to the round trip time. A faster alternative would be to use the same session key repeatedly for the service, which would eliminate subsequent unseal operation on messages received from the same client. The session key could also be re-used for signing, meaning only one TPM operation in total. The disadvantage to doing this is that the key is stored in unprotected memory for a significant period of time. Further optimisation may be possible with virtual TPMs, operating mostly in software.

5   Related Work

Wei et al. [11] split web service middleware into trusted and untrusted parts. Sensitive information in incoming messages is intercepted by a 'message splicer' and only given to the trusted module. This is similar to our solution, but we take the proposals further, allowing users to attest, rather than just hardening the internal structure. Our proposals solve the problem of trusting the server-side message splicer.

Similarly, Jiang et al. [12] mitigate the threat from malicious insiders by using an IBM 4758 secure co-processor. This 'guardian' is responsible for some important functions, and users can establish a secure session directly with it. Our approach expands on this is two ways: allowing conformance with service standards and using a low-cost Trusted Platform Module. Furthermore, our system is designed to minimise threats from both outside and insider attackers.

Watanabe et al. [4] have an alternative approach, separating the communications component - the 'Secure Message Router' - from the application itself. This SMR is a trusted component. This is the opposite of our proposal, and focuses on establishing guaranteed secure communications, rather than service integrity. This might be a way to implement *composite* services, which our architecture does not allow.

6   Conclusion

We have shown that web service middleware is a significant limiting factor in attestation and establishing trustworthiness. Our proposal is to remove it from the trusted computing base of the service, solving both problems and increasing resilience to runtime attack. The back-end platform can then be used to run verified services with critical functionality. We have also outlined a method for establishing a secure session without sacrificing web service standards. From analysis of security benefits against performance overhead, we believe that this architecture is worth considering for any web service with known, high security requirements.

Acknowledgements

John Lyle's work is funded by a studentship from QinetiQ and the EPSRC. We thank Andrew Cooper, Jun Ho Huh and Cornelius Namiluko for their suggestions.

References

1. Schellekens, D., Wyseur, B., Preneel, B.: Remote Attestation on Legacy Operating Systems With Trusted Platform Modules. ENTCS 197(1), 59–72 (2008)
2. The Trusted Computing Group: Website (2009)
3. Lyle, J., Martin, A.: On the feasibility of remote attestation for web services. In: SecureCom 2009, vol. 3, pp. 283–288 (2009)
4. Watanabe, Y., Yoshihama, S., Mishina, T., Kudo, M., Maruyama, H.: Bridging the Gap Between Inter-communication Boundary and Internal Trusted Components. In: Gollmann, D., Meier, J., Sabelfeld, A. (eds.) ESORICS 2006. LNCS, vol. 4189, pp. 65–80. Springer, Heidelberg (2006)
5. Bangerter, E., Djackov, M., Sadeghi, A.R.: A demonstrative ad hoc attestation system. In: Wu, T.-C., Lei, C.-L., Rijmen, V., Lee, D.-T. (eds.) ISC 2008. LNCS, vol. 5222, pp. 17–30. Springer, Heidelberg (2008)
6. Gasmi, Y., Sadeghi, A.R., Stewin, P., Unger, M., Asokan, N.: Beyond secure channels. In: STC, pp. 30–40. ACM, New York (2007)
7. OASIS: Web services security: Soap message security 1.1 (2004),
   http://docs.oasis-open.org/wss/v1.1/
8. Demchenko, Y., Gommans, L., de Laat, C., Oudenaarde, B.: Web services and grid security vulnerabilities and threats analysis and model. In: GRID. IEEE, Los Alamitos (2005)
9. Bhalla, N., Kazerooni, S.: Web service vulnerabilities (2007),
   http://www.blackhat.com/presentations/bh-europe-07/Bhalla-Kazerooni/Whitepaper/bh-eu-07-bhalla-WP.pdf
10. Gray, N.A.B.: Comparison of web services, java-rmi, and corba service implementation. In: Australasian Workshop on Software and System Architectures (2004)
11. Wei, J., Singaravelu, L., Pu, C.: A secure information flow architecture for web service platforms. IEEE Trans. on Services Computing 1(2), 75–87 (2008)
12. Jiang, S., Smith, S., Minami, K.: Securing web servers against insider attack. In: ACSAC, p. 265. IEEE, Los Alamitos (2001)

Dynamic Enforcement of Platform Integrity

Martin Pirker, Ronald Toegl, and Michael Gissing

Institute for Applied Information Processing and Communications (IAIK),
Graz University of Technology, Inffeldgasse 16a, A–8010 Graz
{mpirker,rtoegl}@iaik.tugraz.at,
m.gissing@tugraz.at

Abstract. Modern Trusted Computing platforms offer the basic hardware building blocks to allow effective enforcement of software integrity. In this paper we present a practical software system architecture which uses Intel's *late launch* mechanism to boot a known-good configuration. We restrict the access to data and execution of services to trusted platform configurations, enforcing the integrity of contained applications as specified by the platform operator. Further, we also describe a set of operational procedures to allow flexible and dynamic configuration management. We present our prototype implementation which integrates well with established Linux distributions.

1 Introduction

The concept of *Trusted Computing* extends the standard PC architecture with trust anchors such as the Trusted Platform Module (TPM) [18] and CPU instructions [6] to *dynamically* switch into a trusted hardware state. These hardware primitives can be used to determine the software configuration of a system.

In this short paper we present a practical software architecture which leverages these mechanisms found in commodity hardware to restrict the execution of a security critical software platform to trustworthy platform configurations. We also describe a set of operational procedures which help us retain flexibility in the face of configuration changes. Our implementation integrates well with established Linux distributions.

The components presented here are a part of the hypervisor-layer in the acTvSM virtualization platform we sketched in [14]. It further extends the established trust to any commodity software.

Outline. The remainder of this paper is organized as follows: Section 2 provides an introduction to Trusted Computing and Trusted Execution technologies as well as related work. Section 3 presents our system platform architecture and the process of booting it. We also discuss basic platform operations. Section 4 details the prototype implementation. The paper concludes in Section 5.

A. Acquisti, S.W. Smith, and A.-R. Sadeghi (Eds.): TRUST 2010, LNCS 6101, pp. 265–272, 2010.

2   Background

2.1   TCG's Trusted Computing

Trusted Computing as it is available today is based on specifications of the *Trusted Computing Group* (TCG). The core hardware component is the *Trusted Platform Module* (TPM) [18]. Similarly to a smart card the TPM features tamper-resilient cryptographic primitives, but is physically bound to its host device. The TPM helps to guarantee the integrity of measurements of software components by offering a set of *Platform Configuration Registers* (PCRs), which can only be written to via the one-way *extend* operation. PCRs are reset to defined values at platform boot. A PCR with index $i, i \geq 0$ in state t may then be extended with input x by setting $PCR_i^{t+1} = \text{SHA-1}(PCR_i^t \| x)$. PCRs can be used to exactly document the software executed on a machine by implementing the transitive trust model, where each software component is responsible to measure the following component before invoking it. Ultimately, a *chain of trust* is established where the full Trusted Computing Base (TCB) and configuration of the platform is mapped to PCR values. If such a PCR configuration fulfills the given security or policy requirements, we refer to the system state as a *trusted state*.

The TPM can also *bind* data to the platform by encrypting it with a *non-migratable* key, which never leaves the TPM's protection. An extension to this is *sealing*, where a key may only be used with a specific PCR configuration. Thus, decryption of sealed data can be restricted to a trusted state of the platform.

2.2   Dynamic Switch to Trusted State

Modern platforms from AMD [1] and Intel [6] extend the basic TCG model of a *static* chain-of-trust anchored in a hardware reboot. They provide the option of a *dynamic* switch to a trusted system state. In this paper we focus on Intel's *Trusted Execution Technology* (TXT), which we build our implementation on.

A so-called *late launch* is initiated by the special Intel TXT CPU instruction GETSEC[SENTER]. It stops all processing cores except one. The chipset locks all memory to prevent outside modification by DMA devices and resets PCRs 17 to 22. A special Intel-provided and cryptographically signed *Authenticated Code Module* (ACM) starts a fresh chain-of-trust after setting the platform into a well-defined state. Subsequently, a *Measured Launch Environment* (MLE) [9] is first measured and then executed. Piece-by-piece the MLE decides which system resources to unlock and thus cautiously restores normal platform operation. The ACM is also capable of enforcing specific *Launch Control Policies* (LCPs). Here, the ACM measures the MLE and compares it with the trusted LCP stored in the non-volatile memory of the TPM. Changes to the LCP can only be authorized by the TPM owner. Any other, not authorized software configuration, is not allowed to continue; the ACM will reset the platform.

A late launch is the only way on a TXT platform to initialize the TPM PCR registers 17-22 to all zeros (0x00), as opposed to a standard platform power-on or reboot (0xFF). This allows to seal data to a chain-of-trust which must be anchored in a TXT launch sequence.

2.3   Related Work

An early example of extending the trust from dedicated hardware security modules into applications is given in the Dyad System [19]. AEGIS [2] is an early mechanism to support secure boot on PC platforms assuming a trusted BIOS. The Enforcer platform [11] and IBM's Integrity Measurement Architecture [16] show how to integrate TCG-style static measurements into the Linux environment. While this collects precise information, it does not always allow to identify a limited number of possibly good configurations. Instead of individual files, file system images have been used to transport user software and data with Soul-Pads [3] or Secure Virtual Disk Images in grid services [5] between platforms.

Recently, x86 architectures have been extended to provide the option of a *dynamic* switch to a trusted system state. BIND [17] uses AMD's Secure Virtual Machine (SVM) [1] protection features to collect fine grained measurements on both input and the code modules that operate on it so that the computation results can be attested to. Flicker [12] isolates sensitive code by halting the main OS, switching into AMD SVM, and executing with a minimal TCB small, short-lived pieces of application logic (PALs). PALs may use the TPM to document their execution and handle results. OSLO [10] is an OS loader module which implements a dynamic switch to a measured state in the OS bootchain on AMD SVM systems, whereas `tboot` (Trusted Boot) [8] is a loader which achieves this on Intel TXT platforms. LaLa [4] performs a late launch from an instant-on application to boot a fully fledged OS in the background.

3   Dynamically Enforcing the Integrity of a Platform

We believe that the recent advances allow to turn commodity, off-the-shelf PC systems into versatile platforms which are able to enforce the integrity of software services. Our architecture is built for flexible operation and allows for the practical protection of commodity software. First, we present the security goals we want to achieve and the leitmotifs we want our architecture to follow.

The main objective of our platform is to guarantee that well-defined software configurations are executed. We can achieve this by constructing a chain-of-trust by measuring all components into PCRs. For a deterministic result the measurements must be stable, the number of measurements finite, and their order constant. We believe that for measurements a file-system granularity is sufficient. Of course, also all components involved earlier in the boot process must be accounted for. TXT eases this task, as for instance the BIOS is no longer a link of the chain of trust. We calculate the expected PCR values *a priori* and can then seal data and the desired executable code to this *future trusted state*.

Of course, a security sensitive application and its working data should never be stored on platform storage media in plaintext. Instead, we encrypt the file system by default, and only when the platform attains the good running configuration defined by the system administrator, access and modifications are possible. As unsealing can only occur at runtime, this prevents off-line attacks as well as attacks by running maliciously modified software.

We believe that appropriate usability is needed for practical applications and so we target professional system administrators. We do not want to restrict the choice of software the platform administrator may execute. Our platform should allow to install any application and define it as trusted. The overhead to maintain configuration integrity and to perform updates should be reasonable. Mechanisms to back-up applications and data must exist.

3.1 Integrity Guaranteeing Boot Process

To initialize the system to a predefined configuration, close cooperation of hardware and software is required. We use Intel TXT as physical platform. SINIT is Intel's implementation of an ACM, while tboot is Intel's prototype implementation of an MLE (see Section 2.2). Upon power-on, the platform performs a conventional boot, but does not start an operating system; instead, the MLE is prepared and a TXT *late launch* is performed. The precise, desired software configuration is specified by the administrator in the form of policies stored in the TPM. The LCP is evaluated by SINIT and specifies which MLE is allowed to be executed. tboot's policy is called Verified Launch Policy (VLP), it contains known-good values for measurements of the following Linux kernel and its initial ramdisk file system initramfs. A secure boot is performed into a hardware guaranteed state and the chain of trust is extended over the kernel and initramfs. If the measurements do not match the expected values provided by the VLP, tboot will shut the platform down.

Our start-up code in the initramfs unseals the cryptographic keys needed to mount the platform's file system It also ensures an unbroken chain-of-trust; it measures the filesystem image into a PCR before it is mounted.

To support deterministic PCR measurements, the platform's file system must remain read-only. An overlaid temporary file system provides the needed read-write storage during platform operation. These temporary changes do not survive a reboot of the platform - except by explicit patching or system update (see Section 3.2). This ensures robustness of the system platform image to malicious modifications.

The system platform is a customized Linux operating system. Note that the exact configuration of the software image can be configured freely to the needs of the applications and services it runs.

3.2 Operating the Platform

The basic platform operations which allow the initialization and long-term maintenance of our setup begin with the *Installation*. In order to start from an initial trusted state the software needs to be distributed on a trusted medium. This can be ensured by read-only media such as CD-ROM. Once booted from it, the installation routine wipes the system's harddisk(s) and installs a default configuration of the platform. Immediately, the measurement values for tboot, the platform's filesystem, kernel and initial ramdisk are calculated and appropriate policies are stored in the TPM. Already in this early stage, the platform is ready to do its first reboot into trusted mode. After a successful late launch, the platform runs in *Update Mode*, where it waits for maintenance commands.

In Update Mode the platform is capable of upgrading software packages. At the end of this process, the same procedure is triggered that was run during installation: The fresh system platform image is assembled, compressed and linked in the bootloader menu. As all file system decryption keys are sealed to the old platform state, they must be resealed to the new one. If the kernel or its `initramfs` was updated, a new VLP is written into the TPM. This also applies to a `tboot` update, where a new LCP needs to be written.

The full update procedure outlined in the previous paragraph may be cumbersome for minor configuration changes such as a change of a static IP address in some configuration file. Instead, a "patch" facility allows the remote administrator to provide a patch file on a separate partition. The authenticity of the patch is guaranteed by a cryptographic signature by administrator - the certificate to do so is contained within the platform image. Upon next full system update these patches are automatically integrated into the system. This mechanism allows for easy distribution of pre-configured system platform images in homogeneous datacenters, where machines only vary in small configuration details.

Administrators can reboot the platform with the functions provided by Intel Active Management Technology (AMT) [7] and also access the platform via SSH. Remember that a policy update process requires the TPM owner password. Before the administrator provides this password, she a) must confirm that she is connected to the right platform and b) that the platform is in the correct Update Mode configuration. The first constraint demands that the client must verify that the server always presents the same trusted public key. Second, we seal the SSH daemon's private key to Update Mode. If no external log-in attempt is received, the platform switches into *Application Mode*. This is performed as follows. The SSH daemon is stopped and its private key is removed, and the PCRs are extented to document the state transition and prevent further access to the TPM sealed blobs. Finally, applications are started.

4   Implementation

Obscuring implementation details does not aid the design of cryptographic systems. Only the ability to check the blueprints of a platform gives interested parties the opportunity to evaluate and eventually certify the security level of the architecture. To allow evaluation from the widest possible audience, we base our platform on open-source components. In theory, any Linux distribution can be customized for our architecture. In practise, a large number of patches and changes was needed to assemble a working prototype. We use packages from the x86_64 *Debian Linux* lenny[1] release for the host platform. To support current Trusted Computing hardware we need to add selected packages from the Debian

---
[1] http://www.debian.org/releases/lenny/

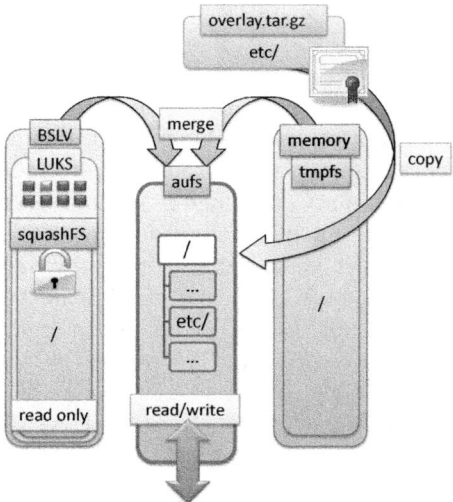

Fig. 1. The writeable platform root file system is merged at boot time from a read-only static image and an in-memory file system. An authentic configuration patch for minor adjustments is integrated.

testing tree. Scripts for installation, initial ramdisk management and rebuilding of the system image are customized to our needs. The system bootstrap scripts for creation of distributable and bootable CDs for initial installation are taken from GRML Linux[2], a distribution specialized for system administrators.

Bootloading is accomplished by using a standard bootloader (GRUB[3]) along with SINIT and tboot [8] to perform a late launch. 64-bit ports of the tools from IBM's *TPM-utils* [15] add the PCR extend and unsealing capabilities in the initial ramdisk environment. The more complex operations such as sealing, unsealing or the policy creation and storing in TPM NV-RAM are performed by custom scripts using *jTpmTools* and *jTSS* from IAIK's "Trusted Computing for Java" project [13]. Computers from the HP dc7900 series serve as our reference hardware platform.

Our platform devides the system harddisk into two partitions. The first partition contains a read-write filesystem hosting all the components necessary for the platform boot process. This encompasses the bootloader, tboot, SINIT and Linux kernel plus associated initramfs images. The remainder of the harddisk storage is allocated as a Logical Volume Manager (LVM)[4] dynamically managed space which is assigned to a single LVM volume group. The individual volumes are transparently encrypted by the Linux kernel's dm-crypt subsystem, using Linux Unified Key Setup (LUKS) for key management.

---

[2] http://grml.org/
[3] http://www.gnu.org/software/grub/
[4] http://sourceware.org/lvm2/

As a running Linux system requires some writable file system, the root "/"
file system of the platform is assembled from multiple layers via aufs[5]. Figure 1
illustrates this process which is performed at boot time. The logical volume
BASELV contains a compressed read-only squashfs image with binaries and
configuration files of the system platform. The boot code in the initramfs measures the logical volume and merges via aufs this squashfs with an in-memory
tmpfs to provide writable, but ephemeral storage. In addition, we copy administrator signed configuration patches, stored on the unencrypted filesystem, after
validation of the signature. Thus, we create a read-write file system which is
based on authenticated images with robust and deterministic hash values. In
Update Mode, we can even (re)create these images and pre-calculate their expected measurement values *in situ*.

5   Conclusion

In this paper we present a practical architecture which uses Trusted Computing
to offer integrity guarantees to a software platform, the applications and the
services it hosts. We enforce any trusted configuration the administrator defined
or updated *in situ*. To overcome the challenge of complexity, we take advantage
of Intel TXT to shorten the chain-of-trust and measure at file system granularity.
We empower administrators to easily customize and update the platform offered.
Our prototype implementation suggests that commodity Linux can be adapted
this way.

Acknowledgments

This work was supported by the Österreichische Forschungsförderungsgesellschaft
(FFG) through project acTvSM, funding theme FIT-IT, no. 820848. We thank
Andreas Niederl and Michael Gebetsroither for insightful discussions and their
help in implementing the prototype.

References

1. Advanced Micro Devices: AMD64 Virtualization: Secure Virtual Machine Architecture Reference Manual (May 2005)
2. Arbaugh, W.A., Farber, D.J., Smith, J.M.: A secure and reliable bootstrap architecture. In: Proceedings of the 1997 IEEE Symposium on Security and Privacy,
   vol. 65. IEEE Computer Society, Los Alamitos (1997)
3. Cáceres, R., Carter, C., Narayanaswami, C., Raghunath, M.: Reincarnating pcs
   with portable soulpads. In: Proceedings of the 3rd International Conference on
   Mobile Systems, Applications, and Services, pp. 65–78. ACM, Seattle (2005)
4. Gebhardt, C., Dalton, C.: Lala: a late launch application. In: Proceedings of the
   2009 ACM Workshop on Scalable Trusted Computing, pp. 1–8. ACM, Chicago
   (2009)

---

[5] http://aufs.sourceforge.net/

5. Gebhardt, C., Tomlinson, A.: Secure Virtual Disk Images for Grid Computing. In: 3rd Asia-Pacific Trusted Infrastructure Technologies Conference (APTC 2008), October 2008. IEEE Computer Society, Los Alamitos (2008)
6. Grawrock, D.: Dynamics of a Trusted Platform: A Building Block Approach. No. ISBN 978-1934053171, Richard Bowles, Intel Press, Intel Corporation, 2111 NE 25th Avenue, JF3-330, Hillsboro, OR 97124-5961 (February 2009)
7. Intel Corporation: Intel active management technology (amt), http://www.intel.com/technology/platform-technology/intel-amt/index.htm
8. Intel Corporation: Trusted Boot - an open source, pre- kernel/VMM module that uses Intel TXT to perform a measured and verified launch of an OS kernel/VMM (2008), http://sourceforge.net/projects/tboot/
9. Intel Corporation: Intel Trusted Execution Technology Software Development Guide (December 2009), http://download.intel.com/technology/security/downloads/315168.pdf
10. Kauer, B.: Oslo: improving the security of trusted computing. In: SS 2007: Proceedings of 16th USENIX Security Symposium on USENIX Security Symposium, pp. 1–9. USENIX Association, Berkeley (2007)
11. Marchesini, J., Smith, S., Wild, O., MacDonald, R.: Experimenting with tcpa/tcg hardware, or: How i learned to stop worrying and love the bear. Tech. rep., Department of Computer Science/Dartmouth PKI Lab, Dartmouth College (2003)
12. McCune, J.M., Parno, B.J., Perrig, A., Reiter, M.K., Isozaki, H.: Flicker: an execution infrastructure for tcb minimization. In: Proceedings of the 3rd ACM SIGOPS/EuroSys European Conference on Computer Systems 2008, pp. 315–328. ACM, Glasgow (2008)
13. Pirker, M., Toegl, R., Winkler, T., Vejda, T.: Trusted computing for the Java™ platform (2009), http://trustedjava.sourceforge.net/
14. Pirker, M., Toegl, R.: Towards a virtual trusted platform. Journal of Universal Computer Science (2010) (in print), http://www.jucs.org/jucs_16_4/towards_a_virtual_trusted
15. Safford, D., Kravitz, J., Doorn, L.v.: Take control of tcpa. Linux Journal (112), 2 (2003), http://domino.research.ibm.com/comm/research_projects.nsf/pages/gsal.TCG.html
16. Sailer, R., Zhang, X., Jaeger, T., van Doorn, L.: Design and implementation of a TCG-based integrity measurement architecture. In: Proceedings of the 13th USENIX Security Symposium. USENIX Association, San Diego (2004)
17. Shi, E., Perrig, A., Van Doorn, L.: Bind: a fine-grained attestation service for secure distributed systems. In: 2005 IEEE Symposium on Security and Privacy, pp. 154–168 (2005)
18. Trusted Computing Group: TCG TPM specification version 1.2 revision 103 (2007), https://www.trustedcomputinggroup.org/specs/TPM/
19. Tygar, J., Yee, B.: Dyad: A system for using physically secure coprocessors. In: Technological Strategies for the Protection of Intellectual Property in the Networked Multimedia Environment, pp. 121–152. Interactive Multimedia Association (1994)

An Improved Memory Integrity Protection Scheme

Yin Hu and Berk Sunar[*]

ECE Department, WPI
100 Institute Road
Worcester, MA 01609

Abstract. In this paper, we proposed an improved memory integrity protection scheme to provide real-time protection service. In addition, we for the first time propose a provably secure scheme that takes advantage of the "error inheritance" property, which can minimize the costly check process that is normally required before every access. The security of the proposed scheme is rigorously analyzed and the performance is measured. The peak performance of the new scheme can be improved by up to a factor of 5 over a previously proposed scheme based on Merkle Trees.

1 Introduction

Integrity is a necessary condition for an entity to be trusted. A compromise of memory integrity can cause a wide range of problems ranging from cheating in games to financial fraud. Many memory integrity protection schemes have been proposed in the past [2,3,6]. However, the efficiency of these schemes is still not good enough for practical applications. The main problem is the overhead introduced by the cryptographic functions. Furthermore, what differentiates the memory integrity protection problem from other security applications that require integrity checks are the so-called *replay attacks*. Extra measures must be taken to prevent replay attacks.

The scheme we propose in this paper is based on an earlier memory authentication scheme introduced in [6]. For easy reference we name this scheme as the HHS scheme in the rest of the paper. In this paper, we proposed an improvement over the HHS scheme which reduces the overhead while retaining the security level. We also propose taking advantage of the so-called "error inheritance" property which allows our scheme to detect earlier attacks without the need to check the integrity before each individual memory access. This feature brings real-time memory integrity protection one step closer to practical reality.

2 Objective

Before introducing our scheme, we will clarify the attacker model and outline some assumptions.

---

[*] This work is supported in part by a gift from Intel Corperation.

A. Acquisti, S.W. Smith, and A.-R. Sadeghi (Eds.): TRUST 2010, LNCS 6101, pp. 273–281, 2010.

The memory in our model is divided into two parts:

- **Protected memory.** This part of memory is protected by higher level of trust service providers.[1]. It is assumed to be secure in this paper. The protected memory is used to store critical data such as the code, the root of the Merkle Tree and the keys. It can also provide a secure cache for the schemes. Our goal is to make this piece of memory as small as possible.
- **Unprotected memory.** This part of memory will be protected by our scheme. The tags, seeds and randomizers used in our protection scheme will also be stored here. Any ordinary process that want to use our integrity protection service must call the *Read* and *Update* (Write) functions provided by our scheme to access the memory.

The attacker in our model can perform any operations that an authorized user can and he can also view and modify the data in the memory directly at any time. Here 'directly' means that the attacker can also access the memory without the participation of the protection scheme. The goal of the attacker is to modify the data directly without being detected by our scheme. The depiction of our model is presented in Figure 1.

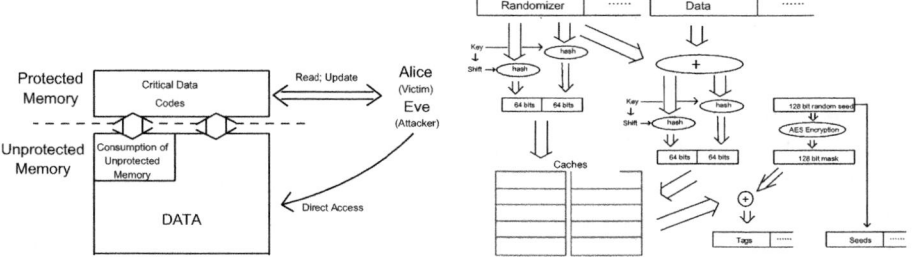

Fig. 1. Outline of the attack model   **Fig. 2.** Outline of the new scheme

The goal of our scheme is to provide real-time integrity protection of the unprotected memory. When an attacker has once modified the data directly in the unprotected memory, the scheme should be able to detect this violation with a high probability even after a few other operations (some *Read* and *Update* calls from the victim process, etc.) Even if the attacker reverses his modification after the victim process has accessed that piece of data at least once (otherwise the attack will be meaningless), this modification should also be detectable by the scheme.

In addition, we assume that the functions of the scheme are treated as atomic such that the attacker cannot perform attacks while the authentication scheme is executing. Also, if an attack is detected by the scheme, an alarm is raised

---

[1] Such as the ARM TrustZone or trusted OS extensions. Some Intel or AMD CPUs provide instructions such as GETSEC[SENTER] on Intel TXT to help performing a measured launch of the operation system with the help of the TPM.

and all the keys are flushed so that the attacker cannot exploit the scheme by repeating the attacks [9].

3   The HHS Scheme

In this section, we will introduce the HHS scheme very briefly. A more detailed introduction can be found in the full version of this paper and it is fully discussed in [6].

The HHS scheme is a combination of the Merkle Tree and the universal hash function family. To prevent replay attacks, the HHS scheme chains the tags together using a Merkle Tree structure [1]. The universal hash function family is a collection of functions that map data to digests. The HHS scheme uses a universal hash function family NH which was proposed for use in the UMAC scheme [4]. It exhibits excellent performance in software [5]. Also, Toeplitz technique [7] [8] is used to strengthen the security.

Tags used in the Merkle tree are generated by adding masks to the hash results. The masks are generated by encrypting a random seed using a block cipher. For this task the AES block cipher is employed. The seeds are randomly generated and saved in the unprotected memory in plaintext alongside the produced tags. This scheme is called the *basic scheme* in [6]. We will refer this scheme as the *HHS Basic Scheme* later.

As also mentioned in [6], caches and parallelism can be used to improve the efficiency. In this paper, our new scheme will also take advantage of the caches and the parallelism and improve the efficiency even greater.

4   Proposed Improvements

In this part, some other techniques that can help improve the efficiency of the scheme will be discussed. They can work together to reduce the overhead to a lower level.

4.1   Error Inheritance

One problem of the HHS scheme, as well as other similar authentication schemes is that the data need a check before every access. For example, if the data is not checked before every access, the attacker can reverse the modification after the read operation however before the next check. In this way, the system will never be able to detect that it has read forged data. However, we can use the *error inheritance* property to eliminate this check. This property was firstly mentioned in [6] but not discussed in detail. In this paper, we will discuss the error inheritance property and make use of this property to improve the scheme. With this property, any injected error that occurs within the execution will carry forward to the future values of the tag. Even if the tags are checked after a large number of cycles it is still possible to detect the injection of an error at one point in time with high probability. Thus, we only need a check before every critical operations instead of before every access. However, if the attacker can control or predict the data, he can compromise the protection scheme. Details of this attack can be found in the full version.

To solve this problem, we keep random masks called randomizers for every piece of data. The randomizers can be generated either by a hardware random source or a PRNG. For each update of the Merkle Tree, instead of the data, the sum of the data and the corresponding randomizer is treated as the leaf of the tree. In addition, the randomizers will also change for each update. If the randomizers are changing randomly, the sum of the randomizer and the data should be unpredictable. In this way, the error inheritance property works.

The protection scheme introduced in [3] also eliminate the checks before each access by using multiset hashing to ensure that data retrieved is same as data saved last time. However, our scheme integrates such protection into the Merkle Tree and the NH we used can reach a higher speed.

4.2 Better Parallelism

Higher levels of the Merkle Tree depend on the results of lower levels. This dependence forms a slow path as the tree grows large and other costly computations are pre-computed. In our scheme, the seed instead of the tags serve as the data for the higher level of the tree. Since the seeds are randomly generated, each level of the Merkle Tree can start updating without waiting for the result of the lower level. Thus parallel computation of the Merkle Tree can be employed. Furthermore, the operations related to the randomizers can be executed in parallel.

4.3 An Alternative Caching Scheme

In the HHS scheme, the masks are cached in a secure cache. In this paper, we make it better by caching the hash result. In this case, no costly AES operation is needed as long as the hash result does not leave the cache. In addition, the incremental update of the hash result and the encryption by the one-time-pad mask are both achieved by addition. Thus, one can actually update the tags without even unmasking the tags. It is not secure to perform such operations in the HHS scheme. However, with a hash cache, this operation becomes secure because the attacker can neither view nor change the tags in the caches. This property can help the scheme to achieve a good peak performance by delaying the costly AES operations to idle times.

5 Putting It All Together

By combining the methods introduced above we can achieve great performance improvements. First of all, the hash results need to be cached to improve the efficiency of the scheme and the new masks are pre-computed or computed in parallel. Let us assume that the masks can be prepared in parallel. The tags of the higher level of the Merkle Tree are calculated by hashing the seeds of the lower level and caches are also used to further improve the efficiency.

The data needs to be randomized to keep the error inheritance property. However, randomizers for every single byte of data will introduce a 100 percent overhead on storing space. The solution is only using randomizers for the frequently updated data. Each data block is associated with a randomizer when entering the cache, the randomizer is only assigned when the tag of that block of data is loaded into the cache. Though a large amount of computation has to be done when there is a cache miss, including a check of the data and the randomizers, the average speed will still be fast with a high cache hit rate.

The higher levels of the Merkle Tree are built similarly using the seeds as data. They do not need such randomizers to maintain the error inheritance property because the seeds are essentially random values which are unpredictable. The resulting scheme is depicted in Figure 2. The detailed algorithm of the scheme may be found in the full version.

6   Security Analysis

The security analysis of the HHS basic scheme is provided in [6]. Here we will discuss the security implications of the proposed improvements.

6.1   Analysis for the Tree of Seeds

In the HHS scheme the Merkle Tree is formed by hashing tags. In the proposed modification the Merkle Tree is formed by seeds.

Theorem 1. *Let A be any adversary who has access to q tuples $(M_i^1, M_i^2, R_i, \tau_i)$, where q is a polynomial in w. Here we have $\tau_i = \mathsf{NH}_{K_1}(M_i^1)|\mathsf{NH}_{K_2}(M_i^2) + \mathrm{AES}_{Ke}(R_i)$ where the addition is computed modulo 2^{2w} separately on each of the two parts of the $\mathrm{AES}_{Ke}(R_i)$, $|$ is the string concatenation operator, and $K_1, K_2, M_i^1, M_i^2 \in \{0,1\}^{2w}$ such that K_2 is the shifted version of K_1. $Ke, R_i, \tau_i \in \{0,1\}^k$ where we have set $k = 4w$. For such an adversary we define P_A to be the probability of A finding M^1, M^2 and τ where $M^1 \neq M_j^1$ and $M^2 \neq M_j^2$ such that $\tau = \mathsf{NH}_{K_1}(M^1)|\mathsf{NH}_{K_2}(M^2) + \mathrm{AES}_{Ke}(R)$ and $R = R_j$ for some $j \in [1, \ldots, q]$. Given the above, P_A is bounded by $P_A \leq q(2^{-2w} + \mathbf{Adv}_A^{AES}(4w))$*

Proof is omitted in this short version. It can be found in the full version of this paper.

6.2   Analysis of Error Inheritance

If the attacker targets the masked hash result, the security level will rely on the strength of AES as shown in the previous section. Alternatively, the attacker may attack the incremental hash process. For an attacker to successfully compromise the incremental update from M to M'' by changing the M to M', he needs to find some valid M''' so that $\mathsf{NH}(M''') - \mathsf{NH}(M) = \mathsf{NH}(M'') - \mathsf{NH}(M')$.

Theorem 2. *Let A be any attacker to the incremental update. With a successful attack A will have:* $\mathsf{NH}_{K_1}(M_1^1)|\mathsf{NH}_{K_2}(M_1^2) - \mathsf{NH}_{K_1}(M_2^1)|\mathsf{NH}_{K_21}(M_2^2) = \mathsf{NH}_{K_1}(R^1)|\mathsf{NH}_{K_2}(R^2) - \mathsf{NH}_{K_1}(M_3^1)|\mathsf{NH}_{K_2}(M_3^2)$ *where the addition is done modulo 2^{2w} separately on each of the two parts, $|$ is the string concatenation operator, and $K_1, K_2, M_i^1, M_i^2, R^1, R^2 \in \{0,1\}^{2w}$ such that K_2 is the shifted version of K_1. R^1, R^2 are random numbers being generated after $M_2^1, M_2^2, M_3^1, M_3^2$ are chosen. For such an adversary we define P_A to be the probability of A finding $M_1^1, M_1^2, M_2^1, M_2^2, M_3^1, M_3^2$ where $M_2^1 \neq M_3^1$ and $M_2^2 \neq M_3^2$ such that the above equation is satisfied. Given the above, P_A is bounded by $P_A \leq 2^{-2w}$.*

Proof is omitted in this short version. It can be found in the full version of this paper.

6.3   Birthday Attacks

The tag in our scheme is computed by adding the mask to the hash result. To perform a birthday attack on our scheme. The attacker may either try to find any two messages that map to the same hash result or try to find two messages that map to the same tag. If the attacker chooses to attack the hash result, since the hash result is protected by one-time-pad, the attacker cannot even check for a collision. In the case that the attacker want to find a collision over the tags, the birthday attack applies. However, the collision probability will be no larger than the hash function. Thus the birthday attack will not provide a more efficient way to compromise the scheme than trying to find collisions of the NH directly.

7   Performance

7.1   Performance Analysis

Since this is a short paper, we will only give out the results. The derivation can be found in the full version. The speed of the outlined schemes when caches are employed are calculated and listed in Table 1. The space demands is listed in Table 3. We can see clearly from the tables a significant peak performance improvement in the scheme with randomizers. However, the unprotected memory needed for the scheme with randomizers is huge due to the extra demand for storing randomizers. However, in practice the cache will be much smaller in practice(consider 2MB CPU L2 cache for GB s of memory) than our assumption. If only one percent of the hash results will be cached instead of twenty percent in the derivation, the unprotected memory demand will drop significantly to about 240 MB.

The estimation for the basic scheme and SHA-1 based Merkle Tree is also present in Tables 2 and 3 for comparison. Note from the tables that on one hand the SHA-1 based scheme has a low unprotected memory requirement and an almost negligible protected memory requirement. On the other hand, it is much slower than our scheme.

Table 1. Speed Comparison (cycles)

l	Full HHS Scheme			Using hash cache			Scheme with randomizers		
	$t_{check\&up}$	t_{check}	$t^{peak}_{check\&up}$	$t_{check\&up}$	t_{check}	$t^{peak}_{check\&up}$	$t_{check\&up}$	t_{check}	$t^{peak}_{check\&up}$
2	743155	889938	741455	890320	889939	741455	446489	1483102	400
3	36068	40862	32768	41301	40862	32768	23584	67077	400
4	11789	8835	6889	9284	8835	6889	6530	14346	400
5	9202	3616	2702	4068	3616	2702	3712	5778	400

Table 2. Speed Comparison II (cycles)

l	SHA-1			Basic Scheme			Scheme with randomizers		
	$t_{check\&up}$	t_{check}	$t^{peak}_{check\&up}$	$t_{check\&up}$	t_{check}	$t^{peak}_{check\&up}$	$t_{check\&up}$	t_{check}	$t^{peak}_{check\&up}$
2	7034100	7034100	7034100	1485378	1483870	1485378	446489	1483102	400
3	431200	431200	431200	103140	100224	103140	23584	67077	400
4	116200	116200	116200	34758	30434	34758	6530	14346	400
5	55700	55700	55700	23084	17352	23084	3712	5778	400

Table 3. Space Demand (MB if not specified)

l	SHA-1		Basic Scheme		Full HHS Scheme		Using hash cache		With randomizers	
	M_p	M_u	M_p	M_u	M_p	M_u	M_p	M_u	M_p	M_u
2	20 B	0.3	35.4 KB	0.71	0.42	0.71	0.42	0.71	0.50	819.9
3	20 B	7.2	15.7 KB	16.0	1.62	16.0	1.62	16.0	3.22	835.2
4	20 B	35.8	3.32 KB	76.8	7.69	76.8	7.69	76.8	15.4	896.0
5	20 B	94.6	1.32 KB	198.7	19.9	198.7	19.9	198.7	39.7	1017.9

7.2   Implementation Results

To evaluate the performance we implemented the proposed schemes on an Intel Core 2 machine with a processor speed of 1.67 G Hz. We developed a simple two level Merkle Tree with combinations of the improvements we proposed. The size of memory to be protected was 32KB. In our experiments, we used a block size of 1KB and a tag size of 256-bit (32B). The cache size is four tags and AES are computed in parallel. We also simulated the HHS Basic Scheme and a SHA-1 based Merkle Tree for comparison.

To evaluate the performance of the schemes in different situations, we measure the speed of our scheme with different cache hit rates. Figure 3 shows the overhead in cycles of the final scheme, the scheme with a hash cache, the scheme

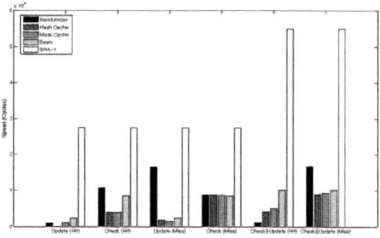

Fig. 3. Performance Comparison

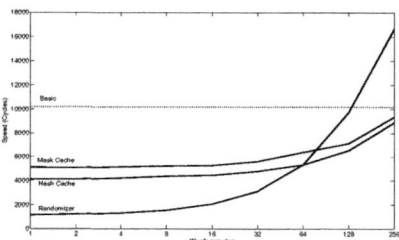

Fig. 4. Cache Performance

with a mask cache, the HHS basic scheme and the SHA-1 based Merkle Tree. For each scheme, the speed of an *Update*, a *Check* and the practical cases (an *Update* for the new scheme; a *Check* followed by an *Update* for other schemes) is provided. As shown in the figure, the scheme with randomizers performs better in the practical cases.

We also measure the average case performance for different cache hit rates. This is achieved by letting the application access memory locations every several words. When this stride, i.e. the number of words, grows the cache efficiency will get worse. Figure 4 shows the performance of each scheme vs. this stride. We can see clearly from the figure that the performance of the new schemes depends heavily on the cache hit rate. However, in most practical cases such as the RAM integrated in a PC, the hit rate should be quite satisfactory considering the CPU cache hit rate.

8   Conclusion and Future Work

In this work we proposed a number of improvements for the dynamic memory protection scheme proposed in [6]. The new scheme can achieve better performance via more efficient caches and better use of parallelism as well as the error inheritance property. When the proposed techniques are simultaneously implemented, the overall performance can be improved significantly. Our implementations show that the peak speed is increased by up to a factor of 5 over the scheme proposed in [6], at the expense of more protected and unprotected memory used to maintain the caches.

We set the integration of the proposed memory integrity protection scheme in a real life application as future work.

References

1. Merkle, R.C.: Protocols for Public Key Cryptosystems. In: Proceedings of the 1980 IEEE Symposium on Security and Privacy (1980)
2. Yan, C., Rogers, B., Englender, D., Solihin, Y., Prvulovic, M.: Improving Cost, Performance, and Security of Memory Encryption and Authentication. In: ISCA 2006 (2006)
3. Clarke, D., Suh, G.E., Gassend, B., Sudan, A., van Dijk, M., Devadas, S.: Toward Constant Bandwidth Overhead Memory Integrity Verification. In: Proceedings of the IEEE Symposium on Security and Privacy (May 2005)
4. Black, J., Halevi, S., Krawczyk, H., Krovetz, T., Rogaway, P.: UMAC: Fast and Secure Message Authentication. In: Wiener, M. (ed.) CRYPTO 1999. LNCS, vol. 1666, p. 216. Springer, Heidelberg (1999)
5. Nevelsteen, W., Preneel, B.: Software performance of universal hash functions. In: Stern, J. (ed.) EUROCRYPT 1999. LNCS, vol. 1592, pp. 24–41. Springer, Heidelberg (1999)
6. Hu, Y., Hammouri, G., Sunar, B.: A Fast Real-time Memory Authentication Protocol. In: Proc. of STC 2008 (2008)

7. Krawczyk, H.: LFSR-based hashing and authentication. In: Desmedt, Y.G. (ed.) CRYPTO 1994. LNCS, vol. 839, pp. 129–139. Springer, Heidelberg (1994)
8. Kaps, J.-P., Yuksel, K., Sunar, B.: Energy Scalable Universal Hashing. IEEE Transactions on Computers 54(12), 1484–1495 (2005)
9. Handschuh, H., Preneel, B.: Key-recovery attacks on universal hash function based MAC algorithms. In: Wagner, D. (ed.) CRYPTO 2008. LNCS, vol. 5157, pp. 144–161. Springer, Heidelberg (2008)

Robust Combiners for Software Hardening

Amir Herzberg and Haya Shulman

Bar Ilan University, Department of Computer Science,
Ramat Gan, 52900, Israel
{amir.herzberg,haya.shulman}@gmail.com
http://www.cs.biu.ac.il

Abstract. Practical software hardening schemes, as well as practical encryption schemes, e.g., AES, are heuristic and do not rely on provable security. One technique to enhance security is *robust combiners*. An algorithm C is a robust combiner for specification S, e.g., privacy, if for any two implementations X and Y, of a cryptographic scheme, the combined scheme $C(X, Y)$ satisfies S provided *either X or Y* satisfy S.

We present the first robust combiners for software hardening, specifically for White-Box Remote Program Execution (WBRPE) [10]. WBRPE is a software hardening technique that is employed to protect execution of programs in remote, hostile environment. WBRPE provides a software only platform allowing secure execution of programs on untrusted, remote hosts, ensuring privacy of the program, and of the inputs to the program, as well as privacy and integrity of the result of the computation.

Robust combiners are particularly important for software hardening, where there is no standard whose security is established. In addition, robust combiners for software hardening are interesting from software engineering perspective since they introduce new techniques of reductions and code manipulation.

Keywords: White-box security, software hardening, robust combiners, cryptographic protocols.

1 Introduction

Many applications rely on secure execution of programs in untrusted, potentially hostile, environments. *White-box security*, refers to ensuring security of programs running in such untrusted environments. Over the last two decades there is a growing interest in white-box security for distributed network applications, e.g., on-line software distribution and licensing, mobile agents, grid computing.

In white-box security the software is at full control of the platform executing the software. The originator loses all control over her software, which is completely exposed to the hosting environment, and the entity controlling the execution environment obtains full access to the program, and can observe and manipulate the execution, code and data. White box security stands in contrast to traditional cryptography, which assumes a trusted platform, i.e., a *black-box*, on which secrets, e.g., private keys, can be stored. In black-box security all

A. Acquisti, S.W. Smith, and A.-R. Sadeghi (Eds.): TRUST 2010, LNCS 6101, pp. 282–289, 2010.

the computations are performed inside a trusted black-box, and secrets (keys) never leave its boundaries. Attackers can only observe the input/output behaviour, but cannot access the code or data, or observe the execution inside the black-box.

Although provably secure software hardening techniques exist for many applications, e.g., [3], they are highly inefficient for practical applications, and due to efficiency considerations, software hardening techniques employed in practice do not have a proof of security. Heuristic implementations, e.g., *obfuscation* (see [4, 5]), are a typical choice in practice, and often implementations gain reasonable security reputation as a result of failed efforts to cryptanalyse them, and as a result of build-break-fix[1] paradigm. Same approach is also taken in black-box cryptography, e.g., instead of implementing schemes with provable security, cryptanalysis secure standards, such as AES [6], are employed, resulting in efficient and practical implementations.

When security of the cryptographic primitive is not proven, robust combiner is a safe choice, to ensure that the overall security of the cryptosystem will be as that of the most secure underlying primitive. In this work we focus on *robust combiners* for software hardening techniques, and present a robust combiner for White-Box Remote Program Execution (WBRPE) schemes, [10] (see Section 2). The authors suggest to apply a build-break-fix cycle to produce efficient, heuristic WBRPE constructions. This process may result in multiple, incomparable candidate practical and efficient schemes. A robust combiner can combine such candidate schemes, and assure security provided at least one of the candidates is secure. Our approach and constructions may constitute a methodology for future heuristic white-box primitives. Robust combiners ensure that the scheme is at least as secure as the stronger one of the underlying candidates. Robust combiners are employed for practical constructions to provide security when the security of the underlying primitives is not known, e.g., the primitive is believed to be secure due to failed crypt-analysis. Robust combiners are especially important in white-box security, where mostly heuristic or cryptanalysis secure solutions are employed, since provably secure solutions are inefficient for practical purposes.

1.1   White Box Remote Program Execution (WBRPE)

In Remote Program Execution, programs are sent by a *local host* (a.k.a. the originator) for execution on a *remote host*, and possibly use some data available to the *remote host*. The local and the remote hosts may be with conflicting interests, therefore the related security issues need to be dealt with. Those include confidentiality and integrity of input programs supplied by the local host and confidentiality of inputs provided by the remote host.

---

[1] A software implementation is published for public scrutiny and undergoes extensive efforts to cryptanalyse it. If a weakness is found, it is being fixed, and the software is tested again for security. Eventually, a software implementation is believed to be cryptanalysis secure, due to failed efforts to cryptanalyse it.

We illustrate the WBRPE scheme in Figure 1. White-box remote program execution (WBRPE) schemes are designed to ensure confidentiality of the input program P and of the output $(P(a))$, and integrity of the output. In addition, WBRPE ensures that the local host does not learn anything about the remote input a, beyond the result of the program applied to it $(P(a))$. All these properties are ensured using software only. The WBRPE is comprised of two phases, the generation phase, run by an offline trusted third party, and the protocol execution phase, run by and between the local and the remote hosts. The trusted third party generates the parameters of the scheme, i.e. the hardening key hk which is sent to local host, and the obfuscated virtual machine (ovm), a 'hardened' program, which is transfered to the remote host. The ovm emulates a trusted (software only) platform, and executes the input programs supplied by the local host in a secure manner. The local host uses the hardening key hk to harden programs P, and sends the 'hardened program' $H_{hk}(P)$ to the remote host for execution. The remote host provides the hardened program and optionally local ('auxiliary') input a into the ovm and returns the hardened result to the local host. The local unhardens with secret key uk: $\mathcal{U}_{uk}(P(a))$ and obtains $P(a)$.

WBRPE can be employed to facilitate a variety of distributed applications, that are sent to remote host for execution, e.g., network gaming, online trading center, voice over IP, and more. In these applications the goal not only to protect the program but also the result of the program, to ensure privacy and to prevent tampering and meaningful modification of the result.

1.2 Our Contribution: Robust Combiner for WBRPE Schemes

We present robust combiners for software hardening, specifically for White-Box Remote Program Execution (WBRPE) [10]. WBRPE cascade combiner is (1,2)-robust; it receives two WBRPE schemes, and produces a third WBRPE scheme that is secure if one of the underlying schemes is secure. In fact, cascade is a robust combiner independently for the confidentiality (indistinguishability) and integrity (unforgeability) properties of WBRPE schems. By cascading two WBRPE schemes, as in Figure 2, if one of the two provides indistinguishability (unforgeability), then the cascade is a WBRPE scheme that provides indistinguishability (unforgeability, respectively).

The combiners we present introduce an additional overhead, since the resulting complexity is the multiple of the complexities of the candidate schemes. Hence when the combiner is applied repeatedly to combine n schemes, the complexity would be exponential in n (although in practice we expect to combine only very few schemes, e.g., two). We leave it as an open question, to investigate more efficient constructions, or to prove lower bounds. In practice, programs are often run (or emulated) inside other programs, i.e., emulators. The basic idea of the WBRPE combiner is the same, the ovm is executed inside another ovm.

1.3 Robust Combiners

The security of cryptographic constructions often depends on unproven hardness assumptions, or on the security of primitives that withstood cryptanalysis

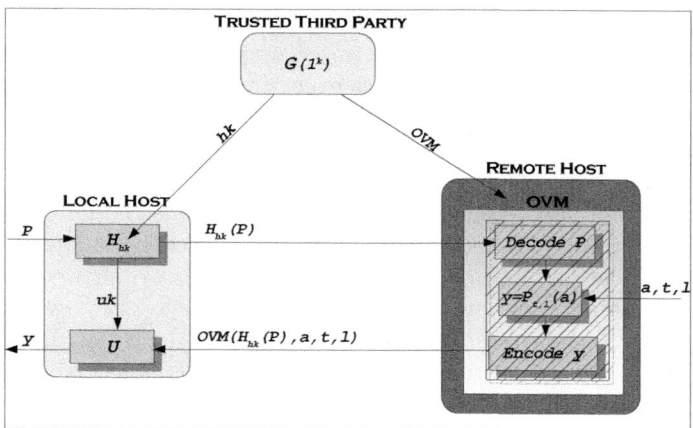

Fig. 1. WBRPE scheme is comprised of three parties the software originator, i.e., local host, the evaluator, i.e., the remote host, and the trusted third party. The trusted party is used during the offline generation phase, to produce the ovm and the hardening key hk. The local host obtains the hardening key hk which it uses to harden programs for execution on remote host. The local host applies the hardening algorithm on the program which results in a one time unhardening key uk and a hardened program $\mathcal{H}_{hk}(P)$, which it sends to the remote. The remote host obtains the ovm from the trusted party and uses it to evaluate hardened programs which it receives from the local host. Intuitively, ovm evaluates the program on the input of the remote host, and outputs the result. ovm can be implemented without decoding the result and this is just an abstract, simplified representation.

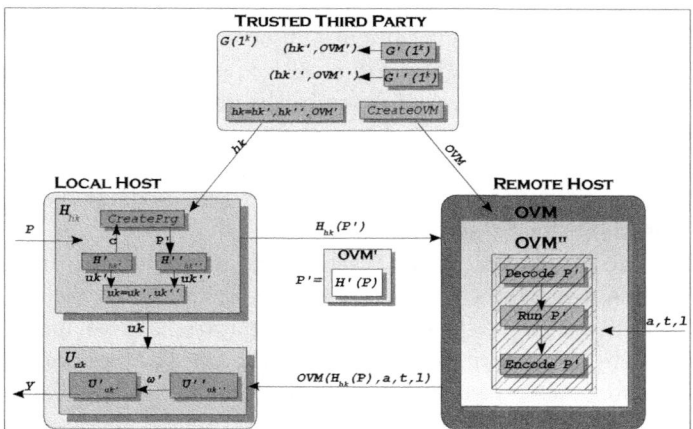

Fig. 2. Cascade WBRPE scheme W, constructed by combining two WBRPE schemes W' and W'', and running input programs inside two ovm's. Thus if the outer (resp. inner) ovm is insecure the program is protected by the inner (resp. outer) ovm.

attacks. A common approach employed to enhance security is to construct robust combiners, by combining two or more cryptographic primitives into one, s.t. the resulting construction is secure even when only some of the candidates are secure. Robust combiners can also be applied to ensure the correctness of the resulting combined scheme and to prevent erroneous implementations or design bugs. Robust combiners for various cryptographic primitives were shown, and alternately, an impossibility of achieving robust constructions for others was presented. The most well-known combiner is the cascade combiner, which is a sequential application of two cryptographic primitives. [7] showed that cascade is a robust combiners of block ciphers, against message recovery attacks. Cascade, and other basic robust combiners, were studied by [11], for encryption, MAC, signature and commitment schemes. Robust combiners were also studied for other primitives, e.g. hash functions [8, 2], private information retrieval (PIR) [12] and oblivious transfer [9].

Robust combiners are especially important in the context of white-box security, where security of practical candidates is not proven. Furthermore, the existing provably secure white-box primitives are either restricted to a limited class of functions or inefficient and as a result not applicable to practical implementations. Therefore, practitioners have to use heuristic constructions, and currently there isn't even a candidate whose security is sufficiently established; therefore robust combining of candidates is highly desirable.

1.4   Software Only vs. Hardware Based Execution Platforms

In white-box security the attacker obtains full access to the implementation. This is in contrast to traditional cryptography where a *black-box* (such as trusted hardware) is assumed to exist, on which secrets can be stored, see [13]. Attacker cannot access this black-box but can only observe the input-output behavior of the cryptographic implementation, e.g. a server performing signature computations on request. The inherent distinction in the attacker's abilities between the two models implies that traditional cryptographic tools are not applicable to remote environments, since they rely on the fact that the secrets used by the software do not reside on the same execution platform as the malicious host, and are not accessible to the attacker.

To support execution in untrusted environment, an additional tamper-resistant hardware module, e.g., a trusted server as in [1], or a smartcard (see [14]) is used, on which the secret data can be stored and the computations involving it performed. In contrast, white box security does not assume a trusted module, and relies on software hardening techniques, rather than depending on (specialized) hardware. In particular, the software is hardened in order to prevent undetected tampering or exposure of secret information, by providing integrity and confidentiality of the execution and of the computations performed.

Although applications that employ hardware benefit from high security promises, there are disadvantages, e.g., high cost, vulnerability to side channel attacks, unreliability and inflexibility of the hardware. In addition the security completely depends on the trust relationship with the additional hardware, thus making it inapplicable to many useful scenarios. Furthermore, in practice hardware alone is often not enough, since even hardware based solutions rely on software to accomplish the overall security. Therefore in order to enable a variety of practical applications secure software only techniques should be provided. In addition to practical importance, understanding the level of security that can be attained by employing software only techniques is intriguing on its own, especially due to prevailing belief that it is difficult to achieve a reasonable level of security by employing software only approach, let alone a level of security comparable to the one that can be accomplished with hardware.

2 Cascade Combiner for WBRPE Schemes

In this section, we present a 'cascade' combiner for WBRPE scheme, and formally define cascade for WBRPE in Definition 1.

Definition 1 (Cascade of WBRPE schemes). *Let $T(\cdot)$ and $L(\cdot)$ be two polynomials. Given two candidate* WBRPE *schemes W' and W'', where $W'' = (\mathcal{G}'', \mathcal{H}'', \mathcal{U}'')$ and $W' = (\mathcal{G}', \mathcal{H}', \mathcal{U}')$, we denote their cascade by $W = W' \circ W''$, where $W = (\mathcal{G}, \mathcal{H}, \mathcal{U})$ with $L(\cdot)$ bounding its output length and $T(\cdot)$ bounding its running time, and $(\mathcal{G}, \mathcal{H}, \mathcal{U})$ are PPT algorithms, presented in Algorithm 1.*

We include the t and l parameters in the construction, in order to prevent the adversary from distinguishing the input programs by their running times or output length. The t and l specified by the remote host are the bounds on the running time and output length of the input program P.

2.1 The WBRPE Cascade Combiner Construction

The construction is presented in Algorithm 1. Given two candidate WBRPE schemes W' and W'', we combine them into one WBRPE scheme $W = W' \circ W''$, see illustration in Figure 2. The main idea behind the combiner is that even if one of the schemes is insecure, e.g., one of the ovm's does not protect the memory contents, or if one of the schemes is incorrect, e.g., exposes the secret input program, then the overall construction will pertain security and correctness. Namely, the resultant scheme preserves indistinguishability, if one of the input candidates preserve indistinguishability. This holds since the inner ovm' is hidden by an outer ovm''. Therefore, even if the outer ovm'' is not secure, i.e., does not 'hide' the programs that it executes, the combined scheme is secure, since the attacker cannot inspect the original input and output. Alternately, if the inner ovm' is not secure, the outer ovm'' protects the computations. Similarly, the combined scheme preserves unforgeability of program and output, if one of the candidates ensures unforgeability of program and output, respectively.

The generation procedure $\mathcal{G}$ of $W = W' \circ W''$, in Algorithm 1, is performed by a trusted third party, and generates the parameters of WBRPE by applying the generation procedures of both candidates ($\mathcal{G}'$ of W' and $\mathcal{G}''$ of W''). The *createOVM* and *createPrg* macros are functions that encode programs as strings,

Algorithm 1. The cascade WBRPE combiner $(\mathcal{G}, \mathcal{H}, \mathcal{U})$ with $createOVM$ and $createPrg$ macros, creating the ovm of the cascade WBRPE and the external program P' supplied as input to $\mathcal{H}''$, respectively. Macros return the code (program) after incorporating their parameters.

$\mathcal{G}(1^k)$ {

    $\langle hk', OVM' \rangle \overset{R}{\leftarrow} \mathcal{G}'(1^k)$

    $\langle hk'', OVM'' \rangle \overset{R}{\leftarrow} \mathcal{G}''(1^k)$

    $hk = \langle hk', hk'', OVM' \rangle$

    $OVM \leftarrow createOVM(OVM'', k)$

    return $\langle hk, OVM \rangle$

}

$\mathcal{H}_{\langle hk', hk'', OVM' \rangle}(P)$ {

    $(c', uk') \leftarrow \mathcal{H}'_{hk'}(P)$

    $P' \leftarrow createPrg(c', OVM')$

    $(c, uk'') \leftarrow \mathcal{H}''_{hk''}(P')$

    $uk = \langle uk', uk'', P, P' \rangle$

    return $\langle c, uk \rangle$

}

$\mathcal{U}_{(uk=\langle uk', uk'' \rangle)}(\omega, P, t)$ {

    $\langle y, P^*, t^* \rangle \leftarrow \mathcal{U}'_{uk'}(\mathcal{U}''_{uk''}(\omega))$

    if $((P = P^*) \wedge (t = t^*))$ return y

    else return $\perp$

}

$createOVM(\mathbf{OVM''}, \mathbf{k})$ {

    return "$OVM(c, a, t, l)$

        $t' = T'(t, l, \mathbf{k}) + 2$

        $l' = L'(l, \mathbf{k})$

        $a' = (a, t, l)$

        return $\mathbf{OVM''}(c, a', t', l')$"

}

$createPrg(\mathbf{c'}, \mathbf{OVM'})$ {

    return "$P'(a')$

        $(a, t, l) \leftarrow a'$

        return $\mathbf{OVM'}(\mathbf{c'}, a, t, l)$"

}

in order to transfer them securely to remote host for execution. The $createOVM$ receives an ovm" and a security parameter k. It then generates and returns an encoding of the ovm program which will be executed on the remote host (the ovm program is encoded as a string). Similarly, the $createPrg$ generates a string encoding the program P'.

The hardening procedure, $\mathcal{H}$ of $W = W' \circ W''$, in Algorithm 1, applies $\mathcal{H}'$ and then $\mathcal{H}''$. This ensures that the overall construction will still protect the input programs even if one of the schemes is insecure. The unhardening procedure $\mathcal{U}$ of $W = W' \circ W''$, in Algorithm 1, receives the ephemeral unhardening keys, i.e. $uk = \langle uk', uk'' \rangle$, and applies $\mathcal{U}'$ and $\mathcal{U}''$, of the given candidates, and recovers the result of the computation of P on a. If the input program P, and the number of computations steps t are provided, the local host can also validate the result. Both validations by $\mathcal{U}'$ and by $\mathcal{U}''$ ensure robustness in case one of the candidates is erroneous.

2.2   Security Analysis

We formally state security in Theorem 1, and show that cascade is a (1,2)-robust combiner for the security specifications of WBRPE. Namely, if one of the candidates satisfies the security specifications of WBRPE, then the cascade satisfies the security specifications of WBRPE, i.e. indistinguishability and unforgeability of the program and result. We use $\varphi = PK$ to indicate public key scheme, and $\varphi = SK$ to define private key scheme.

Theorem 1 (Cascade is a Robust Combiner for WBRPE Schemes). *Let W' and W'' be WBRPE schemes. For $\varphi \in \{PK, SK\}$, the combined WBRPE scheme $W = W'' \circ W'$, is:*

- $WB - IND - CPA - \varphi$ *secure if at least one of W' or W'' is $WB - IND - CPA - \varphi$ secure.*
- $UNF - \varphi$ *secure if at least one of W' or W'' is $UNF - \varphi$ secure.*

The proof of Theorem 1 is in full version of the paper.

References

[1] Algesheimer, J., Cachin, C., Camenisch, J., Karjoth, G.: Cryptographic security for mobile code. In: SP 2001: Proceedings of the 2001 IEEE Symposium on Security and Privacy, Washington, DC, USA, vol. 2. IEEE Computer Society, Los Alamitos (2001)

[2] Boneh, D., Boyen, X.: On the impossibility of efficiently combining collision resistant hash functions

[3] Cachin, C., Camenisch, J., Kilian, J., Muller, J.: One-round secure computation and secure autonomous mobile agents. In: Automata, Languages and Programming, pp. 512–523 (2000),
http://citeseer.ist.psu.edu/article/cachin00oneround.html

[4] Collberg, C., Thomborson, C., Low, D.: A taxonomy of obfuscating transformations. University of Auckland Technical Report, 170 (1997)

[5] Collberg, C.S., Thomborson, C.: Watermarking, tamper-proofing, and obfuscation-tools for software protection. IEEE Transactions on Software Engineering 28(8), 735–746 (2002)

[6] Daemen, J., Rijmen, V.: The Design of Rijndael: AES–the Advanced Encryption Standard. Springer, Heidelberg (2002)

[7] Even, S., Goldreich, O.: On the power of cascade ciphers. In: Chaum, D. (ed.) Proc. CRYPTO 1983, pp. 43–50. Plenum Press, New York (1984)

[8] Fischlin, M., Lehmann, A.: Multi-Property Preserving Combiners for Hash Functions

[9] Harnik, D., Kilian, J., Naor, M., Reingold, O., Rosen, A.: On robust combiners for oblivious transfer and other primitives. In: Cramer, R. (ed.) EUROCRYPT 2005. LNCS, vol. 3494, pp. 96–113. Springer, Heidelberg (2005)

[10] Herzberg, A., Shulman, H., Saxena, A., Crispo, B.: Towards a theory of white-box security. In: Proceedings of Emerging Challenges for Security, Privacy and Trust: 24th Ifip Tc 11 International Information Security Conference, SEC 2009, Pafos, Cyprus, May 18-20, p. 342. Springer, Heidelberg (2009)

[11] Herzberg, A.: Folklore, practice and theory of robust combiners. Cryptology ePrint Archive, Report 2002/135 (2002), http://eprint.iacr.org/

[12] Meier, R., Przydatek, B.: On robust combiners for private information retrieval and other primitives. In: Dwork, C. (ed.) CRYPTO 2006. LNCS, vol. 4117, pp. 555–569. Springer, Heidelberg (2006)

[13] Mitchell, C., et al.: Trusted Computing. Trusted computing, p. 1 (2005)

[14] Spalka, A., Cremers, A.B., Langweg, H.: Protecting the creation of digital signatures with trusted computing platform technology against attacks by Trojan Horse programs. In: Proceedings of the 16th International Conference on Information Security: Trusted Information: The New Decade Challenge, pp. 403–419 (2001)

The PUF Promise

Heike Busch[1], Miroslava Sotáková[2], Stefan Katzenbeisser[1], and Radu Sion[2]

[1] Technische Universität Darmstadt
[2] Stony Brook University

Abstract. Physical Uncloneable Functions (PUF) are systems whose *physical* behavior to different inputs *can* be measured reliably, yet *cannot* be cloned in a physical replica. Existing designs propose to derive uncloneability from an assumed practical impossibility of exactly replicating inherent manufacturing variations, e.g., between individual chipset instances. The PUF promise has drawn significant attention lately and numerous researchers have proposed to use PUFs for various security assurances ranging from authentication to software licensing.

In this paper we survey the history of PUFs as well as the existing body of research proposing applications thereof.

1   Introduction

The idea to build secure cryptographic schemes, using tamper-proof hardware instead of relying on unproven number-theoretic assumptions, has been around for a long time [2, 20]. Research in this area has become more intensive recently, when Pappu [23] introduced the concept of *Physical Uncloneable Functions* (PUF) (also called "physical one-way functions"). A PUF is implemented by a physical device which can be seen as a source of randomness and due to uncontrollable manufacturing variations, is impossible to clone physically [4, 6]. The inputs to such a function are usually called *challenges* and specify measurements to be applied to the device. The outputs of a PUF are the corresponding measurement outcomes and are usually referred to as *responses*. Furthermore, the response to a challenge that has not been queried (i.e., the particular measurement has not been performed) should hard to guess. The nature of PUFs suggests making use of them in device authentication, key-agreement, and secure key-storage. For illustration purposes consider a simple authentication protocol in which case Bob, holding the device, wants to convince Alice about it: Alice queries a set of challenges, gets the responses, and stores all these *challenge-response pairs* (CRP). Then she sends the device to Bob, and Bob announces his response to Alice. If the response matches Alice's key, Alice accepts, otherwise she rejects. Since the device is assumed to be uncloneable, an adversary cannot learn the responses, unless it manages to measure the device original. This could possibly happen before Bob receives the device. Nevertheless, if the adversary is limited in the number of CRPs it can measure, it is unlikely to guess the exact set of Alice's challenges, before it is announced. Moreover, the responses of the PUF can be used to generate a secret key in order to use PUFs in key-agreement protocols.

Since several PUF-based challenge-response authentication protocols with PUF implementations have been proposed in [32, 8, 3, 16], the authors in [5] noted that current PUF-based authentication only prevents the impersonation of the client and do not

A. Acquisti, S.W. Smith, and A.-R. Sadeghi (Eds.): TRUST 2010, LNCS 6101, pp. 290–297, 2010.

prevent impersonation of the server in the context of physical attacks. To solve this problem, one needs a mechanism that allows the client to distinguish between challenges selected by the server in the enrollment step and an attacker. Another interesting application of PUFs is protecting software that runs on embedded systems. Instead of building functionality entirely in hardware, many vendors utilize standard computing equipment and differentiate through software. Unfortunately, software can easily be copied and reverse-engineered which is a real problem in professional product piracy, where software is copied from one legitimate device, and installed on many other (unauthorized) products. Many vendors thus want to bind software against a specific hardware platform or even to a specific instance. The latter can be achieved by PUFs as shown by Simpson and Schaumont [26]. The basic idea is to include a mutual authentication protocol between the provider's software (also called Intellectual Property) and the hardware platform. In this scenario, the PUF is part of an FPGA and it is used for hardware authentication and key generation. The FPGA bitstream is distributed in encrypted form, where the key is derived from a response to a specific PUF challenge. Thus, the bitstream cannot be decrypted and run on a FPGA that it has not been personalized for.

2   How Did PUFs Come About

Pappu introduced PUFs in [23] where a Physical Uncloneable Function is realized as a physical system, which is easy to evaluate, but *assumed* hard to characterize. When a PUF is exposed to a physical stimulus, it answers with a *response*. The way the stimulus is applied to the PUF is specified (usually digitally) in the form of a *challenge*, while the response is measured and appropriately digitized. For a "secure" PUF, predicting the output of the physical system is intractable without actually having physical access to the device. Moreover, PUFs exploit natural manufacturing variations which make them uncloneable: even with highly complex manufacturing equipment it is (*assumed to be*) impossible to create a second, completely identical device with the same challenge-response behavior – this holds even for the manufacturer of the original device. Thus, PUFs can be used to produce unique and uncloneable objects without having to trust the manufacturer.

   Note, since the responses of PUFs are noisy by nature the output of a PUF cannot directly be used in applications that require noise-free output with a perfectly uniform distribution (such as cryptographic keys). To deal with this problem, *fuzzy extractors* of Dodis et al. are applied – a secure form of error correction that enables a reliable extraction of an uniform key from a noisy non-uniform input [7]. Since almost all known PUF implementations produce noisy outputs, PUF implementations will have to be complemented with fuzzy extractors and helper data. Some errors can also be avoided by employing a calibration operation, which is driven by PUF CRPs, as described in [35].

2.1   The First Idea – Optical PUFs

As a first way of implementing PUFs, Pappu proposed an optical approach. An "optical PUF" consists of a transparent material, where many light scattering particles are added in a random way during production. Such a device causes a random speckle pattern when shining a laser beam onto it; here, the position and angle of the laser (and, we believe, possibly other parameters such as amplitude and wave-length) represent the challenge, while the speckle pattern is recorded, quantized and encoded to form the PUF response. In the original work, the author uses these challenge-response pairs to identify specific devices or to extract cryptographic keys [23, 24]. To this end, the PUF is measured right after production on a few random challenges (this step is referred to as "enrollment") to obtain a database of valid challenge-response pairs (CRPs) for a particular device. A device can subsequently be identified once it is placed in the field, by measuring the response for one of the challenges selected during enrollment (this process is called "verification"). If the response matches the expected, pre-recorded response, the device is authenticated and the response can be used to derive keys.

Naturally, a PUF should support a large number of CRPs in order to make it infeasible to learn responses to challenges that were not yet issued. In [33] the authors estimate the entropy of an optical PUF ($\geq 4 \cdot 10^6$ per 5cm^2) and the information contained in one CRP. Based on this data, the authors calculate the corresponding number of independent CRPs ($\geq 3 \cdot 10^4$ per 5cm^2), which turns out to be much lower than the number of all possible (not necessarily independent) challenges ($\sim 10^{10}$). As the number of independent CRPs is rather low and they can all be pre-recorded by an attacker who has unlimited physical access to the PUF once, *optical PUFs do not offer security in the information-theoretic sense*. However, in [33] the authors claim that interpolation of the PUF's behavior is computationally costly and therefore, a lot more challenges need to be measured to successfully predict the response for a fresh challenge. To prevent the attacker from exhaustively reading out all the CRPs (meaning, not only the independent ones), a method for decreasing the measurement-rate is proposed. For instance, if 10ms are required to measure one challenge, the attacker can measure about $\frac{1}{100}$ of all challenges ($\sim 10^8$) in a week of uninterrupted access to the optical PUF [33]. As a drawback, developing a reliable measurement apparatus for optical PUFs is a complex problem, which requires costly high-precision mechanics and thus limits their usage.

Due to the internal structure of the PUF it is very difficult to produce a physical clone because it requires a difficult and costly process (e.g. put the particles in the right position). Furthermore, modeling the PUF is very hard since the scattering of the PUF response is very complex. Note, that there are many papers that investigate this topic [23, 24, 33, 35, 17], the effect of changing measurement conditions [35] or the secrecy rate of optical PUFs more in details [17].

2.2 IC-Based Implementations – Silicon, Arbiter, and Ring Oscillator PUFs

Gassend et al. proposed a new instantiation of PUFs that uses silicon technology [12]. Based on the approach of [30], where it is shown that uncontrollable process variations during chip production make chips measurably different, *Silicon Physical Uncloneable Functions* (SPUF) exploit inherent variations in integrated circuits (IC) – that exist even for chips that were produced with identical layout masks [9, 11]. An important advantage of silicon PUFs is that their production does not require any special devices on top of classic chip manufacturing equipment.

Based on the observation that the timing behavior of chips differs [12], Lim et al. introduced *Arbiter Physical Uncloneable Functions* (APUF) [22, 21, 19, 10]. Arbiter PUFs consist of a number of switch delay elements, which are connected in series.

Every element has two inputs and uses a two-to-one multiplexer[1] to swap its inputs depending on one challenge bit: If the challenge bit is 0 both signals go straight trough the element. Otherwise, the top and bottom signals are switched. To compute the output for a specific challenge, a rising signal is given to the two inputs at the same time. Both signals race through the device; at the end, an arbiter circuit determines which signal passed the device faster. Thus, the challenge of the PUF still determines the path that both signals take through the device, while the response will now be a *single* bit $r \in \{0, 1\}$. Since each delay element doubles the number of paths the signals can possibly take, an APUF with n elements can produce 2^n delay paths. To obtain an m-bit response, one can either duplicate the circuit m times or evaluate the device consecutively on m different challenges and paste the results together.

All PUF implementations that are based on delay characteristics in ICs are not protected against environmentally induced noise. Consequently, a PUF produces different measurements for the same stimulus. Furthermore, if the variations of the PUF measurements are to high and the measurement variations are not adequately improvable a PUF may not be uniquely identified. Lim et al. handle the problem of environmentally induced noise by analyzing the coherence between environmental variations and circuit delays such as temperature and power supply [22, 21]. Firstly, the authors measured an *inter-chip variation* which states how many bits of two responses measured by two different PUFs for the same challenge are diverse. The average inter-chip variation of a PUF should be close to 50% whereas the bits of a PUF response are uniformly distributed and independent. Subsequently, the authors analyze the *environmental variation* which states how many bits of PUF responses will change if they are measured from the same PUF (the noise of the PUF response). The average environmental variation of a PUF should be ideally 0%. For an arbiter PUFs, the authors obtained the average inter-chip variation of 23% and an environmental variation of $\approx 4, 82\%$, if the temperature increases greater than $40°C$ from $27°C$, respectively $\approx 3, 74\%$, if the voltage variation increases $\pm 2\%$. This shows that an arbiter-based PUF reduces the environmental variations well enough below the average inter-chip variation of 23%.

Concerning the security of PUFs, it was shown in [22] that the response of an IC-based PUF circuit can be represented as a linear function of a challenge. If an attacker knows all delays of each element of a path through the circuit it can derive (predict) a response for a given challenge by calculating the sum of the delays of each element. Since measuring the delays at each element is a hard problem, an attacker can use machine-learning-techniques to build a software circuit that models the PUF circuit. With this model, the attacker can simulate the PUF and can predict a response for a random challenge. Note, that using the linear delay model implies that the PUF response is ideally statistical distributed. In reality, however, this is not the case due to measurement or environmental variations. Nevertheless, Lim generalized this model to a probabilistic one to model all the environmental variations. The author also suggests methods to modify the arbiter PUF such that the above mentioned model is no longer possible [22].

---

[1] A multiplexer is a device that selects one of many analog or digital input signals and forwards the selected input into a single line.

Adapted from arbiter PUFs, Suh and Devadas look for a higher reliability and an easier way of implementing PUFs on Application-Specific Integrated Circuits (ASIC) and Field-Programmable Gate Arrays (FPGA) [27]. Based on the "self-oscillating" approach in [12], the authors introduce *Ring Oscillator Physical Uncloneable Functions* (ROPUF). These PUFs are based on delay loops, which are commonly used to generate random bit strings. A delay loop, or ring oscillator, is a simple circuit that oscillates with a frequency influenced by manufacturing variations and thus cannot be predicted, yet can easily be determined by a counter. The PUF construction uses n such circuits and compares the frequency of two selected ones: depending on which oscillator is faster, an output of 1 or 0 is produced. To produce an output of several bits, one picks randomly a set of such oscillators according to the challenge; comparing each pair produces one output bit. In this way, one can generate $\Theta(n \log n)$ bits of entropy out of n oscillators. Suh et al. subsequently used their PUF in the development of the AEGIS processor [29, 28], which can resist both *software* and *physical* attacks. In particular, they use the PUF to store secrets in a secure, uncloneable and cost effective way.

Although ring oscillator PUFs are more reliable and easier to implement on both ASICs and FPGAs, arbiter PUFs are faster, smaller and consume less power. Thus, arbiter PUFs are better suitable for resource constrained platforms such as RFIDs, in which context they are also commercially available [36, 37].

2.3   Flip-Flop-Based implementations – SRAM and Butterfly PUFs

As mentioned in the Introduction 1, protecting software that runs on embedded systems is a problem of growing importance. Guajardo et al. [14] revisited the results and improvements by Simpson and Schaumont [26] and instead of treating the PUF as a black-box, they propose a FPGA based IP protection mechanism, which relies on *SRAM-based Physical Uncloneable Functions* (SRAM stands for "static random access memory") [14, 15]. These PUFs consist of a number of memory cells, involving two *cross-coupled*[2] inverters, having two stable states, commonly denoted by 0 and 1. After power up, cells will randomly end up in state 0 or 1; the state that a specific memory cell will reach is mainly dependent on the production process, yet relatively constant per instance. A challenge is represented by a subset of the memory cells to be read-out after power-up; the response is their respective power-up state.

Moreover, the authors analyze how many secret bits can be extracted from the response in SRAM-based PUFs. The secrecy rate is 0.76 bits per SRAM memory cell [14]. Note, currently available ICs can incorporate $\sim 10^6$ to 10^7 SRAM cells. Yet, without any additional mechanism for decreasing the read-out rate, SRAM PUFs are vulnerable to an exhaustive read-out attack.

Since not all FPGAs support uninitialized SRAM memory, Guajardo et al. [18] enhanced the concept of SRAM-based PUFs to *Butterfly Physical Uncloneable Functions* (BPUF). These PUFs provide a new way of exploiting circuit delays. Butterfly PUFs use unstable cross-coupled circuits, just like SRAM PUFs. While SRAM-cells are based on cross-coupled inverters, in butterfly-cells inverters are replaced by latches or flip-flops. Latches are circuits which store information and can be cleared (turns output to 0) or

---

[2] The output of the first inverter is connected to the input of the second one, and in the other way around.

preset (turns output to 1). Like SRAM cells, butterfly cells have only two stable states. To read out the PUF, one of the latches is cleared and simultaneously the other one is preset. This brings the BPUF into an unstable condition. The butterfly-cell falls back into one of the stable states depending on the circuit delays, which are were determined by the manufacturing process. Thus, BPUFs are very similar to SRAM PUFs beside the fact that they do not need any power-up for evaluation. Unlike SRAM PUFs, BPUFs are suitable for all types of FPGAs. Similarly, Gora et al. [13] and Atallah et al. [1] proposed the use of PUFs in binding software against specific hardware.

2.4   Tamper-Evidence – Coating PUFs

Another approach to obtain a stronger PUF is an "active coating" – a covering that is applied to the surface of an object. Posch [25] suggests to protect a device by embedding a unique signature into the coating material used in smart cards. Tuyls et al. [31, 34] apply this idea to PUFs and introduce the concept of *Coating Physical Uncloneable Functions* (COPUF). A coating PUF employs a protective coating, covering an integrated circuit. The opaque coating material is doped with dielectric particles, having random properties concerning their size, shape, and location. Below the coating layer, a comb structure of metal wire sensors is used to measure the local capacitance of the coating. The measured values, which are random due to the randomness present in the coating, form the responses to challenges, each of them specified by a voltage of a certain frequency and amplitude, applied to a region of the sensor array.

Because of the coating the PUF is physically uncloneable since it is very hard to produce a second PUF where all sensors produce the same measurements as the original PUF. However, the coating PUF is unfortunately easy to be modeled and supports only a limited number of CRPs. Since the characterization of the coating is very difficult, coating PUFs can be used e.g. for RFID-tags or key extraction. As for key extraction, [31] succeed to generate on the average 45 uniformly distributed bits by using 30 sensors.

The advantage of coating PUFs is that their production price is very low. Moreover, a benefit of coating PUF is that they are suitable for detecting a certain level of physical tampering. If a device is physically attacked, its response behavior is likely to change; thus, tampering can be uncovered by measuring the PUF with specific challenges. Due to tampering, the responses usually change only locally, which could even allow the determination of specific attack positions on the chip surface.

3   Conclusion

In this paper, we have summarized the history of PUFs by studying PUF approaches in literature. Many constructions have been called *Physical Uncloneable Function*, however, it is difficult to come up with a consistent definition. Indeed, we can deduce some "requirements" for PUFs, such as *unclonability* or *unpredictability*, but in the end the question "what a PUF is", remains difficult. Even the question "which PUF is more suited", is not easy to answer. Current constructions depend heavily on their application and thus follow different, and sometimes contradicting goals (see Section 2.2). In conclusion, *Physical Uncloneable Functions* are a young research area where many interesting problems are open. We believe that PUFs are a promising technology that benefit from many applications.

Acknowledgments. We thank the anonymous reviewers for valuable comments. This work was supported by CASED (www.cased.de). Sion and Sotáková were supported by the U.S. National Science Foundation grants CCF 0937833, CAREER CNS 0845192, CNS 0708025, IIS 0803197, and CNS 0716608, as well as by grants from Xerox, IBM and Microsoft Research.

References

[1] Atallah, M.J., Bryant, E., Korb, J.T., Rice, J.R.: Binding software to specific native hardware in a vm environment: the puf challenge and opportunity. In: VMSec, pp. 45–48. ACM, New York (2008)

[2] Bauder, D.W.: An anti-counterfeiting concept for currency systems. Research report PTK-11990. Sandia National Labs. Albuquerque, NM (1983)

[3] Bolotnyy, L., Robins, G.: Physically unclonable function-based security and privacy in rfid systems. In: PerCom, pp. 211–220. IEEE Computer Society, Los Alamitos (2007)

[4] Boning, D.S., Nassif, S.: Models of process variations in device and interconnect. In: Design of High Performance Microprocessor Circuits. IEEE Press, Los Alamitos (2000)

[5] Busch, H., Katzenbeisser, S., Baecher, P.: Puf-based authentication protocols - revisited. In: Youm, H.Y., Yung, M. (eds.) WISA 2009. LNCS, vol. 5932, pp. 296–308. Springer, Heidelberg (2009)

[6] Chinnery, D.G., Keutzer, K.: Closing the gap between asic and custom: an asic perspective. In: DAC, pp. 637–642 (2000)

[7] Dodis, Y., Ostrovsky, R., Reyzin, L., Smith, A.: Fuzzy extractors: How to generate strong keys from biometrics and other noisy data 38(1), 97–139 (2008)

[8] Frikken, K.B., Blanton, M., Atallah, M.J.: Robust authentication using physically unclonable functions. In: ISC, pp. 262–277. Springer, Heidelberg (2009)

[9] Gassend, B., Clarke, D.E., van Dijk, M., Devadas, S.: Silicon physical random functions. In: Atluri, V. (ed.) ACM Conference on Computer and Communications Security, pp. 148–160. ACM, New York (2002)

[10] Gassend, B., Clarke, D.E., van Dijk, M., Devadas, S.: Delay-based circuit authentication and applications. In: SAC, pp. 294–301. ACM, New York (2003)

[11] Gassend, B., Lim, D., Clarke, D., Devadas, S., van Dijk, M.: Identification and authentication of integrated circuits. Concurrency and Computation: Practice and Experience 16(11), 1077–1098 (2004)

[12] Gassend, B.L.P.: Physical random functions. Master thesis, Massachusetts Institute of Technology, Massachusetts Institute of Technology (2003)

[13] Gora, M., Maiti, A., Schaumont, P.: A flexible design flow for software ip binding in commodity fpga. In: SIES 2009, pp. 211–218 (2009)

[14] Guajardo, J., Kumar, S.S., Schrijen, G.J., Tuyls, P.: Fpga intrinsic pufs and their use for ip protection. In: Paillier, P., Verbauwhede, I. (eds.) CHES 2007. LNCS, vol. 4727, pp. 63–80. Springer, Heidelberg (2007)

[15] Guajardo, J., Kumar, S.S., Schrijen, G.J., Tuyls, P.: Brand and ip protection with physical unclonable functions. In: ISCAS, pp. 3186–3189. IEEE, Los Alamitos (2008)

[16] Hammouri, G., Sunar, B.: Puf-hb: A tamper-resilient hb based authentication protocol. In: Bellovin, S.M., Gennaro, R., Keromytis, A.D., Yung, M. (eds.) ACNS 2008. LNCS, vol. 5037, pp. 346–365. Springer, Heidelberg (2008)

[17] Ignatenko, T., Schrijen, G.-J., Škorić, B., Tuyls, P., Willems, F.M.J.: Estimating the secrecy rate of physical uncloneable functions with the context-tree weighting method. In: Proc. IEEE International Symposium on Information Theory 2006, pp. 499–503. IEEE Press, Los Alamitos (2006)

[18] Kumar, S.S., Guajardo, J., Maes, R., Schrijen, G.J., Tuyls, P.: The butterfly puf: Protecting ip on every fpga. In: HOST, pp. 67–70. IEEE Computer Society, Los Alamitos (2008)

[19] Lee, J.W., Lim, D., Gassend, B., Suh, G.E., van Dijk, M., Devadas, S.: A technique to build a secret key in integrated circuits for identification and authentication applications. In: Proc. of the IEEE VLSI Circuits Symposium, pp. 176–179. IEEE Press, Los Alamitos (2004)

[20] Leighton, F.T., Micali, S.: Secret-key agreement without public-key cryptography. In: Stinson, D.R. (ed.) CRYPTO 1993. LNCS, vol. 773, pp. 456–479. Springer, Heidelberg (1994)

[21] Lim, D., Lee, J.W., Gassend, B., Suh, G.E., van Dijk, M., Devadas, S.: Extracting secret keys from integrated circuits. IEEE Transactions on Very Large Scale Integration (VLSI) Systems 13(10), 1200–1205 (2005)

[22] Lim, D.: Extracting secret keys from integrated circuits. Master thesis, Massachusetts Institute of Technology, Massachusetts Institute of Technology (2004)

[23] Pappu, R.S.: Physical One-Way Functions. Phd thesis, Massachusetts Institute of Technology, Massachusetts Institute of Technology (March 2001)

[24] Pappu, R.S., Recht, B., Taylor, J., Gershenfeld, N.: Physical one-way functions. Science 297(5589), 2026–2030 (2002)

[25] Posch, R.: Protecting devices by active coating. J. UCS 4(7), 652–668 (1998)

[26] Simpson, E., Schaumont, P.: Offline hardware/software authentication for reconfigurable platforms. In: Goubin, L., Matsui, M. (eds.) CHES 2006. LNCS, vol. 4249, pp. 311–323. Springer, Heidelberg (2006)

[27] Suh, G.E., Devadas, S.: Physical unclonable functions for device authentication and secret key generation. In: DAC, pp. 9–14. IEEE, Los Alamitos (2007)

[28] Suh, G.E., O'Donnell, C.W., Devadas, S.: Aegis: A single-chip secure processor. IEEE Design & Test of Computers 24(6), 570–580 (2007)

[29] Suh, G.E., O'Donnell, C.W., Sachdev, I., Devadas, S.: Design and implementation of the aegis single-chip secure processor using physical random functions. In: ISCA, pp. 25–36. IEEE Computer Society, Los Alamitos (2005)

[30] Thompson, A.: An evolved circuit, intrinsic in silicon, entwined with physics. In: Higuchi, T., Iwata, M., Weixin, L. (eds.) ICES 1996. LNCS, vol. 1259, pp. 390–405. Springer, Heidelberg (1997)

[31] Tuyls, P., Schrijen, G.J., Skoric, B., van Geloven, J., Verhaegh, N., Wolters, R.: Read-proof hardware from protective coatings. In: Goubin, L., Matsui, M. (eds.) CHES 2006. LNCS, vol. 4249, pp. 369–383. Springer, Heidelberg (2006)

[32] Tuyls, P., Škorić, B.: Strong Authentication with Physical Unclonable Functions. In: Security, Privacy, and Trust in Modern Data Management, p. 133 (2007)

[33] Tuyls, P., Škorić, B., Stallinga, S., Akkermans, A.H.M., Ophey, W.: Information-theoretic security analysis of physical uncloneable functions. In: S. Patrick, A., Yung, M. (eds.) FC 2005. LNCS, vol. 3570, pp. 141–155. Springer, Heidelberg (2005)

[34] Škorić, B., Maubach, S., Kevenaar, T., Tuyls, P.: Information-theoretic analysis of capacitive physical unclonable functions. Journal of Applied physics 100 (2006)

[35] Škorić, B., Tuyls, P., Ophey, W.: Robust key extraction from physical unclonable functions. In: Ioannidis, J., Keromytis, A.D., Yung, M. (eds.) ACNS 2005. LNCS, vol. 3531, pp. 407–422. Springer, Heidelberg (2005)

[36] Verayo, http://www.verayo.com

[37] IntrinsicID, http://www.intrinsic-id.com

Privacy Requirements Engineering for Trustworthy e-Government Services

Nikos Vrakas[1], Christos Kalloniatis[2], Aggeliki Tsohou[3],
and Costas Lambrinoudakis[1]

[1] Dept. of Digital Systems, University of Piraeus, Piraeus GR-18532, Greece
{nvra,clam}@unipi.gr
[2] Dept. of Cultural Technology and Communication,
University of the Aegean, Lesvos GR-81100, Greece
ch.kalloniatis@ct.aegean.gr
[3] Dept. of Information and Communication Systems Engineering,
University of the Aegean, Samos GR-83200, Greece
agt@aegean.gr

Abstract. Several research studies have applied information systems acceptance theories in order to examine issues related to the acceptance of e-services by users. Their application in the e-government systems has revealed that trust is a prerequisite for their usage. Moreover, it has been proved that privacy concerns are a main antecedent of trust in e-government systems intention of use. Therefore, information systems that are not privacy aware are not trusted and thus not accepted by users. Currently there are many different attacks that can be realized by malicious users for compromising the confidentiality of private data and thus putting at stake the trustworthiness of the systems. The conventional way for preventing such attacks is mainly the employment of Privacy Enhancing Technologies (PETs). However, PETs are employed as ad hoc technical solutions that are independent from the organizational context in which the system will operate. We argue that we need privacy requirements engineering methods for capturing the context dependent privacy requirements and for selecting the appropriate technical, organizational and procedural countermeasures which will help building privacy aware systems that can offer electronic services which users can trust.

Keywords: Privacy Requirements Engineering Methods, Trust, Privacy Attacks, Privacy Enhancing Technologies.

1 Introduction

There are many alternative definitions for the *e-government* concept [1-2]. E-government has been defined as the utilization of the Internet and the World-Wide-Web for delivering government information and services to citizens [3]. Means and Schneider in [4] define e-government as the relationship between governments, their customers (businesses, other governments, and citizens), and their suppliers (again, businesses, other governments, and citizens) by the use of electronic means. Despite

A. Acquisti, S.W. Smith, and A.-R. Sadeghi (Eds.): TRUST 2010, LNCS 6101, pp. 298–307, 2010.
© Springer-Verlag Berlin Heidelberg 2010

the deviations of the various definitions, there are some common characteristics of the e-government concept: a) it is electronic and not paper based, b) it is available 24 hours per day, 7 days per week, and c) it facilitates the provision of information and delivery of services [5]. Several challenges of e-government provision have been recorded during recent years. Gil-García and Pardo in [6] indicate that the primary challenges of e-government include issues of a) information and data sharing, b) information technology usability and ease of use, c) organizational and managerial issues, d) legal and regulatory challenges, and e) institutional and environmental aspects that relate to the institutional framework and policy environment in which government organizations operate. Security and privacy challenges are among these, and specifically belong to the information technology and the legal and regulatory challenges' categories.

Therefore, despite the major effects that e-government solutions may provide to public administration and citizens' service, a major challenge lies on investigating types and conditions of e-government services that are readily acceptable to the public [7]. Thus, a crucial consideration regards the factors that citizens, business or other government institutions consider when they decide to use such a service. The examination of the issues related to user acceptance for a system or an electronic service can be accomplished through the application of information systems acceptance theories, such as theory of reasoned action [8], theory of planned behavior [9], motivational theory [10] or innovation diffusion theory [11], and technology acceptance model [12]. Several authors have used these theories in order explore the factors influencing intention to use e-government services and have concluded that trust issues are quite significant in e-government services' acceptance [13-16]. In addition, Lean et al. in [17] conclude that *privacy concerns are a main antecedent of trust in e-government systems intention of use*. This is also in line with surveys [18] revealing that citizens believe that e-government has the potential to improve the way government operates, but they have concerns about sharing personal information over the internet, fearing that the data will be misused and their privacy diminished.

Trust is defined by [19] as the "willingness of a party to be vulnerable to the actions of another party based on the expectation that the other will perform a particular action important to the trustor, irrespective of the ability to monitor or control that other party". Two main types of trust can be recognized: institutional trust and interpersonal trust. *Institutional trust* deals with third party guarantors that provide certification about the trustworthiness and expected behavior and escrows that guarantee expected outcome of the interaction [20]. *Interpersonal trust* relates to the consumer's impression, drawn from previous experience or gathered from outside sources of information [21].

Taking into account the findings of the researchers that have highlighted the importance of trust for e-government services' adoption, and also the notice of [22] that "the variable most universally accepted as a basis of any human interaction or exchange is trust" we can conclude that trustworthiness is crucial for the effectiveness of e-government systems. In this paper we address the question of '*how can we design privacy aware systems in order to raise trustworthiness of e-government environments?*"

The structure of the paper is as follows. In section 2 a number of well-known attacks that threaten users' trust are presented while in section 3 the contribution of privacy requirements engineering in designing and implementing trustworthy e-government systems is presented. The paper conclusions can be found in section 4.

2   Direct or Indirect Security Attacks and Privacy Breaches

In e-government environments, the privacy of a user can be compromised through various attacks that in fact take advantage of the vulnerabilities of the deployed protocols. Considering, for instance, the fact that a citizen is able to cast a vote through low resource enabled mobile devices (e.g. smart phones), we assume that the security mechanisms for this type of e-government services should be lightweight. There are documented research results [23-26] highlighting malicious behavior against IP [27] and TCP [28] that are inevitably inherited by the system of reference as described hereafter. Furthermore, the employment of databases and protocols from the application layer (e.g. SIP), introduces many more vulnerabilities [29-31] that a malicious user could exploit in order to disclose private or/and confidential information. It is therefore evident that privacy concerns are raised and that these concerns can deter a user form participating in such e-government procedures.

2.1   Code Injection

A point of crucial importance is clearly the database that holds users' subscriptions and votes. Every database infrastructure that utilizes the SQL language can suffer from SQL injection attacks [29, 32]. Such malicious behavior could lead to confidential information disclosure.

An SQL statement can be injected in a normal query by exploiting the punctuation marks that are responsible for code delimitation and execution according to SQL syntax. More specifically, a statement that could expose the vote of a user "nvra" is the following:

$$\text{SELECT vote FROM users WHERE name='nvra';} \qquad (1)$$

In this example, the attacker can obtain from the table "users" what the user with name "nvra" has voted.

In an e-government architecture there are at least two cases where SQL code could be injected. Firstly, in any text form that a user can enter information by adding the quotation mark """ in the text form and concatenating the malicious code shown in (1). During the parsing of the text form, the code until the end of the statement (in SQL is denoted with the interrogation mark ";") will be executed.

Another case for SQL injection attacks is in SIP signaling messages whenever a procedure (like the voting procedure) is initiated through a mobile device. The code can be injected in the authorization header field of a message during the session establishment or the registration procedure. This is described in detail in [30]. Thus, this malicious act could threaten the required *unlinkability* between users and votes towards a privacy oriented system.

SQL injection can be extremely harmful in cases where the credentials of a user are stored unprotected in a database. A malicious user can inject the SQL code in the SIP message or in the web form "SELECT password FROM users WHERE name='nvra';", in order to obtain the password from the user with name "nvra" which is stored in the table "users". This act can allow a malicious user to access a legitimate users' profile, breaking the *authentication* requirements and thus invading their privacy.

2.2 Man in the Middle

A Man in the Middle (MitM) attack can result in linking users with their personal data (i.e. votes) and disclose the private data of a session. The malicious user acts as an intermediate between the server and the user. This can be achieved through the utilization of the DNS cache poisoning procedure [33].

Firstly, the attacker modifies the binding between the legitimate domain name and the IP, with his own IP in the DNS list. When the legitimate user tries to access the page in order to accomplish the voting procedure, the poisoned DNS returns the IP of the malicious server. Thus, the communication session is established between the attacker and the victim. Afterwards, the malicious server gathers all the requests and by impersonating the user sends them to the real server. The real server responds to the malicious server while the former forwards these messages to the legitimate user. The legitimate user is not able to suspect the faked server while the former can reproduce an exact copy of the real web page. The employment of digital certificates could discourage such behaviors but low resource enabled mobile devices cannot utilize them. Under this context, private information such as vote and user's profile can be obtained illegally by a third party (attacker) breaking the *unlinkability* and *authentication* requirements correspondingly.

2.3 Replay Attacks

A user's private information can be also disclosed through replay attacks. In this scenario, the malicious entity exploits vulnerabilities in cryptographic protocols to gain access to user's account. In this case, not only the vote but the entire user's profile is being exposed.

Such an attack can be launched by a malicious user who firstly monitors, in a passive way, the communication between a user and the web server until the reception of the authentication vector. Afterwards, he incorporates the gathered authentication vectors in his message in order to be authenticated by the server and consequently to gain access to victim's profile. A commonly used message authentication protocol in web applications is the HTTP Digest [34]. The attacker can reuse the captured authentication string to launch a replay attack before the expiration of the nonce (a pseudo-random value that is utilized to prevent the reuse of an authentication string). The specific authentication protocol is also adopted when a user casts a vote from a mobile device that cannot employ stronger and consequently heavyweight authentication schemes. Thus, a malicious user by hijacking the users' profile is able to force disclosure of private data breaking the *unlinkability* and *authentication* requirements as described previously.

2.4 Passive Eavesdropping

The most direct threat to a users' privacy is the eavesdropping attack. An attacker can passively eavesdrop the message transmissions among the communicating entities in order to obtain information that could link a user with an action, preference, address, identity etc. Thus, by eavesdropping the session establishment procedure, a malicious user can determine whether a specific user tries to communicate with the server, for instance the web voting form, breaking one of the most important requirements in such environments: the *unobservability*. Furthermore, the identity of a user can be disclosed while the former communicates with the server either from a mobile device or not. The transmitted signaling messages, which also contain the user's identity, are-up to a point-in clear text so the *anonymity* is also violated.

When the session is initiated from a mobile device, the signaling messages are completely unprotected. Furthermore, the attacker can link the *pseudonym* of a user with his IP address and identity (the ID value from SIP signaling messages): The username of a user is included in the header that is responsible for the authentication (Authorization header field). Authentication is required when the user tries to access the provided services. The server challenges the user while the former responds with a valid authentication string that includes (at least) a hashed concatenation of the user's password, realm and the nonce obtained from the servers' challenge. In this response, the authorization header also includes in clear text the user's username.

An example of the headers in HTTP digest authentication is depicted in Fig. 1. On the left the users access a source from a web browser while on the right the same user accomplishes authentication from a mobile device utilizing SIP. It's clear how an attacker is able to link the user with username "nvra" with a specific action (the request of the e-vote.htm webpage) with his IP address (192.168.2.53) and his private ID (nvra_private@unipi.gr).

```
GET /e-vote.html HTTP/1.1          REGISTER sip:unipi.gr SIP/2.0
Host: localhost                    From:<sip:nvra_private@unipi.gr>
                                   Contact:192.168.2.53
Authorization:                     Call-ID:ak5fj49fhujDUuf0
Digest username="nvra",            Max-Forwards: 30
realm="unipi.gr",                  CSeq: 1 REGISTER
nonce=" 1fe69e629903f",            Authorization:
uri="/e-vote.html",                Digest username="nvra",
qop=auth,auth-int,                 realm="unipi.gr",
response="b97bb34ff31319bb8"       nonce=" 1fe69e629903f",
...                                qop=auth,auth-int,
                                   response="97bb34ff31319bb8"
```

Fig. 1. User's IP, ID, username exposure in HTTP authentication scheme

An eavesdropping attack can provide to the malicious user, not only the signaling parameters but also all the data transmitted between the communicating entities. Whenever a session lacks encryption, the exchanged data and also the media streams are exposed to third parties namely the eavesdroppers. Overall, the eavesdroppers could greatly threaten users' privacy while they are able to violate nearly all fundamental requirements of privacy oriented architectures: *unobservability, anonymity, unlinkability, pseudonymity* and *confidentiality*. The four threat categories that can potentially violate users' privacy are listed in Table 1.

Table 1. Attacks and how they affect fundamental Privacy Requirements

Threat Category	Effect	Privacy Requirements Affected
Code Injection	Authentication Vector / Credential Retrieval	Authentication
	Vote Disclosure	Unlinkability
MitM	Vote and User Profile Disclosure	Unlinkability Authentication
Replay	Vote and User Profile Disclosure	Unlinkability Authentication
Passive Eavesdropping	Session Parameters Disclosure	Unobservability
	Identity Disclosure	Anonymity Unlinkability Pseudonymity
	Data Session Disclosure	Confidentiality
	Media stream Disclosure	

3   Privacy Requirements Engineering

Research efforts aiming to the protection of user privacy fall in two main categories: security-oriented requirement engineering methodologies and privacy enhancing technologies (PETs). The former focus on methods and techniques for considering security issues (including privacy) during the early stages of system development and the latter describe technological solutions for assuring user privacy during system implementation. PETs are usually addressed either directly at the implementation stage of the system development process or as an add-on long after the system is used by individuals. However, PETs focus on the software implementation alone, irrespective of the organizational context in which the system will be incorporated.

Developers and information system specialists must consider privacy as a main technical concern which has to be considered early in the system development lifecycle as a separate design criterion. As a result, privacy as a design criterion has received much attention in recent years by researchers and practitioners alike. Initially, privacy protection efforts have focused on technological solutions for assuring user privacy during software implementation (PETs). However, as it was mentioned before, focusing on software solutions independently from the organizational context in which the system will operate makes it difficult to determine which software solution best fits the organizational needs. Understanding the relationship between user needs and the capabilities of the supporting software systems is of critical importance. This has led to the development of a number of security-oriented requirement engineering methodologies which consider security issues (including privacy) during the early stages of system development, an issue that has also been stated from the Canadian Privacy Commissioner Dr. Ann Cavoukian in the 90s [35].

Based on the privacy threats, mentioned in the previous section, that jeopardize users trustworthiness on the respective system it is understood that privacy-related issues are many and varied, as privacy itself is a multifaceted concept. Privacy comes in many forms, relating to what one wishes to keep private. Review of current research, highlights the path for user privacy protection in terms of eight privacy requirements namely *authentication, authorization, identification, data protection, anonymity, pseudonymity, unlinkability and unobservability* [36-38]. The first three requirements are mainly security requirements but they are included due to their key role in the privacy protection. By addressing these requirements one aims to minimize or eliminate the collection of user identifiable data. Depending on the intended system usage and user needs, one or more of the aforementioned requirements are considered during system development.

The majority of IS development methods manage privacy as one of the system's non-functional requirements. No specific techniques are proposed especially for identifying and implementing privacy requirements. However, the increasing importance of system security in general and user privacy in particular, has resulted in a number of methods that adopt concepts from the field of IS security engineering and use them in order to explicitly represent security requirements (which also include privacy requirements) and they define the way that these requirements can be transformed in specific policies for the system under construction. Methods like the NFR (Non-Functional Requirement Framework), the *i** method, the Tropos method, the KAOS method, the GBRAM (Goal-Based Requirements Analysis Method) method, the RBAC (Role-Based Access Control) method, the M-N (Mofett-Nuseibeh Framework) method, the B-S (Bellotti-Sellen Framework) method, the STRAP (STRuctured Analysis for Privacy) method and the PriS (Privacy Safeguard) method are well-known belong to the above-mentioned category. A description of these methods along with a detailed comparative review can be found in [39]. However, the tendency for a holistic confrontation of security and privacy requirements from the early stages of system design through its implementation phase is expressed in the latest research methods (e.g. PriS, SecureTropos [40-43]).

Specifically, these methods transform the threats identified in section 3 as specific privacy requirements that need to be satisfied in order to protect users' privacy. Furthermore they support the analysis of how these requirements constrain the functionality of the system as well as the examination of specific techniques (mainly PETS) for addressing these requirements. Thus, a privacy-oriented system is realized taking into account both the users' and the organizations' privacy concerns. By applying privacy oriented requirements engineering methods the mapping of users' privacy concerns on the developing system is ensured thus leading to the development of privacy aware systems that users can trust.

4   Conclusions

One of the main criteria that determine users' trust in electronic services is the way that their privacy is protected. This is becoming really crucial, since the greater collection and storage of personal data, the lower the trust of users using the specific applications. Privacy as a social and legal issue, has traditionally, been the concern of social scientists, philosophers and lawyers. However, the extended use of various software applications in the context of basic e-services sets additional technology-related requirements for protecting the electronic privacy of individuals. Most e-services rely on stored data for identifying customers, their preferences and previous record of transactions.

In this paper we argue that in order to build privacy aware systems it is necessary to take into account the peculiarities of the organization that offers the electronic services. To this respect we should utilize privacy requirements engineering methods. Currently we are applying such a requirements engineering methodology to an e-voting service, identifying the privacy requirements and the appropriate privacy enhancing technologies. Our aim is to compare the results that we will get, in terms of the protection mechanisms that will be considered necessary and the degree to which the privacy requirements will be satisfied, with the ad hoc PETs that are usually employed when no systematic method for eliciting the requirements is used.

References

1. Halchin, L.E.: Electronic government: Government capability and terrorist resource. Government Information Quarterly 21, 406–419 (2004)
2. Devadoss, P.R., Pan, S.L., Huang, J.C.: Structurational analysis of e-government initiatives: a case study of SCO. Decision Support Systems 34(3), 253–269 (2003)
3. ASPA: United Nations & American Society for Public Administration (ASPA). Benchmarking e-government: A global perspective. U.N. Publications, New York (2002)
4. Means, G., Schneider, D.: Meta-capitalism: The e-business revolution and the design of 21st century companies and markets. John Wiley & Sons Inc., New York (2000)
5. Holden, S.H., Norris, D.F., Fletcher, P.D.: Electronic Government at the Local Level: Progress to Date and Future Issues. Public Performance & Management Review 26(4), 325–344 (2003)
6. Gil-García, R.J., Pardo, T.A.: E-government success factors: Mapping practical tools to theoretical foundations. Government Information Quarterly 22(2), 187–216 (2005)
7. Lee, J.K., Rao, H.R.: Task Complexity and Different Decision Criteria for Online Service Acceptance: A Comparison of Two e-Government Compliance Service Domains. Decision Support Systems 47(4), 424–435 (2009)
8. Fishbein, M., Ajzen, I.: Belief, attitude, intention and behaviour: An introduction to theory and research Reading. Addision-Wesley, Massachusetts (1975)
9. Ajzen, I.: The theory of planned behavior. Organizational Behavior and Human Decision Processes 50(2), 179–211 (1991)
10. Deci, E.L.: Intrinsic motivation. Plenum Press, New York (1975)
11. Rogers, E.M.: Diffusion of innovations, 4th edn. The Free Press, New York (1995)
12. Davis, F.D.: Perceived usefulness, perceived ease of use, and user acceptance of information technology. MIS Quarterly 13(3), 319–339 (1989)

13. Harris, L.C., Goode, M.H.: The four levels of loyalty and the pivotal role of trust: a study of online service dynamics. Journal of Retailing 80(2), 139–158 (2004)
14. Chang, I.-C., Chang, Y., Hung, W., Hwang, H.: An empirical study on the impact of quality antecedents on tax payers' acceptance of Internet tax-filing systems. Government Information Quarterly 22(3), 389–410 (2005)
15. Belanger, A., Carter, L.: Trust and risk in e-government adoption. Journal of Strategic Information Systems 17, 165–176 (2008)
16. Horst, M., Kuttschreuter, M.T., Gutteling, J.M.: Perceived usefulness, personal experiences, risk perception and trust as determinants of adoption of e-Government services in The Netherlands. Computers in Human Behavior 23, 1838–1852 (2007)
17. Lean, O.K., Zailani, S., Ramayah, T., Fernando, Y.: Factors influencing intention to use e-government services among citizens in Malaysia. International Journal of Information Management 29(6), 458–475 (2009)
18. GAO (General Accounting Office), Electronic government challenges must be addressed with effective leadership and management (2001), http://www.gao.gov/new.items/d01959t.pdf
19. Mayer, R.C., Davis, J.H., Schoorman, F.D.: An integration model of organizational trust. Academy of Management Review 20(3), 709–734 (2003)
20. Warkentin, M., Gefen, D., Pavlou, P.A., Rose, M.G.: Encouraging citizen adoption of e-government by building trust. Electronic Markets 12(3), 157–162 (2002)
21. Felix, B.T., Paul, S.: Online consumer trust: A multiple-dimensional model. Journal of Electronic Commerce in Organizations 40 (2004)
22. Gundlach, G.T., Murphy, P.E.: Ethical and legal foundations of relational marketing exchanges. Journal of Marketing 57, 35–46 (1993)
23. Tanase, M.: IP spoofing: an introduction. In: Security Focus, vol. 11 (2003)
24. Heberlein, L., Bishop, M.: Attack class: Address spoofing. In: National Information Systems Security Conference, Baltimore, pp. 371–377 (1996)
25. Ping, Z., Zhuosheng, J.: Sniffer and Interruption of TCP/IP Communication. Computer Engineering 31, 119–120
26. Bellovin, S.: Security problems in the TCP/IP protocol suite. ACM SIGCOMM Computer Communication Review 19, 48 (1989)
27. Postel, J.: RFC 791: IP: Internet Protocol (September 1981)
28. Postel, J.: RFC 793: TCP: Transmission Control Protocol (1980)
29. Anley, C.: Advanced SQL Injection In SQL Server Applications (2002), http://www.nextgenss.com/papers/advanced_sql_injection.pdf
30. Geneiatakis, D., Kambourakis, G., Dagiuklas, T., Lambrinoudakis, C., Gritzalis, S.: SIP message tampering: The SQL code injection attack. In: Proceedings of 13th International Conference on Software, Telecommunications and Computer Networks (SoftCOM 2005), Split, Croatia (2005)
31. Geneiatakis, D., et al.: Survey of security vulnerabilities in Session Initiation Protocol. IEEE Communications Surveys and Tutorials 8, 68–81 (2006)
32. Cerrudo, C.: Manipulating microsoft sql server using sql injection. Application Security Inc., http://www.appsecinc.com/presentations/Manipulating_SQL_Server_Using_SQL_Injection.pdf
33. Klein, A.: BIND 9 DNS cache poisoning (2007), http://www.trusteer.com/docs/bind9dns.html
34. Franks, J., et al.: RFC 2617: HTTP authentication: basic and digest access authentication (1999)
35. Cavoukia, A.: Privacy by Design, http://www.privacybydesign.ca

36. Fischer-Hübner, S.: IT-Security and Privacy, Design and Use of Privacy Enhancing Security Mechanisms. In: Fischer-Hübner, S. (ed.) IT-Security and Privacy. LNCS, vol. 1958, p. 35. Springer, Heidelberg (2001)
37. Cannon, J.: Privacy, What Developers and IT Professionals Should Know. Addison-Wesley, Reading (2004)
38. Koorn, R., van Gils, H., ter Hart, J., Overbeek, P., Tellegen, R.: Privacy Enhancing Technologies, White paper for Decision Makers. Ministry of the Interior and Kingdom Relations, The Netherlands (December 2004)
39. Kalloniatis, C., Kavakli, E., Gritzalis, S.: Methods for Designing Privacy Aware Information Systems: A review. In: Alexandris, N., Chryssikopoulos, V., Douligeris, C., Kanellopoulos, N. (eds.) Proceedings of the PCI 2009 13th Pan-Hellenic Conference on Informatics (with international participation), Corfu, Greece, September 2009. IEEE CPS Conference Publishing Services, Los Alamitos (2009)
40. Mouratidis, H., Giorgini, P., Manson, G.: Integrating security and systems engineering: Towards the modelling of secure information systems. In: Eder, J., Missikoff, M. (eds.) CAiSE 2003. LNCS, vol. 2681, pp. 63–78. Springer, Heidelberg (2003)
41. Kalloniatis, C., Kavakli, E., Gritzalis, S.: Addressing privacy requirements in system design: The PriS method. Requirements Eng. 13(3), 241–255 (2008)
42. Perini, P., Bresciani, P., Giorgini, P., Giunchiglia, F., Mylopoulos, J.: Towards an agent-oriented approach to software engineering, Modena-Italy (2001)
43. Mouratidis, H., Giorgini, P., Manson, G.: An ontology for modelling security:The tropos project. In: Palade, V., Howlett, R.J., Jain, L. (eds.) KES 2003. LNCS (LNAI), vol. 2773, pp. 1387–1394. Springer, Heidelberg (2003)

Can Competitive Insurers Improve Network Security?

Nikhil Shetty, Galina Schwartz, and Jean Walrand[*]

Electrical Engineering and Computer Sciences
University of California, Berkeley
Berkeley, California 94720
{nikhils,schwartz,wlr}@eecs.berkeley.edu

Abstract. The interdependent nature of security on the Internet causes a negative externality that results in under-investment in technology-based defences. Previous research suggests that, in such an environment, cyber-insurance may serve as an important tool not only to manage risks but also to improve the incentives for investment in security. This paper investigates how competitive cyber-insurers affect network security and user welfare. We utilize a general setting, where the network is populated by identical users with arbitrary risk-aversion and network security is costly for the users. In our model, a user's probability to incur damage (from being attacked) depends on both his security and the network security.

First, we consider cyber-insurers who cannot observe (and thus, affect) individual user security. This asymmetric information causes moral hazard. If an equilibrium exists, network security is always worse relative to the no-insurance equilibrium. Though user utility may rise due to a coverage of risks, total costs to society go up due to higher network insecurity.

Second, we consider insurers with full information about their users' security. Here, user security is perfectly enforceable (zero cost). Each insurance contract stipulates the required user security and covers the entire user damage. Still, for a significant range of parameters, network security worsens relative to the no-insurance equilibrium. Thus, although cyber-insurance improves user welfare, in general, competitive cyber-insurers may fail to improve network security.

1 Introduction

Today, the Internet serves as the primary communication platform for both individuals and businesses. At present, due to the nearly universal connectivity, a huge amount of wealth is accessible online and the Internet has become a preferred destination for criminals. However, the Internet, which was originally conceived to be an academic network, has failed to address many of these security problems. Due to the ease of accessibility and programmability, unwary end

---

[*] This research is supported in part by NSF Grant NeTS-FIND 0627161.

A. Acquisti, S.W. Smith, and A.-R. Sadeghi (Eds.): TRUST 2010, LNCS 6101, pp. 308–322, 2010.

users' computers are routinely infected with malware. These infected computers could be employed for future crimes, resulting in an interdependent security environment.

Technology-based defense and enforcement solutions are available, but a consensus among security researchers [1] is that the existing security problems cannot be solved by technological means alone. Indeed, these security problems primarily result from misaligned incentives of the networked parties with respect to their security. Users under-invest in security since they do not bear the true societal costs of their actions, which causes a negative externality.

Existing research [2,3,4,5,6,7] indicates that *risk management* in general and cyber-insurance in particular are potentially valuable tools for security management.[1] This paper focuses on the effects of cyber-insurers on network security and user welfare, in a general setting with interdependent security and asymmetric information between users and insurers. We believe that these features of the environment induce socially suboptimal network security, and complicate the management of security risks.

In our model, all users are identical. Their wealth is identical and they suffer identical damage if cyber-attack on them is successful. The user's probability of being attacked depends on both the *user security level* and the *network security level*, which individual users take as given. Thus, there is an externality causing individually optimal user security level to be lower than the socially optimal one.

First, we investigate the effects of information asymmetry in the setting with interdependent security. Though our model allows to study both moral hazard (when insurers are not aware of user security levels) and adverse selection (when insurers cannot distinguish different user types), in this paper, we address only moral hazard (see [22] for analysis of adverse selection). We find that cyber-insurance fails to improve the network security level though it may improve user utility, if an equilibrium exists. Second, we assume no information asymmetry between the insurers and the users. We demonstrate that user utility is higher with insurance, but surprisingly, even in this case, the network security level is not necessarily higher. On reverse, for a substantial range of parameters, network security worsens with insurers.

Our assumption of identical users is simplistic, and does not hold in the actual Internet. But, we argue that adding user and insurer heterogeneity to our setting only *increases* informational asymmetries. If insurers could separate users of different types, our results hold for every class of user types in such a heterogeneous environment. If insurers are unable to distinguish between users with different types, the problem of adverse selection arises due to which missing markets are likely, as [23] demonstrate. Finally, the presence of different insurer types also brings the "lemon problem" [24], another manifestation of adverse selection, which also lead to missing markets. Hence, our results will continue to hold in a heterogeneous environment as well.[2]

---

[1] Other papers in this field are [2,8,9,10,11,3,12,13,14,15,16,17,18,15,19,20] For an overview of the related literature, the interested reader is referred to [21].

[2] See [22] where we extend our model to address moral hazard.

The paper is organized as follows. In Section 2, we propose and analyze the base model. In Section 3, we add competitive insurers to our base model, and consider two cases: with non-contractible individual security levels, and with required individual security level included into user's insurance contract. In Section 4, summarize our findings and conclude. The technical details are relegated to Appendix.

2   Model

We consider a network populated by N homogeneous (i.e., identical) users, each of whom possesses a wealth $W > 0$. In the absence of network security problems, user i utility U_i is:

$$U_i = f(W),$$

where the function f is increasing and concave ($f' > 0$, and $f'' \leq 0$), reflecting that user wealth W has a positive but decreasing marginal benefit for the user.

In the presence of network security problems, we assume that a user i incurs a monetary damage $D \in (0, W)$ when he is successfully attacked, and we let p_i denote the probability of successful attack. We assume that the probability p_i depends on two factors: the *security level* $s_i \in [0, 1]$ chosen by user i and the *network security level* $\bar{s} \in [0, 1]$, which depends on the security choices of all network users. We define the network security level $\bar{s}$ as the average security level in the network:

$$\bar{s} = \frac{1}{N} \sum_{i=1,\dots N} s_i.$$

Further, we assume N to be large, i.e., each user has a negligible effect on $\bar{s}$ and takes the network security level as given. Then, we define the probability p_i of a successful attack on user i as

$$p_i = (1 - s_i)(1 - \bar{s}),$$

where the second term $(1 - \bar{s})$ can be viewed as the probability of an attack in the network and the first term $(1 - s_i)$ can be viewed as the probability of success of such an attack on user i.

We assume that, for any user i, achieving individual security s_i entails a cost $h(s_i)$. We let h be an increasing convex function ($h', h'' \geq 0$), with $h(0) = 0$ representing a completely insecure user and $h(1) = \infty$ characterizing the costs required to maintain a "perfectly secure" system. The intuition is that user security costs increase with security, and that improving security level imposes an increasing marginal cost on the user. Additionally, for expositional convenience, we impose $h'(0) = 0$, to ensure positive user investments $s_i > 0$. We assume that the user cannot modify his D by changing his investment h, i.e., users do not self-insure their damages. For e.g., users may backup their data to prevent loss of information. Such self-insurance does not have an externality effect on other users since the advantages of that investment are observed by the user alone [12]. One can also view our D as the residual damages after self-insurance.

Thus, the expected user utility can be expressed as

$$U_i = (1 - p_i) \cdot f(W) + p_i \cdot f(W - D) - h(s_i). \tag{1}$$

To simplify the exposition, we introduce the vulnerability of player i, $v_i = 1 - s_i$ and the network *vulnerability* level $\bar{v} = 1 - \bar{s}$. Then, the expected utility of user i is:

$$U_i = (1 - v_i \bar{v}) \cdot f(W) + v_i \bar{v} \cdot f(W - D) - g(v_i), \tag{2}$$

where $g(v_i) = h(1 - v_i)$. This gives us: $g' \leq 0$, $g'' \geq 0$, and $g(1) = 0$, $g'(1) = 0$ and $g(0) = \infty$.

2.1   Social Optimum

We define the social optimum as a level at which aggregate user utility is maximized. In Appendix, we show that the socially optimal security level is identical for all users: $v_i = v$. Then, $\bar{v} = v$, and from (2), we have:

$$U^{soc} = (1 - v^2) \cdot f(W) + v^2 \cdot f(W - D) - g(v). \tag{3}$$

In any social optimum, $\frac{\partial U^{soc}}{\partial v} = 0$, from which we have:

$$2v^{soc} [f(W) - f(W - D)] = -g'(v^{soc}), \tag{4}$$

and since $\frac{\partial^2 U^{soc}}{\partial v^2} < 0$, the socially optimal vulnerability level is unique.

2.2   Nash Equilibrium

We assume that all parameters are known to users. As discussed above, a user takes the network vulnerability $\bar{v}$ as given and chooses his vulnerability v_i to maximize his utility given by (2). Taking the partial derivative of (2) with respect to v_i, and equating to zero, $\frac{\partial U_i}{\partial v_i} = 0$, we obtain:

$$\bar{v} [f(W) - f(W - D)] = -g'(v_i). \tag{5}$$

From the properties of the function g, the solution of equation (5) is unique, from which vulnerability choice is identical for all users. Hence, in equilibrium, all users have identical security (vulnerability) level, which we denote by v^*. Then, $\bar{v} = v^*$ and the following holds:

$$v^* [f(W) - f(W - D)] = -g'(v^*). \tag{6}$$

As in the case of social optimum, equilibrium vulnerability level is unique. Thus, in equilibrium, user security investments are identical and positive. Optimal investment increases when the damage D increases relative to wealth W. From (2) and (6), the equilibrium expected utility is:

$$U^* = f(W) + v^* g'(v^*) - g(v^*). \tag{7}$$

Comparing (4) and (6), we observe that since the LHS in (4) grows twice as fast as in (6) (see Fig. 1), we must have the following proposition:

Proposition 1. *Individually optimal user security is strictly positive, and it is strictly lower than the socially optimal one ($v^{soc} < v^*$ or $s^{soc} > s^*$).*

The expected per user loss due to network insecurity is:

$$(v^*)^2 D,$$

which is higher than the expected per user loss in the social optimum: $(v^{soc})^2 D$. Thus, in our model, users under-invest in security relative to a socially optimal level and this negative externality results in higher losses to society. In the next section, we will add competitive cyber-insurers to our base model and study how the presence of cyber-insurer affects network security.

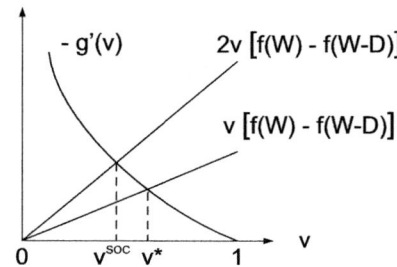

Fig. 1. Nash Equilibrium Vs Social Optimum

3   Insurance

Equilibrium is defined in a way similar to [23], where insurance equilibrium is examined in the markets with adverse selection. Each insurer offers a single insurance contract in *a class of admissible contracts*, or does nothing. A Nash equilibrium is defined as a set of admissible contracts such that: i) all contracts offered at least break even; ii) taking as given the contracts offered by incumbent insurers (those offering contracts) there is no additional contract which an entrant-insurer (one not offering a contract) can offer and make a strictly positive profit; and iii) taking as given the set of contracts offered by other incumbent insurers, no incumbent can increase its profits by altering his offered contract.

The literature referred to such contracts as "competitive," because entry and exit are free, and because no barrier to entry or scale economies are present. Thus, we will consider insurance firms (insurers), who are risk neutral and compete with each other. In addition to these equilibrium conditions, we assume that individual insurers cannot affect the network vulnerability, and thus, take it as given.

Let ρ be the premium charged to a user and L be the amount of loss covered by the insurer. Let user vulnerability be v and network vulnerability be $\bar{v}$. The user pays the premium both when he is attacked and when he is not, but is covered a loss L when the attack occurs successfully. Thus, with probability $v\bar{v}$, the user is successfully attacked and receives utility $\left[f(W - D + L - \rho) - g(v)\right]$

and with probability $(1 - v\bar{v})$, he obtains utility $\left[f(W - \rho) - g(v) \right]$. Denoting $U(v, \bar{v}, \rho, L)$ as the corresponding expected user utility,

$$U(v, \bar{v}, \rho, L) = (1 - v\bar{v}) \cdot f(\tilde{W}) + v\bar{v} \cdot f(\tilde{W} - \tilde{D}) - g(v), \qquad (8)$$

where

$$\tilde{W} = W - \rho \text{ and } \tilde{D} = D - L.$$

The utility in (8) coincides with the no-insurance case if $\rho = 0, L = 0$. When v is identical for all users, we have $\bar{v} = v$, and:

$$U(v, v, \rho, L) = (1 - v^2) \cdot f(\tilde{W}) + v^2 \cdot f(\tilde{W} - \tilde{D}) - g(v). \qquad (9)$$

3.1   Non-contractible User Security

In this subsection, we assume that insurers do not know, and have no control over user security level. This occurs when it is impossible (too costly) for the insurers to monitor the users' vulnerability v. Hence, the contract offered by an insurer will be of the form (ρ, L), i.e., the insurer sets the premium and the amount of coverage, and stipulates that no additional coverage can be purchased.

Note that the user is free to choose his required vulnerability here. Hence, users will choose the vulnerability level to maximize their utility, given the network security level. Thus, in the presence of competitive insurers, users choose which contract to buy, if any, and the corresponding vulnerability that maximizes their utility. In equilibrium, no user wishes to deviate from his equilibrium contract to any other contract or to not buying any insurance. We denote the equilibrium values in this non-contractible security case by the superscript †.

Social Planner. We assume that the social planner's objective is to maximize aggregate user utility with the constraint that the equilibrium contracts must not be loss-making. When social planner offers some contract(s), the users optimal choices could be described as if they play a game as in Section 2.2, but with wealth $\tilde{W} = W - \rho$ and damage $\tilde{D} = D - L$. In Appendix, we show that a social planner will offer a single contract (ρ, L) only. Then, user optimal choice is given by (6):

$$v^{\dagger soc} \left[f(\tilde{W}) - f(\tilde{W} - \tilde{D}) \right] = -g'(v^{\dagger soc}). \qquad (10)$$

To maximize aggregate user utility, the social planner's contract must solve the following optimization problem:

$$\max_{\rho, L} U(v^{\dagger soc}, v^{\dagger soc}, \rho, L),$$

subject to (10) and budget constraint $\rho - (v^{\dagger soc})^2 L \geq 0$. In Appendix, we show that all users buy this insurance. No user deviates to not buying, when other users have bought the insurance.

With the insurance provided by a social planner, user utility is higher, but, the vulnerability $v^{\dagger soc}$ is also higher than in the no-insurance Nash equilibrium:

$$v^{\dagger soc} > v^*. \qquad (11)$$

Competitive Insurance. Insurers offer contracts (ρ, L), and users maximize their utility by choosing the contracts and a corresponding preferred security levels, given the network security. In Appendix, we show that in any equilibrium, the following proposition holds:

Proposition 2. *With competitive insurers present, and non-contractible user security, in equilibrium, the security is always worse than the security in the no-insurance Nash equilibrium ($\bar{v}^\dagger > v^*$ or $\bar{s}^\dagger < s^*$).*

Thus, we demonstrated that although insurers may allow users to reach a higher utility, the network security is strictly lower with insurers. The favorable effect of insurers on user utility is not free of cost for the society. The presence of insurers negatively impacts network security level, which increase the losses from network insecurity. Expected per user loss due to the insurers' presence increases relative to the no-insurance Nash equilibrium by $\Delta^\dagger$ given by:

$$\Delta^\dagger = \left[(\bar{v}^\dagger)^2 - (v^*)^2 \right] D.$$

This is what one expects when insurers cannot monitor user security level. Since user risk is covered, users tend to under-invest in security. Next, we study the case where the insurer has perfect information about, and can perfectly enforce the security of his insured users.

3.2   Contractible User Security

Here, we assume that the insurers can monitor their insured users' vulnerability v at zero cost. Thus, we permit the contracts that specify user's required v. Let (v, ρ, L) be a contract that sets the premium ρ, the coverage L, and requires user vulnerability to be at most v. We denote the equilibrium values in this contractible security case by the superscript $\ddagger$.

Social Planner. We assume that the social planner's objective is to maximize aggregate user utility with the constraint that the equilibrium contracts must not be loss-making. In Appendix, we demonstrate that the social planner offers a single contract (v, ρ, L) only. Thus, $\bar{v} = v$, and to maximize total utility, the contract offered by the social planner must be a solution to the following optimization problem:

$$\max_{v, \rho, L} U(v, v, \rho, L), \text{ s.t. } v^2 L \leq \rho.$$

In Appendix, we show that the solution $(v^{\ddagger soc}, \rho^{\ddagger soc}, L^{\ddagger soc})$ is unique and satisfies:

$$(v^{\ddagger soc})^2 L^{\ddagger soc} = \rho^{\ddagger soc}$$

$$L^{\ddagger soc} = D$$

$$2v^{\ddagger soc} D f'(W - (v^{\ddagger soc})^2 D) = -g'(v^{\ddagger soc}). \tag{12}$$

Thus, the optimal contract makes no profit and offers full coverage. The social planner choice $v^{\ddagger soc}$ is given by (12).

Competitive Insurance. In this case, insurers offer contracts (v, ρ, L). In equilibrium, if the network vulnerability is $\bar{v}$, then all equilibrium contracts must yield equal utility $U(v, \bar{v}, \rho, L)$ for the user. If there exists a contract (v, ρ, L) that an insurer can offer and improve this user utility, it is preferred by the users and users will deviate and buy that contract. Hence, in equilibrium, the contracts chosen by the insurers must maximize $U(v, \bar{v}, \rho, L)$. In Appendix, we prove the following proposition:

Proposition 3. *With competitive insurers present, and security level contractible, in equilibrium, profits are zero ($v^{\ddagger 2} L^{\ddagger} = \rho^{\ddagger}$), and full coverage is offered ($L^{\ddagger} = D$). The equilibrium contract is unique and in this equilibrium, the security is always worse than what will be chosen with a socially optimum insurance ($v^{\ddagger} > v^{\ddagger soc}$). Also, compared to the no-insurance equilibrium, security is worse ($v^{\ddagger} > v^{*}$) except when the damage D is a small fraction of the wealth W. Users are strictly better off with insurers than when no insurers are present ($U^{\ddagger} > U^{*}$).*

When security level is observable by the insurers, insurer presence allows to improve user welfare, but not necessarily the network security. Unless the damage is a small fraction of the wealth, with cyber-insurance, expected per user loss from network insecurity increases compared to the no-insurance Nash equilibrium by $\Delta^{\ddagger}$, where:

$$\Delta^{\ddagger} = \left[(\bar{v}^{\ddagger})^2 - (v^{*})^2 \right] D.$$

Thus, for a significant range of parameters, the losses to society may increase when insurance is available.

4 Conclusion

In this paper, we investigate the effects of competitive cyber-insurers on network security and welfare. We highlight the impact of asymmetric information in the presence of network externalities and address the effects of interdependent security on the market for cyber-risks. The existing literature attributes cyber-insurance a significant role in cyber-risk management; it especially emphasizes positive effects of cyber-insurance market on security incentives. We find that, on reverse, the presence of competitive cyber-insurers, in general, weakens user incentives to improve security.

Though insurance improves the utility for risk-averse users, it does not serve as an incentive device for improving security practices. Indeed, insurance is a tool for risk management and redistribution, not necessarily a tool for risk reduction. To sum up, we argue that a combination of interdependent security and information asymmetries hinder cyber-insurance from performing the function of a catalyst for improvement of network security.

Acknowledgments

The authors would like to thank the members of the NetEcon group at UC Berkeley, specially Mark Felegyhazi, John Musacchio, Libin Jiang, Assane Gueye and Jiwoong Lee for their helpful comments and suggestions.

References

1. Anderson, R., Böehme, R., Clayton, R., Moore, T.: Security economics and european policy. In: Proceedings of WEIS 2008, Hanover, USA, June 25-28 (2008)
2. Böhme, R.: Cyber-insurance revisited. In: Proceedings of WEIS 2005, Cambridge, USA (2005)
3. Gordon, L.A., Loeb, M., Sohail, T.: A framework for using insurance for cyber-risk management. Communications of the ACM 46(3), 81–85 (2003)
4. Majuca, R.P., Yurcik, W., Kesan, J.P.: The evolution of cyberinsurance. Technical Report CR/0601020, ACM Computing Research Repository (2006)
5. Soohoo, K.: How much is enough? A risk-management approach to computer security. PhD thesis, Stanford University
6. Schechter, S.E.: Computer security strength and risk: a quantitative approach. PhD thesis, Cambridge, MA, USA, Adviser-Smith, Michael D (2004)
7. Bolot, J., Lelarge, M.: A new perspective on internet security using insurance. In: The 27th Conference on Computer Communications, INFOCOM 2008, April 2008, pp. 1948–1956. IEEE, Los Alamitos (2008)
8. Boehme, R., Kataria, G.: Models and measures for correlation in cyber-insurance. In: Fifth Workshop on the Economics of Information Security (2006)
9. Kunreuther, H., Heal, G.: Interdependent security. Journal of Risk and Uncertainty 26(2-3), 231–249 (2003)
10. Gordon, L.A., Loeb, M.P.: The economics of information security investment. ACM Trans. Inf. Syst. Secur. 5(4), 438–457 (2002)
11. Hausken, K.: Returns to information security investment: The effect of alternative information security breach functions on optimal investment and sensitivity to vulnerability. Information Systems Frontiers 8(5), 338–349 (2006)
12. Grossklags, J., Christin, N., Chuang, J.: Secure or insure? a game-theoretic analysis of information security games. In: WWW 2008: Proceeding of the 17th international conference on World Wide Web, pp. 209–218. ACM, New York (2008)
13. Varian, H.: System reliability and free riding. In: Workshop on the Economics of Information Security, WEIS 2002, Cambridge, USA (2002)
14. Ogut, H., Menon, N., Raghunathan, S.: Cyber insurance and it security investment: Impact of interdependent risk. In: Proceedings of WEIS 2005, Cambridge, USA (2005)
15. Hofmann, A.: Internalizing externalities of loss prevention through insurance monopoly: an analysis of interdependent risks. Geneva Risk and Insurance Review 32(1), 91–111 (2007)
16. Baer, W.S., Parkinson, A.: Cyberinsurance in it security management. IEEE Security and Privacy 5(3), 50–56 (2007)
17. Fisk, M.: Causes and remedies for social acceptance of network insecurity. In: Proceedings of WEIS 2002, Berkeley, USA (2002)
18. Honeyman, P., Schwartz, G., Assche, A.V.: Interdependence of reliability and security. In: Proceedings of WEIS 2007, Pittsburg, PA (2007)
19. Lelarge, M., Bolot, J.: Economic incentives to increase security in the internet: The case for insurance. In: INFOCOM 2009, April 2009, pp. 1494–1502. IEEE, Los Alamitos (2009)
20. Radosavac, S., Kempf, J., Kozat, U.: Using insurance to increase internet security. In: Proceedings of NetEcon 2008, Seattle, USA, August 22 (2008)
21. Shetty, N., Schwartz, G., Walrand, J.: Can Competitive Insurers improve Network Security (2010) (in preparation), www.eecs.berkeley.edu/~nikhils/SSW-Trust-Long.pdf

22. Schwartz, G., Shetty, N., Walrand, J.: Cyber Insurance with Interdepedent Security and Aysmmetric Information (2010) (in preparation), www.eecs.berkeley.edu/~nikhils/EconSec.pdf
23. Rothschild, M., Stiglitz, J.E.: Equilibrium in competitive insurance markets: An essay on the economics of imperfect information. The Quarterly Journal of Economics 90(4), 630–649 (1976)
24. Akerlof, G.A.: The market for 'lemons': Quality uncertainty and the market mechanism. The Quarterly Journal of Economics 84(3), 488–500 (1970)

Appendix

Social Optimum with No Insurance

In the social optimum, the goal is to maximize aggregate user utility given by

$$U^{agg} = \sum_{i=1...N} [(1 - v_i \bar{v})f(W) + v_i \bar{v} f(W - D) - g(v_i)],$$

where $\bar{v} = \dfrac{\sum_{i=1...N} v_i}{N}$. To optimize this expression, we take the partial derivative w.r.t. v_j for some $j \in 1, \ldots, N$ and equate to zero:

$$\frac{\partial U^{agg}}{\partial v_j} = 0$$

$$\sum_{i=1...N} \left[\frac{v_i}{N} \{f(W - D) - f(W)\} \right] + \ldots$$

$$\ldots \bar{v}\{f(W - D) - f(W)\} - g'(v_j) = 0$$

$$2\bar{v}\{f(W) - f(W - D)\} = -g'(v_j). \tag{13}$$

Since (13) is identical for all j, all users must be assigned an identical vulnerability to maximize the aggregate utility.

Proposition 2

Social Planner. First, we show that the social planner will offer a single contract in equilibrium only. Assume the reverse, and let there exist an equilibrium with network security $\bar{v}$, and at least two equilibrium contracts (ρ_1, L_1) and (ρ_2, L_2). Without loss of generality, let $v_1 > \bar{v} > v_2$.

Then, for any user with contract (ρ_1, L_1) optimal v_1 is the same as in the base model with $\tilde{W}_1 = W - \rho_1$ and $\tilde{D}_1 = D - L_1$, and thus v_1 is identical for all users with contract (ρ_1, L_1) and is given from (5):

$$\bar{v} \left[f(\tilde{W}_1) - f(\tilde{W}_1 - \tilde{D}_1) \right] = -g'(v_1). \tag{14}$$

Using (5), all these users' utility U_1 can be written as

$$U_1 = f(\tilde{W}_1) + v_1 g'(v_1) - g(v_1), \tag{15}$$

Similarly, for all users with contract (ρ_2, L_2) we have:

$$U_2 = f(\tilde{W}_2) + v_2 g'(v_2) - g(v_2).$$

Taking the derivative of $vg'(v) - g(v)$ w.r.t. v, we get

$$g'(v) - g'(v) + vg'' = vg'' \geq 0, \tag{16}$$

which implies that $vg'(v) - g(v)$ increases with v.

Now, consider instead a single contract (ρ, L_1) such that optimal user vulnerability in the base model with $\tilde{W} = W - \rho$ and $\tilde{D}_1 = D - L_1$ is v_1, i.e., from (6),

$$v_1 \left[f(\tilde{W}) - f(\tilde{W} - \tilde{D}_1) \right] = -g'(v_1). \tag{17}$$

Comparing the LHS of (14) and (17), we infer that, since $v_1 > \bar{v}$, $\tilde{W} > \tilde{W}_1$ and hence $\rho < \rho_1$. Comparing the user utility with this single contract (ρ, L_1) with (15), we have

$$U = f(W - \rho) + v_1 g'(v_1) - g(v_1) > U_1 = U_2,$$

since $\rho < \rho_1$. Thus, this single contract (ρ, L_1) permits the social planner to achieve higher user utility and will be preferred to the two contracts (ρ_1, L_1) and (ρ_2, L_2). Hence, we have proven that only a single contract will be offered in the social planner optimum.

Second, we demonstrate that the network vulnerability with the optimal contract $(\rho^{\dagger soc}, L^{\dagger soc})$ is higher than in the no-insurance Nash equilibrium, i.e., $v^{\dagger soc} \geq v^*$. We know that $U^{\dagger soc}$ must be higher than U^* since U^* can always be reached by the planner offering the contract $(\rho, L) = (0, 0)$:

$$U^{\dagger soc} \geq U^*.$$

Next, for any contract (ρ, L) with optimal vulnerability v, similar to (15), the user's utility can be written as

$$U = f(W - \rho) + vg'(v) - g(v). \tag{18}$$

From $\rho > 0$, the monotonicity of $vg' - g$ from (16), (18) and (7), we infer that $U^{\dagger soc} \geq U^*$ holds only if

$$v^{\dagger soc} > v^*.$$

Last, we show that all users purchase this insurance. If a user i deviates to no-insurance, she obtains $U(v_i, v^{\dagger soc}, 0, 0)$, which is highest for $v_i = \tilde{v}$ determined from $\frac{\partial U(v_i, v^{\dagger soc}, 0, 0)}{\partial v_i} = 0$, which gives:

$$v^{\dagger soc} [f(W) - f(W - D)] = -g'(\tilde{v}). \tag{19}$$

Since $v^{\dagger soc} \geq v^*$, comparing the LHS of (19) and (6), we have

$$\tilde{v} \leq v^* \leq v^{\dagger soc}.$$

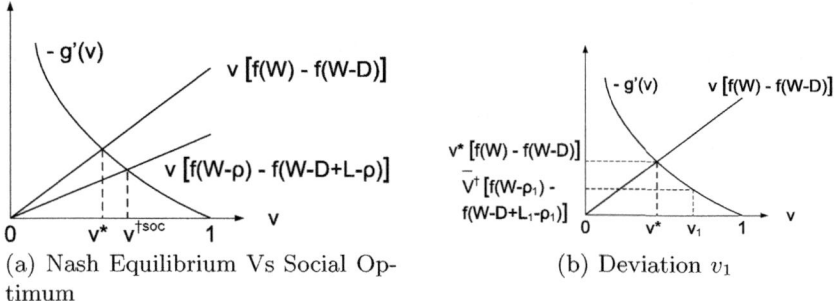

(a) Nash Equilibrium Vs Social Optimum

(b) Deviation v_1

Fig. 2. Competitive Non-contractible Insurance

Next, we write $U(\tilde{v}, v^{\dagger soc}, 0, 0)$ using (19):

$$U(\tilde{v}, v^{\dagger soc}, 0, 0) = f(W) + \tilde{v}g'(\tilde{v}) - g(\tilde{v}). \tag{20}$$

Comparing with (7) using the monotonicity of $vg' - g$ derived in (16), we conclude that, since $\tilde{v} \leq v^*$, the user utility from deviation $U(\tilde{v}, v^{\dagger soc}, 0, 0)$ must be lower than U^*. Therefore,

$$U(\tilde{v}, v^{\dagger soc}, 0, 0) \leq U^* \leq U^{\dagger soc},$$

giving us the required result that no user will deviate and not buy insurance.

Competitive Insurers. In the case of competing insurers, there may exist multiple contracts in equilibrium. However, the resulting network vulnerability $\bar{v}^{\dagger}$ will not be lower than the vulnerability in the Nash equilibrium v^*. Indeed, assume the reverse: $\bar{v}^{\dagger} < v^*$. Let (ρ_1, L_1) be some contract adopted by a non-zero fraction of users in this equilibrium.

From (5), replacing W by $\tilde{W}_1 = W - \rho_1$ and D by $\tilde{D}_1 = D - L_1$, we get an expression for the vulnerability v_1 chosen by users who adopt the contract (ρ_1, L_1):

$$\bar{v}^{\dagger} \left[f(\tilde{W}_1) - f(\tilde{W}_1 - \tilde{D}_1) \right] = -g'(v_1). \tag{21}$$

Note that $\rho_1 \leq L_1$, i.e., the premium must be lower than the coverage, else deviating from this contract to no-insurance gives higher utility to the users. Hence, $\left[f(\tilde{W}_1) - f(\tilde{W}_1 - \tilde{D}_1) \right] \leq [f(W) - f(W - D)]$.

From our assumption that $\bar{v}^{\dagger} \leq v^*$, we observe that the LHS of (21) is lesser than the LHS of (6) which implies that $v_1 \geq v^*$. (See Fig. 2(b).) However, the choice of (ρ_1, L_1) was arbitrary among all the contracts in equilibrium. Hence, the user adopting any contract in equilibrium will choose vulnerability not lower than v^*. This gives us $\bar{v}^{\dagger} \geq v^*$, which contradicts our assumption. Hence, $\bar{v}^{\dagger} \geq v^*$ in the competitive equilibrium as well.

Proposition 3

Social Planner. First, we show that a social planner will offer a single contract in equilibrium only. Indeed, assume the reverse. Let the social planner offer two contracts (The proof for more contracts is similar.) (v_1, ρ_1, L_1) and (v_2, ρ_2, L_2) to a fraction α and $(1 - \alpha)$ of the population respectively. Thus,

$$\bar{v} = \alpha v_1 + (1 - \alpha)v_2.$$

From the budget constraint, we have

$$\alpha\rho_1 + (1 - \alpha)\rho_2 \geq \alpha v_1 \bar{v} L_1 + (1 - \alpha)v_2 \bar{v} L_2.$$

From (8), we observe that the contracts with $L_1 = L_2 = D$ offer users a higher utility. Hence, we will only focus on the contracts (v_1, ρ_1, D) and (v_2, ρ_2, D) for the rest of the proof. In this case, the budget constraint becomes

$$\alpha\rho_1 + (1 - \alpha)\rho_2 \geq \alpha v_1 \bar{v} D + (1 - \alpha)v_2 \bar{v} D = \bar{v}^2 D. \tag{22}$$

From (8), the aggregate utility with the contracts (v_1, ρ_1, D) and (v_2, ρ_2, D) will be:

$$U^{agg} = \alpha[f(W - \rho_1) - g(v_1)] + (1 - \alpha)[f(W - \rho_2) - g(v_2)].$$

Since both f and $(-g)$ are concave functions (and $f' > 0$),

$$U^{agg} < f(W - \{\alpha\rho_1 + (1 - \alpha)\rho_2\}) - g(\bar{v})$$
$$\leq f(W - \bar{v}^2 D) - g(\bar{v}),$$

where the second inequality comes from (22).
$f(W - \bar{v}^2 D) - g(\bar{v})$ is the utility obtained from the contract $(\bar{v}, \bar{v}^2 D, D)$. Hence, there exists the single contract $(\bar{v}, \bar{v}^2 D, D)$ which always provides a higher aggregate user utility than all contracts (v_1, ρ_1, L_1) and (v_2, ρ_2, L_2).

Thus, the social planner offers only a single contract. This contract must be a solution to the following optimization problem:

$$\max_{v, \rho, L} U(v, v, \rho, L)$$
$$\text{s.t. } v^2 L \leq \rho \text{ and } v \leq 1.$$

One can solve this optimization problem to obtain

$$-g'(v) = 2vDf'(W - v^2 D). \tag{23}$$

The details are relegated to [21].

Competitive Insurers. First, we notice that in any equilibrium, due to competition, for any insurer, profit is zero, i.e. $\rho = v\bar{v}L$ for any equilibrium contract (v, ρ, L). If $\rho > v\bar{v}L$, some entrant insurer could offer a contract $(v, \tilde{\rho}, L)$ s.t. $\rho > \tilde{\rho} > v\bar{v}L$. From (8), the contract with a lower premium and same L, v and $\bar{v}$ improves user utility.

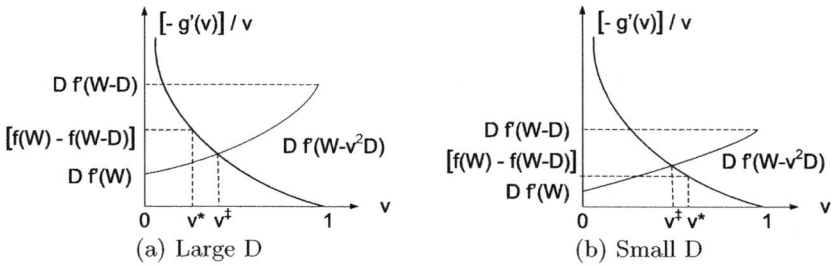

Fig. 3. Competitive Equilibrium with Contractible Security

Second, full coverage, i.e. $L = D$ will be offered due to competition. Indeed, the contract $(v, v\bar{v}D, D)$ offers users the highest utility. To see this, consider the family of contracts $(v, v\bar{v}L, L)$ for $L \leq D$. From (9), the utility $U(v, \bar{v}, v\bar{v}L, L)$ will be $(1-p)f(W-pL)+pf(W-pL-D+L)-g(v)$, where $p = v\bar{v}$. Differentiating w.r.t. L, and equating to 0, we get

$$p(1 - p)f'(W - pL) = p(1 - p)f(W - pL - D + L).$$

If $p \neq 0$ or 1, then $L = D$, which gives the required result. Henceforth, we restrict our analysis to contracts $(v, v\bar{v}D, D)$ only.

Third, in any equilibrium, user utility from deviation to no-insurance gives user a strictly lower utility. Indeed, assume the reverse. Consider a contract $(v_1, v_1\bar{v}D, D)$ that has a non-zero number of users adopting it in equilibrium. If a customer of this contract prefers to deviate to v_i with no insurance, then his utility without insurance must be greater than the utility with insurance contract, i.e., $U(v_i, \bar{v}, 0, 0) \geq U(v_1, \bar{v}, v_1\bar{v}D, D)$. Consider an entrant insurer who offers a contract $(v_i, v_i\bar{v}D, D)$ (full coverage at actuarially fair price). Adopting this contract improves user utility, which conflicts our equilibrium assumptions. Therefore, the utility from deviation to no-contract must be strictly lower than with a contract, and thus, all users strictly prefer to buy insurance.

Fourth, we prove that equilibrium contract is unique. Consider an equilibrium with network security $\bar{v}$. An entrant insurer could offer a contract $(\tilde{v}, \tilde{v}\bar{v}D, D)$ that maximizes $U(\tilde{v}, \bar{v}, \tilde{v}\bar{v}D, D) = f(W - \tilde{v}\bar{v}D) - g(\tilde{v})$. To determine $\tilde{v}$ at which user utility is the highest we differentiate

$$\frac{\partial}{\partial \tilde{v}}U(\tilde{v}, \bar{v}, \tilde{v}\bar{v}D, D) = \frac{\partial}{\partial \tilde{v}}\big(f(W - \tilde{v}\bar{v}D) - g(\tilde{v})\big) = 0,$$

$$f'(W - \tilde{v}\bar{v}D)(-\bar{v}D) - g'(\tilde{v}) = 0,$$

and since the second derivative is always negative:

$$f''(W - \tilde{v}\bar{v}D)(\bar{v}D)^2 - g''(\tilde{v}) < 0,$$

user utility reaches its maximum at a single point $\tilde{v}$ only, which is exactly the contract offered in equilibrium. Thus, we have $\tilde{v} = \bar{v} = v^\dagger$, and in any equilibrium, all users buy an identical contract $(v^\ddagger, (v^\ddagger)^2 D, D)$, determined from

$$-g'(v^\ddagger) = v^\ddagger D f'(W - (v^\ddagger)^2 D). \tag{24}$$

The unique $v^\ddagger$ is strictly less than 1 since $f'(W - D) > 0$. (If $f'(W - D) = 0$, then $f(W) = f(W - D)$ and insurance does not improve user utility and is hence redundant.) Since the RHS of (23) is twice the RHS of (24), we conclude that $v^\ddagger \geq v^{\ddagger soc}$, i.e., the equilibrium security under competitive insurers is worse than under a social planner.

Next, we determine how $v^\ddagger$ compares to v^*. We rewrite (24) as

$$\frac{-g'(v^\ddagger)}{v^\ddagger} = D f'(W - (v^\ddagger)^2 D), \tag{25}$$

and compare with the Nash equilibrium by rewriting (6) as:

$$\frac{-g'(v^*)}{v^*} = f(W) - f(W - D). \tag{26}$$

Note that, from $f'' \leq 0$, we have $f'(W) \leq \frac{f(W) - f(W-D)}{D} \leq f'(W - D)$. Also, $f'(W - v^2 D)$ is an increasing function of v, and $\frac{-g'(v)}{v}$ is decreasing. Hence, if $D f'(W - v^{*2} D) < f(W) - f(W - D)$ then $v^\ddagger > v^*$ else $v^\ddagger \leq v^*$. Thus, if the marginal benefit from full coverage offered at v^* is lower than the average loss of benefit per unit damage, insurance does not improve the security level.

Figure 3 depicts the solution of (25). From the figure, it is clear that only when D becomes small, the network security level in the equilibrium with insurers exceeds security level of no-insurance equilibrium. Note that when D is small, v^* is also large. Thus, competitive insurers improve network security only when equilibrium vulnerability in no-insurance equilibrium is high.

Nudge: Intermediaries' Role in Interdependent Network Security[*]

Jens Grossklags[1], Svetlana Radosavac[2], Alvaro A. Cárdenas[3],
and John Chuang[4]

[1] Center for Information Technology Policy, Princeton University
jensg@princeton.edu
[2] DoCoMo USA Labs, Palo Alto
sradosavac@docomolabs-usa.com
[3] Fujitsu Laboratories of America, Sunnyvale
cardenas@fla.fujitsu.com
[4] School of Information, University of California, Berkeley
chuang@ischool.berkeley.edu

Abstract. By employing an interdependent security game-theoretic framework, we study how individual Internet Service Providers can coordinate the investment decisions of end users to improve the security and trustworthiness of the overall system. We discuss two different forms of intervention: rebates in combination with penalties (pay for outcome) and cost-subsidies (pay for effort).

Keywords: Security Economics, Internet Service Provider Incentives, Enhancing Trust and Security with End Users.

1 Introduction

Unlike earlier worms and viruses that inflicted substantial and immediately noticeable harm on users' network experience and data security, nowadays most malicious software covers its tracks and avoids activities impacting hosts' performance. As a result, users develop limited incentives to upgrade their security software and to remove unwanted code. In economic terms, it is individually rational to 'shirk' or 'freeride' [33]. However, compromised machines lumped together in botnets represent a 'public bad', which is to the detriment of the collective welfare of all network stakeholders. Moreover, the eventual victims of botnet-mediated attacks have little recourse, since the attackers, hiding behind a veil of anonymity or jurisdictional ambiguity, are largely beyond the reach of law enforcement authorities.

This misalignment of incentives in computer security was first highlighted by Anderson, who observed that "where the party who is in a position to protect

---

[*] We thank the anonymous reviewers for their helpful comments to an earlier version of this paper. This work is supported in part by a University of California MICRO project grant in collaboration with DoCoMo USA Labs. This paper is an extended version of a prior abstract contribution [19].

A. Acquisti, S.W. Smith, and A.-R. Sadeghi (Eds.): TRUST 2010, LNCS 6101, pp. 323–336, 2010.

a system is not the party who would suffer the results of security failures, then problems may be expected" [3]. And Varian suggests that liability needs to be assigned to the right parties "so that those who are best positioned to control the risks have appropriate incentives to do so" [32].

Yet, it is far from obvious how to motivate appropriate security efforts or to assign liability to large, dispersed populations of individual consumers, many of whom are unaware of and ill-equipped to deal with technical problems. Trust between different network participants is hard to justify, due both to negative externalities and lack of participant expertise. As such, external incentive mechanisms must be designed to restore faith in other players following appropriate behavior.

2   IT Security Obstacles

In particular, intermediaries such as Internet Service Providers (ISP) would find it desirable if end users pay more attention to security problems and secure their resources since alternative solution and mitigation approaches are not always within reach [4].[1]

For one, cyber-insurance has been proposed as a market-based solution to address the collective security risk. However, the uptake of cyber-insurance policies has been limited. First, the traditional assumption of independent and uncorrelated risks does not apply to the Internet, where security is highly interdependent, and therefore risks can be highly correlated [7]. Second, there is a lack of historical actuarial data or reliable models for cyber-risk evaluation causing high-priced premiums. Finally, those seeking insurance must undergo a series of often invasive security evaluation procedures, revealing not just their IT infrastructures and policies, but also their business activities and partners [5]. Taken together, cyber-insurers and re-insurers are progressing at a "frustratingly slow pace, with major obstacles preventing development into a full-fledged industry" [13].

A similar assessment can be made about the deployment of novel network-based countermeasures [3]. Significant hurdles arise due to the various interdependencies and the associated positive and negative externalities between the different stakeholders of Internet communications [8]. ISPs are generally (technically) capable of undertaking some actions from the physical infrastructure level up to the application layer, but only *within their domains.* And, typically, a service provider does not have purview and control over an entire end-to-end path [10]. Accordingly, the benefit that providers can derive from a deployment

---

[1] An ISP has strong motivations to improve the security of its subscribers' machines [30]. If infected, it may be used to launch attacks across the network, leading to abuse notifications from other network operators, and increasing the risk of blacklisting [9]. Further, malware infections might motivate customer service calls that can easily wipe out the profit margin for the customer for the month. It has been estimated that the cost of incoming (outgoing) customer calls to (from) customer service centers is about 8 (16) Euros per call [30].

of new technology may depend on the number of other entities taking the same measure (including the sharing of security information [12]).

Finally, organizations and businesses that provide network access to their users (i.e., employees or students) frequently install security client software that monitors and controls network access.[2] However, the majority of consumer-oriented ISPs shy away from direct technical intervention involving access to the users' home resources. We are only aware of one US consumer ISP experimentally testing a similar approach.[3] However, several ISPs utilize redirection and quarantining techniques to encourage users to engage in clean-up efforts [21].

ISPs reluctance for active end user management can be partly explained with the fact that securing network communications is a complex task [26], that needs to be managed in a cost-effective manner. Higher-tier ISPs can limit their involvement by exercising market power to delegate security diligence to lower level ISPs [23]. Therefore, ISPs who find themselves lower in the pecking order may find it necessary to police their networks when they are facing disconnection threats, higher transit rates, or a projected shortage of (last-mile) connection capacities. Our work addresses the needs of such service providers by considering different avenues to impact users' decision processes to secure their resources.

3   Understanding Consumer Incentives

A major source of complexity for ISP decision making is the diversity of subscribers. While some providers may be exclusively focused on residential end users, others have a customer base that is a mixture of individual residences, small businesses, and large corporations [9]. In practice, these different subscriber types are subject to different threats and interdependencies, and respond differently to economic incentives.

First, enterprise and residential subscribers are subject to different security interdependencies. Enterprise subscribers (i.e., businesses and content providers that are connected to the ISP) usually deploy their own sub-networks with a *perimeter defense* to shield the interior of the network from scrutiny by competitors and criminals. However, a breach of the perimeter will often cause correlated damages in the interior of the network. Residential end users, on the other hand, are subject to different interdependencies. Their security efforts (or lack thereof) contributes to the general hygiene and *cumulative defense* readiness of the network. For example, if more users invest in spam reduction efforts, install firewalls or anti-malware software, and regularly apply system patches, the overall level of harm to all users can be reduced. Fig. 1 shows a typical ISP with a mixture of residential and enterprise subscribers.

---

[2] For example, some organizations utilize the Cisco Clean Access network admission control software.

[3] Comcast customers in one service area will receive pop-up notices on their desktop informing them about security problems [22].

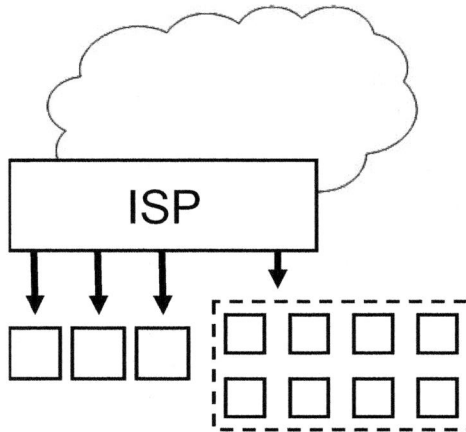

Fig. 1. ISP with residential and enterprise subscribers

Second, enterprise and residential subscribers face different incentives to invest in security. An enterprise can better quantify the monetary impact of a security breach that leads to business disruption or data compromise. At the same time, it is also a more attractive target because a single breach of the perimeter can often yield a number of compromised machines that can then be used by the attacker to commit further crimes. Consequently, enterprises are more likely to respond to intrusions, and to incentives to invest in security. Individual residential subscribers, in contrast, often fail to pay attention to security. Consequently, they may also be less aware of, and less responsive to, changes in incentives and the legal/technical environment concerning security [2,6].

3.1   Basic Model

We now describe a model for evaluation of different security-enhancing proposals that an ISP may consider undertaking. We are building on our security games framework proposed and formally analyzed in previous work [16,17,18].

We consider an ISP with $N \in \mathbb{N}$ users connected to its network. Facing a variety of attacks, end users undertake two different types of security precautions.

Table 1. Parameters for consumer incentives model

Parameter	Interpretation
V	Value from network participation ($V \geq 0$)
b	Cost of protection ($b \geq 0$)
c	Cost of self-insurance ($c \geq 0$)
p	Probability of attack ($0 \leq p \leq 1$)
L	Loss from security breach ($L \geq 0$)

On the one hand, a subscriber i may choose a self-insurance level $0 \leq s_i \leq 1$, for example, by purchasing and utilizing a backup solution. On the other hand, each user selects a protection level $0 \leq e_i \leq 1$ by adopting different preemptive technologies such as firewalls, intrusion detection systems, and anti-malware software [33]. Table 1 summarizes important parameters of the game. The utility function of each subscriber has the following structure [16]:

$$U_i = V - pL(1 - s_i)(1 - H(e_i, e_{-i})) - be_i - cs_i, \qquad (1)$$

where the *security contribution function*, $H(e_i, e_{-i})$, is used to capture different security interdependencies. It characterizes the effective security level given agent's i investment in protection e_i, subject to the protection levels chosen (contributed) by all other players e_{-i}. We require that H be defined for all values over $[0,1]^N$; in particular, $H : [0,1]^N \to [0,1]$.

In the earlier part of this section, we introduced two important types of security interdependencies that are relevant in the ISP context, i.e., perimeter defense and cumulative security. Below we match these problem scenarios to mathematical formulations introduced in prior work (see also Fig. 2) [16].

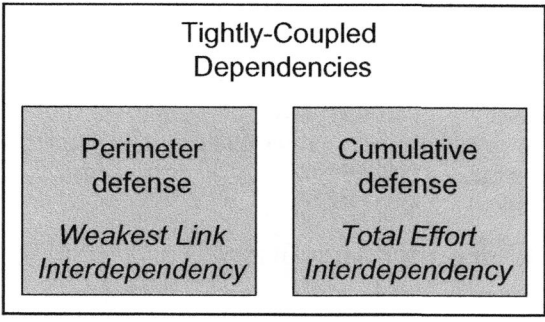

Fig. 2. Overview of security interdependencies

3.2 Perimeter Defense and Cumulative Defense

In Fig. 1 the enterprise subscriber utilizes a perimeter defense that separates its subnetwork from the rest of the ISP network. A perimeter defense is vulnerable if an attacker can identify a weakness that leads to its circumvention. Subsequently, hosts behind the common defense are left defenseless after a breach occurs. This tightly coupled dependency (i.e., in which a single breach can lead to the compromise of the complete subnetwork [11]) can be modeled by considering the minimum effort of any agent to be decisive for the success of the perimeter defense ($H(e_i, e_{-i}) = min(e_i, e_{-i})$) [16].

End users are subject to cumulative interdependencies. Consider, for example, a share of users that under-utilize options for protection, or act carelessly by responding to spam messages. Then all users in the network will suffer incrementally from the clogging of bandwidth, increased spam activity, etc. This effect can be modeled with the total effort security contribution function ($H = \frac{1}{N} \sum_k e_k$) [16].

A complete economic analysis of the base case (i.e., with homogeneous end users and an exogenous attacker) for these two interdependency scenarios is available in our previous work [16]. Our technical analysis showed that several key obstacles may prevent network participants from providing high security efforts:

Strategic uncertainty: In both interdependency scenarios, there is a multiplicity of equilibria for protective and self-insurance actions. For example, in the weakest link security game, agents may choose between full self-insurance and various protection equilibria if $b < pL$, $c < pL$ and $b < c$. The co-existence of these types of equilibria may cause coordination failures if a single agent deviates from a protection strategy to select self-insurance.

Rational underprotection: The ISP would prefer that all agents invest fully in protection; however, agents may rationally decide otherwise. For example, in the weakest link security game, agents have no reliable rational basis to differentiate between a zero-effort strategy (passivity) and a high effort level (protection) given $b < c$. Similarly, in the total effort game, users consider the value of their contributions relative to the size of the network, i.e., they only consider protection if $bN < pL$.

Security passivity: End users rationally select a zero-effort level for both protection and mitigation if they perceive the security costs to be too high. The consequences of lax security are: increased security compromises, service calls, and abuse notifications to the ISP.

4   Shaping Consumer Incentives

In this section, we discuss economically-motivated strategies that an ISP may use to influence customer behavior and to respond to the key obstacles outlined above. More specifically, we attempt to analyze strategies and mechanisms ISPs may utilize to allocate additional security investments for achieving a significant improvement in overall system security, while taking into account given user interdependencies and incentives.

Our attention is focused on lightweight approaches that carry only a moderate cost to ISPs and will not seriously impact the economic well-being of end users. For example, in practice ISPs may attempt to influence users with educational measures about computer security risks and prevention technologies. Similarly, service providers may encourage the installation of certain security packages to impact the status quo of end user risk mitigation.

Recently, researchers in psychology and economics have proposed the concept of nudges to influence consumer behavior. Such interventions create a choice architecture that impacts user behavior in predictable ways without dramatically changing economic incentives (e.g., without excluding certain options) [28]. In particular, security problems that are related to difficult to value goods such as private information or personal data (i.e., photos, diary entries) pose significant decision making problems for individuals who could benefit from a helping hand [1].

We believe that nudging techniques may be of great benefit to end user security problems. In the following, we want to explore two canonical approaches to influence consumer decision making. While we are working within a framework of rationally acting agents we suggest that our results can be used to determine subtle nudges that are more powerful because they are respectful of economic incentives. For example, if we want to steer individuals towards an easier to use security product one should make sure that the usage will create the largest possible benefit to the consumer and to overall network security.

4.1   Rebates and Penalties: Pay for Outcome

Pay for outcome represents a situation where an ISP offers a flat rebate to users who agree to being subject to a monetary or non-monetary penalty, P, when security compromises occur. Similary, an ISP may deliver a bonus, B, to users for positive security outcomes (i.e., a breach is not occuring).

Mathematically, we can express these policies in the following way. First, let us consider an additional penalty in the case of a security breach:

$$U_i = V_P - pL(1 - s_i)(1 - H(e_i, e_{-i})) - pP(1 - H(e_i, e_{-i})) - be_i - cs_i$$
$$= V_P - pL(1 - s_i + P/L)(1 - H(e_i, e_{-i})) - be_i - cs_i$$

For the bonus payment we get:

$$U_i = V_B - pL(1 - s_i)(1 - H(e_i, e_{-i})) + pBH(e_i, e_{-i}) - be_i - cs_i$$
$$= V_B - pL[(1 - s_i) - H(e_i, e_{-i})(1 - s_i + B/L)] - be_i - cs_i$$

The penalty, P, can be implemented, for example, in the form of a reduction of network throughput or a quarantine [21], while the fee remission can take the form of a monetary benefit, or reduced subscription costs. Such a policy needs to be well-balanced since most users are not inclined towards penalty-based systems. The recent protests (that even included the involvement of politicians) against plans to (re-)introduce usage-based pricing systems may serve as evidence [25].

4.2   Cost Subsidies: Pay for Effort

We now look at the problem of subscriber incentives from a different perspective by considering the opportunities of network operators to offer security products to its subscribers at a chosen cost or to subsidize alternative security tools and software. Currently the impact of such practices is limited. A 2008 survey suggests that only 19% of Internet users in the United States and 12% in Europe acquired their most recent security software product from their ISPs [24].[4]

---

[4] The survey polled 1500 consumers in the United States, France, Germany and the United Kingdom.

Further, only few ISPs offer services that fall into the category of self-insurance (such as online backups or replication).[5]

Cost subsidies (or even increases) may affect protection and self-insurance investments. In the presence of pay for effort policies, the utility function changes to:

$$U_i = (V_F) - pL(1 - s_i)(1 - H(e_i, e_{-i})) - (b + E)e_i - (c + S)s_i$$

We denote as E the cost modificator for protection, and as S the influencing factor for self-insurance cost.

4.3   Numerical Sensitivity Analysis

We defer a full analytic discussion of these two policies to future work, and instead present selected results from a numerical sensitivity analysis. In particular, we study the impact of small nudges (i.e., positive and negative) on selected security relevant variables in the two interdependency scenarios.

First, let us consider the perimeter defense scenario. From prior work we know that security contributions in the weakest-link interdependency are highly fragile, and the defection of a single individual (to a lower protection level) can severely impact overall system security [16,31]. We also found that a threshold value ($e_{min} = \frac{pL-c}{pL-b}$) exists that determines the lowest security contribution that a rationally acting defector may consider. The higher the threshold level the less damage we would expect to overall system security.

In Figures 3 and 4 we present the expected influence of the two nudging policies on the protection investment threshold value. On the y-axis we plot the protection threshold level, and on the x-axis the strength of the nudging policy. In particular, we use a common scale for pay for outcome and pay for effort strategies by an ISP. Our approach is to use similar sized intervention investments to influence either a baseline loss with a pay for outcome policy, or to influence a baseline protection cost with a pay for effort policy. The nudges can be either positive or negative to represent bonuses and penalties, respectively. For brevity, we do not plot the impact of pay for effort nudges directed at self-insurance costs. A negative value on the x-axis corresponds to a reduction in cost (pay for effort bonus) or a positive pay for outcome intervention, respectively.

Our numeric examples include a scenario with small attack probability paired with large maximum loss (Figures 3.a and 4.a), and a situation with a relatively large attack probability paired with low maximum loss (Figures 3.b and 4.b). We find that this distinction has relatively little impact. However, the graphs show that pay for effort nudging is fruitful in the presence of comparatively low

---

[5] For example, Earthlink discontinued its Weblife service that included an online backup process in early 2008. See, for example, http://www.dslreports.com/forum/ r19475297-EarthLink-WebLife-will-be-Discontinued-January-7-2008 for the shut-down announcement. Several non-ISP alternatives have emerged such as offerings by security companies (e.g., Symantec's SwapDrive), information storage companies (e.g., EMC's Mozy) and electronic commerce and content providers (e.g., Amazon Simple Storage Service).

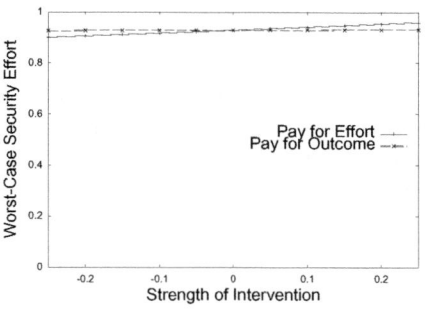 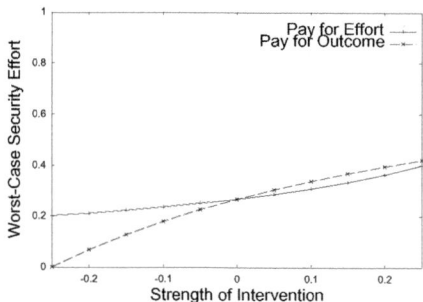

(a) Small attack probability, p=0.1, and large baseline maximum loss, L=10

(b) High attack probability, p=0.8, and small baseline maximum loss, L=1.25

Fig. 3. Perimeter defense with an expensive self-insurance option: Worst case security effort that represents a rational strategy for individual subscribers when protection cost are significantly lower than self-insurance cost (Baseline protection cost b=0.25, fixed self-insurance cost c=0.8, Value of connection V=1)

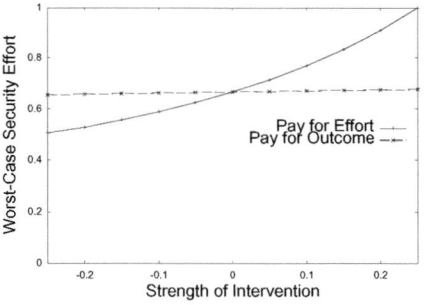 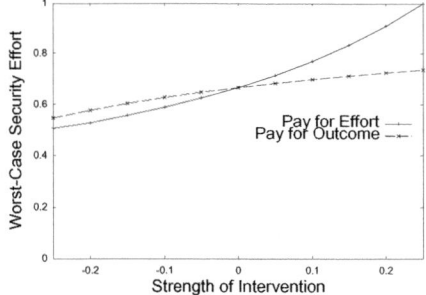

(a) Small attack probability, p=0.1, and large baseline maximum loss, L=10

(b) High attack probability, p=0.8, and small baseline maximum loss, L=1.25

Fig. 4. Perimeter defense with a less costly self-insurance option: Worst case security effort that represents a rational strategy for individual subscribers when protection cost are only somewhat lower than self-insurance cost (Baseline protection cost b=0.25, fixed self-insurance cost c=0.5, Value of connection V=1)

self-insurance costs (see Figure 4). In general, pay for outcome interventions can be more effective than pay of effort, however our graphical analysis does not reveal any high impact scenarios.

In the cumulative security example we are mostly concerned with the decreasing incentives to invest in protection when the network grows in size [16]. Users evaluate $bN < pL$ to decide whether a protection investment is beneficial. Whereas an ISP would prefer that individuals simply calculate $b < pL$, individual users have the incentives to free-ride on others' protection efforts. A rebate/penalty policy can contribute to the betterment of the security outcome. However, it is immediately obvious that a penalty would need to be in proportion with the size of the network to have a noticeable impact.

Therefore, we observe that a moderately sized pay for outcome intervention has little impact on the maximum number of agents that would willingly contribute to security in a network. Similarly, pay for effort interventions only work at the margin, when a cost subsidy essentially provides security products free of charge (see Figure 5).

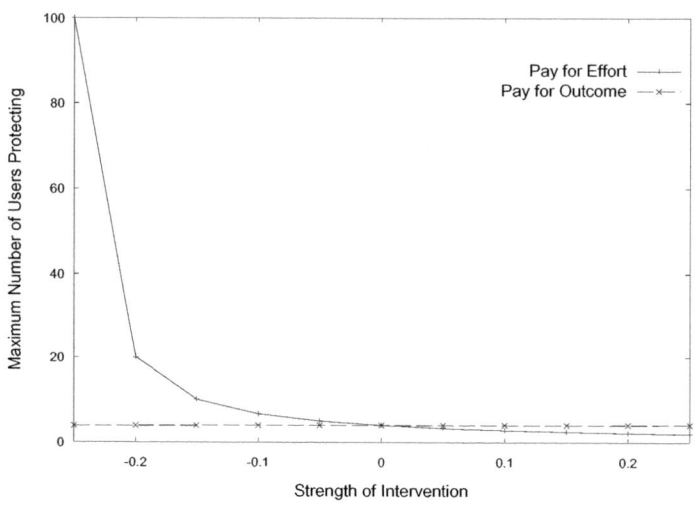

Fig. 5. Cumulative security: Maximum size of the network so that all agents are still willing to contribute to protection (Baseline protection cost b=0.25, fixed self-insurance cost c=0.5, attack probability p=0.1, baseline maximum loss L=10, Value of connection V=1)

5   Discussion and Implementation

We find that pay for effort and pay for outcome policies can influence the basic security trade-offs in the **perimeter defense** case. The major obstacle for a penalizing policy is that users who are located behind a perimeter are usually not in direct contact with the ISP. However, a homogeneous penalty can be applied with selective throttling or temporary disconnection of the subnetwork. Several technologies exist to conduct such traffic management. For example, network operators frequently employ tools to throttle the spread of propagated threats [29]. Similarly, tools can be used to rate-limit certain application flows to implement (approximate) differentiated policies even if the exact individual is unknown to the ISP. However, users may deploy evasive utilities in the presence of such policies. For example, P2P applications trying to avoid rate limitations spread their communication flows over thousands of TCP ports, challenging simple penalty policies that employ port-based identification [14]. The next steps in the arms race are deep-packet inspection (DPI) mechanisms which are, however, met with user resistance. Recently, a major UK ISP stopped the deployment of an advertisement-enabling DPI technology [35].

ISPs may wish to influence, more directly, users located behind a perimeter. A practical approach is to leverage Service Level Agreements (SLA) to manage a variety of rebate/penalty and cost subsidy policies with their institutional subscribers [34].[6] In this way, ISPs can advice corporate customers on security management, and corporate and institutional customers can implement policies in the most suitable manner. For example, they may enforce certain security standards with clearly stated consequences that have evolved within the organization.[7]

In the **cumulative security** scenario, the impact of simple policies is severly limited when the number of users increases. That is, the penalty needs to be proportional to the damages caused in the whole network [33]. In theory, this penalty would never be paid since agents would rationally infer that full protection is the optimal strategy. In practice, it is unlikely that a user would be willing to accept such a risk. Consider the current struggle concerning 3-strikes rules threatening residential users with disconnection if their account is repeatedly used for copyright-infringing activities.[8]

From a behavioral perspective, penalties only have to be large enough to influence consumer sentiment. In fact, in laboratory experiments it has been shown that quite subtle changes can often lead to dramatically different outcomes [15].

Two policies remain relatively effective but may be unattractive for the ISP. First, offering protection at zero cost overcomes the disincentive caused by the network dimensions. Second, a network operator may choose to tackle the problem by compartmentalizing the network into smaller chunks. Several technical solutions exist, e.g., one physical network may be separated into several smaller logical domains (i.e., virtual subnetworks or local area networks). Virtual networks can also be used to separate ports (and therefore groups of applications) which indirectly impacts network size.

So far we discussed how ISPs can encourage protection investments; however, the effectiveness of the policies is unclear if individuals suffer from **strategic uncertainty**. In particular, in both interdependency scenarios users may have some reverberant (and fully rational) doubt about others' willingness to cooperate instead of choosing to shirk, or to select self-insurance [31]. In the perimeter defense scenario, the provision of 'free' security technologies alone cannot reli-

---

[6] Currently, some security service companies draft SLAs to manage security expectations, e.g., http://www.isp-planet.com/technology/mssp/2003/mssp2a.html.

[7] See, for example, the University of Pennsylvania's Disconnection Policy: http://www.upenn.edu/computing/policy/disconnect.html

[8] The currently proposed version of the French 3 strikes law allows sanctioning of users including prison sentences.

ably overcome coordination uncertainty. But, increasing the penalty or reducing the gap between the security investment costs removes the incentives for users to haphazardly coordinate on a lower level of protection. Hamman *et al.* study a similar penalty strategy in an experiment and find that it elicits higher effort levels [20]. However, not all subject groups responded to the penalty when facing the weakest link interdependency, and the effect disappeared almost immediately after the removal of the penalty. Therefore, if the economic incentives cannot be made permanent, then the policy should be associated with a methodology to raise awareness and to instill an intrinsic motivation for effective security practices [27].

Finally, when studying the numerical results it is immediately apparent that the two scenarios may call for different interventions. ISPs that have a user base consisting of both residential and institutional customers may find it therefore difficult to overcome strategic difficulties caused by the multiplicity of equilibria. To effectively address this problems ISPs may be forced to segment their customer groups into different virtual or physical networks. Separating commercial customers constitutes a feasible technique since they often require dedicated lines and services.

With our analysis we have started a discussion about the opportunities and limitations of simple intervention mechanisms that do not necessitate the differential treatment of customers and the associated implementation obstacles. We believe that such easy-to-deploy policies may help overcoming the impasse between the apparent lack of effective protection investments in interdependent networks and the financial viability of cyber-insurance.

References

1. Acquisti, A.: Nudging privacy: The behavioral economics of personal information. IEEE Security & Privacy 7(6), 82–85 (2009)
2. Acquisti, A., Grossklags, J.: Privacy and rationality in individual decision making. IEEE Security & Privacy 3(1), 26–33 (2005)
3. Anderson, R.: Why information security is hard – An economic perspective. In: Proc. of the 17th Annual Computer Security Applications Conference (ACSAC 2001), New Orleans, LA (December 2001)
4. Anderson, R., Böhme, R., Clayton, R., Moore, T.: Security economics and European policy. In: Proceedings of WEIS 2008, Hanover, USA (June 2008)
5. Bandyopadhyay, T., Mookerjee, V., Rao, R.: Why IT managers don't go for cyber-insurance products. Communications of the ACM 52(11), 68–73 (2009)
6. Besnard, D., Arief, B.: Computer security impaired by legitimate users. Computers & Security 23(3), 253–264 (2004)
7. Böhme, R., Kataria, G.: Models and measures for correlation in cyber-insurance. In: Proc. of the Fifth Workshop on the Economics of Information Security (WEIS 2006), Cambridge, UK (June 2006)
8. Clark, D., Wroclawski, J., Sollins, K., Braden, R.: Tussle in cyberspace: Defining tomorrow's Internet. In: Proc. of ACM SIGCOMM 2002, Pittsburgh, PA, pp. 347–356 (August 2002)

9. Clayton, R.: Using early results from the 'spamHINTS' project to estimate an ISP Abuse Team's task. In: Proc. of CEAS 2006, Mountain View, CA (July 2006)
10. Feamster, N., Gao, L., Rexford, J.: How to lease the Internet in your spare time. ACM SIGCOMM Computer Communications Review 37(1), 61–64 (2007)
11. Fultz, N., Grossklags, J.: Blue versus red: Towards a model of distributed security attacks. In: Dingledine, R., Golle, P. (eds.) FC 2009. LNCS, vol. 5628, pp. 167–183. Springer, Heidelberg (February 2009)
12. Gal-Or, E., Ghose, A.: The economic incentives for sharing security information. Information Systems Research 16(2), 186–208 (2005)
13. Geers, J., Goobic, J. (eds.): Cyber insurance. The CIP Report 6(3), 1–11 (2007)
14. Gerber, A., Houle, J., Nguyen, H., Roughan, M., Sen, S.: P2P, The gorilla in the cable. In: NCTA 2003 National Show, Chicago, IL (June 2003)
15. Goeree, J., Holt, C.: Ten little treasures of game theory and ten intuitive contradictions. American Economic Review 91(5), 1402–1422 (2001)
16. Grossklags, J., Christin, N., Chuang, J.: Secure or insure? A game-theoretic analysis of information security games. In: Proceedings of the 2008 World Wide Web Conference (WWW 2008), Beijing, China, pp. 209–218 (April 2008)
17. Grossklags, J., Christin, N., Chuang, J.: Security and insurance management in networks with heterogeneous agents. In: Proceedings of the 9th ACM Conference on Electronic Commerce (EC 2008), Chicago, IL, pp. 160–169 (July 2008)
18. Grossklags, J., Johnson, B., Christin, N.: When information improves information security. In: Proceedings of the 2010 Financial Cryptography Conference (FC 2010), Canary Islands, Spain (January 2010)
19. Grossklags, J., Radosavac, S., Cárdenas, A., Chuang, J.: Nudge: Intermediaries' role in interdependent network security. In: Proceedings of the 25th Symposium on Applied Computing (SAC), Sierre, Switzerland (March 2010)
20. Hamman, J., Rick, S., Weber, R.: Solving coordination failure with "all-or-none" group-level incentives. Experimental Economics 10(3), 285–303 (2007)
21. Kirk, J.: ISPs report success in fighting malware-infected PCs (June 2009), http://www.pcworld.com/businesscenter/article/166444/isps_report_success_in_fighting_malwareinfected_pcs.html
22. Mills, E.: Comcast pop-ups alert customers to PC infections. CNet (October 2009), http://news.cnet.com/8301-27080_3-10370996-245.html
23. Norton, W.: The art of peering: The peering playbook (2002)
24. Pritchard, W., Wong, K.: Infrastructure software: Latest survey results. Report by Cowen and Company (December 2008)
25. Singel, R.: Congressman wants to ban download caps. Wired.com (April 2009)
26. Shrestha, V.: ISP security. In: Tutorial provided at SANOG5 ISP/NSP Security Workshop (February 2005)
27. Siponen, M.: A conceptual foundation for organizational information security awareness. Information Management & Computer Security 8(1), 31–41 (2000)
28. Thaler, R., Sunstein, C.: Nudge: Improving Decisions About Health, Wealth, and Happiness. Yale University Press, New Haven (2008)
29. Twycross, J., Williamson, M.: Implementing and testing a virus throttle. In: Proc. of the 12th USENIX Security Symposium, Washington, DC, pp. 285–294 (August 2003)
30. van Eeten, M., Bauer, J.M.: Economics of malware: Security decisions, incentives and externalities. In: STI Working Paper (May 2008)
31. Van Huyck, J., Battallio, R., Beil, R.: Tacit coordination games, strategic uncertainty, and coordination failure. American Economic Review, 80(1):234–248 (1990)

32. Varian, H.: Managing online security risks. New York Times (June 2000)
33. Varian, H.: System reliability and free riding. In: Camp, L., Lewis, S. (eds.) Economics of Information Security. Advances in Information Security, vol. 12, pp. 1–15. Kluwer, Dordrecht (2004)
34. Verma, D.: Service level agreements on IP networks. Proceedings of the IEEE 92(9), 1382–1388 (2004)
35. Williams, C.: BT abandons Phorm: Not looking good for ad tech. The Register (July 2009)

How the Public Views Strategies Designed to Reduce the Threat of Botnets

Brent Rowe[1], Dallas Wood[2], and Douglas Reeves[3]

[1] RTI International, 114 Sansome St., Suite 500, San Francisco, CA
[2] RTI International, 3040 Cornwallis Road, Research Triangle Park, NC
[3] Department of Computer Science, North Carolina States University, Raleigh, NC

Abstract. Botnets pose a growing threat to the nation's critical digital infrastructure and general level of cybersecurity. Several strategies for reducing the threat of botnets have been outlined in the cyber security literature. These strategies typically call for both Internet Service Providers (ISPs) and home Internet users to adopt a greater share of the responsibility for overall security. However, to date no study has attempted to determine how accepting the public would be of these strategies. This study takes the first step in filling that gap. The results of this pilot survey suggest that, in general, individuals would be willing to spend additional time each month meeting security requirements set by their ISPs. The results also suggest that although only 50% of respondents would be willing to pay their ISP more per month to protect themselves from cyber threats, more people would be willing to do so if they perceived ISPs as being effective or very effective at reducing such threats. The findings provide important guidance for policy makers and ISPs seeking to gain support for such strategies.

Keywords: Botnets, cybersecurity, digital infrastructure, economic incentives, Internet Services Providers, threat reduction strategies.

1 Introduction

In recent years, cybersecurity threats have been growing in terms of economic importance. Prior to the 1990s, the damage inflicted by malicious software programs (malware) was restricted by the fact that data were primarily exchanged through mediums such as floppy diskettes. As a result, installing malware typically required some form of physical access to a target computer. Over the past 20 years, however, the Internet has dramatically increased the ease and potential damage of cyber attacks.

Recent estimates suggest that sophisticated hackers are stealing hundreds of millions of dollars each year. In 2009, $560 million in losses was reported to the FBI-backed Internet Crime Complaint Center [1], and most experts put the total impact on businesses (including inefficiency costs) and individuals (e.g., identity theft) as being much higher. A 2005 FBI survey estimated total annual losses of $67.2 billion per year to U.S. organizations [2].

In May 2009, President Barack Obama released a 60-day, comprehensive, "clean-slate" review to assess U.S. cybersecurity policies and structures. This review

A. Acquisti, S.W. Smith, and A.-R. Sadeghi (Eds.): TRUST 2010, LNCS 6101, pp. 337–351, 2010.

concluded that "the architecture of the Nation's digital infrastructure, based largely upon the Internet, is not secure or resilient. Without major advances in the security of these systems or significant change in how they are constructed or operated, it is doubtful that the United States can protect itself from the growing threat of cyber-crime and state-sponsored intrusions and operations (p. i)" [3].

One of the most significant cybersecurity threats today is the growth in botnets—collections of compromised computers that are used by hackers to attack critical infrastructure enterprises, steal personal information (e.g., social security numbers and bank account information), and spread spam, as well as conduct other illegal activities. Botnets are growing both in size and complexity, and at the same time automated techniques are allowing their operators to acquire and use their resources much more efficiently. As a result, botnets have been identified by network operators and cybersecurity industry leaders as one of the greatest anticipated threats in the near term [4], [5].

Economists, computer scientists, and legal experts have suggested a variety of actions to be taken by individuals and organizations to reduce the threat of botnets. In particular, Anderson et al. [6], Lichtman and Posner [7], and others suggest that Internet service providers (ISPs) could significantly reduce the proliferation of botnets by taking certain actions to better secure their customers. However, no study has been conducted that attempts to determine how the public would react to these strategies if implemented. Given that these actions might reduce ISPs' profits, various private and public (subsidies) payment structures must be considered. It is also important to understand the public's response to these payment structures in order to help private stakeholders (e.g., ISPs) and public stakeholders (e.g., policy makers) determine how to adequately pay for certain strategies.

This report presents the results of a survey administered to a convenience sample of 20 home Internet users. The survey was conducted as a pilot test of a survey instrument being designed for a study funded by the Institute for Homeland Security Solutions (IHSS), a consortium supported by the Department of Homeland Security. This pilot survey and the larger ongoing survey effort are designed to provide initial insights into how the public would react to particular cybersecurity strategies. Specifically, this report focuses on strategies that ISPs could take to help reduce the proliferation of botnets, as suggested by Anderson et al. [6], Lichtman and Posner [7], and others. The lessons learned in this analysis will provide the intellectual basis for a nationally representative survey that will be conducted later in 2010.

2   The Growing Threat of Botnets

Botnets are vast collections of computers (known individually as bots) that have been infected with malicious software allowing them to be controlled remotely by individuals known as "bot masters." Typically, individual bots are personal computers owned by home Internet users that are unaware their computers are being remotely controlled.

Botnets can be used to conduct a variety of illegal activities. Among the most potentially disruptive (and costly) of these activities are Distributed Denial of Service (DDOS) attacks, where hundreds to thousands of bots attempt to access a single Internet system or service causing it to become busy and deny service to legitimate users. DDOS attacks can be used to make public websites inaccessible and can also affect e-mail connectivity, Internet-based telephone systems, and other operationally significant functions [8].

Although typically DDOS attacks are associated in the media with attacks on popular media and social network sites, such as Twitter [9], DDOS attacks pose a more worrisome threat to critical digital infrastructure enterprises. In 2010, McAfee released a commissioned report on the threat that cyber attacks pose to critical digital infrastructure [8]. Based on a survey of 600 information technology (IT) and security executives from critical infrastructure enterprises spread across the United States and 13 other countries, this study found that approximately 30% of U.S. enterprises surveyed reported large-scale DDOS attacks on a monthly or more frequent basis. Additionally, the consequences of these attacks can be dramatic. Among the 600 executives surveyed, nearly two-thirds indicated that large-scale DDOS attacks had impacted their operations in some way. Specifically, among respondents,

- 26% reported that the attack had a serious or sustained impact on IT networks with some effect on operations;
- 23% reported that the attack had effects on operations, causing reputational damage or service interruption;
- 12% reported that the attack had a serious sustained effect on operations, such as environmental damage, floods, etc; and
- 4% reported that the attack caused a "critical breakdown" in operations.

McAfee attempted to quantify the costs of cyber attacks by asking respondents to estimate the losses they would incur from the downtime following a major cyber attack. Respondents estimated that 24 hours of downtime resulting from a major attack would cost their own organization, on average, $6.3 million.

In addition to DDOS attacks on critical infrastructure enterprises, botnets can also be used to carry out a variety of other illegal activities, such as collecting personal information from unsuspecting users or spreading spam that is either annoying or malicious in nature. According to online security vendor MessageLabs (now owned by Symantec), one single botnet, called Cutwail, was responsible for 29% of all spam sent between April and November 2009 [10].

According to recent estimates, approximately 9.4 million computers around the world are infected with bot software [11]. According to the 2009 Arbor Worldwide Infrastructure Security report, which surveyed 132 ISP network operators around the globe, these botnets and the DDOS attacks that they can be used to conduct are considered the largest anticipated threat over the next 12 months. And the threat they pose is only expected to increase with time as botnets become more sophisticated.

Botnets are becoming both easier to create and harder detect. According to a 2009 MessageLabs report, botnets are evolving to become more autonomous and intelligent—with each node containing built-in, self-sufficient code allowing it to coordinate with the bot master and extend its own survival [10]. Another more worrisome trend is that botnets are also becoming easier to access: the cyber security markets are becoming so efficient that it is possible to rent botnets [12].

To both limit economic damage and prevent more catastrophic results, for example to critical digital infrastructure, U.S. policy makers are considering a variety of direct (regulations) and indirect (research and development spending) methods to improve the cybersecurity of the United States. As part of this process, U.S. policy makers need a detailed understanding of the stakeholders involved with providing cybersecurity and their incentives for providing security against botnets.

3   Stakeholder Incentives for Providing Security Against Botnets

Three primary stakeholders are in a position to take action to reduce the threat of botnets[1]: targets of botnet activities, who can improve their defenses; home Internet users, who can take steps to prevent themselves from becoming bots; and ISPs, who grant home users access to the Internet. These stakeholders could take a more active role in improving cybersecurity.

It seems intuitive that the first avenue for reducing the threat of botnets is for individuals or organizations that are the target of botnet attacks to protect themselves sufficiently from such an attack. Inasmuch as these stakeholders bear the full cost of these attacks, they therefore have the most incentive to either prevent them or mitigate their impact on day-to-day operations. For example, these organizations could mitigate a DDOS attack by purchasing bandwidth larger than the attack itself or using packet filters to weed out the bad traffic [13]; and individuals could use spam filters and otherwise improve their host-level security to prevent their personal data from being stolen.

However, because target organizations have the most incentive to protect themselves against attack, it would seem reasonable to suspect that these same individuals and organizations have already made many of the most cost-effective investments (given the information they have and their budget constraints) in defensive technologies; yet the problem of botnets remains. Even if further investments are made, it is doubtful that the most robust defenses will be enough to protect against all attacks. A 2006 iDefense Security Report concluded that "ultimately, many defenses, once employed can later be circumvented by the attacker. It has always been and remains easier for an attacker to adapt their attack vectors or simply increase the number of attacking bots than it is for defenders to mitigate the attack, to increase resources, or to recover" [13].

Further, legal recourse for organizations that are attacked by botnets is not well established. Although successful efforts have been waged in U.S. courts and elsewhere to shut down botnets—for example, by Microsoft [14]—it is often difficult, impossible, or prohibitively time-consuming to determine who coordinated a botnet attack. In many cases, the perpetrator(s) are located outside of the United States. As such, the victims are often unable to utilize a primary government support mechanism, criminal prosecution, civil lawsuits, and the awarding of damages; thus, the costs can be more

---

[1] Note that software vendors, among others, could also play a role in reducing the threat of botnets by improving software quality. However, this report only focuses on strategies that could more directly reduce the impact of botnets, such as strategies that would incentivize action by stakeholders that are both most affected by botnets and most able to make security improvements that could directly affect the proliferation of botnets.

significant. Moreover, if the perpetrators cannot be identified or they are located outside the United States, they may not face sufficient negative costs (e.g., fines or imprisonment) to incentivize them to change their activities. Consequently, if the threat of botnets is to be reduced, other stakeholders must take on some of the responsibility to improve cybersecurity.

A second avenue for improving cybersecurity would be for home Internet users to take steps to prevent themselves from becoming bots. Specifically, home users can engage in good Internet use practices—such as being careful which e-mail attachments are opened and which websites are visited—or by using a variety of up-to-date security software, hardware, and/or services.

However, there are three principal reasons not to expect that home users will adequately secure their computers on their own. First, home users typically do not experience the negative consequences of their own insecurity. Our research suggests that users are only interested in adopting security products or services if they believe they are being prevented from enjoying the Internet—for example, communicating (send and receive messages), shopping, being entertained, conducting financial activities, or conducting business activities. Although some botnets do mine the data (e.g., on financial activities) on bot computers and this can slow the performance of a bot computer, bots are primarily used to wage attacks against other organizations and/or groups of individuals. As a result, home users have minimal incentives for protecting themselves against becoming bots [6] or to simply assess the security level of their computers.

Second, evidence is starting to accumulate that suggests that even if home users were more altruistic, they do not have the proper understanding of how botnets work to adequately protect themselves. Specifically, according to Wash [15], the mental models home Internet users have for understanding how cyberattacks work leaves them ill-equipped to deal with the dangers of botnets. Wash states that the extent to which home users pursue various security activities will depend on the way in which they conceive security threats. For example, individuals that view viruses as simply being "bad" (i.e., spam wastes people's time but is generally harmless) and/or that hackers only pursue "big fish" (e.g., large companies, financial institutions) are unlikely to expend significant resources on substantive security measures.

Lastly, even if home users were more knowledgeable of cybersecurity threats, they still may underinvest from a private perspective and, even more likely, from a social perspective because they may not know who to trust when seeking security advice or considering the purchase/adoption of various security products or services. Measures of effectiveness are particularly elusive in the area of cybersecurity. Although security vendors and ISPs providing security services offer products and services that espouse certain security benefits or features, no objective effectiveness metrics currently exist for users to facilitate making security investment decisions. Thus, the complexity of making cybersecurity decisions may cause many home Internet users to simply not adopt any solutions.

Without objective metrics to compare security solutions, it is unclear how vendors and ISPs can most effectively earn or create trust among customers or potential customers. For example, attempting to increase fear as a mechanism to earn trust could be problematic. One ISP interviewed for this study[2] indicated that only 50% of their

---

[2] Participation by this ISP required that their name be kept confidential.

customers have downloaded a security software package that is free with their subscription. Although the customers would almost certainly be more secure if they downloaded and used this software,[3] the ISP was hesitant to push customers to adopt the software, as they are concerned that this might cause customers to become more fearful of cybersecurity in general, which could result in a decrease in Internet usage by their customer base and thus a decrease in the ISP's revenue. Note that this ISP felt that the cost of the security software package (reported as approximately $1 per license download fee paid by the ISP to the software vendor) was more than justified by the resulting benefits, including increased customer retention and improved network performance (additional bandwidth).

If home Internet users are to take a more active role in protecting their computers from botnets, they likely will need to receive a stronger incentive to care about this threat and to trust vendors offering various security products and/or services. Beautement and Sasse [16] found that in organizational settings, users are more compliant with security policies when they understand the reasons behind them. Education, training, and technical assistance are likely to be important, but security vendors and the government need to be circumspect about pushing out marketing or education campaigns that increase the fear of cybersecurity, which could decrease the use of, and thus the overall value of, the Internet.

The final avenue for improving security against botnets that will be considered here is for ISPs to take a more active role in reducing the threat of botnets. Specifically, because ISPs provide home users with access to the Internet, they can observe traffic flowing into and out of their networks. As a result, they are in a prime position to observe (either with or without looking within users packets) traffic spikes or atypical Internet behavior that could be associated with malicious traffic cause by bots, with or without looking within users' packets. A number of automated tools and products exist to make this process relatively efficient and scalable. ISPs can respond to signs of infection or misbehavior by cutting off Internet access to infected users or quarantining them until their machines have been repaired (e.g., [6], [17], [18], [19]).

However, currently most ISPs do not take such an active role in securing their customers. Although there has been an upward trend in the number of ISPs that actively try to improve the security of their customers, according to the 2009 Worldwide Infrastructure Security report, only 28% of the ISPs surveyed said that they use automated techniques for quarantining infected or malicious subscribers [4]. The majority of ISPs do not currently use these automated systems because they have insufficient incentive for fighting botnets that operate across multiple networks. As noted by Lichtman and Posner, ISPs are currently immune from any liability for the damages caused by their subscribers [7]. Therefore, if more ISPs are expected to take an active role in reducing the threat of botnets, they will need to receive an additional incentive for doing so.

4   Improving Incentives for Providing Security against Botnets

The previous discussion makes it clear that improving incentives for home Internet users and ISPs to stop bots could significantly impact the general level of cybersecurity.

---

[3] Unless customers already use another security software package.

One prevalent strategy discussed throughout the cybersecurity literature is to hold ISPs accountable for their role in the propagation of botnets. Specifically, ISPs are currently immune from any liability for the damages caused by their subscribers that are unwittingly being used as part of a botnet. Lichtman and Posner [7] suggest that courts hold ISPs accountable by explicitly assigning them some share of the responsibility in the damages caused by botnets operating over their networks.

However, in a commissioned report for the European Network and Information Security Agency, Anderson et al. [6] suggest that there are serious difficulties with the approach of imposing liability on ISPs. Specifically, they cite several stumbling blocks, such as the potentially high transaction cost of lawsuits and the difficulty of valuing the monetary losses associated with individual events. Instead, they recommended that ISPs be charged a fixed-penalty charge if they do not quarantine infected individuals in a timely manner once they have been notified of their activities.

In either case, imposing financial costs on ISPs for allowing botnets to operate over their networks would certainly provide an incentive to step up their efforts to quarantine infected or malicious subscribers. In addition, Lichtman and Posner suggest that once ISPs are held accountable for the traffic traveling across their networks, they will take a more active role in ensuring their subscribers protect themselves from becoming bots. Specifically, they note that "ISPs have a direct contractual relationship with their subscribers and so surely a liable ISP will require each of its subscribers to adopt rudimentary precautions…[b]etter still, these contract terms can be enforced by technology, which is to say that an ISP can block any subscriber whose virus definitions are horribly out of date or whose firewall is malfunctioning" [7].

If the U.S government were to impose some version of a penalty on ISPs for not reacting to botnets on their networks, and if in response, ISPs set security requirements for their customers, as Lichtman and Posner predict, it would be a significant step forward in solving the three obstacles that currently face home users in terms of providing more security. First, this creates a clear incentive for home users to keep their computers secure. Second, this will provide home users with access to the knowledgeable technical assistance they need to be fully informed about cybersecurity threats. Third, these requirements will help improve home users security decisions by providing them with information on trusted security solutions.

Although these strategies have been discussed extensively in the literature, no study has been conducted to determine how the general public will react to such policies. For example, it might be expected that individual users would be upset if their Internet connection was unexpectedly disrupted because they were identified as a possible bot. Similarly they may be unwilling to spend the extra time or money that ISPs adopting these policies might impose on home users.

Thus, the present study aims to take the first step in filling this gap in the literature. The following section describes a small survey that was conducted to better understand the public's reaction to these various strategies for reducing the threat of botnets.

5   Survey of Public Reaction to Strategies to Reduce the Threat of Botnets

In February 2010, we administered a pilot survey to a convenience sample of 20 home Internet users. The survey was designed to gain an initial understanding of how the public would react to four specific strategies for reducing the threat of botnets that are based on the existing cybersecurity literature, as described above. Specifically, we asked respondents if they would be willing to

1. pay an additional monthly fee to fund ISP efforts to reduce cybersecurity threats to their computer;
2. pay an additional monthly fee to fund ISP efforts to prevent their computer from being used, without their knowledge, to send spam or to attack other computers;
3. spend time each month complying with ISP-determined security requirements (participating in online security training, updating security software, etc.); and
4. allow ISPs to disconnect them from the Internet if it appeared that their computer was infected with malicious software.

This survey aimed to better understand individuals' perceptions of these security and potential ISP-based security solutions. The lessons learned from this pilot will be used to create a more robust survey that will be fielded to a nationally representative sample of U.S. Internet users between May and July 2010. This full sample survey will use a more sophisticated methodology than the one utilized in the pilot survey. Specifically, we will use stated preference discrete choice experiments to measure individuals' responses to these and other ISP security strategies, and to quantify their willingness to accept the costs (in terms of time, money, etc.) associated with these strategies. Similar approaches have been used in numerous security-related research projects, including one recently completed by Robinson et al. [20].

5.1 Summary Statistics

A summary of responses to the scenarios presented above are reported in Table 1. If respondents said yes that they were willing to spend more time or money to improve cybersecurity, we asked them (in an open-ended format) to estimate how much time or money they would be willing to spend. A summary of the valuations made by responses is provided in Table 2.

As the data in Tables 1 and 2 indicate, 70% of respondents indicated that they would be willing to spend additional time each month participating in online training, updating security software, etc., making this the most popular strategy proposed. On average, respondents indicated that they would be willing to spend 20 minutes each month complying with these standards.

The second most popular strategy proposed was paying an additional fee each month to fund ISP efforts to reduce cybersecurity threats to their customers. Among the respondents, 50% said they would be willing to pay this fee. Specifically, they said they would be willing to pay, on average, $8.40 per month to fund these efforts.

The remaining two strategies, paying an additional fee to fund ISP efforts to prevent one's home computer from being recruited into a botnet and allowing ISPs to disconnect them from the Internet, were approximately equal in popularity, garnering support from 45% of the respondents. Respondents that said they would be willing to fund ISP efforts that prevented their computers from being used as bots by paying, on average, $3.80 per month for this service.

Table 1. Summary results of public reception to cybersecurity strategies (N=20)

Question	Yes	No	No answer	Total
Would you be willing to pay an additional fee each month to fund ISP efforts to reduce cybersecurity threats to your computer?	50%	50%	0%	100%
Would you be willing to pay an additional fee each month to prevent your computer from being used, without your knowledge, to send spam or to attack other computers?	45%	55%	0%	100%
Would you be willing to spend additional time participating in online security training and following your ISP's instructions for securing your computer (e.g., updating your security software) if your ISP required you do to do so in order to continue to receive Internet service?	70%	30%	0%	100%
Would you be willing to allow ISPs to prevent you from accessing the Internet, if it appeared your computer was being controlled by another person to send spam or attack other computers?	45%	50%	5%	100%

Table 2. Quantifying willingness to pay for reductions in cybersecurity threats and willingness to spend time complying with ISP-determined security requirements

	Median	Mean	Standard Error of Mean	N
Additional fee respondent said they would be willing to pay each month to fund ISP efforts to reduce cybersecurity threats to their computers.	$5.00 per month	$8.40 per month	3.3	8
Additional fee respondents said they would be willing to pay each month to prevent their computer from being used, without your knowledge, to send spam or to attack other computers.	$2.00 per month	$3.80 per month	1.7	5
Additional time respondents said they would be willing to spend to participate in online security training and comply with ISP's instructions for securing their computers.	27.5 minutes per month	20.4 minutes per month	3.2	12

Note: Not all respondents who indicated they supported a particular strategy were willing to provide estimates of how much time or money they would be willing to spend if such a strategy was pursued.

5.2 Impact of ISP Trust on Support for Strategies

Although ISPs and policy makers may be interested in discovering which strategies are most popular among home Internet users, information on what factors influence support for a given strategy may be particularly useful. One of the most obvious factors that may potentially influence support for these strategies is how effective respondents believe these strategies will be. Specifically, respondents may be less willing to spend their time and money on strategies they do not believe will be effective. Therefore, as part of this survey, we asked respondents to report how effective they believed each of the cybersecurity strategies would be at reducing cybersecurity threats. A contingency table comparing respondent's answers to these two questions is provided in Table 3.

Table 3. Comparison of support for each strategy with perceived strategy effectiveness

	Strategy 1. Willing to pay an additional fee each month to fund ISP efforts to reduce cybersecurity threats to their computer.			**Strategy 2.** Willing to pay an additional fee each month to prevent their computer from being used, without their knowledge, to send spam or to attack other computers.			**Strategy 3.** Willingness to spend additional time complying with ISP-determined security requirements.			**Strategy 4.** Willing to allow ISPs to prevent them from accessing the Internet, if it appeared their computer was being controlled by another person to send spam or attack other computers.		
	Yes	No	Total	Yes	No	Total	Yes	No	Total	Yes	No	Total
Effective	5	1	6	2	4	6	9	2	11	5	3	8
Ineffective	1	7	8	3	5	8	4	3	7	3	3	6
Total	6	8	14	5	9	14	13	5	18	8	6	14

Note: To obtain a better understanding of the influence that perceived effectiveness has on an individual's willingness to accept a given strategy, we have removed individuals that did not know how effective they believed these strategies would be at reducing cybersecurity threats.

As this table illustrates, 5 of the 6 people (83%) that said they support Strategy 1 also thought that ISPs would be very or somewhat effective at reducing such threats. However, only 2 of the 5 (40%) individuals that said they support Strategy 2 thought ISP efforts would be effective. Among respondents, 9 of the 13 (69%) of the individuals that said they supported Strategy 3 thought this strategy would be effective; and 5 of the 8 people that supported Strategy 4 (63%) thought this strategy would be effective.

These results suggest that the more individuals trust that Strategies 1, 3, and 4 will be effective, the more willing they are to support them. Ideally, we would test this hypothesis using regression analysis, but because the sample size for this pilot survey was only 20 respondents, we cannot expect statistically significant results. Instead, we tested to see whether these variables are independent of each of other or not by using the Exact Test for Independence (as described in Marasculio and McSweeny [21]).

To illustrate how this test was conducted for this study, we describe our calculations for Strategy 1. First, we outline the hypothesis we wish to test:

H_0: the willingness to pay an additional fee each month to fund ISP efforts to reduce cybersecurity threats to their computer is independent of the perceived effectiveness of these efforts.

H_1: H_0 is false.

Next, we define the variable of interest. First, suppose that X_{10} was the number of people that answered yes they would be willing to pay an additional fee to ISPs for protection from cyberthreats to their computer (6) and that X_{01} was the number of people that indicated ISPs are effective at reducing cybersecurity threats (6). Then the number we are most interested in for the purposes of this test is X_{11} or the intersection of these two groups of people (5).

Lastly, we construct the probability distribution we use for hypothesis testing. Because X_{01} equals 6, X_{11} could take any one of these possible values when performing the exact test: $\{0, 1, 2, 3, 4, 5, 6\}$. The exact probabilities for each of these values of X_{11} were computed using the hypergeometric formula; the results are illustrated in Figure 1.

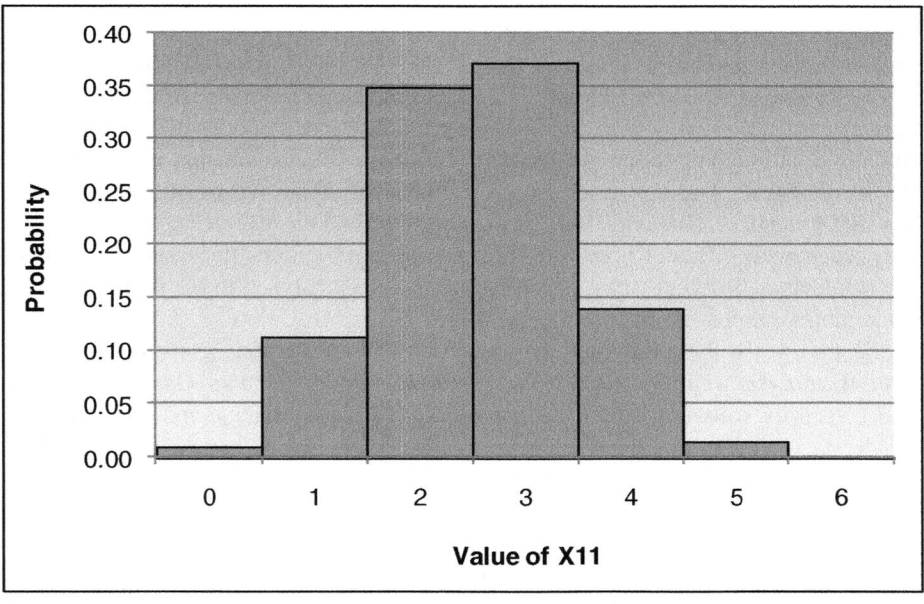

Fig. 1. Probabilities for X_{11}

Table 4. Results of exact test of independence by strategy

	Right-tail P-value	Two-tail P-value
Willing to pay an additional fee each month to fund ISP efforts to reduce cybersecurity threats to their computer.	1.6%	2.6%
Willing to pay an additional fee each month to prevent their computer from being used, without their knowledge, to send spam or to attack other computers.	76.2%	100.0%
Willingness to spend additional time complying with ISP-determined security requirements.	27.2%	32.6%
Willing to allow ISPs to prevent them from accessing the Internet, if it appeared their computer was being controlled by another person to send spam or attack other computers.	52.9%	100%

As Figure 1 indicates, the probability that X_{11} could be greater than or equal to 5 is less than 2%. Therefore, we reject the null hypothesis that these two variables are independent. Similar right-tail and two-tail P-values for all four strategies are presented in Table 4. Looking at these values, we can see that we can only reject the null hypothesis for Strategy 1. We cannot reject the null hypothesis that the willingness to accept any other strategies is independent of their perceived effectiveness for any of the three remaining strategies. This could suggest that effectiveness is unrelated to support for Strategies 2 through 4; however, further data collection and analysis are required before definitive conclusions can be drawn.

5.3 Lessons Learned

The findings from this pilot study suggest that whether individuals trust that ISP strategies are effective can significantly impact their support for these strategies. This raises several important questions that will be explored in the full sample survey. First, we intend to investigate what factors influence individuals' perceptions of ISP strategy effectiveness. For example, does providing more information about security threats or strategies used to reduce them influence the amount that individuals trust these strategies? And how does this affect their willingness to pay for or spend time on ISP strategies? This issue will be explored by fielding several versions of the survey, each with different preamble information that explains the issues and risks to respondents in different ways. Survey results will be analyzed to see if this influences individuals' responses.

Second, we will explore how individuals' trust varies among groups that could affect their cybersecurity—e.g., ISPs, operating system vendors (Microsoft, Apple, etc.), security software vendors, other software vendors, banks, and other websites. Understanding who Internet users trust and why could help to better determine how to increase trust of ISPs as security providers. We will analyze the variance in levels of trust by asking several questions regarding individuals' feelings toward these various stakeholder groups.

In addition to the results presented earlier, the pilot study has provided other insights that will be used to improve the larger survey. Specifically, we found that users can be relatively ignorant of what security tools are currently on their computers and to what threats they may be vulnerable. This finding is consistent with results from other surveys, such as the National Cyber Security Alliance's 2009 study [22]. We plan to use these lessons to simplify the survey and focus on issues that are most familiar to individuals: their perceptions of cybersecurity versus their actual cybersecurity.

6 Conclusion and Next Steps

Botnets pose a growing threat to the nation's critical digital infrastructure and general level of cybersecurity. This study takes the first step in filling a gap in the existing literature by using data from a pilot survey of 20 home Internet users to evaluate how the public will react to various policies that have been proposed as means of reducing the threat of botnets and what factors influence their support for these strategies.

The principal factor evaluated in this study was whether support for a particular strategy was influenced by how effective individuals perceived each strategy to be. The evidence suggests that if home Internet users trust that ISPs are effective at reducing cybersecurity threats, they will be more willing to pay additional fees to ISPs to fund efforts to reduce such threats to their computers. Specifically, respondents that supported this strategy were willing to pay, on average, an additional $8.40 per month to their ISPs. However, more data needs to be collected before definitive conclusions can be drawn.

If the results of the pilot survey are confirmed with further study, this will provide ISPs and policy makers with a clearer guidance for building support for funding ISP efforts to reduce threats and other cybersecurity strategies. Specifically, our evidence suggests that ISPs and policy makers will need to devote resources to building trust among home Internet users that these are effective strategies.

In the next steps of this study, we will collect data from a nationally representative sample of home Internet users and use more sophisticated valuation methods (such as discrete choice experiments) for determining which factors influence public support for these policies. We anticipate that the results of the larger study will provide important input for both private stakeholders (ISPs and security vendors) and public stakeholders (the U.S. government) concerning what personal characteristics and what educational and marketing strategies will motivate home Internet users to spend more of their time and their monetary resources to protect themselves (and others) from cybersecurity threats.

Acknowledgment

This project is funded through a subcontract with the Institute for Homeland Security Solutions (IHSS). IHSS is a research consortium established to conduct applied research in the social and behavioral sciences. The Human Factors Division is the Department of Homeland Security (DHS) sponsor for IHSS. More information about IHSS is available at http://www.ihssnc.org.

References

1. Homeland Security News Wire (HSNW): U.S. Cybercrime Losses Double (2010), `http://homelandsecuritynewswire.com/us-cybercrime-losses-double` (as obtained on April 7, 2010)
2. U.S. Government Accountability Office. Report to Congressional Requestors. Cybercrime. Public and Private Entities Face Challenges in Addressing Cyber Threats. GAO-07-705 (2007), `http://www.gao.gov/new.items/d07705.pdf` (as obtained on April 12, 2010)
3. The White House. Cyberspace Policy Review: Assuring a Trusted and Resilient Information and Communications Infrastructure (2009), `http://www.whitehouse.gov/assets/documents/Cyberspace_Policy_Review_final.pdf` (as obtained on April 12, 2010)
4. Arbor Networks: 2009 Worldwide Infrastructure Security Report (2010), `http://www.arbornetworks.com/report` (as obtained on February 21, 2010)

5. Swartz, J.: Cybersecurity CEO Keeps Watch Over Threat. USA Today, July 23, p. 6B (2007)
6. Anderson, R., Bohme, R., Clayton, R., Moore, T.: Analyzing Barriers and Incentives for Network and Information Security in the Internal Market for e-Communication (2008), http://www.enisa.europa.eu/act/sr/reports/econ-sec (as obtained on February 21, 2010)
7. Lichtman, D., Posner, E.: Holding Internet Service Providers Accountable. University of Chicago John M. Olin Law and Economist Working Paper No. 217 (2006), http://www.law.uchicago.edu/files/files/217-dgl-eap-isp.pdf (as obtained on April 12, 2010)
8. Baker, S., Shaun, W., Ivanov, G.: In the Crossfire: Critical Infrastructure in the Age of CyberWar (2010), http://csis.org/event/crossfire-critical-infrastructure-age-cyber-war (as obtained on February 21, 2010)
9. Buskirk, E.: Denial-of-Service Attack Knocks Twitter Offline (2009), http://www.wired.com/epicenter/2009/08/twitter-apparently-down/ (as obtained on February 21, 2010)
10. Swabey, P.: The New Cybercriminals (2010), http://www.growthbusiness.co.uk/channels/growth-strategies/technology-in-business/1147068/the-new-cybercriminals.thtml (as obtained on February 21, 2010)
11. Symantec: Symantec Global Internet Security Threat Report: Trends for 2008 (2009), http://eval.symantec.com/mktginfo/enterprise/white_papers/b-whitepaper_Internet_security_threat_report_xiv_04-2009.en-us.pdf (as obtained on February 21, 2009)
12. British Broadcasting Company (BBC): BBC Team Exposes Cyber Crime Risk, http://news.bbc.co.uk/2/hi/programmes/click_online/7932816.stm (as obtained on February 22, 2009) (last updated March 12, 2009)
13. iDefense: Distributed Denial of Service and Botnet Attacks (2006), http://complianceandprivacy.com/WhitePapers/iDefense_DDoS_20060428.pdf (as obtained on February 21, 2010)
14. Cranton, T.: Cracking Down on Botnets (2009), http://microsoftontheissues.com/cs/blogs/mscorp/archive/2010/02/24/cracking-down-on-botnets.aspx (as obtained on April 07, 2010)
15. Wash, R.: Mental Models of Home Computer Security. Presented at the Symposium on Usable Privacy and Security (SOUPS), Pittsburgh, PA, July 23-25 (2008)
16. Beautement, A., Sasse, A.: The Economics of User Effort in Information Security. Computer Fraud & Security 2009(10), 8–12 (2009), http://www.sciencedirect.com/science?_ob=ArticleURL&_udi=B6VNT-4XMCXV1-8&_user=775537&_coverDate=10%2F31%2F2009&_rdoc=1&_fmt=high&_orig=search&_sort=d&_docanchor=&view=c&_searchStrId=1292011789&_rerunOrigin=google&_acct=C000042938&_version=1&_urlVersion=0&_userid=775537&md5=d0b7627564e032d681962cdb844a7afb (as obtained April 12, 2010)
17. Evers, J.: ISPs Versus the Zombies. Cnet News.com (July 19, 2005), http://news.cnet.com/ISPs-versus-the-zombies/2100-7349_3-5793719.html (as obtained on February 21, 2010)
18. Huang, Y., Xianjun, G., Whinston, A.: Defeating DDoS Attacks by Fixing the Incentive Chain. ACM Transactions on Internet Technology article 5, 7(1), 1–5 (2007), http://portal.acm.org/citation.cfm?doid=1189740.1189745 (as obtained on April 30, 2009)

19. Richards, J.: Make Firms Bear the Cost to Improve Information Security, says Schneier. Computer Weekly (May 22, 2007), http://www.computerweekly.com/Articles/2007/05/22/223959/make-firms-bear-the-cost-toimprove-information-security-says-schneier.htm (as obtained on February 21, 2010)
20. Robinson, N., Potoglou, D., Woo Kim, C., Burge, P., Warnes, P.: Security, at What Cost? Quantifying People's Trade-offs across Liberty, Privacy and Security (2010), http://www.rand.org/pubs/technical_reports/2010/RAND_TR664.pdf (as obtained on April 9, 2010)
21. Marasculio, M., McSweeny, M.: Nonparametric and Distribution-Free Methods for the Social Sciences. Waldsworth Publishing Company, Belmont (1977)
22. National Cyber Security Alliance (NCSA) and Symantec. 2009 NCSA/Symantec Home User Study (2009), http://www.staysafeonline.org/files/pdfs/2009HomeUserStudy/Home%20User%20Study%20FINAL.pdf (as obtained on April 12, 2010)

Axiomatic and Behavioural Trust

Clark Thomborson

Department of Computer Science
The University of Auckland, New Zealand
cthombor@cs.auckland.ac.nz

Abstract. Academic discourse on trust is fractured along disciplinary lines. Security theorists routinely use a definition of trust which, apparently, has little in common with any of the definitions of trust that appear in the sociological and psychological literature. In this essay, we extend a recently-proposed framework for the technical analysis of secure systems, so that its notion of trust is roughly congruent with the sociological theories of Parsons, Luhmann, Barber, Lewis and Weigert. This congruent extension suggests some ways in which a computerised system might, appropriately, inspire trust in its non-technical users.

Keywords: Trust, security analysis, trust management.

1 Introduction: Two Types of Trust

My recently-proposed security framework [1] provides terminological and definitional support for security analysts in diverse subfields, retaining the common elements of their modelling approaches in the framework while excluding the subfield-specific detail. The definitions and taxonomic classifications in the framework are, for the most part, cross-products of dichotomised variables. For example, the four concepts of security, functionality, trust, and distrust are quadrants in the two-dimensional space defined by two binary variables: feedback and assessment. Functionality and trust involve positive feedback to the owner of a system, whereas security and distrust involve negative feedback. Trust and distrust, as defined by Luhmann [2] and others, are not based on assessment – instead they are characterised by an uncertainty or lack of information about some (presumed, relied-upon) "good" or "bad" contingency. Functionality and security, by contrast, are an owner's assessments of likely future positive or negative feedbacks from their system.

Our approach to the understanding of trust can be viewed as a harshly simplified version of a functional, cybernetic sociological theory. As such, it cannot offer any startling new insights to sociologists, but our reductions and simplifications may be helpful in clarifying the definitions and distinctions made in the conceptual models developed by Luhmann, Barber, and others. However the main goal of this essay is not to contribute to the sociology of trust, but instead to offer support for interdisciplinary discussions of the nature and functions of trust. Technologists can gain useful insights about trust, we argue, from the prominent

A. Acquisti, S.W. Smith, and A.-R. Sadeghi (Eds.): TRUST 2010, LNCS 6101, pp. 352–366, 2010.
© Springer-Verlag Berlin Heidelberg 2010

sociologists of the latter part of the twentieth century. We also suggest, from our technological perspective, some experimentation that sociologists and psychologists might conduct, if they wish to elucidate the structural foundations of trust and the primary factors in an individual's trusting decisions.

We start our exposition by distinguishing two subtypes of trust within our framework. This distinction will allow us to discuss the most important mode of secure-systems analysis, wherein some range of system behaviour is proved to be impossible. Such security proofs are rigorous deductions on a set of axioms, where each axiom constrains the behaviour of the "trusted" elements of the system. Theorems are of the following form: no matter how the untrusted elements of a system (mis)behave, the system will still have some desirable security property. In the context of such proofs, "trust" is thus an axiomatic property, one which is ascribed to certain elements of a system by its modeller. In order to reconcile this notion of trust with our framework, we must define two subtypes of trust.

Behavioural trust statements are either made by, or ascribed to, a set of actors in a model. Such statements are confident (but still somewhat uncertain) descriptions or predictions, by a *trust analyst*, of some desirable behaviour by one or more actors in the model.

Axiomatic trust statements are axioms of a system model, defining the desired behaviour (as judged by the owner of the system) of one or more actors in the system. Axioms are uttered, or assented to, by a *trust modeller* who is, at least notionally, external to the model defined by the axioms.

We have identified four ways in which an actor in a modelled system may gain the externality required to act as trust modellers within their own system. The modeller who created their system may have provided an *oracle* which provides axiomatic advice to actors in a model, in some language that can be interpreted by these actors. Any actor in a system may construct a *subsystem* along axiomatic lines. Any actor in a system may adopt an *induced axiom* by uttering or assenting to statement which they hold to be true beyond reasonable doubt. If an apparent contradiction arises, the contrary evidence is investigated carefully before the axiom itself is questioned. An example of an inductive axiom is $E = mc^2$. Finally, an actor may derive some *deduced axioms*, i.e. lemmas or theorems, from their current set of axioms by a process of logical deduction.

We note that axiomatic trust statements are formally correct. Their validity is questioned only when a set of axioms is discovered to be logically inconsistent by a novel deduction, or when a novel set of observations (e.g. of the behaviour of photons near the Sun) clearly invalidates an induced axiom such as Newton's law of gravitation. By contrast, the validity of every behavioural trust statement is formally uncertain – it is directly contingent on future observations. This is Luhmann's distinction between "confidence" and "trust" [3]. Luhmann also defines the meta-axiomatic concept of "familiarity", in order to discuss the language in which the modeller expresses her axioms. The modeller has "confidence" in the validity of their axioms; anyone who formally analyses this modeller must base their analysis on axioms which describe the modeller's "familiar" language. We do not adopt Luhmann's triad of definitions because they are more detailed than we require for our discussion, and because we have already defined trust in a broader way: as the system owner's unassessed expectation of positive feedback from their system.

We distinguish distrust from trust, by considering the difference between the fears and desires of the owner of the system. Although this essay is devoted to an exploration of trust, we define, in passing, an *axiomatic distrust statement* as an anti-requirement on a system, specifying what it shall not do. A *behavioural distrust statement* is the expectation of an system analyst, regarding the likely "bad" behaviour of one or more actors in that system. Clearly: an analyst who distrusts some behavioural aspect of an actor will endeavour to avoid depending on that actor in the relevant contexts. Such active avoidance, when enacted, becomes a security provision, that is, a system modification whose expense or inconvenience is justified by the owner's assessment of a reduction in harm. As such, a distrusting decision is clearly distinguishable from the functional motivation of a trusting decision, and is deserving of a separate analysis. Later in this essay, we will return to the issue of decision-making with respect to security (costs or other harms), functionality (benefits), trust (uncertainty about benefits), and distrusts (uncertainty about harms).

We define a *model* to be any simplification of a real-world system which is too complex for a direct analysis. A competent modeller will search for radical simplifications which make their model maximally analysable, while doing as little damage as possible to the accuracy and precision of the model predictions. A logically-inclined modeller defines a model by constructing its axioms. An experimentalist defines a model by constructing it from the material at hand, that is, from the malleable elements of the system in which the experimentalist is an actor. We imagine that almost all of the models people use in their everyday lives are of the experimental variety: they are incompletely axiomatised. However every model, as defined here, has a purpose of simplified representation; so we argue that every modeller has uttered at least one (perhaps only vaguely apprehended or understandable) axiom when constructing their model.

Luhmann asserts that everyone in our ever-more-complex modern world is, increasingly, engaging in such a process of model-making and analysis, because such analytic simplifications are required to thrive and perhaps even to survive:

> We are now in a position to formulate the problem of trust as a gamble, a risky investment. The world is being dissipated into an uncontrollable complexity; so much so that at any given time people are able to choose freely between very different actions. Nevertheless, I have to act here and now. There is only a brief moment of time in which it is possible for me to see what others do, and consciously adapt myself to it. In just that moment only a little complexity can be envisaged and processed, thus only a little gain in rationality is possible. Additional chances of a more complex rationality would arise if I were to place my trust in a given future course of action of others (or for that matter in a contemporary or past course of action, if I can only establish it in the future). If I can trust in sharing the proceeds, I can allow myself forms of co-operation

which do not pay off immediately and which are not directly visible as beneficial. If I depend on the fact that others are acting, or are failing to act, in harmony with me, I can pursue my own interests more rationally—driving more smoothly in traffic, for example [2].

We do not attempt to express all of Luhmann's theory of trust in our framework, however we have adopted what we see as the primary elements of his theory. In particular, we do not insist that the primary motivation for every behavioural trust statement is the Luhmannian purpose of uncertainty reduction during decision-making. Such an insistence would limit the scope of our modelling to actors who are sentient and purposeful entities. We see no analytic advantage – and we see some disadvantages – in ascribing a purpose to a computerised actor which is making predictions about future events. We survey a few other theories below, regarding the purpose or function of trust.

In Parsons' AGIL theory [4], every group has a primary functional imperative of pattern maintenance. If the axioms of Parson's theory are adopted (as axiomatic trust statements) in a model within our framework, then a social group's self-descriptions are behavioural trust statements about itself. These self-descriptions are an emergent behaviour of the group, and are developed by intersubjective processes. Every group is expected, by a Parsonian analyst (in our radically simplified model of Parsonian theory!), to mount a spirited defense if the validity of a self-descriptive statement is questioned or threatened.

In a game-theoretic analysis, a behavioural trust statement is a confident description of an player's current tactics and strategy. The rules of the game itself are axiomatic trust statements. If the analyst is acting as a player in the game, then their behavioural trust statements have a clear Luhmannian purpose of uncertainty-reduction. However if the analyst has some other motivation for their analysis, for example intellectual curiosity or a desire to help a player improve their game-playing abilities, then the Luhmannian purpose of uncertainty-reduction seems an insufficient motivation for the analysis.

In some computer-mediated economic markets such as eBay, behavioural statements are automatically generated to express the market-controller's radically simplified estimate of the "reputation" of a vendor or buyer. Participants in such markets are encouraged to rely on such statements, when deciding whether or not to take the risk of closing a transaction. The primary purpose for eBay's utterance might be profit-expansion rather than uncertainty-reduction, but until a teleological system is specified, such speculation is pointless.

A modelling framework must be agnostic on disputed axioms, if it is to aid communication between modellers who have different belief structures or goals. For this reason, we do not presume that a axiomatic trust statement must be consciously constructed by an analyst before it is used by an actor in some model. Instead, the analyst may construct the axioms describing a model of an actor (or a set of actors) on the basis of their prior behaviours.

Similarly, we do not insist that an analysis must be conducted along rational lines. Depending on the axioms in the model, the analysis might be conducted along emotive or faith-based lines. Furthermore, the analysis might, or might not, be conducted by a single person. A psychological analysis of trust requires a model whose axioms support an analysis of individual actor's trusts. A valid sociological analysis of trust, even if is axiomatised, requires an intersubjective process to develop and interpret the axioms.

We now review the theoretical frameworks of a few prominent sociologists, not in the hope of finding an undisputed set of axioms for a system analysis, but in order to discover whether our framework can help elucidate and harmonise these theories, and whether we can discover any inconsistencies or limitations.

2   Barber's Subtypes of Trust

Barber, in his influential monograph, identified three fundamental forms of trust statements [5]. His "general and comprehensive definition of trust" includes an "expectation of the persistence of the moral social order." He also offers "two more specific meanings [of trust], each of which is important for the understanding of social relationships and social systems": an expectation of technically competent role performance, and an expectation of fiduciary obligation and responsibility.

We note that Barber's general definition is an axiomatic trust, under the presumption that a general collapse of the moral and social order is just about unthinkable. His specific meanings are behavioural trusts, because they are reliances on specific individuals or organisations. It seems possible for an individual to place axiomatic trust in an institution such as the Catholic Church, even though they distrust the moral and social order of their immediate environment. Thus Barber's theory of trust seems questionable as a psychology of trust, but his general definition seems an appropriate axiomatisation of a societal trust, and his specific definitions are a subtyping of our behavioural trust.

We now briefly describe the structural (morphological) aspects of our framework, for this is necessary before we can describe how our framework supports a Barberian analysis of a trustworthy profession.

In our framework, a system model consists of a set of actors A in a network of pairwise relationships R between actors. That is, every model is a graph with vertices A and edges R. If an analyst wants to employ our framework to perform a Barberian analysis of the trusting behaviours of a particular political system, a profession, or a family, they should start their modelling procedure by identifying a representative set of actors and relationships.

Only three types of relationships are defined in our framework. An actor is *superior* to another actor, when the analyst wants to express the power that the first actor has to observe and control the second actor. An actor is a *peer* of another actor, when the analyst wants to model the friendly conversations and consensual agreements which can be made between actors who – at least in this context – have no great imbalance of power. Finally, an actor is an *alias* of another actor, when the analyst wants to model either the multiple role-playing abilities of a person, or the multiple aspects of a subsystem (whether it be mechanised, in whole or in part) depending on its observer and the context.

An adequate model of a complex social arrangement, of the sort diagrammed by Granovetter, has multiple aliases for each person who is represented in the model: one alias for each of their interpersonal relationships.

We consider a specific example to illustrate the modelling process. An idealised professional society can be modelled as a set of peers who, collectively, enforce some membership criteria. Any peer who has been found to violate these criteria can be expelled, or they may be chastised (perhaps only in private conversation within the peerage) and allowed to retain their membership. It is in the collective self-interest of the professionals to be considered, by the general public, to be trustworthy. The professionals may regulate themselves effectively; they may have a laissez-faire attitude; and they may be a solidary group which actively defends any member against an ethical complaint raised by one of their clients. Since a client is not able to monitor the conversations among the professional peerage, they have no way of knowing, for certain, whether the peerage is effectively enforcing any fiduciary responsibilities or technical competencies. However if a potential client trusts the professional peerage to enforce these two Barberian "specific meanings" of trust, then (if they follow the Barberian axioms when making their trusting decision) this client will confidently accept professional services from any member of the peerage.

Formally, a profession is a system with at least two sets of actors: the professionals P and their potential clients C. Barber's analysis of trust in the professions includes a third type of actor, a government with jurisdiction over the professionals and clients. When modelled in our framework, a government is an actor that is superior to each professional and client. Because the professionals are not acting as functionaries in the government, we introduce aliases for the professionals and clients so that we can represent the type of power (possibly only an informational advantage) that is wielded by a professional over their client.

Our complete model is shown in Figure 1. The professionals (p, q) and client c, each have a primary alias (p_0, q_0, c_0) that has power over itself – these arcs represent the self-control and self-reflection abilities of any sentient individual. We indicate that c is accepting professional services from p by introducing aliases c_p and p_c, with p_c being a superior to c_p. Conflicts of interest may arise in any aliased relationship. For example, p_c may give advice to c_p which c_0 is not happy to accept; and c_p's relationship with p_c may put p_c (the professional persona of p) into conflict with p_0's self-interest.

The professional society is modeled as a peerage (on aliases p_p and q_p) in our framework. The line connecting the peers is intended to suggest a communication network, such that anyone on the network can send messages to anyone else on the network. Peerages, if they organise themselves, can develop a way to form a collective opinion, possibly using some subsidiary actor or device (drawn below the network) to collect the votes. In the case of Figure 1, the peers have collectively hired a Lobbyist, who is under the control of the peers and transmits messages on their behalf to an alias G' of the government. The Lobbyist in this Figure is apparently insentient, for it has no self-control arc – it is may be just

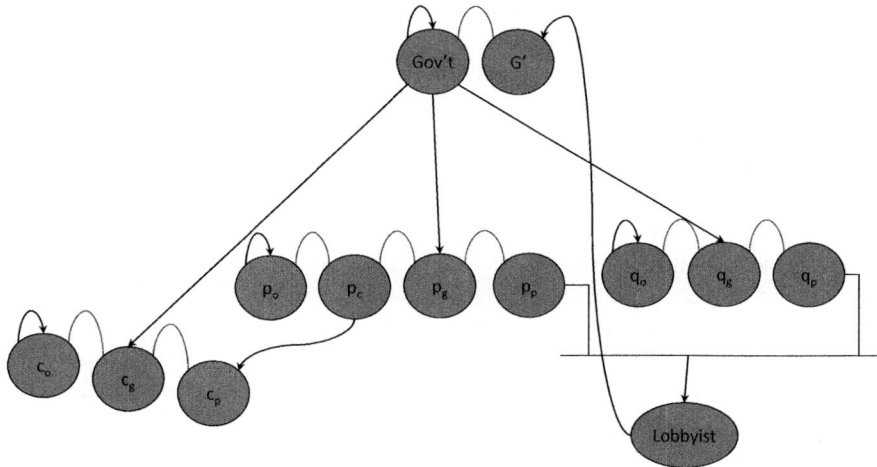

Fig. 1. A client, two professionals, a lobbyist, and a government. The professional peerage consists of actors p_p, q_p, and the Lobbyist. The governmental system is a hierarchy, with c_g, p_g, and q_g as inferior actors. Some amount of self-control, i.e. some form of free will, is possessed by the personal actors c_0, p_0, q_0, and the group actor Gov't. The Gov't may accept advice from the Lobbyist, and the client c_p may accept advice from the professional p_c.

an email-forwarding system. Alternatively, the modeller may be simplifying an already complex system by suppressing the alias representing the self-interest of the Lobbyist, because it is not relevant to the modelled situation.

In our framework, peers have no direct power over each other, aside from ostracism from their peerage. In the system of Figure 1, peers have some indirect power over each other, because they can lodge a complaint against a peer to the Government through their citizen alias p_g or q_g. Also, peers might petition the government for an intervention via their Lobbyist – if the other peers do not prevent the transmission of this petition via their (partial, shared) control over the Lobbyist.

We are now ready to discuss Barber's analysis. He points out that a client's trust in the fiduciary or technical behaviour of the profession P is increasingly problematic, for several reasons. For example, the Lobbyist for the professional society may exert inappropriate control over the government G, through some branch G' of the government that is effectively under the control of the Lobbyist. The governmental branch G' in Figure 1 is thus a distrusted actor, from the perspective of the client c; but it might be highly trusted by the peers.

Barber argues that "trust alone is not enough to ensure [the professionals'] effective performance in the public welfare." In terms of Figure 1, Barber is arguing that the client must, somehow, be assured that the Lobbyist is not effectively in control of the government, and that their government is competently discharging a fiduciary responsibility by regulating the peerage. Barber indicates, by example, some ways in which these assurances can be made. It is impossible to do justice to his essay in this brief summary. However, roughly speaking, his general prescription is for professional groups to accept governmental regulation as a counterbalance to professional self-interest. In a revision to Figure 1, we might follow Barber's advice by adding a Regulator that is inferior to the Gov't. This Regulator, to be effective, must have at least some observational power over the peerage. If a peer misbehaves, then the government can punish the guilty citizen (p_g or q_g). The Regulator may, in addition, have some direct control over the decisions of the peerage. The Regulator can be given full observation rights by granting them a non-voting membership in the peerage; and the Regulator can be given veto rights over the Lobbyist by making the Lobbyist an inferior of the Regulator rather than an inferior of the peerage (as in Figure 1). However if the Regulator has any observation or control power, the professionals must trust the Regulator not to abuse this power, for example by inappropriately vetoing a proposed action of the peerage, or by inappropriately revealing a peer's confidential information to Government (and potentially to the general public through the Government's control over the citizenry). Barber argues that professions will enjoy an increased level of trust from their clients by a well-crafted governmental regulation, if it is openly and fairly administered. Clients may be expected to seek (and to follow) professional advice much more readily if its source is trusted.

We conclude that our framework is adequate to capture the main line of Barber's discussion about trust in the professions, and that our structural diagrams may be used to clarify the ways in which a governmental Regulator could monitor or control a profession.

Our framework provides only marginal support for Barber's three types of trust. His general and comprehensive definition of trust is roughly congruent to our axiomatic trust, but seems problematic (as a "general and comprehensive" definition) in any case where an individual places little trust in the moral and social order, but does trust specific individuals or institutions. Barber's "two more specific meanings" roughly fit within our definition of behavioural trust, with expected behaviours of technical competency being in one of Barber's subcategories, and expected behaviours of fiduciary obligation and responsibility being in the other.

Inferiors must trust superiors not to abuse their power. Barber's subtyping suggests that one form of abuse can be ascribed to an inappropriate control of a superior's other aliases (especially their self-interest persona, e.g. p_0 of the professional p in Figure 1) over the actions taken by their superior-role persona (e.g. p_c). The other type of abuse (insufficient technical competency) can be ascribed to an inadequately provisioned superior-role persona.

Peers must trust each other. Barber's typology will help us distinguish conflicts of interest (where a peer's duty to a peerage is contrary to their self-interest or other responsibilities, i.e. to their government) from the functional inadequacy of a peer.

Individuals must trust themselves. Barber's typology is a sociological theory rather than a psychological one, so some difficulties may be expected in this extension of his theory. Even so: Barber's distinction suggests the following psychological analysis. An individual's trust in their personal competency (e.g. as determined by p_0 in the case of our professional p of Figure 1) can be distinguished from their trust in their management of their conflicts of interest (as determined by all the other aliases of p in Figure 1). When the self-trust in competency is violated, an individual is unable to help themselves (or to refrain from hurting themselves) due to some personal inadequacy. When the conflict-of-interest self-trust is violated, an individual is in the painful position of being expected (by external controllers and observers) to harm themselves (or neglecting to help themselves) in order to discharge their responsibilities to others. This is the fundamental conflict of humanist psychology, but as far as we know, it has not been previously identified as arising in Barber's theory of trust.

We conclude that Barber's subtyping distinctions can be made in our framework, if the axiomatic system of the model clearly distinguishes an individual's responsibility to themselves from their responsibilities to others, and if personal inadequacy can be distinguished from externally-imposed constraints. The latter distinction is commonly made but problematic, in the highly reduced context of human-computer interaction. An unpleasant incident must be attributed to either operator error or to a poorly-designed (or buggy) program, before operator training or program revision can be chosen as the more appropriate resolution.

3   Emotional and Rational Trust

Lewis and Weigert argue that trust has "distinct cognitive, emotional, and behavioral dimensions which are merged into a unitary social experience" [6]. In this essay, we have argued that the behavioural dimension of trust is a primary consideration in a framework, such as ours, which prescribes a structural approach to modelling. However we note that the antithesis of behavioural trust is the axiomatic trust required, in the observer of another actor's behaviour, to ascribe any meaning to, or consequential implication of, this behaviour. Our axiomatic trust is essentially an attribute of the observer, and our behavioural trust is an attribute of the observed. The dichotomising variable is the viewpoint: observer versus observed.

The cognitive and emotional dimensions of trust, as defined by Lewis and Weigert, are complementary. They demonstrate this complemantarity by imposing a three-level scale on each of these two dimensions, forming the 9-category cross-product of Table 1.

We would recommend this table to any technologist who is trying to persuade a non-technical person to use a system. In our experience, technologists tend to operate in the top row of this table, although some will bristle if they are "accused" of having an ideological trust in their analytic methodology or results. By contrast, anyone who is unable to understand a technical analysis is limited to the bottom row of the table, whenever they consider using a technically-complex system. A technologist is likely, in my experience, to adopt a strategy of cognitive argument: essentially attempting to educate the potential user so that they can operate in the second row in Table 1. Education is certainly appropriate, if

Table 1. Nine types of trust, classified by emotionality and rationality [6]

Emotionality / Rationality	High	Low	Virtually Absent
High	Ideological Trust	Cognitive Trust	Rational Prediction
Low	Emotional Trust	Mundane, Routine Trust	Probable Anticipation
Virtually Absent	Faith	Fate	Uncertainty, Panic

the system is not sufficiently foolproof to be used safely by a complete novice. However, if the technologist operates in a requirements-elicitation frame, rather than in a strictly educative frame, then the potential user's desires and fears may reveal some novel requirements for their system and especially for its user interface.

The sociology of distrust has received much less attention than the sociology of trust, even though many theorists have argued that it is best treated as a separate topic. We note that Lewis and Weigert have characterised the near-absence of both cognitive and emotional trust as "uncertainty, panic". We hypothesise that the level of distrust is what distinguishes a state of uncertainty from a state of panic. If the prospect of continued inaction is distrusted intensely, and none of our options for purposeful action are trusted, then energetic but unpurposeful behaviour is the best option under a cognitive analysis, and a state of panic seems the most likely emotional response. However, in a situation where inaction is not distrusted, a lack of trusted options for the next action is not a cognitive stress. The emotional status of our hypothetical individual seems underdetermined, but one possibility is that they are taking a serene step on their path to Nirvana. We conclude that Lewis and Wiegert's intriguing table offers fertile ground for future experimentation regarding the interactions of trust and distrust, in their cognitive and emotional manifestations.

4   Trust, Distrust, and Decision-Making

In this section, we state and explore a hypothesis about the psychology of a human decision. This hypothesis is grounded in the taxonomic theory of our framework, as extended here. We invite correspondence from sociologists, psychologists, and market researchers who can point us at any article in which some variant of our hypothesis has been validated or invalidated.

Within our framework, it is natural to model rational decision-making as occurring on three dimensions. On the economic dimension, the decision-maker will assess whether the expected benefit of an option exceeds its expected cost. On the optimistic dimension, the decision-maker will assess whether their confidence (a behavioural trust statement) in the favourable outcome of an option is sufficient to overcome their fundamental uncertainty about this favourability. Finally, on the pessimistic dimension, the decision-maker will assess whether their sense of control over their expected future status exceeds their level of distrust about this expected status, for each of their options.

We hypothesise that options are considered serially, with a binary go/no-go decision taken on each. There may be multiple rounds of decision-making before a visible action is taken, depending on the perceived urgency and importance of the decision. Experimentally, it will be simplest to work with single-round (i.e. urgent or unimportant) decision-making before attempting to unravel the complexities of a multiple-round decision.

Any option with an expected net benefit, which is sufficiently trusted, and whose analysable downsides are sufficiently controlled, would (we presume) provoke a "go" decision. By contrast, if an action has a poor benefit, is insufficiently trusted, and has many uncontrolled downsides, then it seems a clear "no-go".

If there is any disagreement on the three dimensions, then two of the three assessments must agree. We postulate that a decision that is unfavourable on two dimensions would never be taken, except when the decision-maker is in a state of panic. We would define this state to arise when the prospect of inaction is highly distrusted. A panicked individual will, we presume, take the first option for action unless it is even more distrusted than the status quo.

If there is only one argument against taking an action, and the status quo is not distrusted, we would expect some humans to take the action. The outcome would depend, we presume, on a personality type. Economists will weight the first dimension most heavily; Optimists will pay most attention to their attractions; and Pessimists will pay most attention to their fears. We doubt that this personality typology is novel, since it seems rather obvious; but we are not aware of the relevant experimental literature.

To illustrate a possible use of our hypothesis, we imagine that we are advising a technologist who has designed a system which they firmly believe would be beneficial for most people to use. The technologist seeks our help in understanding why so few people are using their wonderful system. We would advise this technologist to offer twenty-five randomly-selected people a chance to use the technology, and to classify their responses into five categories. Under our decision-making hypothesis, we would expect the classification to be unambiguous except in a few cases where the prospective user expresses multiple reasons for deciding against using the system.

Category -1: The prospective user refuses to use the system, and the technologist is unable to classify their reason for refusing.

Category 0: The prospective user decides to use the system.

Category 1: The prospective user decides against using the system, because they see no expected net benefit in using the system.

Category 2: The prospective user decides against using the system, because they have insufficient trust in the system.

Category 3: The prospective user decides against using the system, because they distrust it.

If category -1 is frequent, we would advise the technologist to engage a more emotionally-communicative interviewer. We would also question the validity of our theory of decision-making, as well as the efficacy of our instructions to the technologist.

If category 0 is frequent, we would advise the technologist to review their advertising campaign. The current advertisements may be insufficiently distributed; they may be much less effective than the direct-sales approach (as conducted by the technologist); and they may be targeted at an audience that differs significantly from the population the technologist interviewed.

If category 1 is frequent, the technologist should attempt to improve the economic performance of the system, and they should look for ways to communicate this performance to their prospective but non-expert users.

If category 2 is frequent, the technologist should attempt to develop a radical simplification in the user interface of our system, so that the prospective user is not faced with a difficult task when developing their own behavioural trust statements about the system. As noted by Luhmann and many others, statements of the form "trust me" or "trust my system" unlikely to increase trust, for they tend to call trust into question. Trust is fundamentally non-assessed. Descriptions of how well the system will respond under adverse conditions (malfunctions or attacks) are arguments against distrust, not arguments for trust.

If category 3 is frequent, the user's distrust is the key variable. If the fears are articulated sufficiently clearly that the relevant system behaviours can be understood by the technologist, then the technologist can look for ways to demonstrate that the system is foolproof in these respects. If the system is not already foolproof against such malfunctions, then improving the design in this respect should be a high priority. If the technologist's search for a clearly-demonstrable architectural control proves infeasible, then economic, social, or legal safeguards should be explored. It will be important to know, at this juncture, whether our prospective users are, generally, trustful of architectures, economies, legalities, or societies. A user's distrust will not be lessened if we point out that the behaviour they fear can be controlled by a power they distrust!

5   Individual, Institutional, and Social Controls

We close this essay with a brief exploration of a taxonomic categorisation developed recently by Riegelsberger et al. [7]. After surveying a broad range of sociological enquiry, these authors propose a unifying framework. They consider one trusting relationship at a time. Accordingly, their framework has just two actors: a trustor and a trustee. The trustee has some power to harm or help the trustor, which we would represent in our framework by a directed arc from the trustee to the trustor.

The Riegelsberger framework defines trust as a three step process. In the first step, the trustor and the trustee exchange some information regarding the nature of the possible trusting relationship. Of particular interest in the framework are the "trustworthiness" signals from the trustee, which are dichotomised into symbols (pure information, uttered by the trustee) and symptoms (observations, either direct or indirect, by the trustor of the trustee's non-verbal behaviour).

In the second step, the trustor either withdraws or engages with the trustee.

In the third step, the trustee either fulfills the trustor's expectations, or it does not fulfill them. Riegelsberger's framework is focussed on the trustee's motivations for fulfilling or non-fulfilling. These motivations would be the result of security controls on the trustee in our framework, and fall into three categories.

The first category of security controls on the trustee's behaviour are *relational controls*. We do not adopt Riegelsberger's label of "temporal" for this category, because (as argued below) the temporal dimension of control in our framework dichotomises all three of Riegelsberger's categories. Relational controls arise because a trustor may maintain a record of their prior relations with the trustee. The retrospective form of this control is expressed if a trustor decides to withdraw because of their prior experience with the trustee. The prospective form of this control is expressed if the trustee's current decision is affected by the trustor's (presumed) record-keeping ability. The trustee may fear that the trustor will withdraw in the future, and the trustee may desire future engagements with the trustor. The commercial importance of relational controls is demonstrated by the prevalence of customer relation management (CRM) systems in modern enterprises. Gartner's estimated revenues for the global CRM market in 2008 was USD $9.15 billion.

Riegelsberger's second category are the *social controls* on a trustee. These controls arise because a trustor may be a member of a social group: a peerage in our framework. A peer may share their impressions of a trustee within the peerage. A trustee would thereby gain a reputation within the peerage for trustworthiness in certain respects, and they may also gain a reputation for untrustworthiness in some respects. The retrospective form of social control arises when the peerage defines and enforces (by solidary action) a normative control through their shared communications, mutual trust, and collective power to decide whether to engage with the trustee. The prospective form of this control arises when the trustor's behaviour is affected by their fear or desire for their relationship with the trustee's peers. The prospective form also arises when the peer group has formed a reputational estimate of the trustee, by a process analogous to the pricing of goods in an idealised free market, and when the prospective trustor uses this reputational information in their decision.

The third form of control on the trustworthiness of a trustee are the *institutional controls*. These controls arise when the trustee is subject to control by a hierarchy. The prospective form of these controls are architectural in nature: these arise when the trustee is effectively unable, due to a prior control exerted by the hierarchy, to refrain from fulfilling the trustor's expectations. In our framework, architectural controls may be the axioms of an intentional system design, the unintentional consequences of an unaxiomatised design, or (in a model with theological axioms) laws of nature, random constraints arising in a randomly-defined system, or a god's decrees. The retrospective form of these controls arise when the trustee is subject to legal or regulatory sanctions. Any trustee who restricts their actions because of a behavioural trust in their hierarch's institutional control has transformed that hierarch's retrospective control into a prior restraint, i.e. an architectural control.

We conclude that the broad outlines, as described above, of Riegelsberger's framework are highly congruent with our framework. Before conducting this analysis, we were unaware of the importance of each actor's self-control arc in a security analysis, and our taxonomy of control did not clearly cover the individual controls. These can be considered a subcase of the architectural and legal controls, in that they are exerted by a hierarch who rules only himself. However we now believe individual controls are important enough, and easily enough to overlook, to deserve the following elaboration in our framework.

A trustor may have *individual trust* in their ability to engage with trustworthy trustees; this ability is dependent on their memory and judgement. A trustor may have *social trust* in the beneficial influence of their peerages' reputation system on trustees, and also in their ability to use the reputation system to select trustworthy trustees. Finally, a trustor may have *institutional trust* in the beneficial influence, on trustees, of a government, corporation, or any other system or organisation that can control (via rewards, punishments, enablements, and disablements) the trustee's actions.

Three types of distrust are also possible. An individual may mistrust their ability to avoid untrustworthy trustees, they may mistrust their peerages' reputation systems, and they may mistrust their legal systems and other hierarchical controls.

Our analysis of Riegelsberger's framework suggests the following hypothesis about social capital. Any sufficiently uniform population, i.e. a society such as a functional nation, will (we suspect) be biased in their decision-making toward considerations of individual, social, or institutional trust. Assessments of trust as a form of social capital may thus be misleading, unless these three types of trust are taken into consideration in the assessment. We are not conversant with the relevant literature, and would welcome pointers.

We briefly consider two limitations of Riegelsberger's framework. The three-step trust process does not include a dispute resolution mechanism, or any other explicit method for handling the cases in which a trustee's perception of a non-fulfillment disagrees with a trustor's perception of a fulfillment. Riegelsberger's framework is silent on this question, however dispute-avoidance and dispute-resolution issues are very important considerations in the practical design of trusted systems. In our framework, trustworthiness cannot be judged in any model that lacks axioms defining trustworthiness; and if the underlying ethic is deontological or consequentialist, then the axioms must establish the ground truth of a fulfillment. Anyone observing a real-world system may use a different set of axioms when constructing a model of that system; and this difference will generally result in a different ground truth for each model. In a trustor-centric model, the ground truth of a trustor's trustworthiness might be established by an ethic, by polling the trustors, or by requiring every trusting relationship to have a trusted third party who, in case of dispute, establishes the ground truth regarding fulfillment. In a trustee-centric model, either an ethic or trusted third party is required.

Riegelsberger's framework is based on sociological research, so it is understandably sparse in its characterisation of technical requirements on designed systems. These have been studied extensively, see e.g. [8]. The "quality in use" concept of ISO 27000 is, essentially, a trustor-centric definition of trustworthiness ability that was developed by an intersubjective process involving hundreds (possibly thousands) of active contributors. A trustworthiness motivation may be demonstrated by an ISO 9000 accreditation.

6   Our Hopes

We hope that this essay will inspire technologists to consider a broader range of trust-enhancement strategies, when they attempt to develop trustworthy systems which actually inspire trust. We hope our essay will provoke sociologists, psychologists, and market researchers to consider how their theories and experimental results on trust and decision-making might be expressed in a sufficiently reduced fashion to be both understandable and useful to technologists. We also have a fond hope that our technologically-inspired, and highly reductionist, musings on the fundamental nature of trust will help to clarify future sociological or psychological studies.

References

1. Thomborson, C.: A framework for system security. In: Stamp, M., Stavroulakis, P. (eds.) Handbook of Information and Communication Security, pp. 3–20. Springer, Heidelberg (2010)
2. Luhmann, N.: Trust and Power. Wiley, Chichester (1979)
3. Luhmann, N.: Familiarity, confidence, trust: Problems and alternatives. In: Gambetta, D. (ed.) Trust: Making and Breaking Cooperative Relations, pp. 94–107. Blackwell, New York (1988)
4. Parsons, T.: Suggestions for a sociological approach to the theory of organizations, part 1. Administrative Science Quarterly 1(1), 63–85 (1956)
5. Barber, B.: The Logic and Limits of Trust. Rutgers University Press (1983)
6. Lewis, J.D., Weigert, A.: Trust as a social reality. Social Forces 63(4), 967–985 (1985)
7. Riegelsberger, J., Sasse, M.A., McCarthy, J.D.: The mechanics of trust: A framework for research and design. International Journal of Human-Computer Studies 62(3), 381–422 (2005)
8. Côté, M.A., Suryn, W., Georgiadou, E.: In search for a widely applicable and accepted software quality model for software quality engineering. Software Quality Journal 15(4), 401–416 (2007)

The Leap of Faith from Online to Offline: An Exploratory Study of Couchsurfing.org

Jun-E Tan

Wee Kim Wee School of Communication & Information,
Nanyang Technological University,
31 Nanyang Link, Singapore 637718
june.tan@gmail.com

Abstract. This paper takes an interpretative approach to study trust in a hybrid online/offline community, based on exploratory research on the case of Couchsurfing.org, a hospitality exchange network that enables travelers to locate locals who would offer them free accommodation or tips regarding the country traveled. The theoretical framework used was Möllering's idea of "suspension" and the leap of faith [1], which looks at trust in terms of dealing with irreducible vulnerability and uncertainty. Qualitative data was collected by doing participant observation and interviewing 15 Couchsurfers about their views on trust. Möllering's theoretical framework is found to be useful to transcend the idiosyncrasies of observing online profiles. It is also demonstrated through understanding the interpretations of the actors within the system, rich insights are yielded about the context of trust and the actors' reactions.

Keywords: Trust, Leap of faith, Couchsurfing.org, online/offline community.

1 Introduction

Given the prevalence of new media and information communication technology, the issue of trust in computer-mediated communication has garnered a fair amount of interest from multiple disciplines. From a holistic level, trust is viewed as fundamental to human society, to increase cooperation and reduce complexities [2], and to build social capital [3], among other important functions. In the current globalized setting, the issue of trust becomes progressively complicated as relationships and networks are increasingly diversified across different contexts. New media facilitates interactions and exchanges with the mediation of technology, transcending physical and cultural boundaries, creating new horizons and contextual situations for trust research.

Corritore et al. suggests that there are generally two approaches to study online trust, i.e. individual-to-individual trust mediated by technology, and technology as the object of trust [4]. Most researchers study the latter, typically in the interest of informational or transactional websites [4][5]. This paper chooses to focus on the former, examining the manner of how trust is formed between people who are often separated in spatial and temporal dimensions, relying on textual information with limited nonverbal cues. Specifically, I intend to use a theoretical framework of Guido

A. Acquisti, S.W. Smith, and A.-R. Sadeghi (Eds.): TRUST 2010, LNCS 6101, pp. 367–380, 2010.

Möllering's idea of "suspension" and the leap of faith as a guide to study online profiles as the avenue of trust and trustworthiness, focusing on the actors who construct and evaluate these profiles [1].

Couchsurfing.org is used as a case study to collect data and apply the theoretical framework. Couchsurfing.org enables travelers to utilize the network to locate interested locals who would offer them spare couches or beds in their homes as free accommodation, usually for a period of a few days. As the largest hospitality exchange network in the world, it has about 1.8 million members worldwide, spanning across 236 countries and 70,588 cities as of April 2010. Further statistics show that Couchsurfing.org has created about 2 million friendships and about 1.9 million successful hosting/surfing experiences. [1]Couchsurfing.org was chosen as a case study because it relies upon trust as the core of its existence, given the immense amount of trust needed to admit a stranger to one's home or to enter into a foreign territory.

At a methodological level, this study answers Möllering's call for more interpretative and qualitative studies on trust. Möllering argues, and I agree, that the methodological strategy employed by trust researchers requires "a *process perspective*, obtaining a rich (typically qualitative) picture of actual trust experiences, understanding the *embeddedness* of the relationships under investigation and taking into account the *reflexivity* not only in trust development as such but also in the research interaction itself. The general orientation should be to get away from measuring predefined variables and get closer to the respondents' idiosyncratic experiences and interpretations." ([1], p.152, emphasis in original) Also, the significance of the study lies in its focus on a research area much neglected by contemporary research on trust online, i.e. the interpersonal interaction through computer mediation. Much of the research to date look at trust in terms of e-commerce, which are important in their own right, but I argue that the advent of Web 2.0 and increased interaction among users through social network sites and other avenues justify more scholastic attention on interpersonal relationships online.

The analysis done within this paper is preliminary, as an initial part of a larger study on trust in transnational hybrid communities crossing virtual and real worlds of the actors. The literature review covers some background on studies on trust and trust-related concepts, Möllering's theoretical framework to be applied, and some past research on Couchsurfing.org. For this pilot study, 15 Couchsurfers were hosted at the researcher's apartment as a form of participant observation, and also to collect insider perspectives by in-depth interviews. Most data drawn for this paper is from the in-depth interviews, and covers open-ended research questions to discover the respondents' self-definition of trust, the manner in which online profiles are assessed, and their world views with regards to trust and Couchsurfing.org. Through interviews with the actors, rich insights are discovered on the motivation to trust and the situational context which breeds trusting behaviour. The exploratory nature of this study is meant to yield initial insights of the case study for further research to build upon.

---

[1] Statistics accessed online from the homepage of Couchsurfing.org (http://www. Couchsurfing. org) on April 1, 2010.

2   Literature Review and Background

2.1   Trust, Offline and Online

Rousseau et al. in a widely accepted definition explains that trust is "a psychological state comprising the intention to accept vulnerability based upon positive expectations of the intentions or behaviour of another." [6] The critical components here are "positive expectations" and "the intention to accept vulnerability". Möllering goes on to refine the understanding of "accepting vulnerability" as stated by Rousseau et al., explaining that accepting vulnerability does not mean that trustors are willing to be hurt. Instead, trustors have "highly optimistic expectations that vulnerability is not a problem and no harm will be done" [1].

Bhattacharya, Devinney and Pillutla outline key themes of how trust is viewed, which is useful to further concretize the concept [7]. Firstly, trust exists in an uncertain and risky environment, without which the concept would be trivial. Secondly, trust reflects expectancy, a prediction of the trustee's behaviour. Thirdly, they argue that any definition of trust must account for the strength and importance of trust. Fourthly, trust is situation and person specific, in other words, context must be taken into account. Lastly, the expected outcome of trusting behaviour is generally positive or nonnegative. They then conclude with another definition of their own, i.e. "Trust is an expectancy of positive (or nonnegative) outcomes that one can receive based on the expected action of another party in an interaction characterized by uncertainty."

Researchers have provided useful angles to dissect the multiple dimensions of the complex concept of trust, summarized by Corritore et al. to cover generality, kind, degree, and stage [4]. *Generality* is a continuum from general to specific trust, i.e. to have overall trust in another entity; or to have trust that the entity would act in a certain way in a certain situation. *Kinds* of trust include slow and swift trust, as well as cognitive and emotional trust. Slow trust is built over a long term relationship whereas swift trust exists in relationships quickly built and quickly ceasing to exist, such as ad-hoc collaborations. Cognitive trust is trust based on rational reasoning, and emotional trust is driven by positive feelings towards the object of trust. The *degree* of trust refers to the depth of trust, whether it is basic, guarded or extended trust. Basic trust is "the underlying, background form of trust that is a precondition of social life"; guarded trust looks at trust "protected by formal contracts, agreements and promises"; and extended trust is trust based on openness, "given in relationships that are so deep that formal contracts are unnecessary" (ibid, p.744). It is argued that trust is developmental, therefore there are different *stages* of trust, progressing from deterrence-based (initial trust maintained by contracts and laws), knowledge-based (having knowledge of object of trust and its predicted behaviour), and finally shared identification-based (similar to the idea of extended trust elaborated above).

The literature on trust over the last few decades is extensive, but more recent studies on online trust are more in line with the purpose of this paper. The studies on online trust naturally build upon studies of trust in the offline world, like how communications online extend that of the offline, in terms of facilitating exchanges and social interactions [4]. Many works equate online trust with e-commerce, typically a B2C framework [8][4][5]. For instance, Wang and Emurian claim that in the context of online trust, "the trustor is typically a consumer who is browsing an e-commerce website, and the trustee is the e-commerce website, or more specifically, the merchant that the website represents"[5]. This perspective is getting increasingly outdated with the advent of Web 2.0, which emphasizes upon participation, collaboration, information sharing and ultimately, communication among end-users of the Internet. Examples of platforms of this paradigm shift include Social Network Sites, blogs, wikis and etc.

Therefore, I see a need for studies of trust that bridge the gap between users of a system. Previous studies inclined towards e-commerce would still hold valuable perspectives to build upon, on underlying principles that would foster trust across web systems regardless of function. One such example is the guidelines provided by Schneiderman to foster trust in online applications such as e-commerce, e-services, online communities and other websites [9]. These guidelines include providing vital information for users within the system, such as patterns of past performance, references from past and current users, third party certifications and clear privacy and security policies. The responsibilities and obligations of all entities within the system should also be clarified, with clear specifications of guarantees and compensation policies (if any) and support for dispute resolution and mediation services. In other words, Schneiderman argues for open and transparent governance in web systems to build trust. Elsewhere, Ba argues that the uncertainty of the online environment and information asymmetry are two major barriers to online trust, which is true for all online systems [10].

2.2 "Suspension", the Leap of Faith

According to Möllering, current literature on trust can be categorized into three major branches, i.e. reason, routine and reflexivity [1]. Reason is the rationalist paradigm that people trust by judging the trustworthiness of the other party. Routine is the "taken-for-grantedness" of trust, its source being presumably reliable institutions. The reflexivity approach taken by some researchers adopts a process view of trust-building, where actors work together to build trust gradually.

Möllering's thesis is that although these studies have attempted to explain trust, they have somehow missed the point. Firstly, if trust is viewed as a matter of rational choice, there will be a paradox of the element of trust being superfluous, if trust can be entirely explained by reason. Secondly, if trust is something that is taken-for-granted, based on existing institutions, where did that trust come from? And thirdly, if trust is an ongoing reflexive process in which trust is built eventually, this element of certainty that trust will be built would also render the idea of trust redundant. Therefore, Möllering believes that there is a missing element in the picture, which is "suspension", also known as the leap of faith.

> "'Suspension' is the process that enables actors to deal with irreducible uncertainty and vulnerability. Suspension is the essence of trust, because trust as a state of positive expectation of others can only be reached when reason, routine and reflexivity are combined with suspension." (p.110)

It is suspension that links reason, routine and reflexivity to trust, and trust thrives in an environment where there is irreducible uncertainty and vulnerability. Actors of trust have to take a leap of faith knowing that there is risk involved. Möllering suggests three major ways to come to terms with suspension. The first is "trust as fiction", suggesting that the trustor and trustee work together to create fiction in the trustor's mind, to enable him to trust. The second is what he terms as "bracketing", i.e. actors manage to live with the fact that there are gaps and missing pieces, and make the leap of faith anyway. The third, "the will to believe", posits that the actor exercises agency through his will to either suspend uncertainty and vulnerability or not.

Other scholars have found Möllering's model to be useful (e.g. [11]), and his book on trust was also critically acclaimed by various researchers [12][13]. This will be the theoretical framework used loosely to guide this exploratory study. I will base the actions of the actors on the assumption of irreducible uncertainty, to explore the interpretations of the actors within the system.

2.3   The Case: Couchsurfing.org

Background. Couchsurfing.org is a social network site, fulfilling the criteria set by boyd and Ellison [14], i.e. "web-based services that allow individuals to (1) construct a public or semi-public profile within a bounded system, (2) articulate a list of other users with whom they share a connection, and (3) view and traverse their list of connections and those made by others within the system." It falls under a subset known as hospitality exchange networks. Hospitality exchange networks are not a new phenomenon – the oldest such network is Servas International, founded in 1949 by an American named Bob Luitweiler. With the tagline "With every true friendship we build the basis for World Peace", Servas International set a common theme also used by newer hospitality exchange networks, to promote intercultural understanding and to reduce intolerance among people of different cultural backgrounds [15]. Other networks include Hospitality Club (founded in 2000, with about 330,000 members); GlobalFreeloaders.com (founded in 2005, with about 60,000 members). Hospitality exchange is grounded on reciprocity, negotiating thin lines between "guest" and "parasite", hospitality and home [16].

Couchsurfing.org is registered under CouchSurfing International Inc, a non-profit organization registered in New Hampshire, USA. It was founded by Casey Fenton, who was inspired to build the website after a successful attempt to stay in a stranger's place for free while travelling to Iceland. Before leaving for his weekend trip to Iceland, he randomly emailed 1,500 students in the University of Iceland to search for potential hosts, getting 50-100 favourable responses as a result. Two years after the inception of the website, Couchsurfing.org experienced a severe database loss, and Casey Fenton announced the closure of the website. However, with the help of volunteers, the website was rebuilt and maintained to date, with Couchsurfing.org serving about 1.8 million members as of April 2010.

How it Works. To use the services provided by Couchsurfing.org, one becomes a member or a "Couchsurfer" by registering an account in the system. No identification details (such as passport numbers etc.) are solicited, and the closest piece of information for identification that the user provides is her email. The user then personalizes her profile to include particulars such as demographic details or auxiliary information such as personal philosophy, interests, taste in music and etc. As with other SNSs, the profile is the virtual face of the user and makes the first impression on her online identity.

One can choose to be a host (offering hospitality) or a guest/surfer (receiving hospitality). There are different shades of hospitality that a host can provide, such as offering free accommodation for a few nights, showing a surfer around town or answering questions on tourist attractions. The modus operandi for a surfer to locate a host is through using the CouchSearch function in the website, filtering the hosts according to characteristics such as couch availability, location and etc. A request is then sent to the host, establishing initial contact, containing some self-introduction and information of when the surfer intends to visit. The host then visits the profile page of the surfer, and after some further communication, makes the decision to accept or reject the request. Similar to other SNSs, Couchsurfers can "add friends", i.e. make a connection with another user within the system, and also give testimonials. It is strongly encouraged by Couchsurfing.org that friend connections and testimonials should only be given to other users that one has met face to face.

Trust is the essential ingredient to the success of Couchsurfing.org, therefore several measures are taken to build that trust. In the website, touted under "Safety Features", are three major ways that trust is built through the system – verification, vouching and references. The *verification* process is optional, and begins when Couchsurfers submit their name and address into the system, along with a small donation through their credit card. The submitted name and address of the user will be verified with the credit card details, and a postcard sent to the user's address with a verification code which the user needs to key into the system. With that, the identity and location of the user are authenticated. *Vouching* is an interesting concept whereby a core group of presumably trustworthy people within the system "vouch for" people that they believe are trustworthy. A user can only vouch for another after she has been vouched for at least three times. With that, the network of trust is expanded slowly to the periphery. *References*, a mechanism often used in SNSs and other online sites in general, supports giving feedback regarding another user within the system after there is face-to-face contact. The system also relies on general reciprocity, i.e. direct reciprocation of hospitality from a guest to his host is not required.

Empirical State of Trust. A small survey held by Heesakkers with a sample size of 101 provides a rough indication of how surfers judge the trustworthiness of their hosts – the most important indicator appears to be positive references, followed by contact through email and the number of friend connections [15]. The result of the survey is congruent with the statistics mentioned above, that only a minority of the Couchsurfers are verified (5.9%) or vouched for (7%), suggesting that users may have to rely on other means of trust mechanisms. Further analysis on vouching patterns show that connections that are vouched can be best predicted by direct interaction between two individuals, from their friendship degree, followed by the overall couchsurfing experience between the individuals, and also how the individuals met [17]. It was also found out that vouches are highly reciprocated, in 74.6% of the cases – which may reflect mutual trust, or simply the pressure to reciprocate.

Bialski's study of friendships based on Couchsurfing brings up an interesting point relating trust and space [18]. Based on Actor Network Theory which argues that inanimate objects have agency created by meaningful interpretation, Bialski explains that space becomes an actor, instead of being only a setting for action to take place. In the Couchsurfing framework, where time spent together is typically limited, space is the factor that builds trust. In her ethnographic study, she elaborates:

"Just as [Actor Network Theory] suggests, this apartment was now a space of meaning, an actor which allowed me to behave in a certain way, and having a close, intimate discussion with a relative stranger made me in no way feel awkward because I was already intimately acquainted with an actor (her apartment) who she was intimately acquainted with, quite similarly to a triadic system of trust, where I would feel closer to a friend-of-a-friend than with a complete stranger. In Sara's case, the apartment was that friend-of-a-friend whom I had already met." (ibid, p. 58)

Space also creates a context for expected behaviour – the host expects the guest to act a certain way in her area of control, and the guest honours the trust and respects the host's ownership and control of the space; both trust each other not to harm themselves within the space. With both actors behaving in a predictable manner, trust is then able to be built and accumulated in a relatively short time span. To expand on her point, Bialski draws upon the Couchsurfing database, showing that Couchsurfers who met through hosting/surfing activities tend to have higher trust on each other, compared to Couchsurfers who met through activities or gatherings in public spaces. To this she attributes the importance of the meeting being held at a meaningful space, i.e. the host's home and personal territory.

3 Research Methodology

The broad research questions asked in this exploratory study are aimed to understand the perspectives of the actors, firstly to confirm the basic assumption made about the existence of trust within their actions, secondly to understand their world views about trust and the contextual situation of Couchsurfing.org, and thirdly to discover the strategies used in the assessment of trustworthiness through online profiles.

Data collection was conducted over a three-month period (November 2009 – January 2010), within which the researcher hosted 15 Couchsurfers from all over the world. To keep the sample random, I did not talk to any of the Couchsurfers that I already knew, but chose to interview only the Couchsurfers who requested to stay with me, after reading my online profile. It was specifically stated on my profile that I was doing research on Couchsurfing, so that participants knew that they were going to participate in my research project. This was done with the intention of gaining trust of potential respondents and to ensure compliance with ethical requirements of non-deception. I tried to accommodate all that I could, and only turned down requests when I was already hosting someone else at the time, therefore the sample selection was relatively free of bias.

From the 15 respondents, 7 were female and 8 were male. The age range was 18-34, average age being 27. Most of the respondents were educated to tertiary level, and most were individual travelers, though sometimes there were overlaps in their periods of stay, resulting in up to two surfers at my living room simultaneously at times. Only in one case I had a party of three Couchsurfers staying over, and the interview was conducted in a focus group style to save time. The countries represented within the sample are Singapore, Indonesia, Taiwan, Switzerland (2), Slovakia, Estonia, Germany, Poland (3), USA, Brazil, Nigeria, Australia. In the interest of protecting respondent anonymity, no names are mentioned in this study. Respondents are referred to by their nationality, gender and age.

The Researcher and the Research Settings. To provide a clearer context, I will provide some details about myself and my "couch", which is actually a spare mattress (or two) on the floor of my living room. I am 27, female, and Malaysian. Travelling is my passion and I discovered Couchsurfing about two years ago when I was travelling and hitchhiking around New Zealand. I have couchsurfed six times in various countries: New Zealand, Malaysia, India and the United States. I have hosted about 25 people to date in my rented two-room apartment in Singapore, which I share with a flatmate (Taiwanese male, 30 years old). Our living room has a large floor space that is able to accommodate at least three people comfortably. My flatmate owns a large screen LCD television and a Play Station 3, which he keeps in the living room. We do not have a spare key to give to the guests, though they are free to leave the flat anytime they want (even when we are not in the flat) because the main door locks automatically upon closing. Apart from interviews, often an hour or two in length, research participants were hosted in the same way as I would host other Couchsurfers who were not part of the sample (who came after the data collection period had ended). The average number of nights stayed is 3 nights.

I recognize that, by acting as a host to my research participants, I may be subjecting them to a situation of power imbalance, as they rely on my hospitality and free accommodation. This is addressed by giving them an informed consent form, where the participants are briefed about their rights as research subjects, such as issues of confidentiality and the ability to terminate the interview at any time that they please with no ramifications. Participant observation appears to be the most effective way to gain an insider's point of view, yielding contextual and nuanced insights that quantitative surveys are unable to depict. Constant self-reflexivity and caution were exercised to ensure that data collection would be done as mindfully and unobtrusively as possible.

4   Findings and Analysis

4.1   Trust as Defined by the Subjects

> "For you to be able to go in and close your eyes and sleep with a stranger in your house, man, it's trust." - (Nigerian male, 34)

It was unanimously agreed that doing Couchsurfing involves a lot of trust. This question was asked to confirm that the participants interpreted their acts as acts of trust. When asked to elaborate about trust, responses were varied and hesitant, as most respondents had not thought about what trust actually meant to them. Here are some of the responses:

> "I guess trust means that, you're allowed to be vulnerable with somebody. [...] So you have allowed yourself to be put into a position where the other person can hurt you, whether that's mentally, physically, financially, whatever. But you do it anyway, knowing that they could potentially hurt you, and I think that's trust." (American male, 26)

"Trust, it means that I can share everything with another person, and I can be free, I can just do and say whatever I want, and I can count on him or her. I know that he or she can do whatever he wants, and I won't feel bad about anything. It's like freedom. [...] It's knowing the other person and to have the security to do whatever I want and I know that I won't disappoint the other person." (Estonian male, 21)

"I guess it's the feeling of being safe, and the feeling that you don't have to worry, safe as in your well-being, and I guess your possessions also, not to have worries that you're going to lose something or something like that." (Indonesian female, 32)

"Trust is feeling safe, and feeling safe enough to open yourself to other people, other things, like, new people, new experiences, new cultures, new way of life, to feel safe enough and comfy enough. To be yourself. Yeah, I think it's about feeling safe, it's very important. Where no one will harass you any way, and you will feel comfy and peaceful." (Polish female, 26)

Most interpretations of trust appear to stem from the feeling of security. From the responses, it can be seen that trust is defined in relation to what the respondents prize, be it relationships, value systems, personal well-being, and etc. The importance of trust is explicitly or implicitly expressed. It is generally regarded that trust is something good, as some incorporate trust as part of their identity, as being trusting as a person; a catalyst to certain acts such as giving out the house keys; as basis to a relationship and etc. Trust is also discerning, not "blind" (Slovakian male, 26); it is something dynamic and contextual. It is noteworthy that Couchsurfers appear to be clear that the trust in operation within the context of Couchsurfing does not apply elsewhere, because "not everybody is a Couchsurfer" (Polish male, 28). It is also specific to the act of surfing or hosting, and does not extend further to lending money, for example.

4.2 The Idiosyncrasies of Trust in Online Profiles

Given that Couchsurfers have no prior knowledge of their hosts, the online profiles and the message correspondences are the only ways of establishing initial trust. From the interviews, it seems that trustworthiness is assumed to exist in other members of the community. When asked about how they assess profiles, the filtering that usually happens is based on the consideration about whether they might like the other person, or the level that they think they might "click". Therefore demographic factors are mentioned, especially age, and occasionally gender.

It is interesting to observe that trust is so intrinsic in the system that in some cases the Couchsurfers don't think about it. An example would be the 21 year old Estonian male Couchsurfer, saying that "I don't really worry about security or the safety, because it seems like, so natural that, the person is trustworthy somehow. I haven't thought about it. I don't worry about it, I guess." In comparison, female Couchsurfers are more likely to think about personal safety, being more vulnerable to attacks, especially of a sexual nature. Therefore most make the choice to surf with only other females, couples or families instead of surfing with males. After eliminating the most obvious fear factor, female Couchsurfers do not differ with their male counterparts in reading profiles.

Profiles contain personal photos and descriptions, as well as trust mechanisms such as references from previous encounters, and whether the user is verified or vouched or not. It is found that the manner of which profiles are read is extremely idiosyncratic. Every Couchsurfer has his/her own way of making judgments about trustworthiness. References are most widely referred to; even so, a Couchsurfer has admitted that he occasionally "forgets" to read the references, after going through the personal description and pictures. Some put pictures as a must for profiles, some do not look at pictures. Some read the entire profile diligently, some just skim through and prefer to leave their judgment to the face-to-face encounter. There are bits of information considered as important by individual Couchsurfers, such as humour, perceived friendliness, and etc. Elements of reason, routine and reflexivity (as discussed in the literature review) can be traced within their thought processes, but it is clear that they are unable to form a coherent picture of trust.

4.3 Making the Leap of Faith

To rise above the idiosyncrasies of profile reading, Möllering's idea of suspension is useful to guide the observation of how different people have different strategies of coming to terms with irreducible vulnerability and uncertainty. For Couchsurfers who put a high emphasis on profile reading, they are able to rely on references left on the profile by previous encounters to form an image in their minds about that person, aiding them to make the decision to trust. To illustrate the point is the quote below:

> "An empty profile is like a nobody. It's like, I don't know this person. Even if it's a filled profile, it could be all invented, it could be all like, fake. I don't know who wrote it. I mean, ok, this person at least made the effort to write it, that's a good thing, but if nobody else is talking about this person, I can't say who it is. And I'm not sure if it's true what this person said." (Swiss male, 26)

However, as mentioned before, there are other respondents who are content with reading the personal description to form the image, helped instead by the profile owner to create the fiction needed for acting "as if" the profile owner is trustworthy. Whether he/she is trustworthy or not is of course another matter. Another situation is demonstrated by the following quote:

> "It's up to how I trust myself, and you know, that's the point. If I know like, I have my backpack here, I'm 80 kilos, I'm a sportsman, I know who I am, I know how to talk, I know this and that, and I know how to find my way, it's like I'm really confident about my personality, what I can do and what I can't do. I know myself pretty well, *then* I'll be able to trust. But if I don't feel confident, if I don't know who I am, I don't know like, where to go, I'm lost with my personality, then I will not be able to trust. So it's really up to my personality. More than to a picture or anything, in a profile. So I would trust you and I would trust a person who has a picture with tattoos with a mad face or something. No difference." (Swiss male, 23)

This quote demonstrates the second strategy to make the leap of faith, where the actor "bracket out irreducible social vulnerability and uncertainty as if they were favourably resolved" (Möllering, 2006, p.115). In the eyes of this Couchsurfer, he is aware of the potential risks but he chooses to focus on himself as being able to handle it, and performs the act of trust. Another example would be the Nigerian male Couchsurfer (34) who was confident that he would be safe, because "God is watching over him".

The third type of strategy offered by Möllering is when the actor has the will to believe. This is especially evident in a community where many identify themselves as being trustful people. Many of the respondents expressed that they were very trusting, quoting remarks from friends and family. An interesting example is this case of a German female respondent (25) who expressed that her biggest fear would be when someone broke her trust, she would lose her ability to trust like how she does now, and hence lose a part of who she is. With this strong identification towards being a trustful person, she has a great will to trust and to maintain that trust.

From the interviews, there is one interesting case that shows interplay of these different strategies of handling suspension. One of the respondents, a Brazilian female Couchsurfer (33) disclosed that she had been held at gunpoint and kidnapped 12 years ago. She described herself as a trustful person, which I infer to mean that she has the will to trust – but her traumatic experience makes it difficult for her to create trustworthy images in her mind about the people that she has to trust. In order to do Couchsurfing, she then has to negotiate within herself whether to take the leap or not. At the beginning of her stay with me, she mentioned that her next host was a man; but after talking about potential risks through the interview, she then informed me that she had changed her mind about staying with that man – i.e. she decided not to take the leap after all.

4.4 Safety – in Terms of What?

This study had commenced with a strong focus on personal safety in terms of risk, therefore the orientation of the questions asked was directed towards that. Further on in data collection, it became apparent that the risk of being robbed, kidnapped or etc. was not the only concern on Couchsurfers' minds, and in some cases it was not even the most important.

It was observed that "open-mindedness" cropped up in virtually all the interviews in terms of being an important characteristic of the Couchsurfer's own identity, a welcomed trait in a potential host, and an underlying attribute of the self-selected community of Couchsurfers. Some Couchsurfers described reading profiles and looking for manifestations of open-mindedness, such as having travelled widely, hosted people of different nationalities and getting references about being open to other cultures. In the meanwhile, it was also observed that most Couchsurfers did not regard themselves as "typical" of their nationality. A link can be established between both phenomena – that Couchsurfers feel somewhat alienated from their home culture and seek acceptance from an online/offline community.

Intrigued, I questioned one of the respondents about "open-mindedness" and its importance to her in terms of trust, when she mentioned the concept. Her answer is quoted as follows:

> "I want to trust that people won't judge me. And that not only that I will be physically safe with them, that they will be friendly to me and nice to me, and not make me feel bad about who I am and what I am doing. That's why open-mindedness is so important. But that's it, that's the other half of trust I guess [the first half being personal safety]. It's both physical safety and psychologically feeling comfortable." (Australian female, 31)

The Nigerian male Couchsurfer (34) had similar concerns about being prejudiced against because of his skin colour, therefore "open-mindedness" was a distinct element looked for when he was reading profiles of potential hosts.

Aristarkhova, cited by Molz [16], argues that online communities are united by a "principle of homogeneity" whereby certain similarities among members of the community work to cancel out individual differences, to bind the community together. She believes that community focuses on difference in order to eliminate or assimilate it, i.e. to differentiate between "us" and "them". Molz argues that since the fundamental themes of hospitality networks reflect a "cosmopolitan desire for and openness to difference" (p.75), the communities do not reject difference per se, but filters the "right" kind of difference from the "wrong". Qualities perceived to be desirable include the ability to reciprocate in kind, a verifiable identity and a clean profile, as well as a certain attitude, that of a "cosmopolitan disposition to the world" (p. 76). Undesirable qualities would be freeloading attitude or strangers who "threatens rather than serves the cosmopolitan fantasy" (p.77). Said "cosmopolitan fantasy" reflects the cosmopolitan as a highly mobile, curious, open-minded and reflexive subject who sees utility in difference and celebrates it.

The cosmopolitanism mentioned by Molz corresponds with the in vivo concept of "open-mindedness", and the online profile may be viewed as a curriculum vitae of sorts, to showcase the open-mindedness or cosmopolitan disposition of its owner. During Couchsurfing interactions, people try to present themselves as being open-minded, and check themselves when they appear to be racist – therefore racism, or other forms of discrimination is now a taboo. An example is provided:

> "But well, I think it's good to see that somebody was there before and when I look for Jakarta for travel, I am checking if there is European people writing. I didn't know about Jakarta at all, and if there were only Indonesian people writing, I don't know like, if I can tru—well, it's just like, an imaginary thing. If it might be a plan to rob, or something. It will be really clever though, if you want to rob somebody, just invite him to your place, and you can have his backpack and his camera and everything. I didn't know at all about Jakarta, Jakarta's a huge city, that's why I checked, and if there's this Italian dude saying, he's very nice or she's very nice, blablabla, then it's ok. Just one, it's enough." (Swiss male, 23)

In the above conversation about reading profiles, the European Couchsurfer checked himself when he thought he might be making a racist remark, from saying "I don't know if I can trust opinions of Indonesian people" to being rather apologetic and saying something more neutral.

5 Conclusion

Möllering's idea of suspension for trust is useful as a guiding framework to enable the researcher to rise above the idiosyncrasies of trust in reading online profiles, to link dealing with irreducible vulnerability to the matter of trust, instead of explaining it away with reason, routine and reflexivity. Through "suspension", the actions of the Couchsurfers can be better understood, by means of understanding the strategies used to make the leap of faith, and how the Couchsurfer can decide *not* to make the leap, hence withdrawing trust.

The interpretative approach taken to handle the subject of trust is important in allowing the actors of trust to articulate what trust means to them. It was found that actors define trust as having security based on what they prize, and further probing revealed that trust within the system did not only involve physical safety, but also the feeling of being accepted as part of the larger, open-minded community. This demonstrates an important lesson of focusing on the actors' interpretation of the social reality that they live in, especially in studying concepts as elusive and abstract as trust. An ethnocentric and positivist approach would typically focus on the obvious (in this case, personal safety), thus missing out on subtle but essential nuances of the meanings attributed by the actors to the contextual situation. It is sufficient to study the guest in this exploratory study, and continuing research will address the corresponding dyad of the host in terms of trust invested in the system.

This study is also interesting to facilitate further study on trust issues on hybrid online/offline communities, because actors negotiate trust through online profiles and then renegotiate it through face-to-face encounters, and after the encounter they are able to leave references in the online world, thus reinforcing trust in the community. Through identifying what is regarded as important trait within the online/offline community, i.e. "open-mindedness" in this case of a transnational community, I can then further research on trust and the manifestations of "open-mindedness" as a form of cultural capital within the actors' social reality of online profiles and offline interactions.

References

1. Möllering, G.: Trust: Reason, Routine Reflexivity. Elsevier Ltd., Oxford (2006)
2. Luhmann, N.: Familiarity, confidence, trust: problems and alternatives. In: Gambetta, D. (ed.) Trust: Making and breaking cooperative relations, pp. 94–107. Basil Blackwell, Oxford (1988)
3. Putnam, R.: Bowling Alone: The Collapse and Revival of American Community. Simon & Schuster, Inc., New York (2001)
4. Corritore, C., Kracher, B., Wiedenbeck, S.: On-line trust: concepts, evolving themes, a model. Trust and Technology 58, 737 (2003)
5. Wang, Y.D., Emurian, H.H.: An overview of online trust: Concepts, elements and implications. Computers in Human Behaviour 105 (2005)
6. Rousseau, D.M., Sitkin, S.B., Burt, R.S., Camerer, C.: Not so different after all: A cross-discipline view of trust. Academy of Management Review 23, 393 (1998)
7. Bhattacharya, R., Devinney, T.M., Pillutla, M.M.: A formal model of trust based on outcomes. Academy of Management Review 23, 459 (1998)

8. Shankar, V., Urban, G.L., Sultan, F.: Online trust: a stakeholder perspective, concepts, implications and future directions. Journal of Strategic Information Systems 325 (2002)
9. Shneiderman, B.: Designing trust into online experiences. ACM Commun. 43, 57 (2000)
10. Ba, S.: Establishing online trust through a community responsibility system. Decision Support Systems 323 (2001)
11. Brownlie, J., Howson, A.: 'Leaps of faith' and MMR: An empirical study of trust. Sociology 39, 221 (2005)
12. Kidd, J.B.: Book Review – Trust: Reason, Routine, Reflexivity. Knowledge Management Research & Practice 4, 254 (2006)
13. Nooteboom, B.: Book Review Organization Studies 27, 1907 (December 1, 2006)
14. boyd, d.m., Ellison, N.B.: Social Network Sites: Definition, history and scholarship. Journal of Computer-Mediated Communication 13 (2007)
15. Heesakkers, P.: Participate in creating a better world, one couch at a time: An explorative study on the phenomenon of Couchsurfing. Thesis published by NHTV Breda University of Applied Sciences (2008)
16. Molz, J.G.: Cosmopolitans on the couch: Mobile hospitality and the Internet. In: Jennie Germann Molz, S.G. (ed.) Mobilizing Hospitality: The Ethics of Social Relations in a Mobile World, Ashgate, Hampshire, pp. 65–80 (2007)
17. Lauterbach, D., Truong, H., Shah, T., Adamic, L.: Surfing a web of trust: Reputation and reciprocity on Couchsurfing.com. In: IEEE International Conference on Computational Science and Engineering, vol. 4, p. 4, pp. 346–353 (2009)
18. Bialski, P.: Intimate Tourism: Friendships in a state of mobility – The case of the online hospitality network. Thesis published by University of Warsaw (2007)

The Role of Soft Information in Trust Building: Evidence from Online Social Lending

Stefanie Pötzsch[1] and Rainer Böhme[1,2]

[1] Department of Computer Science, Technische Universität Dresden, Germany
stefanie.poetzsch@tu-dresden.de
[2] International Computer Science Institute, Berkeley, California
rainer.boehme@icsi.berkeley.edu

Abstract. We analyze empirical data of Germany's largest online social lending platform *Smava.de* to exemplarily study the contribution of unstructured, ambiguous, or unverified information to trust building in online communities. After controlling for the influence of hard information, we find that textual statements that appeal to social behavior actually affect trust building. However, the evidence is less clear for voluntarily disclosed personal data. Lenders generally seem to give more weight to hard information so that disclosing personal data promises little benefit while potentially exposing borrowers to privacy risks.

Keywords: Trust Building, Soft Information, Online Social Lending, Social Behavior, Reciprocity, Personal Data, Privacy, Empirical Study, Content Analysis.

1 Introduction

It is widely accepted that trust between people can be established through interpersonal communication and interaction over time. Computer-mediated communication is characterized by a lack of physical presence and consequently a reduced exchange of social and contextual cues. This makes it particularly challenging to build up trust in online communities and online social networks. Understanding *how* trust is developed between members of online communities, and *which factors* influence trust building in these settings, is subject to ongoing research [BOG+02, HDR04, SGGG09].

Our contribution here is to draw on empirical data from online social lending, an instance of online communities, in order to study the role of different types of information in trust building. Online social lending, also known as *peer-to-peer lending*, has grown rapidly after the launch of the first commercial platform, UK-based *Zopa.com*, in 2005. The idea of social lending is to provide a marketplace for unsecured personal loans. An online platform lets borrowers advertise credit projects to individual lenders, who decide independently in which project they invest. Credit risk is shared in project-specific pools of lenders; each member funds a small share of the financed amount. As a compensation for taking risk, interest is paid to the lenders, whereas platform operators typically charge fixed (i. e., risk-free) fees. The exact market mechanism differs between platforms and has recently been subject to research in mechanism design [CGL09]. Independent of the specific mechanism, matching borrowers' demand with

A. Acquisti, S.W. Smith, and A.-R. Sadeghi (Eds.): TRUST 2010, LNCS 6101, pp. 381–395, 2010.
© Springer-Verlag Berlin Heidelberg 2010

lenders' supply online sidesteps the traditional role of banks as intermediaries in credit markets. This has a plethora of consequences, which we largely disregard in this study.

Our main interest in this new way of organizing credit markets is that it offers an excellent research opportunity to empirically and quantitatively analyze the role of soft information, such as personal data and statements appealing to social behavior, on trust building. In online social lending, the level of trust can be approximated by credit conditions, a measurable dependent variable absent or at least problematic in many alternative approaches. In addition, credit project descriptions contain different types of information, which allows us to disentangle the specific influence of so-called 'hard' and 'soft' information. After some necessary theoretical background in the following subsections, the focus of this paper is to present and discuss evidence from data collected on *Smava.de*, the largest social lending platform serving residents of Germany. Using publicly available field data is not only convenient, but also promises high external validity, in contrast to artificial environments of typical laboratory experiments.

1.1 Social Factors in Online Social Lending

Unlike assumed in classical economic theory, which is potentially applicable to businesses and banks, it is broadly accepted that individuals' behavior is not only motivated by the rational economic consideration of profit-maximization. According to Granovetter's theory of *social embeddedness*, individuals' actions are neither determined by completely rational decisions nor by solely following social norms. Rather, social relationships between people form the basis for interpersonal trust and thereby influence individuals' actions [Gra85]. Likewise, participants in online social lending do not adhere to strictly objective principles for risk assessment and they do not (only) seek to maximize their expected financial wealth. Anecdotal evidence suggests that online social lenders exhibit pro-social and even altruistic behavior. For instance, the not-for-profit platform *Kiva.org* allows individuals to invest capital in small and medium-sized businesses (SMB) operating in developing countries. Although lenders receive zero interest on their investment, the platform counts 675.000 members who have invested about US\$ 120 million between fall 2005 and February 2010 [Kiv]. This example highlights the presence of investors' social motivations on this micro-finance market.

Pro-social behaviors, such as helping others, showing compassion, being honest, trustworthy, and reliable, are believed to be the basis for good social relations and to form the 'glue' of a society. It is important to stress that pro-social behavior need not be completely altruistic; it may also be motivated by expectations of *general reciprocity*. This refers to the social phenomenon that individuals tend to help others when those reciprocate such behavior, i. e., also help others in general [Kol00]. Tangible or intangible – whatever kind of reward lenders expect, borrowers will usually 'pay' it later. Therefore *trust* in borrowers' reliability and their future behavior is vital for online social lending. Trust is defined, for instance, by Schlenker et al. [SHT73] as

> "a reliance upon information received from another person about uncertain environmental states and their accompanying outcomes in a risky situation."

In the case of online social lending, trust can be built by providing information about borrowers and their envisaged credit projects. Observe that such information has a dual nature. First, taking the economic perspective, in credit markets with imperfect information, *information asymmetries* preclude lenders from distinguishing between good and bad risks [Ake70]. Detailed information on borrowers and their credit projects help to reduce uncertainty and thus to establish a trust relationship between lenders and borrowers. Second, from a social-psychological point of view, by communicating personal data, it is possible to convey *interpersonal cues*. These cues may also influence trust building positively, since they allow a potential lender to infer the social background of a borrower and the social proximity between lender and borrower. Both can be used to form expectations about the norms that guide a borrower's future behavior [RSM05].

It remains to be discussed what constitutes 'soft' information. In an essay specific to information on (traditional) credit markets, Petersen distinguishes soft information from hard information by its difficulty "to completely summarize in a numeric score" [Pet04], that is, by its subjectivity, ambiguity, and incomparability. He also acknowledges that it is impossible to draw a sharp line and therefore the concepts 'hard' and 'soft' rather represent end points of a continuous scale than binary categories. Petersen's definition is general enough to subsume alternative distinctions, e. g., by the nature of semantic encoding (hard information corresponds to structured and soft information to unstructured data), or by the verifiability of information (unverified information is difficult to summarize in a valid score, hence it counts as soft information). According to this definition, and due to the aforementioned ambiguity of social cues, any such expression shall be treated as soft information and is therefore relevant to this study.

1.2   Related Work on Online Social Lending

Online social lending has recently attracted the interest of scholars in economics and social sciences. Unless otherwise stated, all prior empirical work is based on data of *Prosper.com*, the major online social lending platform serving US residents.

Ravina [Rav07] as well as Pope and Syndor [PS08] look at discrimination in credit decisions made on social lending platforms. They report effects of race, age, gender, and weight on credit conditions, though not always statistically significant. Credit conditions were operationalized by the (inverse) interest rate, or the probability of (full) funding success. The predictors were either extracted from structured data of the project description or manually assigned by evaluating text or pictures. Herzenstein et al. [HADL08] measured the level of detail of the project description on a 3-step ordinal scale and found it to be a major influencing factor for funding success after controlling for fundamental financial parameters, such as amount, starting interest rate in an auction market, and the (endogenous) duration of the listing. In terms of predictive power, the researchers distinguished between demographic factors (e. g., gender), financial factors (e. g., credit score), and effort measures (e. g., length of project description). The first category was found to have only very little effect on funding success, whereas the latter two categories were found to be influential.

The closest predecessor of our study is Greiner and Wang's interpretation of trust building in online social lending [GW07]. Our study differs from their work in the data source (*Smava.de* instead of *Prosper.com*) and the focus on soft information. By contrast, Greiner and Wang consider the inclusion of genuinely hard information, such as possession of a bank account, credit score, home ownership, group membership, or the availability of pictures, as indicators of institutional-based trust, respectively economic or social cues. These factors appear as control variable in our setup. Greiner and Wang derive eleven hypotheses for specific predictors and find support for seven of them. In a follow-up study [GW09], the problem has been reframed in the theory of *social capital* (see Sobel for a survey [Sob02]) to derive five hypotheses on the influence of the borrower's interaction with other members of the online community around *Prosper.com*. While the results are less clear-cut (indicators of social capital seem to matter most for borrowers with bad creditworthiness, and are generally unstable over time), this study fits well into research bringing together online social lending and social network theory.

Several authors try to identify decision pattern and peer-influence within the social network of registered users of a social lending platform. An early study found that endorsement by group leaders – typically lenders – has the most positive effect on both funding success and total number of bids [RRW07]. This indicates that a personal recommendation can be more important than hard facts, such as credit scores. This finding was confirmed by Berger and Gleisner [BG09], who analyzed the role of group leaders as new "financial intermediaries." Freedman and Jin [FJ08] as well as Herrero-Lopez [HL09] analyzed whether the social network *between borrowers* can contribute to reducing information asymmetries and thus is helpful for making good investments. The authors report empirical evidence that a borrower's affiliation with a reputed group increases the chance of full funding and results in lower interest rates. When looking at the realized default rates, however, the picture becomes more complicated: according to a study by Everett, mere group membership tends to *increase* default rates [Eve08]. Only when distinguishing between groups with supposedly strong and weak interpersonal relations (alumni of one school versus mere profession), a positive outcome (i. e., lower default rate) is observable for groups with strong interpersonal relations. Everett interprets this as evidence for social sanctions [BC95].

Brinceno Ortega and Bell [BOB08] take the platform *Zopa.com* as a case study for a sociological discussion in the context of structuration theory. They argue that the platform as an intermediary between borrowers and lenders empowers its members not only to share information, but to construct "their own financial identities" through collaboration between borrowers and lenders. However, the authors do not underpin their theory with empirical evidence from the analysis of user-generated content, such as profiles, credit project descriptions, and forum messages, on *Zopa.com*.

A first empirical study of online social lending on *Smava.de* from a privacy angle is reported by Böhme and Pötzsch [BP10]. Since voluntarily disclosed personal data constitute soft information, we will update our preliminary results of [BP10] with a meanwhile extended data set and briefly discuss privacy implications in this paper, too.

2   Hypotheses and Data

It is generally accepted that trust reduces transaction costs in arbitrary economic relationships (see for example Dyer and Chu for empirical cross-country evidence [DC03]). Applied to the case of online social lending, this means borrowers who appear more trustworthy to lenders can expect better chances to get their projects funded, and if so at better conditions. In order to demonstrate their trustworthiness, borrowers can introduce themselves by providing personal data in their credit project description and explaining their envisaged project. We hypothesize accordingly:

H1. *Borrowers who disclose more personal data pay lower interest rates.*

As pointed out in Sect. 1.1 above, aside from economic motivations, social behaviors also do play a role in online social lending. Therefore we will study whether emotional statements, direct appeals for help, and the indication of general reciprocity (i. e., statements of the borrower that he also has helped others in the past or will do so in the future) influence lenders' investment decision. Our second hypothesis is:

H2. *Borrowers who explicitly appeal to the social behavior of lenders pay lower interest rates.*

Testing these hypotheses is impeded by the conceptual and practical challenge to extract the independent variables, namely disclosure of personal data and appeals to social behavior, from the borrowers' credit project descriptions. Moreover, the effect of such soft information on credit conditions is small compared to the influence of hard information, like credit score and maturity. So effort is required to control for as much hard information as possible to make subtle effects of soft information observable.

2.1 Data on Credit Projects

Our raw data consists of 1530 credit projects advertised on the largest German social lending platform *Smava.de* between 01 November 2008 and 31 October 2009, representing a total credit amount of 13 million euro (US$ 18 million). This is about 50 % of all loans arranged on the platform from its launch in March 2007 until March 2010.

We have limited the time range to obtain a densely populated sample and avoid singularities in the data during the long launch phase of *Smava.de*. It also helps to avoid heterogeneity before and after the collapse of Lehman Brothers in September 2008, the climax and turning point of the financial crisis. Aside from language issues, homogeneity over time was a major reason for preferring *Smava.de* as data source over the much larger US-based platform *Prosper.com* (loans of US$ 190 million since February 2006). Data of the latter exhibit breaks and instability over time due to several business interruptions, rule changes, and lawsuits with financial supervisors between fall 2008 and spring 2009 [Eis09].

Of our 1530 credit projects, 79 (5 %) were not fully financed and excluded from the analysis to make interest rates – the dependent variable in this paper – better comparable between projects. Note that this ratio is as high as 78 % for *Prosper.com* [RRW07], so studies based on this data source cannot exclude partially funded projects without introducing a substantial bias. In our study, we further excluded another 228 projects which got fully funded within the first two minutes after the creation of the credit project. This can happen because *Smava.de* began to offer so-called *instant loans* in July 2009. In these cases, lenders' decisions are automated and hence do not take into account any soft information.

Smava.de implements the following market mechanism: the platform lets potential borrowers propose credit conditions (amount, interest rate, and maturity of three or five years), checks their identity, and publishes on its website verified demographic information (age, gender, state) along with a credit score and a rough debt service-to-income ratio (so-called *KDF* indicator), as well as a user-provided project description and optional pictures. Lenders can review this information and contribute to its funding in step sizes of 250 euro. When the project is fully funded or after two weeks, whatever is earlier, the (partial) loan is granted via a commercial bank, who partners with *Smava.de* to comply with the German financial supervision regulations. Apparently the bank has no say in the credit decision and immediately securitizes the loan, thereby transferring credit risk to the pool of borrowers. The platform also partners with SCHUFA, the leading German credit bureau, which provides the credit scores, and with a debt collection agency to handle distressed debt. Borrowers can revise the interest rate upwards if their initial offer receives little response.

Borrowers and lenders can appear on the platform under self-chosen nick names, however their full identity is known to and verified by *Smava.de* using the *Postident* procedure. For this service, employees at post offices identify natural persons by their passport or national identity card before relaying a certified document to the recipient. Postident is offered throughout Germany and it is the standard procedure to sign up for online-only bank accounts or online auction sites. In fact, 81.5 % of all borrowers on *Smava.de* appear under fantasy nick names, whereas only 4 % voluntarily chose a nick name that resembles a combination of a first and last name.[1] The remaining borrowers use a nick name that either reveals a common first (10.8 %) or last (3.6 %) name.

Smava.de arranges both non-commercial and commercial credit projects. However, due to a cap of the loan amount at 25,000 euro (US$ 34,000) and the fact that no collateral is provided, all credit projects classified as commercial originate from small non-incorporated businesses. The trustworthiness of these entrepreneurs is most likely assessed by the standards of private persons rather than by checking the financial strength based on corporate balance sheets. Hence we include both types of projects in our analysis and estimate an indicator variable to capture potential differences.

2.2 Content Analysis

We conducted a content analysis [Hol69] to measure the amount of personal data and the occurrence of appeals to social behavior in credit project descriptions. Variation in personal data disclosure can be found in the textual project descriptions, the optional categories of the borrower profile page, and possibly associated pictures. Appeals to social behavior were measured by flagging the occurrence of precisely defined arguments in the textual descriptions. The categories include:

- emotional statements, such as arousing pity about the borrower's situation;
- helping tendency, i. e., direct appeals for help; and
- remarks on (general) reciprocity, such as claims that the borrower has helped others in the past or will help others in the future.

We further coded for each credit project whether it contains a reference to alternative funding by commercial banks and whether the costs were already incurred, e. g., when the *Smava.de* credit is requested for the conversion of other liabilities.

---

[1] Of course, we were unable to verify whether these nick names correspond to the actual names, but we see little indication to believe the contrary.

Two trained coders independently rated the textual descriptions and assigned it to categories without knowing our hypotheses. The underlying code book distinguishes between ten categories of personal data, namely the borrower's name, contact information (address, phone, e-mail, etc.), financial situation, education, profession, further special skills or knowledge, housing situation, health, hobbies, and information about close relatives (children or partner). Each category has several sub-categories that encode in which detail borrowers disclose personal data of the respective category. The coders also rated on a 7-point scale whether their overall perception of a borrower based on all available information was positive, neutral or negative; and how credible they found the whole credit project. Due to resource constraints, 125 of the available credit projects were not coded in full detail. This explains the differences in the number of cases as indicated in the result tables. Nonetheless, a subset of projects has been coded by both coders to calculate the intercoder reliability. Calculated according to the popular formula by Holsti [Hol69], our overall reliability of 90 % is reasonably good.

2.3 Auxiliary Data

To control for fluctuations in the broader economic environment, we have added monthly data on the average effective interest rates charged by German commercial banks for consumer credit of comparable maturity (Bundesbank time series code: SUD114). Since this indicator alone could barely explain the time-dependent fluctuations in the level of interest rates on *Smava.de*, we decided to include monthly fixed effects. We further created three dummy variables to capture fundamental changes on *Smava.de*. First, the platform increased fees for both borrowers and lenders in February 2009. The second intervention was the extension of the *bidding assistant* in May 2009. The bidding assistant places bids on behalf of a lender and distributes a given amount of investment capital on several credit projects. The new assistant allows lenders to define a fine-grained loan portfolio in which they wish to invest. Note that a new credit project can only receive up to 50 % funding from lenders' bidding assistants. The rest of the total amount needs to be invested by manual bids. The third change during the period of our study was the introduction of *instant loans* (in German: "Schnellkredit") in July 2009. Such projects can be fully financed by bidding assistants and the platform suggests an interest rate so that supply matches demand. Although these projects were excluded from our data set, we use the dummy variable to control for a potential influence of this new service on the overall market environment.

3 Results

To study the effects of personal data and appeals to social behavior, a set of predictors representing both hard and soft information in credit project descriptions is regressed on the final interest rate of all fully funded projects. Table 1 shows two specifications of the regression model along with estimates and statistical significance tests. Model 1 is estimated with predictors for hard information only and model 2 extends it by predictors reflecting soft information. The overall goodness-of-fit measured by the adjusted R^2 statistic is very high – also in comparison to similar analyses in the literature, e. g., [GW07]. However, the additional variance explained by soft information is marginal.

3.1 Hard Information: Financial Key Indicators and Economic Environment

Not surprisingly, the credit score turned out to be the most influential predictor. Since the models are fitted without intercept, the estimates for SCHUFA grades can be directly interpreted as average interest rates for the respective grades. Due to the linear regression model, the estimated coefficients are additive contributions to the final interest rate. For example, the baseline interest rate of 8.2 % p. a. for average borrowers of SCHUFA grade D is further significantly revised upwards by on average 0.3 percentage points for debt service-to-income ratios above 40 %. To protect borrowers and lenders alike, *Smava.de* does not arrange credit projects from borrowers with debt service-to-income ratios above 67 %.

Table 1. Regression models for interest rate p. a.

Predictor	Model 1		Model 2	
Credit score				
SCHUFA grade A (good)	5.90 ***	(0.813)	6.16 ***	(0.821)
SCHUFA grade B	6.68 ***	(0.813)	6.96 ***	(0.821)
SCHUFA grade C	7.71 ***	(0.811)	7.99 ***	(0.819)
SCHUFA grade D	8.22 ***	(0.810)	8.47 ***	(0.817)
SCHUFA grade E	9.36 ***	(0.819)	9.59 ***	(0.827)
SCHUFA grade F	10.09 ***	(0.815)	10.38 ***	(0.824)
SCHUFA grade G	11.93 ***	(0.811)	12.18 ***	(0.819)
SCHUFA grade H (bad)	13.33 ***	(0.815)	13.62 ***	(0.824)
Ratio of debt service over net income				
20–40 %	0.21	(0.138)	0.21	(0.138)
40–60 %	0.30 **	(0.132)	0.27 **	(0.132)
60–67 %	0.63 ***	(0.133)	0.61 ***	(0.133)
Time-dependent factors				
Average commercial bank rate	0.55	(1.130)	0.40	(1.142)
Dummy for fee raise (1 Feb 2009)	0.76	(0.704)	0.57	(0.707)
Dummy for bidding assistant (6 May 2009)	−0.65 **	(0.299)	−0.70 **	(0.300)
Dummy for instant loans (16 July 2009)	−0.36 *	(0.187)	−0.32 *	(0.187)
Fixed effect: Nov 2008	1.19	(1.101)	1.18	(1.113)
Dez 2008	1.04	(0.893)	0.98	(0.903)
Jan 2009	0.22	(0.868)	0.11	(0.876)
Feb 2009	−0.24	(0.288)	−0.20	(0.289)
Mar 2009	0.72 **	(0.364)	0.81 **	(0.367)
May 2009	−0.01	(0.302)	0.04	(0.301)
June 2009	−0.46	(0.460)	−0.43	(0.466)
July 2009	−1.55 ***	(0.475)	−1.45 ***	(0.476)
Aug 2009	−2.18 **	(0.917)	−2.06 **	(0.922)
Sep 2009	−1.42 ***	(0.408)	−1.39 ***	(0.408)
Oct 2009	−1.70 ***	(0.395)	−1.66 ***	(0.395)

... table to be continued on the following page ...

Table 1. (*continued*)

Predictor	Model 1	Model 2
Properties of the credit project		
Maturity (dummy for 5 instead of 3 years)	0.49*** (0.082)	0.47*** (0.082)
Amount (multiples of 250 euro)	0.01*** (0.002)	0.01*** (0.002)
Average bid (steps of 250 euro)	−0.14*** (0.049)	−0.14*** (0.049)
Commercial loan (i.e., SMB)	−0.00 (0.103)	0.06 (0.108)
Revision of initial interest rate	−0.09 (0.090)	−0.06 (0.090)
Project-specific picture	−0.18** (0.090)	−0.15* (0.091)
Picture in borrower profile	0.11 (0.124)	0.10 (0.132)
Borrower demographics		
Self-employed	0.13 (0.097)	0.18* (0.097)
Age (absolute deviation from median)	0.02*** (0.004)	0.02*** (0.005)
Gender (female)	−0.00 (0.078)	−0.02 (0.080)
Soft Information		
Voluntary disclosure of personal data		
Borrower profile completed		0.12 (0.112)
Name and contact information [0..20]		0.00 (0.038)
Financial situation [0..13]		0.00 (0.029)
Profession and qualifications [0..23]		−0.05*** (0.016)
Housing situation [0..4]		−0.02 (0.032)
Health [0..5]		−0.00 (0.067)
Hobbies [0..4]		0.02 (0.043)
Partner, family members [0..19]		−0.00 (0.018)
Argument style		
Statements that arouse pity		0.42** (0.188)
Direct appeal for help		−0.22* (0.122)
Reference to own helpfulness (reciprocity)		−0.09 (0.177)
Claimed eligibility for bank loan (competition)		−0.22* (0.128)
Costs already incurred (necessity)		0.16* (0.082)
Model fit: adjusted R^2 (number of cases)	98.72 (1098)	98.74 (1098)

Standard errors in round brackets; significance levels: *** $p < 0.01$, ** $p < 0.05$, * $p < 0.1$.

Controlling for changes on the platform over time, the results indicate that the average interest rate decreased after the modification of the bidding assistant, as did the introduction of instant loans. The fee rise caused no measurable change in interest rates, but cautious interpretation is advisable since the true effect size might be suppressed by a confounded monthly fixed effect. With regard to all monthly fixed effects, observe the spike in March 2009 and the declining rates in the last four months of the sample period. The latter can be explained by two reasons. First, the monetary easing in the aftermath of the financial crisis has increasingly been passed on to consumers (although it is somewhat surprising that this development is not captured by the official statistic).

Second, increased media coverage presenting social lending in general (and *Smava.de* in particular) as investment alternative may have led to over-supply of credit.

Regarding the properties of credit projects, we found evidence that higher rates are charged for higher amounts and longer maturities, whereas upward revisions of the initial interest rate are not penalized. Corroborating the literature (e. g., [GW07, HADL08]), credit conditions were found to improve significantly if project descriptions are illustrated with borrower-provided pictures. However, pictures in the borrower profile, albeit only one click further apart, have no significant effect. Projects attracting higher average bids are associated with lower interest rates, even though this should not be interpreted as causal relationship since bid statistics are partly endogenous.[2]

In the demographics section, we find evidence for discrimination by age in the predictable direction: very young and very old borrowers have to pay higher rates. The age coefficient is estimated for the absolute deviation in years from the sample median of 43 years. No evidence is found for discrimination by gender, whereas being self-employed tends to be associated with higher interest rates.

3.2   Soft Information: Personal Data Disclosure and Appeals to Social Behavior

Voluntarily disclosed personal data was measured for different categories and subcategories, as indicated in Table 1 (numbers of subcategories in square brackets). In contrast to our hypothesis H1, the data suggests that disclosure of personal data is barely influential. Interest rates decline marginally, but statistically significantly, if borrowers disclose detailed personal data about their education, profession, and qualifications. Disclosure of personal data belonging to other categories has no influence on the average interest rate. Hence, H1 is not supported in its generality by our results.

In order to test H2, we precisely coded the argument style of borrowers and included these variable as predictors in model 2. We found more significant effects than for the predictors associated with H1, however not always in the expected direction. For example, emotional statements arousing pity are penalized with higher interest rates. Lenders seem to expect that borrowers who happen to maneuver themselves into pitiful situations might not show exceptional effort when it comes to repaying their debt. Conversely and in line with H2, interest rates tend to decline when direct appeals for help appear in the project description and – to a much lesser extend and statistically indistinguishable from random fluctuations – when references to (general) reciprocity are made. Similar to H1, H2 is not supported in its generality by our results.

The effect of two additional pieces of soft information not covered by specific hypotheses is measurable and turns out to be in line with (common sense) expectations. Borrowers who claim to be eligible for a bank loan, and thus convey that they appear trustworthy to a financial institution, are charged lower interest rates. Conversely, revealing the fact that the costs were already incurred, thus admitting an unfavorable bargaining position, is penalized with tighter credit conditions.

---

[2] We have included this predictor nonetheless in order to remove heterogeneity from the data. To rule out that this variable unduly proxies soft information on project quality, we removed this predictor in a separate analysis without observing noteworthy changes in the results.

3.3 Discussion of Results and Plausibility Checks

The lack of clear support for our hypotheses about the effect of soft information on credit conditions in online social lending suggests some reflection on potential measurement issues. While we are not too surprised by the measurable effects (though partly in the opposite direction) for variables associated with H2, we were initially concerned by the apparent irrelevance of personal data disclosure in six out of seven categories and decided to conduct plausibility checks for the predictors associated with H1.

For example, we tabulated our coders' overall perception of borrowers (based on all available information from the borrower's profile and the project description) against voluntary disclosure of any personal data. Table 2 shows that the overall perception is positive for the majority of credit project descriptions that contain personal data. Whereas, if no personal data is disclosed, the impression is only neutral on average. Table 3 shows a similar analysis for a credibility rating: 79 % of the credit project descriptions that contain any voluntarily disclosed personal data are rated as credible by our coders. This ratio is only 40 % if no personal data is provided. Contingency tests indicate that the difference between borrowers who do not disclose personal data and those who do is highly significant for both tables. Hence, disclosing personal data seems to improve credibility and leads to a more positive perception. Therefore one would expect that the so-increased trustworthiness should be rewarded with better credit conditions.

An alternative explanation for the marginal effect of soft information, notably disclosure of personal data, is a general change of conventions on the *Smava.de* marketplace over large parts of our sample period. All three indicators displayed in Figure 1 (a) witness a development towards vanishing selectivity in individual credit decisions: loans

Table 2. Overall perception of borrowers (variable coded for 790 cases)

| | *Voluntary data disclosure in project description?* | |
Overall perception	no ($n = 163$)	yes ($n = 627$)
positive	19.02 %	66.03 %
neutral	52.15 %	28.55 %
negative	28.83 %	5.42 %

Contingency test $\chi^2(2)=141.47, p < 0.001$.

Table 3. Credibility of credit project descriptions (variable coded for 1096 cases)

| | *Voluntary data disclosure in project description?* | |
Credibility	no ($n = 186$)	yes ($n = 910$)
(Very) credible	40.32 %	79.45 %
neutral	40.32 %	13.96 %
(Very) incredible	19.35 %	6.59 %

Contingency test $\chi^2(2)=119.44, p < 0.001$.

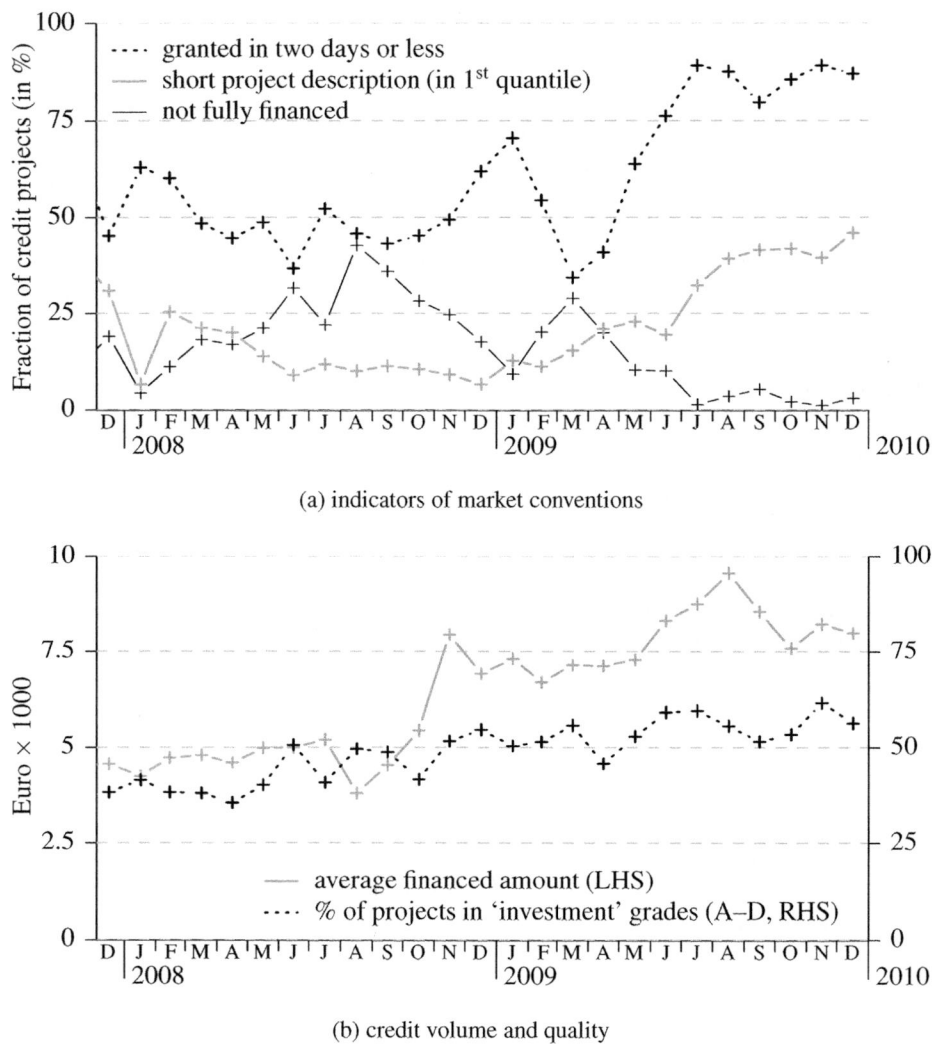

(a) indicators of market conventions

(b) credit volume and quality

Fig. 1. Change of conventions on the *Smava.de* marketplace: scrutiny on loan approval declines (a) while credit quality remains flat and alloted volumes grow (b); time series of selected indicators, aggregated per month from all approved projects

are approved at ever faster pace, almost every project gets fully financed in the second half of 2009, and, most remarkably, credit project descriptions appear to have declined in relevance so much that many borrowers do not bother anymore to elaborate them. Whereas less than 10 % of project descriptions were classified as "short" according to our indicator in December 2008, this ratio rose to almost 50 % one year later. All this would not be remarkable if it occurred as a result of a general change of the type of credit projects arranged on the platform towards less risky, smaller loans as the growing platform attracts larger parts of the population. However, indicators in Figure 1 (b) prove the contrary: average loan amounts actually rose and credit quality did not improve substantially. This calls for more scrutiny in credit decisions rather than less! Without deeper analysis, we can only speculate about the reasons behind this development (e. g., supply exceeding demand, impact of the bidding assistant and instant loans, externalities incentivizing indiscriminate approval of risky projects, etc.). It is evident, however, that one or more factors create a dynamic that marginalizes the influence of soft information on *Smava.de*. While this might be good news for privacy advocates, who can safely advise borrowers and urge platform operators minimize the disclose of personal data, it remains to be seen how this development affects trust between the participants in online social lending and long-term trust in the specific platform and the business model as a whole.

Of course, our results suffer from the usual limitations of empirical field research. Explorative data analysis suggests that there is still some unexplained heterogeneity, and we might have overlooked a third variable that changes the picture. Moreover, our indicators of soft information are, by definition, approximations at best and – despite internally reliable – not necessarily valid for the concepts we are trying to quantify.

4 Concluding Remarks

Trust building in online communities and online social networks is challenging due to the lack of interpersonal interaction and a very limited exchange of interpersonal cues. In this paper we drew on empirical data of the largest German social lending platform *Smava.de* to study the role of soft information as supporting factor in trust building between borrowers and lenders. From a purely economic point of view, it is not overly surprising that hard information strongly influences credit decisions in online social lending, as already shown by other authors (see Sect. 1.2). Our study differs from related work in its focus on soft information, the quantification of which involved an extensive manual content analysis with categories so far unexplored for online social lending. Following Granovetter's ideas of social embeddedness, we analyzed in particular, whether borrowers who disclose personal data or write appeals to social behavior in their credit project descriptions are rewarded with lower interest rates.

Our results indicate that communicating personal data indeed supports a positive and trustworthy overall perception of the borrower, but the impact on credit conditions is marginal: only data in the category education, profession, and qualifications show a small and significant effect. Appeals to social behavior create stronger effect in varying direction. On the one hand, lenders reward direct appeals for help. This can be interpreted as evidence for pro-social behavior. On the other hand, if borrowers overdo and try to arouse pity or admit a weak bargaining position, they are penalized with even higher interest rates. Further, claims of borrowers to be trusted by banks seem to improve their trustworthiness and lead to significantly better credit conditions.

To conclude, besides hard economic facts, lenders on *Smava.de* do consider soft information in their evaluation of their borrowers' trustworthiness, though to a limited extent and apparently with decreasing weight over time. In particular, voluntarily disclosed personal data is less honored than thought. This calls for a deeper analysis on the relation between trust and privacy. Other directions for future work include the refinement of our measurement methods, the collection of data to evaluate social proximity as a factor in trust building, and the replication of our study in contexts that are less susceptible to the increasingly indiscriminate credit decisions observable in Fig. 1 (e. g., other platforms, sample periods, subsets of credit projects). It also remains relevant to study the role of soft information in trust building for other applications. If our results can be confirmed, this may provide insights on how technical systems for trust propagation and trust computation should be designed to mimic trust building between people.

Acknowledgements

Thanks are due to Hagen Wahrig and our coders Ulrike Jani, Kristina Schäfer, and Michael Sauer for their excellent research assistance. Part of the research leading to these results has received funding from the European Community's Seventh Framework Programme (FP7/2007-2013) under grant agreement No. 216483. The second author was supported by a post-doctoral fellowship of the German Academic Exchange Service (DAAD).

References

[Ake70]   Akerlof, G.A.: The market for "lemons": Quality uncertainty and the market mechanism. The Quarterly Journal of Economics 84(3), 488–500 (1970)

[BC95]   Besley, T., Coate, S.: Group lending, repayment incentives and social collateral. Journal of Development Economics 46, 1–18 (1995)

[BG09]   Berger, S., Gleisner, F.: Emergence of financial intermediaries in electronic markets: The case of online P2P lending. BuR - Business Research 2(1), 39–65 (2009)

[BOB08]   Ortega, A.C.B., Bell, F.: Online social lending: Borrower-generated content. In: Proc. of Americas Conf. on Inf. Systems (AMCIS), vol. 380 (2008)

[BOG⁺02]   Bos, N., Olson, J., Gergle, D., Olson, G., Wright, Z.: Effects of four computer-mediated communications channels on trust development. In: Proc. of ACM CHI, Minneapolis, MN, pp. 135–140. ACM Press, New York (2002)

[BP10]   Böhme, R., Pötzsch, S.: Privacy in online social lending. In: AAAI Spring Symposium on Intelligent Privacy Management, Palo Alto, CA, pp. 23–28 (2010)

[CGL09]   Chen, N., Ghosh, A., Lambert, N.: Social lending. In: Proc. of ACM EC, Palo Alto, CA, pp. 335–344. ACM Press, New York (2009)

[DC03]   Dyer, J.H., Chu, W.: The role of trustworthiness in reducing transaction costs and improving performance: Empirical evidence from the United States, Japan, Korea. Organization Science 14(1), 57–68 (2003)

[Eis09]   Eisenbeis, H.: The government crackdown on peer-to-peer lending. The Big Money (March 2009), http://www.thebigmoney.com/print/1674

[Eve08]   Everett, C.R.: Group membership, relationship banking and default risk: The case of online social lending (August 2008), http://ssrn.com/abstract=1114428

[FJ08]   Freedman, S., Jin, G.Z.: Do social networks solve information problems for peer-to-peer lending? Evidence from Prosper.com (November 2008), http://ssrn.com/abstract=1304138

[Gra85]   Granovetter, M.: Economic action and social structure: The problem of embeddedness. The American Journal of Sociology 91(3), 481–510 (1985)

[GW07]   Greiner, M.E., Wang, H.: Building consumer-to-consumer trust in e-finance marketplaces. In: Proc. of Americas Conf. on Inf. Systems (AMCIS), vol. 211 (2007)

[GW09]   Greiner, M.E., Wang, H.: The role of social capital in people-to-people lending marketplaces. In: Proc. of Int'l Conf. on Inf. Systems (ICIS), vol. 29 (2009)

[HADL08]   Herzenstein, M., Andrews, R., Dholakia, U., Lyandres, E.: The democratization of personal consumer loans? Determinants of success in online peer-to-peer lending communities (June 2008), http://ssrn.com/abstract=1147856

[HDR04]   Hung, Y.-T.C., Dennis, A.R., Robert, L.: Trust in virtual teams: Towards an integrative model of trust formation. In: Proc. of Hawaii Int'l Conf. on System Sciences. IEEE Computer Society, Los Alamitos (2004)

[HL09]   Herrero-Lopez, S.: Social interactions in P2P lending. In: Workshop on Social Network Mining and Analysis, Paris, France (June 2009)

[Hol69]   Holsti, O.R.: Content analysis for the social sciences and humanities. Addison-Wesley, Reading (1969)

[Kiv]   Kiva.org. Facts & Statistics, http://www.kiva.org/about/facts

[Kol00]   Kolm, S.-C.: The logic of good social relations. Annals of Public and Cooperative Economics 71(2), 171–189 (2000)

[Pet04]   Petersen, M.A.: Information: Hard and soft. Mimeo (2004)

[PS08]   Pope, D., Syndor, J.: What's in a picture? Evidence of discrimination from Prosper.com (September 2008),
            http://wsomfaculty.case.edu/sydnor/prosperpaper.pdf

[Rav07]   Ravina, E.: Beauty, personal characteristics and trust in credit markets (December 2007), http://ssrn.com/abstract=972801

[RRW07]   Ryan, J., Reuk, K., Wang, C.: To fund or not to fund: Determinants of loan fundability in the Prosper.com marketplace (January 2007),
            http://www.prosper.com/Downloads/Research/
            Prosper_Regression_Project-Fundability_Study.pdf

[RSM05]   Riegelsberger, J., Sasse, M.A., McCarthy, J.D.: The mechanics of trust: A framework for research and design. Int'l Journal of Human-Computer Studies 62(3), 381–422 (2005)

[SGGG09]   Scissors, L.E., Gill, A.J., Geraghty, K., Gergle, D.: CMC we trust: The role of similarity. In: Proc. of ACM CHI, pp. 527–536 (2009)

[SHT73]   Schlenker, B.R., Helm, B., Tedeschi, J.T.: The effects of personality and situational variables on behavioral trust. Journal of Personality and Social 25(3), 419–427 (1973)

[Sob02]   Sobel, J.: Can we trust social capital? Journal of Economic Literature 40(3), 139–154 (2002)

Software on the Witness Stand: What Should It Take for Us to Trust It?

Sergey Bratus[1], Ashlyn Lembree[2], and Anna Shubina[1]

[1] Institute for Security, Technology, and Society, Dartmouth College, Hanover, NH
[2] Franklin Pierce Law Center, Concord, NH

1 Motivation

We discuss the growing trend of electronic evidence, created automatically by autonomously running software, being used in both civil and criminal court cases. We discuss *trustworthiness requirements* that we believe should be applied to such software and platforms it runs on. We show that courts tend to regard computer-generated materials as *inherently trustworthy* evidence, ignoring many software and platform trustworthiness problems well known to computer security researchers. We outline the technical challenges in making evidence-generating software trustworthy and the role Trusted Computing can play in addressing them.

This paper is structured as follows: Part I is a case study of electronic evidence in a "file sharing" copyright infringement case, potential trustworthiness issues involved, and ways we believe they should be addressed with state-of-the-art computing practices. Part II is a legal analysis of issues and practices surrounding the use of software-generated evidence by courts.

Part I: The Case Study and Technical Challenges

2 Introduction

Recently the first author was asked to serve as an expert witness in a civil lawsuit, in which the plaintiffs alleged violation of their copyrights by the defendant by way of a peer-to-peer network. Mavis Roy, of Hudson, New Hampshire, had been charged by four record labels with downloading and distributing hundreds of songs from the Internet.

The principal kind of evidence that the plaintiffs provided to the defendant's counsel (the second author), and which, judging by their expert witness' report, they planned to use in court to prove their version of events that implied the defendant's guilt, was a long **print-out of a computer program**.

Furthermore, the timing pattern of the computer program's recorded actions led us to believe that the program produced the print-outs in an **automatic** fashion rather than as a result of a human operating it *interactively* via a human-computer interface with the operator selecting appropriate actions, stopping to

A. Acquisti, S.W. Smith, and A.-R. Sadeghi (Eds.): TRUST 2010, LNCS 6101, pp. 396–416, 2010.

inspect the results, making determinations, forming hypotheses, and planning further actions.[1]

Thus it appears that the *only* entity to "witness" the alleged violations and to produce an account of them for the court – in the form of a series of print-outs – was in fact an autonomous piece of software, programmed by a company acting on behalf of the plaintiffs and RIAA, and running on a computer controlled by this company.

A Sci-Fi writer might say that the program in question was acting as an autonomous "robotic investigator" (or a "robotic witness"), selecting targets for its investigation and recording its investigative actions in the print-outs as evidence to be used in court. We understand that such evidence has already made appearance in many so-called P2P file sharing cases filed by the Recording Industry Association of America (RIAA) across the US.[2]

Clearly, **software entrusted with such an important function must be held to special, higher standards of trustworthiness.** As any computer scientist (and, indeed, any programmer) knows, bugs and misconfigurations are inherent in software, including – despite the programmers' vigorous efforts to the contrary – in mission-critical software, and can be deadly.[3] Defining such standards in a way consistent with the state-of-the-art knowledge of the technical, legal, and social aspects of the problem poses a multi-disciplinary research challenge. In particular, the following aspects — at least — must be considered:

- **Software trustworthiness.** How much can the software be relied on to be error-free and to operate as expected? Such questions are central to Computer Science in general, and to Computer Security in particular, and an acceptable answer should involve a consensus by computer security experts.
- **Trier-of-fact perceptions.** There is a certain common expectation of precision and impartiality associated with computer systems by non-specialists. However, computer practitioners themselves joke that "computers make very fast, very accurate mistakes", and exchange cautionary stories of ubiquitous computer "bugs".[4] This phenomenon of human trust and the potential trier-of-fact bias should be investigated by legal scholars and sociologists.
- **Software as a witness?** Witnesses in court make their statements under oath, with severe consequences of deviating from the truth in their testimony. Witnesses are then cross-examined in order to expose any biases or conflicts of interest they might have. Computer-generated evidence comes from an

---

[1] As a forensic examiner would do when analyzing a hard drive's contents with software like *Encase* or a network packet trace with software like *Wireshark* that makes no judgments or determinations of its own but merely presents information to the human expert.

[2] For information and defense attorney perspective on these cases see, e.g., http://recordingindustryvspeople.blogspot.com/

[3] E.g., the RISKS Digest http://catless.ncl.ac.uk/risks abounds with dramatic examples.

[4] The above-mentioned RISKS Digest is recommended reading in the Computer Security course at Dartmouth College and other leading higher education institutions.

entity that cannot take an oath ensuring its intent of providing the truth (only programmers directly responsible for creating that entity can do so), nor receive an adversarial examination (which would reasonably apply only to the code and function of the software). Ensuring equal responsibilities for "direct" human witnesses and those who are responsible for the creation of the computer-generated evidence requires research by legal scholars.

In this case study we consider the technical aspects of what we believe it should take computer science experts to deem the output of autonomously operating software *trustworthy*, considering both the extreme malleability of such outputs and the need for mitigating the effects of unintended bugs and misconfigurations.

The structure of this case study is as follows. We subdivide and consider the questions posed above, using our experience with the plaintiff's computer-generated evidence in the above-mentioned "file sharing" case, expert opinions of computer scientists in similar previous cases, and other court decisions. Then we explain the connection of the desired trustworthiness properties with the concepts of Trusted Computing (TC) and sketch a design of how TC techniques can help achieve the stated trustworthiness goals.

3   Summary of the Roy Case

Mavis Roy, of Hudson, New Hampshire, had been charged by four record labels with downloading and distributing hundreds of songs from the Internet. The four members of the Recording Industry Association of America (RIAA) brought a case against Roy in U.S. District Court, following a letter from the record companies' attorneys that directed her to a web site where she could pay by credit card to settle the case. Since she did not have a computer in her house at the time she was alleged to have downloaded the music, she ignored the request, thinking it was a scam.[5]

3.1   Case Materials

The subpoena. Ms. Roy's ISP received a subpoena issued by the plaintiff's lawyers. The ISP was asked to identify the subscriber based on an *IP address* and a moment in time (*date, hour, minute, and second*). The ISP disclosed the subscriber account information, including name, phone number, and mailing address.

Basis for the subpoena and lawsuit. The materials received by Ms. Roy defense lawyer included, besides the subpoena, printouts of several kinds of software-generated logs and the plaintiff's expert witness report[6] that contained an interpretation of these logs.

---

[5] See the press release of the Franklin Pierce Law Center's Consumer and Commercial Law and Intellectual Property and Transaction Clinics, http://www.piercelaw.edu/news/posts/2009-06-18-victory-in-downloading-case.php

[6] *Declaration and Expert Report* by Dr. Doug Jacobson from January 29, 2009.

The latter report contained statements that the computer with the IP address in question was "registered" to Ms. Roy and engaged in file sharing. The basis for this expression was unclear, since the defendant, as far as we know, never had to register her computer or any specific computer with her ISP (which typically only requires the customer to register the MAC address of the *cable modem* at service activation time), and no MAC addresses at all were present in either the ISP response to the subpoena or any other case documents. Many other statements and conclusions of this and similar plaintiff's expert witness reports have been disputed by expert witnesses[7], but their analysis is beyond the scope of this paper, in which we focus on the content and presentation of the evidence itself.

All logs (titled "Evidence for <number>" were provided as text files in PDF format, summarized in Table 1. The filenames followed the common pattern of RoyMNHOxxx.PDF; the first column of the table contains the unique (xxx) part of the filename. Samples from these files are shown in Figures 1– 9.

The choice of format, especially for representing packets as ASCII printouts of their (printable) bytes, complicated analysis of data and introduced additional ambiguity. For example, one can only guess what actual bytes corresponded to non-printable characters, rendered in printouts as a thick black dot; checksumming or cryptographic hashing of such packet captures is impossible, and, as far as we know, was not performed. The most voluminous log (785 pages long, and over 83% of the total submitted pages) contained no relevant information about packets other than their length and was thus of little help for cross-validating other logs.

In particular, the IP addresses contained in such packets – a crucial part of the subpoena – could not be readily verified, nor could other relevant TCP/IP information, such as the Time-To-Live (TTL) values, which could have helped to validate the network path, be readily extracted.

In all of these documents, the assumption that decoding of such information by the generating software was performed without error was apparent. Yet, at least in the case of the document that apparently purported to contain the traced route to the IP in the subpoena, the software obviously failed to operate correctly, as can be see in Figure 7. The reason for this could have been either internal code faults or network configuration faults, or both; we discuss this further in Section 5.2.

---

[7] A selection of such arguments can be found in

1. *Expert witness report* by Dr. J.A. Pouwelse in UMG Recording Inc., et al. v.Lindor, available from http://www.ilrweb.com/viewILRPDF.asp?filename= umg_lindor_080215ExpertWitnessReportPouwelse
2. *Declaration* of Jason E. Street in Arista Records, LLC, et al. v.Does 1–11, available from http://www.ilrweb.com/viewILRPDF.asp?filename=arista_does1-11_070806DeclarationJaysonStreet
3. *Expert witness report* by Dr. Yongdae Kim in Capitol v. Thomas, available from http://beckermanlegal.com/pdf/?file=/Lawyer_Copyright_Internet_Law/virgin_thomas_090303DeftsExpertWitnessReport.pdf

Table 1. Evidence materials in Roy case

xxx:	Purport	Description	Page count
054	"Download Info For <filename>"	ASCII printout of IP packets with IP addresses decoded	124
178	"IP byte log for user at address <IP> for <filename>"	One line per packet: "timestamp, StartByte, %d, EndByte, %d, TotalBytes %d"	785
963	"Shared file matches for user at address <IP:port>"	Filename, length, checksum	1
964	"RECEIVED PACKET <timestamp>"	ASCII printout of IP packet	9
973	"Initializing analysis of user <IP:port>"	Log of actions such as "Attempting to match files", "Choosing files to download", "Initiating download of <filename>"	4
977	"Tracing route to <IP>", "DNS Lookup for <IP>"	Failed traceroute	1
978	"Log for User at address <IP> generated on <timestamp>"	File name and SHA1	11
989	"Total Recognized Files Being Distributed"	File name and size	8

```
RECEIVED CONTENT PACKET: 4/24/2007 5:51:57 AM EDT (-0400 GMT)
Packet Source: 75.68.28.28
Packet Destination: xxx.xxx.31.78
Packet Data: (bytes 0-1459)
ÿû°●●●●●●ị●●●●●●
Å●●●●●□●●●●●●4ƒ€●●LAME3.87 (beta 1, Sep 27 2000)
ŮŮŮŮŮŮŮŮŮŮŮŮŮŮŮŮŮŮŮŮŮŮŮŮŮŮŮŮŮŮŮŮŮŮŮŮŮŮŮŮŮŮŮŮŮŮŮŮŮLAME3.87 (beta 1, Sep 27 2000)
ŮŮŮŮŮŮŮŮŮŮŮŮŮŮŮŮŮŮŮŮŮŮŮŮŮŮŮŮŮŮŮŮŮŮŮŮŮŮŮŮŮŮŮŮŮŮŮŮŮŮŮŮŮŮŮŮŮŮŮŮŮŮŮŮŮŮŮŮŮŮŮŮŮŮŮŮŮŮŮŮŮŮŮŮŮŮŮŮ
ŮŮŮŮŮŮŮŮŮŮŮŮŮŮŮŮŮŮŮŮŮŮŮŮŮŮŮŮŮŮŮŮŮŮŮŮŮŮŮŮŮŮŮŮŮŮŮŮŮŮŮŮŮŮŮŮŮŮŮŮŮŮŮŮŮŮŮŮŮŮŮŮŮŮŮŮŮŮŮŮŮŮŮŮŮŮŮŮ
ŮŮŮŮŮŮŮŮŮŮŮŮŮŮŮŮŮŮŮŮŮŮŮŮŮŮŮŮŮŮŮŮŮŮŮŮŮŮŮŮŮŮŮŮŮŮŮŮŮŮŮŮŮŮŮŮŮŮŮŮŮŮŮŮŮŮŮŮŮŮŮŮŮŮŮŮŮŮŮŮŮŮŮŮŮŮŮŮ
ŮŮŮŮŮŮŮŮŮŮŮŮŮŮŮŮŮŮŮŮŮŮŮŮŮŮŮŮŮŮŮŮŮŮŮŮŮŮŮŮŮŮŮŮŮŮŮŮŮŮŮŮŮŮŮŮŮŮŮŮŮŮŮŮŮŮŮŮŮŮŮŮŮŮŮŮŮŮŮŮŮŮŮŮŮŮŮŮ
ŮŮŮŮŮŮÿû²●ŷ●ð●●ị●●●●●●
●●●●●●□●●●●●●4€●●●
ŮŮŮŮŮŮŮŮŮŮŮŮŮŮŮŮŮŮŮŮŮŮŮŮŮŮŮŮŮŮŮŮŮŮŮŮŮŮŮŮŮŮŮŮŮŮŮŮŮŮŮŮŮŮŮŮŮŮŮŮŮŮŮŮŮŮŮŮLAME3.87 (beta
1, Sep 27 2000)
```

Fig. 1. Sample of RoyMNH054

```
Title: Jay-Z - The Blueprint - 09 - Never Change.mp3

IP Byte Log for user at address 75.68.28.28 for file: Jay-Z - The Blueprint - 09 - Never
Change.mp3
4/24/2007 5:51:57 AM EDT (-0400 GMT), StartByte, 0, EndByte, 1459, TotalBytes, 1460
4/24/2007 5:51:57 AM EDT (-0400 GMT), StartByte, 1460, EndByte, 1778, TotalBytes, 319
4/24/2007 5:51:57 AM EDT (-0400 GMT), StartByte, 1779, EndByte, 3238, TotalBytes, 1460
```

Fig. 2. Sample of RoyMNH0178

3.2   Case Outcome

The case was settled in June 2009. Under the terms of settlement, the case is
dismissed with prejudice and neither side is paying the other any money.

```
Shared file matches for user at address 75.68.28.28:6346

    File Name: Lionel Richie - Hello.mp3    3,994,588    3YYBJ5XUVRJ5CBEGZVBMOI2I2RTKM7BD
    File Name: Happy Hardcore - Eminem - Without me (techno remix).mp3    8,145,307
    ECANFLBNEPOBOAGY67ICSCU6BV54VT7F
    File Name: Eminem - Drips.mp3    6,856,322    TXY5Q4TH4VSKFTSIRJZSJGJ37KW772BX
    File Name: Jay-Z - The Blueprint - 09 - Never Change.mp3    5,729,094
    R2SILUFH7W6ZBEW27NTHP2UACCGUBN2J
```

Fig. 3. Sample of RoyMNH0963

```
RECEIVED PACKET: 4/24/2007 5:49:13 AM EDT (-0400 GMT)
Packet Source: 75.68.28.28:6346
Packet Destination: xxx.xxx.31.78:3245
Packet Data:
• ÛŠð‡•••CÍ‹•••E••Û•Ÿ@•r•¦²KD••Ø• N•Ê-•H‡ÇÐœÊ•P•ŷJE%••••••••••••••••••••••••C••• Ê•KD••ã••••••••UG•
02-busta rhymes-touch it  dirty .mp3•171 Kbps(VBR) 44 kHz
3:38•urn:sha1:2HVBST4FHJ3RCSAKI6RRRUSKQHLRCRW3•ÃÂCTE•¿ŝž%••••••¦»@•04-50 cent-the ski_mask way-
whoa.mp3•182 Kbps(VBR) 44 kHz 3:06•urn:sha1:STYQXPSR7WUOYONF2RGNZO73BA6KBW4M•ÃÂCTE•    Ia-•••••
ª Ž8•06-50 cent-put a hole in yo back-c4.mp3•183 Kbps(VBR) 44 kHz
2:42•urn:sha1:UJL2BCGCQVXDOO32HHQNZV2FBMRB3IOM•ÃÂCTE•Á•{+••••••¼¬^•2 Pac & Dr. Dre -- California
Love.mp3•128 Kbps 44 kHz 6:27•urn:sha1:AIQEQZ2VCPMRA3CNZX5JXXI5BN6OEX6Y•ÃÂCTE•hÀy7••••••ñ?•2 Pac
- Baby Don't Cry.mp3•128 Kbps 44 kHz 4:21•urn:sha1:CCL3CQGS2AOADXIQALYCNPVGIHLUAIBD•ÃÂCTE•="2?•
••••••s[•2 Pac - No More Pain.mp3•128 Kbps 44 kHz
```

Fig. 4. Sample of RoyMNH0964

```
4/24/2007 5:49:32 AM EDT (-0400 GMT)    Initializing analysis of user 75.68.28.28:6346
(ArchiveID: 760387)
4/24/2007 5:49:32 AM EDT (-0400 GMT)    Rule Name: Rec 2 Gnutella c
4/24/2007 5:49:32 AM EDT (-0400 GMT)    System Build Version: 1.30.3560
4/24/2007 5:49:32 AM EDT (-0400 GMT)    Scanner Name: DC014 (agent ID 323)
4/24/2007 5:49:32 AM EDT (-0400 GMT)    Total Recognized Audio: 218
4/24/2007 5:49:32 AM EDT (-0400 GMT)    Total Recognized Video: 19
4/24/2007 5:49:32 AM EDT (-0400 GMT)    Total Recognized Software: 1
4/24/2007 5:49:32 AM EDT (-0400 GMT)    Total Recognized Documents: 1
4/24/2007 5:49:32 AM EDT (-0400 GMT)    Total Recognized Files Being Distributed: 480
4/24/2007 5:49:32 AM EDT (-0400 GMT)    ================================================

4/24/2007 5:49:44 AM EDT (-0400 GMT)    Connection Type: Direct

4/24/2007 5:49:44 AM EDT (-0400 GMT)    Attempting to match files
4/24/2007 5:50:04 AM EDT (-0400 GMT)    Found Match: Lionel Richie - Hello.mp3
4/24/2007 5:50:11 AM EDT (-0400 GMT)    Found Match: Happy Hardcore - Eminem - Without me
(techno remix).mp3
4/24/2007 5:50:12 AM EDT (-0400 GMT)    Found Match: Eminem - Drips.mp3
```

Fig. 5. Sample of RoyMNH0973

```
4/24/2007 6:14:52 AM EDT (-0400 GMT)    Successful download of Jay-Z - Vol.1 In My Lifetime - 11
- Real Niggaz.mp3
                                        First Packet Received: 4/24/2007 5:54:27 AM EDT (-0400
                                        GMT)
                                        First Download Packet Received: 4/24/2007 5:54:27 AM
                                        EDT (-0400 GMT)
                                        Last Download Packet Received: 4/24/2007 5:56:28 AM EDT
                                        (-0400 GMT)
                                        Last Packet Received: 4/24/2007 5:56:22 AM EDT (-0400
                                        GMT)
                                        Bytes Completed: 4,948,606
                                        Copying file: Jay-Z - Vol.1 In My Lifetime - 11 - Real
                                        Niggaz.mp3
                                        Logging Jay-Z - Vol.1 In My Lifetime - 11 - Real
                                        Niggaz.mp3
```

Fig. 6. Sample of RoyMNH0973-1

```
Evidence for Log Ref ID: 126582810

Tracing route to 75.68.28.28...

1                  20ms
2                  20ms
3                  20ms
4                  20ms
5                  20ms
6                  20ms
7                  20ms
8                  20ms
9                  20ms
10                 20ms
11                 20ms
12                 20ms
13                 20ms
14                 20ms
15                 20ms
16                 20ms
17                 20ms
18                 20ms
19                 20ms
20                 20ms
21                 20ms
22                 20ms
23                 20ms
24                 20ms
25                 20ms
26                 20ms
27                 20ms
28                 20ms
29                 20ms
30                 20ms
Trace complete.

DNS Lookup for 75.68.28.28:

1          c-75-68-28-28.hsd1.nh.comcast.net
DNS lookup complete.
```

Fig. 7. Excerpt from RoyMNH977: failed trace route

```
Log for User at address 75.68.28.28:6346 generated on 4/24/2007 5:51:55 AM EDT (-0400 GMT)
Total Recognized Files Being Distributed: 480
-----------------------------
Total Recognized Audio Files: 218
Total Recognized Video Files: 19
Total Recognized Software Files: 1
Total Recognized Document Files: 1
-----------------------------


File Name: 02-busta rhymes-touch it  dirty .mp3
      Sha1: 2HVBST4FHJ3RCSAKI6RRRUSKQHLRCRW3

File Name: 04-50 cent-the ski mask way-whoa.mp3
      Sha1: STYQXPSR7WUOYONP2RGNZO73BA6KBW4M
```

Fig. 8. Sample of RoyMNH0978

4   Witness Trustworthiness: Human vs. "Machine"

Humans' testimony not assumed to be impartial. When human witnesses take the stand, the triers-of-fact are expected to generally consider the possibility that they, despite the oath, may render an untruthful or factually incorrect account of events and circumstances due to a conflict of interest or bias. A possibility of bias may also exist despite the witnesses' genuine desire to render a truthful testimony. Similar considerations apply to expert witnesses.

```
Log for User at address 75.68.28.28:6346 generated on 4/24/2007 5:51:55 AM EDT (-0400 GMT)
Total Recognized Files Being Distributed: 480
------------------------------
Total Recognized Audio Files: 218
Total Recognized Video Files: 19
Total Recognized Software Files: 1
Total Recognized Document Files: 1
------------------------------

File Name: 02-busta_rhymes-touch_it__dirty_.mp3 (4,674,820 bytes)

File Name: 04-50_cent-the_ski_mask_way-whoa.mp3 (4,242,342 bytes)
```

Fig. 9. Sample of RoyMNH0989

In short, a human witness' testimony is not automatically assumed to be trustworthy. Specific court procedures such as cross-examination and deposition by the opposing lawyers have evolved for challenging such testimony, in particular, for exposing any potential conflicts of interest to triers-of-fact who, based on their experiences, may or may not consider them significant enough to distrust the testimony.

Biases and conflicts of interest become particularly important in the case of expert witnesses, where triers-of-fact do not have direct and specific knowledge of the subject matter and must therefore rely on the impartiality of the expert's representations, or, in the very least, weigh the relative credibilities of the opposing expert witnesses, as exposed by cross-examination.

The illusion of "machine" impartiality. However, when computer-generated data is introduced as evidence in court, there appears to be a strong assumption that such evidence is somehow impartial and as such more trustworthy than testimony given by a human witness or an expert witness.

For example, in the *UMG vs. Lindor* case, similar to the Roy case we studied, the court seems to have assumed that the discovery request for software, source code, and algorithm were sought solely to address selection of Lindor as a defendant and *not whether the software-generated output could be distrusted or doubted as a complete and objective testimony of events "observed" or caused by the software.*

In particular, the court concluded that "the software, source code, or algorithm that MediaSentry uses to obtain screen shots is irrelevant to the question of whether the screen shots accurately depict copyright violations that allegedly took place on defendant's internet account."[8]. The court referred to MediaSentry materials as "objective data" and seems to have assumed that "the screen shots attached to the complaint fairly and accurately represent what was on a computer that allegedly was using defendant's internet account at the time of the interception"[9] – essentially because the evidence was generated and presented in a computer format!

It may be inferred that the court *assumed that the software and algorithm were infallible* and therefore fairly and accurately represented what was on [Lindor's] computer.

---

[8] UMG Recordings, Inc. v. Lindor, U.S. Dist. Court, E.D.N.Y., Docket No. 05-CV-1095 (May 16, 2008 Order on defendant's motion to compel) ("Lindor Order")
[9] Lindor Order at 5. See also Part II for discussion of Lindor.

We can only hypothesize that this comes from the perceived properties of the nature of a "machine" as something that repeatedly and reliably performs mechanical actions, or "computer" as an "idiot savant", in the public mind, as well as from daily experience with commodity electronic devices. As a society, we have been persuaded to trust machines and to rely on them, and thus to view them – despite occasional breakdowns and errors, even dramatic ones – as inherently trustworthy, all things considered.

This attitude ignores the crucial fact that computer software and systems can be and have been programmed and configured to incorporate biases and malfeasant logic that skewed their functionality and reporting output to suit the interests of their programmer or vendor. In other words, putting a bias or an expression of an ulterior motive into the form of a computer program is not unthinkable; it is not even very hard (but, as we will show, much harder to detect than to commit).

A computer scientist understands that the language of a computer program does not somehow make it impossible for the speaker to "tell a lie", intentionally or unintentionally, but, on the contrary, is as open to malfeasance or honest error (such as programmers' overconfidence) as any other kind of human expression. However, the public perception appears to be that computer technology inherently adds trustworthiness to human activities, by making it harder for the humans involved to distort reality and fall to deception or self-deception.

However, there are dramatic examples to the contrary. For example, according to news reports, the programmer of red light traffic cameras in Italy conspired "with 63 municipal police, 39 local government officials, and the managers of seven different companies in order to rig the system so that it would turn from yellow to red quicker, therefore catching more motorists."[10]. The intentional, strong bias programmed into the system was only discovered because the unusually high number of reported fines drew an official's suspicion; had the bias been less pronounced, it might have not been detected at all.

Moreover, a bias or deviation from trustworthy behavior need not be malicious or intentional. Programmers and operators may genuinely believe that their systems are operating correctly and as intended, whereas in reality they may be subject to subtle or catastrophic errors. We discuss examples of such errors in the next section.

4.1   The Need for Code Examination

We take the position that **the code of the software must be made available for detailed examination by experts**, especially in such cases as Roy, where *reliability of software-generated evidence cannot be checked or increased by using alternative resources* (e.g., by using competing products for re-testing the same forensic sample, see discussion of the reliability of repeatable vs unrepeatable tests by courts in Part II.).

---

[10] http://arstechnica.com/tech-policy/news/2009/02/
italian-red-light-cameras-rigged-with-shorter-yellow-lights.ars

One important consideration in such cases that involve *transient events* captured only by a single instance of software (and all the more so when the software is plaintiff's) is that the defendants are foreclosed from exonerating themselves by providing independent sources of evidence or causing independent tests to be performed (such as with exonerating DNA evidence). Thus we believe that special-purpose "witness" software that produces a record of transient events must itself be captured in an attestable form tied to the produced output, and its source code examined as explained below.

In cases where a possible conflict of interest is involved (e.g., when the software vendor might profit from a false positive bias or "overdetection" of violations) the code examination must be conducted in great detail to exclude the possibility of subtle bugs resulting in such bias. Although not easy or cheap, such analysis is effective and can be effectively taught (cf. "Hack-the-vote" project [1], in which students at Rice University competed in introducing and detecting such biases into e-voting software).

The Daubert criteria connection to trustworthiness examination of code. Federal courts apply the "Daubert standards" (discussed in Part II) to admissibility of expert testimony. Considering that autonomous evidence-producing software includes and represents an expression of expert domain knowledge, an analogy can be drawn between the goals of these standards and of code examination for trustworthiness.

Namely, this trustworthiness examination of software should establish:

- *absence of bias*, as discussed above;
- *competence* of the programmers – which can only be conclusively judged via a source code review, the long "invisibility" and subsequent impact of flaws left in legacy binaries by less that competent programmers being notorious;
- *methodology's* reliability – even if competently programmed, the program's algorithms themselves may be flawed.

We briefly discuss the second and third items in the following section, to show that even in the absence of any malicious intent or negligence the trustworthiness of software is not assured. We note that courts have ordered code review in several cases, e.g., State vs. Chun, as discussed in Part II.

4.2   Reasons to Distrust Computer Programs

Many researchers have struggled to come up with techniques for answering the following two questions.

1. Can a computer program be trusted to behave in the desired way?
2. Did a certain computer program produce a certain output?

There are several reasons these problems are hard.

First, programs frequently contain bugs that are hard to find through code inspection (and that may not be detectable without code inspection). An array of techniques and tools have been designed to automatically inspect source code of programs. These techniques and tools range from checkers that detect simple known problems (such as the UNIX utility lint, which, among other things, checks C code for "=" used instead of "==") to *model checkers*, such as SPIN [2], designed for the purpose of detecting concurrency problems when multiple processes interact.

Although these checkers are very useful in detecting certain sets of problems, manual code inspection remains the only way that can, in theory, check for all possible failures. In practice, however, such an exhaustive inspection typically has prohibitive time costs and is likely to overlook the more complicated problems. Many bugs in open source software have existed for months or years, despite examination by the open source community. Complicated attacks on complicated algorithms are generally unpredictable (since, if they were predictable, they would not have been ignored when the algorithms were designed).

Second, the programmers may have made implicit (and incorrect) assumptions about the environment in which the program would be run. Cases where such assumptions led to real-world failures are described in nearly every issue of RISKS digest.

Third, the program may have either been malicious from the start or subverted by an attacker. If the program was modified or replaced, code examination would be of little use in deciding on its trustworthiness.

Finally, code inspection may be of no use if the compiler, the interpreter, or the OS itself is suspect, as Ken Thompson, one of the original developers of UNIX, pointed out in his Turing award lecture [3]. As a demonstration of this idea, Ken Thompson suggested building a compiler that would take source code of a legitimate program and compile it, adding a backdoor. If someone attempted to replace the malicious compiler, he would have to compile the new compiler using the malicious compiler, and the malicious compiler would turn the new compiler malicious as well.

The above considerations suggest that the question of whether a program can be trusted can not be answered lightly.

4.3   Beyond Code Examination

Further, we believe that code examination alone does not by itself assure the trustworthiness of *an output presented as evidence*. At least the following additional conditions must be assured:

1. the correctness of external inputs of interest at the time of the output's generation, such as the *wall clock time* needed to establish the events' timeline, can be attested, in particular,
2. the configuration of the platform, the operating systems, and of supporting software can be attested, and
3. the specific version of the code must be linkable with the particular evidentiary output.

We believe that the platform on which such software is to be run must be able to **attest** the above properties. In particular, it must be able to attest the platform's configuration at the time of the evidence generation, as well as measure the running version of the software at that time.

5   The Need for Attesting Configuration

In this section we discuss the two fundamental challenges of ensuring the trust-worthiness of the evidence-generating system *at the time when autonomous software generates evidence*, a point important for legal analysis. We argue that on a Trusted Computing platform, this issue can and should be addressed by *attestation of the system's configuration*.

Broadly speaking, such attestation is necessary to argue that the channels over which the system receives external, trustworthiness-critical inputs are themselves not compromised or misconfigured, and are not a source of errors introduced into the software's operation.

5.1   Ensuring Accurate Wall Clock Time

An accurate *timeline* is critical to many kinds of both criminal and civil cases. Prosecution's versions of the timeline are routinely contested by the defense. Forensic specialists, in particular, are advised to keep accurate, timed records of their activities.

Computer-generated evidence will almost certainly contain timestamps; in the Roy case, the timestamp of the alleged filesharing activities was one of the two principal elements of the subpoena that directed the ISP to name the defendant and thus subject her to a considerable invasion of privacy and other hardships.

Thus, a natural question to ask is, **"How trustworthy are computer-generated timestamps?"** The answer is common wisdom among computer scientists: not very trustworthy, *unless* either a rigorous clock synchronization mechanism is in place or the system has the benefit of a high-precision external clock (which may synchronize with the true wall clock time by its own means such as GPS or the atomic clock time signal).

It should be noted that when – as it was in the Roy case – electronic evidence involves correlation of events by **two** clock readings (e.g., that of the evidence-generating software/platform and of an ISP's DHCP log server), **both** clocks should be held to the same trustworthiness standards. In this article we concentrate on the requirements to the former, but it should be understood that the latter may also be the source of disastrous timeline errors. For example innocent customers' homes have been reportedly raided by the police due to an ISP's timestamp handling errors "blamed on confusion ... over international time zones"[11], mostly likely due to a software error.[12]

---

[11] http://www.theregister.co.uk/2009/07/23/intercept_commisisoner/

[12] Whereas the article quotes a UK government official as saying that "better checks and balances have been put in place", the fault appears to be with the algorithm or process for handling and correlating the timing data, rather than with actual or potential abuse of power.

Clock synchronization is a research problem. Clock time synchronization in computers across networks is an important practical and research problem and should not be taken for granted. Dedicated network protocols such as the Network Time Protocol (NTP)[13] are used to synchronize computer system time with dedicated *time servers* trusted to have the accurate time (maintained, e.g., by the US NIST). Network security professionals stress the importance of correct network time synchronization.[14]

The problem of time synchronization is far from trivial. An MIT's Media Lab 1999 survey of NTP network time servers concluded that "only 28% of the Internet based stratum 1 clocks actually appears to be useful", and over a third had deviations of over 10 seconds, and some deviated by hours, days, and even years.[15]

Even though network time keeping practices have improved over the years, the issue still attracts attention of researchers and practitioners: the original survey quoted above was followed by at least five since.[16]

Trustworthiness of timestamps must be attested. The above considerations suggest that special steps must be taken to assure the correctness of timestamps on a platform where an evidence-producing software runs, at the time it runs. Since commodity platforms possess neither high quality clocks nor built-in means of synchronization with superior clocks, the actual source of correct time for a commodity platform must be *external*.

This external clock can be either a directly connected device, or a network-accessible time authority (e.g., via NTP). In either case, **the means of synchronization must be configured as a part of the OS configuration process,** and **the configuration active at the point of evidence generation must be attested.**

These requirements, which become self-evident after the above consideration, can be viewed as a design guideline for Trusted Computing platforms and software stacks, one that these architectures should be well-equipped to handle.

5.2 Ensuring Correct View of the Network

Whenever software-generated evidence involves data derived from its network connections – be it the primary subject-matter of its reports, or simply its NTP functionality – the trustworthiness of a system running this software crucially depends on the correctness of its network configuration.

This can be seen from the fact that mapping out and compromising the target systems' *trust relationships* is the methodological foundation of network security assessment and penetration testing (and constitutes core functionality of classic network security tools as *Nmap*, *Nessus*, and *Core Impact*). Moreover, man-in-the-middle attacks on these relationship are the mainstay of attack

---

[13] http://www.ntp.org

[14] http://www.linuxdevcenter.com/pub/a/linux/2003/01/02/ntp.html

[15] Nelson Minar, *A Survey of the NTP Network*, http://www.eecis.udel.edu/~mills/database/reports/ntp-survey99-minar.pdf

[16] See, e.g., http://www.ntpsurvey.arauc.br/globecom-ntp-paper.pdf

trees and the reason why vulnerabilities in protocols used to establish network trust such as DNS attract great attention and scrutiny among computer security practitioners.[17]

In the Roy evidence, the evidence-generating system apparently attempted to test the network path taken by the packets, by performing a standard "traceroute" action. However, the results shown in Figure 7 cannot be considered realistic – they neither contain any IP addresses or host names of intermediate hops, nor show realistic hop timings even if we assume that the per-hop tests were actually performed, as it is entirely unrealistic to expect uniform 20ms times on each hop.

This raises the question of whether other actions of the software suffered from whatever caused the apparent failure of the route tracing. This illustrates our point that **full, attested network configuration** is necessary for judging the evidence-generating system's trustworthiness.

6   Conclusion and Challenges

Even though software-generated evidence tends to be regarded as inherently trustworthy by courts, we argue that a number of hard technical problems must be solved in order for such evidence to actually become trustworthy. We believe that the research community must rise to the challenge presented by these inter-related technical, legal, and sociological issues, and develop the – currently lacking – trustworthiness criteria based on the state-of-the-art trustworthy computing approaches.

Part II: Software and Hardware as Witnesses in Trial

7   The Law's Approach to Machines, Software, and Their Reports as Witnesses

A constitutional, country-wide, specific rule has yet to be clearly established in the United States on the issue of the admissibility of, reliability of, and cross-examination of the validity of the underlying theory or algorithm contained in software used as evidence, the machine used to create a report, the source code used on the machine, or the humans operating, maintaining, and otherwise in contact with the machine and source code. However, it can be concluded that, by and large, defendants in the United States will have to demonstrate their need to obtain pre-trial records and testimony on these people, things, and topics and may bear the initial burden in challenging their admission into evidence at trial. A review of cases admitting evidence and expert testimony based on evidence reveals that distrust of the machines used to create evidence and the software running on these machines is a fairly rare commodity, despite technical challenges to accuracy of such machines and their source code.

---

[17] E.g., Dan Kaminsky's report of a vulnerability in DNS at BlackHat 2007.

Defendants in criminal cases benefit from rights under the Bill of Rights of the U.S. Constitution, including, relevant to this discussion, the Sixth Amendment right to confront witnesses against them, known as the Confrontation Clause. The Sixth Amendment provides in relevant part as follows: "In all criminal prosecutions, the accused shall enjoy the right . . . to be confronted with the witnesses against him." U.S. Const., Amend. VI. This constitutional right is available whether the defendant in a criminal case is in state or federal court[18]. The Confrontation Clause - which requires the production of the witness against a defendant at the trial on the criminal matter so that that witness may be cross-examined – represents one of many ways to test the reliability of evidence, but it is the only method guaranteed to defendants. In short, if the Confrontation Clause is implicated, the defendant's task in challenging the evidence is made easier than if the defendant must rely on the rules of evidence, discussed infra.

If the Confrontation Clause is triggered, the prosecution must produce at trial[19] the witness who made the out-of-court statement so that that witness may be cross-examined by the defendant. Failure to do so renders the out-of-court statement inadmissible.[20] The Crawford case provides an example of exclusion of an out-of-court statement. Michael Crawford stabbed a man named Kenneth Lee who allegedly tried to rape Mr. Crawford's wife Sylvia earlier that night. Michael Crawford was convicted of assault with a deadly weapon after the prosecution played for the jury a tape-recorded statement by Mrs. Crawford, recorded immediately after the incident during police interrogation, which discredited Mr. Crawford's argument that he acted in self-defense. Before the case came to the U.S. Supreme Court, the Washington Supreme Court upheld Mr. Crawford's conviction and had determined that the recorded statement was reliable.[21] Due to the marital privilege, Mrs. Crawford was unavailable to testify at trial and unavailable to be cross-examined by the defendant outside of trial. The U.S. Supreme Court held that the recorded statement of Mrs. Crawford, made out-of-court, should not have been admitted as evidence since it was a testimonial statement[22] and Mr. Crawford would not have an opportunity to

---

[18] See Melendez-Diaz v. Massachusetts, ___ U.S. ___, 129 S.Ct. 2527 (2009) (citing Pointer v. Texas, 380 U.S. 400, 403 (1965) for the proposition that the Sixth Amendment is applicable to the States via the Fourteenth Amendment).

[19] If the prosecution cannot produce at trial the testimonial witness against the defendant, the out-of-court statement by that witness is inadmissible unless - generally speaking – the prosecution establishes that the witness is unavailable to testify and the defendant has had an opportunity to cross-examine the witness. Crawford v. Washington, 541 U.S. 36, 5457 (2004).

[20] See prior footnote.

[21] State v. Crawford, 54 P.3d 656, 663 (2002) (overturning the lower court's decision that the statement was unreliable, State v. Crawford, 107 Wash.App. 1025 (Wash.App. Div. 2 2001)).

[22] The out-of-court testimonial statement may be either a sworn document or unsworn and will still invoke the Confrontation Clause requirement. Crawford v. Washington, 541 U.S. 36, 52, n.3 (2004).

cross-examine Mrs. Crawford during trial, in violation of his constitutional right under the Confrontation Clause.

Citing an 1828 dictionary to bolster the U.S. Constitution's framer' intent in light of a series of English cases, U.S. Supreme Court Justice Antonin Scalia, writing the majority opinion in Crawford v. Washington, 541 U.S. 36 (2004), equated the meaning of "witnesses" to be those who "bear testimony."[23] Triggering of the Confrontation Clause is determined based on whether an out-of-court statement is testimonial or non-testimonial. "Testimony" was defined in the 1828 dictionary as follows: "'[a] solemn declaration or affirmation made for the purpose of establishing or proving some fact.' "[24]

Being a human being providing a statement during police interrogation, Sylvia Crawford was easy to identify as a witness bearing testimony, generating a constitutional requirement that she, in essence, be produced as a witness at trial. Whether that constitutional requirement applies to machines, operators of machines, and/or the makers of the machines and their source code remains an open question.

The recent U.S. Supreme Court case Melendez-Diaz v. Massachusetts, the majority opinion for which was also written by Justice Scalia, held that the analyst in the state forensic crime lab who provided a certificate that a particular substance was cocaine must be brought to trial by prosecutors (to enable cross-examination by the defendant) in order to render his certificate of the substance admissible. Under prior law, such lab technician certificates were considered reliable, and therefore not subject to the method of testing that reliability found in the Confrontation Clause, namely, cross-examination of the human signing the certificate presumably reporting results following the use of lab equipment that need be calibrated, operated correctly, possibly with a series of repeated tests, and possibly confirmed with a alternative test method reflecting an alternative underlying principle or algorithm to test for cocaine. See id. at 2537-38 (speculation as to the lab technician's method and techniques in reaching the reported conclusion). The analyst's actions, choice of equipment and tests to use, and methodology were unknown in this case, because none of that information had been admitted; merely the certificate stating the substance was cocaine was admitted in the trial court.

The Melendez-Diaz court eschewed the contrary views that reliability of such lab results need not be tested. Citing a 2009 report prepared by the National Academy of Sciences for a number of error-provoking factors present with such testing, the court found that "[f]orensic evidence is not uniquely immune from the risk of manipulation." Id. at 2536 (citing National Research Council of the National Academies, Strengthening Forensic Science in the United States: A Path Forward (Prepublication Copy Feb. 2009)). Some of the findings of the report were that labs are not neutral, but administered by law enforcement personnel, providing incentive to alter evidence and that the "[f]orensic science

---

[23] Crawford v. Washington, 541 U.S. 36, 51 (2004) (citing 2 N. Webster, An American Dictionary of the English Language (1828)).

[24] Id.

system . . . has serious problems." The latter problem involves lack of competency or failure to exercise sound judgment by the analyst. The court cited a study of wrongful, overturned convictions which "concluded that invalid forensic testimony contributed to convictions in 60% of cases." Id. at 2537 (citing Garrett & Neufeld, Invalid Forensic Science Testimony and Wrongful Convictions, 95 Va. L.Rev. 1, 14 (2009)). The court also cited the National Academy of Sciences report for the proposition that, among other information crucial to creating reliable results, sound methodologies in published material are lacking across forensic science disciplines, resulting in, among other problems, unreliability in even commonly used forensic tests such as fingerprinting and firearms analysis. Id. at 2538. The National Academy of Sciences report suggests that the development of a sound methodology would require published material leading to a general acceptability of the methodology, with published material available to analysis with regard to techniques, research, and types and numbers of potential errors. Id.

In the case U.S. v. Washington, 498 F.3d 225 (4th Cir. 2007), cert. den'd., 129 S. Ct. 2856 (2009[25]), the Fourth Circuit declined to determine that data generated by a lab machine was testimonial. The machinery consisted of a Hewlett Packard chromatograph and a computer using Hewlett Packard ChemStation software. The Fourth Circuit upheld the prosecution's presentation at trial of the supervising director of the lab to interpret the machine's data report and neither the three lab technicians who used the machinery and software nor the machines themselves (not discussing the possibility to cross-examine Hewlett Packard's software engineers). The court pointed out that the Confrontation Clause's cross-examination requirement applies to "(human) 'witnesses.'" Id. at 230, n.1.

There appears to be no right under the Confrontation Clause for a defendant in a criminal case to cross-examine the software developers or machine designers. See, e.g. U.S. v. Washington, discussed supra (and cases cited therein holding, respectively, that time stamp on fax print out, header on print out of Internet images, and computerized telephone trace report are not testimonial statements); see also State v. Chun, 943 A.2d 114, 148 (NJ 2008) (determining that the print-out from a breath alcohol measurement device and associated software and hardware is not a testimonial statement). However, recent U.S. Supreme Court precedent acknowledges defendants' constitutional right to cross-examine analysts using devices and software. It is unclear whether such a right can be extended to software programmers and, if so, under what circumstances.

Once the realm of constitutional protections is left, the burdens on the defendant to find evidence bearing on the reliability of the evidence increase. For example, while a prosecutor bears the burden to prove the chain of custody for evidence, he need not prove every step in the chain of custody, and any lacking evidence merely goes to the weight that may be given to the evidence, not to the admissibility of the evidence.

---

[25] The U.S. Supreme Court denied certiorari, declining to review the Fourth Circuit's decision in this case, four days after it issued its opinion in Melendez-Diaz v. Massachusetts, __ U.S. __, 129 S. Ct. 2527 (2009).

One of the gatekeeping tools available to defendants to prevent unreliable evidence from becoming admissible is the hearsay rule found in the rules of evidence.[26] "'Hearsay' is a statement, other than one made by the declarant while testifying at the trial or hearing, offered in evidence to prove the truth of the matter asserted." Fed. R. of Ev. Rule 801(c). "A 'declarant' is a person . . ." Fed. R. of Ev. Rule 801(b). Generally speaking, hearsay is inadmissible. Fed. R. of Ev. Rule 802. Excepted from the hearsay rule are records made in the regular course of business, Rule 803(6) and reports prepared by public offices pursuant to a duty to so report except for law enforcement personnel reports for criminal cases, Rule 803(8). Also excepted from the hearsay rule are statements containing material facts which may not otherwise be procured through reasonable efforts and have equivalent circumstantial guarantees of trustworthiness. Rule 807. Data reports - so long as they may not be considered "testimonial" – are often sought to be admitted into evidence under the business records exception (and sometimes other exceptions) to the hearsay rule. State v. Chun, 943 A.2d 114, 166 (NJ 2008) (also indicating that machines do not have an intent to generate a false positive); see Thomas v. U.S., 914 A.2d 1, 13 (D.C. 2006); see also Crawford v. Washington, 541 U.S. 36 (2004).

Given the possible interplay between the Confrontation Clause and the business records exception to the hearsay rule, prosecutors should separate testimonial (i.e. a solemn affirmation made for the purpose of establishing or proving a fact) statements, which are inadmissible in criminal cases without the defendant's ability to cross-examine the witness, from data logs prepared in the ordinary course of business which are designed to render a conclusion at the time the data is generated. A continuum of types of reports and logs could be envisioned which leads to a difficulty to deciding at what point a piece of evidence is a data log and at what point it is a testimonial statement. This struggle is apparent in the cases, and yet a review of the cases fails to illuminate where the line dividing the two will gel.

Also, data logs prepared in anticipation or in preparation for litigation generally do not fall within an exception to the hearsay rule, see Thomas v. U.S., 914 A.2d 1, 13 (D.C. 2006). Consequently, defendants may subpoena witnesses to testify on the facts surrounding production of the data logs so long as the defendant establishes a lack of reliability justifying the subpoena. See State v. Chun,

---

[26] Each court has its own rules governing admissibility of evidence into trial. Federal courts follow the Federal Rules of Evidence and state courts are free to adopt their own rules of evidence. Generally speaking, however, state rules of evidence closely follow the Federal Rules of Evidence. Much of the discussion about admissibility of evidence revolves around the interpretation of the rules of evidence, in particular, interpretation of the hearsay rule and expert testimony rule. Although state courts may use federal decisions interpreting the Federal Rules of Evidence as guidance for interpreting their state rules of evidence, see, e.g., N.H. Rules of Ev., Rule 102, their decision - except where rights granted by the U.S. Constitution control - need not follow the federal decision. See, e.g., Alice B. Lustre, J.D., Post-Daubert Standards for Admissibility of Scientific and Other Expert Evidence in State Courts, 90 ALR5th 453 (2001).

943 A.2d 114, 166 (NJ 2008). This shift of burden can be difficult to overcome. See UMG Recordings, Inc. v. Lindor, U.S. Dist. Court, E.D.N.Y., Docket No. 05-CV-1095 (May 16, 2008 Order preliminarily denying defendant's motion to compel production of source code by MediaSentry in allegedly detecting allegedly unlawful copyright infringement).

In the area of source code and hardware design matters, defendants bear the additional difficulty of needing to overcome the creator's allegations that the code/design is proprietary and consequent unwillingness to produce the code/design. In both State v. Chun and UMG v. Lindor, the source code developer initially fought discovery of source code due to the allegedly proprietary nature of the code. In Chun, a case involving source code used in Alcotest, a device and software used to detect blood alcohol level for use in driving while intoxicated cases, the German code developer did produce the code, which was subsequently evaluated by defendants' experts, resulting eventually in a requirement to modify the code to correct errors. By contrast, the software code used to allegedly detect and allegedly produce accurate screen shots of the defendant's computer was not produced in the Lindor case. Even if it had been, the code involved would have been subject to a confidentiality restriction, such that evaluation of the code had to occur on an (expensive, time-consuming, and inefficient) defendant-by-defendant, case-by-case basis. Unlike the code evaluation conducted by experts in the public eye in the Chun case, the code used in the Lindor case - if the court had compelled its discovery, which it did not – could not be tested for reliability in such a way that subsequent defendants could use it.

When determining whether expert testimony is admissible, reliability of the methodology used by the expert is crucial to the decision. See Daubert v. Merrell Dow Pharmaceuticals, Inc., 509 U.S. 579 (1993). One of the key ways to determine whether a new technology's methodology is reliable is whether it is generally accepted after an opportunity for peer review and has reliable results. See id. If no duplication of the forensic testing by another methodology is possible (such as is the case in the alleged detection of peer-to-peer network sharing of copyrightable works, which occurs at a specific instant in time and in the case of deterioration of samples, such as blood alcohol content samples and autopsies (which may not be repeated)[27]), reliability of methodology is difficult to determine.

Despite these concerns, some courts have admitted computer forensic evidence. See, e.g., UMG Recordings, Inc. v. Lindor, 531 F.Supp.2d 453 (2007) (admitting opinion of plaintiff's expert on facts bearing on copyright infringement claim despite failure of the methodology to comport with Daubert factors in light of expert's own testimony that others in the industry would interpret the data the same and court's conclusion that data relied upon by expert was "objective data" provided by plaintiffs' private investigator and ISP records); Galaxy Computer Servs., Inc. v. Baker, 325 B.R. 544 (E.D. Va. 2005) (admitting expert testimony that former officers of corporation deleted files from

---

[27] Crawford, at n.5.

computer after conspiracy and other claims were brought against them following specially-educated and seasoned computer forensic specialist's analysis of hard drives); see also Marjorie A. Shields, J.D., Admissibility of Computer Forensic Testimony, 40 ALR6th 355 (2008) (describing eight cases where the computer forensic testimony was admitted and only one where the testimony was not admitted; in the case where the testimony was not admitted, the alleged expert was unable to even open the AVI files that he was supposedly hired to opine did not exist and were not pornographic (this inability to open the files following his initial inability to locate the files on the computer)). This suggests that in practice there is a low threshold for computer forensic evidence, which places significant burdens on defendants to challenge reliability of this evidence. See also David L. Faigman, David H. Kaye, Michael J. Saks, Joseph Sanders, 5 Modern Scientific Evidence: The Law and Science of Expert Testimony 41:13 (Nov. 2009) (citing State v. Bastos, 985 So.2d 37 (Fla. Dist. Ct. App. 3d Dist. 2008), in which the court refused to order a turnover of source code absent a particularized showing of discrepancy; People v. Robinson, 53 A.D.3d 63, 860 N.Y.S.2d 159 (2d Dept. 2008) (similar); State v. Underdahl, 749 N.W.2d 117 (Minn. Ct. App. 2008) (similar)); but see State v. Chun, supra (allowing thorough evaluation of source code); but see House v. Com, 2008 WL 162212 (Ky. Ct. App. 2008) (ordering disclosure of source code).

In conclusion, while the recent expansion of rights to defendants in criminal cases to require prosecutors to bring lab analysts into court for cross-examination and to produce documents establishing the proper calibration of machines and training of operators of machines is a positive step in the testing of reliability of computer-aided forensic evidence and resulting expert testimony, these rights have yet to gain much benefit for defendants in civil cases faced with the admissibility of evidence and expert opinion that very possibly lack peer-tested methodologies, trustworthiness, and/or competency. A survey of civil court cases suggests a lenience toward admitting evidence and opinions and allowing the jury to sort out the weight to be afforded, which can unfavorable prejudice defendants in civil cases. When a defendant in a civil case can end up with a verdict of $1.92 million[28] for sharing 24 copyrighted songs on a peer-to-peer network, civil cases begin to look as if they should require the reliability and confrontation standards available to defendants in criminal cases.

Acknowledgements

The first and the third author would like to thank Sean Smith, Denise Anthony, and Thomas Candon, who encouraged our interest in social aspects of security.

---

[28] "Music Labels Win $2 Million in Web Case," New York Times (June 18, 2009). The verdict was later reduced to $54,000. "Judge slashes "monstrous" P2P award by 97% to $54,000", Nate Anderson, Ars Technica (January 22, 2010), http://arstechnica.com/tech-policy/news/2010/01/judge-slashes-monstrous-jammie-thomas-p2p-award-by-35x.ars.

We are also grateful to our colleagues at Dartmouth's PKI/Trust Lab and the Institute for Security, Technology, and Society for their support.

The second author would like to acknowledge the support of her colleagues and the administration at Franklin Pierce Law Center.

We would like to thank Ray Beckerman and anonymous TRUST reviewers for helpful comments.

References

1. Bannet, J., Price, D.W., Rudys, A., Singer, J., Wallach, D.S.: Hack-a-vote: Demonstrating security issues with electronic voting systems. IEEE Security and Privacy Magazine 2(1), 32–37 (2004)
2. Holzmann, G.J., et al.: The model checker SPIN. IEEE Transactions on software engineering 23(5), 279–295 (1997)
3. Thompson, K.: Reflections on trusting trust. In: ACM Turing award lectures, p. 1983. ACM, New York (2007)

Token-Based Cloud Computing*

Secure Outsourcing of Data and Arbitrary Computations with Lower Latency

Ahmad-Reza Sadeghi, Thomas Schneider, and Marcel Winandy

Horst Görtz Institute for IT-Security, Ruhr-University Bochum, Germany
{ahmad.sadeghi,thomas.schneider,marcel.winandy}@trust.rub.de

Abstract. Secure outsourcing of computation to an untrusted (cloud) service provider is becoming more and more important. Pure cryptographic solutions based on fully homomorphic and verifiable encryption, recently proposed, are promising but suffer from very high latency. Other proposals perform the whole computation on tamper-proof hardware and usually suffer from the the same problem. Trusted computing (TC) is another promising approach that uses trusted software and hardware components on computing platforms to provide useful mechanisms such as attestation allowing the data owner to verify the integrity of the cloud and its computation. However, on the one hand these solutions require trust in hardware (CPU, trusted computing modules) that are under the physical control of the cloud provider, and on the other hand they still have to face the challenge of run-time attestation.

In this paper we focus on applications where the latency of the computation should be minimized, i.e., the time from submitting the query until receiving the outcome of the computation should be as small as possible. To achieve this we show how to combine a trusted hardware token (e.g., a cryptographic coprocessor or provided by the customer) with Secure Function Evaluation (SFE) to compute arbitrary functions on secret (encrypted) data where the computation leaks no information and is verifiable. The token is used in the setup phase only whereas in the time-critical online phase the cloud computes the encrypted function on encrypted data using symmetric encryption primitives only and without any interaction with other entities.

Keywords: Cloud Computing, Hardware Token, Outsourcing.

1 Introduction

Enterprises and other organizations often have to store and operate on a huge amount of data. Cloud computing offers infrastructure and computational services on demand for various customers on shared resources. Services that are offered range from infrastructure services such as Amazon EC2 (computation) [1]

---

* Supported by EU FP7 projects CACE and UNIQUE, and ECRYPT II.

A. Acquisti, S.W. Smith, and A.-R. Sadeghi (Eds.): TRUST 2010, LNCS 6101, pp. 417–429, 2010.

or S3 (storage) [2], over platform services such as Google App Engine [13] or Microsoft's database service SQL Azure [21], to software services such as outsourced customer relationship management applications by Salesforce.com.

While sharing IT infrastructure in cloud computing is cost-efficient and provides more flexibility for the clients, it introduces security risks organizations have to deal with in order to isolate their data from other cloud clients and to fulfill confidentiality and integrity demands. Moreover, since the IT infrastructure is now under control of the cloud provider, the customer has not only to trust the security mechanisms and configuration of the cloud provider, but also the cloud provider itself. When data and computation is outsourced to the cloud, prominent security risks are: malicious code that is running on the cloud infrastructure could manipulate computation and force wrong results or steal data; personnel of the cloud provider could misuse their capabilities and leak data; and vulnerabilities in the shared resources could lead to data leakage or manipulated computation [8]. In general, important requirements of cloud clients are that their data is processed in a confidential way (*confidentiality*), and that their data and computation was processed in the expected way and has not been tampered with (*integrity and verifiability*).

Secure outsourcing of *arbitrary* computation and data storage is particularly difficult to fulfill if a cloud client does not trust the cloud provider at all. There are proposals for cryptographic methods which allow to perform specific computations on encrypted data [3], or to securely and verifiably outsource storage [18]. Arbitrary computation on confidential data can be achieved with fully homomorphic encryption [12], in combination with garbled circuits [30] for verifiability [11]. While this cryptographic scheme can fulfill the aforementioned requirements, it is currently not usable in practice due to its low efficiency as we discuss later in §4.2.

Another line of works tries to solve these problems by establishing trusted execution environments where the cloud client can verify the integrity of the software and the configuration of the cloud provider's hardware platform. This requires, however, secure software such as secure hypervisors for policy enforcement and attestation mechanisms for integrity verification. The use of trusted computing-based remote attestation in the cloud scenario was recently discussed in [7]. Trusted Virtual Domains [5,6] are one approach that combines trusted computing, secure hypervisors, and policy enforcement of information flow within and between domains of virtual machines. However, those approaches require trust in a non-negligible amount of hardware (e.g., CPU, Trusted Platform Module (TPM) [29]) which are under the physical control of the cloud provider. According to the specification of the Trusted Computing Group, the TPM is not designed to protect against hardware attacks, but provides a shielded location to protect keys. However, the TPM cannot perform arbitrary secure computations on data. It can protect cryptographic keys and perform only pre-defined cryptographic operations like encryption, decryption, and signature creation. In particular, if data should be encrypted it must be provided in plaintext to the TPM, and if data should be decrypted it will be given in plaintext as output.

Unfortunately, the TPM cannot be instructed to decrypt data internally, perform computations on the data, and encrypt it again before returning the output. A virtualized TPM [4] that is executed in software could be enhanced with additional functionality (see, e.g., [25]). However, such software running on the CPU has access to unencrypted data at some point to compute on it. Hence, if the cloud provider is malicious and uses specifically manipulated hardware, confidentiality and verifiability cannot be guaranteed by using trusted computing.

A hardware token which is tamper-proof against physical attacks but can perform arbitrary computations would enable the cloud client to perform confidential and verifiable computation on the cloud provider's site, given that the client trust the manufacturer of the token that it does not leak any information to the provider. For example, secure coprocessors [27,31] are tamper-proof active programmable devices that are attached to an untrusted computer in order to perform security-critical operations or to allow to establish a trusted channel through untrusted networks and hardware devices to a trusted software program running inside the secure coprocessor. This can be used to protect sensitive computation from insider attacks at the cloud provider [17]. If cloud providers offer such tokens produced by trustworthy third-party manufacturers, or offer interfaces to attach hardware tokens provided by clients to their infrastructure (and by assuming hardware is really tamper-proof), cloud clients could perform their sensitive computations inside those tokens. Data can be stored encrypted outside the token in cloud storage while decryption keys are stored in shielded locations of the trusted tokens.

The token based approach is reasonable because both, cryptographic coprocessors and standardized interfaces (e.g., smartcard readers or PCI extension boards) exist that can be used for such tokens. Of course, for trust reasons, the token vendor should not be the same as the cloud provider. However, the whole security-critical computation takes place in the token. Hence, such computation is not really outsourced to the cloud because the function is computed within the token. Some applications, however, require fast replies to queries which cannot be computed online within the tamper-proof token. For example, queries in personal health records or payroll databases may occur not very frequently, but need to be processed very fast while privacy of the data should be preserved.

In this paper, we focus on cloud application scenarios where private queries to the outsourced data have to be processed and answered with low latency.

Our Contributions and Outline. First we introduce our model for secure verifiable outsourcing of data and *arbitrary* computations thereon in §2.1. Cryptographic primitives and preliminaries are given in §3. In §4 we present architectures to instantiate our model: The first architecture computes the function within a tamper-proof hardware token (§4.1) and the second architecture is based on fully homomorphic encryption (§4.2).

The main technical contribution of our paper is a third architecture (§4.3) that combines the advantages of the previous architectures and overcomes their respective disadvantages. Our solution deploys a resource constrained tamper-proof hardware token in the setup pre-processing phase. Then, in the online phase only symmetric cryptographic operations are performed in parallel within the cloud without further interaction with the token.

In particular, we adopt the embedded secure function evaluation protocol of [16] to the large-scale cloud-computing scenario.

Finally, in §5 we compare the performance of all three proposed architectures and show that our scheme allows secure verifiable outsourcing of data and *arbitrary* computations thereon with low latency.

2   Model for Secure Outsourcing of Data and Arbitrary Computations

We consider the model shown in Fig. 1 that allows a client C to verifiably and securely outsource a database D and computations thereon to an untrusted (cloud) service provider S.

A client C (e.g., a company) wants to securely outsource data D and computation of a function f (represented as a boolean circuit) thereon to an untrusted service provider S who offers access to (cloud) storage services and to (cloud) computation services. Example applications include outsourcing of medical data, log files or payrolls and computing arbitrary statistics or searches on the outsourced data. In addition, the evaluation of f can depend on a session-specific private query x_i of C resulting in the response $y_i = f(x_i, D)$. However, S should be prevented from learning or modifying D or x_i (*confidentiality and integrity*) or to compute f incorrectly (*verifiability*).[1] Any cheating attempts of a malicious S who tries to deviate from the protocol should be detected by C with overwhelming probability where C outputs the special failure symbol $\perp$.[2]

While this scenario can be easily solved for a restricted class of functions (e.g., private search of a keyword x_i using searchable encryption [18]), we consider the general case of arbitrary functions f. Due to the large size of D (e.g., a database) and/or the computational complexity of f, it is not possible to securely outsource D to S only and let C compute f after retrieving D from S. Instead, the confidentiality and integrity of the outsourced data D has to be protected while at the same time secure computations on D need to be performed at S *without* interaction with C.

2.1   Tamper-Proof Hardware Token $\mathcal{T}$

To improve the efficiency of the secure computation, our model additionally allows that C uses a *tamper-proof hardware token* $\mathcal{T}$, integrated into the infrastructure of S, that is capable of performing computations on behalf of C within a shielded environment, i.e., must be guaranteed not to leak any information to S.

---

[1] S might attempt to cheat to save storage or computing resources or simply manipulate the result.

[2] As detailed in [11] it is necessary that S does not learn whether C detected an error or not to avoid that S can use this single bit of information to construct a decryption or verification oracle.

As $\mathcal{T}$ needs to be built tamper-proof and cost-effective, it will have a restricted amount of memory only. In many cases the available memory within $\mathcal{T}$ will not be sufficient to store D or intermediate values during evaluation of f. If needed, $\mathcal{T}$ might resort to additional (slow) secure external memory (e.g., [10]).

The token $\mathcal{T}$ could be instantiated with a cryptographic coprocessor built by a third-party manufacturer whom $\mathcal{C}$ trusts in a way that $\mathcal{T}$ does not leak any information to $\mathcal{S}$. A possible candidate would be the IBM Cryptographic Coprocessor 4758 or its successor 4764 which is certified under FIPS PUB 140-2 [27,15]. Such cryptographic coprocessors allow to generate secret keys internally and securely transport them to $\mathcal{C}$ or to another token for migration purposes, and authentication to verify that the intended software is executed within the shielded environment. (For details on migrating a state (key) between two trusted environments (cryptographic coprocessors) we refer to [4,25].) As such tokens based on cryptographic coprocessors can be used for multiple users in parallel, their costs amortize for service provider and users.

For extremely security critical applications where $\mathcal{C}$ does not want to trust the manufacturer of cryptographic coprocessors offered by $\mathcal{S}$, $\mathcal{C}$ can choose his own hardware manufacturer to produce the tamper-proof hardware token $\mathcal{T}$ and ship this to $\mathcal{S}$ for integration into his infrastructure. We note that this approach is similar to "server hosting" which assumes outsourcing during long periods; this somewhat contradicts the highly dynamic cloud computing paradigm where service providers can be changed easily.

3 Preliminaries

In this section we introduce the cryptographic building blocks used in the architectures presented afterwards in §4.

3.1 Encryption and Authentication

Confidentiality and authenticity of messages can be guaranteed either symmetrically (using one key) or asymmetrically (using two keys).

The symmetric case can be instantiated with a combination of symmetric encryption (e.g., AES [22]) and a message authentication code (e.g., AES-CMAC [28] or HMAC [20]). These schemes use a respective symmetric key for encryption/authentication and the same key for decryption/verification.

Alternatively, public-key cryptography (e.g., RSA or elliptic curves) allows usage of separate keys for encryption/authentication and other keys for decryption/verification. This could be used for example to construct an outsourced database to which new entries can be appended by multiple parties without using shared symmetric keys (cf. Fig. 1).

Notation. $\widehat{x}$ denotes authenticated and $\overline{x}$ encrypted and authenticated data x.

3.2 Fully Homomorphic Encryption

Fully homomorphic encryption is semantically secure public-key encryption that additionally allows computing an arbitrary function on encrypted data using

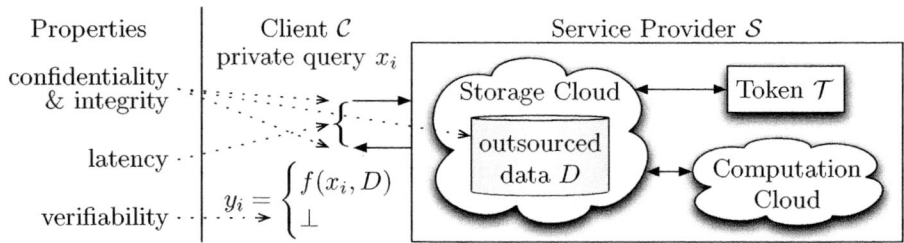

Fig. 1. Model for Secure Outsourcing of Data and Computation

the public-key only, i.e., given a ciphertext $[\![x]\!]$, a function f and the public-key pk, it is possible to compute $[\![y]\!] = \text{EVAL}_{\text{pk}}(f, [\![x]\!]) = [\![f(x)]\!]$. Constructing a homomorphic encryption scheme with polynomial overhead was a longstanding open problem. Recently, there are several proposals starting with [12] and subsequent extensions and improvements of [9,26]. Still, all these schemes employ computationally expensive public-key operations for each gate of the evaluated function and hence are capable of evaluating only very small functions on today's hardware. Recent implementation results of [26] show that even for small parameters where the multiplicative depth of the evaluated circuit is $d = 2.5$, i.e., at most two multiplications, encrypting a single bit takes 3.7s on 2.4GHz Intel Core2 (6600) CPU.

Notation. We write $[\![x]\!]$ for homomorphically encrypted data x.

3.3   Garbled Circuit (GC)

The most efficient method for secure computation of arbitrary functions known today is based on Yao's garbled circuits (GC) [30]. Compared to fully homomorphic encryption, GCs are highly efficient as they are based on symmetric cryptographic primitives only but require helper information to evaluate non-XOR gates as described below.

The main idea of GCs as shown in Fig. 2 is that the *constructor* generates an encrypted version of the function f (represented as boolean circuit), called *garbled circuit* $\widetilde{f}$. For this, he assigns to each wire W_i of f two randomly chosen garbled values $\widetilde{w}_i^0, \widetilde{w}_i^1$ that correspond to the respective values 0 and 1. Note that $\widetilde{w}_i^j$ does not reveal any information about its plain value j as both keys look random. Then, for each gate of f, the constructor creates helper information in form of a *garbled table* $\widetilde{T}_i$ that allows to decrypt only the output key from the gate's input keys (details below). The garbled circuit $\widetilde{f}$ consists of the garbled tables of all gates. Later, the *evaluator* obtains the garbled values $\widetilde{x}$ corresponding to the inputs x of the function and evaluates the garbled circuit $\widetilde{f}$ by evaluating the garbled gates one-by-one using their garbled tables. Finally, evaluator obtains the corresponding garbled output values $\widetilde{y}$ which allow the constructor to decrypt them into the corresponding plain output $y = f(x)$.

Notation. We write $\widetilde{x}$ for the garbled value corresponding to x and $\widetilde{f}$ for the garbled circuit of function f. Evaluation of $\widetilde{f}$ on garbled input $\widetilde{x}$ is written as $\widetilde{y} = \widetilde{f}(\widetilde{x})$.

Security and Verifiability of GCs. GCs are secure even against malicious evaluator (cf. [14]) and demonstration of valid output keys implicitly proves that the computation was performed correctly (cf. [11]). A fundamental property of GCs is that they can be evaluated only once, i.e., for each evaluation a new GC must be generated.

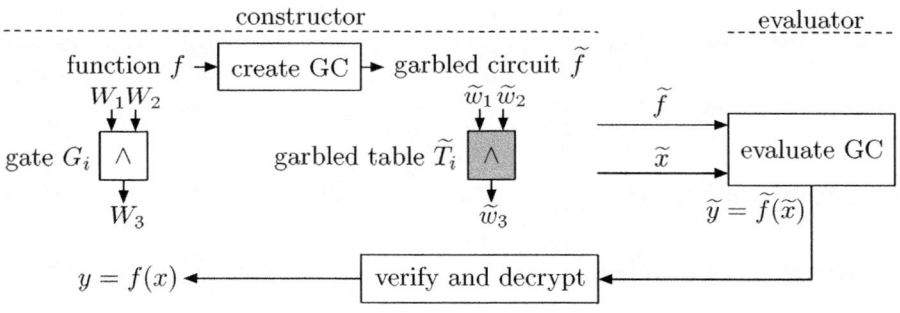

Fig. 2. Overview of Garbled Circuits

Efficient GC construction. The efficient GC construction of [19] provides "free XOR" gates, i.e., XOR gates have no garbled table and negligible cost for evaluation. For each 2-input non-XOR gate the garbled table has size $4t$ bits, where t is the symmetric security parameter; its creation requires 4 invocations of a cryptographic hash function (e.g., SHA-256 [23]) and 1 invocation for evaluation. The construction is provably secure in the random-oracle model.

Efficient creation of GCs in hardware. As shown in [16], GCs can be generated within a low-cost tamper-proof hardware token. The token requires only a constant amount of memory (independent of the size of the evaluated function) and performs only symmetric cryptographic operations (SHA-256 and AES). Generation of the GC for the aforementioned AES functionality took 84ms on a 66MHz FPGA neglecting the delay for communicating with the token [16].

Efficient evaluation of GCs in software. The implementation results of [24] show that GCs can be evaluated efficiently on today's hardware. Evaluation of the GC for the reasonably large AES functionality ($22,546$ XOR and $11,334$ non-XOR gates) took 2s on an Intel Core 2 Duo with 3.0GHz and 4GB RAM [24].

4   Architectures for Secure Outsourcing of Data and Arbitrary Computation

In this section we present several architectures for our model of §2.

4.1   Token Computes

A first approach, also used in [17], is to let the token $\mathcal{T}$ compute f as shown in Fig. 3. For this, $\mathcal{C}$ and $\mathcal{T}$ share symmetric keys for encryption and verification. The encrypted and authenticated database $\overline{D}$ and the authenticated function $\widehat{f}$ is stored within the storage cloud of service provider $\mathcal{S}$. In the online phase, $\mathcal{C}$ sends the encrypted and authenticated query $\overline{x}_i$ to $\mathcal{T}$ and the storage cloud provides $\overline{D}$ and $\widehat{f}$ one-by-one. $\mathcal{T}$ decrypts and verifies these inputs and evaluates $y_i = f(x_i, D)$ using secure external memory. If $\mathcal{T}$ detects any inconsistencies, it continues evaluation substituting the inconsistent value with a random value, and finally sets y_i to the failure symbol $\perp$. Finally, $\mathcal{T}$ sends the authenticated and encrypted response $\overline{y}_i$ back to $\mathcal{C}$ who decrypts, verifies and obtains the output y_i.

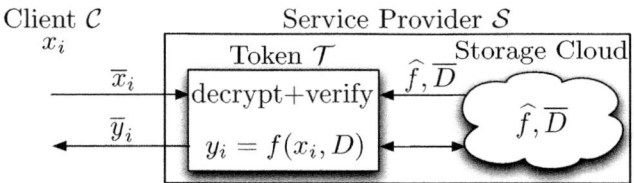

Fig. 3. Architecture: Token Computes [17]

Performance. In this approach, the latency of the online phase, i.e., the time from sending the query x_i to receiving the response y_i, depends on the performance of $\mathcal{T}$ (in particular on the performance of secure external memory) and cannot be improved by using the computation cloud services offered by $\mathcal{S}$.

4.2   Cloud Computes

The approach of [11] shown in Fig. 4 does not require a trusted HW token but combines garbled circuits for verifiability with fully homomorphic encryption for confidentiality of the outsourced data and computations. The main idea is to evaluate the same garbled circuit $\widetilde{f}$ under fully homomorphic encryption and use the resulting homomorphically encrypted garbled output values to verify that the computation was performed correctly:

During setup, $\mathcal{C}$ generates a garbled circuit $\widetilde{f}$ and encrypts its garbled tables with the fully homomorphic encryption scheme resulting in $[\![\widetilde{f}]\!]$ which is sent to $\mathcal{S}$ and stored in the storage cloud. To outsource the database D, the corresponding garbled values $\widetilde{D}$ are encrypted with the fully homomorphic encryption scheme and $[\![\widetilde{D}]\!]$ is stored in $\mathcal{S}$'s storage cloud as well.

In the online phase, $\mathcal{C}$ sends the homomorphically encrypted garbled query $[\![\widetilde{x}_i]\!]$ to $\mathcal{S}$ who evaluates the homomorphically encrypted garbled circuit $[\![\widetilde{f}]\!]$ on $[\![\widetilde{x}_i]\!]$ and $[\![\widetilde{D}]\!]$ using the homomorphic properties of the fully homomorphic encryption scheme. As result, $\mathcal{S}$ obtains $[\![\widetilde{y}_i]\!] = [\![\widetilde{f}(\widetilde{x}_i, \widetilde{D})]\!]$ and sends this back to $\mathcal{C}$. After decryption, $\mathcal{C}$ obtains $\widetilde{y}_i$ and can verify whether the computation was performed correctly. Otherwise, $\mathcal{C}$ outputs the failure symbol $\perp$.

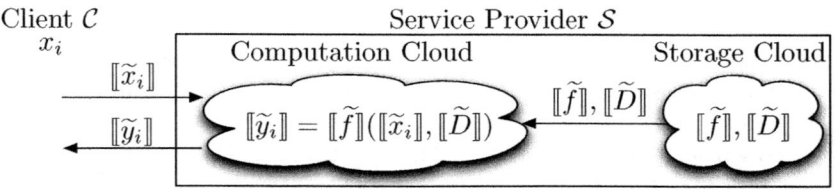

Fig. 4. Architecture: Cloud Computes [11]

Performance. The advantage of this approach is that it does not require any trusted hardware and hence can be computed in parallel in the computation cloud. However, the performance of today's fully homomorphic encryption schemes (in addition to the overhead caused by evaluating a garbled circuit under fully homomorphic encryption) is not sufficient that this approach can be used for practical applications in the near future (see §3.2).

4.3   Token Sets Up and Cloud Computes

Our approach combines a tamper-proof hardware token $\mathcal{T}$ used in the setup phase only with efficient computations performed in parallel in the computation cloud as shown in Fig. 5. The basic idea is that $\mathcal{T}$ generates a garbled circuit during the setup phase and in the time-critical online phase the garbled circuit is evaluated in parallel by the computation cloud.

In detail, our architecture consists of the following three phases:

During *System Initialization*, client $\mathcal{C}$ and the tamper-proof hardware token $\mathcal{T}$ agree on a symmetric (long-term) key k (cf. §2.1). Additionally, $\mathcal{C}$ provides $\mathcal{S}$ with the authenticated function $\widehat{f}$ (represented as boolean circuit) and the authenticated and encrypted data $\overline{D}$ who stores them in the storage cloud.

In the *Setup Phase*, $\mathcal{T}$ generates for protocol invocation i an internal session key k_i derived from the key k and i. Using k_i, $\mathcal{T}$ generates a garbled circuit $\widetilde{f}_i$ from the function $\widehat{f}$ and a corresponding garbled re-encryption $\widetilde{D}_i$ of the database $\overline{D}$ which are stored in the storage cloud: According to the construction of [16], the GC can be generated gate-by-gate using a constant amount of memory only. For each gate of $\widehat{f}$, $\mathcal{S}$ provides $\mathcal{T}$ with the description of the gate. $\mathcal{T}$ uses the session key k_i to derive the gate's garbled input values and the garbled output value and returns the corresponding garbled table to $\mathcal{S}$. In parallel, $\mathcal{T}$ accumulates a hash of the gates requested for so far (e.g., by successively updating $h_i =$

$H(h_{i-1}\|G_i)$ where H is a cryptographic hash function and G_i is the description of the i-th gate) which is finally used to verify authenticity of $\widehat{f}$ (see [16] for details). Similarly, $\mathcal{T}$ can convert the authenticated and encrypted database $\overline{D}$ into its garbled equivalent $\widetilde{D}_i$ using constant memory only: For each element $\overline{d}$ in $\overline{D}$, $\mathcal{T}$ decrypts and verifies $\overline{d}$ and uses the session key k_i to derive the corresponding garbled value $\widetilde{d}_i$ of $\widetilde{D}_i$. Finally, $\mathcal{T}$ provides $\mathcal{S}$ with an encrypted and authenticated OK message $\overline{\mathrm{OK}}_i$ that contains the session id and whether the verification of $\widehat{f}$ and all elements in $\overline{D}$ were successful ($\mathrm{OK}_i = \langle i, \top \rangle$) or not ($\mathrm{OK}_i = \langle i, \bot \rangle$).

In the *Online Phase*, $\mathcal{C}$ derives the session key k_i and uses this to create the garbled query $\widetilde{x}_i$ which is sent to $\mathcal{S}$. Now, the computation cloud evaluates the pre-computed garbled circuit $\widetilde{f}_i$ in parallel using the garbled query and the pre-computed garbled data $\widetilde{D}_i$ as inputs. The resulting garbled output $\widetilde{y}_i$ is sent back to $\mathcal{C}$ together with the OK message $\overline{\mathrm{OK}}_i$. Finally, $\mathcal{C}$ verifies that both phases have been performed correctly, i.e., $\overline{\mathrm{OK}}_i$ for the setup phase ($\mathrm{OK}_i = \langle i, \top \rangle$) and valid garbled output keys $\widetilde{y}_i$ for the online phase.

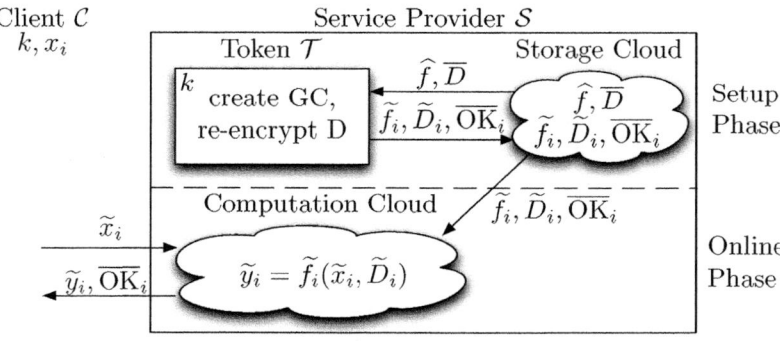

Fig. 5. Our Architecture: Token Sets Up and Cloud Computes

Performance. Our entire architecture is based solely on symmetric cryptographic primitives and hence is very efficient. When $\mathcal{T}$ has access to a hardware accelerator for GC creation (i.e., hardware accelerators for AES and SHA-256), the performance of the setup phase depends mostly on the speed of the interface between the token $\mathcal{T}$ and the storage cloud [16]. The size of $\widetilde{f}_i$ and $\widetilde{D}_i$ is approximately t times larger than the size of $\widehat{f}$ and $\overline{D}$, where t is a symmetric security parameter (e.g., $t = 128$). To evaluate the GC in the online phase, one invocation of SHA-256 is needed for each non-XOR gate while XOR gates are "free" as described in §3.3. GC evaluation can be easily parallelized for many practical functions that usually perform the same operations independently on every entry of the database, e.g., computing statistics or complex search queries.

Extensions. Our architecture can be naturally extended in several ways: To further speed up the setup phase, multiple tokens can be used, that in parallel

Table 1. Complexity Comparison

Architecture	$\mathcal{T}$ Computes (§4.1)	Cloud Computes (§4.2)	$\mathcal{T}$ Sets Up and Cloud Computes (§4.3)
Computation by $\mathcal{C}$	$\mathcal{O}(|x_i| + |y_i|)$	$\mathcal{O}(|x_i| + |y_i|)$	$\mathcal{O}(|x_i| + |y_i|)$
Communication $\mathcal{C} \leftrightarrow \mathcal{S}$	$\mathcal{O}(|x_i| + |y_i|)$	$\mathcal{O}(|x_i| + |y_i|)$	$\mathcal{O}(|x_i| + |y_i|)$
Storage in Cloud	$\mathcal{O}(|f| + |D|)$	$\mathcal{O}(|f| + |D|)$	$\mathcal{O}(|f| + |D|)$
Computation by $\mathcal{T}$	$\mathcal{O}(|f|)$ (Online)	none	$\mathcal{O}(|f|)$ (Setup)
Computation by Cloud	none	$\mathcal{O}(|f|)$ (Online)	$\mathcal{O}(|f|)$ (Online)
Online Latency	$\mathcal{T}$ evaluates f	Cloud evaluates $[\![\widetilde{f}]\!]$	Cloud evaluates $\widetilde{f}$

create garbled circuits and re-encrypt the database for multiple or even the same session. The function and the database can be updated dynamically when an additional monotonic revision number is used. Such updates can even be performed by multiple clients $\mathcal{C}_i$ by using public key encryption and signatures as described in §3.1.

5   Conclusion

Summary. We discussed a model and several possible architectures for outsourcing data and arbitrary computations that provide confidentiality, integrity, and verifiability. The first architecture is based on a tamper-proof hardware token, the second on evaluation of a garbled circuit under fully homomorphic encryption, and the third is a combination of both approaches.

Comparison. We conclude the paper with a qualitative performance comparison of the proposed architectures and leave a prototype implementation for their quantitative performance comparison as future work.

As summarized in Table 1, the asymptotic complexity of the presented architectures is the same: the client $\mathcal{C}$ performs work linear in the size of the inputs x_i and the outputs y_i, the storage cloud stores data linear in the size of the evaluated function f and the outsourced data D and the computation performed by the token $\mathcal{T}$ respectively the computation cloud is linear in the size of f. Hence, all three schemes are equally efficient from a complexity-theoretical point of view.

However, the online latency, i.e., the time between $\mathcal{C}$ submitting the encrypted query x_i to the service provider $\mathcal{S}$ until obtaining the result y_i differs substantially in practice.

For the token-based architecture of §4.1, the online latency depends on the performance of the token $\mathcal{T}$ that evaluates f and hence is hard to parallelize and might become a bottleneck in particular when f is large and $\mathcal{T}$ must resort to secure external memory in the storage cloud.

The homomorphic encryption-based architecture of §4.2 does not use a token and hence can exploit the parallelism offered by the computation cloud. However, this architecture is not ready for deployment in practical applications yet, as fully homomorphic encryption schemes are not yet sufficiently fast enough for evaluating a large functionality such as a garbled circuit under fully homomorphic encryption.

Our proposed architecture of §4.3 achieves low online latency by combining both approaches: $\mathcal{T}$ is used in the setup phase only to generate a garbled circuit and re-encrypt the database. In the online phase, the garbled circuit $\tilde{f}$ is evaluated in parallel by the computation cloud.

Acknowledgements. We thank the anonymous reviewers of the Workshop on Trust in the Cloud held as part of TRUST 2010 for their helpful comments.

References

1. Amazon Elastic Compute Cloud (EC2), http://aws.amazon.com/ec2
2. Amazon Simple Storage Service (S3), http://aws.amazon.com/s3
3. Atallah, M.J., Pantazopoulos, K.N., Rice, J.R., Spafford, E.H.: Secure outsourcing of scientific computations. Advances in Computers 54, 216–272 (2001)
4. Berger, S., Caceres, R., Goldman, K.A., Perez, R., Sailer, R., Doorn, L.v.: vTPM: Virtualizing the Trusted Platform Module. In: USENIX Security Symposium (USENIX 2006), pp. 305–320. USENIX Association (2006)
5. Bussani, A., Griffin, J.L., Jasen, B., Julisch, K., Karjoth, G., Maruyama, H., Nakamura, M., Perez, R., Schunter, M., Tanner, A., Van Doorn, L., Herreweghen, E.V., Waidner, M., Yoshihama, S.: Trusted Virtual Domains: Secure Foundations for Business and IT Services. Technical Report Research Report RC23792, IBM Research (November 2005)
6. Cabuk, S., Dalton, C.I., Eriksson, K., Kuhlmann, D., Ramasamy, H.G.V., Ramunno, G., Sadeghi, A.-R., Schunter, M., Stüble, C.: Towards automated security policy enforcement in multi-tenant virtual data centers. Journal of Computer Security 18, 89–121 (2010)
7. Chow, R., Golle, P., Jakobsson, M., Shi, E., Staddon, J., Masuoka, R., Molina, J.: Controlling data in the cloud: outsourcing computation without outsourcing control. In: ACM Workshop on Cloud Computing Security (CCSW 2009), pp. 85–90. ACM, New York (2009)
8. Cloud Security Alliance (CSA). Top threats to cloud computing, version 1.0 (March 2010),
   http://www.cloudsecurityalliance.org/topthreats/csathreats.v1.0.pdf
9. Dijk, M.v., Gentry, C., Halevi, S., Vaikuntanathan, V.: Fully homomorphic encryption over the integers. Cryptology ePrint Archive, Report 2009/616 (2009), http://eprint.iacr.org; To appear at EUROCRYPT 2010
10. Garay, J.A., Kolesnikov, V., McLellan, R.: MAC precomputation with applications to secure memory. In: Samarati, P., Yung, M., Martinelli, F., Ardagna, C.A. (eds.) ISC 2009. LNCS, vol. 5735, pp. 427–442. Springer, Heidelberg (2009)
11. Gennaro, R., Gentry, C., Parno, B.: Non-interactive verifiable computing: Outsourcing computation to untrusted workers. Cryptology ePrint Archive, Report 2009/547 (2009), http://eprint.iacr.org
12. Gentry, C.: Fully homomorphic encryption using ideal lattices. In: ACM Symposium on Theory of Computing (STOC 2009), pp. 169–178. ACM, New York (2009)
13. Google App Engine, https://appengine.google.com
14. Goldwasser, S., Kalai, Y.T., Rothblum, G.N.: One-time programs. In: Wagner, D. (ed.) CRYPTO 2008. LNCS, vol. 5157, pp. 39–56. Springer, Heidelberg (2008)

15. IBM. IBM Cryptocards, http://www-03.ibm.com/security/cryptocards/
16. Järvinen, K., Kolesnikov, V., Sadeghi, A.-R., Schneider, T.: Embedded SFE: Offloading server and network using hardware tokens. In: Financial Cryptography and Data Security (FC 2010), January 25-28. LNCS, Springer, Heidelberg (2010)
17. Jiang, S., Smith, S., Minami, K.: Securing web servers against insider attack. In: Proceedings of the 17th Annual Computer Security Applications Conference, ACSAC (2001)
18. Kamara, S., Lauter, K.: Cryptographic cloud storage. In: Workshop on Real-Life Cryptographic Protocols and Standardization (RLCPS 2010) - co-located with Financial Cryptography, January 2010, LNCS. Springer, Heidelberg (to appear 2010)
19. Kolesnikov, V., Schneider, T.: Improved garbled circuit: Free XOR gates and applications. In: Aceto, L., Damgård, I., Goldberg, L.A., Halldórsson, M.M., Ingólfsdóttir, A., Walukiewicz, I. (eds.) ICALP 2008, Part II. LNCS, vol. 5126, pp. 486–498. Springer, Heidelberg (2008)
20. Krawczyk, H., Bellare, M., Canetti, R.: HMAC: Keyed-hashing for message authentication. RFC 2104 (Informational) (February 1997), http://tools.ietf.org/html/rfc2104
21. Microsoft SQL Azure, http://www.microsoft.com/windowsazure
22. NIST, U.S. National Institute of Standards and Technology. Federal information processing standards (FIPS 197). Advanced Encryption Standard (AES) (November 2001), http://csrc.nist.gov/publications/fips/fips197/fips-197.pdf
23. NIST, U.S. National Institute of Standards and Technology. Federal information processing standards (FIPS 180-2). Announcing the Secure Hash Standard (August 2002), http://csrc.nist.gov/publications/fips/fips180-2/fips-180-2.pdf
24. Pinkas, B., Schneider, T., Smart, N.P., Williams, S.C.: Secure two-party computation is practical. In: Matsui, M. (ed.) ASIACRYPT 2009. LNCS, vol. 5912, pp. 250–267. Springer, Heidelberg (2009)
25. Sadeghi, A.-R., Stüble, C., Winandy, M.: Property-based TPM virtualization. In: Wu, T.-C., Lei, C.-L., Rijmen, V., Lee, D.-T. (eds.) ISC 2008. LNCS, vol. 5222, pp. 1–16. Springer, Heidelberg (2008)
26. Smart, N.P., Vercauteren, F.: Fully homomorphic encryption with relatively small key and ciphertext sizes. In: PKC 2010. LNCS. Springer, Heidelberg (2010); Cryptology ePrint Archive, Report 2009/571, http://eprint.iacr.org
27. Smith, S.W., Weingart, S.: Building a high-performance, programmable secure coprocessor. Computer Networks 31(8), 831–860 (1999); Special Issue on Computer Network Security
28. Song, J.H., Poovendran, R., Lee, J., Iwata, T.: The AES-CMAC Algorithm. RFC 4493 (Informational) (June 2006), http://tools.ietf.org/html/rfc4493
29. Trusted Computing Group (TCG). TPM main specification. Main specification, Trusted Computing Group (May 2009), http://www.trustedcomputinggroup.org
30. Yao, A.C.: How to generate and exchange secrets. In: IEEE Symposium on Foundations of Computer Science (FOCS 1986), pp. 162–167. IEEE, Los Alamitos (1986)
31. Yee, B.S.: Using Secure Coprocessors. PhD thesis, School of Computer Science, Carnegie Mellon University, CMU-CS-94-149 (May 1994)

Oblivious Transfer Based on Physical Unclonable Functions

Ulrich Rührmair

Computer Science Department
Technische Universität München
85748 Garching, Germany
ruehrmai@in.tum.de
http://www.pcp.in.tum.de

Abstract. Oblivious transfer (OT) is a simple, but powerful cryptographic primitive, on the basis of which secure two-party computation and several other cryptographic protocols can be realized. In this paper, we show how OT can be implemented by Strong Physical Unclonable Functions (PUFs). Special attention is thereby devoted to a recent subclass of Strong PUFs known as SHIC PUFs. Our results show that the cryptographic potential of these PUFs is perhaps surprisingly large, and goes beyond the usual identification and key exchange protocols.

1 Introduction

Motivation and Background. Electronic devices are becoming increasingly mobile, cross-linked and pervasive, which makes them a well-accessible target for adversaries. Mathematical cryptography offers several measures against the resulting security and privacy problems, but they all rest on the concept of a secret binary key: They presuppose that the devices can contain a piece of information that is, and remains, unknown to an adversary. This requirement can be difficult to uphold in practice: Invasive, semi-invasive, or side-channel attacks, as well as various software attacks including viruses, can lead to key exposure and full security breaks.

The described situation was one motivation that led to the development of *Physical Unclonable Functions (PUFs)* [1]. A PUF is a (partly) disordered physical system S that can be challenged with so-called external stimuli or challenges C_i, upon which it reacts with corresponding responses R_i. Contrary to standard digital systems, a PUF's responses shall depend on the nanoscale structural disorder present in it. It is assumed that this disorder cannot be cloned or reproduced exactly, not even by the PUF's original manufacturer, and that it is unique to each PUF.

Due to their complex internal structure, PUFs can often avoid some of the shortcomings associated with digital keys. It is usually harder to read out, predict, or derive their responses than to obtain the values of digital keys stored in non-volatile memory. This fact has been exploited for various PUF-based security protocols, for example schemes for identification [1] and key exchange [2].

A. Acquisti, S.W. Smith, and A.-R. Sadeghi (Eds.): TRUST 2010, LNCS 6101, pp. 430–440, 2010.

Oblivious Transfer. Oblivious transfer (OT) is a two-player cryptographic primitive which was originally introduced by [3] [4]. Several variants exist, which are reducible to each other [5] [31]. The version considered in this paper is a one-out-of-two oblivious transfer or $\binom{2}{1}$-OT [5]. This is a protocol with the following properties: At the beginning of the protocol, one party Alice (the "sender") holds two secret bits b_0 and b_1 as private input, and another party Bob (the "receiver") holds a secret choice bit c as private input. After execution of the protocol, the following conditions must be met: (i) Bob has learned the bit b_c, i.e. those of the two bits b_0 and b_1 that was selected by his choice bit c. (ii) Even an actively cheating Bob cannot derive any information about the other bit $b_{c\oplus 1}$ as long as Alice follows the protocol. (iii) Even an actively cheating Alice cannot learn c if Bob follows the protocol.

Since its introduction, a large class of cryptographic schemes has been realized on the basis of OT, including bit-commitment, zero-knowledge proofs, and general secure multi-party computation [6] [7] [8] [9] [10]. This makes OT a very versatile and universal primitive. The fact that OT can be realized within a certain cryptographic model is often seen as an indication of the model's large cryptographic potential. For these reasons, the feasibility of OT in the context of quantum cryptography [11] [12], within the Bounded Storage Model (BSM) [14] [15], or in noise-based cryptography [16] [17], has been well-investigated in earlier publications.

Our Contribution. In this extended abstract, we describe a protocol that implements oblivious transfer on the basis of two types of Physical Unclonable Functions: So-called Strong PUFs and SHIC PUFs (see Section 2). The protocol seems to indicate the large potential of these PUFs beyond the known schemes for identification [1] and key exchange [2].

The protocol can be executed between two players Alice and Bob under the following prerequisites: (i) Bob had previous access to the Strong PUF/SHIC PUF in a pre-setting phase. During this phase, he established a list of challenge-response-pairs (CRPs) of the PUF, which is unknown to Alice. (ii) At the time of protocol execution, the Strong PUF/SHIC PUF has been transfered to Alice. Only Alice has access to it and can measure CRPs of the PUF.

Since it is known from other publications that OT is a symmetric primitive [31], our technique allows OT in both directions under the above provisions, without re-transferring the PUF from Alice to Bob (see Sec. 3.3).

Organization of the Paper. In Section 2, we give some background on the two specific PUF types which are relevant for this paper (i.e., Strong PUFs and SHIC PUFs). We also briefly discuss their implementation. In Section 3 we describe and analyze our protocol for oblivious transfer. We conclude the paper in Section 4.

2 Background on PUFs

We now give some background on the two PUF types relevant for this paper. Since SHIC PUFs are a special form of Strong PUFs, we start with an explanation of the latter.

2.1 Strong PUFs

A Strong PUF [1] [18] is a (partly) disordered physical system S, which can be excited with a finite number of external stimuli or challenges C_i, upon which it reacts with corresponding responses R_{C_i} [2]. The pairs (C_i, R_{C_i}) are usually called the challenge-response pairs (CRPs) of the PUF. Three security relevant properties of a Strong PUF S are the following:

(i) Due to the disordered microstructure of S, it must be practically infeasible to fabricate a physical clone S' of S, which has the same challenge-response behavior as S. This restriction shall even hold for the original manufacturer of S.

(ii) Due to the large number of possible challenges that can be applied to S, it must be practically infeasible to exhaustively measure all CRPs of S within a limited time frame on the order of weeks, months, or even years.

(iii) Due to the complicated internal interactions of S, it must be practically infeasible to devise a computer program that correctly predicts the response of S to a randomly chosen, previously unknown challenge with high probability. This should hold even if many other challenge-response pairs of S are known.

Together, conditions (i) to (iii) imply that the responses R_{C_i} of S can be determined correctly (with high probability) only by someone who has got direct physical access to the single, unique PUF S. Implementation examples of Strong PUFs include complex optical scatterers [1] or integrated circuits whose outputs depend on their internal, individual runtimes delays [21] [22] [23]. Also analog cellular arrays have been proposed recently [24].

It has been realized relatively early, however, that machine learning techniques are a natural and powerful tool that can potentially challenge the above security condition (iii). Successful attacks on several Strong PUF candidates have indeed been reported in [20] [21] [25] [26]. To rule out a potential susceptibility to algorithmic modeling attacks, SHIC PUFs have been introduced.

2.2 SHIC PUFs

SHIC PUFs are pronounced as "chique PUFs" and have been suggested in [27] [28] [29]. The acronym "SHIC" stands for Super High Information Content. They are Strong PUF (i.e. they possess the above properties (i) to (iii)) and have the following additional features:

(iv) They contain an extraordinarily high amount of response-relevant random information and have a very high information density.

---

[1] Strong PUFs also have been referred to simply as PUFs [19], as Physical Random Functions [19] [21] [22] , or, almost equivalently, as Physical One-Way Functions [1].

[2] Please note that the terminology "R_{C_i}" slightly deviates from the standard terminology "R_i" for PUFs. The new terminology is introduced here in order to make the description of Protocol 2 less ambiguous.

(v) Their read-out speed (i.e. the frequency by which they produce responses) is limited to low values. This limitation should not be enforced by an artificially slow access module or the like, which could potentially be circumvented or cut off by suitable invasive means. Rather, it must be an inherent property of the PUF's design and its physical properties.

(vi) The CRPs of a SHIC PUF are mutually independent. The pairwise mutual information of any two responses of theirs is zero.

SHIC PUFs can be imagined as a huge read-only memory with a very high random information content and an *intrinsically slow read-out speed*. A challenge C_i to a SHIC PUF is the analogue to the address in a classical memory, and the corresponding response R_{C_i} is similar to the bit-value stored under that address. A possible realization with concrete numbers for information content, information density and read-out speed will be discussed in Section 2.3.

Strong PUFs vs. SHIC PUFs. As emphasized earlier, all SHIC PUFs are Strong PUFs, but they possess the further properties (iv) to (vi) above. SHIC PUFs thus have the advantage that their security does not depend on the computational power and the machine learning capabilities of the attacker. As all their CRPs are independent of each other, they withstand prediction even by attackers with unlimited computational power until a complete read-out has been accomplished. Their security only depends on the CRPs known to an adversary vs. the overall number of CRPs of the PUF.

2.3 Realization of SHIC PUFs

Even though this is not the main topic of this manuscript, we will briefly discuss the practical realization of the theoretical concept of a SHIC PUF. One potential candidate are ALILE-based Crossbar PUFs, which have been introduced in [27] [28] [29]. We will only provide a short overview of this approach; much further detail can be found in [27] [28] [29].

Generating Randomness by the ALILE Process. Any SHIC PUF must contain a very large random information content. There are many physical processes that generate large entropy in solid-state systems, but one example that can eventually lead to integrated electrical realizations of SHIC PUFs is a process known as ALuminum-Induded Layer Exchange (ALILE) [27] [28] [29]. It is a simple, crystallization-based method that employs only inexpensive starting materials (amorphous silicon and aluminum). It result in polycrystalline films with p-type conduction, which exhibit a very large level of disorder and randomness (see Fig. 1 a). By adjusting the process parameters, the size, number and density of the crystallites can be tuned as desired. The randomness causes individual electrical properties in different subregions of the surface.

Crossbar-based Read-Out. One method that was investigated in [27] [28] [29] is to read out the information from ALILE structures by so-called crossbar architectures. Slightly simplifying, a crossbar consists of two sets of parallel wires, which are attached to the top and to the bottom of the crystallized structure. The bottom set of wires is arranged in a 90° angle to the top set, as shown in Figure 1. If source and drain voltages are applied at exactly one top and one bottom wire, current flows through the polycrystalline film area at the virtual crossing of the two wires. $I(V)$ curves with a strongly rectifying behavior [29] are observed, which depend on the individual, random configuration in the polycrystalline substrate at the crossing. They can be converted into a few bits of individual information per crossing [27] [28].

Crossbar architectures are among the simplest functional nano devices and possess a very regular geometry. They can hence be fabricated with very small inter-wire distances, leading to high information densities. Concrete realization parameters we tried to make plausible by measurement on single diodes and by crossbar simulations in [28] are 10^5 top wires and 10^5 bottom wires, which leads to an information of around 10^{10} bits per cm^2. This assumes that the footprint of one crossing is 100 nm $\times$ 100 nm [28]. A single CRP of such a structure would have a length of around around $1 + 2 \cdot \log_2 10^5 \approx 35$ bits.

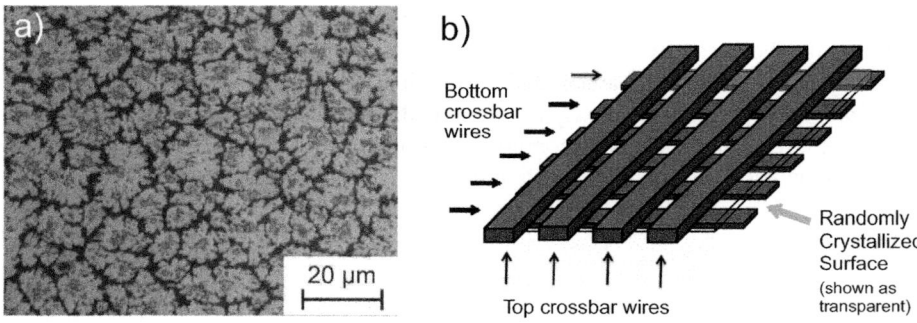

Fig. 1. a) A polycrystalline film resulting from the ALILE process, illustrating the high entropy and disorder in the structure. The green areas are silicon crystallites, possessing a random distribution and strongly irregular shape. b) The schematics of the crossbar read-out circuitry.

Inherently Slow Read-Out Speed. Up to now, we have mainly described a memory-like structure with a high information content and density. Also large arrays of SRAM cells or Butterfly PUFs could fulfill these criteria, albeit presumably at lower information densities. The perhaps most unusual characteristic of Crossbar PUFs is that they promise to guarantee an inherently slow read-out speed [28]. To achieve this property, the Crossbar PUF must be built in one large, monolithic block, not from separate blocks as modern semiconductor memories. The wires are intentionally designed to have only a low, limited current-carrying capacity. Simulations conducted in [28] showed that in such large blocks, depending on the fabrication parameters, several milliseconds must elapse before the sense current/voltage stabilizes. This leads to read-out speeds of around 100 bits/sec [28].

The two apparent strategies to accelerate read-out would be to increase the sense current/voltage, or to conduct a parallel read-out at several crossings. But both approaches lead to a higher current load in the monolithic crossbar, which is proportional to the achieved speed up. They therefore quickly overload and destroy the limited wires [28]. Removing the original wires of the crossbar, which very densely cover the whole crystallized system, and replacing them with a faster read-out mechanism seems practically infeasible without destroying the PUF's structure and current-voltage characteristics. This makes the PUF's original responses unreadable [28].

3   The Protocol

We now provide a protocol for $\binom{2}{1}$-OT on the basis of Strong PUFs, which is inspired by techniques originally presented in [14]. Since SHIC PUFs are a subclass of Strong PUFs, the protocol works for both PUF types interchangeably — using SHIC PUFs only causes some small advantages in the resulting security features (see section 3.3). As a subprotocol, we employ interactive hashing [13] [14].

3.1   Interactive Hashing

In a nutshell, interactive hashing [13] is a cryptographic two-player protocol, in which Alice has no input, and Bob's initial input is an m-bit string S. At the end of the protocol, Alice knows two m-bit strings U_1 and U_2, with the properties that (i) $U_b = S$ for some bit $b \in \{0, 1\}$, but Alice does not know the value of b, and that (ii) the other string $U_{b \oplus 1}$ is an essentially random bitstring of length m, which neither Alice nor Bob can determine alone. A protocol for interactive hashing can be constructed as follows.

Protocol 1:   INTERACTIVE HASHING

Prerequisites:

1. Alice holds no input, Bob holds an m-bit string S as input.
2. Let G be the following class of 2-universal hash functions:

$$G = \{g(x) = a * x \mid a \text{ is an element of the set } \{0, 1\}^m\},$$

where $*$ denotes the scalar product between the vectors a and x.

Protocol:

The protocol consists of $m - 1$ rounds. In the j-th round, for $j = 1, \ldots, m - 1$, Alice executes the following steps:

1. Alice chooses a function g_j uniformly at random from the set G. Let the m-ary binary vector a_j be the description of G. If a_j is linearly dependent on the $a_1, \ldots, a_{m-1}$, then Alice repeats step 1 until a_j is linearly independent.
2. Alice announces g_j to Bob.
3. Bob computes $b_j = g_j(S) = a_j * S$ and sends b_j to Alice.

At the end of the protocol, Alice knows $m - 1$ linear equations satisfied by S. Since the a_j's are linearly independent, there are exactly two different m-bit strings U_1 and U_2 that satisfy the system of equations set up by Bob. These solutions can be found by Alice via standard linear algebra. U_1 and U_2 have the property that exactly one of them is equal to S, but obviously Alice has no chance in telling which one it is. For further details see [13] [14].

3.2 Oblivious Transfer

Protocol 2: $\binom{2}{1}$-OBLIVIOUS TRANSFER BY STRONG PUFs

Prerequisites:

1. Bob holds a Strong PUF S. We assume without loss of generality that the responses R_C^S of S consist of a single bit. [3]
2. Alice and Bob have agreed on an encoding scheme $E(\cdot)$ with the following properties:
    (a) $E(\cdot)$ efficiently encodes finite tuples of PUF-challenges C_i of the form $T = (C_1, \ldots, C_k)$ as finite binary strings.
    (b) $E(\cdot)$ is reversed by a decoding scheme $D(\cdot)$, such that $E(D(T)) = T$ for all tuples T of the form $T = (C_1, \ldots, C_k)$ (with the C_i being challenges of S).
    (c) $D(\cdot)$ uniquely associates a tuple $T = D(x)$ with any finite binary string x.
    Similar encoding schemes can be found, for example, in [32] or [14].
3. Alice holds two bits b_0 and b_1, which are unknown to Bob.
4. Bob holds a choice bit c, which is unknown to Alice.

Protocol:

1. Bob chooses a tuple of challenges $T = (C_1, \ldots, C_n)$ uniformly at random, and determines the corresponding responses $R_{C_1}, \ldots, R_{C_n}$.
2. Bob sends or transfers the Strong PUF S to Alice.
3. Alice and Bob get engaged in an interactive hashing protocol, where Bob's input is $E(T)$.
4. The output of this interactive hashing protocol, which is both known to Alice and Bob, are two strings U_0 and U_1. One of these strings U_0, U_1 is equal to $E(T)$. Let us call the index of that string i_0, i.e. $U_{i_0} = E(T)$.

    Note: Bob knows i_0, since he knows both U_0, U_1 and $E(T)$.

5. Bob sets the bit $c' = i_0 \oplus c$, and sends c' to Alice.
6. Alice determines by measurement on the PUF S the values

$$R_{Z_1}, \ldots, R_{Z_n},$$

where the Z_i are the elements of the tuple $D(U_{c'})$ (which, by the properties of $D(\cdot)$, are all challenges of S). Furthermore, she determines by measurement on S the values

$$R_{Z_1'}, \ldots, R_{Z_n'},$$

where the Z_i' are the elements of the set $D(U_{c' \oplus 1})$.

---

[3] If a response consists of multiple bits $b_1 \cdots b_k$, we can, for example, take the XOR of all these bits, or employ fuzzy extractors.

Note: At this point of the protocol, Alice has chosen two sets of PUF-responses $R_{Z_1}, \ldots, R_{Z_n}$ and $R_{Z_1}', \ldots, R_{Z_n}'$. Bob knows exactly one of these sets, namely the one that is equal to $R_{C_1}, \ldots, R_{C_n}$. The other set is unknown to Bob. Furthermore, Alice does not know which of the two sets of responses is known to Bob.

7. Alice forms the two strings s_0 and s_1 according to the following rules:

$$s_0 = b_0 + R_{Z_1} + \ldots + R_{Z_n} \quad \mathrm{mod}\ 2,$$

and

$$s_1 = b_1 + R_{Z_1}' + \ldots + R_{Z_n}' \quad \mathrm{mod}\ 2.$$

8. Alice sends s_0 and s_1 to Bob.
9. Bob obtains the bit b_c he selected through his choice bit c as

$$b_c = s_c + R_{C_1} + \ldots + R_{C_n} \quad \mathrm{mod}\ 2.$$

3.3 Discussion

Security. The security of the protocol depends on the fact that Bob does not know both sets $R_{Z_1}, \ldots, R_{Z_n}$ and $R_{Z_1}', \ldots, R_{Z_n}'$ in step 7. If he did, then he could learn both bits b_0 and b_1. This is where property (iii) (see page 432) of Strong PUFs and SHIC PUFs becomes relevant. Due to this property, Bob cannot know all CRPs of the Strong PUF/SHIC PUF, but only a fraction γ with $0 < \gamma < 1$. Since one of the sets $R_{Z_1}, \ldots, R_{Z_n}$ and $R_{Z_1}', \ldots, R_{Z_n}'$ is chosen at random in the interactive hashing protocol, the probability that Bob knows the corresponding CRPs is γ^n, i.e. it is exponentially low in the security parameter n of the protocol. The fact that Alice does not learn Bob's choice bit c stems from the security properties of the interactive hashing protocol, which prevents that Alice learns which of the two strings U_1 or U_2 is equal to Bob's private input S [13] [14].

The security difference in using Strong PUFs and SHIC PUFs in Protocol 2 is that by its definition and property (vi), a secure SHIC PUF would fulfill the essential requirement (iii) (see page 432) independent of the computational power of the adversary. Secure SHIC PUFs hence could guarantee the protocol's security also against cheating parties with unlimited computational potential.

Practicality. The communication and storage requirements are mild: Bob must store only n CRPs, and the protocol has around m rounds for the interactive hashing. The latter can be reduced to a constant the techniques described in [15].

In order to cope with potential noise in the PUF responses, presumably standard PUF error correction such as helper data (see [2] [27] and references therein) could be used. In that case, a few steps of the protocol should be adjusted. Firstly, Bob measures and stores noisy data R_{C_i} in Step 1. Alice likewise obtains noisy responses R_{Z_i} and R_{Z_i}' in Step 6 of the protocol, and extracts helper data W_{Z_i} and W_{Z_i}', together with secrets S_{Z_i} and S_{Z_i}'. In Step 7, Alice uses the secrets S_{Z_i} and S_{Z_i}' (instead of the values R_{Z_i} and R_{Z_i}') to "encrypt" the bits b_0 and b_1. In Step 8, she transmits the corresponding helper data W_{Z_i} and $W_{Z_i'}$ together with the strings s_0 and s_1. Of these two sets of helper data, Bob uses the one that matches his data set R_{C_i}. He derives identical secrets as Alice from the R_{C_i}, and uncovers the bit b_c from $s_{i_0 \oplus c}$.

Symmetry. Oblivious transfer is known to be a symmetric primitive [31]: Given an OT protocol where Alice is the sender and Bob is the receiver, one can construct the "reverse" OT protocol where Alice acts as receiver and Bob as sender. The construction of [31] is generic, and independent of the concrete implementation of the OT.

Therefore, Protocol 2 can also be used to implement OT in the other direction, i.e. from Bob to Alice, without re-transferring the PUF from Alice to Bob. This is an important practicality asset: In many applications, the physical transfer of the PUF in one direction is executed naturally (e.g. in a hardware shipped from a manufacturer to a customer, or on a bank card carried to an automated teller machine (ATM) by a customer). Once accomplished, this allows oblivious transfer in both directions and secure two-party computations, e.g. between the manufacturer and the hardware.

4 Summary

We discussed a protocol for oblivious transfer on the basis of Strong PUFs and SHIC PUFs. It allows OT and secure two-party computation between two players, provided that (i) Player A had previous access to the PUF, and (ii) only Player B holds physical possession of the PUF at the time of the protocol execution. These circumstances occur frequently in practice, for example between a central authority on the one hand and mobile hardware systems, decentral terminals, or security tokens (including bank cards, ID cards, access cards, and the like) on the other hand. The protocol does not use any computational assumptions other than the security of the PUF.

References

1. Pappu, R., Recht, B., Taylor, J., Gershenfeld, N.: Physical One-Way Functions. Science 297, 2026–2030 (2002)
2. Tuyls, P., Skoric, B.: Strong Authentication with Physical Unclonable Functions. In: Petkovic, M., Jonker, W. (eds.) Security, Privacy and Trust in Modern Data Management, Springer, Heidelberg (2007)
3. Rabin, M.O.: How to exchange secrets by oblivious transfer. Technical Report TR-81, Harvard University (1981)
4. Even, S., Goldreich, O., Lempel, A.: A randomized protocol for signing contracts. In: Rivest, R.L., Sherman, A., Chaum, S. (eds.) Proc. CRYPTO 1982, pp. 205–210. Plenum Press, New York (1982)
5. Crépeau, C.: Equivalence between two flavors of oblivious transfer. In: Pomerance, C. (ed.) CRYPTO 1987. LNCS, vol. 293, pp. 350–354. Springer, Heidelberg (1988)
6. Yao, A.C.-C.: How to generate and exchange secrets. In: Proc. of the 27th IEEE Symposium on the Foundations of Computer Science (FOCS), pp. 162–167 (1986)
7. Goldreich, O., Micali, S., Widgerson, A.: How to play any mental game, or a completeness theorem for protocols with honest majority. In: Proc. of the 19th Annual Symposium on the Theory of Computing (STOC), pp. 218–229 (1987)

8. Goldreich, O., Vainish, R.: How to solve any protocol problem – an efficiency improvement. In: Pomerance, C. (ed.) CRYPTO 1987. LNCS, vol. 293, pp. 73–86. Springer, Heidelberg (1988)

9. Kilian, J.: Founding cryptography on oblivious transfer. In: Proceedings, 20th Annual ACM Symposium on the Theory of Computation, STOC (1988)

10. Crepeau, C., van de Graaf, J., Tapp, A.: Committed oblivious transfer and private multi-party computations. In: Coppersmith, D. (ed.) CRYPTO 1995. LNCS, vol. 963, pp. 110–123. Springer, Heidelberg (1995)

11. He, G.P., Wang, Z.D.: Oblivious transfer using quantum entanglement. Physical Review A 73(1), Part A, 012331 (2006)

12. Wehner, S., Schaffner, C., Terhal, B.M.: Cryptography from noisy storage. Phys. Rev. Lett. 100(22), 220–502 (2008)

13. Naor, M., Ostrovsky, R., Venkatesan, R., Yung, M.: Perfect zero-knowledge arguments for NP using any one-way function. Journal of Cryptology 11(2), 87–108 (1998)

14. Cachin, C., Crepeau, C., Marcil, J.: Oblivious transfer with a memory-bounded receiver. In: Proceeding of the 39th Annual Symposium on Foundations of Computer Science (1998)

15. Ding, Y.Z., Harnik, D., Rosen, A., Shaltiel, R.: Constant-Round Oblivious Transfer in the Bounded Storage Model. Journal of Cryptology (2007)

16. Crepeau, C.: Efficient cryptographic protocols based on noisy channels. In: Fumy, W. (ed.) EUROCRYPT 1997. LNCS, vol. 1233, pp. 306–317. Springer, Heidelberg (1997)

17. Wullschleger, J.: Oblivious Transfer from Weak Noisy Channels. In: Reingold, O. (ed.) TCC 2009. LNCS, vol. 5444, pp. 332–349. Springer, Heidelberg (2009)

18. Guajardo, J., Kumar, S.S., Schrijen, G.J., Tuyls, P.: FPGA Intrinsic PUFs and Their Use for IP Protection. In: Paillier, P., Verbauwhede, I. (eds.) CHES 2007. LNCS, vol. 4727, pp. 63–80. Springer, Heidelberg (2007)

19. Gassend, B.: Physical Random Functions, MSc Thesis. MIT, Cambridge (2003)

20. Lim, D.: Extracting Secret Keys from Integrated Circuits, MSc Thesis. MIT, Cambridge (2004)

21. Gassend, B., Lim, D., Clarke, D., Dijk, M.v., Devadas, S.: Identification and authentication of integrated circuits. Concurrency and Computation: Practice & Experience 1611, 1077–1098 (2004)

22. Lee, J.-W., Lim, D., Gassend, B., Suh, G.E., van Dijk, M., Devadas, S.: A technique to build a secret key in integrated circuits with identification and authentication applications. In: Proceedings of the IEEE VLSI Circuits Symposium (June 2004)

23. Majzoobi, M., Koushanfar, F., Potkonjak, M.: Lightweight Secure PUFs. In: IC-CAD 2008 (2008)

24. Csaba, G., Ju, X., Ma, Z., Chen, Q., Porod, W., Schmidhuber, J., Schlichtmann, U., Lugli, P., Rührmair, U.: Application of Mismatched Cellular Nonlinear Networks for Physical Cryptography. In: IEEE CNNA (2010)

25. Majzoobi, M., Koushanfar, F., Potkonjak, M.: Testing Techniques for Hardware Security. In: IEEE International Test Conference (2008)

26. Rührmair, U., Sehnke, F., Soelter, J., Dror, G., Devadas, S., Schmidhuber, J.: Modeling Attacks on Physical Unclonable Functions (submitted 2010)

27. Rührmair, U., Jaeger, C., Hilgers, C., Algasinger, M., Csaba, G., Stutzmann, M.: Security Applications of Diodes with Random Current-Voltage Characteristics. In: Financial Cryptography and Data Security (2010)

28. Rührmair, U., Jaeger, C., Bator, M., Stutzmann, M., Lugli, P., Csaba, G.: Applications of High-Capacity Crossbar Memories in Cryptography. IEEE Transactions on Nanotechnology (to appear 2010)

29. Jaeger, C., Algasinger, M., Rührmair, U., Csaba, G., Stutzmann, M.: Random pn-junctions for physical cryptography. Applied Physics Letters (to appear 2010)
30. Suh, G.E., Devadas, S.: Physical Unclonable Functions for Device Authentication and Secret Key Generation. In: DAC 2007, pp. 9–14 (2007)
31. Wolf, S., Wullschleger, J.: Oblivious Transfer Is Symmetric. In: Vaudenay, S. (ed.) EURO-CRYPT 2006. LNCS, vol. 4004, pp. 222–232. Springer, Heidelberg (2006)
32. Cover, T.M.: Enumerative Source Encoding. IEEE Transactions on Information Theory 19(1), 73–77 (1973)

Author Index